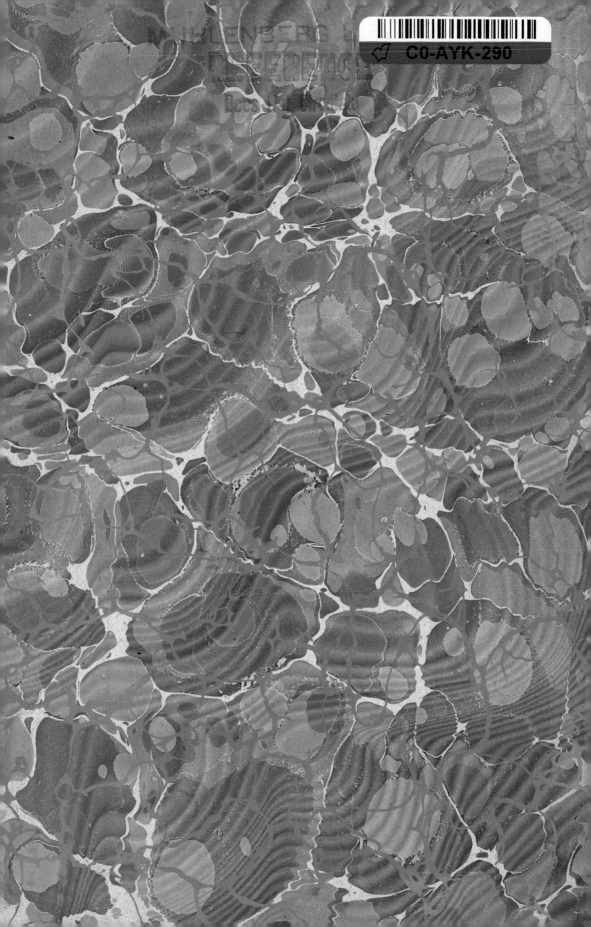

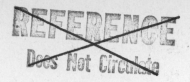

THE MYTHOLOGY OF ALL RACES

—

Volume IV
FINNO-UGRIC
SIBERIAN

VOLUME I. *Greek and Roman*
WILLIAM SHERWOOD FOX, Ph.D., Princeton University.

VOLUME II. *Eddic*
AXEL OLRIK, Ph.D., University of Copenhagen.

VOLUME III. *Celtic, Slavic*
CANON JOHN A. MacCULLOCH, D.D., Bridge of Allan, Scotland.
JAN MÁCHAL, Ph.D., Bohemian University, Prague.

VOLUME IV. *Finno-Ugric, Siberian*
UNO HOLMBERG, Ph.D., University of Finland, Helsingfors.

VOLUME V. *Semitic*
R. CAMPBELL THOMPSON, M.A., F.S.A., F.R.G.S., Oxford.

VOLUME VI. *Indian, Iranian*
A. BERRIEDALE KEITH, D.C.L., Edinburgh University.
ALBERT J. CARNOY, Ph.D., University of Louvain.

VOLUME VII. *Armenian, African*
MARDIROS ANANIKIAN, B.D., Kennedy School of Missions, Hart-
ford, Connecticut.
ALICE WERNER, L.L.A. (St. Andrews); School of Oriental Studies, London

VOLUME VIII. *Chinese, Japanese*
JOHN CALVIN FERGUSON, Ph.D.,
(*Adviser to the President of the Republic of China*)
MASAHARU ANESAKI, Litt.D., University of Tokyo.
(*Japanese Exchange Professor at Harvard University, 1913–1915*)

VOLUME IX. *Oceanic*
ROLAND BURRAGE DIXON, Ph.D., Harvard University.

VOLUME X. *American (North of Mexico)*
HARTLEY BURR ALEXANDER, Ph.D., University of Nebraska.

VOLUME XI. *American (Latin)*
HARTLEY BURR ALEXANDER, Ph.D., University of Nebraska.

VOLUME XII. *Egyptian, Indo-Chinese*
W. MAX MÜLLER, Ph.D., University of Pennsylvania.
SIR JAMES GEORGE SCOTT, K.C.I.E., London.

VOLUME XIII. *Index*

PLATE I

Grave–Houses in Russian Karelia

(See page 32.)
Water-colour by V. Soldan-Brofeldt.

PLATE I

GRAVE-HOUSES IN RUSSIAN KARELIA

(See page 32.)

Water-colour by V. Soldan-Brofeldt.

THE MYTHOLOGY OF ALL RACES

IN THIRTEEN VOLUMES

CANON JOHN ARNOTT MacCULLOCH, D.D., EDITOR

GEORGE FOOT MOORE, A.M., D.D., LL.D., CONSULTING EDITOR

FINNO-UGRIC, SIBERIAN

BY

UNO HOLMBERG, PH.D.

DOCENT OF THE UNIVERSITY OF FINLAND, HELSINGFORS

VOLUME IV

ARCHAEOLOGICAL INSTITUTE OF AMERICA

MARSHALL JONES COMPANY · BOSTON

M DCCCC XXVII

PRINTED IN THE UNITED STATES OF AMERICA BY
THE PLIMPTON PRESS · NORWOOD · MASSACHUSETTS
BOUND BY THE BOSTON BOOKBINDING COMPANY

EDITOR'S NOTE

IN place of a preface, Dr. Holmberg has asked me to say that much in his account of Finno-Ugric and Siberian Mythology is the result of personal acquaintance with various tribes. In the summer of 1911 he lived among the heathen Votiaks. In the summer of 1912 he travelled in Siberia (District Turuchansk) among the Siberian Arctic peoples. And in the summer of 1913 he lived among the Cheremias.

J. A. MacCULLOCH

Editor

EDITOR'S NOTE

IN place of a preface, Dr. Holmberg has asked me to say that much in his account of Finno-Ugric and Siberian Mythology is the result of personal acquaintance with various tribes. In the summer of 1911 he lived among the heathen Votiaks. In the summer of 1912 he travelled in Siberia (District Turuchansk) among the Siberian Arctic peoples. And in the summer of 1913 he lived among the Cheremiss.

J. A. MacCULLOCH
Editor.

CONTENTS

FINNO-UGRIC

	PAGE
Editor's Note	V
Introduction	XV

Chapter I	The Belief in Souls	3
II	Death and Burial	17
III	Memorial Feasts for a Particular Dead Person	37
IV	General Memorial Feasts	60
V	The Life Beyond	72
VI	Animal Worship	83
VII	The Seides of the Lapps	100
VIII	Family Gods	113
IX	Heroes	139
X	Household Spirits	159
XI	Forest Spirits	175
XII	Water Spirits	191
XIII	Gods of Sky and Air	217
XIV	Fire	235
XV	Deities of the Earth and Vegetation	239
XVI	Deities of Birth	252
XVII	Sacrifices to Nature Gods among the Volga Finns	262
XVIII	The Shaman	282

SIBERIAN

Introduction		299
Chapter I	World Pictures	306
II	The Origin of the Earth	313
III	The Pillar of the World	333
IV	The World Mountain	341

viii CONTENTS

PAGE

V THE TREE OF LIFE 349
VI DESTRUCTION OF THE WORLD 361
VII THE CREATION OF MAN 371
VIII THE FALL OF MAN 381
IX THE ORIGIN OF THE MOSQUITO 386
X THE HEAVEN GOD 390
XI THE SONS OF GOD 402
XII THE GREAT MOTHER 413
XIII THE STARS 417
XIV THUNDER 439
XV FIRE 449
XVI THE WIND 457
XVII THE EARTH 459
XVIII THE "MASTERS" OF NATURE 463
XIX DREAMS, SICKNESS AND DEATH 472
XX THE REALM OF THE DEAD 483
XXI SHAMANISM AND TOTEMISM 496
NOTES, FINNO-UGRIC 527
NOTES, SIBERIAN 545
BIBLIOGRAPHY, FINNO-UGRIC 563
BIBLIOGRAPHY, SIBERIAN 581

ILLUSTRATIONS

FULL PAGE ILLUSTRATIONS

PLATE   FACING PAGE

I Grave-houses in Russian Karelia — Coloured . . *Frontispiece*

II A Karsikko or Memorial Tree 26

III 1. Lapp Grave 36

      2. Graves of the Northern Ostiaks Erected over the Ground 36

IV At the Grave. Ingermanland 56

V Sacrificial Tree of the Dead among the Eastern Votiaks — Coloured 58

VI Bear Worship of the Voguls 84

VII Masker's Frolic at the Vogul Bear Feast 96

VIII The Holy Rastekaise Mountain in Utsjoki — Coloured 104

IX 1. Lapp Seides Made of Tree-stumps or Posts, roughly Carved in Human Form 110

      2. The Rastekaise Mountain with two Sacred Stones 110

X 1. Samoyed Stone Family-god Clothed and Lifted on a Tree Trunk 114

      2. Family Gods of the Ostiaks 114

XI Votiak Kuala or Sanctuary of the Family-gods . . . 118

XII 1. Votiak Case for the Voršud or " Luck-protector " . 122

      2. Votiak Village or Great Kuala 122

XIII Voršud Case Venerated by the Votiaks — Coloured . 126

XIV 1. Remains of an old Votiak Sacrificial Kuala . . . 130

      2. Voršud Case of the Votiaks, with other Sacrificial Apparatus 130

XV. 1. The Little Kudo or Dwelling of the Kudo-spirit within a Cheremiss Hut or " Great Kudo " . . 136

      2. Cheremiss Kudo 136

XVI 1. Ostiak Holy Place with Images of Gods or Spirits 140

      2. Ostiak Place of Sacrifice 140

XVII 1. Votiak Sacred Grove or Lud with Surrounding Fence and Gate 146

      2. Storehouse of the Ostiak Idols near Vasyagan . . . 146

PLATE   FACING PAGE

XVIII   1. Votiak Lud-kuala, formerly a Storeplace for Offerings, Sacrificial Vessels, etc.   150

          2. Votiak Lud-kuala, Birsk District   150

XIX   1. The Image of the Samoyed " Master of the Forest ", Carved on a Tree-trunk   156

        2. Cheremiss Horse-sacrifice to the Keremet-spirit in Time of Sickness   156

XX   The Aino Episode in Kalevala — Coloured . . .   192

XXI   1. Votiak Sacrifice to the River Buj after the Breaking-up of the Ice   200

        2. Votiak Sacrifice to the River Buj after the Breaking-up of the Ice   200

XXII   The Eastern Votiaks Sacrifice a White Goose to the Ilcaven God   204

XXIII   Ostiak Sacrifice of a White Animal to the Heaven-god   208

XXIV   The " World-pillar " of the Lapps   212

XXV   Sacrificial Meal among the Russian Karelians . .   216

XXVI   Old Sacrificial Grotto of the Thunder-god among the Finnish Lapps   220

XXVII   Drawings on a Lapp Drum   224

XXVIII   Drawings on a Torne-Lapp Drum   228

XXIX   Ostiak Sacrifice   232

XXX   Cheremiss Sacrifice to the Field-gods   242

XXXI   The " Feeding " of the Sickle among the Cheremiss — Coloured   248

XXXII   The Sacrifice-grove among the Cheremiss — Coloured   262

XXXIII   Cheremiss Sacrificial Loaves, Bowls and Coins at the Festival to Nature-gods   268

XXXIV   Cheremiss Sacrificial Prayer   272

XXXV   A Cheremiss Priest Praying to the Accompaniment of a Stringed Instrument — Coloured . . .   276

XXXVI   Cheremiss Priests at the Festival to Nature-gods . .   280

XXXVII   1. Lapp Shaman's Bowl-drum. Front, Back and Side Views   284

           2. Lapp Shaman's Sieve-drum. Front, Back and Side Views   284

XXXVIII   The Living Sacrifice-tree Bound with the Sacrifice Girdle — Coloured   288

PLATE   FACING PAGE

XXXIX Samoyed Shaman   294

XL An old Turkish Image and Memorial Stone in
    North Mongolia   302

XLI Boat-gods and Boats of the Yenisei Ostiaks . . .   308

XLII Tortoise-shell Shaped Stone Representing the
    World-bearing Tortoise   338

XLIII Old Turkish Memorial Image and Landscape in
    North Mongolia   352

XLIV Old Turkish Memorial Image in North Mongolia   372

XLV Phallus before a Mongol Monastery   396

XLVI 1. Dolgan Shaman Pillars Representing the Nine
    Storeys of Heaven   400

    2. Yakut Trees Representing the Storeys of Heaven   400

XLVII Hides of Buriat Offerings   410

XLVIII Shaman Drums from the Minusinsk District . . .   432

XLIX Shaman Drums from the Minusinsk District . . .   444

L Mongol Shaman with his Drum   452

LI Mongol Stone Heap (obo)   458

LII Dress and Drum of a Mongol Shaman   462

LIII Shattered Tomb of a Yakut Shaman   466

LIV Mongol Seer Prophesying from a Shoulder-blade .   470

LV Yenisei Ostiak Shaman with Drum. Front and
    Back Views   476

LVI Buriat Shaman-tomb and Ongons   482

LVII 1. Buriat Shaman with his Hobby-horses   488

    2. Hides of Buriat Shaman-animals   488

LVIII Dress of a Yakut Shaman. Back View   494

LIX 1. Breast Cloth of a Yakut Shaman   504

    2. Lebed-Tatar Shaman   504

    3. Drum of a Lebed-Tatar Shaman   504

LX 1. Dress of a Yakut Shaman (Bird Type). Front
    View   508

    2. Dress of a Yakut Shaman (Bird Type). Back
    View   508

LXI Dress of a Tungus Shaman (Bird Type). Front
    and Back Views   512

LXII Dress of a Yenisei Ostiak Shaman (Animal Type).
    Back View   518

LXIII Drum of a Yakut Shaman, Showing Inner and
    Outer Sides   522

ILLUSTRATIONS IN THE TEXT

FIGURE   PAGE

1   Ostiak Grave-house with Coffin of the Deceased   31
2   Graveyard in Russian Karelia   33
3   Lapp Christmas Custom   67
4   Lapp Seide-stone   101
5   Lapp Sacrificial Posts   108
6   Sun Ring   225
7   Moon Ring   227
8   Lapp Sacrificial Board of the Thunder God   230
9   Drawing of Heaven on Shaman Drums   250
10   Sacrificial Bread   267
11   Sacrificial Accessories   274
12   Shaman Hammer   289
13   Dolgan Shaman-pillars with Figures of Birds   334
14   Two-headed Birds of Iron which Hang on the Dress and
      Drum of the Yenisei-Ostiak Shaman   335
15   A Kalmuck World-picture   347
16   Signs of a Twelve-divisioned Period   437
17   The Tungus Thunder-bird   439
18   North-Siberian Tombs   480
19   Koori and Buču, Spirit-birds of a Golde Shaman   509
20   Dolgan Shaman-attributes and the World-tree with the
      Two-headed Lord of the World   511
21   Head-dress of a Yenisei-Ostiak Shaman (Reindeer or Stag
      Type)   513
22   Head-dress of the Soyot Shaman (Bird Type)   513
23   Tungus Shaman-boot (Bird Type)   513
24   Tatar Shaman (Bird Type) in Minusinsk District   515
25   Left Boot of Yenisei-Ostiak Shaman (Bear Type) with all
      the Bones of the Bear's Left Legs   517
26   Shaman Drum with Bird-shaped Hand-grip   520
27   Hobby-horse of a Buriat Shaman   521
28   Relics of a Buriat Shaman Found in the Earth   521

MAP

FACING PAGE

Finno-Ugrians, Siberians   2

FINNO-UGRIC MYTHOLOGY

BY

UNO HOLMBERG

PH.D.

DOCENT OF THE UNIVERSITY OF FINLAND, HELSINGFORS

INTRODUCTION

IN THE course of thousands of years the Finno-Ugric race, which once possessed a common home and a single language, was divided, for reasons which we no longer know, into a number of smaller peoples; and these, intermingled with alien stocks, and influenced by divergent civilizations, are found as widely separated from each other as are the Baltic and the River Ob, or as the Arctic Ocean and the Danube.

The nearest to the Finns, both in linguistic and in geographical aspects, are the Esthonians (about 1,250,000 in number), who live south of the Gulf of Finland; the Livonians, an almost extinct people who dwell on the northernmost point of Courland and give Livonia its name; the Votes (about 1000) and the Vepses (about 26,000), the former of whom inhabit western Ingermanland (now part of the Russian Government of Petrograd) in the vicinity of the city of Narva, while the latter are to be found south-west of Lake Onega. Among the Finns themselves, who number about 3,500,000, various linguistic groups are distinguishable: Tavastlanders in the west, Karelians in the east and along the Finno-Russian boundary, between Lake Ladoga and the White Sea, the Russian Karelians, the most northerly of whom seem to be mentioned in the old Norse sagas under the name of Bjarmar; the Ingrians of Ingermanland are also included among the Karelian stocks. In the seventeenth century Finnish Karelian families migrated as far as the Russian Governments of Novgorod and Tver; and some of the Finns are found in Scandinavia. At the beginning of our era all the peoples mentioned above — i.e., the so-called Baltic Finns — may still have spoken approximately the same language.

From many borrowed words we may infer that at an early period Finnish influence prevailed among the Lapps, who, about 30,000 in number, inhabit a wide region which extends from Trondhjem in Norway to the White Sea in the east, and who thus belong to Norway, Sweden, Finland, and Russia. Anthropologically, however, the Lapps appear to belong to a race different from the Finnish, although their language is held to be Finno-Ugric. Of the remaining Finno-Ugric peoples, those most nearly related to the Baltic Finns are the Mordvins, who number about 1,400,000, and whose language falls into two distinct dialects — Moksha and Erzya. The Mordvins are divided into a multitude of small clans throughout the vast region in inner and eastern Russia south of the great curve of the Volga, and along that river and its tributaries in the Governments of Tambov, Nizhniy-Novgorod, Pensa, Simbirsk, Saratov, Kazan, Samara, Ufa, and Orenburg. At an earlier date, however, the Mordvins appear to have inhabited a more uniform region, and one which was so far to the west that they were in contact with the Lithuanian peoples, as is shown by the Lithuanian loan-words in their language.

Next to the Mordvins, the nearest kindred of the Finns are the Cheremiss, who number about 400,000 and dwell for the most part along the central Volga in the Governments of Vyatka, Kazan, Nizhniy-Novgorod, and Kostroma. From the character of the regions which they inhabit, the Russians usually designate those living to the left of the Volga as "Meadow Cheremiss," and those to its right as "Hill Cheremiss." During the last century a portion of the Cheremiss also colonized a large district to the east on the Kama in the Governments of Ufa and Perm; and these are generally termed "Eastern Cheremiss."

Near to the Volga Finns is the dwelling-place of the Votiaks (about 450,000 in number), who, with their kinsfolk, the Siryans (to the number of about 300,000), constitute the so-called Permian linguistic stock. The former live chiefly in the Governments of Vyatka and Kazan, but have in part later migrated across the Kama into the Governments of Perm, Ufa and Samara. The latter dwell north of the Votiaks in the vast expanse along the rivers and streams of north-eastern Russia.

All the peoples whom we have thus far mentioned form a single great linguistic group, from which the so-called Ugrian stock seems to have separated at an early date. To them belong the Voguls (about 5000 in number) on both sides of the Ural in the Governments of Perm and Tobolsk, and also the Ostiaks (of whom there are about 19,000) on the Ob and its tributaries. Their nearest congeners are the Hungarians, or Magyars, who number about 10,500,000, and who, breaking off from the parent stock in the migrations of the peoples, wandered to their present land of Hungary toward the close of the ninth century.

Of all these Finno-Ugric peoples only the Hungarians, the Finns, and the Esthonians have been in a position to attain a superior degree of civilization. Some — especially the Lapps, the Ostiaks, and the Voguls — who live principally by fishing and the chase, or else are nomads wholly dependent on the reindeer for food and raiment, stand on the humble level of primitive folk. The same statement holds true of the Samoyeds, whose vast territory lies on the tundras along the Arctic Ocean, stretching from the region of Archangel in the west to Cape Chelyuskin, the northern-most promontory of Siberia, in the east. As their language clearly shows, they have been in closest relation to the Finno-Ugric peoples. In conformity with their principal dialects, several groups of Samoyeds are usually distinguished, the most numerous being the Yuraks, of whom there are about 12,000, and who dwell furthest to the west, between Archangel and the mouth of the Yenisei. East of them are the Yenisei Samoyeds and the Awam Samoyeds, who are but few in number and are a dying race. The tundras between the Ob and the Yenisei, as well as the forest regions in the northern part of the Government of Tomsk and the adjoining portions of the Governments of Tobolsk and Yenisei, are the home of the so-called Ostiak Samoyeds, of whom there are about 4000; and the northern slopes of the lofty Sayan Mountains are the habitat of the scanty remnants of the Kamass stock, which, though once so numerous, is gradually becoming either extinct or Tatarized.

Of the remaining Finno-Ugric peoples only the northern Siryans are nomads relying upon the reindeer for support; for all the others agriculture constitutes the principal means of livelihood, even though it is very primitive in many places.

In different regions and at various periods the Finno-Ugric stocks have been subject to heterogeneous civilizing influences, as is shown, among other evidences, by their language. The eastern branches have long lived in contact with the Turco-Tatars, the chief focus of civilization in the east having apparently been the Bolgar kingdom on the Volga, for the Turkish people which established itself on the central portion of that river about 600 A.D. sustained far-reaching connexions with all the nations that dwelt about it. Their descendants are the Chuvashes, the greater part of whom inhabit the Governments of Kazan, Simbirsk, Ufa, Saratov, etc.; and among them the investigator may find traces of the relatively high pagan civilization of the Volga Bolgars, as well as of their ancient religious concepts and customs. In 922 the Bolgars embraced Islam; but in 1236 the Tatars put an end to their power and for a time remained the ruling race in eastern Russia. Through this people Arabo-Muhammadan civilization made its way in some measure among the eastern Finno-Ugric stocks; but despite this, the ancient paganism of the Bolgars has left deep traces, particularly as regards the religious concepts and customs of the Cheremiss. At a later period Russian folk-belief also penetrated everywhere side by side with Russian colonization.

The Baltic Finns and Lapps, on the other hand, received

their deepest impress from the Teutonic race; and the Scandinavian Lapps, in particular, borrowed from their neighbours a host of religious beliefs and usages which actually cast light on the ancient Scandinavian religion as well. The Baltic Finns, moreover, came in close contact with the Lithuanians, traces of whose language, as already noted, are likewise found among the Mordvins; and these latter, at a time subsequent to that of their separation from the Baltic Finns, were influenced by some Indo-European people from whom they actually received their name for " God " (Pas, Pavas; cf. Sanskrit Bhagas, Old Persian Baga, Old Church Slavic Bogu). The ancestors of the Finno-Ugric peoples, however, were in contact with the forefathers of the Indo-European stocks at a very remote period, as is shown also by certain mythological designations; while numerous borrowed words demonstrate that the Magyars have been subjected to Turco-Tatar, Slavic, and (later) Teutonic influences.

Though all the Finno-Ugric peoples have now come into contact with Christianity, this religion is held only superficially in many places among the stocks that live in Russia. The ancient sacrificial customs still survive, despite the fact that in some localities the saints' days of the Christian Church are substituted for the pagan days of sacrifice. Occasionally — as among the Siryans, the Russian Karelians, and the Orthodox Esthonians — certain saints have begun to take the place of ancient gods in receiving propitiation by means of sacrificial gifts. A like custom prevailed among the Finns during the Roman Catholic period, and even later. At a very early date the Magyars, the Baltic Finns, and the Siryans were led to accept the Christian faith; but among the Volga Finns missionary activity did not begin until after the fall of Kazan in 1552, and first began to bear visible fruit in the eighteenth century. Even at the present day there are some thousands of unbaptized Cheremiss and Votiaks, part of whom (at least among the former) cling with great tenacity to the beliefs and customs which they have inherited from their fathers. Baptism of the Ostiaks, Voguls and Samoyeds began in the eighteenth century. Though only a small number of unbaptized are still to be found among the Ugrians, nevertheless the sacrificial rites of paganism survive in many places; and it was not until the eighteenth century that Christianity gained firm footing among the Lapps.

Simultaneously with missionary labours, interest was awakened in recording and describing the ancient heathen beliefs and customs of the people. Of these accounts the least complete are those which deal with the religions of the peoples that were earliest converted to Christianity. Such is the state of affairs, for example, with the Magyars, who began to surrender their ancient faith about the year 1000; whereas the Ostiaks and the Voguls of the present day may throw light upon the early religion of the Ugric stock. One of the most important of the oldest sources is G. Novitskiy's *A Brief Description of the Ostyak People*, written in 1715, but not published till 1884. The foremost collectors and investigators in this domain have been the Finn M. A. Castrén and the Hungarians A. Reguly and B. Munkácsi, who have published large works in Hungarian and German; the German O. Finsch, the Russians N. L. Gondatti and S. Patkanov, and the Finns K. F. Karjalainen and A. Kannisto, who lived for several years among the Ostiaks and the Voguls respectively, engaged in linguistic studies. Castrén also collected data for the elucidation of Samoyed religion; a little older source is a description of the Yuraks by the Russian Archimandrite Veniamin, published in 1850. Concerning the latter a young Finnish linguist, T. V. Lehtisalo, has gathered new material. In similar fashion another Finn, K. Donner, has undertaken the task of investigating the language, customs, etc., of the eastern Samoyeds.

The oldest accounts of the religion of the Siryans are contained in the biography of their apostle, St. Stephen, who died in 1396, the chief importance of this lying in the fact that for many subsequent centuries no one made any notes whatever regarding their religion during a period when the Siryans were adopting Orthodox doctrine and Russian folk-beliefs in ever increasing measure. Here also the collecting of the ancient beliefs is still in progress, the foremost name in this connexion being that of the indefatigable Siryan scholar, V. Nalimov, who has sought to gather together such scanty remnants as may yet be obtained in obscure districts.

We possess far more knowledge of the ancient faith of the Votiaks, the kinsfolk of the Siryans, although the earliest sources date only from the eighteenth century. During recent decades the literature on this subject has become relatively abundant. The most valuable authorities are the Finns T. G. Aminoff and Yrjö Wichmann, the Russians N. Pervuchin, B. G. Gavrilov, G. Vereščagin, P. Bogayevskij and J. Vasiljev, the work of the scholar last named having also appeared in German, the language in which Max Buch wrote his ethnographical account of the Votiaks.

Records of the Cheremiss religion were gathered by A. Olearius during his travels in 1636, and of the numerous studies which have been subsequently made in various districts the most valuable is from the pen of the Cheremiss G. Jakovlev and V. M. Vasiljev.

The ancient faith of the Mordvins fell for the most part into oblivion until modern scholarship discovered it. As early as 1740 and the following years the Mordvins adopted Orthodoxy, but it was not until the middle of the nineteenth century that valuable and trustworthy accounts of the vanishing remnants of their paganism began to appear. This religion has been described by the Russians P. Melnikov, V. Mainov and others; Mainov's work, which was also published in French, has been used by scholars, although it is unreliable to the highest degree. By awakening interest among the people themselves, the Finnish linguist H. Paasonen has endeavoured to do all that is still possible by way of collecting material and elucidating the ancient Mordvinian religion; nor should we forget the Russian scholar I. N. Smirnov, who, in his great ethnographical treatises on the Cheremiss, Votiaks, Siryans and Mordvins, has sought to gather whatever was then known regarding their religious life.

The character and the development of the ancient faith of the Volga Finns receive some measure of elucidation from the religious beliefs, customs, and usages of the Chuvashes, hence a knowledge of their religion is of great moment in Finno-Ugric studies. The most valuable account of their religious life is afforded in the works of the Russian V. Magnitskij and of the Hungarian G. Mészarós.

The Lapps being the last of the western stocks to adopt Christianity, we possess relatively voluminous accounts of their paganism. The most important contribution was collected by missionaries in the Norwegian and Swedish Lapp districts toward the close of the seventeenth and the beginning of the eighteenth century; and during recent years all the chief sources have been published by K. B. Viklund, J. Qvigstad, E. Reuterskiöld and I. Fellmann. Certain earlier investigators, however, had already gathered accounts of this heathen faith for their descriptions, the first being J. Schefferus's *Lapponia* (1672), which was translated into several languages; while somewhat later E. J. Jessen (1767) and Knud Leem (1767) issued their well-known delineations. The abundance of material has been still further enriched in our own time, and has induced a number of scholars to describe the ancient religion of the Lapps, notably J. A. Friis, G. von Düben, J. Fritzner, Axel Olrik, E. Reuterskiöld, etc.

The oldest records of the early faith of the Esthonians and Livonians are preserved in the Chronicle of Henry the Lett, written at the commencement of the thirteenth century; and the chief later sources are J. Gustlaff's description of the sanctuary at Wōhanda (1644) and Joh. Forselius' collection of the ancient beliefs, customs, and usages of the Esthonians, published in German by J. W. Boecler (1685), the language in which F. J. Wiedemann issued a general survey of Esthonian religion. Very recently a voluminous and important collection of folklore has been made by J. Hurt, M. I. Eisen, O. Kallas, and others.

The very oldest reports of the ancient religion of the Finns are extremely brief. In an Old Norse saga recounting the expedition of certain Vikings to conquer the land of the Bjarmar along the White Sea in 1026 we find the first occurrence of the word Jómali, which is plainly identical with the Finnish Jumala (" God "); but the earliest record of real value concerning the Finnish heathen pantheon dates only from the beginning of modern times. To his translation of the Psalter (1551) Bishop Agricola prefixed a versified introduction which included a short list of the old gods of the Tavastlanders and Karelians; and for a long period this catalogue constituted the sole source until, in the seventeenth century, the historian H. G. Porthan began to seek illustration of the ancient civilization and religion of the Finns from Finnish magic songs, in which he believed that he might find trustworthy survivals of Finnish paganism. With the help of these songs, C. E. Lencqvist wrote his *De superstitione veterum Fennorum theoretica et practica* (1782), and Christfrid Ganander his *Mythologia Fennica* (1789), which long remained the most important and the most utilized source for investigation along these lines. An interest in comparative study was already aroused in Ganander, who gave consideration to the Lapp religion, which, he was convinced, would also elucidate the Finnish, and for certain names of deities he even sought to find analogues in Scandinavian mythology.

Real depth of interest in all Old Finnish investigation was, however, first awakened by Elias Lönnrot's publication of the Finnish epic of the *Kalevala* (in 1836 and 1849); the elucidation of the ancient religion of the Finns was the task of the

famous linguist, Castrén. Before the completion of the work
which he had planned, Castrén had travelled extensively
among the Lapps, Samoyeds, and Siberians; and during this
time it became clear to him that a correct comprehension of
the religious beliefs and customs of the ancient Finns required a knowledge of the religions and the cults of the other
stocks belonging to this family. His work on Finnish mythology appeared first after his death in 1853, and the chief
merit of the contribution is that it constitutes the earliest attempt at a comparative study of Finno-Ugric religion.

Castrén's presentation of Finnish mythology is based chiefly
on the *Kalevala*, which is compiled from Finnish folk-songs.
With all the caution with which its collector, Elias Lönnrot,
endeavoured to proceed, it is plain that the popular songs
which he employed, and which were later recorded in countless variants, must themselves form the basis of all investigation. Yet even in the study of this purely popular material
due account must be taken of the manner in which it developed during its centuries of migration and extension, whether
from western Finland or from Esthonia (by way of Ingermanland) to eastern Finland and the Government of Archangel,
where we find the most highly evolved and the most com-
posite variants. In the utilization of this material the geographical method, which was discovered by Julius Krohn, and
which was later applied by Finnish scholars to the study of
the national sagas as well, must be applied. We must also
note that most of the Finnish magic songs and a large part of
the epic poems in the *Kalevala* arose in the Middle Ages, during the Roman Catholic period, hence they can be used for
the interpretation of pagan times only under the restrictions
of a vigilant and critical caution.

Some of the names of heroes in the *Kalevala* were con-
strued by Castrén as having been originally appellations of
divinities, and his view long prevailed. More recently, however, the historical explanation has again been adopted. For

example, the old bard Väinämöinen has been interpreted as
a sage or hero whose appellation, like the names of other
heroes mentioned in the *Kalevala*, may also be used to designate a giant or a divine being; and in like manner the smith
Ilmarinen presents a contamination of the name of the Finno-
Ugric air-god, Ilmari (Votiak Inmar), with the name of the
hero Ismaroinen, who figures in the folk-songs of Ingermanland as the maker of the Golden Maid.

With the aid of newer and richer sources Julius Krohn
planned the preparation of a comparative presentation of all
the beliefs and usages of the Finno-Ugric race; but at his
premature death only four chapters had been completed, these
being published in Finnish in 1894 by his son, Kaarle Krohn,
under the title *The Pagan Worship of the Finnish Stock.*
This already antiquated work has been translated into Hungarian, with some additional material, by the Magyar scholar
A. Bán. Among later comparative presentations mention
should be made of M. Varonen's *Ancestor-Worship among the
Ancient Finns*, published only in Finnish, H. Paasonen's *Über
die ursprünglichen Seelenvorstellungen bei den finnisch-ugrischen Völkern und die Benennung der Seele in ihren Sprachen,*
and the present writer's *Die Wassergottheiten der finnisch-
ugrischen Völker.*

During the last few years, the publication of complete descriptions of the religions of the different Finnish stocks has
begun at the initiative of Kaarle Krohn. Under the collaboration of several specialists, the following volumes have already
appeared in Finnish: Kaarle Krohn's *Religion of the Finnish
Songs* (1914–15), the present writer's *Religion of the Permians* (1914), *Religion of the Cheremiss* (1914), and *Religion of the Lapps* (1915), and K. F. Karjalainen's *Religion
of the Ugrians* (1918).

example, the old bard Väinämöinen has been interpreted as a sage or hero whose appellation, like the names of other heroes mentioned in the Kalevala, may also be used to designate a giant or a divine being; and in like manner the smith Ilmarinen presents a contamination of the name of the Finno-Ugric air-god, Ilmaz (Vogul Jumer), with the name of the hero Ismaroinen, who figures in the folk-songs of Ingermanland as the maker of the Golden Maid.

With the aid of newer and richer sources, Julius Krohn planned the preparation of a comparative presentation of all the beliefs and usages of the Finno-Ugric race; but at his premature death only four chapters had been completed, these being published in Finnish in 1894 by his son, Kaarle Krohn, under the title The Pagan Worship of the Finnish Stock. This already antiquated work has been translated into Hungarian, with some additional material, by the Magyar scholar A. Bán. Among later comparative presentations mention should be made of M. Varonen's Vainajain-Palvelus among the ancient Finns, published only in Finnish; H. Paasonen's Über die ursprünglichen Seelenvorstellungen bei den finnisch-ugrischen Völkern und die Benennung der Seele in ihren Sprachen, and the present writer's Die Wassergottheiten der finnisch-ugrischen Völker.

During the last few years, the publication of complete descriptions of the religions of the different Finnish stocks has begun at the initiative of Kaarle Krohn. Under the collaboration of several specialists, the following volumes have already appeared in Finnish: Kaarle Krohn's Religion of the Finnish Songs (1914–15), the present writer's Religion of the Permians (1914), Religion of the Cheremiss (1914), and Religion of the Lapps (1915), and K. F. Karjalainen's Religion of the Ugrians (1918).

-Ugrians
Siberians

Tiaks

Yenisei-

Ostiaks

edes

Dolgans

Tungus

Yakuts

Yukagirs

Chuktchee

Koriaks

Kamtchadals

Tungus

Giliaks

Buriats

tars

Tungus

Goldes

Mandshu

Dahurs

mucks

Turks

mucks

Uigurs

Mongols

FINNO-UGRIC MYTHOLOGY

CHAPTER I

THE BELIEF IN SOULS

THE BELIEF of the Finno-Ugric people regarding the soul presents a very primitive concept. According to the Lapps, life does not cease altogether at death, but in some form continues as long as the skeleton remains, an example of this conviction being afforded, for instance, by their bear-feast; and in like manner they hold that the gods let new flesh grow on the sacrificial victim's bones, all of which are preserved with great care.[1] If we may draw inferences from the sacrificial ceremonies, this belief was formerly general throughout the Finno-Ugric stock. As an instance of the concept which holds that the soul vanishes when the body is annihilated we may cite the Vogul custom whereby, lest the bear should do grave harm to any one, the injured man, instead of worshipping the animal, endeavours to free himself from it by completely destroying all parts of its body. Charuzin, who describes this usage, remarks that by it they purpose " to kill the victim's soul together with its body."[2]

This concept is likewise found in the cult of the dead. In his account of the burial rites of the Pite Lapps the missionary Graan records that for several years after the death of any of their number they crumbled barley bread into small bits and strewed it on the graves " until the sinking of the grave-mound showed that the body had decayed."[3] Among the Ostiaks, in like manner, the belief has been found that after the body has decayed the dead no longer survive.[4] Even at a very late period the Ingermanland Finns were wont to go to the burial places to weep and to carry food to the graves of their tribesmen so long as it was conceivable that the bodies had not yet crumbled; for after that they believed that "the soul itself ceases to exist."[5] If the deceased is supposed to be dangerous, the corpse is cut in pieces or even burned to ashes; and in a village in the Circle of Birsk the Votiaks pursued a like course after the lapse of several years in the case of a death which the sorcerers declared to have given rise to a severe epidemic. To this day the Ostiak Samoyeds fear certain corpses which are believed to go about at night and injure the living, though they become powerless as soon as the sun rises. A whole host of stories tells of contests between such corpses and living men; but they may be prevented from rising out of their graves by being pierced with a stake and pinned fast to the ground.[6]

Side by side with this belief in a soul inseparably connected with the body, the Finno-Ugrians seem to have held that each limb and organ likewise had its separate soul. Accordingly, at a sacrifice a small portion of all the parts of the victim's body was taken and dedicated, together with the bones, to the deity. Souls or (more properly) soul-powers are hidden especially in the most important organs, such as the heart, the liver, and the blood; and the circulation of the blood has obviously given rise to the Cheremiss belief that the "soul" or the "life" (*tšon*) can wander about within the body. If a blow which reaches some part of the body proves to be mortal, the "soul," according to this view, has been in that portion just at the fatal instant; but even though a man's skull were fractured, the Cheremiss maintain that death would not ensue if the "soul" chanced not to be in the head at the moment.[7] The concept of the material character of the qualities of the soul is also evidenced by the belief that one may acquire them for his own by devouring the organs containing

the soul-qualities of another. Gondatti states that the ancient
Vogul heroes ate the hearts and livers of their slain enemies
"that their strength might be transferred to their own bodies
and that the foe might never again be able to rise from the
dead."[8] Beliefs regarding the potencies hidden in the heart
recur in a Chronicle of 889, which states that the Hungarians
cut the captives' hearts in pieces and ate them as some sort
of remedy; and to this day the sacrificial priest of the Cheremiss prays God to protect men against "those who cut out
the heart and the liver." The same belief was doubtless held
by the forefathers of the Finns, for among their Esthonian
kinsmen it was still flourishing in the thirteenth century, since
the Sakkala peasants are said to have torn the heart from the
breast of a living Danish Crusader, and after roasting it, to
have divided it among themselves and eaten it "in order to
be brave against the Christians." By drinking another man's
blood the Voguls and others believe that soul-powers pass
from one body into another.[9] Even in such insignificant parts
of the body as the hair, nails, and teeth a soul (or soul-power)
is believed to lie concealed. How else could the means of
guarding the soul against falling into evil hands be explained?
Novitskiy expressly relates that a Vogul sacrificial priest
warned his people against the Russian missionaries in the following words: "Take care, my friends . . . when they start
to cut your hair, they cut off your souls." In this connection,
it may be mentioned that the Ostiaks believed that by scalping
an enemy they could prevent his ghost from walking.[10] Even
those objects which have been in contact with a man sustain a
certain relation to the soul. Among causes of illness the Lapps
recognize the power of a dweller in the underworld to take
to himself some article of attire which has been in contact
with the sick, such as cap, gloves, or boots;[11] and from this
is deduced the magical theory of *pars pro toto* which finds
application likewise in rites of sacrifice.

In close relation to the remains of the deceased stands his

shape, or shadow, which can occasionally free itself from the body even during life. Of a man who is unconscious the Cheremiss says that his " shape " or " shadow " (*ört*) has left him; and in like manner, if any one gives him a severe fright, he declares: " Thou drivest mine *ört* away." If a Cheremiss dreams of a city, he is convinced that his *ört* has wandered thither by night; otherwise, he argues, he could not have seen the city exactly as it is. Dreaming is also called " the *ört's* wandering "; and when the man awakes, his *ört* returns to his body.[12]

The *ört* of the Cheremiss corresponds to the *urt* of the Votiaks. If the *urt* does not succeed in coming back to its abode before the man wakes, he falls ill, is pale, and begins to pine away, so that a sleeper must not be aroused suddenly.[13] In general the disappearance of the soul is regarded as a cause of grave illness, and in such a contingency it is advisable to have recourse to a magician or shaman in order that he may seek the lost soul and bring it back to the body. Sometimes it happens that the " soul " of the dying goes to the nether world, but returns after a while; and then the man recovers. Thus an Ostiak song tells of a hero who, in battle, received a sword-stroke on his head and lost consciousness. For a time his " shadow " ascended to heaven, only to return when his dead brother's " shadow " informed him that his hour was not yet come.[14] A very wide-spread belief holds that the shaman's " shadow " can go to the underworld to seek aid there.

The closeness of the connexion between a man's body and his " shadow " is shown by an account of Lapp shamanism which dates from the thirteenth century. This states, among other matters, that during a shaman's journey in the nether world a hostile " shadow " struck out the stomach of his " shadow," the mishap being clearly visible in the magician's real body, which was lying in the tent;[15] and several similar instances will be cited in a subsequent chapter on the shamans.

Death does not in the least sever the bond of union between the " soul " and the corpse. When asked why the bones of the sacrificial victim are not broken, the Finnish Lapps answered: " On certain nights the victims which we have offered wander as ' shadows ' from burial-place to burial-place together with the folk of the underworld." [16] The general concept is that after death the " shadow " takes up its abode where the body has been buried.

In Finno-Ugric belief man has also another soul which can release itself from the body, and which is called " breath." The source of this concept is to be found in the last expiration of the dying. At death the Ostiak *lil*, Vogul *lili*, Hungarian *lekek*, Siryan *lol*, Votiak *lul* (" expiration," " soul "), and the Esthonian *leil* (" expiration," " soul," " steam," cf. Finnish *löyly*, " bath-vapour ") leaves its abode through the mouth or nostrils; and " the breath's departure " is a common synonym for death. Obviously the " breath " was originally understood to be simply a vital function which revealed itself as respiration or vapour; and Nalimov states that, in Siryan belief, at death the *lol* evaporates in the air like vapour.

The Finnish stocks are convinced that when the soul liberates itself from the body, it can appear not only in a quasi-human shape — which is the form which it most frequently takes — but may also assume some other guise, often that of an animal. Nalimov has noted a Siryan tradition which tells how, while a woman slept, her *lol* came forth from its abode and in the form of a little mouse danced about on her breast. For a time her mouth was hidden by the coverlet; but the soul again transformed itself into vapour and thus re-entered the body, so that the sleeper could wake up. [17] The Votiaks believe that one of the forms in which the soul appears during sleep is that of the bat; and an old Votiak declared that the reason why these creatures are never seen by day is because men are then awake; they appear only at night, when men are asleep. If a bat approaches any one, it is a sign that it is in reality the soul of some kinsman or acquaintance; and the old man just mentioned even related a tradition that the bat is, as a matter of fact, a soul-bird. " A man went to rest, but his companions sat up in the yard. They saw how a bat flew round certain places; and when the sleeper awoke, they asked him what he had dreamed. The man declared that in his slumber he had wandered to the very places where the bat had flown, and from this his comrades inferred that the bat which they had seen was the soul of the sleeping man." Sometimes the soul also appears in the form of a little grey butterfly. In the Circle of Birsk the present writer heard it said that when the *urt* leaves a man's body because of severe fright, the services of a witch are sought, and she begins to spy after it with a white cloth in her hand. After she has hunted everywhere, she finally notices a little grey butterfly, and when she has caught it in her cloth, she takes it into the room and at night binds both cloth and butterfly about the sufferer's neck. On the following morning observation of the shapes assumed by molten tin dropped into water determines whether the captive soul-butterfly is really the sick man's *urt*.

In like manner the soul of a sleeping man moves about as a butterfly in a tradition recorded by the present writer from the Circle of Mamadysh. " Two men went to the forest to cut down trees, and at midday, while they were resting, one of them fell asleep, whereupon his comrade saw the *lul* issue from his mouth in the form of a butterfly and go to a pail of water which they had with them in the woods. From the water it flew to a cavity in a linden, thence back to the water-vessel, and from there to the sleeper's mouth. Waking from his slumber, he said to his companion: ' I was asleep and dreamed that I floated over a river on whose farther shore was a tree in which was a hollow containing many pieces of gold.' After finishing their work the men returned home, but a little later the comrade, who had seen where the sleeper's soul moved about the tree, went by night to the forest, sought out the tree, and there found a number of coins." [18]

The "souls" of the dead have power of motion like those of the living. When a little grey butterfly was seen to come in by the window during the memorial feast in honour of a Votiak child's father, its mother said to it: "His soul has come in the form of a butterfly." It is also believed that the souls of the departed may find concealment in the guise of other sorts of insects, this explaining the Cheremiss custom that whenever many caterpillars begin to appear in the grain-fields, sacrifice is made to such of the departed as have died without leaving kinsfolk. A belief in soul-mice among this same people is implied by a similar offering which is given if many mice begin to be found in the yard. [19] According to the Ostiaks, the deceased transforms himself into a beetle and is thus revealed to the living; and a like idea seems to have been known to the Finns, as is evident from a peculiar custom. Maidens are wont to take beetles in their hands and ask them whither they go to wed, hither or thither or "in the swart earth's bosom." If then the beetle flies to the churchyard, it is an omen of death. Similar beliefs occur among other European peoples.

Certain Finno-Ugric peoples are also convinced that the departed appear as birds, and the Lapps tell how a dead man who had been buried on a small island and who haunted it by day flew across the water in the form of a great bird. [20] Like wicked men the dead may likewise manifest themselves as wolves; and when the Votiaks drive away spirits which roam about at Easter, one of their cries is: "Go, wolves, go!"

"Souls" may also be seen in other guise than that of animals, and the belief is very general that a man's soul may wander around as a whirlwind. In the Circle of Birsk the present writer heard the Cheremiss tell how a wayfarer hurled his knife into such an eddy, which, with the knife, immediately vanished. The man continued on his journey till evening came, when he was about to pass the night in a hut along the road. There, to his amazement, an old man sat with a knife in his cheek; whereupon the traveller forthwith recognized his own knife and perceived that the master of the bothie was the old man who had wandered about as an eddy of wind. The soul of the living as well as of the dead can likewise fly around as a "fire-serpent," in other words, as a meteor. According to the Cheremiss its course can be stayed by tearing off the wristband of one's shirt or the band of one's lime-bark shoes, or by splitting a wooden pitch-fork, together with which the meteor falls to the ground and is changed back into the man who flew about as the "fire-snake." In Siryan belief the soul (*ort*) of the departed may even manifest itself as a blue flame burning on the ground (*ort-bi*, "*ort's* fire").

Shadow-souls may sometimes lose their original meaning by being transformed into the *Doppel-gänger* or tutelary genius of the person in question. Thus the Siryan *ort*, in the form in which the popular mind now most usually conceives it, recalls the guardian spirit of the man rather than the real shadow-soul. Every one has an *ort* which constantly dwells near its protégé, acting as a guardian-spirit; it appears in dreams, generally in the shape of the person in question, and occasionally pinches blue spots in one's skin. In some places its abode is believed to be wholly separate from the man, whence the assertion is made, for example, that it has its home in birds. Yet one of the proofs that the *ort* was originally nothing else than the man's "shadow" is found in the belief that, after his death, his soul is blended with his *ort*, so that both form one and the same being. It is further believed that the *ort* of the deceased reveals itself in the form of the departed for forty days after death, and then vanishes.[21] As a portent of someone's death the *ort* manifests itself chiefly in the shape of a bird; and the same belief is found among the Voguls: "The *urt* lives in the forest. When a human being must die, his *urt* cries out; when a little child comes to his last hour, the *urt* speaks with a child's voice; if an adult passes away, the *urt's* voice is that of an adult. Its exterior is parti-coloured, and its wings resemble those of a bat." Shamans can always see it near them. Should any one hear its call, he turns to it with the words: " If one of my kins-folk is to die, draw thou nigh to me." If some relative is actually the person in question, the *urt* approaches the inquirer; but otherwise it withdraws from him. According to Friis, the Norse Lapps called such a bird, heard by night lamenting with a human voice, a Šuöje-lodde (" Šuöje-bird "), the word Sueje being used in the Swedish Lapmark to denote the shaman's " tutelary genius," the appellation having apparently meant primarily " shadow." The spectres of shamans are especially liable to metamorphosis.[22]

The tutelary genius of a man is called Haltia (" Ruler ") by the Finns; and each individual has his own, which pre-cedes him. A man might be blessed with such a potent Haltia that, for example, it would reach home a little earlier than the man himself, whose approach it announced with clamour and crash. A man's Varjohaltia (" Shadow-ruler ") could inform him beforehand of coming events, as, e.g., whether he would reap a good or a bad harvest. It was be-lieved in some districts that a child made its own Haltia when it was three days old; before the expiration of that time it was dangerous to leave the infant alone, for a changeling might be substituted in its stead. That the Haltia manifested itself in the form of the culprit is obvious from such phrases as " it was not he, but his Haltia," or " the dead themselves do not walk, it is their Haltias which appear as ghosts."

The Saattaja (" guide ") — an expression which is com-paratively rare — and the Onni (" fortune ") seem to denote precisely the same being as the Haltia; and a man's " fortune," which might be propitious or the reverse, never left him till death. Like the Haltia the " fortune " precedes the man and announces his coming. When any mischance happened on the road, the "fortune" warned its owner as he returned homeward, his ears beginning to ring, or his eyes or nose to itch, etc. The Haltia of the Finns has its analogue in the Rådare or Rå ("ruler") of the Swedes, and their Saattaja finds its counterpart in the Fylgja of the Scandinavians.[23]

The word employed by the Finno-Ugrians and peoples influenced by them to denote "shadow-soul" often means originally "shadow," "appearance," and "image." When the Yurak Samoyeds make images of the sun, moon, or human beings, they call them "shadows"; and the Vogul term for a man's "soul" (*is*, Finnish *itse*, "self") is also employed when they speak, for instance, of the "shadow" of a tree or of a house. The Ostiaks call their "earthly gods" and the wooden figures of these deities by a name (*tongk*) which originally meant "shadow"; and the word *haamu*, which signifies "shadow-soul" in Finnish, means "form," "figure" in Lappish and "countenance" in Mordvinian; while in Cheremiss the Tatar loan-word *tys* is occasionally employed to denote the "shadow-soul," though properly it signifies "countenance" or "image," as when it is applied, for example, to the leaden figure representing the sacrificial animal, as we shall see later. The Mordvinian word for "soul" (*tšopatsa*) is also applied to the image of a god.

If "soul" or "image" were thus an identical concept, it would be natural to infer that the prototype would be intimately affected by whatever happened to the image. Originally the Finno-Ugric peoples were extremely cautious in regard to the delineation of themselves, and to this day many of them are most reluctant to permit themselves to be photographed or otherwise pictured. A certain anxiety also lurks in the words which a Cheremiss girl repeats when she sees herself in a mirror: "Take not from me my appearance or image"; and this fear is especially associated with showing a mirror to a small child. By injuring their enemy's image the Lapps believed that they could cause their foe himself to feel pain. In the notes of the missionary Randulf we read the following account: "When the Lapp wishes to injure a man with whom he is angry, whether he dwells close by or far away, he employs for this purpose a little bow made of reindeer horn, together with the arrows belonging to it, one blunt and one pointed. If he desires to make his enemy's hand, foot, or other member useless, he shoots the blunt arrow into the corresponding part of the body of an image supposed to represent the person in question; but if his intention is rather to cause an open wound or a constant subcutaneous pain, he shoots the sharp arrow into the relevant portion of the effigy." [24]

Generally speaking, persons of superior importance, such as primal ancestors, shamans, and heroes, survive their bodies in images or "shadows" which are made after them.

Just as men speak of the "shadow" or "soul" of a human being or of an animal, so various things are supposed to possess a "soul," which can free itself from the object to which it belongs. Thus, for example, everything which grows has its "soul." According to the Votiaks, the "soul" (*urt*) of the corn can assume the form of a little butterfly, precisely like the soul of a man; and the Cheremiss speak, furthermore, of the "soul" (*ört*) of the earth, fire, water, etc. When "souls" vanish out of the earth, it can no longer produce vegetation; if the "soul" of the water disappears, it begins to sicken and is turbid and nauseous to the taste; and if a man drinks of such water, he falls ill. Even the bothie or hut has its "soul," which flees if men are noisy and quarrelsome in the room. "You are driving the 'soul' of my bothie away," cries the Cheremiss if any one commits a breach of the peace in his home. When the "soul" has fled, the bothie is no longer "happy," and "life is heavy there"; while no "soul" is found in a deserted, uninhabited house. In the fantasy of the Cheremiss the "bothie-soul (*pört-ört*) cannot assume any shape whatsoever. When asked what he means by the "soul" of the bothie, he answers that it is not any distinct entity, but the "luck," "joy," or "health" of the hut. Both farm-yard and threshing-floor have their "souls." When the former possesses it, "the cow-yard re-joices; the cattle thrive and multiply." Of the latter it is said that "where the 'soul' flourishes, even small quantities of seed yield a blessing; but if it leaves the place, great heaps of seed wholly lack their proper usefulness." If no seed is found on the threshing-floor, neither is any "soul" dis-coverable there.

According to the belief of the Finno-Ugrians, the very smallest things have a "soul." This explains the custom of breaking objects intended for the dead, such as wooden spoons and bowls, clay pots, and the like, "so that the departed may take them with him to the invisible world." Doubtless this reflects the concept that even things have an invisible part which is separated from the visible by being broken; in other words, an object must be deprived of its life in order that its "soul" may leave it. Or, as in Mordvinian usage, the ob-ject which is given to the dead may simply be scraped with a knife, its "soul" being thus released. At the offerings in their groves the Cheremiss violently shake the objects em-ployed for the occasion; and when we recollect that the sacrificial victim which shivers, like the man who is frightened, loses its "shadow," we understand what beliefs are connected with this peculiar custom. Just as there is a "tutelary genius" of a man's "shadow," so there is a "nature god" of a "nature soul"; and water, earth, forest, tree, house, and the like possess a Haltia, just as we have seen the Finns apply the term to the *Doppel-gänger* of a man.

The name must also be reckoned in the category of belief in souls, and this explains, among other matters, why the Votiaks call the rite of choosing a name "the seeking of the soul" (*urt kuton*).[25] When a child cries a great deal or falls ill, or when a "mark" caused by the dead rises on its skin, this is interpreted to mean that it has chanced to receive a wrong name. To remedy this, sundry magic ceremonies are employed to determine what new name the child should receive in order that it may thrive and recover. From the names which are enumerated during these rites, and which have usually been borne by departed forefathers, the inference may be drawn that the "soul" or "spirit" which is sought for the child is the soul of some ancestor. That this was actually true in the beginning is shown by the corresponding beliefs and ceremonies of the Lapps. They held that a pregnant woman could indicate, either in dreams or through shamans, which of the kindred dead was willing to live anew in the child. The name was given by an old woman, who baptized (a later custom) the child, saying: "I baptize thee with the name of such and such a departed one. Mayest thou have the same fortune and happiness that he (or she) had in this world." In addition they believed that, with the name, the child received the "guardian spirit" which had once belonged to the former bearer of the name. "Guardian spirits" could also appear in visible form, as in that of a fish. Sacrifice should be offered to the dead whose name was given to the child. If the right name was not immediately found, the appellation of the child might afterwards, in case of sickness, be changed several times.[26] According to the Northern Ostiaks, after a number of years the spirit of the deceased could be born again to earthly life in a child belonging to his kindred; and then the name of the dead man must be found in order that the child might thrive and be strong.[27] Side by side with this custom another is met with among the Eastern Finno-Ugrian peoples, according to which a name was given to a child from the first object or phenomenon to attract the attention of the parents or the midwife at its birth.[28]

That the giving of the name was a custom of immemorial

antiquity among the Finno-Ugric peoples is shown by the fact that the word for "name" is common to them all, so that the Finnish term *nimi*, is actually used also in Samoyed (*nim*). Probably it is the same word which also occurs in the Indo-European languages (*naman, ὄνομα, nomen, name,* etc.).

CHAPTER II

DEATH AND BURIAL

AMONG all the Finno-Ugric peoples, the customs and beliefs connected with death, though varying locally, will be found to possess certain general affinities.

The most significant ceremonies arise out of a desire to do everything possible for the departed on their last journey, and from precautionary measures by the living against the dead, as these are believed to seek companions with whom to enter the other world.

Immediately the " breath had departed," the Finns opened the smoke-outlets, in Russian Karelia the boards forming the roof of their chimneyless houses even being lifted three times, so that the soul might quicker fly away. The Esthonian custom was to open the doors. If a wind arose while someone lay dying, it was called " the wind of the dead." [1] The Permian peoples believed that on the death of a shaman, a storm was sure to arise. [2]

When a death occurs, the relatives of the deceased gather round the body. Forgiveness is implored of the dead one. The Cheremiss say: " Forgive me, be not angry with me if I have used hard words against thee." [3] Probably after a Russian custom, the Mordvins and the Ingrians, etc., immediately life has departed, place a bowl of water on the window-sill, " so that the soul can cleanse itself." [4] More general is the custom of cutting the throat of a hen when death occurs. When this is done by the Chuvash, they say: " soul for soul and body for body " or also " this hen shall lead thy soul." The Eastern Cheremiss slaughter the fowl first at the gate, as they follow the dead to its grave, and they

observe whether the hen remains within the courtyard or flies
headless out into the road.   The former is accounted a sign
that a new death will soon occur in the house.   At the spot
where the hen is killed, it is believed that the deceased meets
with the spirits of his departed relatives, which come forth to
meet the new arrival.   The reason for the actual act of
slaughtering has been interpreted in different ways.   Some
say that the hen gathers together in the other world the
nails of the departed, which have been scattered about in this.
In other places, it is the custom to say to the dead at the
slaughtering: "Save with this blood thine own blood from
death!"   With the first drops of the hen's blood, the Cheremiss paint the eyebrows of the dead.   The fowl is not prepared for food, but is left lying on the road for dogs to feast
on.[5]   A later custom is the preparing of the flesh of the
fowl, slaughtered at the moment of death, for the funeral
repast.   A relic of the hen-sacrifice is found among the Finns
in Savolax, who, when the coffin is being borne away, cast a
living hen on to it, to prevent the dead from taking the
"poultry-luck" away with it.[6]

The dead must be escorted as soon as possible to the peace
of the grave.   The first service consists of the washing of the
body of the dead, a practice followed by all the tribes, though
it cannot be regarded as a purely Finno-Ugric custom.   The
person carrying out the washing is often chosen during the
lifetime of the deceased.   In some places, the left hand only
is used during the performance.   If any one of the persons
engaged in the washing is displeasing to the deceased, the
latter holds himself stiffly, clenches his fists, etc.   Where the
body remains soft and plastic, the washers are all agreeable
to the dead.   The corpse must be clad in clean garments, even
down to its underclothing.   The Volga Finns, like the Baltic
Finns, accoutre their dead as for a long journey.   A hat is
placed on the head of the corpse of a male, and clean foot-
wrappings are wrapped round its feet, which are fitted with

lime- or birch-bark shoes; other clothes are placed with it
also. The Votiak wife lays a clean suit of undergarments
by her dead husband to enable him to change when necessary.
The husband gathers into his wife's coffin kerchiefs for the
head, towels, and trinkets worn on the breast. Many garments and kerchiefs of all descriptions are placed in the
coffin of a young girl, "as the men who have died unmarried
are thought to be quicker in proposing marriage to girls with
a bountiful marriage portion." A staff is placed in the hand
of an old man. Naturally, all the tribes fit out their dead
according to their scale of living, means and opportunities.
The more northern peoples appear to have used very simple
wrappings in which to swathe their dead. To conclude from
remains dug up, the Lapps, in olden days, used only wrappings
of birch-bark. In certain districts, both Lapps and the Northern Ostiaks were accustomed to swathe their dead also in rein-
deer- or bear-skins.

In addition to clothing or protective swathings, the dead
had to be supplied with provisions for the journey, and with
money, weapons, and all kinds of implements and household
articles. Among the objects laid with the dead may be mentioned fire-tools, bow and arrows, an axe, a knife, fishing-
gear, skis, a sickle, pots, dishes, wooden spoons, boats and
vehicles, etc. The corpse was supplied with everything it was
supposed to need. With women, distaffs, pieces of cloth,
scissors and needles were laid; with children, toys. The lame
received their crutches, a shaman his drum, a hunter his dog
and his spear. Above all, the Volga Finns never forget to
give the dead for their last journey the tools needed for the
making of bast shoes. Smaller objects were laid in the coffin
of the dead, larger ones were placed around the grave. In
some places among the Cheremiss it was further deemed
necessary to place a rod in each hand of the corpse, so that in
the underworld it could protect itself against attacking hounds,
serpents, or evil spirits.

Among the articles and coins laid in the dead man's coffin by the Ostiaks were also some which were sent along with the deceased to some relative who had died earlier. It is said of the Cheremiss, that some of them poured nuts into the pocket of the dead man, saying while this was being done: " Greet our kinsmen when you arrive; we send sweets to their children; when you meet them, divide the sweets amongst them." [7]

A noteworthy custom among all the Finno-Ugric peoples is the breaking-up of all the objects which the dead receive with them. That a like usage was followed in Finland, appears from a report from Savolax, according to which, on the placing of the corpse on the sleigh, some object from among the most valuable in the house had to be dashed in pieces, with the remark: " This you may have, but nothing else." In this way the spirit of the dead was prevented from returning after the burial with any demands for his property. Similarly, in Ingria, when the master or mistress of the house was borne out, the spoon of the deceased was carried three times round the coffin, after which the spoon was broken and the pieces thrown after the coffin, with the words: " There hast thou thy portion, more thou shalt not receive." This was done that the dead might not appear afterwards and demand more at the division of the inheritance.[8] Apparently it was believed that by "killing" an article, its "soul" or " shadow " was released to follow the deceased into the world of shadows.

An important part in the burial ceremonies is played by all kinds of protective measures, performed by the survivors obviously with a view to protecting themselves against dangers which the dead are believed to be able to cause. The belief of the Lapps that the dead wishes to take along with him " his family, his children, and his dependants " is common to all the Finno-Ugric peoples.[9] A very widespread measure of protection is to cover, immediately death occurs, the eyes and mouth of the deceased. To prevent the dead from doing harm to its own with its glance during the time the corpse lies in the house, the Samoyeds cover its eyes with copper-coins or with small stones. The Ostiaks cover the face of the deceased with a cloth, in addition to covering the eyes, nose, and mouth with silver or copper coins, or with brass buttons.[10] The Cheremiss close the eyes and mouth of their dead, and cover the eyes, ears, and nostrils with little bunches of thread. The Chuvash act in the same way, saying: " If the dead over there ask of thee if there are others to come after thee, answer them: ' My ears heard none, my eyes saw nothing, my nostrils knew no scent.' " [11] Missionaries relate that when the Lapps covered up their dead in shrouds, they were very careful to cover up the body completely.[12] This was most likely done for fear that the soul of the deceased, which was supposed to dwell in the body even after death, would otherwise leave its dwelling-place and come to frighten those left at home.

The Cheremiss are so cautious that as soon as signs of imminent death are forthcoming, they remove the sick from their beds to a litter of straw. According to the Hill-Cheremiss the person dying on a bolster of down must reckon up the number of feathers in the coming life, and similarly, those dying on hair-mats must count the hairs of the same.[13] Obviously, the removal of the sick to the litter of straw has its origin in the fear that death contaminated a bed.

As a means of protection articles made of metal have been used widely. The Finns cast a copper coin in the water in which the corpse is washed. It was believed in some places, that unless one gave a copper coin to the person who washed the corpse, his hand would become diseased.[14] Among the Scandinavian Lapps, the one washing and covering up the dead had to bear, on his right arm, a ring of brass, given to him by some relative of the deceased " so that no evil could befall him." [15] In Russian Lapmark the coffin and the grave of the deceased are prepared by such men whose womenfolk

are not pregnant, or have ceased to suckle their children;
otherwise, the child might be smitten with a mortal illness.[16]
A further very widely spread custom was that no one, often
not even the neighbours, might go about his ordinary occupations while the corpse was still in the village, but that everyone had to be prepared, if necessary, to serve the dead.
According to the Samoyedic idea, it is extremely reprehen-
sible to go hunting or fishing during a similar period; they
forbid even the crossing of a stream.[17] Among the Esthonians it is strictly forbidden to chop wood, to heat the bath-
house, to wash clothes, to sweep the floor, and to comb
one's hair while the body is in the house. Neither is it suitable to visit friends or to receive visitors. Even to sell, or
give away anything from the house is forbidden during this
period.[18]

If the corpse is kept over night in the house, no one may
undress, but must, instead, watch by the body, as " if one were
to lie down and sleep, it would be easier for the deceased to
take one's soul along with him to the kingdom of the dead."
Singing and shouting are also forbidden while the dead is in
the house. The Cheremiss declare that the relatives and
neighbours of the dead must sit silently watching by the dead,
in order to see if the spirit of the deceased should return to its
dwelling-place. If there is a mirror in the room, it must be
turned round or covered, in order that the dead may not, by
means of the mirror, look out a comrade for itself among
those present.[19]

To prevent the dead from visiting their old home, many
means of leading them astray are used. The Lapps and the
Samoyeds do not bear out their dead through the door, but
directly out under the canvas tent from the spot where they
were stricken by death; in order that the dead and the living
may not come in each other's way. The Lapps declare that
were they to bear out their dead through the door, a new death
might be expected soon after.[20] The Ostiaks removed their

dead through the windows.[21] The Votiaks attempt to deceive their dead by removing the door through which the corpse is carried from its hinges and passing it through an opening on the side of the hinges.[22] The Volga Finns were in the habit of placing the coffin on the end of a log and spinning it round three times in a contrary direction to that of the sun. Often the footmarks of the funeral procession are swept away.[23] The most general protective or cleansing measure is the strewing of ashes: thus both the Lapps and the Baltic Finns used to throw ashes and fire after those following the hearse.[24] In some places, all tables, benches, etc., in the house were thrown down on their sides at the removal of the coffin.[25] Against infection from death, articles of steel, axes and knives, or heated stones, glowing cinders, ashes, salt, flour, etc., were placed on the spot where death had stricken its victim.[26] A custom of the Baltic Finns is to hammer in a nail in the place where death occurred, or where the corpse was washed, often, also, into the threshold over which the coffin was borne. The people say, that if a nail has been driven in where a death has taken place, no sickness need be feared if one happened to receive a shock there.[27]

The Russian Lapps leave their homes open and empty after the death of a member of the family. In earlier times, the nomad families would remove altogether to some other place. A mark, such as for example, a stone, would be left to mark the place of death.[28] A more prevalent custom is to smoke a room, or to beat the walls with branches. When the Voguls smoke out their homes, they create a din at the same time, shriek, jingle sleighbells, and pound in every corner to drive away death. Among the Ostiaks the fire may not be allowed to go out for five nights when a male dies, and four nights when a female.[29] The dread felt for death is increased by the belief that the relatives of the dead man who have died earlier come to take him away. The Lapps declare that they have actually seen these with their own eyes in the twilight.

Generally, however, these spirits of dead relatives are invisible to human beings, but animals can see them.[30]

When the Lapps transport their dead for burial the corpse is always placed in the last sled,[31] and among the Ostiaks at Tremyugan the escort never goes after the coffin, but before.[32] The escort may not in any circumstances look behind it. Neither may the other inhabitants of the village look at the funeral procession through their windows. The Cheremiss go so far as to hide their windows with coverings in order " not to follow the dead one." [33]

Measures of protection are carried out also on the return from the burial. To prevent the dead from following the trail of the escort, all footprints are swept over at the burial mound.[34] According to Lehtisalo, the Yuraks, on their return from a burying, are in the habit of going three times round the grave in widening circles. In addition, a gateway is erected "towards the night," or towards the north, with the saying: "Here is thy way, wander thine own way." Returning from a burial, one may not look back. To cleanse oneself utterly from the contact with the body, a gateway of two sticks is erected before the door of the tent. Through this the relatives of the dead must pass, taking with them all their belongings.[35] The Votiaks strike at one another at the cemetery gate with branches of fir, saying to the dead: " Go to thy home, do not remain with us." Or a branch of juniper is waved with the cry: "Come not with us, go to your home! " [36] In some places, a channel is cut by dragging an axe or some other sharp instrument across the way or round the escort of the dead. When the house is reached again, a fire is usually made, over which one must jump, or the hands are rubbed with ashes, or a bath is taken. In Finland the coffin was sometimes carried to the cemetery between two fires of straw " so that the soul should not return home to disturb the sleep of the living." [37]

The sleigh, or carriage, in which the corpse is transported, is either left at the cemetery, or must stand for at least three days in the village street before it can be used again.[38]

The Eastern Cheremiss have a custom, according to which they fell a tree on their return from a burial, leaving a stump about a yard high. This is generally done about half-way between the cemetery and the village, " so that the dead, when looking around, may notice the stump, and realize that his old home is still far away, and so return to his grave." [39]

About half-way between the cemetery and a village, one sees very often among the Volga Finns, a place by the way-side where all kinds of objects, clothes, etc., have been placed on the ground or hung up in the trees. To this place the clothes worn by the deceased at his death, the bark-sponge used in washing him, the shavings from his coffin, and objects regarded as having become infected with death have been carried. The Cheremiss say that were one to burn up the shavings gathered after the making of the coffin the deceased would break out in blisters or an eruption on his face. At these widely-feared places, the Votiaks sacrifice at times of serious illness. Also after certain memorial-feasts held at home, the bones of the sacrificed animal are taken to the above-mentioned place, where they are hung up in the trees. Thus, in some districts, sacrificial gifts have been laid down at this place instead of at the cemetery, where they really should be, and in many places even to this day, are laid. In the District of Mamadysh the Votiaks have erected little posts with a small table in front, to the memory of such dead as have died in strange places, " so that their souls may return to their native village." On the table, sacrificial food is placed on the anniversary of such deaths.[40]

Among the Finns in Savolax and Karelia, a tree, the *karsikko*, on the road leading to the cemetery, was stripped of its lowermost branches as a memorial of the dead. Often, a cross would be carved on the tree together with the initials of the dead, and sometimes also the year of death. Or these might be cut on a piece of board which was then fastened to the tree. The practice of carving a cross for each corpse borne by was carried out with the intention of preventing the dead from coming any nearer to their former home. Offerings were also made, or at least, everyone had to drink spirits to the memory of the dead. Strips of clothing, bindings, etc., were also often hung here.[41]

A similar custom prevailed amongst the Esthonians. In some districts the crown of a young tree was chopped off, in others a cross was carved in a tree by the way, or a nail hammered in, so that the soul of the dead should not approach any nearer home from the cemetery.[42]

It is said to have been the custom in Savolax for a settler to mark out near his home a suitable thicket of firs to the memory of the dead. In a thicket of this description, which was called *karsikko*, a tree was denuded of its branches at each death of a dependant of the house, whether an adult or a child. Immediately such a tree was found in the thicket, offerings were made there to the dead. This statement, the origin of which is to be found only in K. H. Hornborg's description, is not supported by actual folk-custom. Hornborg seems to have confused the *karsikko* of the dead with the so-called *elättipuu* (Swedish *vårdträd*), a tree planted in the vicinity of the house when first built, and to which sacrifices of first-fruits were offered, and every autumn that of a sheep. From this tree no branches were ever cut.[43] A growing fir or pine in Finland has its branches removed so that only the top remains in honour of one who for the first time is about to begin a long journey or some more important enterprise, such as hunting or fishing; and in Russian Karelia this is done also in honour of a bride. But to this *karsikko*-tree no sacrifices were offered.

Some kind of protective measure is probably also at the root of many customs, regarded nowadays merely as signs

PLATE II

A Karsikko or Memorial Tree, on the way to the cemetery in Finnish Karelia, hung with offerings and stripped of its lower branches in memory of the dead. (See pages 25–26.)

After photograph by V. Mainov.

of mourning. The Ostiaks regard it as not correct for the relatives to go barefooted during the first week after a death. According to another report, Ostiak women wear their linen and head-kerchiefs inside out for five months (or fifty days) if the deceased is a man, and four months (or forty days) if a woman.[44]

A custom now regarded as a mark of mourning is the Ostiak's refusal to gird his belt around him for five or four days, the time depending on the sex of the deceased. In some districts this is done "so that the dead shall feel itself lighter and freer." The Lapps have the same custom during the trance of the shaman and child-birth. Probably, the thought behind this Ostiak custom is that the journey of the dead to the other world will be unhindered by knot or band. For a similar reason, perhaps, the Samoyed and Ugrian women allow their hair to fall unbound during a burial.[45]

A method of expressing sorrow among the Ostiaks was to scratch wounds that bled on one's own face. Novitskiy writes of this (1715): "When anyone's father or mother, a husband or a wife, or any other member of a family dies, the relatives following the corpse to the grave seek to express their sorrow by tearing their hair, and, as far as is in their power, scratching wounds on their faces; the bleeding locks of hair are thrown by them on to the corpse."[46] Among the Mordvins also the wounding of one's face was regarded as a means of expressing sorrow.[47] These last, like the Orthodox Finns and the Siryans had the custom of singing "weeping-songs" to the memory of the dead. In the villages were often to be found women who made a profession of weeping at graves. The singing of special weeping-songs seems with these to be derived from the Russians, amongst whom the custom is general. The "weeping" at the grave is, however, apparently of older origin. In an old source it is written of the Voguls: "They wail and cry greatly after the dead." The Ostiaks customarily use the relatives of the dead as "weepers." The dead man is praised very greatly at the same time, and his works are admired.[48]

A strange custom of inquiring from the dead, who shall be the next to die, is often connected with the burial ceremonies. When the coffin has been borne out of the house into the yard, the Cheremiss place on it a bunch of pieces of thread of varying lengths, from which each of the participants in the ceremony draws out a thread, saying: "Although thou perhaps didst die too early, do not take me with thee, see how long my thread is, let my life be equally long."[49] After burning the straw on which the dead has departed this life, the Esthonians look among the ashes for footmarks from which to make out whether a human being or an animal will be the next to die from the same farm.[50] The Finns kept an eye on the horse that drew the hearse; if it lifted its left foot first, it was a sign that someone from the village would soon follow the dead.[51] The Ostiaks attempt to obtain answers from the corpse to certain questions, by lifting the lid of the coffin in which the dead lies. Before they transport the dead to the graveyard, they tie a rope round the coffin at the place where the head of the corpse should be, and by the grip thus formed one of the persons present tries to lift the coffin, each time he does so directing a question at the deceased, for example: "Was it a spirit, that took thee?" or "Shall we all live to the next year?" and should the answer to this last question be in the negative: "Tell me, who will be the next to die?" after which the names of all present are called out at each attempt to lift the coffin. Should the coffin appear to be heavy, it is regarded as an answer in the negative; if the contrary, as assent.[52]

It is, further, the duty of the survivors to take care of the dwelling-place of the dead. According to the most widespread custom now, the dead are buried in a coffin in the ground. The coffin, called the "house" of the dead, is made of boards; at each side the Karelians, Volga Finns, etc., make a little square hole, the "window," "through which light reaches to the house of the dead," and "through which they can observe what happens around them." When the Cheremiss makes the coffin, he says: "Now do I make thee a house, be not angry if it please thee not." [53]

When the Cheremiss lift the corpse into the coffin, they speak a few words to the memory of the deceased and wish him a happy destination: "Farewell (with the name of the deceased)! Over there may you enjoy a light, happy, good and warm existence. Leave us not, but come and inform us in our dreams, how joyful and pleasing thy life beyond the grave has become!" Other wishes are also expressed: "Let us not die too early, return not to us, make friends for thyself among the other dead!" [54]

To an unmarried young man the parents say: "In this life we had not time to give thee away in marriage; choose for thyself a good wife over there." In certain districts the unmarried dead are escorted to the cemetery with the ceremony attaching to a wedding. The horses are harnessed in gleaming harness, a large bell is fixed to the bent bow of wood over the horses' necks, all the comrades and friends of the youthful dead follow them to the graveside. When a young virgin dies, the Cheremiss lay away with her, her needlework and decorations, and in addition a *charpan*, the headgear of a married woman, "so that the deceased, when she celebrates her wedding beyond the grave, will be able to array herself as a married woman." While the relatives fit her out, they say with tears in their eyes: "Here you had not time to be wedded, marry an honourable man over there!" [55]

In some Districts (Urzhum, etc.,) a thread is snatched from the garments of the deceased, or they merely take hold of the coffin, with the remark: "Take not the house, the cattle, the seed, the fortune with thee; leave thy luck with us!" [56] The Eastern Votiaks have a custom according to which one of the relatives of the dead tears a white cloth,

which he has brought with him to the cemetery, into two
pieces; the part remaining in the left hand, he leaves on the
breast of the dead, the piece in the right hand is taken home
and bound fast to one of the rafters or attached to the wall,
in which places it is allowed to hang a year. With the act
of tearing, they say: " In the same way as a part of this
cloth remains here while the other part goes home with us,
mayst thou not altogether depart from us."[57]

A custom of the Volga Finns, met with also among the
Ostiaks, is that when the face and the whole body of the dead
have been covered with cloths brought by the friends of the
deceased, a thread, of the length of the deceased's body, is
laid from its head to its feet, or at times, even three threads
of different colours, " along which the dead can climb up to
heaven." By some, this is called the " swing " of the dead.
Sometimes a thread of the length of an adult is laid by a
child; " so that it may in the other world grow to the length
of the thread." [58]

The Cheremiss regard it as essential that the persons watching by the body through the night should also follow it to
the grave. On the way to the cemetery all who meet the
procession must wish the dead a happy existence, warmth
and light. While the body is being lowered into the grave,
the coffin is lifted up three times, with the saying: " Fear
not! " The grave is thereafter filled in again, during which
process the relatives of the dead in turn wish it a happy existence and a calm dwelling-place, and beg that it will not
frighten those near to it, but will protect its former home,
its family, and its herds. In a Karelian " weeping-song " for
the graveside, the wish of the dead is expressed, that when
the grave is filled in, a tiny crack, like the way of a mole,
will be left for the soul to move through.[59] When the Volga
Finns return from the graveside each one present sweeps a
little more earth on to the grave from its sides, saying:
" May the earth be light over thee! " In both ends of the

grave a little branch is stuck into the earth, and threads for the dead are bound to these. For young girls kerchiefs are bound to a pole planted in the grave, or to the surrounding trees. A three-branched candle is lit on the grave.[60]

The coffin in which the dead is borne to the grave is, however, of comparatively late origin. The Eastern Votiaks and Cheremiss prepare the dwelling-house of the dead first at the grave, to which the dead is escorted in full panoply, on a sleigh in the winter, and on a carriage in the summer. During the journey the widow of the dead sits or lies alongside it. At the cemetery a low grave is dug, twigs of fir or birch-leaves being strewn at the bottom; at the sides and ends a couple of stout boards are then placed, between which the dead is intended to be laid on its back. As a roof to this "house," in one side-wall of which a window is introduced, two boards are used.[61] Formerly and in many places at the present time, especially during the winter, the Samoyeds and the most Northern Ostiaks had a custom according to which the dead were not buried in the earth, but in a dwelling-place erected over the ground. Among the Ostiaks and Voguls a tomb of this description built over the ground resembles a

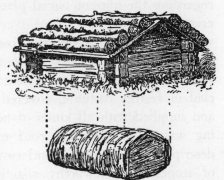

FIG. 1. OSTIAK GRAVE-HOUSE WITH COFFIN OF THE DECEASED

little low house. The roof, sloping on both sides, is made of birch-bark and narrow logs; often this house of the dead is furnished with a window.[62] Among the Lapps burial-houses are also found, the roofs of which rise above the ground; the dead being bedded in them on a layer of moss, reindeer-hair, etc.[63]

A further relic of the times when the above-mentioned custom of burial over the ground was prevalent among the Finno-Ugric peoples, is the custom, met with among the Finns in Karelia, of building, even after the dead had begun to be buried in the earth, a little house of thin, round logs, carpentered together, and furnished with a roof and windows. This building would seem to have little actual meaning for the dead, since these are buried in the earth, and it must therefore be connected with the old method of disposing of the dead. Perfectly clear examples show how the method of burial has gradually passed from the erection over the ground to burial within it; an intermediate form being the low grave which is not filled in again, but only covered with boards and birch-bark.[64]

The development of the dwelling-place of the dead to the coffin is shown also by the old burial customs of the Finns. In his work on the Iron Age in Karelia, Schwindt mentions regarding the ancient burial-places examined by him, that an erection resembling a house over the ground, joined together with wood, with jutting-out corners, was lowered into the grave; it was at times even fitted with a floor of boards, over which skins were spread. The dead were laid in this building clad in festive costume, covered most often with birch-bark and supplied with all kinds of necessary articles. The building was covered with a roof of boards. A grave of this description was filled in and covered with one or two layers of stones.[65] Noteworthy also is the Volga Finns' custom, mentioned earlier, of furnishing their coffins with a window.

Of early origin would seem to be a custom, preserved among the Ugrians and the Karelian Finns, of burying their dead bedded in a boat or punt. Even at the present time the coffin is called the " punt " (*ruuhi*) in some parts of Karelia. Munkácsi has assumed, that the Ugrian custom of using an oaken punt as a coffin, is a direct outcome of the belief which they held regarding the world of the dead, and especially of the journey there over water. It is argued against this by Karjalainen, that the belief in a land of the dead to be reached over water is not an original belief of the Ugrians. According to this last investigator, the custom of supplying the dead with a boat for their last journey, depends solely on the fact that the dead were regarded as needing a boat in the world beyond, with which to procure their means of existence.[66] In Russian Karelia, remains of boats have been found which had not been used as coffins for the dead, but lie capsized, often shattered into two parts, over the grave.[67]

FIG. 2. GRAVEYARD IN RUSSIAN KARELIA
According to Blomstedt

In the same way as the Ugrians buried their dead in boats, Lapp sleighs were used by the Lapps as coffins. In more remote districts the Lapps, even to the present time, continue to bury their dead in this way: laying sods of earth and stumps of trees around them, as a protection against beasts of prey. It is even related that the dead, on occasion, have been buried in a sitting position in a sleigh to which a reindeer was harnessed.[68]

A very old custom, which seems to have been general in earlier times and of which traces can be found among most of the Finno-Ugric stocks, is the use of a coffin made by hollowing out the trunk of a tree, or a trough, as the protective covering of the dead. Most of the dead were buried between two hollowed logs, of which the lower formed the coffin and the upper one the lid.[69] Among the Siberians such a coffin is erected over the ground upon two or four pillars.

The oldest method of burial of the Finno-Ugrians is also made clear by a word, meaning in Samoyed "corpse" (*halmer*, *kamelo*, etc.), in Mordvin "grave" (*kalmo*, *kalma*), and in Finnish "grave" (*kalma*) and also "death" and "the scent of death." In an explanation of this word Setälä says: "On the grounds of the meaning of the word both in Finnish and in Samoyed, we can assume that its original meaning was 'corpse,' 'the dead one.' The oldest method of burial undoubtedly consisted merely in the laying-out of a body, a habit prevalent, and followed even now, among many peoples, which habit would explain why the same word can have the two meanings 'corpse' and 'grave.'"[70]

Reliable reports on the burning of bodies are to be found solely among the Baltic Finns. In certain ancient remains in Finland, burnt bones have been found in graves. Henry the Lett relates in his Chronicle how the Esthonians, when they returned to their old beliefs during the unsettled period of the Crusades, "took back their wives, whom they had forsaken during the time they stood under the influence of Christianity, exhumed their dead, whom they had buried in cemeteries, and burned them in their old heathen way." The other Finno-Ugric peoples seem to have burned bodies only when the dead were supposed to be dangerous to those surviving. We may concur fully with Varonen, who says: "As, therefore, no reliable proofs exist concerning the cremation of the dead among the Finno-Ugric stocks, except in those branches, which continuously, and for the longest period, have been under Germanic influence, we may conclude that the burning of the dead did not originally form part of the burial-customs of the Finno-Ugrians, and, where it may occasionally be found among them, is merely in the nature of a temporary loan from other peoples." [71]

The Finno-Ugric peoples bury their dead in certain burial-areas, which, among the agricultural tribes, are often fenced in. Every village has its own cemetery, or several villages lying closely together may have a common one. This comes from the fact that from the original mother-village, newer ones have been formed in the course of time, the inhabitants of which continue to use the burial-area of the original village. In the same way as the old villages were family-villages, the old cemeteries were family-cemeteries. That it was not the custom to bury strangers in them is shown, among other proofs, by the custom of the Votiaks, who besides their village-cemetery, sometimes have a special one, often situated by the main road, for the burial of wandering strangers, stricken by death during their sojourn in the village. [72]

Usually, the cemetery is a consecrated thicket or wood, where possible, of firs (Finnish, *kuusikko*), where the Votiaks and the Cheremiss hang up on the trees all kinds of garments, cloths, kerchiefs, etc., presented to the dead, " so that they should not, lying on the ground, be turned to earth." At times, even the solitary graves are ringed round. According to Rytschkov this was done " so that the dead should not leave their dwelling-place and trample down the surrounding fields." [73] The Eastern Cheremiss have, further, a custom of placing on their graves a cuckoo made of wood, and fastened to the end of a long pole. [74] What the meaning attached to this bird may originally have been, the present generation no longer knows. Some say the cuckoo sounds its note for the edification of the dead. Certain Siberian tribes have also a custom of setting up figures of birds on the graves of their dead.

Whether the use of special cemeteries had its origin already in Finno-Ugric times is doubtful. According to tradition, the Lapps, in their earlier periods, did not possess special burial-places, because their dead were buried at any spot. In the summer, when it is extremely difficult, and even, at times, impossible, to transport the corpses to the remote burial-places, the Lapps have to our day buried their dead in the forests and on the uplands, wherever they happened to be dwelling, and then with the arrival of winter removed them to the churchyard.[75]

PLATE III

1. Lapp Grave. (See page 36.)
After photograph by T. I. Itkonen.

2. Graves of the Northern Ostiaks erected over the ground. (See page 31.)
According to Finsch.

CHAPTER III

MEMORIAL FEASTS FOR A PARTICULAR DEAD PERSON

THE duties of the living with regard to the dead do not cease when the latter have been carried to the grave with all honours. The dead continue to need the help and care of the living. If a dead man is not given his rights, he may resent it and, coming back, disturb the peace of his survivors. Such of the dead as haunt their old homes are called by the Esthonians "home-visitors" (Kodukäiat). Generally, they are masters and mistresses who in their life-time were particularly order-loving, economical and strict. They are, of course, seldom seen, but every now and then they are heard making noises to remind their family of their duties, or they may even attack their children if these have not arranged the memorial-feast due to them.[1]

Memorial feasts may be either general ones, celebrated in memory of all deceased relations, or special, in which case a certain deceased relative is the object of remembrance. Of these, the latter seem to be of older origin.

The first memorial feast celebrated in remembrance of a member of the family, takes place on the actual burial-day, so that this first feast is at the same time a burial feast.

Lundius, the missionary, relates of the Swedish Lapps, that when their dead were buried, they drank "funeral beer." When the liquor was handed round, the Lapps first dipped their fingers into it and smeared their faces. Having become intoxicated, they began to praise the dead man, saying that he was shrewd and strong, that he was an able forester, that he understood well his wife and children, that he was a mighty shaman, etc.[2] This wetting of the fingers and smearing of the face can be traced to a corresponding custom among the Norwegian Lapps of whom Randulf, the missionary, relates, that before going to the Lord's Supper, they used to take a glass of beer or gin, if they had any, and dipping three fingers into the drink, make the sign of the cross on their foreheads. At other times they made, with fingers dipped into the drink, three dots on the breast, one with each finger. This was done by the Lapps in order to get their dead relations to protect them.[3] The memorial drink, as well as the three finger-marks, is with the Lapps a later Scandinavian custom.

The custom, however, of killing the reindeer that dragged the dead man to his grave, seems to be an original Lapponian usage. This sacrifice performance is described by Rheen, the missionary, in the following way: — "Three days after the funeral of the dead man, the Lapps take the reindeer which conveyed him to the cemetery, kill it in his honour, and consume it in company with their relations and dependants. They collect all the bones, and having made a chest, put them into it, burying the chest in the earth. They then make an image of wood which is placed on the chest, the image being large or small, according to the size of the dead man." [4] According to Graan, three rods besmeared with blood, on which were placed pieces of the heart and lungs of the reindeer, were also buried with the bones.[5]

Even after the funeral feast, the deceased was remembered by taking some tobacco, or anything else he may have been fond of, to his grave. Rheen mentions that if the deceased was a rich man, reindeer were killed in his honour one, two or even three years after his death. Here also the slaughtered animal's bones had to be hidden in the earth. A black piece of thread had to be sewn into the ear of the reindeer chosen for the sacrifice.[6]

If sacrifices were not made to the dead man, the Lapps

believed that they would be punished with poverty. According to Lundius, the Lapps believe that their reindeer, be they many or few in number, " will die after their master, as they stand or walk, like grass." [7]

If, after the death of the deceased, he was given some charge, *e.g.*, as reindeer-herd, they were obliged to sacrifice to him yearly during that time. J. Kildal relates how the Lapp was able, by means of sacrifice, to make his father or some other near relation from the lower regions guard his reindeer for one, two or three years. After that time he would go back to the dead. [8]

The deceased are also remembered at ordinary feasts. Randulf says that when a Lapp drinks the health of anyone he always pours one part of the liquor, before drinking, on the ground, in honour of the spirits, but in particular of the deceased. [9] Lundius relates that at their feasts, they sacrifice cheese, meat, fish, fat, marrow and other food, which they put into a little trough and bury in the earth together with an image. [10]

Like the Lapps, the Samoyeds have no fixed memorial days or annual feasts in honour of the dead. The reindeer which dragged the deceased to his grave, is here also sacrificed. Most frequently it is impaled on the grave, a meal being sometimes prepared from the meat. [11] Müller says that the Samoyeds tie up a reindeer or two, if the deceased has had any, on the grave, where the poor beasts are left to starve to death. In some districts they believe that the dead need the care of their relatives until the shaman has taken their " shadows " to the world of the dead. When, for some accidental reason, *e.g.*, during illness, they sacrifice a reindeer or a dog to the deceased, the sacrifice is performed after sunset, behind the tent. The head of the sacrificial beast must then be directed to the west. [12]

According to Pallas, the Ugrians of the North take to the graveyard three of the best reindeer of the deceased on the sleighs which follow that on which the corpse lies. Having placed the body in the grave, they tie a strap to each of a reindeer's hindlegs, two men seize the straps and four others pierce the animal with sharpened poles from different directions. In this way one reindeer at a time is killed. When a rich man is buried, several reindeer are killed; a noose is placed round their necks and legs, and thus tied, they are beaten along their backs with poles until they cease to breathe. An animal killed in honour of the deceased is left on the grave; the straps are placed on a stand fixed above the grave and the sleighs are overturned against it. Near the grave the funeral meal is cooked, and when they have eaten enough, the burial guests take the rest home.[13] According to later custom the best-beloved reindeer of the deceased is killed, the meat being eaten, and the bones and horns, together with the sleigh and harness, are placed on the grave.[14]

The funeral feast of the North Voguls is described by Gondatti. Immediately after burying the dead, they cook some kind of cereal or meat-dish, which they then pour out against the coffin. The bottom of the pan is knocked out, after which it is left by the grave. If the deceased has been conveyed by reindeer, the latter are strangled by the grave, the meat being boiled and eaten on the spot, the hide buried, and the bones placed by the dead man.[15]

Like the Lapps, the Ugrians frequently remember their dead, especially during the first period of their life in Hades. In most districts, however, they have no fixed memorial days, but settle these according to agreement with relations. Karjalainen says that the Northern Ugrians celebrate memorial feasts in honour of a dead man for fifty days, and of a dead woman, for forty. The ceremonies are very simple: — they cook some food, and, having kept it at the grave for a while, they eat it at home. At Tremyugan the dead are remembered after one or two months, a half-year, or a whole one, by "setting forth a dish or a trough made of birch-bark." Fish

and meat are cooked and, together with other eatables, placed
in vessels either on the ground by the house against the door
on the side of the hinges, or taken to the cemetery, where
they are put on the ground above the head of the deceased or
below the window of the grave-house, if there is one. On
the ground tea, gravy, gin, and, finally, some cold water are
poured, whence the term "water-pouring" is derived.[16]
According to Munkácsi, the Northern Voguls celebrate
memorial feasts on the third day after death, then, at the end
of "the holy week," and, after that time, thrice a year. They
make a fire by the grave and cook a dish, a small part of which
is placed in a vessel by the grave with the saying: "Do not
remember us, thinking evil thoughts."[17] Where outside influence can be traced, the memorial feasts are celebrated on
carefully fixed days. With the Southern Ugrians, such days
are the ninth, the sixteenth, and thirty-sixth, and a half-year
or a whole year after death.[18]

A strange custom among the Northern Ugrians is the
making of a memorial doll of the deceased, of which Novitskiy says: "A curious irrational and shameless custom is that
which is observed by their women after the death of their
husbands. The widow carves a wooden doll, resembling a
human being, to represent her dead husband, takes some of
her husband's clothes, dresses the doll in them and provides
it with ornaments worn by the deceased, and putting it in the
place where her husband used to sit, cooks for this lifeless
block of wood all the dishes that used to please the deceased.
When they sit down in the place of honour to eat, she places
the image beside her, embracing and kissing the doll as if it
were a living being, fully believing that the deceased sees all
this and that his soul enters this image at times. She keeps
the doll for some time, going on with this nonsense for a
year or even longer, and then buries it with its clothes on in
the earth, exhibiting her sorrow by weeping and wailing."[19]

Castrén and Pallas relate that memorial dolls of this descrip-

tion were made to represent persons who had been in some
way important. The image was kept in the tent of the deceased and was shown the same honours as its precursor. It
was fed at every meal, dressed in the morning and undressed
in the evening, and a widow, who had loved her husband,
even went so far as to place it beside her in bed. According
to Castrén the image was worshipped in this way for three
years, after which it was buried. They supposed that the
body of the deceased had disintegrated during these three
years.[20] In some places the image was kept for five years, if
the deceased was a man, and for four, if a woman. In our
days the image is burned after the course of the said time.
Yet the old idea also remains that the doll should be buried in
the grave of the deceased. Where they are in the habit of
building the so-called grave-houses, the doll is placed in these.
During the time when Finsch was travelling among the
Ugrians, he saw, among the most Northern, small buildings
on their graves of the size of kennels, provided with a door,
and within them a doll, dressed in Ugrian garments. These
dolls noticed by Finsch were plainly such as had been taken
to the graveyard at the end of the memorial-time and placed
in the grave-house.[21]

The memorial doll is also to be found among some Samoyed tribes, though the custom of making images of shamans
seems here to be more widely spread. According to Lehtisalo,
the Yuraks make a wooden image of the "shadow" of the
shaman, which resembles a reindeer-bull. This image is kept
by the wife or son of the deceased in a case, consisting of the
whole-flayed skin of a young calf.[22] The fact that the
"shadow" of the shaman is thus represented, springs from
the idea of the Samoyeds that the soul of the shaman, when
leaving his body, takes on the shape of a reindeer-bull.[23]

Karjalainen suggests that the custom of the Northern
Ugrians of making an image of the deceased has developed
from a usage retained among the Southern Ostiaks and Voguls.

Among the latter, the linen and bed-clothes of the deceased are kept unwashed in his bed, among the former generally under his pillow. These clothes are brought out at the memorial feast and placed in the middle of the bed. A spoon is then placed in the dishes with its handle directed towards the clothes. In some places a widow even keeps her late husband's clothes beside her when going to bed. Karjalainen thinks that this method of representing the deceased has developed into the Northern Ugrians' custom of making a particular image of the dead.[24] Yet it must be remembered that the Lapps, who were not in the habit of worshipping the clothes of the deceased, also used an image every time they sacrificed to them. This image, which does not seem to have been an object for worship at home, but was made only for the occasion of the sacrifice, was not clothed.[25] Among most of the Finno-Ugrian races the clothes of the dead man are nowadays considered as visible representations of himself. This is true of all the Volga peoples. Images are not seen among them nowadays, but according to the most ancient sources, the Mordvins seem to have had memorial dolls, which were worshipped at the memorial feasts. A very common usage is, further, to choose as the representative of the deceased a living man who resembles him in appearance and who dresses himself for the feast in the deceased's clothes. The fact that even the name of the deceased was later made into a visible object of remembrance to the survivors, has been mentioned already when speaking of the *karsikko* of the Finns. The name *karsikko* was also given in North Savolax to a piece of white paper on which were written the name of the deceased and the year of his birth and death, this paper being placed for the funeral day on a cloth spread on the back wall of the hut.[26]

Like the Chuvashes, the Volga Finns celebrate memorial feasts in honour of some particular person on the funeral day, and also on the third, the seventh and the fortieth day

after death. In some districts, the anniversary is also celebrated. These memorial feasts are often celebrated late at
night, and the time for them is calculated by the Volga Finns
not according to days but according to the number of nights.
For this reason they call the memorial feast of the third day,
" the third night," that of the seventh, " the seventh night,"
and that of the fortieth, " the fortieth night." According to an
old custom, some animal, a hen at the very least, must be
killed during each memorial feast, for without bloodshed, as
the Votiaks say, a memorial feast cannot be celebrated.[27]

The Votiaks begin their preparations for the first memorial
feast before the deceased is taken to the burial-ground. As
soon as the dead man is washed and dressed, he is placed on a
bench; the eldest female member of the family puts down
two bowls by the body and makes meat pies. The eldest male
member of the family then takes a pie and breaks three pieces
from it, placing these into one of the bowls; into the other he
pours some gin, saying: " In this life you lived well, live
well also there. Do not torment and worry us. Protect our
cattle well. Protect our children well. Gather the dead
round you. Protect our good cattle from floods and precipices. More I cannot say to you; do not be angry. Live well
in the life over there; do not take hold of us in front or from
behind; do not persecute us." The eldest member of the
family having finished, the others do and say the same.[28]

These ceremonies differ somewhat in different places. In
the district of Sarapul, where they believe that the relatives of
the deceased who died earlier have arrived to meet the new-
comer, they are believed to take part in the feast together
with the deceased. In honour of the latest deceased and of
the others, the men make wax-tapers and the women cook a
hen, if the deceased is a woman, and a cock, if it be a man.
At the door near the fireplace, a trough is placed on which,
as on the head of the bed, little wax-tapers are fixed. Into
the trough pieces of meat are thrown and some gravy poured

when the names of the dead are mentioned, with an appeal to them to eat and drink and to receive the lately deceased with a contented mind into their company.[29] Such customs are common to all the Volga Finns.

When the Esthonians are ready to take their dead to the grave, they cook beans or peas (which fare among the Baltic Finns seems to be a general memorial dish), and pour ladlefuls of these on to the coffin, on which they also place some other food, white bread, etc. In some places they are in the habit of pouring out beer or gin on the ground by the gate while the deceased is being taken away, lest he should suffer from thirst in the life to come.[30]

Most frequently the Volga Finns, however, prepare the funeral meal only when they have returned from the graveyard. Generally no one is invited to such a feast, but it is everyone's duty to know for himself that he must come and honour the deceased. For the feast, everyone brings food with him, no one coming empty-handed, and the attention of the dead is generally called to what each has brought. For the newly-buried a dish is placed on the table at the spot where he is supposed to sit among his own people, but for those who died earlier, a trough is placed by the door. For all the dead, for the nearest relations and also for more distant ones, whose memory still lives in the minds of the survivors, a wax taper is lighted. Even the ruler of the kingdom of the dead and that of the graveyard are remembered. The first cup and the first morsels of food belong to the dead. If anything happens to fall on the floor under the table, no one is allowed to take it up. The food sacrificed to the deceased is afterwards taken into the yard for the dogs. If the latter scorn the food, it is believed that the dead are not satisfied with the feast; should the dogs fight while eating it is considered to be a sign that the dead do not agree among themselves.

For the earlier deceased relations, who have arrived to meet the newly deceased, there has thus been placed a dish of food near the door. This custom is very common, as it is believed that the place by the door is the place of residence of the dead who arrive at the memorial feast.

Even to the graveyard all kinds of food are taken, and there crumbled over the grave of the deceased. In some places, they dig a pit above the head of the dead man, into which they pour gin, a honey-drink or water. When doing this, the Siryans say: " Drink, drink." [31]

Nowadays, the Volga Finns seldom kill larger domestic animals than poultry for the memorial feasts. Formerly, circumstances seem to have been different. Olearius relates that during the first half of the sixteenth century, the Cheremiss, when burying a rich man, killed his best horse, the surviving friends eating the meat of the animal.[32] A hundred years later Müller reports likewise: " When some important person dies, the Chuvash and Cheremiss put up two sticks in the yard, between which they stretch a thick thread. On this thread they place a ring. The young people then shoot at it with bows and arrows at a distance of ten paces, and he who first makes the ring fall, mounts the horse that the deceased used to drive, but in case of the deceased being a woman, any horse he may choose, galloping three times to the grave of the deceased and back. The horse is then killed — the Cheremiss carrying out this in the yard and the Chuvash in the graveyard — the meat being boiled and eaten in memory of the deceased." [33]

Numerous examples show that the Baltic Finns were also in former times in the habit of killing a large domestic animal in honour of the dead. Even in our days they believe, in some places, that if a cow is not killed for the funeral of the host or hostess, it will die in any case. A remainder of the said funeral sacrifice is found in a custom among the Finns, as well as among the Esthonians, of making the clergyman a present of a cow after the death of the host or hostess, as a fee for the burial ceremony. The Esthonians were in the habit of taking an ox to the clergyman after the death of the host, and a cow after that of the hostess. Sometimes the clergyman was expected to prepare a meal of these for the funeral guests. In North Karelia the people were in the habit of tying the cow due to the clergyman to a tree in the graveyard for some time, the clergyman having to take it from there.[34]

The different memorial days are celebrated by the Volga Finns in varying ways, some of them being more solemn than others. Thus, Georgi relates of the Votiaks, that at the first memorial feast, which is celebrated on the third day, the friends of the house of mourning are assembled only to eat pancakes and drink beer, some of which is also poured out in the yard for the dead, but on the seventh day a sheep is killed, and on the fortieth, a cow or a horse.[35]

The memorial feast of the third day among the Siryans (District of Orlov) is described by Dobrotvorskiy. When the guests have arrived, wax-tapers are lighted in the window and on either side of the threshold. The door is opened for a while, when the guests are sitting down at table, to invite the soul (*lol*) of the deceased to the feast. In the farthermost corner, a hat or a kerchief is placed, depending on the sex of the deceased. On the place where the hat has been set down, no one seats himself. On the table beside it, they place a bowl filled with pancakes, porridge, milk and gin. Every guest considers it his duty to put into the bowl of the deceased some of the food displayed on the table.[36]

The memorial feast of the seventh day is, in most places, like that of the third day. Some one of the relatives of the deceased goes to the grave to remember him. At home, they light a candle on the brim of the vessel of food offered to the deceased. When the first pieces of food are dropped into this vessel, everyone utters a few words of remembrance, pointing out that it is now the seventh day of the memorial feast. In other places the seventh day is kept almost as solemnly as the fortieth. The participants in the ceremony go to the grave with two horses to invite the deceased; they kill a hen for him, sometimes even a sheep; in the evening they go to the bath-house with him; all night he is regaled; and not until dawn is he taken back to his new home.[37]

According to a general idea of the Volga Finns and of many other East European peoples, the deceased remains during the course of forty days in a very near relationship to his old home. The Votiaks say that the " soul " of the dead lives at home for forty days after death. It is therefore the duty of his people to show kindness and hospitality to the deceased, particularly during that time. In some places, it is customary, during these forty days, to put down a bowl for the deceased every time the family and servants sit down to take a meal.[38]

The Siryans believe that after the funeral, the deceased returns with the funeral guests to his old home and remains there for the above-named time. For that time, therefore, it has been customary to hang up a towel in some fixed place in the hut, so that the deceased may wipe his face every time he washes himself. No living soul may touch it, as death might be the immediate consequence.[39]

The Mordvins say that the deceased passes over to the realm of the dead forty days or six weeks after his death.[40] The same idea is found also among the Baltic Finns who have been under Russian influence. According to Groundstroem the Votes dared not speak ill of the dead for six weeks, for they believed that the soul of the deceased stayed for that time in his home, mostly under the table. They were careful also not to stretch their legs under the table, as they might easily trample on the deceased.[41] Like the Siryans, the Karelians in the Government of Tver were in the habit of hanging a towel for six weeks on the back wall of the hut, so that the deceased when coming home, might wipe himself.[42] A similar custom is found among the Russians, from whom the Finnish tribes seem to have borrowed it.

As the forty-days' memorial feast is at the same time a farewell feast, it has attained a particular significance and is celebrated more solemnly than the others. Among all the Volga Finns, the ceremonies observed on this occasion were very much alike. The following description was taken down by the author among the Cheremiss in the District of Urzhum, where, on the fortieth day, they kill a sheep, or at times even a bigger animal, all the relations, neighbours and friends of the deceased gathering together. The deceased himself is fetched, with particular ceremonies, from the graveyard, members of his own family being chosen to do this. When the sun is highest in the heavens, the latter put the best horses before a waggon, take meat and drink with them and drive with great speed and tinkling of bells to the burial-ground. The ceremonies had to be as solemn as at a wedding, and all the dead were to know that they were now coming with two horses to fetch " so-and-so " to the " great feast." The horses stop by the grave, where honey, meat, gin and beer, and also bread, cheese and pancakes are placed on a white cloth. Uncovering their heads, those who have come to fetch the deceased now remind him, kneeling, of the great day that has arrived: " Get up (the name of the deceased is mentioned), see what we have brought thee — honey, mead, gin, beer, bread, butter and pancakes, get up and eat! The ' fortieth night ' is nearing, come with us to the village. At home they have killed a sheep for thee, thy widow and children await thee, thy relations want to meet thee. We have not come to thee for nothing, we have come to take thee to the great feast." They then pour out drink on the grave, placing also some food on it and repeating the words usual at memorial-feasts: " May this be thy portion! " The deceased is called on to bring with him the relations who died earlier, all the dead fathers and mothers of the family; even the ruler of the lower world is invited to the feast. When about to start, they place a soft cushion in the waggon for the deceased to sit on. Having regaled the dead man in every way and tasted of the food themselves, they ask him to get into the waggon. The deceased may seem shy, or puzzled, so they assure him: " Thou knowest us, and thy waggon thou knowest, thine own are the horses too." Having shaken up the cushions, the one who gets into the waggon says: " Sit down beside me, we will drive together, we are going home." Though the seat is empty, the Cheremiss believes that the shade of the deceased is there. He often turns to it during the drive and speaks to it. If several persons have arrived to invite the deceased, the horse by which he is taken is at the head of the procession. In some places they drive three times round the grave before returning to the village.

At the homestead, the widow comes to meet the deceased, and kneels with her children by the steps. Before them stands a solemn functionary with bared head, holding bread, cheese and drink in his hands. He speaks kindly to the dead man, calls him by name and asks him politely to step into the hut. The widow and children look at the arriving guests with tears in their eyes. When the deceased is supposed to have stepped out of the waggon, the cushion is taken into the hut to a fixed place where the deceased is asked to sit down. None of the living people seat themselves on that place, and near it all his clothes, even his bast-shoes, are hung on the beams. Pointing to them, the widow says: " Look, here are thy clothes, no one has used them, nothing of them have we lost." They place meat and drink before the deceased, and when they suppose him to have eaten enough, the men take him to see the cattle, the corn-stacks and the farm implements, and it is even customary to take him to the bath-house to have a bath. Some of the relations living a long way off have already arrived, but the feast proper does not begin until the sun goes down.

Then all the relations and friends of the dead man arrive at the yard. A common usage is for every family to bring with them meat and drink of every kind. The member of the family who receives the guests, says to the deceased: " See, thy friend (the name is mentioned) has brought thee this." Besides bringing meat and drink every guest takes also a small wax-taper with him. The festival mood is heightened above all by the numerous wax-tapers which are placed near the back wall on a stand made for the purpose. In the middle burns a thick wax-taper, one metre in length, twisted out of three ordinary tapers. To the right of it stands a row of smaller ones, one for each of the dead man's relations who have departed earlier, and to the left each guest places his taper in honour of the deceased. When they are burnt out fresh ones are lighted. The " great taper " that burns until dawn has also been lighted for the actual guest of the day.

It is this last who is the object of everyone's attention. All eyes are directed towards the cushion on the bench in the interior of the room below the tapers, where they believe that the dead man is sitting. The women vie in carrying meat and drink there; everything cooked is intended for the deceased. Yet the living also get their share. The memorial feast in honour of the dead man is no real festivity unless everyone eats and drinks on this occasion. The Cheremiss believes, just as the Votiak does, that the more sated the guests are, the more so is the deceased. For this last separate vessels are set forth; a separate trough for meat, bread, pancakes, pies and eggs, and a large round stoop made of birch-bark for gin and mead. Every one going up to taste of the meat and drink kneels by the seat of the deceased and throws or pours a little into his vessel, inviting him to eat. A small piece of each part of the slaughtered sheep is also placed in his trough. Old men remain long kneeling before the deceased imploring him to protect the family, and also the cattle from falling down precipices or being torn to pieces by wild animals; asking him, further, to make the corn grow, to ward off insects from the fields, mice from the store-house, etc.

At midnight the living, at least, begin to feel that they have had enough. They are all in good humour, the gin-goblets have been emptied every now and then, and also the " stoop " of the deceased has gradually filled. The bag pipe which until now has lain mute, tucked into the shirt-front of its owner, is now brought out, and one and another invite the " shade " of the deceased to come and dance. No one keeps in his seat, all swing and whirl around. The tired hands can hardly longer make fresh tapers and put them up. Even the widow and children have for a while forgotten their grief. Many old men move now only mechanically, and some of them have already gone to sleep in the corners.

But there are people among them who have strength enough to watch. The dancing and the murmur of the people cease for a moment. Curiosity increases, when some one near the door exclaims: " The dead man is coming," upon which a person, looking very dignified, steps into the hut and takes the seat of the deceased. The widow hastens to embrace him, calling him her husband, the old men press his hand, calling him by the name of the deceased. The Cheremiss choose some one resembling the dead man in size and appearance, and for the night this substitute is dressed in the dead man's clothes. He is called " the representative of the deceased," and every politeness and kindness is consequently shown him. Every one wishes to regale him in the best possible way with meat and drink, especially drink. The " dead man " relates his observations on life beyond the grave and advises his relations to remember him, to live in harmony and avoid quarrelling, to work and to be economical. The survivors, for their part, ask for the protection of the dead man.

The tapers gradually begin one after the other to go out, only the biggest of them is still burning, when one of the old men, coming in, wakes up the sleeping people, saying: " The day is dawning, the dead man wants his rest." The languid people then bestir themselves, as before sunrise the dead man must be conveyed with all honours to the peace of the grave. But first a prayer is said, all kneeling and turning their faces in the direction of the seat of the deceased. He is told that it is now time for him to depart for his home among the other dead. They wish him a pleasant time, advise him to make friends with the "old Cheremiss," by which name they mean those who have departed before. The latter, who are considered to be present, are also addressed with good wishes: "May you have bread and salt over there in abundance, do not go away from us hungry and thirsty, be rich and happy, walk in light, help us too, to live, do not frighten us, do not forget our cattle and do not disperse our family." Then one of them takes the taper-stand, another the food-trough, a third the drinking-vessel, and the others, with the widow at their head, carry the dead man's clothes, and thus they go out into the yard, the "representative" being the foremost. From the yard they step out into the village street, wending their way to the burial-place. The women weep aloud. They do not, however, walk all the way there, but the procession stops at a hill situated outside the village, where the rest of the burning tapers and the food and drinks are thrown down. Even here, they remember the deceased, wishing him a happy existence and exhorting him to live in comfort in the society of those already there, and asking him not to come home, at least not as an uninvited guest. Besides giving him meat and drink, he is presented, on his departure, with a wooden spoon and cup, which are shattered on the spot, for otherwise — so say the Cheremiss — the dead man does not get them.

It is usual among the Hill Cheremiss to kill a horse for the memorial feast of the fortieth day, if the deceased is a man, and a cow, if a woman. During the feast all the meat must be consumed, as it is not right to reserve festival food for the next day. The vessels and tapers of the deceased are here placed by the threshold. When sacrificing to the deceased, his own people say: " In thy memory have we prepared meat and drink; we, thy relations and neighbours, have all assembled. Do not take it amiss if we have not entertained thee enough, forgive us if we have hurt thee in thy lifetime, do not be angry with us, and do not punish us by sending us diseases and other misfortunes. Together with our friends and comrades, we wish you, all ye dead ones, to be satisfied with our feast; now go back to your dwelling, sated, singing and dancing." The deceased is then conveyed with music and singing to a fixed place, where they put up in his honour a little table with one foot. On this table, which is called " the table of the deceased," they place a vessel for food and three spoons. In some parts it is customary to lay a long pole across chasms or rivulets, should any such be in the neighbourhood, so that the dead man may be able to cross them. The pole is called the " bridge of the deceased." This seems to be a symbol of the "bridge of the realm of the dead," across which, according to an idea descending from Iran, the deceased had to wander to the other life.[43]

Among the Eastern Cheremiss in the District of Birsk it is also customary, in some places, to go to bed on the fortieth night. After the music, the dancing, and the entertainment are over, the widow takes to her the cushion on which the deceased is supposed to have been sitting during the feast and says: " Still for the last night will we sleep together." Early next morning the dead man is ceremoniously conveyed with two horses back to the burial-ground.[44]

In the province of Perm the Cheremiss are in the habit of making one of the dead man's relatives ride on horseback to the burial-ground to invite the deceased. Having fulfilled his task, the rider returns to the village at full gallop, crying: " He is coming, he is coming." At the same moment, the waiting crowd rush at the panting horse with knives in their hands, slaughtering it at once. The meat of the horse is then boiled and eaten, but the hide is hung over the grave of the dead man.[45]

Similar ideas and customs are observed also among the Mordvins. The dead man is fetched from the graveyard by the horse promised him for sacrifice. The one who has dressed himself in the clothes of the deceased relates his experiences and describes the work of the dead, saying, among other things, that such and such a person has fine horses, another walks in the forest, this one has lost his property, that one has married, such a one keeps bees, etc. Among other curious customs occurring at funeral festivities, it may be mentioned here that the Mordvins even make the " dead man " fell trees, if he wishes it. They place the man who has dressed himself in the clothes of the deceased on a chair provided with a cushion, put a big knife into his hand and then carry him sitting on the chair out of the hut to the drying-kiln, where, beforehand, they have stuck a twig into the ground. The dead man begins to chop it down with all his might. The " tree " having been felled, the deceased is carried back to the hut, taking the " tree " with him. At dawn the representative of the dead man is taken to the graveyard, where he is carried from the waggon on the cushion on which he has been sitting, and seated on the grave of the deceased with his back to the east. At his feet the others lay pancakes, mutton, etc., asking the dead man to eat together with them for the last time. Then, having eaten, they say good-bye to the deceased, asking him to come again at harvest-time, when also his portion is to be reaped. The deputy bows and hastily steps from the grave.[46]

Of the Siryans it is related that at the memorial feast of a deceased female a woman appears as the principal guest of the feast, and, at that of a male, a man, who, at the close of the feast is the first to go out of the hut, attended by the others with candles in their hands, for, according to their ideas, the deceased withdraws from the hut in the person of his deputy. In some places the latter is accompanied as far as the first cross-road.[47]

In Ingria the people used to go with food to the grave at the " six weeks " festival, in order to invite the deceased to the feast. Having returned home, they put the food on the table with a spoon in it, which no one was allowed to touch. Moreover, the eldest member of the family scattered some salt, peas and slices of egg on the table for the benefit of the dead. During the repast, a woman in the entrance sang a " weeping-song," in which the deceased were implored to join the circle of relations. After the repast these went, in the order in which they left the table, out of the door into the village street, turning their faces in the direction of the grave-yard. At the same time each one stuck a fire-stick or a twig into the ground, as a walking-stick for the dead man.[48]

In Russian Karelia it was customary, when the relations were going to the graveyard to invite the deceased to the feast, to take with them, besides the other horses, one that was with-out a driver and harnessed to an empty sleigh over which was spread a white cloth, for the purpose of conveying the deceased to his former home.[49]

In some districts, among the Siryans and the Volga races, there seems to have been the custom to celebrate also the anniversary with a farewell feast.

According to the Eastern Votiaks the deceased then first leaves his own people, among whom his "soul" (*urt*) has up to that time lived and thriven. To accompany the deceased all the relations arrive; a sheep or a cow is killed for the feast, and some of the food is taken to the grave. The white piece of cloth which on the funeral day had been fixed to a rafter, is also taken there and solemnly buried in the grave. After that day the clothes of the dead man, which up to then had been carefully kept and only produced on the occasion of great memorial feasts, could be given away to the poor.[50]

PLATE IV

AT THE GRAVE.   INGERMANLAND

(See page 56.)

After photograph by J. Lukkarinen.

According to one report the Votiaks believe that if they do not celebrate a memorial feast then, the dead will not give the new-comer a place in their community, but will make him continue to wander about the village, as the deceased had done in the course of the year.[51]

The anniversary is celebrated by the Eastern Cheremiss, in the District of Birsk, in such a manner that all the clothes of the deceased are hung upon his favourite horse, which is then taken to the grave and led three times round it. They light a three-branched candle on the grave, saying at the same time to the dead man that the anniversary has arrived and promising to kill the horse in his honour. Having arrived at the homestead, the horse is killed at once and a memorial meal prepared of its flesh. While sacrificing, the relations say to the deceased: " Eat what we have prepared for thee; we have not harnessed thy horse, we have not used it, now take it with thee." At the end of the feast, the bones of the horse are taken to the graveyard, where they are hung in a tree, but the hide is sold for the benefit of the poor and the fatherless.[52]

In honour of particular persons the Votiaks further cele-brate a remarkable memorial feast, which, however, does not take place at a specially fixed time, but sometimes a year or several years after death.

This festivity, which is generally celebrated late in autumn, is called by the Votiaks a " horse-wedding " or " the wedding of the dead," these names being derived from the fact that it is, above all, a cheerful feast with wedding-songs and wed-ding-presents. The sacrificial animal, which is generally killed in the yard, must be a horse, if the deceased in question is a man, but a cow, if a woman. In some places where the memorial feast is celebrated the first year after death, the animal which the deceased liked best and which he used in his lifetime, is generally sacrificed to him. All his relations are invited, these alone partaking of the sacrificial meal, as it is

against custom to invite strangers. The most important performance consists of the taking of the animal's bones in the
evening, by candle-light, with music and singing, to the graveyard, where they are hung upon a tree.[53]

A curious custom among the Mordvins is the " harvest of
the dead." Already when sowing in spring they pray to the
Lord to let the corn grow for the welfare of the living and
the dead. During the harvest-festival the relatives of the
deceased also reap the portion of the dead man, each of them
cutting only a few straws. The chief part is played by the
widow, who all day wears a belt of straw made by herself.
Cattle are slaughtered for this feast.[54] Among the Siryans,
traces of a memorial feast in the harvest-field have also been
found.[55]

Besides feasts decided on beforehand, particular memorial
feasts are occasionally celebrated for some special reason. According to a general idea, the dead may remind the living in
in a dream, or by all kinds of signs, of their wishes. Memorial
feasts are chiefly celebrated in such cases of illness as have
been declared by a wise man to originate from some one among
the dead. Among the Mordvins, the patient must then creep
on all fours to the grave of the deceased to ask his forgiveness.[56] Should an animal — a horse or a cow — disappear
from the pasture-land, or go astray in the forest, one of the
dead relations, according to the Votiaks, has hidden away
the animal. Wax-tapers are then lighted, and just as at the
memorial feasts, food is sacrificed to the dead, in the hope that
they will not keep the animal, but drive it home. Even little
adversities, such as a failure in distilling brandy, or the loosen-
ing of a wheel on a journey, the restlessness of a baby, etc.,
may become reasons for preparing a memorial feast.[57] A
widow, at least, must always be on the lookout. If the
Cheremiss woman's back aches, she believes that her deceased
husband has had sexual connexion with her during the night.
Then she must light a wax-taper and sacrifice to the dead

PLATE V

SACRIFICIAL TREE OF THE DEAD AMONG
THE EASTERN VOTIAKS

(Government Permission)
(See page 56.)
Water-colour by V. Soldan-Brotfeldt.

man, saying: "Make me well again. Here are pancakes and a candle, eat and do not touch me any more."[58] The customs of Finnish widows are described by Agricola in the following words: "The deceased (Männinkäiset) also received their offerings when widows re-married."

CHAPTER IV

GENERAL MEMORIAL FEASTS

BESIDES memorial feasts in honour of some particular person, general ones are also celebrated, on which occasion all the deceased belonging to the family are remembered. Such feasts are called by the Cheremiss "taper-feasts," because then, as at memorial feasts in general, a number of wax-tapers are lighted. The Volga Finns seem to have two separate memorial feasts each year, namely, one in spring at Easter-time, and another in autumn, at the end of field-labour.

General memorial feasts are here celebrated either in such manner that every family circle remembers its own dead by itself, or that related families assemble at the house of the head of a greater family, to celebrate in common the memory of their mutual dead relations. At times even the whole village, which in that case is a so-called family-village, will celebrate in common the memory of its dead. Nowadays the first-named way would seem to be most in use, but in many places, even up to our days, remainders of the last-named also have survived.

The ceremonies observed at the general memorial feasts recall very much those of the special ones. To every relation kept in memory a wax-taper is lit, meat and drink being also sacrificed. To those no longer remembered a mutual taper is also lighted. When crumbling bread and pouring gin into the trough of the dead the Votiaks say: " Ye long ago deceased, may this food we are sacrificing to you reach you." In some places a farewell feast is still celebrated on the morning of the next day.

When the memorial feast lasts a day and night, the family must see that the dead are not bored in any way and that they do not go away hungry from the feast. In order to amuse their dead relations, the Votiaks, among other things, take them for a walk. They believe that near to every participant in the feast there is a dead person of the same age, who in his life-time was more intimate with him than with anybody else, and it is therefore the duty of every participant to amuse and regale the soul in his vicinity. According to the belief of the Votiaks the deceased does everything that his living relation of equal age does; the more cheerful the participant is, the more cheerful is his dead friend; the more sated he is, the fuller is the deceased. From this it follows that, at the memorial feast, people eat and drink as much as possible, so that the dead need not go away hungry. For the same reason, it is not proper to work on this occasion, so as not to vex the deceased by not only not amusing him, but by actually compelling him to work. Therefore, also, people do not go to bed during a memorial feast, as the deceased who has been in company with the sleeping, might easily sleep too long and thus remain among the living when the other dead are taken to the burial ground.[1]

The most remarkable of all the Volga peoples' memorial feasts is the one celebrated during Easter-week. The night before Maundy Thursday is called " the wandering-night of the dead " by the Votiaks. They believe that all the dead then move about. On the night before, after sunset, these rise from their graves and make for the villages. At night one can even see them, if one turns one's clothes inside out, and, putting a horse-collar round one's neck, goes up on the roof of the house. But during this time the Votiaks take many precautions. Thus, they do not work, nor do they heat the oven, nor may they bring anything to the house, or take anything away from it. In many places, they do not even feed the cattle, at least not with their hands, the food being pushed before the animals with their feet. In some parts the young people are warned not to take even a stick or a distaff into their hands, as the one who does this will be bitten by a snake the following summer. In the night-time everything must be still. Food must be set forth on every table, and it is even carried to the bath-house, where the dead go to have baths. During the feast, they place on a bench by the door pancakes, pies, bread, cheese, eggs, etc., for the dead, and, in addition two empty vessels, on whose brim they fix a little home-made wax-taper for each of the dead relations retained in memory. On the bench spoons are also placed for the invisible hands of the spirits. When throwing food and pouring drink into the vessels set forth for the dead, the Cheremiss say: " Dead people, eat, drink, give us health, peace, success and wealth; multiply our cattle, make our corn grow, give us a good wind for cleaning the corn, and protect us from destruction by fire, water and evil spirits! " In other places the door is opened, and food is thrown over the threshold, with the saying: " Ye deceased, eat and drink, do not be angry, do not go away hungry, may ye live in light in the other world, may the earth on your graves feel light, do not torment us, the sur-vivors, with illnesses, do not attack our cattle and do not worry us with other calamities!" The names of all the relations retained in memory are mentioned at the feast. At the same time the ruler of the graveyard is remembered. Even to the dead that have no surviving relations they light a mutual taper and throw some morsels of food. When the ceremonies are over, the food of the dead is carried out into the yard, where it is eaten by the dogs.[2]

With this feast are frequently connected all kinds of pro-tective ceremonies. Pervuchin relates of the Votiaks that on this occasion they collect all sorts of weapons and go to the nearest forest, shooting and shouting, in order to chase away wolves and other beasts of prey. Having returned, they take a scythe, a shovel or a spade, and some ashes from the hearth and draw a ring round their houses to protect them from evil spirits, who at this time are abroad everywhere. When going to bed, they burn juniper in the hut, and shut the windows, the smoke-hole and the openings under the floor, lest the spirits should get in. In some places the young men sit armed all night on the roof of the hut or the store-house to watch for these. The spirits generally appear in the shape of a cat or a dog, sometimes even in that of a wolf. Next morning, in the yard, a fire of straw is made, over which the members of the family jump one after another, to purify themselves.[3]

The idea that the spirits of the dead walk about early in spring is a common one among the Slavic and other East European peoples. During the Christian era the above festival coincided with the Easter festivities, but, in some parts, the Cheremiss have retained for it a more original time, namely, the first new moon in the month of March.[4]

From the Russians, the above ideas reached the Orthodox Esthonians, who were in the habit of celebrating a similar memorial feast on Easter morning. The hostess spread a clean table-cloth in the yard near the gate, and placing on it every kind of food, milk, cheese, butter, meat, pies, etc., she began calling the dead relations, saying: "Come, (the names are mentioned), come yourselves and bring your children with you, come and partake of our food and our drink! I invite you in hospitable mood, with a tender heart; I serve you first, and help myself afterwards." Having kept silence for a while, in order to give the dead people time to eat and drink, she then began counselling them to return: "Go away, let it be enough of eating and drinking, go where ye were taken, each to his place; lead the children by the hand, go away!" The food of which the deceased had had their portion, was taken back to the hut and placed on the table, round which the family sat down to eat.[5]

According to a general belief among the Baltic Finns, the dead move about in autumn. The month of October is called

by the Esthonians "the time of the spirits" (Hingede aeg)
or "the month of the spirits" (Hingekuu). Occasionally,
this time lasts until November, which not infrequently is
called "the month of the dead" (Kooljakuu). The Catholic
festivities of All Saints' Day and All Souls' Day were more
especially devoted to the dead. During these days it was
not permitted to shout or make a noise, huts were cleaned,
and food was set forth at night for the dead. The festivity
coinciding with the Catholic All Saints' Day was called by the
Finns, Kekri, of which Agricola says: "Kekri multiplied the
cattle."

The oldest description of the Kekri-feast is to be found in
E. Castrén's narration about the neighbourhood of Kajana in
1754. He says that the Kekri-feast or All Saints' Day was
celebrated in two different ways: partly in the pagan manner
in honour of the ancient Finnish god Kekri, partly in the
Catholic way, in honour of all the saints. According to the
heathen custom, a half-year-old sheep was killed either in
the evening before the feast-day or very early the next morning. The sheep was boiled, the bones being kept intact, and
it was not allowed to be tasted, not even to try its saltness,
before the carcase had been served whole on the table. Then
it had to be eaten until the last morsel had gone and no remains were left. By Kekri other spirits also were meant, for
whom all sorts of eatables and drinkables were prepared on
the evening before the feast day, some in the cow-house for
the welfare of the cattle, others in the stable for luck with
horses, others under big trees and by huge stones in the fields
or in the forest, and yet others in all these places at once.
According to the Catholic way, the host received the saints
outside in the yard, in the darkness of the evening before the
feast, taking them to the bath-house, which had been particularly cleaned and heated for their use and provided with cold
and hot water and "bath-brooms." A table with meat and
drink had also been placed there. The host waited on these

guests at certain fixed times, and finally, on the evening of the following day, All Souls' Day, late and in the dark, with bared head, and pouring on the ground some beer and brandy, he took his guests out of the yard. If, after the baths of the "saints," there were straws in the water, it was the sign of a good harvest, but if there were instead chips of wood or bits of coal, it was a presage of famine.[6]

To the celebration of the Kekri-feast belonged, further, the custom of disguising oneself in curious costumes. Masks for the face were made of birch-bark, paper, etc. People, masked in this way, were called Kekritär. The latter wandered unknown from house to house, from village to village, threatening to pull down the ovens of the house, should these uncommon guests not be abundantly regaled and entertained. During All Saints' time it was also customary to regale beggars with food.

As at the New Year's festivities, the people tried to make the spirits reveal coming events. The custom of casting tin, and foreseeing events from the figure formed when the molten tin was poured into water was of this character. Or, on the night before Kekri, they walked under the windows to listen to what was being talked about in the hut, and, from the conversation going on there, to infer what would happen during the following year. Further, in the evening, they would count the sticks in the oven, and if they were all there in the morning, no one needed to trouble himself about possible deaths in the following year, but otherwise there would be as many deaths at the house as the number of the absent sticks indicated. When making bread they took from the straw as many ears of corn (rye) as there were members in the family and pressed them into the bread. The one whose ear was burnt up during the baking, would die before the next Kekri-feast. When the loaves were taken out of the oven, the master of the house cut a piece from one and let it fall on the table. If the piece happened to fall with the crust downwards, life would go well during the year; otherwise some disaster was to be expected. In some neighbourhoods it was, moreover, customary, on the evening before All Saints' Day, to place on the window-sill one grain of salt for each member of the family. He whose grain of salt melted during the night, was to die. It was also customary to burn Kekri-fires, most probably for the purpose of driving away spirits. The fire was burnt on some hill and was made of oakum mixed with straw.[7]

A corresponding feast is known also among the Esthonians and seems to be common among the Baltic Finns, though the wandering-time of the dead has later been influenced by the Catholics, who, since 835, have celebrated the first of November as All Saints' Day and, since 998, the second of November as All Souls' Day. The name *kekri* or *keyri* seems further to be known among the Russian Lapps (*kevre, kovre,* " a sacrifice ").[8]

In Western Finland the belief prevails that the spirits walk at Christmas. Even in our days young people are in the habit of dressing up and masking themselves at Christmas and going about the farms, where they are called " Christmas Mothers." This custom together with the idea behind it is borrowed from Scandinavia. Like the Scandinavians, the Lapps also believed that at Christmas the dead left their underground dwelling and set out to wander through the woods and fells. For this reason, the children had to keep still during that time; if they made a noise, ghosts would appear. When, on Christmas night, the shamans sat at the entrance of their dwelling, they felt the spirits climbing over their legs into the tent. Food, and particularly some water, had to be set out when the spirits came. In order to protect their wells from being destroyed by the spirits, the Lapps used to throw pieces of metal into the water on " the most dangerous evening." If they did not treat the underground people well, these might take a cruel revenge, e.g., suck out the brain from a man's head. These spirits, walking about at Christmas, were called by the Lapps, " the Christmas people." [9]

The keeping of Christmas by the Swedish Lapps in heathen times is described by the missionary Graan, who says that the Lapps then collected morsels from all the dishes prepared for the feast and put them into a small trough of birch-bark, shaped like a little sailing-boat with masts, sails and oars. They then searched out the tallest pine-tree near the tent, and into the tree nearest the pine they put the boat as high up as their hands would reach, but in the trunk of the pine they cut round figures on four sides. Into each of these, every man in the village who had put food into the trough, had to throw three spoonfuls of fat with his left hand. According to Graan they also used to set up a tree, four yards high, with twigs set half-way up it. This tree was smeared with blood from a slaughtered reindeer on Christmas Eve, and on its branches were put morsels of the animal's lungs, heart, tongue and lips. [10]

Fig. 3.
Lapp Christmas
Custom

Mallmer relates that at Christmas they made boats of fir, three-quarters of a yard long, with masts, which were then dedicated to " the Christmas Master." The boat with its masts was smeared with reindeer-blood and here and there the sign of the cross was drawn on it. [11] Högström adds that the sailing-boats were placed in tall trees, not in a hanging position, but resting on branches. Even the pine was marked with the sign of the cross and was smeared a good way upwards from its root with reindeer blood. Moreover, it had been customary, he says, to hang up a trough of birch-bark in tall trees which were carved on two sides and marked with the sign of the cross. Into the trough Christmas food, fish, cheese and milk were laid. On its rim were stuck two spade-like sticks, one foot long (most probably, as oars). This sacrifice was made to a spirit called Ruotta, "to prevent it from piercing the womb of the women." [12]

This sailing-boat sacrifice among the customs of the Lapps, cannot fail to attract attention, as the Lapps themselves did not use sailing-boats. With reason does Fritzner therefore compare the " Christmas people " of the Lapps, who are furthermore worshipped in connection with a foreign feast, with the Icelanders' Jolasveinar, who were also believed to move about at Christmas.[13] Remains of this belief are met with still in our days everywhere in Scandinavia. In Lapland the above-named custom of sacrificing is limited to the Lapps of Scandinavia.

A common feast in honour of the deceased, celebrated at a time agreed upon by the relations, has been retained in East Karelia. This feast was arranged by the owner of a farm agreed on beforehand. Many animals were killed, and the invited relations and friends brought with them food in abundance. For the deceased a cloth was spread in a separate room on a separate table, on which something, a spoon or a dish, had to be laid every day for nine weeks. Into the walls of the room many nails were driven, for the deceased to hang their clothes on. The day before the feast the food was put on the table, round which empty chairs were placed. The windows were opened, after which all the family went to the burial-ground to invite the deceased to the feast. Everyone invited his kinsfolk, the women weeping aloud: " Come and bring with you your relations unto the ninth generation! Kinsfolk, bring all your acquaintances with you!" [14]

According to the oldest sources, the Mordvins were earlier in the habit of celebrating from time to time, after a longer period, e.g., fifty years or so, a great common feast for a large family, in honour of the deceased.[15]

It is customary among the Cheremiss to celebrate a memorial feast also in honour of the unknown deceased who have no relations in life. Such deceased are called Utumö. Nowadays these feasts are customary only among the Eastern Cheremiss. The feast is celebrated in the village community in summer when many insects and larvae have appeared in the fields, hindering the growth of the crops. The guests put on their holiday attire, and the ceremonies, which resemble those at a wedding, are led by a host, who is called the " head of the wedding." The " wedding-women " also appear, wearing round their shoulders beautiful shawls embroidered with silk, and also the " wedding-dancers," who are commanded by a leader with a whip to which a bell is fixed. Further participants in the festivity are a drummer and a bagpiper. As in a wedding-procession — only without a bride and bridegroom — the villagers, carrying with them pancakes, bread, beer and brandy, with the functionaries and pipers at their head, go to the corn-field, round which they drive or walk three times, following the sun. Every now and then the procession stops, a wax-taper is lighted and the festival food is tasted, part of which is also sacrificed to the dead. All the time music is played and wedding-songs sung. In the meantime the old people have started for the burial-ground, where a black ox is to be sacrificed to the Utumö. The killing, the cooking of the sacrifice-meat, and the eating of it take place by the burial-ground, outside its enclosure. Having marched or driven round all the corn-fields of the village, the wedding-procession also arrives at the graveyard. Thinking of the Utumö, everyone places a wax-taper on the fence. A prayer noted down by the author in the District of Birsk runs thus: " Utum man, Utum woman, protect our fields from larvae, from butterflies! A large ox has been killed, come with your family and eat. Do not touch the corn!" After the meal the ox-hide is cut into one narrow strip, long enough to surround the whole of the burial-ground. The bones of the ox and certain parts of the meat are buried in the earth. The sacrifice is, however, not often performed immediately; frequently it is enough to make only a promise, which is done in this way: — a bast-rope is wound by the old people of the village round the tree dedicated to the Utumö in the graveyard. If the rope is wound one, three, five or seven times round the tree, this means that the sacrifice will be performed after so many years. The number must always be an odd one. The old promise-rope is not burnt till the sacrifice is performed. On account of its similarity with the wedding-ceremonies, this memorial feast is called " Utum-wedding."

At times a single family must also perform an Utum-sacrifice. If there are many mice in the store-house, it is, according to the Cheremiss, a sign that the Utumö claim a memorial feast. It is generally not celebrated at once, but the father of the family goes to the forest and hunts up as large a piece of lime-bark as possible, which he then twists into a rope and winds nine times round the aforesaid tree. Thus they need not perform the sacrifice till nine years later. In the wedding ceremonies only the members of the family participate. This time they do not go to the corn-field, but instead wander three times round the farm-yard, going into the store-house, the larder and the cow-house. The sacrifice, which also now consists of a black ox, is performed, cooked and eaten at the burial-place.[16]

Only a few of the innumerable dead can, in the long run, avoid the fate of the Utumö, the identity of which becomes in time quite effaced from the memory of the living. Castrèn says of the Samoyeds that only their shamans remain " immortal." However, some other remarkable persons, such as famous ancestors, princes, heroes, etc., may be retained for a longer time in the memory of their survivors and be worshipped as household-gods and heroes.

The importance of ancestor worship in the social life of the Finno-Ugric races will be further seen from their belief that their deceased ancestors did not only create their customs and found their religion, but even now protect and watch over them. The Votiaks say that if the present people begin to neglect the customs and usages of their ancestors, they will be punished with diseases and years of famine.

The near connexion between the worship of ancestors and an instinctive nationalistic feeling, is very vividly described by the Norwegian missionary Isaac Olsen († 1730) in his account of the Lapp's belief in his underground spirits, whose dwellings, clothes and language are perfectly similar to those of the Lapps living above ground. The underground people exhort the Lapps to " have just such dwellings, ceremonies and customs, clothes and language and other things as the living have seen among the dead, impressing this especially upon the shamans, whose duty it is to instruct the others and educate them by a wise discipline. They speak the Lapp tongue with them, as this language is the best of all, and warn them not to speak any other language than that spoken by their gods, which was created by their first shamans, the spirit-folk, and other ancient beings. This they must do, if they wish to live long and happily, to have success in their trades, and to keep themselves and their cattle in good health." [17]

CHAPTER V

THE LIFE BEYOND

THE MANNER in which life beyond the grave was regarded appears plainly from the burial ceremonies. The Lapps say that they fit out the dead with provisions and various implements " so that these may satisfy their·hunger, go fishing, or chop wood, as they did before, while alive." [1] The " ancient Cheremiss " till and sow their fields over there, practise cattle-raising, hunt, fish, keep bees, marry and go visiting each other. As in their former life, the dead can suffer from cold and hunger. [2] To help protect them from cold, the Voguls, when they have warmed themselves in the open at a fire of logs, leave a few pieces of wood behind in order that the dead may also be able to warm themselves. [3] The dead may even find themselves in situations of mortal danger in the life beyond. The Mordvins and Cheremiss believed that the dead, having lived for a certain period in the underworld, could die a second time. [4]

A general belief is that the life beyond is lived under the earth. The passage occurs in a Vogul song: " The dead people go to the land below "; also, in Ostiak folk-poetry we read: " We arrive at the sea belonging to the man living in the underworld." [5] In its nature this underworld resembles the world we live in in everything, with the exception that, seen with our eyes, everything there would appear inside out or upside down. The Lapps believe that the dead walk there with the soles of their feet against ours. According to the Samoyeds the same rivers and streams exist there, but flow in opposite directions. The tops of trees there grow downward; the sun rises in the west and sets in the east. The life of those over there runs also contrary to ours; they become younger and grow smaller with the years, until they disappear and become nothing or are born into the family again as children. In this way, the " shade " lives as long in the underworld as its predecessor on the earth.[6] The Ostiaks say that the dead dwindle in the end to a little beetle.[7]

The belief that everything is topsy-turvy in the underworld, appears also in the worship of the dead. From this springs the custom of washing the dead, or sacrificing to them, with the left hand. When the Mordvins reap the portion of the dead, they hold the sickle by the blade, throwing it backwards over their heads.[8] To sacrifice backwards, contrary to the sun's motion, with clothes inside-out, or to place the offering upside-down on graves, is characteristic of the Finno-Ugrian cult of the departed. The idea of an inverted world seems to have been derived from the reflection seen in the water.

Just as the villages were formerly family-villages and the graveyards contained only members of the same family in their ground, it is believed that the dead live together in villages, the coffin of each of their inhabitants forming their private " houses." The Volga Finns call the first one to be buried " the graveyard ruler "; he is supposed to keep order in the graveyard-community, and at commemoration feasts a special candle is lit for him and food is sacrificed. That discipline is actually upheld in the underground village is shown by the Votiaks' belief that the dead receive very unwillingly into their ranks newcomers who have been noted in life for evil ways and quarrelsomeness.[9] To meet with death in a strange district is regarded as a great calamity, because the " shade " of the dead one, according to a prevalent belief, is forced to dwell where the body lies, or at any rate in its immediate neighbourhood, and is therefore prevented from joining its relatives. When such a death occurs, certain tribes, including the Voguls, perform a mock burial to entice the dead to the burial-place of its home.[10]

The Finns called the " world beyond " under the earth Manala (orig. *maan-ala* = " underground ") or Tuonela (" the home of Tuoni "). Tuoni, which occurs also in the language of the Norwegian Lapps as Duodna, means " the dead one," later, also " death " and the " life beyond," and is probably a Scandinavian loan-word (cf. Swedish *dana-arf*, " an inheritance falling to the State "). In Tuonela everyone has his own " house," as pictured by a Finnish folk-song in the following words: " Of the finest turf the roof, of fine sand the floor is made, a fathom long is each side-wall, the hinder one a yard in length." That this " house " in Tuonela is the grave itself appears plainly from lines in which the " house " is described as being " carpeted with women's hair, supported by men's bones." In an Ingrian weeping song " Manalan vanhimmat " (" the elders of the underworld ") are mentioned, which " elders " appear to hold some governing rank, as they were not always inclined to permit the dead to pay visits to the world of the living.[11]

In folk-poetry Tuonela seems to be regarded as a common underworld for all. On the way there, one had to cross the " black river " of Tuonela, on which neither sun nor moon shines and over which leads " a bridge " (Tuonen or Manalan silta). These beliefs, probably of later origin, remind one of the Scandinavian river of death, over which one also crossed by means of a bridge. It is probable that they are part of the mediæval views met with also in the literature of the time. Gregory the Great relates how a person being near to death, saw a bridge under which a gloomy, black stream flowed. On this bridge a judgment took place; should any of the unrighteous attempt to pass over it, they fell down into the dark evil-smelling waters. Besides the Christian peoples, the Mohammedans also are acquainted with this originally Persian idea; from these it has reached the Volga Finns. The Chere-

miss believe that the poor dead, in order to reach " the place
of light," must travel slowly along a narrow pole over " the
place of darkness," also called the " resin-cauldron," as there
the souls of the wicked are tortured in burning resin. Only
the righteous come luckily over with the help of the " Prince
of Death," Kiyamat-tora (Arabic *kiamat*, " the resurrection of
the dead "; *tora*, " judge ") or Tamek-vui (Turco-Tatar
tamyk, " the world beyond "; Cheremiss *vui*, " head ") and his
assistant Kiyamat-saus.[12]

A more widely-spread idea in Finnish folk-poetry is, however, that the dead are transported over the river of Tuonela
in a boat. In one song, it is related that, when Wäinämöinen
was on his way to the underworld, the daughter of Tuoni came
with a boat and ferried him over the river. Among the folk-
beliefs the view is expressed that the evil one makes a boat
out of finger-nails clipped on Sundays, in which he carries
the dead off with him to his own place. An identical boat
was called the " corpse-boat " by the Icelanders. Doubtless
all these beliefs about the crossing of a river of death in a
boat are derived from Greek mythology. The furiously-
barking Manalan-rakki (" the underworld's hound ") reminds one of the Greek Cerberos. To the mediæval ideas
belong also Tuonen-portti (" the underworld's gate ") which
corresponds to the Helgrindr in Icelandic poetry.

The common dwelling-place of the dead is called Yabme-
aimo (" the home of the dead ") by the Scandinavian Lapps,
and is governed by Yabme-akka (" Old woman of the dead ").
The Lapps sacrifice to her, and to the dead in general, black
animals, which must be buried alive in the earth. The most
common are said to have been black cats or cockerels. During
the Christian period they believed that the dead, according
to their deeds, could come from Yabme-aimo to God in
Heaven (Radien-aimo, the " Ruler's home ") or to the
" gloomy " Rut-aimo or Ruta-aimo, where the evil Rutu or
Rota tortured the dead. This Rutu was not originally re-

garded as a devil, as it was often the custom to make offerings to him, especially during epidemics. The sacrificial animal itself, a slaughtered horse, buried entire within the earth or in a fissure among the rocks, points to a borrowing from the Scandinavian. According to Randulf, Rutu appeared sometimes to the Lapps as a man dressed in blue. The wolf was called "Rutu's hound." Originally Rota or Rutu (from Old Scandinavian *throte*, "an ulcer") may have been the spirit of the plague.[13]

A mutual belief of both Scandinavians and the Lapps living as their neighbours is, further, the idea that the dead dwelt in certain "holy mountains," [14] where, according to the Lapps, they existed happily, living in tents, keeping themselves in the same way and speaking the same language as the Lapps. They describe the inhabitants of the mountain, who seem to have composed a closed family, and paid visits to one another, riding from mountain to mountain with reindeer, which were sacrificed to them by the Lapps. These "mountain spirits" were the protectors of the living; the Lapps having often many such mountains to which they came when in need. Forbus says that these mountains were not equal in regard to the assistance they could give, "one holy mountain might be of greater help than another, its inhabitants more ready to listen and quicker to act than those of the other." [15] The Lapps inherited these tutelary spirits from their forefathers, or came into possession of them through marriage, and could even raise them themselves by offerings, becoming the more powerful and respected as the number of their "spirits" grew. These spirits would sometimes attempt to take life; by calling the "soul" of a Lapp to themselves before his time had come, they caused sicknesses that could be cured only by the shaman appeasing the "spirits," and leading the sick one's "soul" back to his body again. Leem relates that while a shaman lay in a fit, those present tried to guess which "holy mountain" his soul was at the moment visiting.[16] After death, the Lapps

hoped they would be received into the mountain, the inmates
of which had protected them most during life. "There they
became spirits themselves, and could keep death away from
their relatives and friends for some time." [17] In the more
southern districts, these "mountain spirits," there called
"Saivo man" and "Saivo maiden" (originally a loan-word
from Old Scandinavian *sjö*), have borrowed their characteristics from the Huldre-folk of their southern neighbours. [18]

In West Finland, also, traces of a belief in "mountains of
the dead" may be found. In certain districts the people tell
how the gods have borne away the dead man from the grave
to an adjacent forest-hill, in which he must reside as a penance
for some crime committed during his life. This belief is found
lurking in some Finnish magic-songs, in which the name *hiisi*
(originally "forest" and "hill") appears with apparently
the same meaning, for example: "I call for help from *hiisi*,
I seek for folk from the hill." Hiiden väki ("Hiisi's folk")
means often the same as the Swedish Huldre-folk.

The night being the time chosen by most spirits for moving
about in, the thought arises easily, that the underground world
of the dead lies towards the sunset, or towards the dark north.
In these directions offerings are generally made to the dead.
The Northern Ostiaks and the Voguls are of the opinion, like
many other North Siberian tribes, that the land of the dead
lies hidden somewhere in the Northern Arctic Ocean. According to the Voguls, the land of the dead is under the earth, but
the entrance to it lies far away in the north, where the waters
of the River Ob flow into the sea. Arrived at the entrance,
the road divides itself into three branches, at the mouth of
each of which are signposts, telling which way, according to
the deeds done in life, each soul must take. The ruler of
the land of the dead, who is greatly feared, is called Khul-
ater ("the Ruler of the dead"). In the same place is situated the underworld of the Northern Ostiaks, in which there
are three storeys; in the lowest, said to be of the height of a

dog's tail, live those who have sinned most. The journey to the "world of the dead" appears to be across water; songs relate how the dead are placed sitting in the boat of Khin-ort's ("Prince of sickness") son. In the sagas, a world of the dead is also mentioned, from which the Prince sends his assistants to bring over the dead on a boat. Although the view that the dead are treated in the underworld according to their deeds in life, is unquestionably of later origin, it is still probable that the Ob itself, with its "downward-running" waters, has suggested the idea of a chasm in the dark, mysterious north, where the waters of the river are swallowed up and the underworld opens its gloomy portals. The journey there in a boat receives in these circumstances its natural explanation.[19]

As among the Scandinavians, where the road to Hel led "downward and northward," Finnish poetry tells of Pohjola ("northern home") as being the home of the dead. A corresponding idea to it is the Norrhem of Swedish magic-songs. Where this "gloomy" and "dark" place, as such called Pimentola (*pimeä* = "dark") was supposed to be situated, is made clear by another name, Sarajas (from which Sarantola, etc.), meaning originally "sea" and denoting the Northern Arctic Ocean. The Esthonians called it Maksameri (= the Lebermeer of the mediæval German sagas) and believed it to be a gathering-place for sorcerers, witches, etc. As in Tuonela, so also, according to Finnish folk-poetry, in Pohjola flowed a gloomy river; both names occurring in the same song, and meaning, obviously, one and the same place. This death-river is also envisaged as a turbulent rapid, and is then generally called Rutja's or Turja's rapids, the name of the place denoting a mystic neighbourhood far away in the north. From the songs themselves it would appear that this "awful stream," that "swallows up all waters," where "the trees sink downward their crowns," and where "the reeds fall downward," being therefore of the nature of a vortex, has its origin in the idea of the Maelstrom. Sometimes these "rapids" are said to be a "flaming whirlpool," a name perhaps connected closely with the Aurora Borealis, explained by the Finns as being "the Fire of the Arctic Ocean." Pohjola, to which a "gate" gives entrance, is described in the magic songs as a place breeding sickness and death, or "the man-eating village" where the evil Pohjan-akka or -emäntä ("mistress"; cf. Lapp Jabme-akka) ruled.[20]

Mingled with beliefs from Greek mythology, the paradise of the eastern lands, through the medium of the Russian Orthodox Church, has crept into the views of the Russian Karelians concerning the life beyond. In a "death-song" taken down in the Olonetz Government, and sung the moment the "soul has flown," the journey of the dead to the other world is described in detail. In the opening lines the dead is asked: "Who were they who took thy soul? Were they the Archangels Michael and Gabriel with their angels and apostles? Did they meet thee bearing candles of white wax? Did the chief apostles, Peter and Paul, meet thee bearing golden plates and golden eggs? Did Abraham and Isaac meet thee bearing the keys from Abraham's time with which to open the doors of that distant time? Hadst thou during life (by good deeds) redeemed for thyself the guides to that world? Did they escort thy soul over lands rich with berries, over highly beautiful heaths? Couldst thou with thine own hands pluck the berries? Surely they refreshed thy soul with them, wert thou not over reluctant to give away of thine own berries to others during life?" The song goes on to tell that the way to the other world leads over roaring rapids and swiftly-moving streams: "Did an escort come to take thee over these with oaken boats and oars of gold? Did they come without thy calling, or hadst thou to shout with thy tired voice to them?" Over the river a dense forest grows: "Hadst thou during life redeemed the services of 'the woodcutters, the roadmakers'?" After that come very wide bubbling marshes: "Hadst thou during life redeemed 'the guide over the marsh'?" In the marsh creep the ever-watchful serpents: "Hadst thou during life caused them to sleep?" From the edge of the marsh three pathways lead: "Hadst thou during life redeemed the right to the one on the utmost right?" On that road the soul comes to the blue bridge with parapets of reed, at the end of which is a spring of water with a golden ladle for the cleansing of the besmirched soul. There is also "the bed of fishbone" in which to rest the weary limbs: "Hadst thou redeemed also those during the days of thy life?" "After these, very great stretches of lush grass and wide fields open out before thee. On the grass a table is decked from 'the air to the edge of the air.' On the table many foods of which thou needst not even eat, only to breathe in their direction to satisfy thy stomach. Along the table run 'rivers of milk' and at the place of each soul, a tree has grown giving fruits sweet as honey. At the eastern end of the table is a balance, in which the events of thy life are weighed. Didst thou in life redeem the weighers in thy favour?" [21]

Here we thus meet, in the same song, ideas already known to the ancients. The honey-tree and the "rivers of milk" have prototypes in the tree and rivers of life in paradise.

During the pagan period, separate worlds for the good and the bad dead were unknown. But, already at that time, there seem to have been views that the dead attained to different worlds, not on account of their deeds during life, but according to that which had been the cause of their death. Those who died in battle or as the result of some accident did not go to the underworld but peopled another world up in the heavens. The Cheremiss say that "those who die in battle or are killed by lightning go to heaven." [22] In an old account of the Ostiaks' religion, we read the following words: "If the beasts of the forest tear one asunder, or he is shot in battle, his soul goes upward, but the souls of those dying a natural death at home go downward." In the same manner,

Strahlenberg relates: " those who meet with a violent death or are killed in a fight with the bear, go immediately to heaven, but those dying a natural death in their beds or elsewhere must worship for a long time a stern god under the earth, before they can go up to heaven." [23]   Similar ideas are met with in the folk-poetry of the Ostiaks.   In a song from the Irtysh it is told how the soul of a hero who, in the clash of battle, has received a blow on the head rendering him unconscious, leaves the body to climb by a narrow stairway to heaven, and how he is met by three red-legged squirrels who say to him: " This is our word: we eat our food in the midst of human blood, we drink our drink in the midst of human blood, go back!"   When the soul of the hero returned, consciousness returned also to him.   In another story a hero in heaven is accorded permission by the Heaven god to return to earth to help his comrades who are in a great difficulty. [24]

According to the Finnish Lapps the Aurora Borealis is " the dead in battle, who, as spirits, still continue battling with one another in the air."   The Russian Lapps also declare the Aurora Borealis to be " the spirits of the murdered."   These live in a house, in which at times they gather together and begin stabbing one another to death, covering the floor with blood. " They are afraid of the sun, hiding themselves from its rays."   The Aurora Borealis appears " when the souls of the murdered begin their slaughter."   Hence the Lapps fear it. [25]

The Esthonians also see in the Northern Lights a heavenly war, " Virmalised taplevad " (" Virmalised fight ").   On the island of Ösel they say that during the holy nights when the heavens open, one may see two armed fighting-men, eager to give battle to one another, but God will not allow it, and separates them. [26]   Most probably the Finns also possessed a similar belief; in certain Karelian magic songs Pohjola is sometimes mentioned as the residence of those who " were killed without sickness " and where the inhabitants are said to have " blood-dripping garments." [27]   In a variation on the " song of the Great Oak " that grows so high that neither the sun nor the moon could shine on the earth, and was therefore chopped down " with its crown towards the south and its trunk towards the north," it is further related that the giant tree fell " straight across Pohjola's river " as " an everlasting bridge " for those " killed without sickness." [28] The author is inclined to believe that in this last we meet again the idea of the Milky Way, regarded by some Arctic tribes as being the trunk of a great tree, along which those killed in battle wander. To the same folk-belief may ultimately be traced the Scandinavian belief in Valhall, where the souls of the dead in battle dwell, and, according to *Gylfaginning*, " take on their accoutrements, go out into the yard and fight and kill one another." Other Arctic peoples also have had similar ideas of the Aurora Borealis. The Chukchee in the north-east corner of Asia believe that " the Northern Lights is a dwelling chiefly for those who have died a violent death," [29] and even the Tlingits in North America, according to Veniaminov, the Russian missionary, believe that the souls of the dead dwell, not only in the " underworld " far away in the north, but also up in the sky, where only the souls of those killed in battle may go, and where, as the flames of the Northern Lights, they battle with one another, predicting bloodshed on the earth.[30]

All the dead, however, do not attain to the Life Beyond, wherever this may be regarded as being situated. The souls, especially, of little children, killed and hidden by their mothers, remain as ghosts in the worlds of the living. The Lapps called these Äppäräs (Finnish *äpärä*, " bastard ") and the Ostiaks Vylep or Patshak. The Finnish Liekkiö (" the flaming one ") was probably originally a similar spirit, who, according to Agricola, " ruled over grass, roots and trees." All those lost in forests or drowned in the water, and who were therefore denied the opportunity of resting peacefully in a grave, became similar homeless, restless spirits.

CHAPTER VI

ANIMAL WORSHIP

LIKE many other primitive peoples the Finno-Ugric stocks regard the fruits of the chase and of fishing as holy. While engaged in either of these two occupations their actions, having a significance beyond those needed in ordinary tasks, follow closely certain rules. Their words for game are used with meanings differing from those in everyday use. The bear, especially, has many secret names. The Lapps call him " master of the forest," " the old man of the mountains," " the wise man," " the holy animal," " the dog of God." The Ostiaks have names such as " the fur man," " the dweller in the wilds," for him; the Finns speak of him as " honey-paw," " great forest," etc. They believe that were the actual name of the prey to be used, it might hear it and become angry. On hunting trips and at bear feasts even the different parts of the bear and the hunting gear are given special names. Similarly, on fishing expeditions, a special language is used. The Livonians, for example, when out at sea, retain even to this day the habit of speaking of their fishing gear in strange, mysterious terms.

Cleanliness was essential in both hunting and fishing. Of this, traces can be observed even to-day amongst all the Finno-Ugric peoples. The most general methods of purification, used both for people and for the implements of the hunter or fisher, were smoking over a fire, jumping over fire, washing in water, or being besprinkled with water. The opinion of the Siryans that hunting is a " pure " occupation, animals loving only " pure " people,[1] is common to all the Finno-Ugric stocks. The Ostiaks regard it as improper even for those who stay at home to engage in any dirty work, such as scrubbing floors, or washing clothes, on the day when they know that the hunters have reached the lair of the bear.[2] The Samoyeds do not hunt or fish or even cross the stream when there is a corpse in the village; they also avoid intercourse with women at hunting or fishing times.[3]

In earlier times, when the hunters or fishers among the Lapps set out on an expedition, they did not use the ordinary outlet when leaving their tents, but instead, a special opening in the back of the tent that was regarded as holy and was never used by womenfolk. This opening was called *varr-lyps* ("the bloody backdoor") by the Russian Lapps, the name originating from the fact that the bleeding corpses of the prey were always brought in by it.[4] Missionaries relate that the Lapps threw in by this opening "both the gifts of the forest, viz, birds and animals, and of the sea, viz, fish."[5] Traces of this custom can be observed among the Ostiaks, who, on returning from the forest, carry in the head of the bear through the window and, after the feast-night, carry it out the same way to the storehouse.[6] Of similar origin is likewise a custom among the Finns, whose hunters, when going out in pursuit of a bear, lift the door from its bottom hinges and pass through the opening between the door and the door-post on the side where the hinges are.[7] One had also to set forth with due secrecy on hunting or fishing trips and without meeting anyone, women in particular. A very old custom decrees that no woman may take part in hunting trips, but instead must prepare to meet the returning hunters with special ceremonies, obviously in order thus to avoid dangerous contact. This was especially necessary when the prey was some large animal. When the Lapp brought in the meat of some fallen wild reindeer through the "holy" backdoor, his wife had to have in readiness a liquid prepared from alder-bark, with which the Lapp washed his face while being be-

PLATE VI

Bear Worship of the Voguls

The eyes and nose of the bear are covered over as a protective measure, in the same way as those of the corpse in burial rites. (See page 95.)

After photograph by J. A. Kannisto.

sprinkled by his wife, believing that by this ceremony he could assure himself of better luck among the wild reindeer.[8] Besides the special animals caught in or near the " holy " places, a woman, according to the Lapps, was not allowed to eat of every part of even birds, squirrels, hares, wild reindeer, bears, in short, of any forest animal.[9] It is also to be noted that slaughtering and the cooking of the meat were always left to the men. The more northern stocks, the Lapps and Samoyeds, do their slaughtering for the home-sacrifices also, behind the back of the tent, where women are not allowed to tread.[10]

The bear has always been regarded among the Finno-Ugric peoples as being the most holy of all wild animals. At least the Lapps, Finns, Ostiaks and Voguls held feasts in its honour. Among the Volga peoples, relics of these feasts are no longer found, though many of the beliefs appertaining to the bear are still general among them all. The bear is more intelligent and stronger than a man, say the Votiaks. It understands the speech of men though it cannot talk; when they meet " the old man " in the forest they bare their heads, as is fit and proper, before the master of the forest. Sometimes they bow to it, go down on their knees, etc., as they believe that if one shows due respect to a bear, it will not do them any harm. Enemies are recognized by the bear even after its death, and persecuted by him. For this reason it is unwise to laugh near the body of a bear.

In the life of the community, among the more northern peoples, the bear would seem also to have had some part. The Samoyeds, Ostiaks and Voguls swore their oaths by the bear. A delinquent would bite the hair of the animal, or its nose, claws or teeth, saying: " If I am wrong, so bite me as I now bite thee." [11]

The festival ceremonies of the " holy animal " have been preserved in their most original form among the Lapps; Pehr Fjellström and another unknown author having left us complete accounts.[12] Both descriptions date from the eighteenth century, and were made in the Swedish Lapp territory.

In the autumn the Lapps track the bears and seek their hiding-places for the winter. When they have discovered one of these spots they leave the bear there in peace until it has snowed so much that it is difficult for the animal to move freely. Often the bear is not awakened until March or April, when the Lapp invites his nearest relations and friends to a bear-killing. This is not, however, proceeded with at once, the magic drum having first to be consulted as to whether the hunt will succeed or not. When this matter is clear the hunters arrange themselves in a fighting-line, and march one after the other in a certain order to the winter-quarters of the bear. As first man, marches the one who tracked the bear. To the end of a pole which he bears in his hands a brass ring must without fail be attached. After him comes the interpreter of the message of the magic drum, who in turn is followed by the bravest of the company, their duty being to fell the bear, and lastly the crowd according to rank. Each of them has his own fixed duties in the bear feast ceremonies, one having to cook the flesh, another to carry water, a third to make the fire, and so on. When this procession finally arrives at the lair, the bear is attacked with spear and gun, and having been killed, is dragged out of its hiding-place. To the accompaniment of much merry singing, it is then begged for forgiveness that its sleep was disturbed, and thanked for the little trouble it gave the hunters and that none of the staves or spears was broken.

In all this, the Lapps follow many curious customs handed down from their ancestors. They whip the bear with slender twigs as soon as it has been dragged from its lair, or they lay their skis against it as a token of their victory. It is also customary to weave a ring of fir-twigs round the lower jaw of the animal, to which ring the highest in rank among the crowd fastens his belt and, accompanied by the merry singing of the others, drags the fallen bear a little way from its place. The Lapps also indicate their bravery by swinging their spears threateningly against the dead enemy as though it were still alive. After this play the carcass is covered with branches of fir and left lying there until the next day.

When the hunters approach their home after a successful hunt, they indicate their success by a merry traditional singing at the first sound of which the women in the tent begin to array themselves in festive garments, answering meanwhile the singing of the heroes by a similar singing. According to Fjellström the leader of the crowd usually plaits a twig of fir (*söive-rise*), at the end of which he forms a little ring. With this twig he strikes three times at the backdoor of the tent, saying: " Söive-olmai," if the prey be a male animal, and " Söive-neida " if it be a female. The same name was afterwards given to the hunter and his wife. From another source we learn that the wife of the hunter or some other person gives him a twig of birch, plaited solely for this occasion, to which the womenfolk have to fasten copper rings.[13] According to Randulf, the slayer of the bear informs those at home of his arrival by pushing an alder-branch under the wall of the tent. When the wife notices this, she tries to take hold of the branch, but the man draws it out again, repeating this manœuvre three times, from which the wife understands that " the holy hound of God " has been felled. Before the hunters enter the tent they sing for a while outside, until the women are ready to receive them.[14]

The women, who on no account may go near the bear, or take part in its slaughtering, have now, as the men enter through the sacred backdoor, to cover their faces with a cloth. Should they wish it, they are allowed to cast a glance through a copper ring at those entering; but at the same time, according to an old custom, they must spit the juice of chewed alder-bark in the faces of the hunters, from which the men's faces become quite red. The same thing is done to the dogs which

have taken part in the hunt.   Sometimes both men and women
paint their bodies with alder-bark juice — a ring round the
arms, lines on the breast and a cross on the forehead.   The
women also sometimes paint their faces red.[15]   It is further
the custom for women to decorate their husbands with brass
rings and chains, which are hung on the neck and, under the
garments, round one hand and foot.   The twig described above
is now given into the care of the bear-killer's wife; she wraps
it in a piece of linen and keeps it until the tail of the bear has
been cooked and eaten.   The news of the killing of the bear
having thus been spread, the Lapps feast in honour of the
day on all the delicacies they can command, men and women,
however, eating in separate groups.   Nothing else is even attempted to be done on this day.   Everyone goes to sleep in
the evening in the finery which has during the day fallen to
their lot, the husbands forsaking their usual couches with their
wives and sleeping, like the women, with their own sex only.

The next day measures are taken for the transport of the
bear.   All the men do not go out for this purpose, some of
the hunters remaining behind to prepare a temporary dwelling-
place for the bear.   This is formed of hewn boards and is
covered with branches of fir.   Rooms of this description for
the cutting-up and cooking of the bear are built where the
bear, as, for example, at Jockmock, is not carried to the holy
back-compartment of the tent.[16]   Most of the men, however,
go out to bring in the bear, all of them being, like the reindeer
detailed for the work, decorated with rings and chains of brass,
those of the reindeer being hung round its neck.   It is also
usual to draw a ring with alder-bark juice on the neck of the
reindeer and a cross on its forehead, sometimes also other
figures.   On the way the men sing merrily, and pray to the
bear not to send bad weather to inconvenience them.   During
the whole time care must be taken not to cross over the track
of any woman.   Neither is it advisable for a woman, for the
period, at least, of the ceremonies, to pass over the track left

behind by the bear, and even the use of the reindeer which has dragged in the bear is forbidden to women for a whole year.

As the brave men near their home with their burden they sing arrogantly: "Here come men from Sweden, Germany, England and from all lands"; to which the women reply: "Welcome, ye noble men from Sweden, Germany, England and all lands, ye who have felled the bear." [17]

The bear, brought thus ceremoniously from the forest, is now placed in the cutting-up tent, generally built a stone's throw from the holy backdoor of the dwelling-tent, and often decorated with garlands of hay in honour of the event. Here the carcass is laid down outstretched, alder-bark juice is sprinkled on it, and a small receptacle made of bark and filled with this liquid is set before the bear's nose. The knives are decorated with rings of brass, which, like alder-bark, are used on these occasions for magic protective purposes. Similarly, all vessels used in the ceremonies are decorated. Round the neck of the "holy" animal itself brass rings and chains are bound. The children, who are allowed to be present on these occasions, run frequently into the house to tell the women what they have seen and heard.

During the whole time of the cutting-up the men sing their varying moods, trying to guess the home district of the bear, thanking it for its fur, or pointing out how great an honour has fallen to its part. Further, they beg the bear to tell the other bears of the honour shown it, so that these may more willingly surrender themselves to their hunters. In songs the men also try to guess what the women are doing in the tent, and should they guess correctly, which can easily be ascertained from the children running between the two tents, this is regarded as a good omen.

When the animal has been skinned, the flesh is cut up very carefully lest even the smallest bone should be damaged, or some artery or muscle be broken. The whole of the flesh is cooked at once, the women's part separately. The blood is cooked first and mixed with fat; this is devoured at once as the greatest delicacy. With the blood of the bear, which is believed by the Lapps to possess magical qualities, the hunters also sometimes besmear their bodies, and in some districts they even smear their wives and children and the door and the logs bearing up the tent. The head of the animal with the wind-pipe and all the entrails hanging from it is left untouched until all the flesh has been cooked. It is skinned last, at which operation the thin, hairless region of the mouth is cut out; the person skinning the head is permitted the honour of bearing this skin before his face for a time. The head is cooked, with all its hanging burden of entrails, which are perfunctorily cleaned but not detached from the skull.

While the flesh is being cooked the hunters sit on each side of the fire according to their rank and position. First sits the one who tracked the bear, then the interpreter of the magic drum, the bear-killers, etc., all according to the importance of the duty which they have had to do during the kill. The vessel in which the flesh is cooked must be of brass, or at the very least, ornamented with brass rings. It must be carefully watched during the cooking, as the running-over of the tiniest trifle of gravy into the fire is regarded as a very bad omen. Should the gravy commence to boil too violently it is not regulated by adding water or thinning out the fire, but one of the men must go to the tent to see whether any of the women has caused the trouble by unsuitable behaviour. Should nothing blameworthy be found there, the chief person of the gathering tries to stop the gravy from boiling over by the customary singing.

When the preparation, which may not be seasoned with salt, is finally ready, the chief person deals out to each his share of the meat, which the men sitting in their places begin to devour; the women's share is taken over to the dwelling-tent. In the division of the meat certain rules are followed. Thus, women may not partake of the fore part of the bear, this belonging to the men, and the oldest man of the party must eat from the hind part of the bear the three or four last joints of the backbone.[18] It is also forbidden for women to eat the more noble organs, in especial, the heart, "the holy flesh," which the men devour greedily as the greatest delicacy. The kidneys also are of great merit, not only as delicacies, but as awakeners of love. Some suck in the gall of the bear to harden their natures. It is not, however, advisable to besmear one's boots with fat from the bear, as the latter might thus find out who it was who killed him.[19] When eating bear's-meat, knives or other metal aids may not be used, only the fingers or pieces of wood being allowable. Neither may one save anything for another occasion, but the whole of the meat must be eaten at one sitting.[20]

The men who carry over the women's share to the dwelling-tent are received by the women with showers of alder-bark juice in the face and with glances through a brass ring. This is also done by the women to the children coming from the cutting-up place, their festival-portion undergoing the same treatment. The first bite is taken through a ring of brass, or the ring is at least held before the mouth while eating it. Sticks of wood must all the time be used by the women during the meal, as women may not touch bear's-meat with their hands at all.[21] Lastly the bear's tail, which has been cooked unskinned in a little lard, is brought into the tent. The twig mentioned earlier is brought from its hiding-place, and all the women and children present bind brass rings to it as ornaments.[22] When everything eatable has been chewed off the tail and the last speck of lard sucked from among the hair, the tail is tied to the branch and returned to the men. The women then cover their faces and are kissed and thanked by the men for not having in any way disturbed the bear feast.

In the notes of the unknown author of the eighteenth century we find many of the songs sung at the bear feasts. From them it would appear that the Lapps, like the Voguls and Ostiaks, had some kind of dramatic ceremonies at these feasts, in which the bear also is regarded as appearing. In the name of the bear the Lapps sing: " Now come I from great wide forests, where I lived, to thickly-peopled districts," or: " I thought of returning to my old place, but these young men hindered my journey." [23]

As mentioned earlier, the Lapps do not break the smallest bone of the bear, but prepare a resting-place in a hole dug in the ground of about the size of the animal, on the bottom of which twigs form a soft bed. The bones are all placed in this grave in the order which they occupy in the bear. Should a dog have happened to devour or take away any of the bones, the missing bone or bones are taken from the dog.[24] The skin of the nose, borne hitherto by the flayer of the head, is now put back in its place, likewise the sexual organs and the tail. The rings hung on this last by the women are taken off, being used afterwards, e.g., for decorating the magic drum; or the one who tracked the bear may sometimes receive them as reward for the bear's-meat to which he has invited the others. The final fate of the plaited birch-twig mentioned earlier, kept wrapped in a cloth on account of its supreme holiness, and to the ring in the end of which the tail was bound, is not given. It would appear, however, from the notes left by the Lapp Spirri Nils that " when they have cooked the flesh of the bear they gather together all the joints of the backbone, threading them on a twig in their natural order, later fastening also the head to it." [25] In this way the tail attached to the twig would fall naturally into its place. A vessel made of birch-bark and filled with alder-bark juice is also placed before the nose of the bear. The significance of this vessel is unknown. The custom of the Ostiaks and Voguls of placing food in a vessel before the nose of a fallen bear might be compared with the above. Sometimes, other objects also were laid in the grave of a bear — skis, a plane, a knife, etc.[26]

After having, as above, ceremoniously buried the bear, the Lapps speak in a friendly manner to it, begging it to run about and relate to the other bears the great honour that befell it, so that these may not be afraid and show resistance when being captured. The grave is then covered carefully with logs and branches of fir to prevent dogs or beasts of prey from seizing or disturbing the dead one. In some districts it is the custom to set up a little wooden spear on the bear's grave as a monument.

All the Lapps do not make the graves alike; some make them smaller but deeper, and place the bones upright in them. At the bottom they place the hind-legs, on these in their right order the other bones, and finally the head, by which they place the bark-vessel with its contents of alder-bark juice. According to other reports, the Lapps also tied together the bones of the bear and hung them up in trees at the spot where the bear was killed.[27]

During the whole of the meal-time the bear's skin, which, especially at the head, had been decorated with all kinds of brass ornaments and rings and sprinkled over with alder-bark juice, has been hidden away under branches of fir. It is now taken from its hiding-place and spread out on a snowdrift or against a tree near the tent. And now comes the last of the bear feast games. The women are led veiled from the tent and a bow or a twig of alder is placed in their hands with which they must, following the directions of the men, take aim at the bearskin. Lucky the one who hits the skin, as this is regarded as a sign that her husband will be the next to kill a bear. Should she be unmarried, she can live cheerfully in the certain hope of being one day the wife of a celebrated bear-hunter.[28] The honour of sewing crosses with metal wire on pieces of cloth, which are then hung round the neck of every man who has taken part in the bear hunt, falls also to her lot. Even the reindeer used for dragging the bear is given one of these ornaments. The veils are then taken off the women and they are allowed to look at the magnificent skin of the bear, but even now, only through a ring of brass. The brass ornaments on the skin are not taken away at this conclusion to the festival, but are left on until the skin has dried and is ready for use.

When the bear feast is ended, the men do not at once go into the dwelling-tent, but delay some time still in the cutting-up tent. It is not seemly, according to the Lapps, for a hunter to approach his wife for three days after the killing of a bear. The leader of the expedition must abstain from his wife for five days. They must also purify themselves by peculiar ceremonies, carried out after sunset on the third day after the kill. All who have taken part in the hunt wash themselves with a solution of birch-ash in water and afterwards run three times round the cutting-up tent, jump into the dwelling-tent through the door and immediately out again, in again and out through the holy backdoor of the tent. While running they imitate the growling of the bear. Finally the wife of the bear-killer catches hold of them and asks when the next bear feast is to be. On these occasions she is said always to have mittens on her hands. According to Rheen the purification takes place in such a manner that the men run singing round the fire a few times and then jump one after the other through the door, an old woman throwing hot ashes after each as they do so. After this the men take off their brass ornaments and may without danger return to their wives.[29] To the memory of each bear killed, the Lapps hammered a copper nail in their spears, their gun or the magic drum, the felling of a bear having always been regarded as a great honour.[30]

Like the bear of the forests, the polar bear is also an object of worship among the Lapps. When the drift-ice sometimes brings with it in the spring a polar bear to the shores of the Kola Peninsula, the Lapps quickly capture it. Having succeeded in killing it, they are merry and play like children, e.g., they creep over the bear roaring as it used to do, extolling at the same time their own bravery. They then make a log-fire round which they sit long and sing. Now and then they rise and bow to the bear. Finally they place a piece of salt fish in the mouth of the animal and say: " Thou shalt not tell at home that thou paidst a visit to us and received nothing, the others may come also, them also shall we feed." Their last words express a pious hope that the bear will tell all its relations what brave men the Lapps are.[31]

The bear feast ceremonies of the other peoples mentioned correspond in their main points with those related here. A very common custom is to place the bear or its head or its skin for the period of the feasting in the sacred back part of the dwelling-place, where women are not allowed to go. Somewhat resembling the magic protective use of alder-bark by the Lapps is the Finnish custom of chewing a piece of alder-wood before the skin of the bear is brought into the house " so that the forest shall not infect anything." [32] Thus, among the Ostiaks it is the fashion when the huntsmen return to the village with the bear-skin for the men and women of the village to go out to meet them, some bearing a dish of water and a " smoke " in their hands. The bear-skin is smoked, and sprinkled three times with water. Very general is the use of metal objects as means of protection. More difficult to derive is the Ostiak custom of cutting a picture of the bear on a flat surface chopped out of a tree-trunk and cutting over this as many lines as there were hunters in the kill. While the picture is being made, one of the men strokes the bear's head with dry branches, " waking " it to let it know that they have arrived at the village. A means of protection used often at burial feasts — the covering of the nose and mouth of the dead — is met with among the Ostiaks and Voguls. Round pieces of birch-bark are sewn on to the eyes of the bear, or these are covered with silver or copper coins, and the nose is covered with a piece of tin-plate which is fastened from its sides by threads behind the ears. Thus arrayed, the bearskin is placed in the sacred back part on a low table with the head resting on the forepaws. A many-coloured cloth is spread

over the back. In some districts a hat was placed on the head
of a male animal and a muffler round its neck, while a female
animal was decorated with a small shawl round its head and
a pearl necklace round its neck. Women and children slip
brass rings on to its claws " so that it should not scare them
during berrying time in the summer." On the table all kinds
of victuals and drink are placed before the bear, even the
neighbours bringing these. The skin is allowed to remain for
three or four days in the house, during which time festivals
are held each evening, banquets are eaten and much merriment
made in honour of the bear. The participants must arrive
" purified," and are sprinkled with water as they enter. The
festivals generally begin in the afternoons. Included in the
programme are bear songs in which the birth of the bear, its
adventures with the hunters, and its life after death are described; dances are performed, the dancers wearing bearskins
turned inside out; the bear and its actions are imitated by peculiar movements.[33] Among the Voguls these bear-feast games
have developed into a kind of drama in which masked men appear. The masks are made of birch-bark, generally with huge
noses, and are painted over with charcoal and red earth. Sometimes a beard is affixed to them made of a piece of hairy rein-
deer-hide or oakum. The purpose of the masks is said to be
to hide the actors from the bear so that should the latter be
offended by the play he will not recognize them. For the
same reason the performers alter their voices, talking chiefly
in a shrill falsetto. Everyone tries to make the bear believe
they are not from the village in question, but travellers from
a long way off. Without doubt the origin of the masks is to
be found in the fear that the bear might recognize its killers
after death and avenge itself. To the most original ceremonies, i.e., those picturing the life and hunting of the bear,
others have been added later, some of these borrowing their
form from such modern sources as the Russian baptism ceremonies.[34]

PLATE VII

Masker's Frolic at the Vogul Bear-Feast

The players are masked in order to prevent the bear from recognizing them. (See page 96.)
After photograph by J. A. Kannisto.

At sunrise after the last feast night the skin is borne out through the window to the warehouse-shed where the dish first placed on the table before it in the house is placed in front of it. After two or three days the hunters gather together again in the house and then go into the shed, where each takes a morsel of food from the dish and eats it " for luck." [35]

From the prayers and wishes made by the Ostiaks to the dead bear, it appears plainly that in doing honour to it they wish to honour the whole race of bears. As an example of this the words of the Ostiak woman as she places a ring in the bear's claw may be cited: " When I go to gather berries, go thou round one tree, round two trees." When they set food before the bear-skin they say: " Do not touch my horse or my cow, I placed the dish before thee." [36]

The Finns called the bear feast " the wedding." The house had to be cleaned and everyone clad in his or her best. A young man was arrayed as a bridegroom and a young girl as a bride, or one only of these was chosen: a bridegroom if the bear was a female, and a bride if a male. The head of the bear was placed highest on the table and the rest of the meat in its natural order. In the place of honour sat the bridegroom and bride. The singing of runes in honour of the bear was customary among the Finns, certain of these being sung while the bear was carried to the house. In these the hunters endeavoured to show themselves innocent of the killing of the bear, declaring that the bear had wounded itself or that they had taken its life by accident. Arrived at the house-door the hunters asked singing whether the floor had been scrubbed and the room cleaned, or also singing urged the womenfolk to get out of the way and to beware of the holy bear.[37]

That the object of the ceremonies with the Finns was to ensure good bear-luck in hunting, appears from the oldest account of their bear feast ceremonies. Bishop Rothovius, in his speech at the inauguration of the University of Abo in

1640, relates the following concerning the customs of the Finns: " When they capture a bear, they must hold a feast in the dark, drinking the health of the bear from its skull, acting and growling like the bear, procuring in this way further success."

The skull of the bear had to be left overnight on the table and taken the following morning, ceremoniously as at a wedding, to a certain tree. First went the " bridegroom " and " bride " side by side, after these a man carrying beer in a vessel, after him a singer, then the one who carried the skull, and lastly the rest of the people.

The Samoyeds, who like the Finns specially preserve the skull, hang it up in a tree or place it on the end of a long pole, generally near a road.[38]

Like the bear, other wild animals had also to be treated with honour. More particularly the wild reindeer and other scarce and valuable animals had to be received with special ceremonies. The Ostiaks, when they kill a stag or an otter, often cut pictures of these in a pine near the village as they do with the bear.[39]

An important question is the original purpose behind the Lapps' method of carefully preserving all the bones of beasts of prey. That this care was not only expended on the bones of the bear is shown by an account from the year 1724: " The bones of the bear, the hare, and the wild-cat must be buried in dry sand-hillocks or clefts between rocks where neither dog nor other prowling animal can reach them. This is because these animals lived on dry land; the bones of those living in in the water are hidden in springs." [40] Even today the Lapps in some districts have a custom of throwing the bones of the fish caught by them, as far as possible complete, into the water again.[41] Sometimes the skeletons of wolves were hung up in trees.[42] Similar accounts are preserved of the Samoyeds. These also do not give the bones of forest animals to the dogs, but, as far as possible, preserve them. The Yuraks, for example, hang up the bones of the fox and the skulls of many other animals in trees.[43]   In the slaughtering of domestic animals similar ceremonies were also observed.   The Lapps exercised the same care for the bones of the reindeer, which also they buried carefully in the ground.[44]

Similar usages throwing light on these customs are found among many other primitive peoples.   Thus, for example, we know that the American Indians arranged the bones of the bison which they had killed in their natural order on the prairies, with the intention that the animal might come to life again for the next hunting season.   The Eskimos throw the bones of seals into the water in order to be able to catch them afresh.   In some mysterious way, life is held to exist while the skeleton is in existence.   That this belief was not alien to the Finno-Ugric stocks is shown by the words of an old Lapp who, when asked why he placed the head, the legs and the wings of a capercailzie on a rock, explained that " from them new birds would grow which he could shoot again." [45] The same belief has caused the preservation of the bones of the bear.   The unknown author, whose account has already been cited, remarks in his description of a Lapp bear feast: " They believe that the bear will arise again and allow itself to be shot." [46]

In these circumstances the preservation of those parts of the bodies of useful animals which were supposed to contain the soul or the soul-force cannot originally have been a sacrificial act, but had behind it purely practical motives.   Not until the original conception had paled could these actions have become incorporated in a cult.   Then in the throwing of fish bones by the fisherman into the water, it was easy to see an act of sacrifice to the Water god, and in the burial of animal bones in the forest, a sacrifice to the Forest god.

CHAPTER VII

THE SEIDES OF THE LAPPS

ALREADY in the sixteenth century the stone gods of the Lapps are mentioned in literature. Such gods of stone were kept by the Fell Lapps on the mountains, by the Fisher Lapps on the shores of the fiords, on capes reaching into the sea, on islands, or near rivers and rapids. These stones, called "Seides" by the Lapps, were to be found everywhere in Lapland.

According to accounts by missionaries these Seides had not been fashioned by human hands, but were natural stones, often hollowed out by water, having, as such, often a peculiar form, resembling human beings or animals. Those regarded as the most valuable were the stones resembling human beings. In some places, many Seide stones were placed together in the same sacred place and were then believed to represent a family. Even immovable rocks were at times regarded as Seides. As late as the summer of 1908, a holy place was discovered at Luleå (Vidjakuoika), containing several small mounds about a foot in height, and around these ten Seide stones. When the stones had been put back in their places, it was seen that each mound had had one larger stone on it and several smaller ones around it. These small ones were sometimes not more than two decimetres in height.[1] The Seides of the Fisher Lapps might, at times, be stones altogether surrounded by water.[2]

The Lapps gave a devoted attention to these sacred stones. Wherever possible they were placed on green ground, where the grass grew thick and lush in the summer-time. In addition,

the place where the Seide stood was decorated in the summer
with birch-leaves and in the winter with branches of fir. The
foundation on which the Seide was placed had always to be
kept green, and whenever the leaves
or pine-needles withered, they had to
be renewed.[3]

When the Lapp wished to ask for
something from his stone god, or to
inquire into the future, he went to the
holy place, and baring his head, took
the god in his hand and spoke to it.
While he was relating all kinds of
wishes, he would keep on attempting
to lift the stone. If this proved im-
possible, and the stone grew steadily heavier, it was regarded

FIG. 4. LAPP SEIDE STONE

as an answer in the negative. Even the very smallest stone,
said the Lapps, became heavy when the god was not willing to
give a positive answer. When the Lapp received what he had
wished for, he made an offering as a sign of thankfulness to
the stone, the nature of the offering being inquired after also
in the above-mentioned manner.[4]

This method of turning to the gods was, however, not possible when the Seide was a great rock or a stone embedded in
the earth. Consulting these, the Lapp laid his hand on the
rock and began his questions in the unshakable belief that
his hand would stick to it and not be loosened until he chanced
to hit on the exact event that would happen to him.[5]

The place where the Seide stood and its nearest surroundings were " holy " (_passe_) to the Lapps. The mountain on
which the stone gods were placed, was called in general " the
Holy Mountain " (Passe-vāra). In the same way, the Fisher
Lapps called the rivers and lakes by which their Seides stood,
" the Holy River " or " the Holy Lake." Names such as
these are met with in Lapmark even today.

The fear felt for these holy places forced the Lapps to

observe great caution. According to Leem, they only approached them clad in their festival clothes, beginning to make genuflections at a distance, as they walked. Every year they journeyed to them, and if it was impossible to make new offerings, the bones of former offerings had, at least, to be moved. Dwellings were erected very unwillingly near these places, for fear of disturbing the gods by the crying of children or other noises. When they travelled by a holy mountain they dared not fall asleep as that was regarded as a sign of irreverence. Neither would they speak loudly or shoot birds or any other game within their precincts. If they were wearing anything blue in colour, they would remove this as they approached a holy place. Women had to hide their faces or turn their heads in passing them. Even men were not allowed to wear any garment that had been at some time worn by a woman, not even foot-wear that had lain in the same soaking-vessel as the women's moccasins.[6] Högström adds that it was dangerous for a woman, even at a distance, to go round a holy place. If during any journey she had passed to the right of one of these places, she had, on returning, to pass by on the same side, though it might mean a detour of several leagues.[7] Mallmer relates further, that when a Lapp went aside to make an offering, he tied up all his dogs very carefully, as should one of these cross his track, misfortune might befall him; the wolves, for example, might worry his reindeer to death. When coming out of or going into his tent on these errands, the Lapps never used their ordinary doors, but crept in through a little backdoor which was regarded as so holy that no woman might either leave or enter through it.[8]

Even today these beliefs persist in the more remote districts. In Kola Lapmark there is a holy place, situated near the Finnish frontier and composed of the narrow and steep spur of a mountain, which is the object of the Lapps' superstitious reverence. When rowing past the place in the summer-time, one must be careful to make as little noise as possible, wetting the rowlocks lest these should creak. In the winter one drives by, step by step. One may not glance aside, but must look straight ahead. Having reached a spot about three hundred yards past the place, one must get up out of the sleigh, and — at least when passing that way for the first time — drink spirits in the god's honour; earlier, one should also have spilt a little on the ice as an offering. Not until then may one let one's reindeer run. Should one neglect these precautions or in any other way insult the god, he would cause a fateful blizzard to arise as a punishment, or, as has sometimes happened, bind the culprit with his reindeer and everything to the place so that he was unable to stir from the spot.[9]

By the Mutenia River in the Finnish Lapmark there is also a Seide, of which the people relate that in earlier times, when passing this holy stone, women were not allowed to sit in the boats, but must travel by it along the shore on foot. Near the stone they had in addition to dress themselves in trousers.[10] The Russian Lapps believed, that women on nearing the holy places invariably were stricken with " a certain illness " by means of which, even in strange districts, they could tell the nearness of such places.[11]

One of the best known holy mountains in Finnish Lapmark is the Rastekaise in Utsjoki, on the top of which there are two large stones, and which even today is regarded by the superstitious people with awe. When a storm arises on the mountain they regard it as a sign of the wrath of the god.[12] Travellers relate that the Lapps say this mountain will not willingly show itself to strangers, hiding itself instead in mists.

The Lapp turns to his Seides in all his different needs, for good luck on his journeys, to obtain plentiful fish or game, to ensure the health and increase of his reindeer, but especially when sickness or other misfortunes befall him. At first promises are made of offerings, the promises being then redeemed when the sick become well again. If, in addition, one remembers that the Seides had the power of raising storms, one can understand how powerful and many sided these spirits were.

Whence arose the power of these dumb Seide stones, spreading as it did a reflection of awe even over the ground on which they stood? The Lapps themselves hardly longer knew at the close of their pagan period. Signs are to be found, however, that the Seide-cult has its root in the worship of ancestors. A significant feature is that the Seide is the protecting spirit of a certain family or clan. A report made use of by Schefferus says that " every family and clan has in the land wherein it moves and dwells," its own Seide.[13] A Seide worshipped by a larger clan seems to have been mightier than the Seide of a separate family. Högström relates concerning this, that " the power of these stones is adjudged according to the number worshipping and offering up to them." In another place, he tells of a Seide that had " long been worshipped by a whole village." [14] Family worship — for the Lapp-villages were family-villages — is also pointed to in an account by the missionary Tornaeus: " So many households, one can almost say so many as there were Lapps, so many gods were there to be found, situated in different places by the sea. But one was always the highest and mightiest, and this alone was worshipped by the whole population of a village. It was situated on some hill, or other high place, so that it could be well seen of all, and honoured; but other house and family gods were placed in lower places." [15] The duty of making offerings was bequeathed by father to son. The missionary S. Kildal says, that " when the parents died, the children inherited the holy mountains and the mountain gods." [16]

Among the Scandinavian Lapps, this Seide-cult is connected with their beliefs in holy mountains with underground inhabitants, as described in another chapter. Jessen says expressly that sacrifices to the Saivo spirits were made near a stone.[17] But these spirits were originally the ancestors wor-

PLATE VIII

The holy Rastekaise mountain in Utsjoki in Finnish Lapland, on the top of which there are two large stones. Even today it is regarded with awe by the superstitious. (See page 103.)
Water-colour by V. Soldan-Brofeldt.

shipped by the Lapp families or clans as guardian-spirits. That also in the Swedish Lapmark a dim idea of the origin of the Seide-cult has remained behind, is shown by the following words of the missionary Rheen: " These stones were set up on the mountains, in clefts between the rocks, or by rivers and seas, on places where they at some time or other had heard ghostly noises." [18] The Finnish Lapps have also preserved certain interesting knowledge. A man, who happened to sleep the night near a holy place, saw in his dreams " all kinds of ghosts, animals and human beings." It is also worth mentioning, that near these places one must never speak ill of the dead, as otherwise those underground become angry. [19]

The Lapps believe also that the Seide can appear to its worshipper in human form. In the account of a sacrifice in the eighteenth century, it is stated: " Then a being in human form, like a great ruler, extremely good to look at, dressed in expensive garments and trinkets, appears and sits down to take part in their meal, speaks with them and teaches them new arts, and says that he lives in the stone or mountain to which they sacrifice." [20] To the Lule Lapps the Seide appeared in the form of a well-built, tall man, dressed in black like a gentleman, with a gun in his hand. [21] Also among the Finnish Lapps Fellman heard a story about a man who was about to destroy his Seide because of his poor luck at fishing, but desisted when it appeared before him in human form. [22]

The matter is still further illustrated by the belief that the Seide is a human being turned to stone. [23] The following account was written down in Russian Lapmark. Near the Puljärvi Lake lived an old woman, whose husband, after his death, would visit her in the night. The old woman, who would have nothing to do with the dead, locked her door and smoked out her house, but got no peace from the deceased in spite of these precautions. She related her troubles to a shaman who happened to visit her house. He tried to soothe her, promising to remain overnight. In the evening he tidied the bothie, placing all the woman's belongings on one side and sweeping the other side clean; in the corner he placed a few fish-bones. Soon, both heard the deceased examining the fishing-net outside, after which he came into the bothie, placing himself on the place that had been swept clean, where he commenced to gnaw at the fish-bones. Then the shaman got up and taking the dead by the hand, led him into the yard. Having remained for some time outside, the shaman came back, telling the woman that the deceased would no longer trouble her. "Look up at the sky tomorrow morning," he said when he had finished, and went away. When the woman went out into the yard the next day, she saw something black moving in the sky, and sinking down to the opposite shore of the Puljärvi Lake. The visits of the deceased ceased from that day, but at a slight distance from Puljärvi a Seide had appeared.[24]

The Russian Lapps have generally speaking had the same views of their Seides as of their dead. According to their ideas, they live a similar life to the Lapps, keeping reindeer and dogs, building houses, preparing sleighs, etc. The Lapps say they have heard how the Seide spirits hunt, how their dogs bark and how the snow creaks as they travel on their Lapp sleighs. They believe that the Seides are born and die, and even, at times, celebrate weddings.[25] They are invisible spirits, but have the power, like the dead, of appearing in animal form, especially as birds. Thus, they relate how a Seide often flew up out of a chasm in the mountains in the shape of a raven. With this view of the Russian Lapps may be compared the similar one of the Swedish Lapps that the Seide is a bird, turned into stone as it sank down out of the air; on this account one could often make out the general outlines of a bird in these stones.[26]

If we, finally, remember that many of these Seides might be found together, forming a family, we need not be at all uncertain as to the origin of this ancient cult. It is possible that some of these Seide places were former dwelling or burial places, but that this is not always the case appears, for example, from the following account from the Swedish Lapmark: " They believe that the Seide spirits live in some places, to which on account of the height of the mountain they cannot reach; they, therefore, smear a stone with the blood of the reindeer sacrificed in honour of the Seide and throw the stone high up on the mountain, where the Seide spirit dwells." [27]

How closely connected were the " spirit " and the stone, one may see from the belief of the Lapps, that the Seide stone could move about and that it was dangerous for a human being to pass over the " wander-path " of the holy stone. The stone was also supposed to be impressionable and capable of feeling; when necessary it could be punished by striking it or by hammering out pieces from it. If it began to be regarded as a dangerous neighbour, the Lapps would destroy it altogether by shattering, burning, or throwing it into the water. This was the death of the Seide. [28]

According to an inherited tradition, the Lapps near the Sompio Lake were " so modest and easily satisfied in the choice of their gods, that they worshipped that which first met their glance on going out from the tent — a stone, or the stump of a tree. The next morning the Lapp would have a new god should his first glance in the morning happen to fall on some other object." [29] According to this report, the only one of its kind, the Lapps thus also worshipped the so-called " accidental gods," which certain investigators believe that they have found among a few primitive peoples.

Besides the Seides of stone, the Lapps had also wooden ones. They were either tree-stumps embedded in the ground, or posts driven into it. The wooden Seides do not appear to have possessed any definite shape. It is stated, however, that on an island in the foaming Darra rapids in the Tärne River certain posts resembling human beings have been found. They stood in a line one after another, the first of the height of a man, the other four somewhat smaller; each had something resembling a hat on its head.[30] Among the Finnish Lapps the method of preparing Seides of wood has been preserved. A growing tree was chopped off about a yard or two yards from the ground; the upper end was then shaped into the resemblance of a funnel, and covered with a slab of stone; in this way the tree was prevented from rotting. Pillars of this description are said to have been formed by the Lapps "to the honour of the water," near waters rich in fish.[31]

FIG. 5. LAPP SACRIFICIAL POSTS
According to Appelgren

The "sacrifice-stumps" of the Swedish Lapps were from two to three yards high. They were shaped roughly to resemble a human being, with "head and neck," which were then smeared over with blood. The "sacrifice-stump" was used only once, but "in spite of this, it was never destroyed." For this reason, a missionary might at one and the same place see "a legion of wooden gods." The relations between these and the stone gods is made clear in a note by Högström: " Undoubtedly, they make some definite difference between the times of sacrifice to the different gods; but this I have not been able to ascertain. However, as far as I do know, they worship the stone gods when in the neighbourhood of these, but otherwise gods of wood." [32]   It would appear, therefore, that the wooden pillars were set up only as occasion arose, perhaps to represent some spirit dwelling in a more distant place. The stone Seides were regarded by the Lapps, according to Högström, as being much more holy than those of wood. [33]   These wooden Seides are not, however, to be confounded with the wooden images fashioned to represent Nature gods.

Sacrifices to the Seides were naturally not offered up in precisely the same manner over the whole of the wide Lapland area, but one may observe general main forms of an archaic kind among them.

One of the very best accounts of a sacrifice, which has been preserved for posterity, dates from the seventeenth century and is from the Lule Lapps. When these had decided to make an offering, they bound fast the sacrificial animal behind the tent, thrust a knife into its heart and carefully gathered its heart's blood. The horns and the bones from the head and neck, together with the hoofs, were carried to the holy place in which their Seide stood. When the Lapp had come to the Seide, he took off his hat, bowed low to the idol and smeared it with blood and fat from the sacrifice. The horns were piled in a great pyramid behind the stone, the pile being called the " horn-yard " and containing sometimes as many as a thousand horns. Of the meat of the sacrifice which was eaten by those making the offering themselves, a small piece was cut from every quarter, threaded on to a switch of birch and hung on to the front of the horns. At times the slaughtering might take place at the holy place, the meat being then prepared and eaten there. Besides the bones, the hide of the reindeer was also left on the holy mountain; the head was hung on a tree, where such were to be found in the vicinity of the idol. [34]

The Kemi Lapps had a custom of cutting down a tree near

the Seide stone, calling it the *luete-muor* (" sacrifice tree "). Before the sacrifice the god was asked, by lifting him, what he wished in return for giving assistance in some matter or other. The animal chosen for the offering was bound fast to the tree and slaughtered "after a long speech." Both the stone and the tree were besmeared with blood, and when the meat was prepared, small strips were cut out of it, threaded on to a ring made of young pliable branches and hung up in the sacrifice tree. After which, the sacrificial meal was begun. Should anything be left over, it could not be taken home but must be left at the place together with the animal's hide and horns.[35]

The Norwegian Lapps, before the slaughtering, cut a small piece out of each ear and the tail of the animal and placed them before the god as a preliminary taste. The sacrificial animal was killed by stabbing, and flayed in such a manner that the horns and the hoofs remained fast to the hide. Thereafter, several small sticks were prepared, lines and figures being cut in them. The sticks were called " the sacrifice tree " and were placed smeared with blood near the god; their function was to represent " wax candles." We see from this that the Lapps at that time tried to ape Scandinavian customs. When the meat was carved, a piece from every quarter was cut out for the idol. The fire was made in a fixed spot, near which there had to be, where possible, a spring or brook; the whole of the flesh of the sacrifice was cooked at once. With the fat that rose in the cauldron and with the blood, the sacrificial priest smeared certain curiously-shaped stones, placing them afterwards near the god. Then, with his followers, he finished off the whole of the carcase, taking due care not to spread the bones about, but to leave all on the place of offering, where the hide also was left. During the performance of the sacrifice, the Lapps sang their songs, which they call *luete* (= Finnish *luote*, " magic song," Scandinavian *blót*, " offering ").[36]

Slightly differing from the foregoing was the sacrificial

PLATE IX

1. Lapp Seides made of tree-stumps or posts, roughly carved in human form. (See pages 107–8.) Drawn by Teringskiôld.

2. Rastekaise, a holy mountain of the Lapps, with two sacred stones. (See page 103.) After photograph by L. Hannikainen.

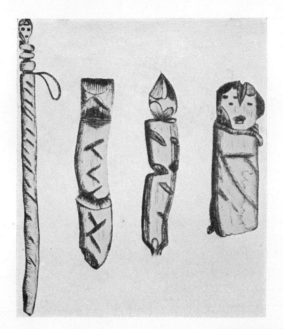

custom of the Russian Lapps, as described by Genetz. Certain features of the performance seem to point to a sacrifice in honour of Nature gods. The sacrifice had to be begun early in the morning and the gods prayed to with the face turned towards the east. After the flesh had been devoured, the hide with horns and hoofs attached was built up with branches of birch and fixed to a pole in a position resembling that of a live reindeer.[37] Up to a few score years ago these Lapps sacrificed as many as twenty-four reindeer at a time. A great sacrificial feast of this description was not, however, celebrated every year, nor were the reindeer killed all at once, but during the space of several days, a few at a time. All the participants in the feast had to cleanse themselves and put on clean garments. The sacrificial food was regarded as being so holy, that one might not spill any even on one's garments. During the ceremony the shaman stood alone, at one side, with his face turned to the east. The reindeer hides that were stuffed with birch-twigs were also placed with their heads to the east. After the ceremonies the priests had to cleanse themselves again.[38]

Besides reindeer, the proper time for sacrificing which was in the autumn, the Lapps also slaughtered other animals in honour of their Seides, such as birds and other game, occasionally also strange domestic animals procured from their neighbours. Sometimes a dog might be offered up entire to the Seide, or living animals, which were imprisoned in chasms in the mountain or grottoes, or were left alive on some solitary island as a gift to the gods. There are even reports of children being sacrificed.[39]

In like manner as the Mountain Lapps sacrificed their reindeer, the Fisher Lapps fed their Seides on fish. When a fisherman went out to fish, he generally went first to the stone, kissed it three times and said: " If I now succeed in catching fish in the sea or the river, I promise thee their intestines and livers." After making a catch, the promise was fulfilled.

Even as late as the middle of the last century, the Norwegian Lapps are said to have sometimes smeared their stones in secret. As sacrifices to the Seides in later periods, there are reports of money being offered up, both in Finnish and Russian Lapmark; also rings of brass, tobacco, etc., all of which objects were placed in small hollows in the stones.[40]

If we follow the development of religious beliefs and customs among other related peoples, we can observe that the Seides worshipped by the Lapps under the naked sky, contain two different classes of spirits, of which the one, the so-called house or family gods, little by little, are generally moved into the dwelling-house of the worshipper; while to the other, to whom might be given the Greek name " heroes," many people began to build special small bothies.

CHAPTER VIII

FAMILY GODS

THE TERM family gods is here meant to express such tutelary genii as are worshipped by each separate family and whose images are kept at home, or in the vicinity of the home, and which the family carry along with them when removing from one place to another. As already stated in an earlier chapter, Tornaeus relates about the Seides of the Lapps by the Torne Lake that among " many gods " there was always one which was the highest and foremost, the principal god, which alone was worshipped by the whole village. It was set up in an elevated place, in order to be seen and honoured by everybody, but those which were merely " family gods," stood in lower places. Whether the Lapps carried their family gods with them during their rovings, is uncertain, and also whether they used to keep them in their tents.

The family gods of the Samoyeds are made of wood or consist of stones only, the latter often of a peculiar form. The father of the family may have as many as fifteen different " dolls," generally dressed in reindeer-skins or in gowns of cloth. These clothes may not be sewn, but are wrapped or tied around the god. When travelling, the gods are conveyed in sleighs made specially for them, and during the journey the " sleigh of the gods " must be the last in the caravan. These images are well kept; they get new clothes every year, and sacrifices are made to them from time to time, though these are, indeed, very often of little value. On the occasion of sacrificing, they are taken out of their sleigh, which is outside the holy back of the tent, and set up on a dais made solely for the occasion, or are carried into the tent and placed in its sacred background. When sacrificing reindeer to them, the Samoyeds besmear the mouths of the images with blood and lard. When they make images of their family gods, the shaman must conjure up a spirit to live in them. Sometimes the gods have, in their vicinity, small arms and tools made of lead, and, for company and help, images of the spirits of animals.[1]

Like the Samoyeds the Northern Ostiaks also preserve and carry their family gods with them in a special sleigh. A more common custom among the Ostiaks and also the Voguls, seems to be the harbouring of them in the dwelling-house itself near the back part of the tent, in a chest or case. Later they have begun to keep them also in a barn, or in the attic. The family gods may be made of wood, metal, hides, etc. Besides all sorts of victuals, such as meat, fish, gin, they receive for clothing, offerings of hides, kerchiefs, pieces of cloth, etc. The feeding of the family gods takes place, among the above-named races, at hours that are not fixed beforehand.[2]

Traces of the social signification of the family gods among the Finno-Ugric peoples, have, however, been best preserved among the Votiaks, who live a settled existence. By acquainting oneself with their beliefs and customs, one can clearly discern that these family gods are really the late forefathers of the family, who are worshipped from generation to generation as the tutelary genii of the family. In their capacity of protectors of the family prosperity, a small building is devoted to them on the Votiak farm. Its name *kuala* or *kua* is of Finno-Ugric origin and corresponds to the Finnish *kota*.

The *kuala* is a barn-like, square building of timber, without a basement. It has neither windows nor ceiling, and the floor consists of hard-stamped earth. In the middle of the floor there is a fireplace bordered with stones, and on this a large iron cauldron is kept, resting either on the stones or attached to

PLATE X

1. Samoyed, stone Family-god clothed and lifted on a tree trunk. (See page 113.)
After photograph by K. Donner.

2. Family-gods of the Ostiaks. (See page 114.)
After photograph by Adrianov.

an iron chain hanging down from the rafters. From the fire-place the smoke goes out through an opening in the wooden roof. The low door was formerly situated on the south side. Sometimes we find the *kuala* divided into two parts, or an extra building erected behind it. The inner part is generally held sacred, and women are not allowed to enter it. At the present time, the Votiaks use the *kuala* only as a depository for household utensils, but in olden times, before their archi-tecture had developed into its present form, the *kuala* was the only dwelling-house of the Votiak family.

A reminiscence of these distant times, of which the Votiaks still speak in their tales, is the custom in some districts of still using the *kuala*, not only as a storehouse, but also as a room for cooking and eating by the family, especially during the warm season. In this case, it is generally fitted up like a dwelling-house; along the walls run solid benches of red-wood, and in the corner nearest the door there is a table round which, in summer, the family assemble to take their meals. At times there will be found, near the door, a cupboard for holding household utensils. The most notable and remarkable object is, however, a shelf of wood in the cupboard, dark with age and situated at the height of a man, on which may be seen in some districts even in our days, a little case with a lid. This little case is the most sacred object of the Votiaks, for in its vicinity the living believe they can approach departed genera-tions. As a sanctuary, the *kuala* has been retained in its former condition, though the Votiaks, now that agriculture has become their principal means of existence, have begun to build more modern dwelling-houses for themselves.

The resemblance of the *kuala* cult to the worship of the spirits of the dead is seen in the fact that the *kuala* sacrifices must always be performed within the particular family. A person belonging to one family will never enter the sanctuary of another family in order to perform a sacrifice. How par-

ticular the Votiaks are in this respect is shown by the fact that
if the family has a foster-son of another family, he must,
during the *kuala* sacrifice, go to the praying-*kuala* of his
own family, even though the latter be situated in another
village. Further, the alien position of a married woman in
her husband's family is shown by the usage of the Votiaks
of calling her by the name of her *kuala*-family as a distinction
from the family which she entered by her marriage. In the
beginning of her married life, she is even for a time obliged to
frequent her own family *kuala*, in order to sacrifice there,
when sickness or other troubles occur. From the above the
signification of the *kuala* cult in the social life of the Votiaks
will be clearly seen. As an uninterrupted tie of union between
those belonging to the same family or tribe, and not only between the living but also between the living and the departed,
this cult unites the present with the dark primeval time. Every
Votiak considers it his holiest duty to know his origin, even
after removing to a strange neighbourhood. This is, indeed,
not very difficult, as every Votiak family has a particular de-
nomination of its own. These family names are words, the
meaning of which has been generally forgotten, such as *možga*,
utša, etc. By the family name kinsfolk may know each other
even in a strange place. This fact is of all the more importance
as the Votiaks consider it a crime to marry within the same
kuala family, obstacles to marriage being confined not only
to the nearest of kin but extended over a comparatively large
circle.

Originally, the Votiak villages were family villages; hence
a village and a family living in it often bear the same name;
at times, a newly built village is called by the name of the
home village. If, in such a village, there are several families,
the village generally takes the name of the oldest family
living in it. Certain instances from the District Sarapul will
show that the Votiaks really have a natural tendency to keep
together almost as one family. Some time ago, in a village

called Norja, sixteen fathers of families still lived in such economic nearness, that in spite of their inhabiting different houses, they took their meals in common. In another village, twenty men, living separately, were subordinate to one common head.[3]

Besides by means of the family name, the Votiaks are united by the stamp with which they mark their property. This mark is generally the picture of some object, such as a goose-foot, an axe, etc. (The Ostiaks at an earlier time used also pictures of animals.)

The mark of the father is left to the eldest son, who lives on in his father's cottage. The other male members of the same family, must therefore, when removing from the paternal home, procure a new mark for themselves, which is generally done by making a trifling addition to or slightly changing the mark of their former home. Having received their own, they do not, however, forget the mark of their fathers, which, at the same time, belongs to the *kuala* sanctuary still in existence in their former home. Left thus as an inheritance by the father to the eldest son, a mark may sometimes be very old. As in the case of the family name, blood relations may also, by means of the mark, know each other in strange parts.

As a family inheritance, the eldest son, after the death of the father, besides the homestead, the mark and the *kuala*, also receives the office of " *kuala* guardian," whose duty it is to perform family sacrifices. Should there be no male heir, the office of " *kuala* guardian " is inherited by the brother of the deceased or by some other of the nearest male relations.

Besides worshipping in the *kuala* sanctuary of the family, which by its master is used at the same time as a storehouse and a kitchen, and in which only the family in question worships, the Votiaks take part in the sacrifices also in the *kuala* whose guardian is, if possible, a lineal descendant of the founder of the village family. Compared with the latter the family sanctuary is called " the little *kuala*." Of little *kualas* there are many to be found in a village, not so many, however, as there are families, for every *kuala* is not a sanctuary. This springs from the fact that every Votiak who has founded a family and home of his own does not mark a sanctuary for himself at once, but continues to worship in his father's *kuala,* and should he have none, in the *kuala* of his grandfather, the guardian of which is a lineal descendant of the latter, and, where possible, an eldest son. Thus we find here another suggestion that the Votiak family was formerly larger than at the present time, comprising several sub-families, who most likely lived in the same complex of houses, obeying the same head.

Of " great *kualas* " there is, on the other hand, only one, if the village is a family village, as are most of the old Votiak villages. If, as often happens when founding a new village, people descended from different families are included in the population, there will be as many *kualas* in the village as there are families. Every " great *kuala* " is called after its respective family: *možga kuala, utša kuala,* etc. The worshippers of the *kuala* are likewise called after their family: *možga pijos* ("*možga* sons"), *utša pijos,* etc. From the number of the great *kualas* one can thus easily find out how many families there are in a village. Especially among the Eastern Votiaks, there are villages formed of several different families which have moved to strange parts as settlers. Where there are several great *kualas* in a village, these are generally to be found in the houses of their guardians; they differ in no way from a private *kuala* and are also used like the last named as store-rooms for household utensils. Should, however, the village be inhabited by one family only, there being consequently only one " great *kuala*," the latter attains an entirely different position from the other *kualas*. In its capacity of the common property of the village, the " great *kuala* " or " village *kuala* " is generally situated in the garden of its guardian, or in a particular enclosure either in the village or

PLATE XI

VOTIAK KUALA OR SANCTUARY OF THE
FAMILY-GODS

(See page 114.)
After photograph by U. Holmberg.

near it. As a village sanctuary, the *kuala* has attained an exclusively religious significance, being sometimes considered so sacred that, for instance, no women are allowed to enter it. Thus, among the Votiaks, it has generally developed into a kind of temple, which development, in the southern parts, at least, has evidently been influenced by the Mohammedan prayer-houses of the Tatar villages.

In the family *kuala*, as in the village *kuala*, the sacrifice shelf is generally situated on the back wall, most often in the left-hand corner there. On holy days, offerings are placed on the shelf, but, generally, it is for the most part empty, when not occupied by articles necessary for the sacrifices. In some instances, there is, under the sacrifice shelf, a cupboard about a yard high, in which are kept, besides the sacrifice utensils, smaller offerings. The Votiaks believe that the "Luck-protector," Voršud, lives near the sacrifice shelf. Formerly, there was, on the sacrifice shelf, a little case with a lid to it made of linden bark, which is still to be found in some parts, e.g., in the Government of Kazan. The size and form of the sacrifice case vary somewhat in different places. For the most part, they are round, but very often we also find oblong and square ones. A sacrifice case may sometimes be found to be very old and darkened by the smoke in the *kuala*, having been handed down as a sacred heirloom from father to son for generations.

In our time, the Voršud case, in both family and village *kualas*, is generally empty. But can it be possible that a receptacle regarded with such superstitious awe, forbidden to women and strangers to approach, was always thus empty? Several authorities, for the most part among the very oldest, relate that they have seen many different objects in these cases: ancient coins, the bones of birds, gaily coloured feathers, squirrel skins, sheep's wool, etc. But again, could these trifles, possessing obviously more the nature of sacrifices than of objects of worship, have been venerated by the Votiaks? When one compares the sacred background of the *kuala* with the corner of the bothies regarded as holy by both the Ostiaks and the Voguls, and the sacrifice case with the god-chest of the latter, which is not empty, but among these more primitive peoples contains images of their tutelary genii, is it not more likely that the Votiaks' sacrifice case was also in former days a similar home for their family gods? In our days, there are certainly no images to be found among them. Even in the oldest sources we find it written that the Votiaks possess neither pictured nor carven images. But the memory of gods who formerly dwelt in these cases has not altogether died out, and the Christian Votiaks place even today a picture of a saint on the same shelf that, earlier, held their spirit offerings.

The scanty traditions, however, give no clear idea of the images of the Votiak family spirits. Assuming that the sacrifice cases, the circumference of which is, on an average, about one hundred and twenty centimeters, and the height about thirty centimeters, have not become very much altered in the course of time, we may conclude that the images were not very large. Most likely they were just such clumsy, dressed wooden dolls as the Votiaks still make for themselves during severe illnesses, in order to remove the illness from the patient to the doll. Such would also seem to have been the images of the Siryans, judging from the fact that in the life of St. Stephen, their apostle, it is stated that their images resembled human beings, had noses, mouths and even feet, and that they were either carved, or hollowed out. As they were made of wood, St. Stephen was able to chop them into pieces with an axe and burn them. There was a great number of them " both in the villages and dwelling houses." [4]

When beginning their sacrifice, the Votiaks place fresh green twigs on the corner shelf of the *kuala*, under the sacrifice case. In autumn or in spring, or, generally during the time when the trees are leafless, they use, when sacrificing, twigs of the silver pine (*Pinus pichta* or *sibirica*), but in the summer birch twigs. The use of green twigs certainly originates from very ancient times, for this custom has also been observed among the Lapps, of whom missionaries relate that they placed birch twigs under their images in the summer, and fir twigs in the winter.

This custom of laying green twigs on the sacrifice shelf, which, together with the sacrificing, belongs to the most important duties of the *kuala* guardians, has, curiously enough, been kept up even in parts where the sacrifice cases, not to speak of images, are no longer to be found. This is particularly the case among the Eastern Votiaks. Among these we seldom find sacrifice cases, but on the other hand we may see, even in our days, on every sacrifice shelf, whether there be sacrifice vessels there or not, twigs more or less faded, according to the time that has passed since the sacrifice. In several places, these twigs, which originally were of quite a secondary importance compared with the images, are regarded with the same superstitious awe as the latter. Only the officiating priest, who on holy days burns the old twigs and places fresh ones in their stead, is allowed to touch them. Certain investigators have supposed that these same twigs have been objects of worship.[5] This is, however, a mistake, though the twigs have at times had the high honour of being removed from their place under the " case " to the " case " itself, and in this way the original idea became confused. That the *kuala* cult is concentrated around the sacrifice shelf and the " case," is proved, above all, by the custom of the sacrificing priest's standing, while praying, with his face turned towards the sacrifice shelf.

We have stated earlier that not every Votiak *kuala* is used as a sanctuary. This it may become only by means of particular inaugural ceremonies, generally performed in the summer. On a day fixed beforehand, the person who intends to obtain for himself a Voršud of his own, invites a few guests, generally two men and two women. The guests having arrived, the young master and mistress, with their guests, proceed to the head of the family who is at the same time the guardian of the Voršud *kuala*, taking bread and gin with them. On arriving, they begin to feast in the house of the chief. The latter invites one of his neighbours and his wife, and these officiate as host and hostess, the host of the feast entertaining the men, and the hostess the women. When the guests have been sufficiently entertained, the host and his wife begin singing wedding songs, in which those present also join. Lastly, the guests go to their neighbours for more hospitality and return to the *kuala* guardian in the evening. On their return, porridge is cooked by the guardian of the family *kuala*. The one who intends to secure a Voršud for himself, now goes to the *kuala*, takes some ashes from the fireplace, and wraps them in a clean white cloth, saying: " I take the smaller and leave the greater." He then places the bundle of ashes on the shelf of the *kuala* and sits down to the sacrificial porridge together with the other guests. After the meal he goes back to the *kuala*, takes the ashes from the shelf, and sets out for home with his guests. During the journey home, the escort of the Voršud play and sing, the mistress of the new *kuala* meanwhile keeping a copper coin in her mouth until they arrive at the homestead. When starting out into the street, on the way home, and on arrival, she dances to the music of a stringed instrument. The ashes conveyed in this manner are now placed on the shelf of the new *kuala*, the master saying: " I, thy master, have brought thee here with reverential ceremonies, be not angry therefore, and when we pray to thee, hear our prayers."

In some places, the feast is held, according to an older custom, in the *kuala* itself, where a functionary, with a loaf received from the guardian of the old *kuala*, turns to the Voršud with the following words: " Voršud, come with us to another place; do not take offence, old ones, deceased ones." Later, he does the same thing with a loaf from the son,

PLATE XII

1. Votiak case for the Voršud or "Luck-protector," with offerings on the sacrifice shelf. (See
page 119.)
After photograph by Y. Wichmann.

2. Votiak village or Great Kuala. (See page
118.)
After photograph by U. Holmberg.

afterwards handing the father's loaf to the son, and the son's to the father. When the son who has separated from the home of his father, has received the bread, he reverently carves a chip from the pot hanger of wood suspended from the ceiling. He takes, further, ashes from the hearth, and conveys these with the chip to the newly founded *kuala* of his new home.[6]

A curious statement is that he who carries the Voršud must not put his foot on the bare ground, but must walk all the time on planks laid on the ground.

Many circumstances in the above descriptions recall the customs followed at a Votiak wedding. The very tunes played on this occasion are wedding tunes. In some places, it is further customary to distribute presents at the *kuala* feast, as at a wedding. In the District of Mamadysh a custom recalling a wedding is connected with the above mentioned ceremonies, namely, that the Voršud is taken to the new home like a bride in a sleigh with two horses and tinkling bells, the women being dressed in wedding costume. That the Votiaks themselves consider the Voršud feast to be a wedding festivity is seen from the name of this feast, *mudor šuan* (" *mudor* wedding "). Among the Votiaks, certain ceremonies recalling those of the *mudor* wedding are now observed at the inauguration of the modern huts used in these days. They also call this festivity " hut wedding " (*korka šuan*), on which occasion as at a wedding a " host " (*törö*) officiates. As the Indo-European races observe similar customs, we may assume that the Volga Finns acquired theirs through a foreign culture. The fact, however, that the above named ceremonies refer to a time when the Votiaks were still living in the old *kuala*, indicates that they date from a comparatively distant time.

The very word *mudor*, which phonetically corresponds to the Finnish *mantere* (" earth foundation "), recalls a different kind of removing ceremony, described by Aminoff. " When leaving his father's home to found a household of his own,

the son descends under the floor of the hut, takes a little earth
from there, and also fire from the hearth of the hut and then
prays to the son of the family spirit to accompany him to the
new home." [7]   A similar custom, when removing, seems to
have been known also among the Siryans in former times.
This appears from the following statement by Nalimov: " Even
in our days, everyone, on leaving home for a long journey,
takes with him a handful of earth from under the earth foundation of his home.   This earth protects him from accidents
and nostalgia." [8]   Similar beliefs are to be found among the
Baltic Finns.   Among the Ingrians a custom has been found of
giving to a bride who is going to a strange neighbourhood, a
bundle containing earth from the earth foundation under the
floor of her native hut, to protect her from nostalgia.   Likewise, they believe that a domestic animal removed to another
farm, will not miss its former home, if, when removing it,
some earth is also brought from the outhouse where the animal
was kept before. [9]

In the earliest times, the founder of a new family, when
parting from the home of his fathers, seems to have received
one or several images of his family spirits, to take with him,
the Lapps believing these to descend as an inheritance from
father to son, like any other property.   On account of the fact
that the Votiaks have not, for a long time, used images, no
exact statements concerning this custom are to be found.   Only
a few traditions and customs point back to this distant time.
Wichmann relates about the District Urzhum, that on leaving
his father's home, a son was given also a part of the contents
of the sacrifice case. [10]   Another writer mentions that the
sacrifice case of the new *kuala* must be made in the old *kuala*,
and before being removed, it must have lain for some time on
the sacrifice shelf of the old *kuala*. [11] This may be the origin
of the words in the above mentioned custom among the Votiaks
when removing the Voršud; " I take the smaller and leave
the greater."   To receive a Voršud from his native home is

of such great importance to the son that if for one reason or another the father quarrels with his son and refuses to give him a Voršud, the son must procure it by robbery. If the son who is angry with his father says, when taking the Voršud: " I leave the smaller, I take the greater," the consequence, according to the interpretation of the magicians, is that the son gets the older Voršud, and, in a religious sense, stands higher than his father. If, after this, any of his younger brothers is in want of a Voršud, he must apply to his brother with his request and not to his father.[12]

After the *mudor* wedding, the *kuala* is a sanctuary; the Voršud lives in it, and from that day, worship is carried out there. To keep up this is the sacred duty not only of that generation, but also of the following, for according to the beliefs of the Votiaks, the sacrifices in a building consecrated as a sanctuary must never be interrupted. He who does not observe this rule, will meet with some great accident. The people tell with terror how such persons have lost their property, have gone mad, etc. If, for instance at the change of guardians, the *kuala* should be removed from one place to another, the building is pulled down, and the timber of the walls is placed in the same order when built anew. The ashes of the hearth, the stones, and the Voršud case are taken with ceremony to the new place, together with the timber. Besides being removed when changing a guardian, the *kuala* may also be taken away for some other reason. Thus, for instance, it once happened that a sacrificial bull, when about to be killed, broke loose and ran away from a " great *kuala*," the sacrificers, in the midst of their devotions, having to leave off and pursue it. The place where the animal was at last caught, was considered to be so pleasing to the *kuala* spirit that the whole building was removed there.[13] If, from any cause, people are obliged to destroy a *kuala*, the sacrifice case and the stones of the hearth may not on any account be lost. As an instance of the superstition of the Votiaks the following legend is mentioned: A man destroyed his *kuala* and built in its stead a barn, leaving the sacrifice case and the stones under the hearth. Once, some young men who had gone there to sleep were awakened suddenly by groans from under the barn, like the wailing of a sick man. The next night the same wailing was heard. At last, the master himself went to sleep there, and found that it was none other than the Voršud who was moaning. He then promised to remove the stones and the case into a new *kuala*, which he did, and thenceforward there was silence in the barn.[14]

Considering that the name of Voršud, at the sacrifice meetings of the Votiaks, is generally used in the singular, most frequently in connection with the *kuala* family's name, as "možga Voršud," "utša Voršud," etc., it would seem as if every Votiak *kuala* had possessed only one family spirit. This was, however, not so in olden times, as is proved by the circumstance that the Votiaks consider themselves able to distribute them among their descendants. In one prayer the name of Voršud is also used in the plural.[15] The idea of several spirits in one *kuala* appears, moreover, in the following legend: A certain Votiak became a Christian and renounced the ancient customs of sacrifice, but did not destroy his *kuala*. After some time the spirits began annoying him; when lying in bed, he seemed to feel a heavy stone pressing on his breast; when he went to the barn to sleep, the spirits came there, too, to annoy him. At last, the man made up his mind to shoot them, and one night he walked about, gun in hand, waiting for them. At midnight three persons in white came out of the *kuala*, the first a beardless youth, the second also young but with the beginnings of a beard, the third, a woman. The man fired, and the vision vanished at once. After that they did not show themselves any more, but removed to another place, sending the man a severe illness as a punishment.[16]

The above story, showing that in one and the same *kuala*

PLATE XIII

Voršud Case Venerated by the Votiaks

(See page 119.)
Water-colour by V. Soldan-Brofeldt.

there were several family spirits, points also to their human origin. According to the belief of the Votiaks, the *kuala* spirits generally appear as human beings. At times, however, though rarely, the Voršud may reveal itself in some other form. In a story of the Votiaks in the District of Glazov, a *kuala* sanctuary is mentioned as having been on the site where the present town of Vyatka is situated. It is related that when the Russian settlers, after having driven out the Votiaks from their then dwelling-places, began pulling down the *kuala*, a bird flew out of the sanctuary, meeting its death beside the church just erected, as if stricken by an invisible power.[17]

The Votiak, having founded for himself a *kuala* of his own, still visits the old *kuala*, and sometimes even the still older mother *kuala*. The first, in comparison with the second, is a " little *kuala*," likewise the second in comparison with the third, while the second, compared with the first, is a " great *kuala*," and in the same way, the third in comparison with the second. According to their *kuala* worship the Votiaks are commonly divided into two groups, to both of which the same person may belong — the family of the " great *kuala* " and the family of the " little *kuala*." To illustrate the present *kuala* cult of the Votiaks and the relations of the different family groups with each other, it may be mentioned that the same Votiak in the village of Oštorma-Yumya in the District of Mamadysh, besides visiting the " little *kuala*," which is situated in his own yard and in whose sacrifices, besides himself, the families of his three younger brothers take part, also frequents the " great *kuala*," situated in the same village and visited by seventy-three families in all. The other families in the village, belonging to other clans, go each their own way to sacrifice. The above mentioned seventy-three families visit also the *kuala* in the neighbouring village or Staraya-Yumya, from which Oštorma-Yumya and certain other villages were originally formed. The " great *kuala* " of Staraya-Yumya is visited, not only by its own villages, but by the seventy-three families of Oštorma-Yumya, and, also, by all the persons living in the neighbouring villages who belong to the same tribe. In later days, however, people have more and more ceased coming from strange villages with their offerings to the " great kuala " of the mother village.

The relationships among the family groups are, of course, not the same in every Votiak village. Sometimes a " little kuala " may be visited by quite a number of families, up to several score, this depending wholly on the zeal of the Votiak families in founding new kuala sanctuaries for themselves.

Those Votiaks, who have removed as settlers, and even those who now remove far from their native place, and who, therefore, cannot take part in the sacrifices of their native village, remember, however, the kuala of their ancestors in their own kualas. Thus for instance, a Votiak family living in the village of Možga in the District of Birsk, remembers the " great kuala " in the native village of the same name in the district of Yelabuga, because their ancestors had removed thence, bringing with them mudor. A remarkable feature of the kuala cult of the Eastern Votiaks is, further, the circumstance that the so-called " little kualas " have come to be neglected; relatives perform their sacrifices only in the mutual family sanctuary, several of which may be found in one village, depending on the number of different families. Under such circumstances, mudor weddings take place only when Votiaks remove as settlers from the old village to a new one.

Reverence for the old home has been best preserved in the oldest native districts of the Votiaks, where, in certain neighbourhoods at present uninhabited, we may see remains of crumbling huts, which are sometimes visited at the command of the sorcerer, for the purpose of sacrificing in cases of severe illnesses. A hut of this nature, which is called " the uttermost kuala," is most probably the oldest home of the family that has been retained in memory.

General, regular *kuala* sacrifices are performed by the Votiaks at somewhat different times in different places, but, according to the most widespread custom, three times a year — in the spring, in summer, and in autumn. Later, it has become customary to sacrifice much oftener in the family *kuala*, in some places on every Christian holy day.

On regular holy days, the Votiaks sacrifice in the "little" as well as in the "great" *kuala*, representatives being sometimes sent also to the greater sanctuary of the mother village. The sacrificial ceremonies in the different sanctuaries resemble each other very much, with the exception of unimportant deviations. On the other hand, the times and order of sacrificing in the *kualas* of different rank vary, sacrifices being sometimes carried out first in the "little *kuala*" and then in the "great *kuala*" and *vice versa*. In some places the sacrificial ceremonies are held late in the evening, in others in the daytime. At times the festivity lasts for two or three days.

The oldest account of a *kuala* sacrifice originates from the province of Ufa and was published by Ryčkov in the eighteenth century. The author relates that the Votiaks sacrifice, " near certain branches of fir regarded by them as representing the family god," a young calf, whose ears they then place on the shelf on which the fir branches lie. The sacrificial animal they kill in the sanctuary itself.[18]

Of the same period is the description by Georgi, who gives a more detailed account of the sacrifice performed at Easter. The author states that both men and women partake in the ceremony, having cleansed themselves first by taking a bath in the bathhouse. Each one brings with him to the *kuala* guardian the objects necessary for the sacrifice. When the meat is cooked, the officiating priest places a portion from every dish and also some beer on a table opposite the door. On the shelf above the table some fir-twigs are laid, and on these he puts a dish with morsels from the sacrifice. These he takes after a while, together with the drinking vessel, in his hand, asking from the Voršud happiness, health, children, cattle, bread, honey, etc.[19]

A later, but much more complete account (1838) describes a sacrifice in the village of Multan. In this account it is stated that the guests bring with them to the sanctuary, bread, cakes, boiled eggs, and, for drink, home-made spirits and beer. Having accompanied the sacrificial animal to the middle of the *kuala* in front of the "image," they place beside it loaves of bread with eggs on them. If very many loaves have been brought, those officiating select three whole ones, but of the others they cut only a piece, placing these slices together with the eggs on the whole loaves. At the same time, one of the Votiaks recites prayers over the victim, and another pours water on it. The prayer done, they begin killing the animal, letting the blood flow into a cup or a trough; the skin is stripped off, the entrails cleaned and the worthless parts buried in a pit. The sacrificial animal is then cut up, its different members being severed so that a piece is obtained from each, the head, the breast, the legs, etc. The meat is boiled in a pan, into which the blood is also poured. When everything is ready, the Votiaks begin drinking the gin and tasting the sacrificial food. At the same time, they sacrifice, three times, food and meat in the fire, pouring into it, also three times, gin and beer from every vessel. Further, all the bones of the sacrificial animal are gathered and put into the fire, only those that will not burn being buried in a pit. The prayer read during the sacrifice contains invocations to the god to protect the family, to multiply the cattle and cause the vegetation to prosper.[20]

In the southern and eastern Votiak Districts, women generally do not appear at the sacrifices, and even when allowed to come, they stop outside the door with their children. This does not seem to have been the original custom. Among the Votiaks of the northern parts, where the ancient original customs have been partly better preserved, women are always

PLATE XIV

1. Remains of an old Votiak sacrificial *Kuala* in a now uninhabited district. (See page 128.)

2. Voršud case of the Votiaks with other sacrificial apparatus. (See page 119.)
From the Nukharka Museum.

present when sacrificing at home. At times they have a representative of their own even at the *kuala* festivals, such representatives, besides the ordinary *kuala* guardian, being chosen from each sex for the purpose of arranging the festival ceremonies. These become the host (*törö*) of the festival and his wife, who sit each at a different table in different corners. While officiating, the host keeps his cap on. The guests arrive in white holiday costume at the sanctuary, where the men take their places to the left of the fireplace, the women to the right. Amusements very often follow the sacrifice: music, singing, etc. The sacrificial priest sings sacrifice songs improvised on the occasion in question.[21]

In our days blood sacrifices at the *kuala* festivals have begun to be scarce. When sacrificing for some special reason they are still necessary, but at the regular festivals it has become customary to sacrifice only bread or porridge. Even if bread only be sacrificed, the Votiaks, in remembrance of the older custom, must still light the sacrificial fire. Once a year however, at least, they must still carry out a blood sacrifice with materials mutually contributed.

At the sacrifices, the Votiaks place one part of the sacrificial gifts on the shelf, while another part is burnt in the fire. When sacrificing bread, they always place it on the shelf in the corner, on which a white cloth is laid for the purpose. Sometimes there is placed on the regular sacrifice bread, which the wife of the *kuala* guardian makes of spring corn, other little pieces of bread from all the other families taking part in the sacrifice. Besides bread, the Votiaks also sometimes put butter, honey, and drink on the Voršud shelf. On the occasion of the blood sacrifice, a little meat porridge, or, when the beast is a big domestic animal, portions of its most important organs, generally boiled in different pans, are placed there. In most Districts it is customary to place the above named offerings on the shelf only as long as the prayer is being said. There are circumstances, however, which indicate that formerly the offerings were also left in their place for a longer time. Thus, for instance, it is customary in the District of Mamadysh, when sacrificing a duck, to leave its head on the sacrifice shelf until after the second or third day after the *kuala* festival, when it is eaten up by the priest. At Easter, a cake or a cup of water is placed on the shelf for the night, sometimes for a whole week, after which period persons belonging to the family eat up the offerings. The women, in general, are not in the habit of eating of the food placed on the sacrifice shelf.

Such portions of the sacrifice as the Votiaks place on the shelf, have also been sacrificed in the fire. Is this dual sacrificial custom of the *kuala* cult to be considered as the original, or are there two different stages of development reflected in these customs? Aminoff considers that the placing on the shelf is an older form of the *kuala* sacrifice, and the throwing into the fire a more recent one.[22] That the fire sacrifice in general is of later date among the Finno-Ugric races is seen clearly from the sacrificial customs of the Lapps.

Besides the blood sacrifices, the purpose of which was principally the feasting of the family gods, the Votiaks, in former times, also carried gifts to their *kuala* sanctuaries which were intended to serve the spirits as clothing, ornaments, or other holy property. We have already mentioned that in the ancient sacrifice cases of the Votiaks, all kinds of objects, such as skins, feathers, coins, etc., have been found, which most likely had been placed there as offerings. In former times, sacrifices of this kind were of course much more abundant and of more value, so that many " great *kualas* " became quite remarkable treasuries. For this reason their doors were well closed in unsettled times, and the services of a special " guardian " were necessary.

Besides the gift offerings, sacrificial coins are kept in the *kuala* sanctuary of the Votiaks, a collection of money being, indeed, embodied in the sacrificial ceremonies, and generally carried out after the feast. This is done in such a manner that every guest either puts his mite into the money box or presses it into the cake that the *kuala* guardian carries in his hands, after the sacrifice. Sometimes the guests bring their money stuck into the sacrificial bread. This common money, of which much more was collected formerly than nowadays, is used only for sacred purposes. With this money they pay for the repair of the sanctuary and for things necessary at the performance of the sacrifices, and in addition for the sacrificial animals.

Besides the above mentioned regular sacrificial festivals, there are others, more or less accidental, celebrated only under certain circumstances, sometimes in the " great *kuala* " and sometimes in the " little *kuala*." Occasional sacrifice festivals are celebrated by the Votiaks when such illnesses or other misfortunes have occurred, as are declared by the sorcerer to originate from the spirits living in the *kuala*. The sacrifice is not killed immediately, but a " sacrificial vow " is made first, which, in case of lack of means, may still be " renewed," before the true sacrifice is offered up. But on no account may it be forgotten or put off to an indefinite future. Particularly is it obligatory to sacrifice when a young girl in the family is to be married. It is related that, in the District Sarapul, when a bride removes to her new home, she is first taken round the fireplace in her old home, the while her father prays, with a measure of gin and another of beer in his hand, promising to sacrifice an ox, a calf, or some other animal to the family spirit.[23] In the District Mamadysh it is customary that, on the wedding day, the young wife makes a sacrificial vow, but the sacrifice itself generally takes place first in the following autumn, when she arrives at her native village with a duck under her arm. The bird is killed and boiled in the " great *kuala*," the sacrifice prayer being said by the " guardian," who points out to the Voršud which of the daughters of the family, having married, has now removed to another family and is therefore bringing an offering to the family spirits of her native home. No other person than the sacrificing priest and the sacrificer herself may take part in the performance. Only after this sacrifice may the wife perform sacrifices in her husband's family *kuala*. In case of illness, however, or some other misfortune, she must, on the advice of the sorcerer, sacrifice to the *kuala* of her family.

We have earlier pointed out similarities between some features of the Voršud cult and those of the worship of the spirits of the deceased. The worship of departed ancestors is, above all, recalled by the close relationship of the Voršud to the family worshipping the same, in whose name it is often addressed in prayer. It is to be noted, also, that the Votiaks turn to the Voršud and to the deceased in exactly the same matters, chiefly in cases of illness, the Voršud and the deceased members of the family being sometimes named side by side in the same prayer.

In comparing the *kuala* sacrifices and the order in which they are performed, with the general memorial festivals of the Votiaks, celebrated in the dwelling-house, we notice that in these, customs are observed that resemble the *kuala* ceremonies. Thus the Votiaks celebrate memorial festivals, besides those at home, within a greater family circle, or at the home of the ancestors of the family, on which occasion they recall together the memory of the deceased members of the family, in particular that of the most important. This corresponds to the Votiaks' curious fashion of distinguishing between the family of the " little *kuala* " and that of the " great *kuala*." Thus, it is no accident that the time of celebrating the regular *kuala* festivals and that of the regular memorial festivals fall so near each other. Evidently, the *kuala* festivals are only a more ancient form of the memorial festivals, in which, instead of poultry, larger domestic animals were used for the sacrifice. As the ceremonies at a later time have become altered to some extent from their earlier form, both have been retained side by side with each other until our days.

Among other Finno-Ugric peoples, the *kuala* cult has not

been preserved to the same extent as among the Votiaks. Many of them do not even use the old building, although it bears a name common among all the tribes of these peoples. Remains of the *kuala* cult, have, however, been preserved among the Cheremiss, amongst whom we may still see, in some parts, in the background of the hut (*kudo*) a time-darkened case which these, like the Votiaks, regard as the dwelling of the *kudo*-spirit. Nowadays we see there, besides offerings, only dried birch leaves which are not even always renewed on the occasion of sacrificing. Most frequently, however, we no longer find a sacrifice case in a Cheremiss *kudo*, but in its former place, the corner shelf continues to be held sacred. No stranger is allowed to approach the sacrifice shelf, as the *kudo*-spirit (*kudo*-Vodyž) may take it amiss, nor does it befit women to approach it, and even the children are afraid of it and avoid it. In order to shield the sacred back part of the sanctuary from injurious contact, the Cheremiss in some parts of the country used to divide the house by a partition.[24] In the District of Urzhum I heard the back part called " the little *kudo*." At times only one or the other back-corner is separated by means of a partition of boards. The " little *kudo*," which is reached from the " great " one through a small door, is, according to the Cheremiss, more sacred than the other parts of the building. Only grown up men may enter there, and not even these unnecessarily. In bygone days there were kept in " the little *kudo*," besides the sacrificial objects necessary at divine service, also arms and implements of the chase. Here were made, besides, their vows of sacrifice, by bringing in the firewood necessary when sacrificing in the forest, and the pan in which the victim was to be boiled. Where there is no longer any *kudo*, the sacrifice case is kept in the storehouse in the entrance to the bathhouse.

The *kudo*-Vodyž of the Cheremiss, when requiring sacrifice, also appears in human form in the dreams of the family members. The offering is then placed in the above named case,

or on the sacred corner shelf. According to the earliest accounts, the Cheremiss slaughtered a black sheep for their god.[25]
Nowadays they bring for the most part only small sacrifices,
such as hens and ducks, for occasional reasons, mostly on account of a certain eye disease (trachoma). At first the sacrificial
vow is fulfilled in such manner that a little meal, some honey,
and cakes or other eatables, are placed on the sacrifice shelf.
The sacrifice itself is not executed until after the lapse of some
time. Then the flour and honey used at the sacrificial vow
are mixed into a dough, of which sacrificial bread is made for
all the members of the family. In the sacrificial meal, which
is prepared and consumed in the *kudo*, only members of the
family partake, strangers not being allowed the tiniest bit.
When beginning the meal, pieces of food are placed on the
sacrifice shelf, near which the head of the family prays, asking
for forgiveness on behalf of the sinner and on that of the
whole family, should any one, unconsciously, in one way or
another, have happened to offend the *kudo*-spirit, and imploring him to protect and keep the family and home. In some districts it is customary to offer up a sacrifice to him at a fixed time,
in the autumn. The bones of the victim are not burnt, but
buried in the earth under the building; a portion from every
part of the body of the sheep used for this being placed on the
sacrifice shelf. In the District of Urzhum a curious custom has
been retained of taking the household god to one's neighbours,
when the spirit, by sending an illness, seems to require a sacrifice.
When not inclined to sacrifice to it, they say: " Do not require
any thing of us, we have boiled the last already; we will take
thee to our neighbour's; there is a silver-horned bull and a fine
woolly sheep, there thou shalt have a treat." Thus speaking,
the Cheremiss takes dust from the " *kudo*-spirit's " case and
sets out for his neighbour's. If he is asked to take a seat there,
and is offered bread and salt, all is well, as then " the spirit "
has been kindly received. Unnoticed, the guest throws the
dust from his hand into the corner and goes away without

PLATE XV

1. The little *kudo* or dwelling of the *kudo*-spirit within a Cheremiss hut, or great *kudo*. (See page 135.)

2. Cheremiss *kudo*. (See page 135.)
After photographs by U. Holmberg.

saying good-bye or asking his neighbour to come and see him. Also among the Hill Cheremiss, amongst whom one very rarely comes across a *kudo*, the belief has been preserved that the *kudo*-Vodyž continues to live in the place of the former *kudo*, and that he who quarrels in the said place or besmirches it, will undoubtedly fall ill.[26]

After marriage, the Cheremiss woman still goes at first for some time to the *kudo* of her old home to sacrifice, should she meet with illness or any other misfortune declared by the sorcerer to have been caused by the spirits of the " old place." Similarly the scattered younger families turn when necessary to the spirits of older *kudo*. Thus, the " little family " remains always dependent on the " great family " in some way or other.[27]

Georgi speaks also about a material image of the family god, stating that " in many houses, perhaps in every house, there is in a corner in a case, a coarse little doll of wood, dressed in male attire." When describing the wedding ceremonies of the Cheremiss, he further relates that " when everything is ready in the wedding house, the family god is placed on the table and the sacrificing priest (*kart*) of the village prays in front of it." Considering that the Cheremiss have not been in the habit of keeping the sacrifice case in the dwelling-house, there is reason to suppose that the family god mentioned by Georgi is the *kudo*-Vodyž.[28]

A similar family cult doubtless existed among the Mordvins, and even among the Baltic Finns. Among the Esthonians, remains of it seem to have been preserved, through alien influence, until modern times. The Voršud case of the Votiaks corresponds, with them, to the " Tõnni vakk " (*vakk* = " case "). On Tõnni or Antony's-day (January seventeenth) one must brew beer or slaughter some animal — the latter being generally a sheep, though a bull is sometimes mentioned. At nightfall, the Tõnni vakk was taken from its recess, candles were lighted on the rims of the case, and it was carried all round the dwelling house, the cattle sheds, and the yard. From each part of the carcase of the sacrificial animal a piece of meat was cut as a sacrifice to Tõnni, and of the gravy a little was also sprinkled on the nearest paths. Lastly the people sat down to eat.

Tõnni's case, which had to be made by the sorcerer, was kept in a place known only by the master, generally in the attic of the storehouse. In this were placed all the year round, for one reason or another, various offerings: — when the corn was threshed, when beer was brewed, when milking a cow that had lately calved, when shearing the sheep, and when spinning yarn or weaving cloth. When slaughtering, they sacrificed meat, blood or fat. The case had to be particularly remembered on the occasion of illness among either human beings or animals. Falling ill was considered to be a consequence of the case having been damaged or of some one, when passing, having made a noise, or because the people had forgotten to sacrifice to it. There is a report even, that the case used to contain a doll-like image. That the Esthonians also had known both a lesser family spirit and a greater one, is shown by a tradition, according to which not only every family but also every village had its common sacrifice case.[29]

There are no reliable statements regarding the corresponding family worship of the Finns. Yet, in the social life of the Karelians there are indications that these belonged to two different families, a smaller and a larger one, the chieftainship of the last named — where its head was not chosen by election — descending from a father to the eldest son of the eldest branch of the family. A result of the worship of the forefathers of the family was most likely the alien position of the wife in her husband's home, for, as with the Votiaks, the women in Finnish Karelia kept their own family name even after their marriage.[30]

CHAPTER IX

HEROES

THERE is every reason to believe that those Lapp Seides, which were worshipped by a larger following, were dedicated to the spirit of some more famous man, the founder of a family, a shaman, etc. Such people were worshipped also among other Finno-Ugric peoples and the Samoyeds. Veniamin relates of the Yuraks that certain of their stone or wooden gods, the latter having a head coming to a point, were worshipped by a great tribe, spread over a wide area, others again by only a very scant congregation. The former are generally situated in the neighbourhood of such places as the Yuraks are accustomed to gather at, to hunt or fish or to seek food for their reindeer. He mentions two such ancient sacred places, visited by great numbers, of which one was situated on the holy island Vajgats. At these meetings the Samoyeds sacrifice reindeer and dogs to their tutelary spirits, besmearing the mouths of the idols with the blood and fat of the sacrifice, and having eaten the flesh, hanging up the head, and even at times, the hide, on a holy tree.[1] Of later origin is possibly a custom of the Eastern Samoyeds of throwing pieces of the flesh of the sacrifice into the fire. Bloodless sacrifices are performed among the Ostiak Samoyeds. These sometimes do not slaughter the sacrificial deer, but content themselves with cutting out the face of the god or other strange figures on its back. After a ceremony of this description the animal is regarded as holy, and may not be used for any purpose or eaten.[2]

The " sacred places " of the Yuraks are not fenced in, neither are buildings to be found on them, the idols standing always under the open sky.[3] On the other hand, special buildings for their idols are met with among the Ostiak Samoyeds. A building of this kind, hidden away in the forest, is described by Donner in the following words: " As the dwelling-place of the gods they use here a building standing on four high supports, resembling greatly the average barns by the River Ob. In the fore-wall there was a little opening and against the back wall stood the god, made of wood and resembling a human being, together with his marital partner. The face was very clumsily carved, the eyes formed of two large blue glass-pearls, imparting a very quaint expression to the old man. The images were dressed in fine furs and had around them a number of weapons made of pewter with which to protect themselves; and, fashioned of the same material, swans, geese, snakes, reindeer and other animals, by the help of which they were supposed to be able to flee on the approach of an unconquerable enemy. Near the door was posted a little man dressed as a Russian policeman, holding a wooden sabre in one hand, while in the other he swung a great sword. The dwelling-place of the gods was furnished with gaudy cloths and expensive furs, and before the image of the ancestor the most varying objects lay on the floor, among other things a great deal of money, of which many coins were a couple of hundred years old. In the branches of the holy trees surrounding the building garments, horns of animals, hides, etc., were hung." [4]

Similar spirits, bound to certain fixed places, are also possessed by the Ostiaks and Voguls in great numbers. The mightiest of these are honoured by a great circle extended over a wide area, others again only by a small one, or merely by the population of a single village. " All places dedicated to idols," says Pallas, " the boundaries of which are exactly defined by rivers, brooks, or other marks, are spared by the Ostiaks, who neither cut down trees nor mow grass, neither hunt nor fish, abstaining even from drinking the water within

PLATE XVI

1. Ostiak Holy Place, with images of gods or spirits.
According to Finsch.

2. Ostiak place of sacrifice.
After photograph by Rabot.
(See page 141 and compare pages 139–140. Yurak.)

their boundaries, for fear of offending the gods. Should they be obliged to traverse these waters by boat, they are careful not to approach too closely to the shores or to touch them with their oars, and if the way through them is very long, they supply themselves with water before reaching the holy place, as they would sooner suffer the worst tortures from thirst than drink of the holy water." [5] These holy places, however, have not definite boundaries, still less are they fenced in, but especially in the southern districts there is a little building resembling a storehouse, intended for the preservation of offerings and the images. Like their house gods, the spirits living at fixed holy places of the Ostiaks and Voguls have all been materialised into images. Most often they have been shaped as wooden figures resembling human beings, at times as rag-dolls made out of stuffed sacks or natural stones; further, they have also been formed of bronze, copper, lead, or even of bones. As assistants these have often images resembling various animals. The storehouses for offerings are generally under the care of a special person, who then also carries out the sacrificial ceremonies and receives the offerings, money, skins, etc. Very often this occupation is hereditary in the same family. [6]

That these powerful and dreaded spirits, regarded as being able to visit people with sickness, were originally human, has not been forgotten by the people. A part of them are said to have been former rulers or heroes, whose mighty deeds are extolled in songs, others are expressly said to be the founders of the clans. Those again that are furnished with images of animals were probably famous shamans. An example of how a powerful spirit is believed to develop out of a man of mark after death is given by an Ostiak folk-poem, in which a Vasyugan hero displays an uncommon nobility of character by burying the body of a dead enemy-hero, erecting his sword on the grave, and consoling him by saying: " In the times of coming daughters, in the times of coming sons, thou shalt be called to life, and thou shalt become an offering-spirit accepting offerings." [7]

At times one may see many images in the same offering-house. Two hundred years ago, Novitskiy visited a " great " god-house, containing five wooden images resembling human beings wrapped round with " clothes." Around this chief building were smaller square store-rooms on posts about the height of a man; in these were preserved the objects used at the slaughter of a sacrifice; axes, knives, etc. Separated from these was another little store-room filled with bones. [8]

The sacrifices of the Ostiaks and Voguls, which may be either annual or occasional, do not materially differ from the corresponding uses of the Samoyeds. According to the oldest sources, the mouths of the images were besmeared with blood and fat, and the hides of the animals, with horns and hoofs attached, hung up in trees. The use of fire as a means of transmitting the offerings, met with also among the Ostiak Samoyeds, is most probably of later origin. Like these last mentioned, the more Eastern Ostiaks have the custom of occasionally offering up so-called bloodless sacrifices, that is to say, sacrifices in which the animal is not killed, its " soul " only being made over to the god. Even children may thus be consecrated to some spirit; the child thus consecrated has to fulfil certain duties during his lifetime, as, for example, to marry a wife, or a husband, from the direction of the compass in which the spirit dwells. [9]

The worshipping of heroes among the Siryans, at the present time totally forgotten by them, is described in the Life of St. Stephen (d. 1396) in the following words: " In Perm many kinds of idols were to be found: some large, some small, others again, of medium size; some were famous and very fine, others were legion; a part were worshipped only by few and were shown little honour, but others again were worshipped by people dwelling far and wide. They have certain idols to whom they travel long distances, bringing them gifts from afar, even from districts three or four days' or a week's journey away." [10]

The brother-tribe of the Siryans, the Votiaks, have even today forest copses, consecrated to their ancient heroes, and called *lud* by them. In earlier times these holy places were hidden in the forests. The oldest authors to mention the Votiaks say that these *lud* were generally in forests of fir. [11] Nowadays, as the forests in East Russia have diminished to a very great degree, having even become quite scarce in some districts, these consecrated groves have become visible, standing out on the open plains as memorials of the former forests. Thus, in the vicinity of the pagan Votiak villages flourish luxurious sacrificial groves, the tall trees of which have been held sacred from generation to generation.

Wherever these *lud* may happen to be, in the forests or open plains, they are always fenced in. In this respect they differ from the holy places of the Samoyeds and the other northern peoples. But common to them all is the superstitious fear felt by the people for them. The Votiaks have nothing else that they hold so sacred as these *lud*. No one enters them without due reason, not even on holy days, without taking an offering there. Cattle may not enter them, branches may not be broken off, not even a stick may be taken away; all disturbance is forbidden, and game seeking shelter there may not be shot at by the hunters. Women and children avoid them altogether; in passing them they turn their heads aside, still less would they ever set foot in them. Neither may a stranger enter the sacred area. The spirit, when angered, vents its wrath relentlessly by causing a severe sickness. Most fear-inspiring, however, is the *lud* in the twilight.

The fence surrounding the sacred grove is either of sticks or boards, or sometimes of plaited branches. As in appearance, so also in height, do they vary in the different districts. A little gate of boards, swinging on wooden hinges, generally leads to the sanctuary, being open only during the performance of sacrifices. The direction of these gates varies so much that it is impossible to conclude that they have been placed to point to any special point of the compass. Wichmann saw in the Elabuga District (Bussurman Mozhga) a *lud* that was divided into two by a fence; into the inner part only the guardian of the *lud* and his assistants were allowed to enter. In this part was the fireplace and a table for the flesh of the sacrifice. In the front part, to which the congregation also were admitted, there was a table for the mutual meal.[12]

In most of the *lud* which the author was able to see during his travels, there was, with the exception of the fence, nothing that might specially draw attention to it. Only in a few sanctuaries was there a rotted bench, a moss-grown stool, or a narrow table, used by the Votiaks as an altar on which to offer up their sacrifices. The offering-table is often placed at the foot of some thick, centuries-old tree, under which the sacrificing priest reads out his prayers. It would appear that the sacrificial ceremonies of the Votiaks were particularly centred round some old tree. Of this, Buch relates also, from the Sarapul District, that in the centre of the *lud* there was an old tree, the lower branches of which were lopped away to allow of a freer approach.[13]

In the larger and much visited groves there was also a store-like building, without a fireplace, called the *lud-kuala* by the Votiaks.[14] One of these the author saw in the Mamadysh District. It was a small hut, unfitted for a dwelling-place, with a roof sloping backwards, and a small door, which, like the gate of the grove, opened towards the west, that is to say, towards the village. Nothing was to be seen in the hut, except a shelf of board in the right-hand back corner. The fireplace was outside the building, between it and the gate. The old inhabitants relate that the *kuala* was not as empty in earlier times as it was then, but was used as a store-place for offerings, sacrificial vessels, towels, coins, etc.

The Votiaks worship in families at the *lud;* the members of one family never come to worship in the *lud* of another family. Should several *lud*-families live in the same village, just as many groves will be found in its vicinity. A grove in which a great clan, i.e., many villages, gathers for a mutual sacrifice, is called a " great *lud*." Every *lud* has its separate " guardian," the post passing down from father to son. Only when a " guardian " is childless, is another member of the family or clan chosen at a meeting of its members to be a sacrificing priest. Sometimes, the magician (*tuno*) chooses a guardian for the sacred grove.

The guardian has no special ceremonial dress at the sacrifices, but it is demanded of him that his apparel shall be neat and clean. Where possible, he must wear a white coat, on his head a white hat, and white wrappings round his feet, and new bark-shoes. Cleanliness is also demanded of the congregation visiting the grove. No one is allowed to enter who has not bathed beforehand.

The Votiaks make a *lud* for themselves for many different reasons. They begin to worship the *lud* spirit, for example, in the hope of being delivered from some serious illness, or, again, they build a fence round a grove, the spirit of which has revealed itself in a dream, giving the exact situation of the same. It is the duty of the dreamer to set out at once to fence in the place shown him in his dream. When the Votiaks move as settlers to a new neighbourhood, too far away for the old *lud* to be conveniently visited, they prepare a new one for themselves. This may not be done in any place without calling upon the services of the magician, who bestrides a young foal that has never been ridden before, and rides without a bit or reins into the forest. The place where the foal stops is the site of the grove. The Votiaks, however, take care that the grove is not situated too far from the village.[15]

Sacrifices are not offered up in a new sacred grove until the " spirit " has been brought from the old place. The " bringing of the spirit " is carried out in the same manner as the *mudor*-wedding. The Eastern Votiaks relate that their forefathers, for the inauguration of sacred groves in strange neighbourhoods, brought with them ashes from the grove of their native village. In the same manner Bogayevskiy says of the Sarapul District, that when the *tuno* has decided on a site for a new grove, the sanctuary is removed there with solemn ceremonies, in which the most important act is the bringing over of ashes from the old place to be placed on the site of the fireplace of the new.[16]

As soon as the *lud* has been inaugurated for its mission, it becomes a sanctuary in which yearly sacrifices must be offered up. This is not only the sacred duty of the founder, but of all his descendants. Miropolskiy says that though the Russians may have laid waste a *lud*, the Votiaks continue to worship the spirit at the site of the former grove.[17] Anyone omitting the proscribed sacrifices is sure to be punished severely by the *lud*-spirit, who is regarded by the Votiaks as stern and exacting.

Doubtless, the Votiaks formerly had images within their sacred groves, although we can no longer determine the appearance of these. The difficulty, for a child of nature, of grasping the idea of a spiritual being when he has nothing material to lay hold of, is shown by a fable of the Votiaks in which it is told how they were at one time so crushed beneath material adversities that the duty of sacrificing lay too heavily upon them and they decided to abolish this rite. A Tatar offered to take away the *lud*-spirit by collecting all the objects gathered together as offerings in the grove. The hopes of the Votiaks were, however, dashed again by their being continuously punished by the spirit. The people believed this to be due to the fact that the Tatar had not taken the offerings far enough away, but had cast them on to the village fields.[18]

Besides occasional offerings, annual sacrifices are offered up by the Votiaks in the *lud*. The annual sacrifices appear to

PLATE XVII

1. Votiak sacred grove or *lud* with surrounding fence and gate. (See page 143.)
After photograph by Y. Wichmann.

2. Storehouse of the Ostiak idols near Vasyagan. (See page 141.)
After photograph by Adrianov.

have been made chiefly in the summer before hay-making time, and in the autumn after the conclusion of work in the fields. The ceremony itself was performed, according to the most ancient custom, in the evening. Occasional offerings are made by the Votiaks after every misfortune, especially during a severe illness, said by the magician (*tuno*) to be a sign that the *lud*-spirit demands a sacrifice. It is the magician's duty to find out what the spirit wishes as a sacrifice on the varying occasions. To begin with, however, a promise of sacrifice is regarded as sufficient. Thus, a few copper coins are bound up in a rag, with the words: " With this money, *lud*-spirit, I buy thee a horse, let the sick not lose his life." Silver coins are then placed in the rag, with the words: " With silver I deck the mane of thy horse." Further, a little meal is strewn there, with the words added: " Besides which I will bake thee a loaf, if thou wilt give health to the sick." The rag bundle is then hung up in some secret place. Should the sickness not improve after this, it is regarded as a sign that the spirit wishes the actual sacrifice immediately.[19]

This promise to the *lud*-spirit is often made by the guardian, who, as soon as he is informed of the matter, goes out into his yard or even into the sanctuary with a loaf of bread or a dish of porridge in his hand, praying in the name of the sick person, that the *lud*-spirit may be appeased and wait until the sick person is himself in a condition to offer up his sacrifice. Sometimes, the promise is again " renewed " before the actual sacrifice. When the *lud*-guardian prays in his own yard, he keeps his face always turned in the direction in which the sanctuary is situated.

The day on which an annual sacrifice is to be performed, is determined by the *lud*-family or *lud*-clan. Before the ceremony, the participants must all cleanse themselves and put on clean apparel. To the preparations belong also the collecting of sacrifice-money by cutting the family-mark of each family on a stick, the marked lines indicating the amount given.[20]

The *lud*-spirit always demanding blood-offerings, a foal is generally used as the victim, but also, at times, a black sheep.

After the conclusion of all these preparations, the actual ceremony is begun. Only the older males go into the sanctuary, carrying with them the vessels, cauldrons, dishes, provisions, and the sacrificial animal. When the crowd arrives at the gate of the sanctuary, they greet the spirit by taking off their head-dress, the guardian himself opening the door and, as the leading person, going first into the grove, the others following silently after. As a beginning fire must be made on the site of the old fires, fallen trees, stumps, or fallen branches being used for fuel. Towels for the wiping of hands are brought with them also and hung up in the branches of the tree. On the altar-table, decked with green boughs and white cloths, the accompanying loaves and pancakes are piled up. When the number of worshippers is very great, the food-offerings are placed on the ground, a white cloth being laid under the wooden bowl of each family.

Before commencing the sacrifice it must be ascertained whether the *lud*-spirit will accept the offering. This is done by pouring fresh spring-water by means of a bundle of twigs, over the sacrificial animal, which must be flawless and of one colour. This ceremony is repeated several times, the *lud*-guardian reading softly a prayer the while, until the animal shivers, which, according to the Votiaks, Chuvashes and Cheremiss, is a sign that the sacrifice is pleasing to the god.

After the " sign " the sacrificing priests begin the slaughtering. Its feet having been bound together, the animal is turned over on to its left side and the blood allowed to run dry from the veins in its throat without any previous stunning of the victim. A few drops of the warm blood are thrown by means of the sacrifice ladle into the fire. During the slaughtering, the *lud*-guardian reads out a prayer, holding the sacrificial bread in his hand. As soon as the animal has been killed, the hide is flayed from it and the carcase divided in a particular way. The chief organs of the body, the heart, lungs, liver, etc., are cooked separately and when prepared are set in a special dish. Later, two small fragments are cut from each quarter of the carcase, from the tongue, lungs, heart, liver, etc., one of which is placed in a dish on the table, the other thrown into the fire. During an earlier period, the pieces now set on the altar-table were hung up in the tree itself, and in some places it is still said to be usual to thread them on to a little twig, to the end of which a strip of lime-bark is bound, probably for hanging up in the tree.[21] As other peoples also, including the Lapps, have been in the habit of cutting small slices from the most important organs of the sacrificed animal, which were then threaded on to a pole and fastened to the holy tree, it is apparent that this must have been an ancient Finno-Ugric custom.

In sanctuaries possessing a building, the offerings are placed on the corner shelf. This is quite to be expected, for if the *lud*-spirits, as may be supposed, were at one time materialised in the form of images, they were certainly situated in the *lud-kuala*, together with the offering vessels and the money. This is further pointed to by the fact that the Votiaks regard the *lud-kuala* as being so sacred, that only the *lud*-guardian may enter it.

From the Life of St. Stephen we may obtain a graphic view of the ancient *lud-kuala* sacrifices. Incidentally, the image-house of the Siryans is mentioned, which was also watched over by a special " guardian." The actual appearance of the build-ing is not described; it is only stated that within were images, sacrificing tables and a great amount of valuables. The saint is praised for the fact, that out of all that was hung up round the gods, either as clothing for them, or for their bedecking themselves, or merely as gifts of sacrifice — skins of sable, ermine, skunk, beaver, fox, bear, lynx, and squirrel — all these he gathered together into a pile, and burnt them, smote the images with an axe on their foreheads and hewed them into small pieces, throwing these on the fire, and burning up everything together, the pile with the skins and the images at the same time. This caused great surprise among the Siryans, who said: " Why did he not take all this as booty for himself? " In another place we read: " In the same manner he forbade his disciples to take away anything from the houses of the idols, neither gold, silver, copper, iron, pewter, nor any of the objects mentioned earlier." [22]

When the *lud*-spirit has received his share of the sacrifice, the food is divided according to the number of families taking part in the sacrifice. Following a very old custom, the whole of the food must be consumed within the sanctuary and at the same time. The hide and the larger bones are, following another old custom, hung up in the holy tree.[23] Nowadays, hides are not seen in the groves of the Votiaks, as not even the fact of their being cut into pieces has been able to protect them from thieves. On the other hand, one can see among the Eastern Votiaks whole skeletons of animals hung up with ropes of bark on the tree. The extreme care with which the flesh of the sacrifice is carved by the Votiaks, who avoid fracturing any bone whatever, and the care with which they join these together in their natural order, appear to be a result of a belief, said by Bechterev to be prevalent among them, that the sacrificed animal does not die, but passes living to the *lud*-spirit.[24]

A noticeable feature in the *lud* worship of the Votiaks is, further, the use of wax candles, not found among the more northern peoples. These candles are often prepared first in the grove, where the wax obtained in bee-keeping is kneaded between the hands round strands of flax.

After the meal, the congregation form up in long rows while the *lud*-guardian prays in a low voice. According to the oldest custom the prayers, like the slaughtering also, should be read with the face turned to the west or the north. The contents of the prayer vary in different districts, depending chiefly on the accidental needs of the sacrificers. The *lud*-spirit is first

PLATE XVIII

1. Votiak Lud-kuala, formerly a storeplace for offerings, sacrificial vessels, etc. (See page 144.)
After photograph by U. Holmberg.

2. Votiak Lud-kuala, Birsk district. (See page
144.)
After photograph by Y. Wichmann.

PLATE XVIII

1. Votiak *lud-kuala*, formerly a storeplace for offerings, sacrificial vessels, etc. (See page 144.)
After photograph by U. Holmberg.

2. Votiak *lud-kuala*, Birsk district. (See page 144.)
After photograph by Y. Wichmann.

asked to protect human beings and animals against sickness and all other evils, and the fields from hail and storms, etc. After each prayer, read by the guardian, the kneeling congregation touch the ground with their foreheads. Sometimes the minds of the worshippers are uplifted by the tones of stringed instruments. While the people are leaving the sanctuary, they bow low to the *lud* and say: " Live happily and protect us." [25] At times the festival is prolonged in the village at the house of the " guardian," where the men and women of the village gather, and where feast-songs are sung in these words: " The *lud*-spirit has wished us peace and given his blessing." The festival may even be prolonged for two or three days.[26]

What the origin of this *lud*-spirit was, the Votiaks themselves do not always know. Many features of the ceremony point, however, to the worship of the dead. Such features are, e.g., the fact that the *lud*-spirit, often called the " ruler " or " lord " (*lud-kuźo, lud-asaba*) or merely *lud*, appears in dreams in human shape, that he is fixed to a certain place, and that he is worshipped by families and is sacrificed to in the evenings with the face turned to the west or the north. The black sacrificial animals are also a sign pointing to the worship of the deceased.

As Georgi already relates, the Votiaks sometimes worship in their *lud* a spirit called Sulton (= Arabo-Turkish Sultan).[27] The same epithet is applied by the Chuvashes to a spirit dwelling in their sanctuaries, which is called by them *kirämät* (?an Arabo-Turkish word meaning " holy "). To Turco-Tatar influence points also the belief of the Votiaks that the *lud*, when desiring a sacrifice, appears in dreams in the guise of a Tatar. The *lud* sacrifices of the Votiaks are, however, not entirely of foreign origin, for signs that these also worshipped their ancestors and heroes are not wanting even in our day. As an example may be mentioned that in Bussurman-Mozhga (Elabuga District) eleven villages celebrate the memory of the founder of their line, Mardan. The brave Mardan had in bygone times come from the north and chosen this village as

his dwelling-place. Every third year they sacrifice a horse to
him and a cow to his wife, and annually, in addition, a sheep is
sacrificed. The words of thanksgiving uttered during the sacrifice to Mardan, are as follows: "Together we sacrifice a horse
to thee. For the fine children and the fine harvest thou hast
given us, we thank thee, Father Mardan." [28]

Further light is thrown upon the *lud* cult of the Votiaks by
the corresponding sacrificial cult of the Cheremiss. Like the
Chuvashes, the Cheremiss call their fenced-in sanctuaries
keremet. Contrary to their attitude towards the groves of the
Nature gods, in which they say sacrifices are made "upward,"
or "towards the sun," sacrifices are here made "downward,"
or "towards the night." The Cheremiss display great dread of
the groves of the "lower spirits," in which, where possible,
coniferous trees must grow. A peculiar feature is that in the
keremet no foreign tongue may be spoken, as the spirit dwelling
there "hates foreign tongues." They often give to their
sanctuaries names such as "the *keremet* of our clan." The
same person may, however, belong to two different *keremet*-
clans. In such cases, the *keremet* groves are generally consecrated to different spirits. At Kurmanaeva (Birsk District)
there is a so-called Sultan-*keremet*, in the sacrifices of which
the people of about twenty-five villages take part. Some villages have no *keremet* at all, while in some places a *keremet*
may belong to a few separate families only. In the Urzhum
District, where this cult has better preserved its original features than among the Eastern Cheremiss, one may see several
sacrifice-trees in the same gloomy fir forest, by each of which
the different families offer up their sacrifices.

Where there is only one *keremet* in a village this is generally
called after the village. At times, the *keremet* may be called
after its founder, or after the place in which it is situated.
Every clan takes care of its sanctuary, where the collective
sacrifices are offered up by a member of the clan chosen for
the purpose, but where any single member also may make offer-

ings on his own account. The Cheremiss make their offerings late in the evenings, as after a sacrifice one may neither go out to visit anyone, nor receive visitors. On the way to the grove, one must, as far as possible, avoid meeting people. The most usual sacrifice nowadays is a foal or a black sheep, but earlier it was very often a black bull.

Like the Votiaks, the Cheremiss at times make only a promise of sacrifice. The usual method is that money, flour, honey, or a little loaf prepared specially for the occasion, are placed in a little bundle, and the worshipper prays to the *keremet*-spirit to be appeased and to soothe the agony of the sick; binding himself to carry out the offering on a suitable occasion. The bundle may be hung up either at home on the wall of the storeroom, or in the *keremet* on the branches of the sacrifice-tree; when the promise is redeemed, the bundle is burned up. Often the promise is accompanied by the hanging-up of the garments of the sick, or the thrusting in of some iron implement, an axe, a sickle, or a knife in the wall of the storeroom, from which they are removed after the promised animal has been sacrificed. When the Cheremiss promise a sheep or a bull, they take a little wool or hair from the promised animal into the grove. If a horse has been promised, they prepare harness of bark, and hang this on the sacrifice tree as a guarantee to the spirit. At the same time a few sticks of wood are piled against the tree. Some who make promises of sacrifice hang up a wax candle with the objects already mentioned. The promised sacrifice is slaughtered, like the others, in the evening, as " should anyone meet the sacrificer, he would immediately fall ill." By means of all the objects that follow the making of a promise of sacrifice, the Cheremiss attempt to assure the spirit that he need not wait very long for the redemption of the promise.[29]

Where a poorer Cheremiss cannot in due time fulfil his promise of sacrifice, he must " renew " the promise by sacrificing some lesser object. Very usual is the sacrificing of a goose, a duck, or a hare, in the place of a horse. In the Birsk District the author had the opportunity of seeing how the population of a village offered up a smaller sacrifice to the *keremet* on account of a cattle-plague. Into the sanctuary only the sacrificing priest and three assistants entered. These had first to take a bath and clothe themselves in clean garments. Immediately when they had arrived at the grove, the assistants made a fire, using for this purpose glowing cinders brought in a pan from the village. Sacrifice bread was kneaded on the spot and baked on a wooden fork over this fire. When the loaf, on which two " noses " had been impressed by three fingers held together, was ready, it was placed at the root of the sacrifice tree. The candles were then made and placed in hollows in the bark of the tree. The actual sacrifice, a duck, lay with feet bound together near the tree. Swinging a burning branch and striking the knife against the blade of the axe, the " priests " prayed side by side, while the others killed the duck by cutting its throat. The sacrificing priest poured a little of the warm blood into the fire, imploring the *keremet* to accept the sacrifice, free the cattle from the plague, and wait until the autumn for the promised horse. When the flesh of the duck was cooked the sacrificing priest carried it to the tree, where he cut off small pieces of the heart, liver, windpipe, neck, breast, back, wings and feet into two bowls, the contents of one being given through the fire to the *keremet*, of the other to the medium of the sacrifice, " the Fire-mother." In each bowl was also laid one of the cut-off " noses " of the sacrifice bread. Before this ceremony, more prayers had been read before the tree, accompanied by the swinging of torches and the clang of the knife against the axe. After the sacrifice of the contents of the bowls, the rest of the meat was eaten; the remnants were thrown into the fire.

At the sacrifices, one hears the Cheremiss in the Urzhum District refer to the *keremet*-spirit as the " Old man," the " Great man," or the " Prince." The best known is a spirit called the " Old Man of the Hill " or as he is also called, after his dwelling-place, Nemda, " the Old man of the Nemda Hill " or " the Prince of the Nemda Hill." Of this worship, Olearius relates in the first half of the seventeenth century that the Cheremiss made pilgrimages to the Nemda brook and sacrificed there. This holy place, he says, is feared greatly by them: " Any one going there without an offering, perishes, as the devil is believed to have his habitation there." [30]

The sacred place mentioned by Olearius, situated in the Yaransk District, is spoken of also in certain accounts dating from the former half of the last century. As the Russian priests exerted much pressure on the Cheremiss at that time on account of their pagan religion, they knew that these were in the habit of making sacrifices at a stone, lying on the bank of the Nemda near the village Tshembulatova, and, therefore, they destroyed the stone. The spirit worshipped by the Cheremiss at the stone, was called by them Tshembulat, from which the village had derived its name.

Nowadays the people no longer gather at the actual dwelling-place of this spirit, but have prepared groves in his name at different places. Thus, the same spirit may be worshipped in the groves of many villages. In the neighbourhoods where tales of the " Nemda Old man " have been best preserved, it is said that he lived by the Nemda brook over which a " bridge " led. Besides a wife he had also officials: a " bookkeeper," an " interpreter," a " guardian of the gate," and a " bridge man," whose office it was to watch over the bridge. To each of these it was usual to make a separate offering, a horse to the Prince himself, a cow to his wife, and to the others some smaller animal.

Many tales go to prove that this " great man " was a former Cheremiss chief. He is said to have ridden a white stallion and fought against enemies: " When he finally succeeded in re-establishing peace on earth, he called together the Cheremiss to a stone, and proclaimed the peace to them. He then lifted up the stone, and placed himself under it, saying to his people: 'Should war break out again, some one must bestride a white stallion, and ride three times round the stone, shouting: " Arise, Chief, there is war on the earth! " ' A Cheremiss did this once out of curiosity, shouted out the necessary words, and immediately the chief arose, sat himself on his horse and rode out to the east and west, to the north and the south, but nowhere could he see signs of war. Then, calling the Cheremiss together again, he said: 'As you have fooled me and called me without cause, you are hereafter my slaves, and must sacrifice a foal to me annually.' "

In some districts he is called " the Northern Ruler " and is said to have command over an invisible army. When sickness is rife among the cattle, the people say: " The Northern Ruler has sent his warriors to cut down our cattle." Even now he is said to ride through the land of the Cheremiss at times, to see how these are progressing. Should anyone meet him without knowing who he is, and thus not get out of his way, an immediate illness is the result, and a horse must be sacrificed to the spirit. The people even speak of his green cloak and his red head-dress. He is specially sacrificed to in times of war.

Besides the widely-known and everywhere highly respected " Nemda Prince " the Cheremiss have other local *keremet*-spirits, the fame of which is not so widely spread. The majority of these have become the objects of worship through their heroic deeds. The Cheremiss remember their feats even today. There are many local heroes, especially in the old dwelling-places of the people. Thus, they make offerings to " the Old man of the castle-hill " and to the " Hero Aren," who fought against the Tatars, but met his death before a gate, ever afterwards called the " Hero gate." At his death the hero said: " Remember me, give me a good horse with me in the grave, and continue the war by slinging stones! " The Cheremiss did as their leader had advised. The stones, di-

PLATE XIX

1. The image of the Samoyed, " Master of the Forest," carved on a tree-trunk. (See page 178.)
After photograph by K. Donner.

2. Cheremiss horse-sacrifice to the keremet-spirit in time of sickness. (See page 157.)
After photograph by U. Holmberg.

rected by the dead hero himself through the air, whistled in a peculiar manner and destroyed the enemy. On the place where the hero had died, a *keremet* was established, in which the Cheremiss sacrifice a foal in cases of sickness, even today. A strange inherited custom is connected with this sacrifice as a memory of those times of war: a stone is cast in the air in the name of the sick person, and by the whining sound it makes, the possibilities of recovery are made known.

Together with their own heroes, who "hate foreign tongues," the Cheremiss, like the Votiaks, sacrifice to a spirit called Sultan. The last named has his own special sanctuaries, as according to the people's view, he cannot be worshipped in the same place as a Cheremiss chief. This may be a relic from the period of power of the Bolgars, when the independence of the Cheremiss first began to waver. In any case the *keremet* cult already described, corresponding with the *lud*-sacrifices of the Votiaks, proves that the Finnish stocks on the Volga have had their own princes at one time in history, the memory of whom they have been able to preserve through the centuries.

Under the alien name of *keremet* the Mordvins also worshipped their heroes and the dwelling-places of these. Their *keremet* also seems to have been a fenced-in forest-grove. Even sacrifice store-houses (*kudo*) and probably also images were kept by them in their sacred places.[31]

That the Mordvins, like the Votiaks and Cheremiss, sacrificed also to the spirits of alien rulers, is shown by the name mentioned earlier, Soltan, or Salhta. The hero cult of the Mordvins is further described by Paasonen as follows: " Among the Erzä in the Kazan and Samara Governments, we find a deity called Staka Pas ("the heavy god"), who is honoured with special sacrifices, and entreated not to launch " his heaviness " (evil generally) upon the people. In some parts, a divine couple, popularly supposed to be husband and wife, and bearing many names — e.g., Onto and Bonto —

are invoked by the epithet of Staka Pas, while elsewhere the "heavy god" is addressed in sacrificial prayers as Kan Pas, Kuvan Pas, and regarded as living "in the black earth." The word *Kan*, the signification of which is now unknown to the people themselves, is simply the Tatar Kan ("prince"), so that Kan Pas means "god-prince"; Kuvan again is most probably derived from the Turkish title *kagan*, which in Chuvash or Bolgar would be pronounced *kugan*, and in Mordvin may easily have become *kuvan*. The Mordvins having been at one time under the rule of the Volga Bolgars, of whom the present day Chuvash are a descendant people, it is quite probable that "the heavy god" was originally the spirit of some Turkish ruler. Similarly, the other heavy gods, Onto and Bonto, etc., are perhaps the rulers of an earlier age.[32]

Of a corresponding sacrificial cult among the Baltic Finns we have no reliable information. We need not doubt, however, that they also had their heroes whom they worshipped. The Esthonians and the Finns have preserved a common name *hiisi*, which originally meant "forest" but later also "sacrificial grove." Hiisi, as the spirit dwelling within these was also called, is generally regarded as an evil spirit, like the *lud* of the Votiaks. An old tale has been recorded in Esthonia, according to which the "Thunder god" thrived best in a forest of leaf-trees, but Hiisi best among coniferous trees. Here the same difference is made between the worship of the Nature god and the underground spirits, as the Cheremiss observe today. The old folk-traditions relate further, that groves of this description among the Baltic Finns were fenced in. That they even possessed sacrifice buildings in their sanctuaries, is shown by the Papal Bull of Pope Gregory IX in the year 1229, in which he allows Bishop Thomas to accept the sacrificial groves and image-houses (*lucos et delubra*), presented to him by the converted heathen.[33]

Doubtless also among the ancient heroes of Finnish song were many who at one time were worshipped.

CHAPTER X

HOUSEHOLD SPIRITS

THE anthropomorphic household spirit of many European peoples was unknown to the forefathers of the Finno-Ugric race. Even now it is rare or unknown among the Ostiaks and Voguls. A later spirit is the Russian Lapland Kyöde jielle ("the One who dwells in the tent") or Pört hozjin ("Household ruler"). Of this latter, it is related that he lives under the fireplace, and may sometimes appear in the shape of a dog. To appease him the Lapps offer up sacrifices to him and are glad when he leaves the house. By the fireside where he dwells, there is a spot where women are afraid to go or to step over. This household spirit is without doubt borrowed from the Russians (*horzjin* = Russian *hozyain*). Through the Finns, the Lapps have made the acquaintance of the Tonto (Finnish Tonttu = Swedish Tomte). [1]

The spirit dwelling in the house is called by the Votiaks Korka-murt ("House man") or Korka-kuźo ("House ruler"). His chief dwelling-place is under the floor, for which reason he is sometimes called "the Ruler dwelling under the floor." As may be concluded already from the word *murt* ("man") this spirit has the outward form of a man. The "House man" shows himself very seldom; when this happens, it is a forewarning of death or other misfortunes. When he does appear he resembles sometimes the master of the house. Generally speaking, he is a kindly and useful spirit, protecting the inhabitants of the house from strange spirits and in every way looking after the interests of the house. He may even at times take part in the household duties. The Votiaks relate that he sometimes spins in the night, if for some reason or other, the womenfolk have been hindered from finishing their day's task. When the " House man " is given cause for anger, he annoys sleepers in the form of the nightmare, tangles hair and beards in the night, and hinders the successful conclusion of tasks. Little children are never left alone in the house, as it is believed that the " House man " can substitute changelings for them.[2]

Whenever the " House man " in one way or another shows signs of being offended, he must be appeased by sacrifices. The sacrifice, which with the Votiaks generally takes the form of a black sheep, must be killed under the floor, where the spirit dwells. In the ceremony, in which the master of the house plays the part of the sacrificing priest, only members of the family may take part, as the flesh of a sacrifice may not be offered to strangers. Pieces of the meat and the bones of the sacrificed animal are buried in a hole dug under the floor, into which the victim's blood is also allowed to run during the slaughtering. The flesh of the sacrifice is cooked and eaten, as a rule, in the house itself. Besides occasional offerings, regular sacrifices are made at certain times to the " House man." Usually, the Votiaks sacrifice to him in the autumn, after the conclusion of agricultural work, a goose or duck and also porridge; the bones of the bird together with the porridge and a spoon are placed under the floor. The person carrying out the sacrifice reads out the following prayer: " Thus do I sacrifice to Thee, O Spirit dwelling under the floor, a goose. Do not frighten us. Be pleased to accept the sacrifice offered. Give to me and my family and dependants peace and happiness." In some places offerings are also made during the summer, at the time when the sheep are driven in to be clipped. Where a suitable victim is not to be found in the flock, the ceremony is postponed to a later date, and at the time a promise only is given along with the porridge, part of which must be buried under the floor.[3]

Above all, the Votiaks regard it as a duty to sacrifice to the "House man" when they first establish themselves in a new house. We find Georgi already relating that the Votiaks, on moving into a new house, sacrifice a black sheep.[4] The removal into a new house has in certain Votiak territory acquired a festival character — the "house-wedding" (*korka-śuan*). All the relatives and friends gather in the house, bringing gifts. The most important ceremony is the killing of the sacrifice under the floor of the new dwelling. In the Sarapul District it is the custom for the master of the house, accompanied by his wife, to step under the floor, bearing pancakes and home-distilled spirits and a young fir about a yard high, and there deliver a promise of sacrifice. The master of the house sets up the green fir tree in a corner, takes a branch of the tree in his hand and kneels down beside it. His wife spreads a tablecloth before him on which she places a pancake. She then pours spirits into a goblet and offers it to her husband. The latter, with the goblet in his right hand and the branch in his left, reads out a prayer, in which he prays that the dwelling now completed may be comfortable to live in even until old age and death, and he promises to sacrifice a black sheep. After the prayer he drinks up the spirits and tastes also of the pancake. The promised sacrifice is made later. While its flesh is being cooked, the master of the house prays on his knees for happiness, riches, and everything that is good for the new home, pointing out that he is now fulfilling the promise given. At times even a bull may be sacrificed. On the day of the sacrifice, nothing may be given away from the homestead, and the animal to be sacrificed may not be killed on the bare earth, but on twigs of fir.[5]

Besides the "House man," the Votiaks sacrifice also to the "Cattleyard man" (Gid-kuźo). This also is an anthropomorphic, kindly spirit, which, in the sheds, looks after the cattle and sees that they duly increase, protecting them from beasts of prey and sickness. The "Cattleyard man" also looks after the provender of the cattle, as the Votiaks believe that he drives away strange spirits of like kind, when these come to their neighbours' sheds to steal provender. He dwells chiefly in the stables. The horses that please him are cared for and fed by him; he will even, at times, plait their manes and tails; but others which he hates, he tortures by riding them to exhaustion during the night. A folk-tale relates how a farmer spread resin on his horse's back, and in the morning, coming into the stable, saw a little old man, about half-a-yard long, sitting stuck fast there.[6] As in the case of the " House man," both occasional and regular sacrifices are offered up to the " Cattleyard man." The Eastern Votiaks are in the habit of sacrificing a capercailzie in the cattle sheds when a cow is sick, and a brace of pike for horses. In some districts it is customary to offer up once for each foal the above fish-sacrifice, so that these may, as horses, shine like the pike. The fish, however, is not cooked, but burned as it is in the cattleyard.

The yearly sacrifices in honour of the " Cattleyard man " occur both in the spring, when the cattle are let loose to pasture, and in the autumn, when they are shut up in the cattlefolds again. In most places, it has now become the rule to give only a promise of sacrifice together with bread or porridge in the spring, the promise being fulfilled in the autumn if the cattle have been healthy out in the pastures and have increased. The sacrificial ceremony, in which only members of the family may take part, greatly resembles the ceremony under the floor, described earlier, the only difference being that the sacrifice intended for the " Cattleyard man " is burned in the cattleyard. Even the animals used are the same as in the sacrifice under the floor. In the prayers, the appeal is for fat horses and milch-cows, enough to fill the whole yard, or one may also say: " Be vigorous and strong, drive out the strange spirit, protect the cattle and banish all evil from the yard! "[7]

The bath-house spirit is called the " Bath-house man "

(Munt'śo-murt) or the " Bath-house ruler " (Munt'śo-kuźo).
He lives in a dark corner of the bath-house and resembles
in appearance a tall, middle-aged man, clad in a white shirt
and shoes of lime-bark, or he may also be tall and have only
one eye. Sometimes this being speaks and cries like a suckling
babe. He appears to human beings only before some misfortune.

The " Bath-house man " plays pranks with the bathers,
sometimes hiding their underclothing, at times binding together
the sleeves of their shirts or turning them inside out, in this
way hindering their dressing. His nature is more evil than
that of the spirits described above. It is not advisable to go
alone into the bath-house, neither is it wise to quarrel there or
speak loudly. Like the " House man," the " Bath-house man "
can also substitute changelings in the place of rightful infants.
In both the foregoing cases, a piece of iron or some other
metal is used as an amulet. This spirit is rarely sacrificed to.[8]

In the threshing-barn lives the " Threshing-barn man "
(Obiń-murt). Sacrifices are offered up to him in the autumn,
so that he may refrain from becoming angry and frightening
folk, but instead protect the threshing-barn from fire and
storm. For these sacrifices a goose or a duck is chosen, or,
at times, a sheep, which is killed by the head of the family in
the threshing-barn, or on the threshing-floor, on to which the
blood is also allowed to drip. The flesh of the sacrifice is
cooked at home, after which all return to the scene of the killing for prayers, the food being also brought there. In the
end, the remains of the sacrifice and the bones are buried under
the threshing-barn. Besides blood-offerings a sheaf of grain
is often left on the beams of the threshing-barn after the
conclusion of the threshing, for the use of the " Threshing-
barn man." [9]

If one compares the household spirits of the Votiaks with
the corresponding ones of the Russians, one cannot detect any
difference even in the nature of the sacrifices. The " Korka-

murt " of the Votiaks is identical with the Domovoy of the Russians. Sometimes he is also given the Russian name Sušetka, which is used especially by the Siryans, whose folk-lore has generally adapted itself to the Russian. The Siryan Sušetka dwells under the floor, like the Votiak " House man," where sacrifices in his honour must be placed. Like these he is a kindly spirit, which looks after and protects the prosperity of the house. If he becomes angry, all kinds of misfortunes are met with, manual labour turns out badly and the cattle grow thin, as the Sušetka neglects to feed them. Sometimes he attacks human beings in the shape of a nightmare or kisses them in their sleep so that painful blisters appear on their lips. At times, he spins and makes a noise as though he were building something, but this is never a good sign, being followed by death, fire, or other misfortunes. When the Siryans remove into a new house, they also endeavour to appease the house spirit with sacrifices. Rogov relates that at a removal, the master of the house takes a picture of a saint from the corner of his old dwelling, goes down with this under the floor and calls to the house spirit in the following words: " Sušetka, my brother, let us dwell also in the new. Love my cattle and my family." In the new home, the picture is placed in a corner, and the house spirit is bidden to take up its dwelling under the floor. According to a general belief among the Siryans, the household spirit does not move into the new house until the fireplace is ready.[10]

As with the Votiaks' " House man," foreign models are to be found for their " Cattleyard man," " Bath-house man " and " Threshing-barn man " among the Russians, from whom the Siryans also here have borrowed their spirits. The " Threshing-barn man " of the Votiaks corresponds with the Siryan Rynyš olyśa (" the one who lives in the threshing-barn ") or the Rynyš-aika (" Threshing-barn man "), the " Bath-house man " of the former with the Pyvśan olyśa (" The one who dwells in the bath-house ") or the Pyvśan-aika ("Bath-house man") of the latter.[11] As the buildings themselves inhabited by these spirits are not originally Finno-Ugric, the spirits also must be of later origin. The dwelling-place of the "House man" under the floor points to the assumption that the Votiaks cannot have worshipped this spirit at the time when they still lived in the old *kuala*-dwellings, where there was no floor. It is worth mentioning in this connection, that the "House man" has never had the *kuala*, in which the Finno-Ugric family gods are considered to dwell, ascribed to it as a dwelling-place.

The anthropomorphic spirit dwelling in the house is called Pört-oza ("House ruler") by the Cheremiss, but when praying to it, two names are used, Pört-kuguza ("House man") and Pört-kuva ("House woman"). The spirit appears at times, especially before some important event, in the form of a man or woman clad in the old Cheremiss fashion. If, for some reason, it becomes angry, it can bring about many kinds of misfortune among the family or in the home; thus it may cause illness. The Cheremiss sacrifice to it, so that it will not be angry or bring troubles upon the house. When appeased, or otherwise contented, it protects the home from robbers, fire, and spirits of sickness, and brings happiness and prosperity to the family. For this reason the Cheremiss pray very often to it. Every evening, when their women retire for the night, they offer up, in the name of the family, the prayer: "'House man,' 'House woman,' give success and health!" Besides those made for accidental reasons, annual sacrifices are offered up to the household spirit. In some districts it is the custom to go under the floor every autumn, bearing beer, porridge, bread or pancakes, to beg for happiness for the home from the spirit, or a sheep may also be annually sacrificed. Sometimes, a black ram is sacrificed to the male spirit, and a black sheep to the female.

Above all, the "House man" and "House woman" are worshipped with bread and pancakes at the removal into a new house, when they are implored to make the new house happy, to give children, and to bring riches and other good things. They are also often prayed to for happiness when the first layer of logs is laid in its place. Even at the grove-sacrifices, when all the gods and spirits are remembered, a drink-offering is presented to the household spirits.

An evil household spirit of Tatar origin is the Šukšendal, which is believed to disturb the peace of the people of the house. It creates disturbances in the night, troubles people in the guise of nightmares, and has sexual intercourse with people in their sleep, appearing in the form of a man to women, and in the form of a woman to the men. Further, it deposits changelings in the place of children left alone in the house. To protect the latter from harm, the Cheremiss mother places a pair of scissors or some other iron object in the cradle. The Šukšendal can not only do harm in the house, but can also molest human beings in the bath-house, where it may even kill a person paying a late visit there.

The cattleyard spirits are the Vit'ša-kuguza (" Cattleyard man "), and the Vit'ša-kuva (" Cattleyard woman "), believed by the Cheremiss to protect the cattleyard. They can appear to the inhabitants of the house in human form. If the " Cattleyard woman " likes the cattle, she causes them to increase, but where the cattle are displeasing to her, she refuses to protect them, neither does she cause their increase, but is instead cruel to them in many ways during the night. Thus, she drives them from place to place and prevents them from grazing in peace. In order to cause her to care for the herds, and refrain from molesting them, the Cheremiss offer up a hen to her. According to their statements, the cattleyard spirit is an old woman, who appears clad in white in the folds among the cattle in the evenings.

A spirit who feeds some animals and worries others — especially horses — by riding on them the whole night through, so that these appear quite worn-out and limp in the morning, is called by the Cheremiss generally Vit'ša-oza ("Cattleyard ruler"). The name is, however, never mentioned by the Cheremiss in their prayers, who turn instead to the "man" and "woman."

The "Bath-house spirit" (Mot'ša-oza), most often regarded as an evil spirit which disturbs the bathers, is not worshipped by the Cheremiss. Only when a new bath-house is heated for the first time, do they set a little butter on the benches, "so that the bath shall be good." The person offering up the butter utters during the ceremony: "'Bath-house man,' eat up the butter!"

The watermill spirit is the Vakš-oza ("Mill ruler"), which has also the power to appear in human form, sometimes as a man, at others as a woman. This last is decorated over the breast with silver coins. The mill spirit lives in the mill under the floor, or behind the water-wheel, and is friendly to the miller, whom it helps. Old millers, notably, are in league with the mill spirit. When the mill spirit is angry and the grinding goes badly, the miller sets out a dish of porridge as a sacrifice under the floor of the mill or in some other suitable spot. In the porridge-offering a pat of butter must be placed and a spoon given along with it. The Cheremiss declare that from the nature of the difficulties that beset him, the miller can interpret the present needs of the mill spirit.

A spirit in the shape of a human being dwells also in the threshing-barn. The "Threshing-barn man" (Idem-kuguza) or "woman" (Idem-kuva) shows itself early in the morning, disappearing when one approaches it. In the ritual in the sacred grove a drink-offering is made to the "Threshing-barn man" and "woman," and they are remembered also in the harvest-festival ceremonies. A blood-offering may even be made to them at the threshing-barn.[12]

These Cheremiss household spirits bear also plain marks of Russian influence, which is equally evident in the corresponding beliefs of the Turco-Tatars in East Europe. Another anthropomorphic spirit is the Kardas-śarko (" Yard-śarko ") of the Erza Mordvins, which lives beneath a stone situated in the courtyard and is generally represented as a male, though sometimes also as a female. But coincidently with these beings who clearly possess human characteristics, certain more primitive beliefs are found among both the Cheremiss and the Mordvins, which may perhaps throw some light on the origin of the household spirits. These peoples had animated the buildings themselves. This appears plainly in Mordvinian folklore; while the parting words of a newly-married girl are: " Dear house, I have sojourned long in thy warm shelter." The household spirit Kud-ava (" House mother ") or Kud-azerava (" House mistress ") is originally the house itself, although these terms may at times be also used with a similar meaning to that of the Russian Domovoy. The more primitive meaning is discernible in the following examples: In a Moksha magic prayer the passage occurs: " House mistress, pardon him who built thee and heats thee." And in an Erza petition of a similar character we read: " House mother, above is thy lime-bark (the roof is thatched with this material), beneath are thy beams." The dwelling-place as a whole, i.e., with the adjoining buildings, designated as *jurt* by the Mordvins, has a special spirit of its own, the Jurt-ava (" Dwelling-place mother "), known also among the Moksha as Jurt-azerava (" Dwelling-place mistress "). In addition, they speak of the " Bath-house mother," the " Mill mother," etc. The protectress of a whole village is the Vel'-ava (" Village mother ").[13] The Cheremiss, amongst whom the dwelling-place and all objects connected with it are also regarded as animated beings, impressionable and capable of feeling, believe that the *kudo*, their ancient dwelling-house, and the more modern *pört*, are fitted like human beings with a " soul " (*ört*) which can depart from its habitation. If one quarrels, shouts, smokes too much tobacco in the house, or keeps the place untidy, the " soul " disappears. " You drive away the soul from my house," say the Cheremiss when anyone disturbs the peace of their homes. Has the soul departed, then the house is no longer "happy," "life begins to be wearisome in it," and "the building has received hurt." When the building creaks in the night, the Cheremiss say "the building's 'soul' moves." In empty dwellings, which have been deserted for some time, there is no "soul," as they no longer "live." The soul of the building cannot in this primitive state take on any definite appearance, but is, as the Cheremiss say, merely the "prosperity," the "happiness," or the "comfort" of the house. An equally indefinite soul have the cattleyard, the threshing-barn, etc. As the "soul" of buildings was believed to be able to deliver itself from its material dwelling-place, it is hardly to be wondered at that gradually the thought arose, that these, like other souls, might at times become visible, e.g., in the shape of some domestic animal, a cat or a dog.[14] Later, the "soul" of buildings may have become identifiable with those of departed human beings or family gods, and thus have borrowed from these last also their human characteristics.

Among the Cheremiss and the Mordvins the bee-garden has also its special tutelary genius. The former call this the Mükš-ört ("Bee-soul"). The Moksha Mordvins worship the Neškeper-ava ("Bee-garden mother") as the protective spirit of the bees; the Erza Mordvins use the name Neške-pas ("Beehive god").[15]

The Baltic Finns, who form a group by themselves, call the household spirit "the Ruler" (Finnish Haltia, Esthonian Haldja). Without doubt, this "Haltia," which according to the Ingrians was "not made nor brought, but was in and through itself," has the same origin as the ört of the Cheremiss.[16] Like this last, the Finnish Haltia needs no food. But one must do honour to him in every way. When settling in a new dwelling, and even when staying anywhere for the night, permission must first be begged of this "Ruler." If any rapping sound be heard in the house, it is regarded as a sign of permission to do so. Similarly, when entering a room for the first time that day, one must always remember to say: " Good morning, Ruler." In this case, also, the answer is a rap.[17]

Every room with a roof-tree had its own Haltia, as this last was supposed to live in the roof-tree. According to another report, he took possession of the house as soon as three logs had been crossed, and when the building was demolished and the logs laid in a pile, the Haltia cried with fear lest he became homeless. But if even one log was taken into use, he removed with this into the new house. " In order that the Haltia should not feel lonely in the new house," the ashes from all the hearths were taken over to the new fireplaces.[18]

According to the prevalent view, the Haltia could become visible at times, but he appeared only before some misfortune. In Ingria the Haltia is said to have appeared at such times in the shape of a dog or a mottled or striped cat. This was a sign of fire.[19] The Haltia of a house was also pictured as a human being. According to a belief prevalent in Finland, the person who died first in the house, or the one who lit the first fire there, became the Haltia of the house. Especially was it supposed to appear in the shape of the first departed master or mistress of the house. As such, it was generally kind to everyone, and had special care, in particular, of the provisions. The male Haltia was of higher rank than the female, just as in life the master had stood above the mistress; but children grew up better where the Haltia was a woman. Both the male and female Haltia were better at the tasks which they had carried out while alive; under the care of a male Haltia the horses flourished, and similarly, cows, sheep, pigs and poultry under that of the female. Other buildings also, and even vessels, had their Haltia. That of the latter was intimately connected with the keel of the vessel. The

Haltia of a church was sometimes regarded as being of equal height with the church.[20]

The Baltic Finns have to a very great extent been under the influence of the Scandinavians. The Finnish Haltia and all the beliefs now connected therewith find their counterpart in the Swedish Rå or Rådare (" ruler "). Of Swedish origin, as may be seen from its name, is the Finnish Tonttu (Swedish Tomte) with human characteristics, concerning which Bishop Agricola says, that he " guided the house." In some districts a special, clean room was furnished for the Tonttu. The room had to contain a table laid with untouched food, which was renewed a few times each week. With the exception of the person who looked after the food, no one was allowed to live in this room.[21]

Of the outhouses, the Tonttu occupied the bathhouse, stables, mill, and above all, the threshing-barn. Every threshing-barn had its Riihitonttu (= Swedish Ritomte) who stole grain from the neighbours' fields and carried it to his own threshing-barn. The threshing-barn Tonttu looked after the threshing-barn, but if he was offended, he began to carry away grain from the house or would soon burn up the whole threshing-barn. He was wished a good-morning in the mornings, and in the evenings, when the fires were lit there, the Tonttu was begged to keep an eye on them, and wished good-night. Should one desire to stay overnight in the threshing-barn, one had to request permission of the Tonttu, and on no account could one lie down near the hearth. He appeared sometimes in grey clothes and wearing a grey hat on his head. Porridge and milk were offered up to him behind the threshing-barn fireplace.

According to some beliefs, the threshing-barn Tonttu was born of the last sheaf of grain that was cut in the fields. The sheaf was placed on the rafters of the barn for the whole year. At times, it was left for many years; and " during this period the spirit was supposed to come forth." When it was desired to ask on Christmas Eve what the next year's harvest would be like, the master of the house had to proceed to the threshing-barn and ask: " Good Tonttu, say what kind of year we may expect." If the threshing-barn creaked in reply, a good year might be hoped for.[22]

Among the household spirits may also be included a being, which gathers all kinds of good things from other places for its owner. The Votiaks, who perhaps have appropriated this spirit from the Russians, call it the " Bearer." It is said to resemble a cat, and assists its owner by bearing grain to him from other people's granaries. The animistic character of this being is shewn by the belief that if the " cat " is killed, the owner of the same dies likewise.[23]

The Finns call this spirit the Para, after the Swedish Bjära or Bära ("Bearer"). In Ingria there are Money-, Bread-, and Milk-Paras. In some districts in Finland also, the Para has brought its owner money and rye, and even, at times, manure from the fields of neighbours. Generally, however, the Para is regarded as the bearer of milk, cream and butter. As such, it was usually believed to have the shape of a cat.[24] The " Butter-cat " of the Scandinavians is identical with the Smierragatto of the Lapps.[25] Anyone who desired to own such a spirit, could, according to the Finns, create one for himself. Its material body was fashioned, for example, out of cast-off female garments, the head of a thread-ball, and the foot of a spindle. Each of these objects had to be stolen. The milk, or other commodities brought by the Para to the house, was carried by it either in its mouth or in its intestines. If the door of the milk-closet was left open during the night, empty milk and butter dishes would be found full in the morning. The Seed-Para left a narrow track through the fields from which it had stolen grain.[26]

The same spirit is called Puuk by the Esthonians (Platt-deutsch Puk; Latvian Puhkis). The Money-Para of the Ingrians, which flies through the air like a meteor, is identical with the Esthonian's Tulihänd (" fire-tail "), or Kratt (ancient Scandinavian *skratti*, " ghost "). The Esthonian Kratt, which, like the Finnish Para, could be manufactured of certain materials, carried money, etc., in a sack. Food was offered up to it — generally porridge and milk. If, during its flight through the air, one succeeded in unloosing all the bindings and buttons of one's garments, the Kratt fell down upon the ground with all its treasures.[27] In Finland also the Kratti was known, where, as Bishop Agricola relates, it " had the care over property."

A spirit flying through the air like a " fire-worm " — a meteor — the Votiaks call by a Tatar name, Ubyr. It is entirely evil in its ways, drinking the blood of sleeping persons; where this has happened blue marks are left on the body. The Ubyr may be either the soul of a living sorcerer, or that of an evil dead person. It can be brought to the ground in the same way as the Kratt of the Esthonians.[28]

On the boundary between the property of two neighbours, dwelt, according to the Finns, Raja-äijä (" Boundary man "). In West Finland they have a saying: " shouts like the Boundary man." It is believed that when the " Boundary man " shouts, there is no echo in response, and that he appears when boundary lines are dishonestly moved. In East Finland, according to ancient report, the people sacrificed on the boundary stones.[29]

The treasures hidden away in the earth had also their " Ruler " (Finnish Aarnion Haltia), and over them, on certain holyday nights, Midsummer's Eve in particular, one could see blue flames.[30]

All the above mentioned beliefs have their counterpart among the Teutons and Slavs.

The Esthonians in Krasna, who have continuously worshipped their old " land gods," sacrifice to the " Father of the home " (Kodojezä) in a corner of their orchards. This holy or " purified " spot could be entered by women once only in their lives, i.e., after their wedding ceremony. It was the duty of the master of the house to look after the place and offer up sacrifices there, choosing as assistant a " pure " person. Besides occasional offerings for some reason or other, the ceremony of the " family-beer " (*perekahi*) was performed every autumn. A portion of all the flesh cooked in the house from sacrifices, would be taken over to the " purified spot." [31]

In order to understand the genesis of the " pure spot " of the Esthonians, it is necessary to glance at a similar custom among peoples related to them. The Votiaks, who no longer possess their older dwelling-house, *kuala*, have the same sacrifices in a corner of their yards as the other Votiaks in their *kuala*. The site of the old *kudo* is also regarded as " holy " by the Hill Cheremiss.[32] May one assume that the family-sacrifice of the Krasna Esthonians to the " father of the home " (a " village god," Küläjumal, is also known) is identical with the autumn sacrifices of the Volga Finns to their family gods? In that case one could understand also the Finns' habit of offering up all kinds of first-fruits at the root of a holy tree or a holy stone in the vicinity of the home. Old sacrificial ceremonies often continue to exist under changed circumstances.

In the offerings to household spirits by the Finno-Ugric peoples it would appear that they most of all felt the need of appeasing the underground spirits. Traces of an old Indo-European custom of sacrificing a human victim under certain buildings, are to be found among the Volga Finns, who sacrificed children under a new watermill.[33] The Mordvins are said to have expressed the following wish at this ceremony: " Be the Ruler of the mill, the Mill mother! " [34] But from this the conclusion can by no means be drawn that the household spirits of the Finno-Ugric peoples, the majority of which spirits are direct loans from neighbouring peoples, were originally human beings sacrificed under their buildings.

CHAPTER XI

FOREST SPIRITS

AS IN olden days, hunting was one of the chief means of existence of the Finno-Ugrian tribes, it is but natural that they should have peopled the forests with all kinds of spirits.

Missionaries relate that the Scandinavian Lapps worshipped a Forest spirit, which was called Leib-olmai (" Alder man "). The Lapps honoured him " in order that he might give them luck in hunting." The following description by Randulf shows that the above mentioned spirit was especially the protector of bears: " Leib-olmai is a bear-man or bear-god, who protects the bear, the holy animal, and who also presents it to the Lapps when they pray and call to him for it." He relates further that where the Lapps had not asked for the assistance of Leib-olmai, they not only lost their prey, but in addition the god might help the bear, when it would rush upon its assailants. Therefore the Lapps consult their magic drums before hunting the bear and pray the spirit not to take the bear's part.[1]

The older sources of information do not mention actual offerings to Leib-olmai nor anything about the manner of offering. Randulf only states that hunting equipment, bows and arrows, were offered up to him. According to J. Kildal, Leib-olmai looks down on the female sex. A woman may not walk round a tent where there is a gun, this being regarded as in some way connected with the Forest spirit. Forbus says further, that the custom of sprinkling extract of alder-bark on the hunters' faces at the bear-feasts, was carried out in Leib-olmai's honour.[2] The name of the Forest god, " the

Alder man," has probably been derived from this magic custom. Judging by this, " Leib-olmai " would seem to be neither more nor less than the genius or race-soul of the bear.

According to Charuzin the Russian Lapps worship a Forest spirit which they call Luot-hozjik (*hozjik* = Russian *chozyaika*, " hostess "). She looks after the reindeer when they wander in freedom in the forests in the summer, keeping them together, showing them good pastures, and protecting them from beasts of prey. From human beings she cannot, however, protect the flocks. She helps the hunters to catch the wild reindeer and the Lapps are not afraid of her. When they drive their reindeer out to pasture in the spring, they pray to this Forest spirit — " Luot-hozjik, protect our reindeer." And in the autumn, should they recover all their flock, they say: " We thank thee, Luot-hozjik for protecting our reindeer." This Forest spirit, which lives on a mountain covered with lichen, resembles a human being in having a human face and walking on human feet, but the body is hairy all over like a reindeer's.[3]

The same Forest spirit may be the one spoken of by Genetz, Mintyš. In one tale a being named Mientuš appears which at times is like a male reindeer, but by casting off its horns is turned into a human being.[4] Originally Mientuš meant " wild reindeer," and is probably their genius as Leib-olmai is that of the bear. Their reindeer spirit the Russian Lapps call Pots-hozjin (" Reindeer-master ") and Pots-hozjik (" Reindeer-mistress "), who have the same duties as Luot-hozjik.[5]

The Russian Lapps also speak about the tutelary genius of the wolf; by treating a wolf very roughly, one could scare this spirit into keeping its wards in check.

Among the Western Lapps the tutelary genius of the migratory birds is the Barbmo-akka (*akka* = " old woman "; cf. *barbmolodde*, " migratory bird "), who brings back the birds to the northern countries from the warm south. Further, the protecting spirit of birds is called "Loddiš-edne ("Bird-mother").[6]

A Forest spirit resembling the Russian Lěšiy is the Eastern Lapps' Miehts-hozjin ("the Master of the forest") who according to Genetz is also called Vare-jielle ("Forest-dweller"). He is a black being with a tail, and does not do any harm to human beings unless provoked. When anyone shouts, sings or makes a noise in the forest, he becomes offended, and bewilders the culprit so that he cannot find his way out of the forest. The "Master of the forest" loves silence above all.[7]

The Western Lapps' belief in "Forest people" has been influenced by that of the Scandinavians. Leem mentions a Ganiš (according to Friis, *Lexicon Lapponica,* = "echo," "*daemon montanus*") which is probably the same being whom Randulf, in his records, names Gidne (Pite Lapp Kine; Lule Lapp Kani). This appears in the forest, and seen from the front resembles a beautiful maiden, but has a long tail behind. The Forest maiden serves the Lapps, bringing the reindeer together when they are spread among the hills and assisting in the milking of reindeer-cows. Sometimes she will even wish for sexual intercourse with a Lapp.[8] In appearance and conduct she reminds one of the Scandinavian "Forest maiden."

Alien already in name is the Gufittar of the Scandinavian Lapps, an underground dwarfish being, who lives in the forest or on the mountains. At times he appears on the earth with fine herds of cattle. He will at such times hang a bell round the necks of the cattle, when one can easily hear where he wanders. One must then go boldly towards him without glancing to either side and show him a piece of iron, or else throw the iron over the cattle, when the Forest spirit will at once disappear under the earth and the cattle become the property of the enterprising person. The Lapp Gufittar corresponds to the Norwegian Go(d)vetter ("a good spirit").[9]

The Uldda of the Scandinavian Lapps is a similar underground being, which also appears on the earth with its cattle. It is said to change children left alone and in various ways to disturb people who have settled on its territory. The Lapps generally pour a drink-offering on the ground for it, either coffee or spirits. The name Uldda shows it to be identical with the Swedish Huldra.[10]

It is uncertain whether the Forest spirits of the Lapps were the object of a special sacrificial cult. Their custom of preserving the bones of certain kinds of game by burying them in the earth or hanging them in trees, cannot truly be described as being of the nature of an offering. On the other hand the Lapps made offerings to their Seides to secure good luck in hunting.

All the Samoyed stocks also know of a Forest spirit, generally called " the Master of the forest." According to Donner the Ostiak Samoyeds sacrifice, among other things, peculiarly shaped arrows to the Forest spirit. A human-like image, often carved on an old tree, is made of the " Master of the forest." When an offering of anything eatable is made, the food is rubbed into the mouth of this image.[11] That there was some connection between the " Master of the forest " and the spirit of the " holy places " appears from the notes made by Lehtisalo among the Yuraks. " The Samoyed may wander freely in the forest, but when passing a holy place, he must sacrifice something, as otherwise the ' Master of the forest ' will be offended."

The Ostiaks call the Forest spirit Unt-tongk (" Wood spirit "), which resembles a human being but is said to be hairy like a wild animal. A spirit of this kind lives in every forest. He gives game to those who remember him with offerings. The usual time for these is in the autumn or in the early spring, at the beginning of the two hunting periods. At Vasyugan an image of the Wood spirit is made. The Northern Ostiaks do not seem to have made offerings to him. In tales the family and daughters of the Forest spirit are spoken of, the latter being able to marry human beings.[12] The Mis-khum (*khum*, "man") of the Voguls can appear as tall as a tree; he leads wanderers astray in the forest.[13] A more evil spirit is Mengk, known to both these related stocks. Of these there are many, both male and female, in the forests. Their way of living resembles ours, and they are often regarded as people from older times, while tales are told of their strength.[14] Over a wide territory and also among the Yuraks the evil Parne is known, dwelling deep in the fastnesses of the forest, and said to have three fingers on each hand, and on each foot three toes with sharp nails.[15]

The Votiaks call the Forest spirit Ñules-murt ("Forest man"). In appearance and customs he is like a human being, but he is often imagined as one-eyed, and is believed to have the power of lengthening or shortening his body at will. Generally he holds his head on a level with the highest tree, and on account of his great height he is called "Great uncle" in the Glazov district. In the forest where he lives he has his household and family, and many treasures — gold, silver and cattle. He moves from place to place in the guise of a whirlwind. Forest spirits also celebrate weddings, which are held twice a year, in the summer and in the winter, the Forest spirits moving then as whirlwinds so that great trees are uprooted. The Forest spirit entices people, more especially children, into his power. Sometimes he will also entice cattle to become lost in the forest, or drag them long distances in the whirlwinds. He is enormously strong, but being a stupid spirit, he is neither dangerous nor dreaded. Very often he is even of great help to people, giving game to hunters and protecting the cattle in the forest.

The Votiaks make offerings to the Forest spirit in the forest during the autumn, preferably under a fir-tree. All the hunters take part in the ceremony. As offerings, brandy, bread, and a bull or a goat are used. In some districts bread is placed on the branch of a tree for the "Forest man."[16] A prayer to the Forest spirit discovered by Aminoff runs: "Give me, 'Forest man,' of thy forest-animals, squirrels, wolves, bears. Give also of thy bees, drive them into my bee-hives. If thou doest this we shall give thee gifts." [17]

The Votiaks also sacrifice to the Forest spirit in order that their cattle may thrive and increase. In the spring when the cattle are driven out to pasture, the head of the family prays to him: "Great uncle, Forest uncle, now drive we our cattle out to pasture and begin our ploughing. Therefore, we sacrifice to thee. Accept our offering. Protect the cattle from beasts of prey and evil people. Our cattle go over twelve rivers, behind twelve meadows. Save and protect them from disease and from all evil." The porridge prepared as an offering for the Forest spirit is taken to him in the forest in a basket made of birch-bark. Also in the autumn when the cattle return home, another offering is prepared, viz., a goose. The Forest spirit is thanked for having taken such good care of the cattle in the forest during the summer. [18]

Occasional offerings are also made to the Forest spirit, as when the foresters go out hunting. In the district of Sarapul, offerings are sometimes made during stormy weather. At these times the offering is an animal, generally a duck. Offerings are further made in cases of sudden illness, according to the directions of the magicians. This last reminds one of the worship of the dead. The number of pancakes, made specially by the hostess for the occasion, must absolutely be an odd number, three, five or seven. When going to perform the offering, it is regarded as a bad omen to meet anyone, for which reason great care is taken to avoid this. After the person making the sacrifice has returned from the place of offering, he must go direct, without speaking, to the fire-place, where he washes his hands in the ashes, after which he may approach his family. [19]

Besides the above mentioned Forest spirits, which are worshipped by the Votiaks, these have still many others to whom offerings are not made. One of this latter kind is the Pales-murt (" Half-man ") known to all the Votiaks. It resembles a human being, but has only half of a human body. Thus, it has only one eye, one foot, one hand and one breast, which is so large that it can suffocate people with it by pressing it into their mouths. In the twilight it frightens the lonely wanderer in the forest with its shrieks.[20]

More evil than the former is a spirit known in the Southern Votiak area, called Šurali, which is also anthropomorphic, but naked and hairy. It has only three long fingers on its hand (cf. Ostiak Parne). It calls all night in the forest, causes people to lose their way, and entices them to itself. At times it rushes suddenly upon people, tickles them or dances with them until they are completely exhausted. Often it will mount a horse in the meadows and ride it madly round the fields until the horse nearly falls.[21]

The Yskal-pydo-murt (" Cowfooted man ") belongs also to the evil Forest spirits, and from its name one can imagine its appearance. To the waist from above it is dressed in ordinary peasant costume, but from there downwards the legs, which are hairy and end in hoofs, are naked.[22]

Fully coinciding with the Forest spirit of the Votiaks is the Vörys-mort (" Forest man ") of the Siryans. The Siryans fear to call him by his correct name, and so all kinds of mysterious names are used for him. Generally, like the Russians, they call him Dyadya (" Uncle "). Like that of the Votiaks, the Siryan Forest spirit also resembles a human being, having his house and family in the forest. He is large in size and taller than the highest tree, for which reason the Siryans often call him " Tall uncle." He rushes from place to place like a whirlwind and sometimes carries both people and cattle with him. Women fear him greatly, as he is believed to seek amorous adventures with them. The Forest spirits of the Siryans celebrate weddings, gathering then, as at human weddings, in great companies. On the whole the " Forest man " is a good spirit, being often of great use. To huntsmen, especially, who live on good terms with him, he shows the way through the wilds, sits by their camp-fires to warm himself, and drives game into their snares. Wherefore the hunters now and then make small offerings to him; sometimes a little tobacco, which they place on a stump in the forest, as " Forest uncle " is known to like tobacco. But other offerings are also made to him, such as squirrel-skins and bread and salt, when the cattle have happened to go astray in the forest.[23]

On making comparisons, one notices that the Siryan and North Votiak ideas of the Forest spirits have been borrowed from the Russians to a very great extent, and resemble the popular beliefs of these down to details, the Russian names being also the local ones. Similarly, Tatar influence is perceptible in the Southern Votiak area. As appears already from the name, the evil Šurali is a loan from foreign sources. The " Half-man," who seems to have been known also among the Ostiaks, corresponds to the Chuvash Ar żori, which has the same meaning, and the " Cowfooted man " to the Tatar Syiyr-ajak (" Cow-foot ").[24]

An anthropomorphic Forest spirit, who can change his height, so that he can be as tall as a pine, is also the Cheremiss Kožla-ia (" Forest spirit ") or as he is sometimes called Targeldeš. In some districts he is said to have only one eye in the centre of his forehead. Sometimes he appears as a forest-animal, a dog, an owl, or also as a hay-stack, a stump, etc. He moves from place to place as a whirlwind. The usual abode of the Forest spirit is the forest, but often he visits the fields and meadows. In the forest he shrieks, or roars with laughter, so that the cattle become frightened. He can speak human languages and call the traveller by his name, and by pretending to be his friend, entice him into his power. People believe him and follow him until they can no longer find their way again. Thus the Forest spirit causes people to become lost. When lost in this way in the forest, one must change the right boot on to the left foot, and *vice versa*, to find one's way home. To fall into the power of the Forest spirit is dangerous, as he tickles people to death. When in a good mood he will go to the huntsmen's log-fires to warm himself, but when angry he puts the fires out. Often he rides full gallop on a horse, frightening people who are picking berries or mushrooms. In stories we are told that the Forest spirit also goes to the villages, where he sits down with the people and takes part in their feasts. He also arranges feasts and weddings in the forests, where he has a magnificent home and a large family, servants and cattle. To see the Forest-people is not a good sign, as very often some accident, sickness, or death follows.[25]

Ovda is another evil Forest spirit who has descended from the Chuvash to the Volga Finns. Besides living in the forest it is said to dwell in chasms in the rocks and in the ruins of old castles. These last named, one often hears called " Ovda's village." Ovda wanders in the forest in the shape of a human being, but its feet are turned backwards. It is naked, with long hair and large breasts which it sometimes throws over its shoulders, and it is also covered with hair. Sometimes it appears as a man, sometimes as a woman. It has a home and property in the forest. In the same way as Targeldeš celebrates a marriage, Ovda also moves then as a whirlwind, so that the trees bend to the ground. Often one may hear it laugh and clap its hands in the forest. Ovda is feared because it approaches people, enticing them to dance or wrestle with it, when it tickles or dances them to death. A human being can overpower the Forest spirit if he knows how to touch it on the left armpit, where there is a hole, the Forest spirit becoming powerless immediately when touched there. Ovda tortures animals out at pasture, as well as people, sometimes mounting a horse and racing it nearly to death. In some places the people say that Ovda will mount a horse and make the poor animal run backwards. The Cheremiss call this spirit also by the Tatar name Šurali. A foreign name for an evil Forest spirit is Alvasta.[26]

When a Cheremiss makes offerings to the Forest spirits he addresses them mostly by the names Košla-Kuguza and Košla-Kuva ("Old man" and "Old woman of the forest"). He asks them for protection in the spring when he sends his cattle out into the forest. When a hunter goes out hunting he cuts a little opening in a tree and puts in a piece of bread for the Forest man, in the hope that the latter will help him by driving game into his path. The "Old man and Old woman of the forest" are further appealed to when a person is lost in the forest or wishes to spend the night there, and in the sacred groves, the people never omit to pour a drink-offering on the ground for the "Forest man and Forest woman." [27]

To the Mordvin Vir-ava ("Forest mother") alien features have also become attached later, which are obviously loans from the Forest spirits of the Russians. More especially in tales, the "Forest mother" is a humanlike being as high as a tree. She has a particular habit of sometimes slinging her large hanging breasts over her shoulders. She has long, freely flowing hair and her legs are as thick as logs. Besides appearing in human guise the "Forest mother" shows herself also in other forms, e.g., as a flame burning on the ground, as a whirlwind, or as any of the forest animals. She visits the villages in the form of a dog, a cat, or a wolf. A general belief is further that the Forest spirit appears at times as a horse flying at full speed through the forest. In stories it is said that the Forest spirit comes to the log fires to warm her long hands.[28]

Among the Baltic Finns also, a Forest spirit resembling a human being is met with. Usually the Finns call the Forest spirit Metsänhaltia ("Forest ruler"), every forest possessing one of these beings. In some places he is believed to be an old grey-bearded man with a coat of lichen. Here also the Forest spirit can lengthen his body so that his head is on a level with the highest tree. When seen, he is of the height of an average human being but on being approached he became longer, so that at a distance of nine paces, he was six yards in height, and at six paces nine yards in height. According to other reports the Forest spirit grew smaller on approach.

Sometimes the Forest spirit appears as a woman. In West Finland the Metsänneitsyt (" Forest virgin ") is said to look like a very beautiful, well-dressed woman, but from behind she is like a stump, a bundle of twigs, a pole or a trough. Sometimes she is fitted with a tail like an animal. The Forest virgin is in love with men, and entices them to cohabit with her.[29]

The Finnish Metsänhaltia has its counterpart in the Skogsrådare of the Swedish Finns, and likewise their Metsänneitsyt in the Skogsjungfru of the latter. The Mets-haldijas (" Forest ruler ") is known also among the North Esthonians, his cry in the forest meaning that something special is about to happen, — a death, —for example.[30]

Bishop Agricola mentions two Karelian Forest or Game spirits — Nyrckes (in folk-poetry, Nyyrikki, " Tapio's son "), who " gave squirrels from the forest," and Hittavainen, who " brought hares from the bushes." The latter is even today known in East Finland; the people say, for example, of a good hunter that: " Hittavainen will bring him game even if he set his traps in the stable-loft." Etymologically these names are not clear.

A peculiar idea of the Finns is that one must make offerings to the Forest spirit at some ant-hill. Here, however, one can note traces of the former belief in certain small anthropomorphic beings, who were supposed to live under the earth (Maahiset, Esthonian Maa-alused, Swedish Älva). It is believed that " those who live under the earth," and who can cause skin-diseases in one who sits down near their abode, are small ant-like beings. Similar beliefs are also met with in Sweden, where such ant spirits are called Alv-myror.[31] Underground people and Forest spirits often play similar parts in folk-belief.

If the forest people were angered, they could keep one in the forest, so that it became impossible to find one's way anywhere. Especially if, when wandering in the forest, one happened to hit on the Forest spirit's track, one was sure to become lost. Those who had thus been bewildered by the Forest spirit were called " forest-bewitched." To find one's way out of the forest the reversing of one's garments was employed. Cattle which had become lost in the forest, were said to be " hidden by the forest " (*metsän peitossa*). The Swedes in Finland called this *skogen håller* ("the forest keeps ").

According to the Cheremiss the anthropomorphic Forest spirits were originally human beings. It is believed that those who die in the forest become Forest spirits or their assistants. When anyone dies in the forest, he becomes a Forest spirit, who on the site of his death frightens people and causes them to lose their way so that they too may die.[32] Even a horse that dies in the forest is believed to move in the night and to attack wanderers. The Cheremiss call it " horse-Targeldeš." [33]

The ceremonies attached to the making of offerings to the Forest spirit by the Votiaks also bring into mind the cult of the dead. In certain districts it is an old custom at the worship of the Forest spirit to remember the dead. Aminoff relates that in the District Vjatka, where hunting still plays an important part in the nourishing of the tribe, offerings are made at the beginning of the autumn hunt to the dead, coincidentally with those to the Forest spirits.[34] It is hardly to be wondered at that the dead should gradually have changed into Forest spirits, when one remembers that burials took place in the forest at an earlier time. A relic of this old custom can still be traced among the Votiaks, who believe the dead to inhabit willingly the depths of the forest. And further, it is only natural that those who have found an unknown grave in the forest should remain there as feared, ghostly beings.

One must, however, also recollect that the ceremonies in honour of the fallen bear and other more remarkable forest animals are of a similar character. That among the Forest spirits there should actually be found the race-souls of tutelary genii of animals appears, e.g., from the beliefs of the Lapps. Originally these animal spirits moved in the material shape of the animal they represented; little by little they became, in the imagination of these people, more humanlike. But even thus changed, they cannot hide their origin — they are hairy, like animals, they have the feet or tails of beasts, etc. The Ingrian wolf-spirit is described in the following tale: " To a village tavern in Sombra there once came a being, who was in all else like a man except that he had a wolf's head, and asked for spirits to drink. He was offered a small bottle which, in the host's opinion, was quite enough for a man. The guest was, however, unsatisfied, and drank first a whole can, and then several small bottles in addition. When he was about to leave, the host, wondering greatly, asked him who he was. The guest answered that he was one who would lead all the wolves out of their country." [35]

But the forest itself and the separate trees contained therein were also regarded as animated among the Finno-Ugric peoples. Charuzin relates that when the Lapp goes to the forest to fell trees, he strikes the trunks first with the back of the axe before beginning to chop them down, or, as the Lapps themselves say, " kills the tree first." Should they omit to do this, they believe that the wood from these trees will crackle and throw out sparks when burning.[36] Mrs. De-mant-Hatt, during her travels among the Lapps, observed that the Lapp girls, when returning from the heights to the forest districts, hurried to embrace and greet the trees. According to the missionary Lundius, the Lapps also worshipped trees, as when they had shot down game from a tree, they laid the feet of the animal in the tree, smearing it also with the blood.[37]

In the same way the Cheremiss also regard the forest in animistic fashion. When they go into it, they greet the trees, ask them the way, and pray to them for a peaceful resting-place for the night. In the morning they give thanks and offer their hands to the tree under which they have spent the night. "The tree understands what men say, and the forest listens to the song of the hunter." The trees are afraid of the lumbermen and tremble when one of these goes by with his axe on his shoulder. When felled, the tree attempts to kill its murderer by falling on him. It is even believed that trees can change their sites. As elsewhere in nature, one may not use ugly or rough words in the forest. The Cheremiss speak also of the tree's " soul " (*ört*). While the soul is in the tree, it is glad and prospers, but when the " soul " moves away, the tree withers. At festivals for the furthering of bee cultivation, an offering of a duck is even made to the " tree-soul." When hanging up a bee-hive in a tree, they say: " Tree-soul (Pu-ört), give luck to the bees," or: " Gather the bees around thee." [38]

Whether the Finno-Ugric peoples worshipped special kinds of trees as such is uncertain. The Baltic Finns, however, seem to have known tutelary genii for the different trees. The Esthonians believe that the spirit of the birchwood never goes into a forest of alder or oak.[39] Milkovič relates of the Erza Mordvins that when they prayed for rain, they turned towards an oak, saying: " Oak god (Tumo-pas), give rain." While doing so, a man would conceal himself in the foliage, whence he would sprinkle those praying with a drink made from honey. The food-offering was hung in a vessel of bark on a branch of the sacred oak.[40] It is possible, however, that not the oak itself, but the Thunder god in the shape of the oak was the object of worship at these ceremonies. The rowan also played a prominent part in the beliefs of the people. Both the Baltic and the Volga Finns believed in its protective powers, though offerings were not made to this tree. According to the Hill Cheremiss evil spirits could not approach the rowan, and for this reason, when anyone was obliged to spend the night in the forest, branches of rowan were placed under the head, and if one were even then afraid of ghosts, one could run to the shelter of a rowan.[41] The same idea is met with also among the Russians, etc.

The common representative of all the trees is the forest itself; when worshipping it the Mordvins call it Vir-ava (" Forest mother " or " Mother forest "). The Tapio of the Finns, of whom Agricola says: " he gave game from the forest," and who in folk-poetry appears in anthropomorphic guise, meant originally merely " forest," as may be seen even today from countless expressions in folk-songs, e.g., " the twig-filled Tapio," or " oak Tapio." This would seem to have been taken over by the Russian Lapps, whose Tava or Tava-ajk (" Tava mother ") is a Forest spirit.[42] Originally, the Hiisi of the Finns, who, according to Agricola, " gave victory over the forest dwellers," meant also " forest " ; but, in a more restricted sense, *hiisi* also signified a sacred grove. Often in magic prayers and songs, the forest itself is appealed to:

> " Good forest, pure forest,
> Watch over my herds of cattle."

Like the animal spirits dwelling in the forests, the animated forest itself aspires to anthropomorphic features. In attempting to simulate a human being, however, it cannot hide its original self. Standing among tall pines, the Forest spirit is as long as these, and moving in the underbrush it again shrinks to the height of this. The Mordvin Forest mother, when in the shape of a human being, has still feet as clumsy and thick as logs, and the Forest virgin of the Finns, beautiful from a front view, appears from behind as a rotted stump or a bushy tree. In the folk-poetry of the Finns, " the King

or Lord or Mistress of the forest " has " a hat of pine-
needles," a " blue mantle," and a " beard of leaves."

An extremely wide-spread belief is that the Forest spirit,
having bewildered human beings and enticed them into its
power, tickles, dances, or smothers them to death. The explanation of this curious idea is to be found in the psychic
state that overwhelms the individual, when lost in the forest,
and, in desperation, he sees no chance of ever finding his way
out.

CHAPTER XII

WATER SPIRITS

COMPARATIVE research shows that the ideas of the Finno-Ugric peoples regarding Water spirits have to a large extent been influenced by impressions from other sources.

In remote times, the Lapps, for success in fishing, seem to have offered chiefly to their gods of stone or Seides, which the Fisher Lapps always put up on the coasts of rivers and seas. Such a Seide stone was called also a " Fish-god." The spirits living in the water itself have never had sacrifices offered up to them to the same degree.

A god, known only at the coasts, is Akkruva, the upper part of whose body the Lapps imagine to be human, the head covered with long hair, the lower part of the body that of a fish. She rises at times from the sea and, sitting upon the water, rinses and combs her hair. Sometimes Akkruva walks up to the mouths of the rivers taking fishes with her, and at such times the catch is excellent. What this sea-spirit, called by Friis Avfruvva, really is, is shown above all by her name — a distortion of the " Havfru " of the Scandinavians, which, like the above mentioned being, had a human upper body whilst the lower body was fishlike.[1]

Limited also to Scandinavian Lapland is the Ravgga, which lives in the water mostly in human shape, its appearance or voice predicting misfortune, tempest or shipwreck. Meriläinen, who calls it in Finnish, Meriraukka, tells that it appears on the shore examining the accessories of a boat, from which, later, somebody will be drowned. When it is seen walking on the shore, the duty of the beholder is to walk round it with a firesteel, when it will stop, or, if it disappears on approach, to wait for its reappearance. It should then be asked why it has appeared, who will be drowned and when. That the Meriraukka is the spirit of a drowned person, is shown by the fact that it keeps in the neighbourhood of the body, the boat, the clothes, etc., of the drowned.[2]

As already pointed out by Fritzner the Ravgga of the Lapps is the same being as the Old Norse *draugr*.[3]

As will be seen from the name, the Lapps have also received from the Scandinavians the evil Nekke or Nik (Swedish Näcken), which is known also in Finnish Lapland, and is further met with among the Finns and the Esthonians.[4]

A Water spirit with a Lapp name, to whom offerings are sometimes made, is the Cacce-olmai (" the Water man "). He is the god of fishing, who brings fish to the hooks or in the nets and lines. In the notes made by S. Kildal we read that at sacrifices men made an image of the Water man and put it into a crevice so that he might give them more luck. On the other hand they sacrificed to the " Water man " so that he should not do them any harm on the water.[5]

The Cacce-olmai of the Scandinavian Lapps corresponds to the Cacce-jielle (" Water dweller ") of the Russian Lapps. This is a dangerous spirit who calls upon and then tries to drag people into the water. The sight of it predicts disaster. A woman who saw this spirit while fetching water from the sea asked him whether his appearance predicted good or bad. She was told that her son would die, which happened also within three days.

Cacce-jielle presents itself to people in different shapes; as an old man, a pretty woman, a naked child, or often also as a fish, which somehow differs from other fishes. It is considered dangerous to kill such a fish. When seeing it one has to sacrifice something, a piece of bread, a coin or brandy. Strange fish are said to be the children of the water spirit.[6]

The " Water dweller " of the Russian Lapps corresponds

PLATE XX

The Aino Episode in Kalevala (V. 45–133)

(See page 210.)
Illustrated by Akseli Gallen-Kallela.

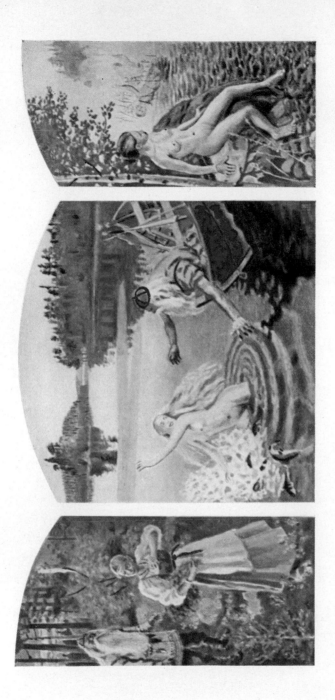

completely to the Vodyanoy of the Russians, whose Water-Nymph, the Rusalka, is called by the Kola-Lapps Cacce-jienne ("Water mother"). In the shape of a naked woman she emerges from the water at dawn to comb her long black hair. When frightened, she throws herself into the water so quickly, that she leaves her comb on the shore in the place where she was sitting. She loves men and entices them to her. The Saiva-neida (" Sea maid ") of the Western Lapps is a loan from Scandinavia.[7]

A Water spirit is also found amongst the Samoyeds, who call it the " Master of the water." Generally he is looked upon as a dangerous spirit, sometimes bringing disease. According to Donner they sacrifice money, etc., to him, especially at the mouths of rivers. In cases of illness they hang clothes on bushes near the water for him. During certain seasons the " Master of the water " is offered sacrifices that he may give fish.[8] As a rule, images are not made of him, only the Yuraks worshipping him in the form of a fishlike image of wood, or choosing a specially shaped dried fish to represent him.[9]

The Ostiaks call the Water spirit Jengk-tongk ("Water spirit"). Patkanov tells that sacrificial feasts are held on the shore, before the beginning of the fishing, to honour the Water spirit and to influence him in the fishermen's favour. Although their Water spirit has no image, almost all the usual sacrificial ceremonies are gone through. For the spirit itself the blood of bigger animals and of cocks is poured into the water. Polyakov says that the spirit was offered brandy and a cock, a lamb or a calf, and that only some drops of the blood of the victim were poured into the water. Also in the autumn, as soon as the rivers are frozen, the Ostiaks sacrifice to the Jengk-tongk on the ice.[10]

Like the Lapps, the Ostiaks sacrificed in older times for luck in fishing chiefly to the spirits of the dead, which are believed to live in certain holy places. Karjalainen points out that the Forest spirit as well as the Water spirit is sacrificed to chiefly in such districts where foreign influences may be noticed. Except in tales, where the Water spirit has been given special features, the idea entertained regarding it, especially in more remote territories, is very vague.[11] At Vasyugan they sacrifice to a certain Fish spirit, Kul jungk (" Fish spirit "), that lives in the water and is said to give fish to its favourites. When the ice has broken up, a fish-like image is made of wood or birch-bark and taken along to the fishing place. Especially of the first catch is the Fish spirit given its share.[12]

The Water spirit of the Voguls, Vit-khan (" Water Khan "), appears to be still less than that of the Ostiaks an object of sacrificial worship, although it is mentioned in folk-lore, e.g., that the spirit or his daughter may marry human beings.[13]

A loan from the Siryans is the Water spirit Kul, an evil being living in deep waters and known both in the western districts of the Ostiaks and in the northern part of the Vogul territory. It has a human shape.[14]

In leaving the Lapps and Ugrians and turning to the other tribes, we pass at the same time from hunting and fishing peoples to agricultural ones. Fishing is no longer of the same importance, although it is in places pursued next to the chief occupation as a good second industry. The importance of the water is nevertheless not diminished by the development of agriculture. The villages are still, as far as possible, situated near to the waters, which besides ways of communication are used also to afford power for mills. Agriculture, moreover, has drawn the attention of man to an important feature of water, namely its secret power of fertilization, without which no vegetation can exist. Man being thus in many respects dependent upon this important element of nature, the result is that the water itself becomes an object of sacrificial cult.

Before considering the animated water itself, we will first glance at those Water spirits, found amongst other Finno-

Ugrian tribes, to which the imagination of the people has given distinct features.

The Votiaks call their Water spirit Vu-murt ("Water man"). In some places he is also called Vu-kuźo ("Water master"). He is a human-like, often naked being, with very big eyes and long black hair. They speak also of the fingers of the "Water man"; these are stones resembling thunderbolts which they believe to be found on the shores of rivers. Usually, the "Water man" lives in deep waters, such as the big rivers and seas, but he also likes to dwell in little brooks and especially in mill ponds. The "Water man" has a house and a family in the water. According to folk-tales he may also seek the company of people, especially at the time of the great fairs. The "Water man" then appears dressed as a peasant, but is easily recognized by the left side of his coat being always damp. Often the "Water man" is an invisible being, and woe to the unfortunate person to whom he then appears, as this is a foreboding of death or other misfortune.

Like the male Water spirit, the female has also features which betray her foreign origin. She is beautiful and her naked body is glistening white. Sometimes in the twilight the wife or daughter of the "Water man" will emerge on the shore to comb her long black hair. In some places she is said to have breasts as big as buckets. The male spirit, like the female one, is a shy being, who immediately throws himself into the water on being observed by a human eye.

Besides appearing generally in human form, the "Water man" may sometimes become visible in the shape of a fish. Fishermen have seen him as a pike, differing from other pikes by his enormous size and by his sleeping with his head in the opposite direction to that of other pikes.

Twice a year, in the spring and in the autumn, the Water spirits have weddings, during which they move in the water merrily and noisily, causing inundations, so that the mill sluices break. The Northern Votiaks have, further, the idea that they come during the winter before Christmas to the villages and occupy the bath-houses; one may sometimes meet them in the twilight on the village street. For this reason the Votiaks are afraid to go out alone without a light. It is also dangerous at these times to make a noise near the water, to rinse dirty clothes, or to ferry singing people over any river. While they are thus on the move they are called the "evil spirits." When Twelfth Day is over, the Votiaks accompany the Water spirits back to the water where they live. On account of this the feast of Epiphany is also called "the following of the Water spirit." During Twelfth Night the young people wander with torches from bath-house to bath-house, to hear their fate and to call to the "Water man"— "Leave us!" The following morning men supplied with axes, sticks, or branches go down to the river, where they knock on the ice saying: "Go away from us." On this occasion they turn to the river itself with offerings: "Preserve us from all disease and accidents." A piece of bread, a spoonful of porridge and a piece of meat are thrown into the water. In some districts it was the custom to sacrifice a duck to the "Water man" through an ice-hole.

The Votiaks' impression of the "Water man" is more that of an evil than a good spirit. He brings ruin to both people and animals, and is dangerous in the winter, because he breaks the ice under the feet of the wanderers so that these sink helplessly into the depths. The "Water man" can also send sickness. If appeased he can, however, be of very great use. For example, he helps the miller in his work, and fishermen by driving fish into their nets. He is also believed to protect and increase the water birds.

Sacrifices are made to the "Water man" for accidental reasons, but also at fixed times. In the autumn the Votiaks sacrifice a duck or a goose in the river, so that no one will drown or be taken ill with ague. At the same time the "Water man" is prayed to, to protect the geese and ducks, and to increase their number. The blood of the bird, its bones and a piece of the meat are thrown into the water, along with bread. Sacrifices are made in addition when sickness occurs, a bird often sufficing for this offering. If the mill sluice is out of order, or if there is fear of a flood, offerings are made to the "Water man." [15]

Among the Siryans the usual name of the Water spirit is Kul, but it is also called Vasa ("Water dweller"). As among the Votiaks the Water spirit possesses here distinct features that hint at a longer period of development. This is true of both the male and the female spirit. The male one is a black, hairy and wet being, who at times sits on the shore shaking himself and sometimes seizing the mill-wheel. Sometimes the people imagine him to be a being with a big head and big round eyes, who at times emerges from the water and comes ashore to comb his dark green hair. He is dressed in a green robe or his body is naked. When he throws himself from the shore into the water a tempest arises and the waves rise high. He swims thus, especially in bad weather, in the water, but at other moments he has been seen rocking on the water or on fishing nets or standing on some pier. Sometimes the water spirit haunts the night, slapping the washing hung out to dry, or crying loudly on the river-bank. He has also been seen at the fish-spearing and recognised by the sudden disappearance of his boat and torch.

As with the male Water spirit, the characteristics of the female one differ in different districts. She is also a long-haired being, who combs her hair with her big paws. There is a tale about a peasant, who found a Water maid sitting naked on a hill, combing her hair, and frightened her so that she threw herself into the water, leaving her comb on the hill. The peasant took the comb to his house, but in the night the Water maid came to claim it back.

The Water spirit may also appear in the shape of a small child, according to the Siryans. The children of the Water spirit are, while young, hairy and of a peculiar appearance, often like fishes, but become later more human in shape. Now and then a child of the Water spirit may stray into the net of a fisherman.

Like the Votiaks the Siryans also know the stony fingers of the Water spirit. These are belemnites, found near the beaches in the land of the Siryans.

At times the Water spirit takes another shape than that of a human being. Thus it may appear, as among the Votiaks, in the shape of a big pike. In the collected works of Nalimov the Water spirit is mentioned as a pike that could speak and had long white hair on its head. By mistake it had gone into the net of a fisherman.

The Siryans also believe the Water spirits to have weddings, when they make much noise and break down the sluices of mills, and that they go and dwell amongst human beings at Epiphany.

The Water spirit of the Siryans is a being much feared. The mere sight of him means tempest, death or other disaster. He entices both mankind and animals to his home.

From the notes of Wichmann it appears that the Siryans offered the " Sea spirit " butter and bread in order that he might give them fish. When fishing one had to be careful not to use bad words, as this incensed the Water spirit, who in his anger would seize the net so firmly, that the fisherman could not move it. Like the fisherman, the miller also has to keep on good terms with the Water spirit. For other purposes also, the Water spirit is sometimes given small offerings. No Siryan will go over water without giving the Water spirit a gift: if nothing else he throws at least a thread from his belt into the water.[16]

According to the Siryans the Water spirits have their origin in the spirits of the drowned, which continue living in the water, where they have entered the service of the Water spirit. Even the name Kul is, as is proved by Setälä, the old name of a Finno-Ugric god who lived under the earth, the cult of which was obviously connected with the cult of the dead.[17] When comparing the present highly developed characteristics of the spirit Kul, which the similarly-named spirit of the Ob peoples, borrowed from the Siryans, does not possess, with the corresponding features of the Water spirit of the Great Russians, it is evident that the first mentioned, even to its details, is a copy of the latter. The name Vasa seems to be only a translation of the Russian Vodyanoy.

A fully corresponding Water spirit of the Cheremiss is their " Water master " (Vüt-oza). He is said to dwell in such waters as do not dry up during the hot season. Usually the Water spirit is here also an evil and feared being. Especially is it dangerous to swim at midday. Where he does not succeed in kidnapping a man, he will take cattle. The male Water spirit appears usually as an old man who is often seen before dawn on the surface of the water near the shore. He is dressed sometimes in rags, and sometimes in splendid clothes; his chest being, for example, sometimes covered with silver coins, but at times he is also naked. The Cheremiss say that the greater a river is in which a Water spirit lives, the richer it is. Should a human being cast his eye on him, he throws himself immediately into the water. Besides his human form, the Water spirit can also show himself in the form of a horse or a bullock. The Water spirits living in the sea show themselves mainly as bulls, and the bellowing of the " water bull " has often been heard from the sea. But the Water spirit can also take the form of a fish, or of other miscellaneous objects. But in whatever form he shows himself, the sight denotes disaster — often death — to the one who has seen him, or to some one belonging to him.

The female Water spirit, " Water master's daughter," has been seen on the shore combing her long hair with a gold or silver comb. Sometimes she becomes entangled in a fisherman's fishing-tackle. Once some fishers found a great being in their net, which dragged it here and there. With great labour they managed to keep hold of their net, and when they finally succeeded in dragging it nearer to the boat, they saw a pretty dark maid, who, however, disappeared immediately from sight. The net became at once lighter and was found to contain no fish at all. Sometimes people are fortunate enough to get a " Water master's daughter " into their power. This happens only when they throw a piece of iron at her or touch her with their hands, as then the water-maid cannot move an inch.

In prayers, the Water spirit is often referred to as " Water old man " (Vüt-kuguza) and " Water old woman " (Vüt-kuva). The Cheremiss worship the " Old man " and the " Old woman " of the water when they go swimming or fishing. The fishermen offer up to these spirits bread or brandy, sometimes even a duck, a goose, or a hen, as they are supposed to drive fish into the fishermen's tackle. In the spring, when the first fish has been caught, the Eastern Cheremiss generally boil it immediately, and eat it without breaking the bones, the latter being thrown back into the water with the following words: " ' Water man,' come and eat fish; I have tasted it already, give us still more fresh fish." [18]

Similar beliefs in human-like Water spirits are met with among the Mordvins. The spirits living in the water are here called Ved-eräj (" Water dweller ") or Vetsa-eräj (" He who inhabits the water "). There are many such spirits, and they are malignant beings, who, like Vampire spirits, lie in wait for newly born children, and devour grain that has been cursed by an enemy.[19]

The Baltic Finns have been under Germanic influence. The Näcken of the Swedes is called Näkk by the Esthonians, and they believe it to live in all deeper waters, such as the sea, rivers, lakes and wells. The deepest spot in the water is particularly its dwelling-place, and also any whirlpool.

The Näkk presents itself in different shapes, as a human being, an animal, or even some inanimate object. Neverthe-

PLATE XXI

Votish sacrifice to the River Buj after the break-
ing-up of the ice. (See pages 214–15.)
(Government permission.)
After photograph by U. Holmberg.

PLATE XXI

Votiak sacrifice to the River Buj after the break-
ing-up of the ice. (See pages 214–15.)
(Government permission.)
After photograph by U. Holmberg.

less, it lives in the imagination of the people mostly as a human being. In this shape, according to the idea of the Esthonians, it is both male and female, and may appear full grown or as a child. The people believe the male spirit to be a grey old man, who at times swims in the water with his enormous, widely opened maw, swallowing everybody who comes in his path, sometimes lifting his head above the water, sometimes seating himself on the shore of a river, lake or sea, or on the cover of a well to watch for people. When appearing in human shape he executes human work. Now and then he is found by night at the fish-spearing places and is recognized by having his torch not in a boat but on a stone slab. One of the most remarkable features of the Näkk is his song, by which he bewitches his hearers, who in this way become his prisoners. In the neighbourhood of Hapsal the belief prevails that when the Näkk sings or plays, men and animals begin to dance in gradually increasing *tempo* until they at last fall into the sea. Although the Näkk appears in human shape, he has, in the tales of the people, fish teeth.

Like the male spirit, the female human-like Water spirit has also the pronounced character that proves development. To distinguish her from the male, the Esthonians call her Näkineiu or Näkineitsi (" Näkk's maid "), Veeneiu (" Water maid ") or Mereneiu (" Sea maid "). Usually, Näkineitsi is a pretty young girl, who sits on the surface of the water, or on a stone on the shore, or in the shadow of a tree growing near to the water, combing her long hair with a golden comb. Her hair is wonderfully pretty, now golden yellow, now grass-green. Occasionally she appears naked, at other times dressed. In some districts the Näkineitsi has a human body and a fish tail.

As with the Näkk, one of the most important features of the Näkineitsi is her song and her music. On the coasts they speak also of the cattle of the water-maid, which are beautiful and fat. The colour of the animals is usually grey, like the sea. Suddenly emerging from the sea, the cattle come ashore, where they are tended by the Näkineitsi until she again disappears with them after awhile. The Livonians tell of blue sea-cows; some of these sometimes go astray from the other cattle and remain on the shore, falling thus into the hands of men.

Besides his human form, the Näkk of the Esthonians also appears in the shape of a young, usually grey horse, sometimes also as a white foal. This emerges from the water, runs all round the shore, approaches children and entices them to sit on its back, whereupon it immediately rushes back into the sea at a gallop. At times it can also appear as an ox, now black, now brown or grey, or as a white calf. The Näkk that has changed himself into an animal, is recognized by his coming from the sea and disappearing into the water. Sometimes he even changes himself into a startled hare, which by running to and fro on a pier tries to entice its pursuer so far, that the latter is in danger of falling into the water. He may also appear as a waterbird, a swan, a goose or a duck. Further, the Näkk is seen in the shape of a fish, which at times comes ashore, winds its tail round a fisherman, and drags him into the water. Often the Water spirit appears also as a big strange-looking or one-eyed fish. Two fisherman had once fished a long time without catching anything when one of them saw two strangely shaped gold-glittering fishes in the water. Neglecting the warning of his comrade he set about catching these fish and got one in his net, but as he was about to lift it from the water there suddenly arose a strong tempest and snowstorm, and at the same moment the fish disappeared from the net. The Näkk can also take the shape of a lifeless object.

In whatever shape the Näkk appears, he is always a dangerous and feared being, whose mere appearance predicts drowning or other disaster. Even if the one who sees him is not himself doomed, one of his relatives will perish in the water.

Some people believe that in all waters where a Näkk dwells, a man will be drowned every summer. When the time for this approaches, a voice is heard from the water: "The hour has struck, a man is wanted." Against his will somebody will then go and bathe and lose his life in the water. Before he drowns, the water becomes agitated, boils and seethes, but calms down as soon as it has got its victim. The Näkk can drown people not only in deep but in shallow places, where the water is only a foot deep.

The Näkk takes his victim either by enticement, by bewitching songs, or by appearing in the shape of the animals or object that a man desires. At times he bewitches the eyes of people so that they no longer recognize their surroundings, but lose themselves and at last are at his mercy. The cattle he entices by changing himself into an animal, mingling with them on their pasture ground, and, on his return into the water, enticing the other animals to follow him.

One who notices the danger in time, may protect himself against the menace of the Näkk. An effective remedy is to mention his name, as on hearing this he flees at once and throws himself into the water. To protect themselves, the inhabitants of the island Mohn, before going into the sea, take a stone from the beach, spit on it and throw it into the sea, saying: "A cake to the Näkk." Women also do this when they go to the sea-shore to watch the sheep, as they believe that the Näkk will not touch them or their cattle if they throw him a cake into the water.[20]

The Näkki of the Finns closely resembles the Näkk of the Esthonians, only a few new features being met with in the former. In West Finland the Water spirit is represented as a man of unusual size. He has been seen in the shape of an immense, long and stout old man standing over the water, so that one foot was on the one shore and the other foot on the other shore of the sea. A miller saw him thus standing over a waterfall, like an unusually big, grey man. Probably this latter type of the Water spirit has been influenced by the traits of the Forest spirit, which appears in mythology more regularly than the Water spirit as a lone being. At times the Water spirit also appears as a dwarf. So he was once seen by fishermen: " in the bag of the net was a small human-like old man, not longer than two spans, with long hair reaching to his throat."

Sometimes he is half-man, half-animal: the upper part human, with horse-feet. He does not seem to appear in complete horse form in the imagination of the Finns. On the other hand he has been seen as a dog with a long beard; sometimes as an enormous buck, which wears net-pouches on its horns. Often Näkki appears also in the shape of an object, at times as a big balk or log, which differs from an ordinary one by having an eye as big as a plate and a mane on its back, or as a tree, fallen into the water, which sinks when one tries to sit on it.

The female Näkki has also many other names such as Näkinneito, Näkinpiika ("Näkki maid"), Vedenneito ("Water maid"), Merenneito ("Sea maid"), Vedenemäntä ("Water mistress"). According to the ideas of the people this Water spirit is a pretty being. In Österbotten they believe that the female Näkki is a beautiful woman with glittering white body and very long curly hair. On the coast of Österbotten and in Nyland the Water maid is further known by her breasts as big as buckets, which are thrown over the shoulder when bathing.

When the Water maid appears, she is always busy in some way. Now she washes her face or her breasts, now she combs her hair, splashes gaily in the water, washes her clothes on a stone on the shore or on a rock in the sea, or goes sometimes on land to watch the water cattle in the grass on the beach.

The idea that the Water spirit possesses magnificent cattle in the water is very general in Finland. Often it has been noticed how stately cows emerge from the sea, which on the approach of a man go back into the water and dive down.

PLATE XXII

The Sacrificing "Upward"

The Eastern Votiaks sacrifice a white goose to the
Ilcaven god. (See page 220.)
Water-colour by U. Soldan-Brofeldt.

When the Water spirit disappears with his cattle at sunrise, it may happen that an animal is left on the shore. According to the general belief of the people, this can be seized by walking round it once or thrice with a piece of iron in the hand, as then it can return no more to the water, but belongs to man. In vain the spirit cries from the water for his lost animal. It is very advantageous to possess a cow of the Water spirit, not only because it is pretty, but also because it gives much milk; it is however to be noted, that it always gives only the same quantity that was milked the first time.

At times the cow of the Water maid is like a fish. Once in Karelia a fish with horns and feet was caught in the net of a fisherman, who, after some wondering at its appearance, threw it ashore, with the result that in the night the plaintive cries of the Water woman were heard.

According to the Scandinavian Finns, besides the Water spirits, the Maahiset (" those living under the earth ") also possess big cattle that man may seize, if he throws something made of steel upon them. As the Water spirits rise from the water, so the " Undergrounders " emerge from the earth and disappear therein. In North Finland and in Russian Karelia the same power is given to the cows of the Manalaiset (" the deceased ").

Now and then the Water spirit also appears in the shape of a big fish of unusual species or strange shape. Once some boys caught a big salmon-trout, which had lost itself on a low river-bank. At home they were told, however, that the fish was a Marras, and they were instructed to take it back to the water, because they would otherwise drown on the same spot where they had caught the trout. Lencqvist already mentions the Marta as an omen of death.

The Finnish Näkki is, like the Esthonian Näkk and the Swedish Näcken, always an evil and feared being. That children may take care when near the water, they are frightened by words such as " Näkki comes." A usual means of protection against Näkki when bathing is a form of witch-craft in connection with certain words. On stepping into the water the bather once, thrice, or even nine times, scoops water on to the beach with his hand or throws a stone, taken from the water, or earth from the sea-bottom, on the shore, saying: " Näkki ashore, I into the water." After bathing the pro-ceeding is reversed, the water or the object used previously is now thrown back in the river or the sea, with the saying: " Näkki into the water, I on land." Another means of pro-tection against Näkki is to put into the water a piece of metal or a metal object while one is bathing. Similarly, animals also have to be protected against the evil caused by Näkki. When bathing a horse they used to put into the water some one of the above-mentioned metal objects or bind a fire-steel to the tail, or hang a bell on the neck of the horse. More particularly had this to be done with an unshod horse, be-cause Näkki is believed not to seize a shod horse.

Similar ideas and means of protection are general also amongst the Swedes.

Of foreign origin is also an idea of the Finns, that the Water spirit is a musician, whose wonderful music anybody can learn. The proper moment to approach it for this purpose is Midsummer Night, or before the Eves of Lent and Easter. The spirit may be seen on a rock in a waterfall, on one that has never been under water, or on one that is always sur-rounded by water. The person wishing to learn has to take a violin with him. When the Water spirit has emerged from the waterfall, he will seat himself on the same stone as the man, turning his back to him, and start to teach him. As a reward the man has to promise himself to the Water spirit and during the lesson bind himself fast to the master, but with caution, so that the ties break or become undone when the spirit suddenly precipitates himself into the water. Should the fetters not loosen, the pupil falls into the power of the Water spirit. The one who succeeds in passing through the trial becomes a great player, who can make people dance even against their will. Sometimes his violin develops the wonderful quality of playing by itself and even its pieces will play when the violin is at last broken.

The wonderful music to be learnt from the Water spirit is known round all the Scandinavian countries.

Corresponding to Näkki is the Vetehinen ("Water dweller"), known originally only in Russian Karelia, Ingria, and East Finland, who in the imagination of the people appears as a human-like being with marked characteristics. Vetehinen is also regarded as a malignant being. He causes a disease (eruption) and, like Näkki, seizes people and animals as sacrifices. Protection against him, as against Näkki, is found in metal objects. The idea of Vetehinen does not however completely cover that of Näkki, which latter is exclusively the cause of drowning, because the Karelians worship the former also as the giver of luck in fishing.[21] Foreign influence is to be noted already in the name of Vetehinen, of which Castrén says that both in idea and etymologically there is a correspondence to the Water spirit, which the Russians call Vodyanoy.[22]

The Mordvinian Ved- or Vetsa-eräj corresponds in name to the Water spirit of the Votes, the Järv-elaj ("Sea dweller").[23] Only through their literature do the Finns know anything now of the old Water spirit of the Tavastlanders, Ahti, about whom Agricola says, that he "brought fishes from the water." In the old popular poetry he appears as a water dweller, and in a song about the origin of frost, the following description occurs: "then thou caused a strong frost, when thou made Ahti freeze in the sea."[24] The etymology of the name is not clear. According to Daniel Juslenius (1745) Wäinämöinen was also a Water spirit; Agricola does not, however, mention him thus, but says only that he "composed songs." Both Ahti and Wäinämöinen appear in folk-poetry as mighty heroes.

Over all Finland and also amongst the Finnish Lapps and

Northern Esthonians the dark Vedenhaltija (" Water ruler ")
is known. He is supposed to appear before a disaster in human shape, and he corresponds completely to the Swedish
Sjörå, Sjörådare, etc.

The belief that the drowned are transformed into Water
spirits is general among most of the Finno-Ugric peoples.
The Esthonians, for instance, believe that the size and shape
of a Näkk depend upon the person drowned. If an adult
had fallen victim to the water, his Näkk would appear as a
full-grown person; if a child, the spirit would appear as a
child. When swimming in places where people had been
drowned, one might easily get cramp, because the spirits of
the dead seized the living by their feet and dragged them
down. Like the Siryans, the Esthonians sometimes call the
water spirit by a name that originally meant the spirit of the
dead: Kull or Koll (cf. the Lapp Ravgga). The spirit living
in a river is called Joe Kull (" River Kull ").[25]

A similar being, although not originally of Cheremiss origin,
is their Pele koleše (" Half-dead "), which floats on the surface of the water with its face turned upwards like someone
drowned. A person who tries to save it falls a victim himself
to the water. The Cheremiss have a general idea that where
a corpse lies, there its " soul " (ört) remains. The fishermen
at Belaya told me how a young Cheremiss mother, who, on
her way back from a feast, had been drowned by falling
through thin ice, rises early in the morning on the beach to
express her sorrow for the babe she had left. The fishermen
had heard her plaints: " My breasts are filled with milk, my
little child cries at home! "[26]

Further evidence of the transformation of drowned people
into Water spirits, to whom one sacrifices for luck in fishing,
are the Soiem tongk (" River spirits ") of the Konda Ostiaks,
" which are drowned people." According to Paasonen, every
family has a common idol-house for its members lost thus,
where they are given offerings twice a year, in spring and in

PLATE XXIII

Ostiak sacrifice of a white animal, or of one covered with a white cloth, to the Heaven-god. (See page 220.)

After photograph by K. F. Karjalainen.

autumn, before the beginning of the fishing season; the latest of the deceased receiving a cock, while to those transformed earlier, clothes are given. The drowned appear during the course of the year following their death to the priest and are then escorted to the god-house, receiving at the same time a shirt or a kerchief as an offering.[27] But from the examples given it becomes evident that the "souls" of the different species of fish, or their tutelary genii are also contained in the Finno-Ugric Water spirits. The Yurak Samoyeds make an image of a fish-like "Water master" or they choose as such a dried fish of peculiar appearance. The Ostiaks make an image of a fish when they worship their "Fish spirit," and with other peoples also the Water spirit often appears in the form of a rare fish. The Pite Lapps speak of a Water spirit with horns.[28] Sometimes these "spirit-fish" can be detected only by their position. The Water spirit of the Permian tribes appears as a large pike which is recognised by the fact that it is larger than others, and that when sleeping it holds its head against the current of the water, or towards the shore, or contrary to the other fish. The "Water dweller" of the Russian Lapps often appears as a turbot or a flounder, which contrary to the habit of these fish comes inshore. Sometimes the Fish spirit strives after more human-like features.

The Siryans say that the "Water dweller" when young resembles a fish, but as it grows begins to resemble a human being. A "spirit-pike" could speak and had long light hair on its head.[29] In Pite Lapland a white fish was caught that had scales all over its body, except on its breast, which reminded one of a woman's breast.[30] In a tale from the Finnish coast, a Water spirit was found by the people, which from the front was like a most beautiful young maiden, but on its back was covered with scales and had also fins. It is believed in addition that in the Baltic there are water-dwellers with a human body and a fish-tail. Even when a spirit appears altogether as a human being, it has generally some fish-like feature, such as the large maw of a fish, fish-teeth and round eyes. Another significant fact is that it moves with the other fish, taking them with it from the sea to the rivers, and also that it wanders into the fishers' traps. There is a story of such a half-fish, half-female being in the Karelian folk-songs which Lönnrot uses in the Aino episode in *Kalevala* (viii. 45–133).

The Finno-Ugric peoples also envisage the water itself animistically. The Cheremiss say that the " water lives," it moves from one place to another, serves people and carries their boats. Donner relates, that the Samoyeds, when they are out in their boats and come to a new river, wash their heads with its water. A large river they call " Mother." [31] This custom is met with also among the Siryans, who, when they go out fishing, sacrifice bread to the Vorikva River saying: " Vorikva-mother, carry us without danger, protect us, and give us a whole boatful of fish." [32] The Votiaks and Mordvins, when praying, use also the name " Mother " to their rivers and brooks as the Russians speak of the " Volga-mother," etc.

The Volga and Baltic Finns have the same belief, i.e., that lakes can move from one place to another. This may happen as a consequence of someone offending the water by polluting it. They say that when the sea wanders, a black bull goes bellowing before it, so that people may know to get out of its way. [33]

In a little village in the District of Birsk there is a lake that has the same name as the village, Cherlak. The people say it has two sisters, Azelekel and Kandralekel, which are also two lakes in the District of Belebey. Cherlak Lake is the youngest sister and is called the " Cherlak girl." Sometimes it is asked to visit the older sisters, and to take with it water, fish and sea birds. Some time ago it paid a visit to them, the lake being in the meanwhile so dry that cattle were able to pasture on its bed, the only water being in a hole. The village was quite unhappy over the shortage of water and decided to offer up a sacrifice to the " Cherlak girl." They thought first of offering her a black bull, but this did not please the lake as the animal did not shudder when water was poured over it. In the end they offered a black heifer, which she accepted with pleasure. Clad in clean clothes, the people around sprinkled water on one another from the water that was left in the hole, praying to the " Cherlak girl " to return to its old place. The heifer's bones and pieces of its flesh were wrapped in its hide and hidden in the water hole. On this occasion the following prayer was read: " Water-mother, protect the water, give the Cherlak girl good health, bring her and all kinds of fish back to her place, bring her with all kinds of sea-birds, give the water good health. Make Azelekel and Kandralekel return her former riches to the Cherlak girl! " When it had received the sacri-fice, the water began to return, but in the beginning it was muddy and foul. The village sacrificed a black lamb for the health of the water, and then " the water became clean and even fish and sea-birds began to appear." Sometimes, the elder sisters also come from Belebey to visit the " Cherlak girl," when it becomes flooded. An old Cheremiss related that during his lifetime it has happened twice that a strange lake has visited another.

The Cheremiss and Mordvins generally call the animated water " Water mother." Probably the Esthonians' Vete-ema (" Water mother ") and Mere-ema (" Sea mother ") have the same origin, although the ideas connected with them are now in close relation to the Wasser-mutter of the Teutons. The Livonians' Mier-iema (" Sea mother ") is a similar goddess.[34] Agricola says that the Karelians worshipped Veden emä, who " drove fish into their nets."

In the magic prayers of the Mordvins the " Water mother " has already certain anthropomorphic features: silky hair, and a plait decorated with silver wire, at times also her children and family are mentioned. One finds, however, in some prayers words like these: " Water mother, Boyar mistress, thou comest from the sea and spreadest thyself over the whole country, thou wanderest over thine own land, thou floatest over thine own ways, thou doest much good, thou receivest many genuflexions, thou flowest glowing like gold, shining like silver." [35]

It is quite evident that the " Water mother " in the votive prayers is the animated water itself. As an example one might give the following prayer written down by Melnikov among the Christian Mordvins. " Water mother, give all Christian people good health. Give health to those who eat thee and those who drink thee, to those who bathe in thee a light and merry heart; give the cattle also who drink thee good health." [36]

Smaller offerings are also made to the water when going out to fish, or in sickness, i.e., ordinary skin diseases which are believed to come from the offended water. The real water-cult is, however, connected with agriculture. Mutual sacrifices have been made to the Water mother, chiefly to obtain fruitful rains. Like the earth, the water is given a black sacrificial animal, generally a bull or a sheep. The Cheremiss have a custom of sprinkling water on one another at such ceremonies. Black sheep, or hens that happen to be near the water, are also sprinkled with it. A part of all the sacrificial food is thrown into the water, in addition to the bones and a portion of each part of the carcase, which, wrapped in the hide, are also thrown in. At the close everything used at the sacrifice is rinsed in the water. If a sacrifice should bring too much rain, the offerings that have been thrown into the water must be taken up again, and buried in the earth to make the rain cease.[37]

A water cult of this description was known among the Votiaks, Mordvins and Baltic Finns. J. Gutslaff (1644) relates about the Esthonians that they worshipped a brook (Wõhhanda), which they believed could produce a fertilising rain,

PLATE XXIV

The " World-pillar " of the Lapps, consisting of
two high stones and a squared log of wood.   (See
page 222.)

According to Leenis.

or when the brook so desired, torrential rains, hail, or frost. An old man said that the weather could be arranged with the brook's help. If one wished for rain and stormy weather, one threw something into the water, but if one wished for fine weather, one cleaned out the brook. An example was given of a pair of oxen which, while out at pasture, fell into the water and were drowned, with the result that a terrible rainstorm arose and only ceased when the carcases were dragged out of the water.[38] Often, " rain is made " without sacrifice, by wetting people, the walls of houses, cattle, and the fields. Among the Votiaks, the " Thunder mother " has in many districts usurped the place of " the Water " at the large common sacrifices. Among the Mordvins it has been noted that in some places they had a custom, when sacrificing for rain, of going round a little lake three times, carrying a duck, which was afterwards cooked and eaten in honour of the water. Sometimes the finding of rain-giving springs is difficult. But if rain comes soon after a sacrifice to a spring or brook, one can be certain of having found a good sacrificing-place. Droughts are often caused by rain-giving springs becoming choked. These have then to be cleaned out in order to obtain rain.[39]

When the fructifying powers of rain were noticed, the belief arose that rain could also fructify human beings and animals. To the general custom of taking a newly married woman to the brook near her husband's home, in order to conciliate the strange water, the rite of sprinkling her with water has been added. This custom can be explained partly by the belief that one must come into contact with the new water oneself in order to become acquainted with it. The Siryans have a custom according to which a newly married pair should go to the nearest stream three days after their wedding, when the wife sacrifices money and pieces of cloth and thread, or bread and cheese to the " mother " river, after which she washes her hands and face in the water. With

most of the agricultural Finnish races it is regarded as necessary to drench the bride completely with water. If weddings
are celebrated in the winter, when it is of course too cold to
do this, the Votiaks and Ingrians consider it their duty to
drench all the winter's brides together in the spring. It is
not quite clear why this wetting is done, but some light may
perhaps be thrown on the matter by a Mordvinian custom.
According to this the bride goes the day after the wedding to
the stream or well, not only to pour water over herself, but
to beg the " Water mother " to give her children. Bishop
Makariy says that when the bride sacrifices money, linseed,
bread and salt to the water, she begs it to wash her clothes
and give her children. The same author says that barren
Mordvin women also pray to the " Water mother " for her
assistance. Usually such sacrifices were made at midnight,
when both husband and wife went together in secret to the
shore. According to Butuzov the Erza woman also prayed
in the following words: " Water mother, pardon me, if I have
offended thee and therefore cannot give birth to children."
The German belief that children come from the water
(" Kinder-brunnen ") is also explained by the above.[40]

Rivers and seas were also prayed to for an increase of water-
birds. Aminoff says that the Votiaks sacrificed a duck to the
water, so that it might richly increase their geese and ducks.[41]
Wichmann has discovered the following prayer: " To Mother
Ybyt (a river) I give a goose. Produce many geese when
their time comes." [42] The Mordvins also pray to the " Water
mother " to increase their cattle.

The Votiaks and Mordvins, like the Russians earlier, each
spring when the ice begins to break up, celebrate great festivals with sacrifices of horses in honour of the water. Among
the Votiaks this feast is called " to follow the ice." In 1911
the author had the opportunity of being present at one of these
feasts at the river Buy, one of the tributaries of the Kama.
After a young foal had been killed and cooked on the shore

of the stream, the people knelt down with their faces towards the water, while the officiating priest read out a long prayer, begging prosperity from the river. During the prayer the bones, hide, and small pieces of the different parts of the carcase were thrown into the water, together with the animal's new halter, the blood having been already drained there by means of a channel dug into the bank. The animal sacrificed is changed each year, being one year a brown foal, the next year a black bull. The people believe firmly that if they do not sacrifice to the river, it will flood their corn-fields, or make great gaps in the banks, or cause fogs, storms and disastrous hail-storms. In one village this same spring, the sacrifice had been neglected, and in punishment hail had ruined the corn-fields.

The Cheremiss believe that the water has also a " soul " (*ört*) that can depart to other places. They say that when the water's " soul " disappears, the water becomes muddy and foul. Illness follows from drinking such water. The close relation between the Water spirit and the water itself with its " soul," is shown by the belief that if the " Water master " leaves, the water dries up, and that a spirit can rule over two different waters, causing each to fill or dry up as it removes from one to the other. The undefined Pamaš-oza (" the Spring's master ") of the District Uršum is also apparently a nature-soul. It becomes angry if anyone comes to take water from the spring with unclean vessels, or if any one shouts, quarrels, speaks indecently or spills water over his clothes. It punishes such people by giving them boils or some other skin disease; and they must then cook porridge at the edge of the spring and ask for pardon.[43]

Doubtless the undefined Veden Haltia (" Water ruler ") of the Finns is of the same origin. An indication of this is the strange magic custom, that when the water in a well is spoilt or run dry, fresh water is brought from another well, in the belief that by thus renewing the water in the well, a new

Haltia is secured. To lakes also in which the fishing water is spoilt or where the Haltia is not good, " new water " and a " new Haltia " are brought. Considering that in the above-mentioned proceeding, which is also known among other tribes, e.g., among the Chuvashes, the water, by the addition of new and better water, is provided with new soul-power, we may assume that the Haltia here is to be understood in the sense of the nature-soul. It is further to be observed that origi-nally each sea, lake or river had only one Haltia.

These examples should show, that besides the spirits of those drowned and the tutelary genii of the fish, the water itself, furnished with a soul, is included among the Water gods of the Finno-Ugric stocks.

PLATE XXV

SACRIFICIAL MEAL AMONG THE RUSSIAN KARELIANS

(See page 229.)

After photograph by I. K. Inha.

CHAPTER XIII

GODS OF SKY AND AIR

THE SUPREME deity among the Finno-Ugric stocks is the Heaven god, who is called by different names, the original signification of which is the same among all the peoples.

In the Finnish language there are two words, Jumala and Ilmarinen, both of which were originally names for the god of the sky. The former, which is found in Icelandic literature as early as 1026 (Jómali), has in our time come to denote "god" in general (*deus*), like the loan-word Jubmel or Ibmel in the Lapp tongue, except among the Cheremiss, where in its present form of Jumo it has preserved its original meaning. In this last language the word has also a third meaning which may be taken to be the very oldest, i.e., the "sky" or the "air." A similar example of a word meaning "heaven" or "the Heaven god" gradually coming to denote generally "god," is provided by the Turco-Tatar Tängere. The second Finnish word also, Ilmarinen (diminutive of *ilmari*), which later became the name of a hero in the *Kalevala*, comes from a word originally meaning "sky" or "air" (*ilma*). The word Ilmari formed by adding a suffix, is met with also among the Votiaks, Inmar (the god of the sky), and originates therefore from the Finno-Permian period, over a thousand years before the birth of Christ. Contemporaneously, and with the same meaning as the word Inmar, there is another word in the Votiak, In(m) (= Finnish Ilma); the same word being also found among the Siryans, Jen (now meaning the Christian God), and among the Ostiaks, Ilem or Item. These last-named have also other names for this god, such as Num-Tūrem (Tūrem = " sky," " air," " world," etc.), which has its counterpart in the Vogul Numi-Tōrem. The word Tūrem has been compared by Castrén with the Lapp Tiermes (the god of thunder). Both the sky and the Heaven god are called Num by the Samoyeds.

Knowing that the highest god, as appears already from his names, was at one time merely the animated sky, it is not surprising that, especially in earlier times, the people's ideas of him were dim and uncertain. The most usual qualities attributed to him are " great," " high," " good " ; in the southern districts the Ostiaks call him Sängke (" light "), probably a shortening of Sängke-Tūrem. As there was no actual conception of his being, there were no attempts to materialise him. Characteristic for all the above-mentioned peoples is the following description of the Samoyeds: " They never make images of Num, therefore they do not know how to sculpture him." [1]

Only in folk-poetry do we find the Sky god anthropomorphised. Here, we find the Cheremiss relating that he is a man-like being, living in the sky. Like the people down below, he practises agriculture, he has green pastures and much excellent cattle. As befits a good Cheremiss farmer, he even keeps bees. In the sacrificial prayers he appears as a worldly ruler with a large train of lesser deities, to whom at times sacrifices are also made. Like a rich and powerful ruler, the god of the Ostiaks and Voguls dwells in the highest story of heaven in a house glittering with gold and silver; he is said to have seven sons and many assistant spirits, some of which have wings. The idea of a heavenly suite is, however, of later origin, a fact that appears also from the names borrowed from the Turco-Tatar.[2]

It is quite natural that the sky with its light and rains, and other wondrous forces and phenomena affecting so closely the whole of our earthly existence, should have early become the object of the curiosity of primitive peoples. It would seem, nevertheless, that however animated the sky was regarded as being, no sacrifices were originally offered up to it. This is witnessed to by the fact that even today, sacrifices to the Heaven god are extremely rare among the more northern peoples, e.g., the Eastern Samoyeds and the Northern Ostiaks, for whom the god himself is too far away to be at all interested in human life.[3]

The worship of the Heaven god is more closely connected with agriculture, which, more often than any other occupation, raises its glance to the sky. That he is a god of agriculture, is shown plainly by the fact that sacrifices are made to him chiefly that the fields may become fruitful. According to certain peoples, his period of worship is the summer months only; as the Votiaks, for example, believe that Inmar may be sacrificed to, like the " Earth mother," only up to the beginning of winter, after which it is regarded as unsuitable to do so.[4] Quite apparent is the opinion that the sky is a procreative power. In their prayers, the Votiaks call Inmar, " the procreator and nourisher," the Mordvins address their " god dwelling on high " (Erza: Vere-pas) generally by the name " procreator," Moksha: Shkaj or Shka(j)-bavas, Erza: Shki-pas (from *ška-ms,* " to procreate," " to give birth to," words to be found now only in folklore; *bavas* or *pas,* " god," an Indo-Iranian loan-word). The word *škaj* may at times denote only and solely " the sky," as in the phrase, *škajs mazems* (" the sky reddens ").[5] The Voguls believed that the Heaven god " sends down " even animals; in a prayer to Numi-Tōrem occur the words: " Send down, our father, the fishes of the sea, let down the game of the forest! " [6]

In later times the Heaven god among the Volga Finns has, under the influence of Christianity and Islam, become a much more powerful god, to be worshipped in all the necessities imposed by life. Even now, however, he is turned to solely in the case of material needs. Extremely characteristic is the belief of the Votiaks as described by an unknown author: " Inmar is, according to them, only a good spirit, who protects their lives and gives them food and clothing, having nothing whatever to do with the mutual relations between mankind." [7] Thus, the Heaven god did not originally, in the view of the Finno-Ugric stocks, watch over the morality of the people, as the spirits of the dead were supposed to do.

By the side of the male Heaven god, generally termed the " Father," the peoples by the Volga and the Ob speak in their sacrificial prayers of a female deity, the " Mother of heaven," regarded as the guardian-spirit of child-birth and as such later merged into the Virgin Mary. This " Mother of heaven," pictured in folk-tales at times as the wife of the Heaven god, and met with also among the Turco-Tatars, originates from pagan times.[8]

In sacrificing to the Heaven god, the peoples by the Volga and the Ob follow similar customs, previously common also to the surrounding peoples, of keeping the faces, both of the sacrificing priests and the sacrificial animal, turned in the direction of the rising sun, contrary to the custom in the worship of the dead of turning in the opposite direction; the Cheremiss and the Votiaks having also different expressions for the two ceremonies, i.e., " sacrificing upward " and " sacrificing downward." The sacrifice to the Heaven god must, as far as possible, consist of a white animal. Where this is not possible, the Ostiaks place a white cloth over the animal's back. A feature of note is also that the sacrificial-tree of the Heaven god, must, as with other Nature gods, be a leaf or " white " tree, those of the dead being invariably coniferous, or " dark " trees.[9] Most often burnt offerings are offered up to the Heaven god, but there are traces of other methods having been used. As the smoke from the sacrifice could not reach the sky from the plains, the sacrifice was performed on a hill or other high place. In the oldest accounts of the Samoyed re-

PLATE XXVI

Old Sacrificial Grotto of the Thunder-
God Among the Finnish Lapps

(See pages 230–1.)
After photograph by T. I. Itkonen.

ligion it is stated that the Yuraks offered up white reindeer
to Num on the highest mountains.   When the animal was
slaughtered, it was held, as during the rest of the ceremony,
with its head turned to the east.   The flesh was eaten uncooked.
The skull, together with all other bones, was left on the place
of sacrifice; the first-named being generally stuck on a pole
with its nose towards the east.[10]

In looking at the night sky, the attention of people was
drawn to a certain fixed point, round which the heavens, as
seen from the earth, seemed to revolve.   This regular motion
of the sky, which we know to be due to the movement of the
earth round its axis in the opposite direction, awakened among
primitive peoples the idea that the sky at this point, i.e., at the
North Star, is affixed to some object bearing or supporting the
heavens.   For this reason, the Samoyeds (Turuhansk District)
call the North Star the " nail of the sky," " round which the
heavens revolve." [11]   The ancient Finns had also a corresponding but now forgotten term, as proved by the name of the
North Star, borrowed by the Lapps from the Finns, Bohi-
navlle (" the nail of the north "); its counterpart among the
Esthonians being the Põhjanael.   The connection of these
beliefs with the sky is described by Holzmayer in the following words: " In the middle of the sky, or in the north, the
heavens are affixed to a nail in such a manner that they are
able to revolve round the nail, the revolving causing the
movement of the stars.   As the North Star is situated in the
very centre, it is called the ' nail of the north.' " [12]   This nail
is, at the same time, regarded as supporting the sky.   Turi
relates that the Lapps believe the Boahje-naste (" north
nail," " north star ") to support the sky, and that when Arc-
turus, supposed to be an archer, shoots down the Boahje-naste
with his arrow on the last day, the heavens will fall, crushing
the earth and setting fire to everything.[13]

The Lapps believed also, however, in a more reliable support for the sky than a nail.   Missionaries relate that the

Lapps sacrificed to their highest god Veralden rade (" Ruler of the world ") so that " he should not let fall the sky," erecting at the altars a tree either split in two or forked naturally, or also, at times, a high pillar, called the " pillar of the world " (Veralden tshuold) for the god to "support the world with, and keep it in its present form and condition, that it might not grow old and fall from its former nature." The tree was besmeared with blood from the sacrifice.[14]   A "pillar of the world" of this description was seen by Leem in the vicinity of the Porsanger Fjord at an old site of sacrifice, where there were two great stones and, on their eastern side, a very high square log with its lower end stuck in the ground. In the top of the log there was an iron nail.[15] That these pillars of the Lapps had a heavenly counterpart is shown by the fact that in some places, the name of the North Star is " pillar of the world " (Veralden tshuold).[16] It is probable that the Lapps obtained both their ideas and their sacrificial customs from the Scandinavians (Cf. Teutonic Irminsûl, " world-pillar "); the " nail " may be compared with the Scandinavian Veraldar nagli, the " world-nail." [17] The corresponding belief of the ancient Finns is found nowadays only in the phrase, known also to the Esthonians, and used of people living to a very old age, that these live " to be a pillar of the world " (Finnish Maailmanpatsas or Maasampa, Esthonian Ilmasamba). The Ostiaks, amongst whom this " pillar " was also known, and who even worshipped it as a deity, have, as we shall see, in this respect been under Turco-Tatar influence.[18]

Like the sky itself, the heavenly bodies and certain phenomena in the air were regarded as animated beings, although not all of them were the objects of worship. In Ostiak poetry " the Sun mother " and the " Moon old man " are often mentioned, but sacrifices to them are rare; only at Vasyugan was a piece of cloth with a ring attached offered up to the sun, when the latter had caused a sudden fainting fit.[19]

Among the Samoyeds, only the Yuraks, according to Lehtisalo, worship the sun, " the kindly eye of the heavens," and the moon, " the evil eye of the heavens," to which they even sacrifice at the New Year's Festival in July, " when the wild geese arrive again." A " shadow " (image) is made of them, similar in form to these bodies. Besmeared with the blood of the sacrifice, these images are set up on long poles.[20]

Much more general is the worship of the sun and the moon amongst the agricultural peoples. The Cheremiss and the Votiaks sacrifice white animals to the sun (" the Sun mother "), both at annually recurring ceremonies, and also for occasional reasons, e.g., when a long drought dries up the grass and ruins the harvest, or for certain sicknesses. During the prayers, the priest keeps his face towards the sun.[21] Why the Eastern Cheremiss should sacrifice animals to the moon (" the Moon mother ") is uncertain.[22] A very important part is also played by " the rising and setting Sun god " and " the wandering Moon god " in the religion of the Mordvins. In honour of the former, public sacrificial festivals were held, but the Mordvins worshipped it at other times also, bowing whenever a ray of sunlight fell on the window. Sacrifices to the sun were set up in high places, so that the sun on rising could take possession of them. The Mordvins also took oath before the sun.[23] Of sun-worship by the Finns, there are no reliable accounts. The custom of the East Karelians of going at dawn to the eastward slopes of their fields, to a " purified place," where they bowed three times, saying: " My dear sun, my provider, give peace, health, look over everything, watch over everything," may, however, be mentioned.[24] The new moon was also accorded a welcome by many Finno-Ugric peoples. The Mordvins say, like the Russians: " Be greeted, new moon; to me health, to thee a whole loaf." The silver and golden horns of the Moon god are also spoken of.[25] According to Agricola, the Finns believed that at eclipses, the

" animals " (*kapeet*) " ate up the moon," and lunar markings were explained by saying that Rahkoi " makes the moon black in parts." In Northern Finland " the man in the moon " is called Rahkonen.

More apparent is the worship of sun and moon among the Scandinavian Lapps, on whose magic drums they are often pictured. When the Lapps sacrificed to the sun they made a wooden image, one end of which they formed like a globe and furnished with thorns, or they used only a large, wooden ring decorated with figures; these objects were besmeared with the blood of the sacrifice. The animals offered up to the " Sun virgin," were always female, and where possible, white. At the very least, a white thread had to be sewn through the right ear of the sacrificial reindeer. When the sacrifice had been killed, the Lapps cut a piece from all its quarters, threading them on to a switch bent into a ring. This object they then hung up on a high sacrificial-board behind the tent. The Lapps also sacrificed to the sun by taking three switches of birch, plaiting them together up to about half-way, where they bound a tape. These switches they besmeared with blood from the sacrifice. Afterwards a ring was made of a birch-bough and laid in the middle of the board as an image of the sun, and inside this a small piece of the lungs, heart, tongue and lips of the sacrifice. On the ring they set up the blood-smeared switches. The bones of the sacrifice were also often placed within a ring on the offering-board.[26]

Like the Norwegian peasants, the Lapps living in Norway had a custom of besmearing their doors with butter when the sun, after the darkness of winter, first threw its rays on them from the horizon.[27] Another annual sacrifice was performed at the lightest period of the summer. On Midsummer's Eve the Norwegian Lapps hung up a ring of leaves or grass, called the " sun-ring," in honour of the " Sun virgin." A porridge of meal, mixed with butter, " sun-porridge," was also cooked and eaten. On beginning this sacrificial meal,

PLATE XXVII

DRAWINGS ON A LAPP DRUM ACCORDING TO RANDULF'S DESCRIPTION

1. The Thunder-god, Hora-galles. 2. "Man of the world." 3. Wind-old-man. 4. The shaman of the heaven. 5. Rutu, disease-god. 6–7. Sacrificial animals. 8. The bear of the heaven. 9. Two lines separating heaven from earth. 10–12. The festival men. 13. The sun. 14. The Christian's road with church, house, cow and goat. 15. Sacrificial horse. 16. The shaman of the underworld. 17. Underworld with a church and a house. 18. Juksakka. 19. Sarakka. 20. Madderakka. 21. Sea with fish. 22. Lapp village. 23. Leibolmai. 24. The bear. (See page 230.)

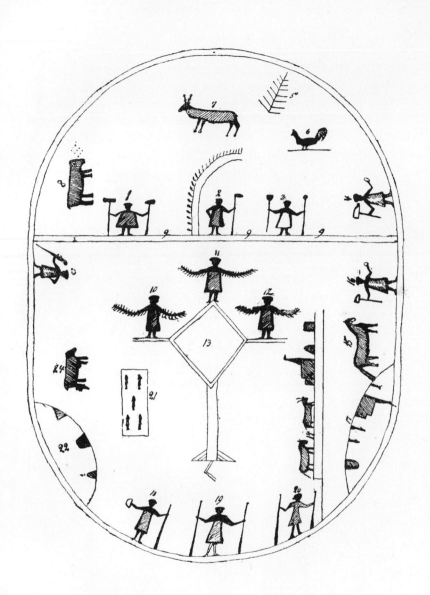

eaten by the men together with their wives, the Lapps bowed their knees and prayed the sun to " pour its merciful rays over the reindeer, and everything else they needed to live on." After the meal, they did the same, praying for " a merry milking-summer and good luck for the reindeer herds." [28] Besides reindeer, sheep and goats could be used for sun-sacrifices. At times even a spinning-wheel and flax were set up on the altar to the Sun goddess.[29]

Magic acts were also at times connected with the prayers. Missionaries relate that Lapps who had gone astray during the day among the mountains, would go on their knees and call to the sun not to set, using at the same time a wooden object with a handle, in which a round hole had been cut. This object they held up in their hands against the sun, so that it might shine through it.[30]

FIG. 6.
SUN RING

Without doubt, much in the sun-worship of the Lapps may be referred to the corresponding customs of their Scandinavian neighbours. Thus, for example, the " sun-porridge " and the spinning-wheel and the flax are certain proofs of foreign influence.

The Lapps turned to the moon as well as to the sun with worship. The Christmas new moon, in especial, called " the holy moon," was worshipped with separate ceremonies. Immediately the new moon had risen, complete silence was observed in the Lapp home, the women being forbidden to spin, the men to perform any noisy labour. As an offering to the moon a ring of copper was placed in the roof-hole of the tent so that the moon could shine through this into the tent. If for any reason this old custom was broken, it was believed that the moon became angry, and had then to be placated by sacrifices.[31] In some districts it was the custom to sacrifice a half-year-old reindeer calf, the hide of which was hung up in the tent in honour of the moon. Of the reasons for this worship, an unknown author writes the following: " The Lapps hang up a ring of copper tied to a copper chain in the roofs of their tents before the door, in such a manner that the rays of the moon can fall on the ring of copper; believing, i.e., that the moon can help the reindeer-cows to give birth easily to calves and also protect them from all injuries during the time they are with calf." [32]

Besides the Christmas new moon, the Scandinavian Lapps formerly worshipped with special ceremonies the February-moon also, which they called Kuova-manno. Högström relates how he heard from an old Lapp woman in Swedish Lapmark that in earlier days it had been the custom at a certain time in February (probably the time of the new moon) to bind hay, used by the Lapps in their foot-wear and mittens, to the horns of the reindeer. The Kuova-manno was then adjured with alarm and din to eat. [33] Certain marks of honour have also in other districts in the northern lands fallen to the first two months in the year, e.g., in Iceland the first (*thorri*) and the second (*goa*, Lapp *kuova*) new moons were worshipped. [34]

These, the coldest months of the year, are also mentioned in a Finnish tale, in which January is called Iso tammi ("the great oak") and February Pikku tammi ("the little oak"), the latter saying to the former: "If I were in thy place I would freeze the foal in its mother's womb, the hands of the housewife to the dough, and the feet of the swine to the ground, but though I freeze in the night, water runs from my eye during the day." A similar myth seems to have existed among the Teutons. In one of their proverbs "the little Horn" (das kleine Horn = February) says to the "great" (das grosse Horn = January): "hätt ich die Macht wie du, liess ich erfrieren das Kalb in der Kuh." [35]

When the Scandinavian Lapps sacrificed to the moon, they acted in the same manner as when sacrificing to the sun; the sacrificial animals were also similar, never black and never males. The magic act mentioned earlier, appeared also in

their moon-cult, the wooden object, however, being furnished
with a smaller hole for the moon to shine through, for the
purpose of preventing the moon from withdrawing
its light during the long, dark winter-time.[36]

Among the Baltic Finns and the Lapps, the
Thunder god had waxed more and more powerful, until at the close of the pagan period in Finland he had pushed aside even the Heaven god;
this development has, however, in the light of
comparative research, taken place under foreign
influences.

Fig. 7.
Moon Ring

Like the North Siberian peoples in general, the Samoyeds
regard the Thunderer as a great bird, in the company of which
the soul of the shaman can travel over sea and water. Sacrifices to this Thunder bird have not been noted, excepting
among the Yuraks, who sacrifice to it during the before-men-
tioned New Year's Festival at about the time of the first
thunderstorms, making then out of birch-wood, a goose-like image of the Thunder god.[37] In some districts the Ostiaks also
believe the Thunderer to be a " black, loudly-screaming bird,"
but call it also " the winged old man," to the honour of whom,
in the more southern districts, they devour " thunder-por-
ridge," when the first thunder is heard, bowing in the direction
in which the thunder travelled.[38] We know also the Siryans
to have greeted the first thunder of the Spring.[39] The Votiaks call thunder " the Thunder mother," but have no definite
idea of its form. In their sacred groves, they sacrifice horses,
as the Cheremiss do, in order that the Thunderer may spare
their fields from hail and give fruitful rains. The last-named
speak of two separate beings: the " Lightning god " and the
" Thunder god "; a common sacrifice is, however, made to
them. The so-called " summer lightning " they believe to
ripen the crops. A magic means of stilling a thunderstorm is
used by the Eastern Cheremiss, who, during the storm, throw
an axe into the yard, sacrificing at the same time the wool of

a white sheep in the fire, and praying that the thunder should pass by.[40]

The Mordvins have a Thunder god with anthropomorphic characteristics. The Moksha call him, like the phenomenon itself, At'am (a derivative of *at'a*, " grandfather," " old man "), the rainbow At'amjonks (*jonks*, " bow," " crossbow "). The Erza, who worshipped thunder in the communal sacrificial feasts, and at oaks or other trees struck by lightning, call the Thunderer Pur'gine, a word derived from the Lithuanian Perkunas.[41] Probably through the Letts this word has travelled also to the Esthonians, who called the thunderbolt, according to an old lexicon of the year 1660, *perckun nohl*. Together with the old name of the Scandinavian Thunder god Fjorgynn, the Finnish Perkele (" devil ") comes from the same root. The Esthonians' *kou, kouk* (" thunder ") must be regarded as cognate with the Lithuanian *kaukas* (" ghost ") and *kauk-spennis* (" thunderbolt "). The Norse Thor has been recognized in the battle-cry of the Esthonians about 1200 A.D.: " Tar abitha! " (" Tar help! ") and in the name Tuuri, which appears in a Karelian magic song. It is uncertain whether Turisas (? " father Tur "), who, according to Agricola, " conferred victory in war," is also the same god.

Like all the other peoples dwelling around, the Esthonians (Äi, " old man "; Äiä-hoog, " thunder-shower "; Äikene, " the little old man," " thunder ") and the Finns (Isänen, " the little father "; Ukko, Ukkonen, " grandfather," " thunder ") have regarded the Thunderer as an old man. Descriptive names are the Finnish Pitkäinen, Pitkämöinen (from *pitkä*, " long "), the Esthonian Pitkne, Piker, etc.[42]

The cult of the Thunder god played so important a part in the life of the Finns, that we find Agricola describing it as follows: " Ukko's goblet was drunk at the sowing of the spring seed; Ukko's chest was also brought, and then maid and wife drank to excess, and, moreover, many shameful things were done there, as was both heard and seen." This god was wor-

PLATE XXVIII

Drawings on a Torne-Lapp Drum

1. Ilmaris. 2. Diermes. 3. Reindeer. 4. The sun. 5. The son of God. 6. God-Father. 7. The cathedral. 8. The angel. 9. St. Anne. 10. St. Mary. 11–13. The lords of Christmas. 14. The moon. 15–17. Peasants go to church. 18. The church. 19. The wife of devil. 20. Disease-devil. 21. The loose-going devil. 22. The fire of hell. 23. The tar-kettle of hell. 24. The grave. 25. The devil in chains. (See page 232.)

shipped because it " brought thunder showers and the year's harvest." Dating from Agricola's time (c. 1550) is a petition still preserved, written in Swedish by peasants from the east of Finland, in which the fine for drinking " Thordns gilde " is described. " Ukko's chests " (Ukon vakat) are also mentioned in the report of an ecclesiastical inspection held in 1670. Vestiges of the sacrificial feast connected with the same, described by Agricola, have been noted in quite recent times. The " chests " were made of birch-bark, and sacrifices of food intended for Ukko were placed in them and carried to " Ukko's mountain." For the sacrifice itself the best sheep in the flock was taken and slaughtered on a given day. Its flesh was boiled and portions of the meat, together with other victuals, were put into the chests, and along with a large quantity of beer and spirits, taken to the holy mountain, where they were left untouched until the next day. Ukko was supposed to eat his share during the night, and in the morning what remained of the victuals was eaten by the worshippers, part of the liquors, however, being poured on to the ground to ensure a summer free from drought.[43] These festivals have been held in Finland very nearly to our time. The most detailed accounts come from Ingria, where the Ukko festival was held on the days of St. Peter and St. Elias (twenty-ninth June, twentieth July, old style). Sacrificial beer was poured on to the ground to Ukko to invoke fruit-giving rains, or the ground was sprinkled with water with magic ceremonies.[44] Sacrifices of bulls are reported from Esthonia in an account of the year 1644, which contains the following prayer: " Piker, we, praying, give a bull, two-horned, four-footed, for the sake of the ploughing and the sowing: stalks of brass, ears of gold. Push elsewhere the black clouds, over the great swamp, the high forest, the wide plain; air of mead, rains of honey to our ploughmen, sowers! Holy Piker, look after our fields: fine straw beneath, fine ears above, fine grain within! " [45]

Agricola mentions also the wife of the Thunder god, Rauni, whose name occurs in a song as Röönikkä, and was also known to the Finnish Lapps as Ravdna. In the same manner as to the Thunder god himself, the Lapps sacrificed reindeer to Ravdna, most often in grottoes in the mountain consecrated to her. Just as, among many peoples, the oak was the favourite tree of the Thunder god, the rowan was Ravdna's favourite, growing in her grottoes.[46] In Finnish folk-poetry also the rowan and its berries are described as being " holy." The name of the Thunder goddess seems originally to have applied to the tree, being, as such, a loan-word, from the Scandinavian (Icelandic *reynir*, Swedish *rönn*).[47]

FIG. 8. LAPP SACRIFICIAL BOARD OF THE THUNDER-GOD
According to Rheen

In the Finnish magic songs the Thunder god, like the Scandinavian Thor, is given a hammer as a weapon. Armed in the same manner was the Tora-galles or Hora-galles ("Thor-man") of the Scandinavian Lapps, who was pictured on the magic drums with one or two hammers in his hand. In their own language, the Lapps called the Thunder god Tiermes, who had a " bow " (*tiermaz-juks*, " rainbow ") and an " arrow " as arms. With either his hammer, or with his bow and arrow, the Thunder god was regarded as driving away evil spirits who everywhere hide themselves at his approach. When the Lapps, to frighten away these beings, invoked thunder, they beat on their drums and shouted. At times, Hora-galles had as assistant a man-servant.[48]

The missionary Rheen describes how the Swedish Lapps sacrificed to the Thunder god: " When the magic drum has indicated that a sacrifice to Thor must be made, the reindeer-bull chosen as a sacrifice is bound fast behind the tent, where the women are not allowed to go. The animal is killed by being stabbed with a knife in its heart. The blood is preserved to be smeared on the image of Thor. As many reindeer as the Lapp sacrifices, so many images of Thor does he set up. The images are prepared out of the stumps of birch trees, the root being made into the head, the trunk into the rest of the body; a hammer is placed in its hand. After the slaughtering of the votive reindeer, the Lapps build up behind their tents an offering-board, about three yards high, setting pretty birch branches around it. These are also strewn on the ground from the tent to the board. On this board the blood-besmeared images of Thor are set up, certain marks resembling crosses being also made on the latter. Behind the images, the horns and skull and the feet are set up. At the same time a small piece of flesh is cut from each quarter and placed in a little wooden case, into which also a little fat is poured, on the dais before the image. In the right ear of the reindeer chosen for sacrifice to Thor, a grey woollen thread must be sewn as a mark." [49]

At times the Lapps offered up, besides reindeer, large wooden hammers to the Thunder god. Forbus says that a hammer, two fathoms long and beautifully carved, was made in his honour and smeared with blood from the sacrifice; [50] S. Kildal relates that such hammers were laid in mountain grottoes.[51] The Finnish Lapps regarded clefts in the mountains as suitable places in which to sacrifice to the Thunderer.[52]

The Wind god is called by the Votiaks in their prayers, simply " the Wind." A goose is sacrificed to it in the sown fields at the time of the general field-sacrifices, and it is appealed to not to blow overmuch, spoiling in that way the seed, but to blow mildly over the sown fields. The colour of the votive goose is not particularized, but it is not seemly to sacrifice to the wind anything black or white. In some places it is the practice to sprinkle blood in the air. Occasional sacrifices are also made to the wind, particularly during storms. Besides this cult in the fields for the sake of the seed, it is worshipped at times in the stock-yards, to the intent that the violent autumn storms of the steppes should not destroy the straw-roofed cattle-sheds or do injury to the cattle.[53] For similar purposes, the Cheremiss and the Mordvins sacrifice to the " Mother wind " or " Wind mother." The last-mentioned say: " When the children of Wind mother are noisy, the storm begins." [54]

The Esthonians say that the Wind god dwells in the forest on a shaded branch, whence it sets the wind blowing; according to its dwelling-place, it is called Metsmees (" Forest man "). A more general name is, however, " Wind mother," who " weeps " when the rain falls during a storm, and " dances " in whirlwinds.[55] At the sowing of flax, doves or a cock are sacrificed to the " Wind mother." [56] In Finnish magic prayers the appeal is to the wind itself, though, sometimes, also to the " Wind woman," etc. According to Agricola, Ilmarinen was, later, worshipped as the Wind god, " giving calm and bad weather, and furthering travellers." A figure of Ilmaris, " the ruler of the storm, and of bad weather," has been found also on the magic drum of a Finnish Lapp.[57] Usually, the Lapps called the Wind god the " Wind man," in the cult of whom one can discern Scandinavian influence. The missionary Randulf describes the Wind god

PLATE XXIX

OSTIAK SACRIFICE

(See page 233.)
After photograph by K. F. Karjalainen.

of the Lapps as follows: " Their third great god the Lapps call the ' Wind man,' who is identical with Aeolus. They picture him (on their magic drums) with a spade in his right hand, with which spade he shovels back the wind to blow. This god they call on both when out with their reindeer on the mountains for the stilling of a wind harmful to their herds, and when, while fishing out at sea, a storm arises that places them in danger of their lives. They promise then to lay sacrifices on his altar." [58]

At the sacrifices to the Wind god, a peculiar bundle of twigs, sometimes formed of birch (Finnish *tuulenpesä*, " the nest of wind "), had to be set up at the sacrificial altar, and smeared with blood from the sacrifice. Boats and spades were also offered up to him.[59]

Randulf speaks of a kind of wind-magic, formerly invoked very often by the Lapps: " When they are angered with any-one, they call to the Wind god to blow, binding this appeal by incantations into three bundles. On opening the first of these, a moderate storm arises; with the second, a storm strong enough to make sailing dangerous even for a vessel with a main-sail reefed half-way; but when they open the third, a shipwreck is the inevitable result." This magic means of in-voking wind, reports of which are found as early as the thir-teenth century, and which was used both by the Finns and the Esthonians, is obviously adopted from the Scandinavians.[60]

The wind is personified also among the Ugrians, the Ostiaks calling it the " Wind old man," to whom huntsmen sacrifice at Vasyugan a small piece of white cloth at a birch-tree, to secure good luck for themselves in hunting.[61]

The agricultural peoples sacrifice also to the Frost god. The Votiaks sacrifice a grey lamb or a duck to the " rime-frost," when during the cold spring nights the rime appears on the fields. In some districts, an annual sacrifice is even made at Easter-time.[62] In their prayers, the Cheremiss speak of the " Frost man " and the " Frost woman." But despite these names, they are not regarded as anthropomorphic beings. Some districts call the morning-frost the " Frost man," and the evening-frost the " Frost woman." They sacrifice a grey ram to the " man," and a grey sheep to the " woman." Sacrifices are made to them both annually and also at other times for accidental reasons. The appeal in the prayers is for the frost to refrain from spoiling the seed.[63]

The Mordvins had a custom of placing porridge for the " Frost man " in the smoke-outlet on the Thursday before Easter. The prayer recited on this occasion runs: " For thee have we prepared porridge, protect our spring-sowings! " The Russians had an absolutely identical custom.[64]

There are no reliable accounts of sacrifices to the Frost god among the Baltic Finns, although the frost is personified in the Finnish magic songs. But the most Southern Lapps in Scandinavia worshipped the " Frost man," who is said to be " the god of weather, snow and ice," and to whom they sacrificed, so that " the ice should not harm the reindeer and that the blizzard should cease." [65] The word, recurring in the name, which means " rime-frost in the grass " and is found only in the more southern dialects, points to a connection with the customs of the agricultural peoples.

With the gods of the air, the " Cloud mother " of the Cheremiss should also be reckoned, being remembered at the great sacrificial feasts with a drink-offering, which is poured into the fire. The clouds are living beings, according to the Cheremiss. " If they were not alive, how could they move about and wander whither they will? " they say. " One can call them towards oneself, or beg them to travel away to other neighbourhoods." [66] The " twilight " they worshipped only by not performing any work, or at least any work that causes a din, after sunset, lest the " twilight " should punish them. A similar belief exists among the Volga Tatars.[67]

CHAPTER XIV

FIRE

"FIRE is the friend of man," say the Cheremiss, "it warms the house and cooks the food, but if it has reason to be angered, it jumps from the fireplace and burns up the house and the village." One cause for the fire's anger, is the spitting into it by any person, another the "wounding" of it by any sharp instrument, another the stirring of it with an "unclean" stick. Further, if one throws the wood on to the hearth, or addresses the fire with evil words, it may become vexed. Probably, from the very earliest times, fire was regarded as something pure that cannot endure defilement. The most common punishment to befall the culprit is a kind of skin-disease. The fire must then be appeased by small sacrifices. The Cheremiss use the following words: "Forgive me, 'Fire mother,' perhaps I have spat in thee or wounded or defiled thee. Make me well again." The worst punishment the fire is capable of is the breaking loose of fire. At such times, the Cheremiss go round the fire, sacrificing to the "Fire mother" a black hen, or milk from a black cow. During this, the "Fire mother" is prayed to not to destroy the village, and also in the future to protect the people from loss through its agency.[1]

The Ostiaks call the fire "Fire girl" or "Fire woman" in their prayers, this deity being as easily wounded as the Fire god of the Cheremiss and the other Volga peoples. To appease it, the Ostiaks sacrifice to the fire victuals, cloths of red or a fire-like colour, and pieces of stuff. Despite these sacrifices, intended as clothing for the "Fire girl" or the "Fire mother," it is merely the animated fire itself that is

the object of worship.² The Mordvins say: " the Fire mother
' flames,' " the Ostiaks speak of " the many-tongued Fire
mother," and in a Cheremiss prayer the passage occurs: " Fire
mother, thou whose smoke is long and whose tongue is sharp." ³

The Cheremiss speak also, at times, of the soul (*ört*) of
the fire, which disappears if water is poured over the fire, a
method of putting it out which is regarded as unseemly,
among them the wood being merely drawn to one side so
that the fire goes out of its own accord.⁴ This " soul " of the
fire can appear to men in some shape or other. According to
the Finns, the " Ruler " of the fire appeared in the night as
glittering sparks before some accident. The Esthonians believe that the " Fire mother " appears in the shape of an
animal as a warning of a coming fire; a " Fire cock " or " Fire
cat " has been seen to move over the roof of a house shortly
before a destructive fire.⁵

In the tales of the Ostiaks, the " Fire spirit " can even take
on human form. A man who had used the fire badly, saw
the " Fire girl " sitting naked and covered with wounds on a
stone. According to another tale, every hearth has its own
" Fire maiden "; these can visit one another, tell each other
their experiences and ask advice of one another.⁶ Similar
tales are met with among the Turco-Tatars.

The holiness of the domestic hearth is seen from the custom
of bearing fire, burning brands, or ashes from the old home to
the new. According to an earlier view, the fire should never
be allowed to go out, and even today the Cheremiss light
their sacrificial fires with brands from the hearth. Were the
fire to go out of its own accord, it was deemed an omen of
misfortune. The people seem, however, to have believed
that the power of the fire diminishes, if it is allowed to burn
too long. The Volga Finns had therefore a habit of renewing
their fires once a year by lighting a " new fire," or a " wood
fire," by rubbing two dry sticks against one another. The
" new fire " is supposed to contain a specially purifying magic

power. For this reason, the Cheremiss extinguish all their village hearth fires on an agreed date in the hottest part of the summer, at the close of the " evil time," draw forth a " new fire," and make a fire of logs somewhere on the edge of the village, over which the people have to jump; the cattle, even, are driven through it. To render this last more easy, the site for the fire is chosen at the gateway to some meadow, the gate itself, having for reasons of magic, branches of rowan bound to it. From this log-fire, which generally burns for two or three days, every householder carries home " new fire " to his hearth, smoking out his stockyard at the same time.[7]

For occasional reasons also a similar fire may be made. The Mordvins sometimes lit such fires even at the forty days' feast for the dead, at which those present cleansed themselves by jumping over the fire.[8] A more widespread custom is to use this method of purification during the course of some epidemic in the neighbourhood. At such times a furrow is also ploughed round the village, or a plough carried round it. That also the Spring and Midsummer-Eve bonfires of the Finns originally possessed a prophylactic significance appears from an account from Ingria, according to which the bonfires were intended to be made on the pasture land visited by the cows.[9]

The stocks living along the Volga have further a custom of worshipping fire as an intermediary between the gods and men. Sacrifices thrown into the fire are not always intended for the " Fire mother," but it is intended that she should hand on these offerings to their true recipients. In the sacred groves of the Cheremiss one can hear the priests say to the fire: " Bear with thy smoke our sacrifices to God, and recite to him our prayers! " As a reward, a sacrifice is then given to the fire also.[10] These beliefs and customs are undoubtedly, however, like so much else in the fire cult of the Finno-Ugric peoples, of foreign origin, probably Iranian. A more original custom is that of the Lapps, as described by Randulf: " To none of their idols do the Lapps offer up burnt sacrifices, i.e., they do not destroy their sacrifices by fire, excepting those to the sun, which are burnt up to show the heat and fire of the sun, and are made on a particular stone, consecrated for the purpose." [11]

In their magic songs the Finns describe how mankind came to obtain fire. In some, the origin of fire is said to be from heaven, as appears from the following words: " Where has fire been cradled, where rocked the flame? — Over there on the navel of the sky, on the peak of the famous mountain." Its birth there is also pictured in the following: " Fire struck Ismaroinen (Ilmarinen), fire flashed Väinämöinen, he struck fire without a flint, tinderlesss he secured it, struck it with a black snake, with a mottled serpent, on the open plain of water, on the wide-spread waves." In a variation the Thunderer appears as the giver of fire: " Pitkämöinen struck fire, among the rocks of the sea, from a many coloured serpent." [12] That the serpent here is the lightning is obvious.

In another song it is described how a net is woven to catch a " red salmon " in the bowels of which fire is bound. That this tale is very old is shown by the method of preparing the net as described in the Finnish song: " A net was made of lime-bark, it was woven of heather," or " the net was woven of bast, of juniper threads was it spun." [13] An interesting counterpart to this tale is to be found among certain North American tribes on the North-West coast in which fire is also found in the bowels of a salmon. [14] The colour of the salmon has perhaps, in the fantasy of these people, awakened the idea of connecting it with fire.

CHAPTER XV

DEITIES OF THE EARTH AND VEGETATION

AMONG the non-agricultural Finno-Ugric peoples, offerings to the earth are rare. The Ugrians often mention in their folk-poetry " the black or hairy Earth mother,"
but sacrifice to her only when suffering from certain sicknesses,
believed to come from the earth.[1]   Much more important
is the " Earth mother " among the stocks living along the
Volga; these sacrifice to her black animals, most often cows and
sheep, the bones of which are carefully buried in the earth
" so that the earth shall be able to produce corn and grass."
The blood is also allowed to run into the earth.   Besides
annual sacrifices, additional ones are performed when, for
example, the fields do not grow in spite of rain.   When sacrificing to the earth, the Cheremiss say: " Eat, Earth mother,
and give us corn."[2]   The following prayer has been taken
down among the Votiaks: " O Earth mother, we thank thee
for that thou hast nourished us during the past year, be not
grudging now either with thy gifts, produce corn for us also
during this summer."   These last also pray that the earth
might not be offended, when men are obliged to wound her
with their ploughs.   Very late in the autumn, sacrifices may
not be made to the earth, as then, the Votiaks say: " the earth
sleeps."[3]   Equally primitive is the " Earth mother " of the
Mordvins, who is turned to in the following words: " That
which we sow in thee, allow to come up."[4]   The Mountain
Cheremiss worship also the " Yard mother " and the Mordvins
the " Field mother " and the " Meadow mother."[5]

" Earth-luck or field-luck " can be stolen from another by bearing to one's own field a sod or a little earth from the field of some one more fortunate. When the Siryans do this, they say: " Good luck, follow me, give me a good subsistence." [6] As soon as the Cheremiss sees that his " field-luck " has been stolen, he finds out who has robbed him of this. Should he discover that a field which formerly produced a scanty harvest has improved, he believes he has found the culprit and goes in the dusk to carry the lost " field-luck " back with him in a bark-shoe, saying to it: " Let the corn grow, do not go away if someone tries to steal thee, but remain always in my fields." [7] The Chuvashes " steal earth " with wedding-like ceremonies, choosing even a living " bridegroom " for the Earth mother.[8] This custom would seem to have been known also among the Votiaks.[9] According to Mordvinian folk-lore, these were afraid that even in the hoof of a horse, the " Field mother " might be taken to a strange field.[10]

Coincidently with these material views, the Cheremiss talk also of the " ' soul ' (*ört*) of the earth," which may disappear from the tilled earth, taking the fruitfulness of this away with it.[11] Like the Votiaks, they believe this also of the " field-soul." When this happens, it is essential to discover whither the " field-soul " has gone, and if possible, procure its return. The Votiaks also call the productive power of the field, which can free itself from the latter, the " corn-soul," and they believe that this can, like the soul of a human being, become visible in the shape of a little, grey butterfly.[12]

In the course of the author's sojourn among the Eastern Votiaks, he had the opportunity of hearing how the vanished " soul " of a cornfield is sought after. Besides the actual " seer," six other persons are chosen for this purpose, three youths and three maidens, who, clad in white, ride round the village fields on white horses, to seek the above-mentioned butterfly. Having found this, the whole suite returns well-pleased, singing and playing a song special to this occasion, to the sacrificial site on the edge of the field, where the oldest men in the village have, meanwhile, slaughtered a white sheep as a sacrifice. After the completion of the sacrificial meal, during which the soul-butterfly is kept enclosed in a white cloth, the one whom the butterfly had most obviously neared during the search, receives the " corn-soul " into his care, taking it to his granary for a time, after which the butterfly is again ceremoniously escorted to the cornfield and there set free. After the recovery of the " corn-soul," it is believed that the badly-grown corn will improve.[13]

The " soul " of the corn can easily develop into a separate deity of corn. In the " Corn mother " of the Mordvins, to whom a duck of a yellow, or corn-resembling, colour is sacrificed, there are already noticeable signs of a change into an anthropomorphic goddess. But in no case need one be uncertain as to the origin of this goddess, for though the " Corn mother " appears in a popular lyric as singing songs in the festive attire of a Mordvin woman, she goes on to speak of herself thus: " I was sown in the morning twilight, reaped in the evening twilight, thrown into the granary in order to be brewed into small beer at Easter, and baked into pastries at Christmas." [14]

That the corn-seed as such was worshipped appears from a Votiak custom connected with the feast of the spring seed. After having sowed the first measure of oats in his field, the Votiak farmer fills his measure again, sets it on the ground before him, and, addressing the measure of seed, prays, with a loaf in his hand, for a good harvest. To assist the growth of the crops, magic is also used in this ceremony. Into the first measure, besides the seed, hard-boiled eggs are placed. Whilst sowing, the farmer flings these also into the air, where they are caught amid much competition by young girls. Lucky the one who gathers most in her lap, as this is regarded as a good omen. Should the gatherers of the eggs often trip or fall, it is regarded as a sign that the grain will also bend

over during the summer on account of the heaviness of the ears.
The sowing of eggs in this manner is an old custom common to
all the East European and many other peoples, and one can
discern in it a wish expressed in terms of magic, that the seed
sown should give grain of the size and the agreeable taste of
hen's eggs, a wish often expressed also in prayers.[15]

Other means of magic, for the growth of the corn and the
bringing forth of fruitful rains, are connected also with the
spring seed festival of the Cheremiss. After the offering up
of sacrifices at a " pure spot " in the fields, the people gather
closely together, holding their shirts or their blouses stretched
out before them, while the sacrificing priest sows oats over
them. The one who receives the biggest share of the seed
as his part will reap the biggest harvest in the autumn. It
is, further, customary to sprinkle water over the crowd " in
order to ensure warm and refreshing rains during the
summer." [16]

The Votiaks sacrifice early in the spring " to the honour
of the grass." At a spot where the bare earth first showed
through the melting snow of the past winter, porridge in a
dish is laid on three such places. In these porridge-dishes hay
and a spoon are placed. During the ceremony prayer is made
to Inmar for a good harvest of hay. The Votiaks living in
the Glazov District sacrifice at the same time a white bull, the
tail of which is cleaned of hair and soaked in water until it
becomes tough. It is then taken by one of the young men
who, pressing his chin on his breast, waves it behind him, bellowing meanwhile like a bull. This youth, who is called the
" bull-calf," is offered home-distilled spirits to drink by some
of the surrounding crowd, while others again try to prevent
him from drinking it. The " bull-calf " becomes incensed at
this and charges at the crowd, waving the tail behind him,
pursuing the flying people.[17]

A perfect counterpart to the Russian Polevik (field-spirit)
is the anthropomorphic " Meadow man " of the Votiaks, who

PLATE XXX

is supposed to be of the size of a child, but has the power, like the forest spirit, of becoming longer or shorter according to the length of the grass. For this reason it is difficult to see the spirit. It is said to be clad in a white garment, and to live chiefly in the pastures, where it looks after and protects the animals. The only sacrifice to this spirit is one when the cattle are first let out to pasture, offered up with the words: "Protect the cattle well, follow them nicely to the meadow, do not give them into the power of the beasts of prey."[18]

The Baltic Finns doubtless also, as an agricultural people, worshipped the "Earth mother," who appears in the folklore of both the Finns and the Esthonians. In the Finnish magic songs, the "Field old woman," the "Meadow old woman," and others, are spoken of. That the "Earth mother" received here a black sheep as sacrifice, is indicated by the belief, that, if a field produces too little, the milk of a black sheep must be sacrificed to it.[19] The "Earth bridegroom" mentioned in many poems may be a relic of some ancient ceremony in which the "Earth mother" was honoured with a wedding. At the Ingrian festival of the Thunder god, a song was sung of some deity of vegetation, called Sämpsä or Pellervo (from *pelto*, "field"), in the absence of whom nothing could grow. The "Winter son" was first sent after him, who driving with his wind-horse, caused only disaster, and was, therefore, killed; the "Summer son" finally succeeding in bringing Sämpsä. In Finland this god was represented as being conveyed from an island, sleeping upon a corn-ship, with his mother as his wife. These ideas seem to emanate from the Scandinavian cult of Frey. The name Sämpsä (a Teutonic loan-word, German *Simse* or *Semse*, "bulrush") signifies a species of fodder-grass (*Scirpus sylvaticus*, the wood club-rush), one of the earliest products of the spring, which is gathered for the cattle when the snow melts, and the roots of which are readily eaten by children.[20]

According to Agricola, the Karelians worshipped deities of

the different kinds of grain: Rongoteus who "gave rye";
Pellon Pekko (the "Pekko of the fields") who "furthered
the growth of barley"; Virankannos who "tended the oats";
Egres who "created peas, beans, and turnips, and brought
forth cabbages, flax and hemp"; Köndös who "reclaimed land
and tilled fields." Of these names, the first is to be found in
several old songs, as Runkateivas or Rukotivo, the name being
regarded as a Teutonic loan-word (cf. Icelandic *rugr*, "rye";
tivar, "gods"). Later the Rye god is associated with St.
Stephen (Ruki-tehvana or -tahvana, "rye-Stephen"); in
a magic prayer Rukotivo appears beside St. Stephen as the
"ruler of horses" (cf. Halmstaffan, "straw-Stephen" in the
Christmas customs among the Swedes).[21] Ägräs or Ägröi is
known even today to the people, who call by that name two
turnips growing together. When a double turnip was found,
it had to be carried by itself, on the shoulders, or in a basket
of bark, to the turnip-cellar. On the way, one had to fall
three, or in places, even nine times on one's knees or flat on
to the ground, as though one were tottering under the weight
of some too heavy burden, and each time one had to shout:
"I cannot bear it, holy Ägröi, oh, how heavy it is!" In the
prayers recited at the turnip-cellar, a good turnip year was
asked for.[22]

Originally, Ägröi was not only the deity of turnips, but the
god of twins in general. Ceremonies resembling the above
are also performed by the Votiaks when they find a double
ear of grain in the fields. Gavrilov relates that the custom was
to hang the ear over a stick, round which clean, white linen
was wound, and then bear it by two men to an empty chest
in the granary, the men acting during the journey as though
they bore something heavy. Spectators and passers-by had to
be avoided on the way. If this was done, one became rich
little by little, said the Votiaks.[23]

Pekko, the god of barley, was worshipped by the orthodox
Esthonians under the name of Peko, his image being prepared

in wax and preserved as the common property of the village, in each farm in turn for the duration of a year. The feast of Peko was held in the spring, when vegetation awakes to life. Before Whitsuntide, each worshipper of Peko had to bring corn, from which Peko's host prepared festival-beer. On the eve of Whitsuntide, after sunset, the worshippers gathered, bringing food with them, in a room, in the corner of which Peko stood on a beer-barrel surrounded by burning wax candles. On separate sides of the corner beer-vessels and loaves of bread were spread in rows along the walls. In the front row of the kneeling congregation the host of the feast and his assistants grouped themselves. After all had prayed, each for himself, the host took a little beer in a cup from each vessel, pouring it back again with a prayer of blessing for its owner and his family. Afterwards the congregation ate and drank to the honour of the god. A mutual prayer against hail was finally sung at dawn. The remains of the feast were divided amongst the poor. The wax remaining in the candles was added to Peko's head; the greater the amount of wax gathered there, the more prosperous the summer became.

According to another report the worshippers of Peko gathered together after sunset with their food-knapsacks on their backs at the house of Peko's guardian, who had previously carefully closed all the windows and lit the roof-lamp. The guardian, followed by two men, went to bring in Peko with a sheet in his hand, Peko being kept in the granary. The god was wrapped up in the sheet, brought into the house, and placed under the hanging-lamp. Everyone sat down with his back to Peko and began to eat out of his food-sack. Having finished, all rose up without even then turning towards Peko, and made fast their food-sacks again. They then marched nine times round Peko, singing: " Peko, our god, shepherd our herds, look after our horses, protect also our corn from snow, from hail! " Leaving Peko in the room, they then went on to wrestle. The one receiving the first bruise cried out with a loud voice that blood was shed, on which all hurried to acclaim him as the guardian of Peko for the next year. The image of Peko was taken the same night in the dark to the new guardian's granary.[24]

The name Pekko or Peko is to be traced to the same Scandinavian word from which Beyggvir or Byggvir, the name of Frey's servant, and the Swedish *bjugg* ("barley") are derived.

In North Tavastland in Finland, it was believed that the hop-field also had its own "ruler"; the Esthonians calling it the "Hop king" or the "Hop-field master." This last people still speak of the "Flax mother," preserved in the linen-chest "in order that the linen should flourish well."[25] Counterparts to these deities of particular kinds of plants of the Baltic Finns are met with among the Teutons.

A very general belief amongst the majority of European peoples is that the cornfield is protected by its tutelary spirit, especially during the period of ripening. During the ripening-time of the rye, the Volga Finns say that one may not dig in the earth or go into the rye-fields, and that one must avoid all noisy work and work causing evil smells, such as, for example, the carting of manure or the making of tar. Neither may one dress in startling colours. The most exacting time is noon, when one may, even not talk aloud. As a punishment for unseemly behaviour, hailstorms and thunder, which ruin the crops, are dreaded. The hot "evil time," said to last a couple of weeks, is concluded among the Cheremiss (Kazan Government) by so-called *sürem*-ceremonies, in which occurs an odd custom of blowing long horns of wood made specially for the occasion. These are taken later to a tree, round which one goes in a procession with the horns held in the hand, and where the sacrificing priest with cakes in his right hand and a vessel of beer in his left, recites a prayer. Should one of the horns break during the ceremony, it is regarded as a sign of hail.

The more Northern Cheremiss blow these horns later in the autumn after the conclusion of field-labour, keeping them for the next year in a secret place. During the "dangerous time" one may not blow them. It is further related that the members of a wedding-procession, when escorting the bride to the village of the bridegroom, attempt to steal these horns from her home, believing that they carry with them "corn-luck." [26]

The Mordvins believe that if absolute silence is observed during the flowering of the rye, one can hear from the "corn-mother" what kind of a harvest to expect. One has only to go out in the stillness of the night and listen; should one hear whistling from the field, then a good year may be expected, but if one hears weeping and wailing, it is a sign of a year of famine. [27]

According to the Siryans a female spirit dwells in the rye-fields, called Pölöznitsa (from Russian Poludnitsa, "Mid-day-goddess") and punishes all who in any way harm the rye during the time of flowering. A blue flower (*Centaurea cyanus*) which grows among the corn, is called "Pölöznitsa's eye." [28] The Esthonians speak of the spiteful "Corn virgins" who wander in the fields, and of a "Corn wolf" (also "Pea wolf" and "Bean wolf"), with which they frighten the children. [29] The Finns also represented the corn-spirit in the form of an animal; in Österbotten, they say that the person to cut the last stalk of the crop on the rye-field or oat-field "catches a hare." [30] Among the Esthonians the animated last sheaf goes by the name of "rye-pig." [31]

Like the Teutons and Slavs, the Baltic Finns have retained a habit of preserving the last sheaf of the corn-field, regarding this as a kind of corn-deity. The Finns are said to have placed a sheaf left from the previous autumn on the rafters of the threshing-shed whence it was brought at Christmas-time into the dwelling-house. There the grain was separated from the ears and the straw thrown up to the ceiling, where

part of it remained clinging to the rafters. The spring sow-
ings were begun with the grain obtained in this way; the
straw which adhered to the ceiling being also hidden in the
corn-field.[32] A more widespread custom found also among the
Volga Finns, was to preserve the last sheaf undisturbed till
the next year, in order that the corn should thrive. Among
the Esthonians such a sheaf was called "threshing-shed
father." [33] The Swedes in Finland constructed a human-like
"Christmas old man" (Jul-gubbe) of straw at Christmas-
time, which was then put in the place of honour at the head
of the table and was treated with drink.[34] A corresponding
straw doll was prepared by the Finns on Kekri or Keyri (All
Saints' Day) and was called the "Keyri old man" (Keyri
ukko).[35] At both festivals there was further a custom of
placing straw on the floor of the dwelling-room and of baking
of new flour an especially large cake, sometimes faintly resembling an animal (Esthonian "Christmas pig" or "Christmas bull"); the cake being kept on the table during the
holiday, but afterwards taken to the granary, where it was
preserved among the grain until sowing-time. According to
an older custom this loaf was baked from grain dried in the
open air.[36] Compared with Christmas, the Kekri of the Finns
represents an older festival of new bread and a new year, as
the agricultural peoples, also of Finnish stock, earlier celebrated this festival as the time for the baking of the fruits
of the new harvest (Finnish *vuodenalkajaiset*, "the beginning
of the year"; Votiak, *vil'ar*, "New Year"). A straw doll
is known also among the Esthonians. According to a statement made in 1694 the peasants on Shrove Tuesday evening
made of straw a human-like figure, *metsik*, dressed as a man
or a woman, which was put upon a stick and carried to the
wood, where it was bound on the tip of a bush in order "that
the corn and flax should grow well." The custom was in
some districts connected also with New Year and other times.[37]

The Cheremiss conclude their harvest with a ceremony,

PLATE XXXI

THE "FEEDING" OF THE SICKLE AMONG THE CHEREMISS

(See page 249.)

Water-colour by V. Soldan-Brofeldt.

called " the feeding of the sickle." The people of the farm take bread, cheese, etc., out with them to the field, and kneel down before a few remaining stalks of oats, the master of the house reading a prayer in which a good harvest is prayed for from the gods. After this, the food brought out is tasted, and then all kneel down again. The master of the house now collects all the sickles used in the harvest, piles them up on the unreaped stalks, which he thus presses to the ground and then, beginning at the point, winds them round the sickles down to the root. Finally, by lifting the sickles he pulls out the oat-stalks by the roots, saying meanwhile: " Sickles, the whole summer have you laboured, may the food you now have eaten bring strength to you," or " Sickle, take strength, the whole summer hast thou laboured, take strength. Thy share have we spread out, our share mayest thou not touch! " The master of the house, followed by the family, then takes the sickles, wrapped in oat-straw, to some attic in the house or a barn, whence they are taken out first at the next summer. The last stalks are called " the sickle's share." [38]

It is quite natural that among the more northern peoples, who exist chiefly by hunting and fishing, deities of vegetation are not found. The " grass mother " of the Russian Lapps, seeing that grass is of very little consequence even to the reindeer, who live on moss, is probably of late origin. This may also be true regarding the Rana-neidda (" Rana virgin ") of the Lapps, who lived in heaven and ruled over the mountains which first became green in the spring. When sacrificing to her " in order that the reindeer should get grass in time," a spinning-wheel or a spindle was placed against her altar, both of which were besmeared with sacrificial blood. The spinning-wheel sacrifice, which cannot originally have been a Lapp custom, shows that "the greatest of all goddesses," who besides the grass, called forth also the leaves in the spring, is a Scandinavian goddess (Frigg).[39]

The Norse Frey can be recognised in the Scandinavian

Lapps' Veralden-olmai (" World's man "). The missionary Randulf compares him with Saturn and says that the Lapps " paint him on their magic drums in such a manner that a curved line with many little outspringing thorns is drawn over his head; this symbolizes the fruitfulness of sea, land and cattle. They pray to him to make the earth fruitful with corn, that they might on reasonable terms brew beer and

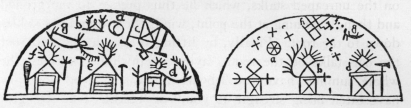

FIG. 9.   DRAWINGS OF HEAVEN ON SHAMAN DRUMS

Left: c and e, Thunder-gods; d, God of Fertility; f, Wind-god.
Right: d and f, Thunder-gods; b, God of Fertility; e, Wind-god.

From Rudbeck's *Atlantica*.

spirits and everything prepared from corn. This is indicated by the hoe which they fit into his hand. At the same time they pray that he would render the sea bounteous in order that they might procure much fish (this is done especially by the Sea Lapps), and that he would make their reindeer fruitful, so that they might bear many calves, and that he would make the moss of the uplands, which is eaten by, their reindeer, grow richly, that they might obtain much reindeer butter, cheese, etc. Altogether they pray to Veralden-olmai or Saturn, for everything that grows or is born." [40]

In the cult of this god of fruitfulness the sexual organs played an important part. Noraeus relates that the Swedish Lapps sacrificed to it on St. Matthew's Day in the following manner: " They gathered together the horns of the reindeer they, had slaughtered, but the bones of one reindeer, from the smallest to the biggest, were extracted and the blood of the same reindeer sprinkled over these bones, which were then buried in the earth; erecting thereafter amongst them an image made of birch-wood, also sprinkled with blood, on the breast of which, under the face, the *membrum genitale* was attached." When the Lapps were asked why they did this, they answered that they were following the ancient habits of their forefathers and sacrificing to the earth, firstly, because the earth kept alive their reindeer; secondly, that it might not send diseases that hurt the feet of the reindeer in summer; and thirdly, that the earth, besides nutrition, would give their reindeer a powerful pairing-lust, sacrificing for this purpose the above-mentioned organ, in order that the number of reindeer might increase greatly, as the time of the feast of St. Matthew was the best pairing-time of the reindeer.[41]

Besides reindeer, in the ear of which a red thread was tied, the Scandinavian Lapps sacrificed also the implements needed in agriculture — hoes and spades, to the " World's man." [42] Even without these customs, one can see from the name of the god that he is none other than the Scandinavian Frey, who is also called " Veraldar god " by Snorri Sturlason.

CHAPTER XVI
DEITIES OF BIRTH

THE DEITIES of birth among the Lapps were Madderakka and her three daughters Sarakka, Juksakka and Uksakka.

Madderakka (*akka*, " old woman ") although called the mother of other deities, seems at least in later times to have been regarded as of less importance than these others. Sidenius says that the Lapps sacrificed to her only " so that she would allow her daughters to serve women." He points out, however, that among some she was believed to help her daughters herself in their duties.[1] Jessen relates that she creates the body of the child,[2] and Randulf tells that she renders both women and cattle fruitful.[3]

On certain magic drums appears also a male counterpart to Madderakka, the so-called Madderatshe (" Madder father "), who is, however, little known and has most probably only later appeared at the side of the female Madderakka.[4]

This latter — the first part of whose name, according to Setälä, corresponds to the Finnish word *mantere* (" the earth ") — lived, according to the Lapps, together with her three daughters, in the earth beneath the Lapp tent. For this reason, sacrifices to them were placed in the ground.[5]

At the birth Sarakka of Saredne (" Sar mother ") seems to have played the most important part. Her name may possibly be derived from the Lapp word *saret* (" to cleave "). Skanke gives Sarakka another significant name, Sadsta-akka, in which the word *sadsta* is said to be identical in meaning with the Lapp word *suorek-muora* (a piece of wood split at one end into two parts).[6] Both names of this deity remind one of a magic method of assisting childbirth and rendering it easier, a method palpably touched on by Forbus when he puts the following question to the Lapps: "Have you not chopped wood in honour of Sarakka in time of birth?"[7]

From the questions by Forbus it is further apparent that these pieces of wood, cleft in honour of Sarakka, were regarded as holy; they were not used as fuel, and were not even allowed to be touched.

Sarakka was worshipped chiefly in childbed. Besides women, she helped also reindeer at the birth of their calves, assuaging their pains. For this reason the Lapps endeavoured to stand well in the favour of the deity. How intimately Sarakka followed the course of the birth-pangs of her wards is seen from the belief of the Lapps that she felt the same agony as the one in childbed. Like Madderakka, Sarakka was also believed to create the body of the infant.[8]

The protection of Sarakka was sought by the Lapp women also during menstruation. According to Forbus the women took off their collars and belts at such times "in honour of Sarakka." This custom is unquestionably derived from the magic belief that during these periods, as also during childbirth, nothing knotted may be worn on the body. During menstruation women were regarded as unclean and were not allowed to move about freely. When the said period was over, a woman would wash her head in water, in a pan which she then scoured with meal and used for the baking of a cake which women only were allowed to eat.[9]

A purification-meal in honour of Sarakka was eaten also after the successful birth of a child. Jessen relates that women in childbed drank "Sarakka's brandy" before deliverance and, together with other women, ate "Sarakka's porridge" after giving birth. In the porridge three sticks were placed; the first one was cleft and had three rings hanging from it, the second was black, and the third white. These were all laid for three days at the door of the tent. If it were found that the black stick had disappeared, it was believed to indicate that either the mother or the child would die. If, on the other hand, the white one was lost, both would live.[10] S. Kildal relates that in some districts a miniature bow and arrow were placed in the porridge so that the child, if a boy, would become a good hunter when grown up.[11] Forbus explains that the weapons were placed in the porridge in three different parts, the shaft, the bow, and the arrow. The accident of lifting out any of these parts with the spoon while eating was fraught with significance. The bow was hung later on the child's cradle; but if the pieces placed in the porridge had unluckily not been fished out in the spoons, they were thrown away. Among the questions written by Forbus is the following: "Have you still the little bow that you had to bear on thy body?"[12]

Just as the cleft stick seems to be connected with the name of Sarakka, the bow placed in the porridge is connected with another name, Juksakka ("Bow old woman"). Of this last-named deity Solander says that she helps women at the production and birth of children. The most important duty of Juksakka was to change the girl-child in the womb to a boy-child.[13] To gain her help in this, sacrifices had to be offered up to her. According to Leem the Lapps sacrificed continually to her because they desired boys rather than girls, as these last were of no use in the chase. Juksakka, who is sometimes pictured on the magic drums with a bow in her hand, seems to have taken care that the Lapp boy became a good hunter.[14]

The third of Madderakka's daughters was Uksakka ("Door woman"), who was believed to live in the ground under the door of the tent. As a watchman at the door she protected people at their goings in or out. At childbirth she received the newcomer on his arrival in the world. Later she watched over the first steps of the child to prevent its falling and hurting itself. The Lapps sacrificed drink to her in the ground at the door of the tent, where she was supposed to dwell.[15]

Jessen adds that a special, consecrated building was erected for Madderakka and Sarakka. On some magic drums Sarakka's tent can be seen.[16] As the Lapps do not customarily erect special dwelling-houses for their deities, there is reason to believe that the so-called "tent of Sarakka" is a relic of the times when a woman in childbirth was not allowed to stay in the common tent, but had a special tent erected for her. Such, for example, is the custom among the Samoyeds and Ostiaks even today.

When the Lapps sacrificed to the deities of birth, they did this in a manner differing from the ordinary sacrifices. Olsen tells us that the Lapp mother, when convinced that she was with child, secured beforehand a little dog, which she kept by her until the time of giving birth had come. A little while before lying down for the approaching birth this dog had to be sacrificed "in order that God might help her and everything go well, and that both she and the child would preserve their lives and health, and live merrily and well afterwards." [17] After the birth a reindeer or some other domestic animal bought from the neighbouring peasants was sacrificed. Among such animals, goats, calves, sheep, lambs, pigs, cats and cockerels are mentioned.[18] On the head of the sacrificial animal "a linen kerchief or a woman's linen hat" had to be bound.[19] Jessen points out that the sacrificial priest also wore on these occasions a white linen hat, besides the linen apparel usually worn at votive ceremonies in Norwegian Lapland.[20] The dog, together with the other animals, had to be buried alive in the ground, only the cock being shut in in a grotto of stone, where it could live and crow for a time, before dying of hunger.[21] With the exception of the cock, male animals were never sacrificed to the deities of birth.[22] From Randulf's notes it appears that the Lapps also sacrificed spinning-wheels and spindles to them.[23]

Certain customs had also to be observed after the calving of a cow. According to Leem, the "first milk" had to be milked on to the ground. In the purification ceremonies flour was used, being scattered over both the cow and the calf, and flour had to be added also to the milk, before a male person might partake of it.[24] Doubtless, the flour was here of the same significance as at the ceremony for women. The custom here pictured by Leem can only have prevailed among the more Southern Lapps, who had, in places, begun to keep cows.

Many features in the above beliefs and customs show plainly that they cannot have been of Lapp origin, for instance, the special dress of the sacrificial priest, but, above all, the use of flour in so important a degree, points to derivation from an agricultural people. There would seem to be, therefore, good grounds for comparing Sarakka's porridge with the Old-Scandinavic "Norna porridge" (Norna greytur), the first meal eaten after childbirth by the women of the Färö-Islands. Troels Lund shows that among the Scandinavians also it was the custom to place in the porridge for women in childbed, "three sticks," with which the luck of the child was supposed to be intimately connected.[25] The sacrifice of spinning-wheels and animals bought from the neighbouring peasants, and clad with linen kerchiefs, points, too, with certainty to the fact that these customs have been borrowed by the Lapps. On several of the Lapp magic drums the deities of birth are seen pictured as three females, their number corresponding with that of the Scandinavian Norns. It should be observed also that Madderakka's three daughters are known only among the Scandinavian Lapps. One of the daughters, Uksakka, has a counterpart in the Swedish Dörr-Käring ("Door old woman"), who even to our times lives in the beliefs of the people in Västerbotten, as "a light-fearing spirit, dwelling near the door." One had to be careful of her in going out with a lighted candle, as she would blow it out.[26]

More widely known also among the Finnish Lapps, is the mother, Madderakka.[27] She might also find her counterpart in the Swedish Jordegumma (" Old woman of the earth "), which word now means " midwife," but in earlier times may well have been the name of a deity who, dwelling in the earth, assisted at childbirth. Similar changes in the meaning of a term may be observed in the Lapp tongue. At Gellivara the word *sarak* has been noted as meaning also " midwife." [28] It is not, however, necessary in all the Lapp customs connected with birth to see only borrowed beliefs. The Yurak Samoyeds also worship a deity living in the earth and assisting at births, and, like the Lapps, they bury a dog alive to secure her help at the said event.[29]

Among the ancient Finns the deities of birth were called Luonnotar (*luonto*, " nature ") or Synnytär (*synty*, " birth "), and were three in number, corresponding thus with the Scandinavic Norns and the Roman Parcae. In a magic song a man says: " I am created by three Luonnotars." These three deities appear also in the songs on the origin of iron, in which it is described how their milk was allowed by them to run into the earth, one dripping forth black milk, the second white, the third blood-red; the first giving birth to smithy-iron, the second to steel, and the third to refuse iron.[30] Often, the Virgin Mary, who in the Catholic period has played an important part in the beliefs of the people, is also in the magic songs given the name Luonnotar and Luojatar (*Luoja*, " Creator "), and is appealed to in childbirth; the " sweet milk of Mary " is supposed to cure all kinds of sickness. At times she is imagined to have many breasts, like her prototype, the Ephesian Artemis, and is said to have " a hundred horns on her forehead, a thousand nipples to her breast." [31] In magic songs she " spins a blue thread with a blue spindle." It is difficult to distinguish how much in the above beliefs is from an older time, and how much from the Catholic period (" the three Maries "). Both the origin and the name of the

Esthonian Rõugutaja, of which all that is known is that she was believed to help at births, are uncertain.[32]

The Cheremiss and the Votiaks have a custom of sacrificing a white sheep at the birth of a child to the deity of birth, called Kugu shotshen-ava (the " Great birthgiving mother ") by the former, by the latter Kildisin (*kildini*, " procreate," " give birth to "; *in*, " heaven, god "), or Kildisin-mumy, (" Kildisin mother "). According to an account from the eighteenth century, the Votiak women prayed to the goddess, Kaldyni-mumas, for children, and virgins for a happy marriage.[33] Another account from the same period states that this deity was the fructifier of women and animals.[34] Generally, however, the Votiaks speak of special deities of fruitfulness, the Kildisin of the earth, of the corn, and of children, who receive their own special sacrifices. Similarly, the Cheremiss worship the Shotshen of children, animals, corn, bees, etc., as separate deities. In the place of Shotshen (= Hill Cheremiss Shatshektshe), the Turco-Tatar loan-words Puir-sho (" procreator ") and Perke (Kazan Tatar, *bärägät*, " success ") are used with the same meaning.[35]

From the sacrifice of the white sheep, one may conclude that both the Cheremiss and the Votiak deities of birth, who " carried the soul to the child," were deities of Heaven. The word Kildisin means also literally the " procreating Heaven." According to Ryčkov the female Kildisin was the mother or wife of the Heaven god, Inmar. In their folklore mention may also be found of " Inmar mother." [36] The Jumon-ava of the Cheremiss (*jumo*, " Heaven," " Heaven god "; *ava*, " mother," " wife "), to whom female animals were sacrificed in the sacred groves, was worshipped also as the deity of childbirth and marriage.[37] Another heavenly deity was the Nishke-ava (properly, Ine-shki-ava, " the Great birth-giving mother "), probably identical with the little-known Azer-ava (" Mistress ") of the Moksha Mordvins, who was, according to an old account, a " corn-begetter " and " a dweller in the high place, in the upper parts of the atmosphere." [38]

The other deities of fruitfulness were sacrificed to in the same manner as to the " souls " of the things they were supposed to fructify, thus, for example, a black sheep to the " Earth-fructifier," the bones being buried in the earth. The " Cattle-fructifier " was worshipped by the Cheremiss especially when the cows had borne calves; friends and neighbours being invited to a " cow's-milk feast." The host poured water on the oven and prayed that the calf might grow to be the size of the oven. The bystanders were also sprinkled with water with an accompanying prayer that god would let the cow give much milk. At the sacrifice-porridge, which was mixed with butter, the host prayed that the " Cattle-fructifier " would give " as much cattle as there are hairs on the cow, so that one end of the herd might be still on the village-road when the other end had entered the cowsheds." [39]

Other magic ceremonies are also connected with the cult of procreation. As an example of these, the following custom of the Eastern Cheremiss may be described. When the sheep have not increased satisfactorily, a festival is proclaimed, to which boys and girls are invited. As a sacrifice a wild bird is shot, but for lack of this a hen may be used. The host takes the bird and the hostess the implements necessary at the sacrifice, and a journey to the sheepfolds is made, the boys and girls following them, creeping on all fours. The hostess induces the children to keep after her, enticing them like sheep, the movements and voices of which the children seek to imitate. The boys butt at the girls, imitating rams. Arrived at the sheepfold the host makes a fire, round which the so-called sheep crawl baa-ing three times, following the hostess. They then rise, and the bird is cooked and eaten in the sheepfold, the bones being thrown on to the roof of the fold and prayers offered up to the " Sheep-fructifier." The

Cheremiss, from whom the author took down the above account, remarked that is not customary to invite many boys to this ceremony, but chiefly girls, lest too many rams be born in the flock.

A being dwelling in Heaven is also the deity to whom the Ostiaks and the Voguls pray for children, and who gives aid to their wives in childbed. At Vasyugan she is called Puges, " daughter of the Heaven god," and is said to live in the heights in a golden house, in the roof of which hang seven cradles. When she rocks one of these seven times a " soul " is created, but if the cradle should overturn during its movements, a " soul " is born that will not live long. The road to this dwelling goes over seven seas to a mountain consisting of seven stories. In the districts around Surgut, this deity with the seven cradles is called Vagneg-imi (*imi*, " old woman "), said in the old stories to be " the mother of the seven sons of the Heaven god." In her hand she holds a wooden staff, from which hang threads for each person born. When a child is born the goddess makes a knot in one of the threads, the distance between this and the staff indicating the length of the child's life, a matter not to be altered whatever sacrifices are offered up to the deity. The " Kältas mother " of the Northern Ostiaks and the " Kaltes mother " of the Voguls, who protects both the one giving birth and the child, and who is said at a birth to " write down in a golden book," or on a " gold-embroidered seven-forked tree," the fate of the child just born and the length of his life, reminds one, as far as the name is concerned, of the Kildisin of the Votiaks. In folklore, the " Kaltes mother," often furnished with the epithet " the golden," appears as the daughter or wife of the Heaven god Tōrem, and as the mother of his children. Under the name of " Tūrem mother," the Northern Ostiaks also worship their great soul-giving deity.[40]

In certain districts images are made of this deity of childbirth. Possibly an idol of this description, worshipped for

long distances around, has given rise to many exaggerated
tales of the " Golden old woman," mentioned for the first
time in an old Russian Chronicle, and afterwards, often under
the name of Zlota baba, in the older geographical accounts.
In the seventeenth century she is seen pictured, sometimes
with a child in her arms, on many maps, on which she represented the districts round the Northern Ural, little known at
that time.[41]

Of the ceremonies observed by the Ostiaks at the birth of a
child, only the fact that special consideration is attached to
the placenta need be mentioned. We find Pallas already relating that it was laid in a basket of birch-bark, together with
fish and meat, as a sacrifice, and carried to the forests where
it was hung up in a tree. This custom survives today. Karjalainen says that the Ostiaks around Tremyugan call the placenta, in which they believe they can make out human features,
" the nourishing-mother of the child," and, before the birth,
sew a little shirt for it, to which is further attached a kind of
belt and a headdress, the whole being placed together with
the placenta in the above mentioned basket. Before the basket is carried into the forest, fish, meat, and other victuals are
set before it, and the women bow, saying: " Nourishing-
mother of the child, eat! " The food used at this ceremony
may only be eaten by women. At Vasyugan, if the newly-born
is a boy, a little bow with two tiny arrows is tied to the
basket.[42]

Similar beliefs about the placenta were prevalent also among
the Slavs, and are met with even today among many primitive
peoples.

CHAPTER XVII

SACRIFICES TO NATURE GODS AMONG THE VOLGA FINNS

ALTHOUGH sacrifices to Nature gods are not bound to be made at particular holy places, but may be performed anywhere, in the farm-yard, or at a " pure " spot in the fields, generally certain sacred groves are kept also for them. These groves resemble very much the already, described *keremet*-groves, though they are not always fenced in like these last. Among the Cheremiss, who call them *küs-oto* (" sacrifice-grove "), they are often very large in area. As far as possible, groves to the Nature gods consist of leafy trees; the Cheremiss say that the most suitable tree is the lime, though oak and birch will do at a pinch. Sacrifices are made with the face turned to the east, or " upward."

Often, each village has its separate grove, called " the village-grove." In addition, the Volga Finns have had more important groves, in which the villages of a whole district offered up mutual sacrifices. Both the Votiaks and the Cheremiss call a district, bound in this way to sacrifice together, by, a loan-word *mer* (Russian *mir*, " village-community "), but the latter (Urzhum District) also by their own word *tište-kerge* (*tište*, " ownership-mark," *kerge*, " district "), probably from the fact that the villages connected therewith have had a common ownership-mark. From this, one may conclude that the greater sacrifice-district originally consisted of villages and families belonging to the same clan. Even today, one may observe in certain neighbourhoods, that although the villages belonging to one of these sacrifice-areas may be relatively distant from one another, similar usages and customs are ob-

PLATE XXXII

THE SACRIFICE-GROVE (Küs-Oto) AMONG
THE CHEREMISS

(See page 263.)
According to A. Reinholm.

served, while in a much nearer village belonging to another sacrifice-area, widely differing customs are followed. Each *mer* has its special name, often after the village near which the grove is situated. It is possible that these villages were the mother-villages of the clan. Besides its connection with sacrifices, the term *tište-kerge* has also a communal significa-tion among the Cheremiss. During periods of great trouble, war, or famine, several *mer* may, according to the directions of a " seer," assemble to still greater mutual sacrificial feasts, lasting sometimes for a week or two, in some very old grove, where the number of animals sacrificed may rise to a hundred and the sacrificing congregation to a thousand or so. It is obvious, that such great gatherings have great significance politically; even today the often very widely-scattered vil-lages are bound together and prevented from being assimi-lated into the foreign tribes living around them by these gatherings.

In the groves sacred to Nature gods there are no buildings for the preservation of sacrificial offerings or idols. It is probable that these peoples never made images of their Nature gods.

The great festivals in honour of the Nature gods are gen-erally held during the most beautiful time in the summer, before the hay-making, or also after the harvest. Often the *mer*-festivals are not annual like the village-festivals, but are celebrated after the lapse of a longer period, e.g., after three or five years.

When intending to hold a mutual sacrificial festival, the different villages belonging to the area send representatives, i.e., priests, to a meeting, at which the precise day for its celebration is fixed upon, as well as the animals to be sacrificed and the procuring of these. The animals must be of one colour, healthy, and not too old, at the most in their second year. Moreover, they must be " untainted " animals, i.e., animals that have not been used for labour or for procreation.

According to the Cheremiss, not even a goose or duck may be used that has sat on eggs. Should an animal shiver when it is looked at, this is regarded as a good omen. When the sacrificial animal has been decided on, a long, narrow towel is bound round its neck, as a sign that it has been set aside for a sacred purpose. The towel is not taken away until the sacrifice begins, when it is hung up in the sacrifice tree for the period of the ceremony.

Funds for the procuring of the victim are collected from all the farmers belonging to the area, regardless of whether these intend to be present at the festival or no. Although there is no question here of an obligatory tax, but of voluntary gifts, each head of a family deems it his duty to subscribe to the mutual sacrifice, according to his means and present condition. The handling of and accounting for the funds is entrusted to a special functionary, the so-called " cashier." The number of sacrifices depends on the prosperity of the people; the sacrificing priests discuss together and decide which of the gods is to be sacrificed to in each separate case.

In every village there are one or more priests, called among the Cheremiss *kart* (" old man "). In the choice of these *kart*, who keep their positions until their death, or until the weakness of old age, the trustworthiness of the candidate, his knowledge of the sacrificial ceremonies, and his ability to recite prayers are taken into consideration. Often, a former assistant to some *kart*, who has already filled a lower position in the priesthood, is chosen to be the follower of one of these. Where there are several priests, the Cheremiss call the oldest or most capable of these the " great *kart*," the others being " small *kart*." At the sacrifices of several villages, the many priests of the area are, without further choosing, participators in the ceremony, discussing among themselves the order of the same and which god each separate priest shall pray to. When one of these priests, who in the sacred grove stand in line, each under his own sacrifice tree, resigns, the new-comer does not take his place, but instead the neighbour to the one leaving moves up one place in his holy office, followed by those coming after him, so that the newcomer may step into the place at the end of the line. Each priest has the right to choose his own assistant.

To obtain a clear and complete view of the ceremonies at a great festival in honour of the Nature gods among the agricultural Volga Finns, we should follow closely the programme of one of these festivals at any one place. As the old heathen customs have best been preserved among the unbaptized Cheremiss, we shall consider a great *mer*-festival among these (Birsk District, Tsherlak village) at which the author was present in 1913.[1]

On the morning of the festival the functionaries concerned in the same go earlier than the rest of the congregation to the grove. They do not, as yet, step right into the sanctuary, but remain at first in a kind of forepart to the grove itself, where a provisional little tent-like hut has been erected. Here the treasurer accounts for the means collected during the festival. This forepart is chiefly intended for the congregation, who remain here during the holy ceremonies, discussing the news of the day, telling fairy-tales, enjoying refreshments, etc., or drying their garments, washed in the brook in the vicinity of the grove. Into the sanctuary itself no one may go who has not previously bathed in this brook and clothed himself in clean, preferably white, holiday garments. This is a daily duty to each participator in the festival for the whole period of the same. In the forepart may also be seen the sacrificial animals and the sacrificial objects awaiting their turn to be put into use.

In a Cheremiss grove, in which several gods are offered up to, each god has his own " sacrifice tree "; these trees stand in a row a few paces distant from each other. On the extreme east is the tree of "the great Jumo," at which the ceremonies are begun. As the ceremonies at each tree resemble one another closely, we shall follow only the one at the tree of the Heaven god.

Having bathed in the brook, the sacrificing priests bear all the objects needed at the ceremony to the foot of the tree of the Jumo. Every one has his own particular duty, one bringing water from the brook, another chopping down old stumps and gathering fallen branches for fuel. Others prepare from lime-bark sacred objects necessary at the sacrifice, a girdle, a bridle, a peculiar " tassel," etc. At the beginning a fire must be made on the site of former fires. Fire must be brought from the village in a pot, as the Cheremiss believe that one may not light a sacrificial fire with a match. Over the fire-place an erection of young limes is set up, on which in earlier times, as one may judge from the name " cauldron-holder," cauldrons for sacrifice were hung, but in the present time it is generally so weak that it can hardly bear a small pan for porridge; the meat-cauldrons are placed on a foundation of birch-logs. The trunks of both the above-mentioned trees must be laid so that the thick end is towards the sacrifice tree.

The chief priest now digs up the copper coins, buried during the foregoing festival in the ground at the foot of the tree. To the left, before the tree, a candlestick of wood (" silver candlestick ") is stuck into the ground, in which a little yellow candle, formed in the grove, is placed. Although this candle is thin and unpretentious, it is called in the prayers " the great silver candle." To the right of the sacrifice tree, a little round pillar is also stuck into the ground, and a little wooden bowl placed on it. Into this, a drink made of honey is poured, but, judging from the name " resin-bowl," it must formerly have contained resin. Further, against the living " great " sacrifice tree, a " little " one is set up, which is bound to the former with bast; the " little " tree is a young lime chopped off at the root. If the " great " sacrifice tree is an oak or a birch, the " little " tree should also be an oak or a birch.

Before the great sacrificial cauldrons are laid on the fire, porridge is cooked in a smaller vessel, which is then lifted on to the roots of the sacrifice tree, being placed next to the "resin-bowl." In the vessel a small spoon like a shaving of lime-bark is placed, called, despite its unpretentiousness, "the silver spoon." Before all this, white cloths are spread on the ground bestrewed with lime-branches, and on these, in rows, the sacrificial "butter and milk" loaves are placed touching one another. Of the sacrificial bread, baked by the priest himself early in the morning at the village, there must be nine loaves, one "large" and eight "small." In the middle and at the edge these loaves have a mark made by the three finger-tips; the mark on the edge is called the "nose" (*ner*) and the one in the middle "the body" (*kap*). On the "large" loaf there are also lines, those on the sides being called "wings," and those on the opposite end to the "nose" the "(bird's) tail." On this loaf, therefore, a bird is formed. The loaves are placed on the cloth with the "noses" towards the tree, the "large" loaf on the extreme right. Behind the loaves, nine wooden bowls are laid parallel with these. Later, a drink made of honey is poured into them, the drink being prepared for the festival by young maidens. Sometimes the loaves and the bowls are arranged in two rows. Both are dedicated to certain deities: the "large" loaf and the bowl behind it to the "great Jumo," the others to other gods who do not seem to be exactly defined, but vary, even at different festivals in the same grove.

FIG. 10. SACRIFICIAL BREAD

The candle is now lit with a brand from the fire and a young foal is led into the sanctuary. To the right of the fire, about ten paces away from this, a post of birch-wood is driven into the ground and to this the sacrificial horse is bound fast with a bridle made solely of lime-bark (" the silver bridle "). To this ceremony belong also a footsnare of plaited lime-bark with which the forefeet of the sacrifice are bound during the sacrifice.

The first sacred act is the casting of pewter. The *kart* places himself to the left of the fire, holds the blade of an axe vertically over a vessel of water and says: " O bless and protect us, great god, give us health, prosperity and riches! We on our side brought and set up for thee a sacrifice; if thou on thy side wilt accept a horse with shining hair and gleaming mane, with silver tail and silver hoofs, may its head and feet be formed in the cast pewter! " Here the assistant pours the molten metal on the blade of the axe, having heated the former, praying as he did so, in a little iron ladle. With great curiosity, the priest examines the shape formed by the metal as it fell into the water. Should there be nothing in its shape that resembles the sacrifice it is thrown into the fire and a new lot melted; but if there is, this shows, as the Cheremiss believe, that the god is willing to accept the animal. The pewter figure which is called the " picture " or " shadow " of the sacrifice is set for the while on the " large " sacrificial loaf.

The axe is now laid on the ground before the sacrifice tree. The *kart* takes a knife in his right hand and a burning brand in his left, and places himself by the axe with his face towards the tree. Swinging the brand in the air, he speaks now also of the shining sacrificial horse, adding: " With the scent of smoke and the clang of iron, we call thee to our feast, thou merciful! " When he has finished this prayer, he rings three times on the axe with the knife. Thereafter he goes to the horse and touches its forehead and neck three times with the brand, saying: " Accept a good foal, with shining hair and silver tail! "

He then takes the knife and a green lime-branch and stands to the left of the fire, where he whittles a little of the thick

PLATE XXXIII

CHEREMISS SACRIFICIAL LOAVES, BOWLS AND
COINS AT THE FESTIVAL TO NATURE-
GODS

Ufa Government.   (See page 267.)
After photograph by U. Holmberg.

end of the branch, after which he moves over to the sacrifice tree where, with the knife in his right hand and the branch in his left, he recites the following prayer: "O bless and protect us, great god! With a large sacrifice loaf and with a great vessel filled with honey-drink, with a great silver candle, with a great resin-bowl, with a great sacrifice tree, with a great sacrifice girdle, with a great 'tassel' and with a great sacrifice pewter we approach thee. If thou art satisfied with thy people and the priests, let the shaving of lime-wood fall right." As he says this, he shaves off a piece from the branch, the position of which on the ground is then closely examined by the priests together. Should the thicker end be towards the sacrifice tree or to the east, it signifies that the god is kindly disposed and satisfied with the people and the priests; in the opposite case, the sacrificing priest, following the direction of the sun, goes round the fire, placing himself again to the left of it, where he whittles the branch again and, standing before the sacrifice tree, does as before.

Where the first shaving has signified good luck, it is placed in the porridge-pan, to the right of the "silver spoon." As the *kart* whittles the second he pronounces a prayer, the beginning of which is the same as in the foregoing, but finishes with a new wish: "If thou art pleased with the work of our hands (i.e., with the objects needed at the ceremony) let the shaving fall right!" Its position is examined again, and if a lucky omen is now also discovered in it, it is laid beside the other in the porridge-pan. A third shaving must still be whittled. With the help of this the sacrificial foal, which has to shiver when sprinkled with water, is examined to see whether it is acceptable to the god. The prayer accompanying this begins also like the former, but ends with the words: "If thou art satisfied with the shivering horse with shining hair and gleaming mane, with the silver tail and silver hoofs, let the shaving fall right." The third shaving also is laid in the porridge-pan.

The assistant of the sacrificing priest now pours fresh water into a wooden bowl, takes this in his right hand and green lime-branches in his left and goes to the foal, after having encircled the fire in the direction of the sun. The head of this, on which the "silver bridle" has been set, should be turned towards the sacrifice tree. The *kart* himself stands before the tree and prays again: "O bless and protect us, great god! We on our side have brought and set up a sacrificial horse, with shining hair and gleaming mane and silver tail, accept it on thy side with good feeling, and shake from it the touch of human hands!" During the prayer the assistant pours water on the animal's back through the lime-branches, beginning from the head. That the purpose of this is to purify the animal appears from the accompanying prayer. During this ceremony, as during all others, the other participants kneel with bared heads and wait reverently for the shudder which the touch of the water is bound to cause in the animal, and which is regarded as a sign of acceptance of the sacrifice by the god. Should the desired result not be accomplished at the first attempt, it is repeated a second, third, or even more times. Each time the *kart* recites the same prayer before the tree. While waiting for the sign, the reasons why the god will not accept the offering are examined. The assisting priests look to see that the fire is made on exactly the site of former fires, that the erection over the fire is rightly placed, so that the saplings have their thin ends upward, and the horizontal ones their roots towards the sacrifice tree. The positions of the objects on the altar are also looked to. Finally, the bridle is set right on the foal's head. If the candle has gone out, it is lighted anew. The assistants of the officiating priests try their luck at sprinkling, one after another, even attempting to obtain the desired result by sprinkling in the animal's ear. While the *kart* prays, the person from whom the animal was brought, kneels also before the tree. While waiting the result, all present, kneeling, pray half-aloud: " O good, great god, let the sacrifice shake and shiver! " The sprinkling may not, however, be repeated an unlimited number of times, but the animal, after a ninth attempt, is taken out of the grove and a new one procured in its place. When the victim, sometimes at the first attempt, does shiver, all rise from their knees, thanking the god, and the slaughterers begin their work immediately. The animal's feet are bound together with a rope of lime-bark, and it is then thrown over on to its left side; the head must also now be in the direction of the tree. A smaller hole is dug in the ground at the head, and, in order that the blood shall not flow on the ground, is covered with lime-branches. The *kart* now places himself before the tree and says: " We on our side have brought and set up a sacrifice for thee, accept thou it on thy side and let the rising ' soul ' (*tšon*) be a foal with shining hair, etc." Meanwhile the slaughterer cuts the veins of the neck open, with an old-fashioned knife used only at sacrifices, so that the blood streams through the lime-branches into the hole. The first warm drops are taken by the *kart* in a little wooden spoon, after which he goes as before round the fire to the tree and prays: " O good, great god, with fresh blood we turn to thee. Send peace and justice to all peoples living under the sky! " Having said which, he throws the blood up into the tree, goes again to the foal and fills the spoon with blood as this continues to flow out of the wound. This time he steps to the left of the fire and with his face to it says: " Thou, 'Fire-mother,' with fire and steam, with thy sharp tongue carry up the sacrifice to the great god! " At the same time he throws the blood into the fire. Afterwards, the offering-girdle, intended later to be placed round the tree, is drenched with blood; both sides of the girdle are drawn over the wound. The " bridle " and the " footsnare " are taken off and for the time hung up on the post to which the foal had been tied, and the flaying of the foal, in which four men take part, begins. Now also, the head of the victim must be kept towards the tree. The candle at the foot of the tree burns all this time, a new one being used to replace the old one as soon as needed.

Immediately the flaying is begun, the nose or the part containing the lips is cut off as a special sacrifice, and purified by being scorched in the fire. The head, from which the lower jaw has been removed, is similarly scorched. The flesh is cut from the limbs without damaging the bones. Regarding the different parts of the meat, the Cheremiss follow a certain order. The so-called *šüvö*-pieces are placed separately in the cauldron at the cauldron-stand which is nearest to the sacrifice tree. These are the nose, or the parts around the mouth, the tongue, the brain, the throat, the back of the neck, the breastbone, the heart, five ribs from the right and three from the left side, a piece from each hip, the knees of the hind legs, the stomach, liver, kidneys, and the intestines. The remainder is boiled in two cauldrons behind this first. When the flesh has been divided among the cauldrons, the hide is spread on the ground to the right of the sacrificial altar, with the head towards the tree. Spread on the ground, the hide resembles a horse, thrown over on its left side. The parts unfit to eat are placed in the hole with the blood. Later, the contents of this hole are burned up in a fire which is built over it. While the flesh is being cooked, this taking about two or three hours to do, the people remain in the forepart of the grove, to which new people continue to come from the surrounding villages. Only the *kart* with his assistants remains at the sacrificial fire. This is the time to gird round the " little " tree with the sacrificial " girdle," which must be twisted three, five, seven, or nine times (an odd number) round the tree. Between the tree and the girdle a bunch of green twigs is placed and the above-mentioned " tassel " is attached to the same, the pewter figure being made fast to this.

A separate sacrifice must now be made to the " messenger of Jumo." A white sheep is led into the grove and bound

PLATE XXXIV

CHEREMISS SACRIFICIAL PRAYER

Ufa Government. (See page 276.)
After photograph by U. Holmberg.

PLATE XXXIV

CHEREMISS SACRIFICIAL PRAYER

Ufa Government.   (See page 276.)
After photograph by U. Holmberg.

fast to another post. The sacrifice of this is made before the same tree and is performed by the same *kart*. The ceremonies are also the same as with the foal, except for the casting of the pewter, the clinking of the knife against the axe, and the whittling. At the slaughtering the blood is thrown into the tree and fire. For the flesh of the sheep a fourth cauldron is laid further behind on the stand. The skin is stretched out against that of the foal, with the head towards the tree and the legs stretched out to the right. At this time the *kart* pours the honey-drink in the wooden bowls on the altar and cuts out from the loaves the marks made on them by three fingers, leaving them still, however, in their places.

When the sacrifice flesh is at last ready, the *šüvö*-pieces are laid in a row in a special trough. From each piece of flesh a piece is cut out and placed in a round wooden dish, which is then placed at the foot of the tree. The pieces laid in the dish are called *orolek*. In addition, quite small pieces are cut from these parts of the flesh, and laid in two small wooden bowls (*šüvö-korka*) of which one is dedicated to the accepter of the sacrifice, Jumo, and the other to the intermediary, the Fire god. Pieces are cut from the tongue at its root and from its apex, from the head at several different places, such as the upper and lower jaws, the parts round the eyes, and from the gullet. In each of the bowls the loosened pieces of bread are also placed, the *kap*-parts in the first, and the *ner*-parts in the second. A little porridge is also placed in each. Small slices are also cut from the following parts in this order and threaded on to a thin pointed stick of lime-wood: the after-intestine, the right and left hips, the kidneys, the middle of the breast, the heart, the aorta, the back of the neck, the throat, the tongue, the lips, and from the liver. On examining more closely the order of these twelve parts one notices that they stand towards each other pretty much in the same relation as in the body of the animal. This stick with meat-slices, called *šopšar*, the *kart* places in the sacrificial girdle with

these words: " O, bless and protect us, great god! The shining
sacrificial horse, etc., etc. — accept it with good feeling; with
the great *šopšar*-meat we approach thee, give us health, prosperity, riches, and peace! " The flesh remaining in the trough
from the first cauldron, together with the left part of the
" large " loaf and five small ones, is cut up at once to be eaten.

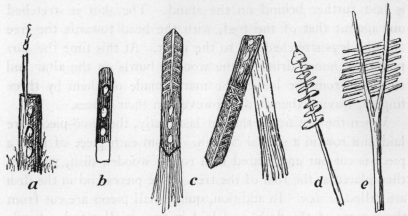

FIG. 11. SACRIFICIAL ACCESSORIES

a, Silver Candlestick. b, Silver Spoon. c, Sacrificial Tassels. d, Šopšar.
e, Šuldeš.

The right-hand part of the " large " loaf and three small ones
are placed in the *orolek*-piece dish. When the sheep's flesh is
ready, pieces are cut from it as in the foregoing and placed
in two *šüvö*-ladles. No flesh-stick is made from them, nor is
orolek-flesh divided from the rest.

The sacrificing priest begins again to recite a prayer, holding
a knife in his right and a burning brand in his left hand, at
the close of the prayer ringing three times with the knife
against the axe, which lies on the ground before him, and
saying: " O bless and protect us, great god! With the large
sacrificial loaf, with the great mead-dish, with the great silver
candle, with the great candlestick, with the great resin-bowl,
with the great sacrificial tree, with the great sacrificial girdle,
with the great ' tassel,' and with the ' great pewter,' we ap-

proach thee; grant to us health, happiness, riches and peace. Give family-happiness in the house, cattle-luck in the stock-yards, grain-luck in the threshing-barn, bee-luck in the hives, money-luck in the money-chest, give all kinds of luck and progress! " After which he throws the brand into the fire and seizing the lime-branch which he had earlier whittled, goes as usual round the fire, whittles a little from the end, and placing himself before the tree, says: " If thou wilt grant family-luck in the house, let the shaving fall right." As he says this, he lets fall a shaving, the position of which is then examined as before. The fifth shaving is whittled to a question regarding cattle-luck. The sixth for the threshing-barn, the seventh for the bee-hives, the eighth for the money-chest; whereafter the *kart* whittles a ninth, saying: " If thou, like the rising morning mist, wilt give all kinds of blessings to us, likewise long life, let the shaving fall right! " These six shavings are also laid by the others in the porridge-pan with the bark upward.

The bough from which the shavings have been pared is taken by the *kart* a third time round the fire, after which he stands to the left of the fire, saying as he stares into the fire: " O great, good god! As the lime-bush in the meadows is glad, grant to us health, happiness, wealth and peace! But to those who regard not god as a god, the Czar as a Czar, a man as a man, and to the one who says he can work evil to others, give not, O god, to him that which he prays for. They who pluck ears of rye (for magical reasons), they who pluck out hairs from the cattle, they who ' cut the heart and liver,' hound them from one end of the world to the other. Health, happiness, give; peace and riches present to all the peoples living under the air! "

Having said this he strikes off with the knife the top of the bough, so that it falls into the fire. Thereafter he splits both branches of the bough, threading on them (see Fig. 11, e) the afore-mentioned shavings in the order in which they were whittled. The object thus obtained, *šuldeš*, is besmeared with the porridge and placed in the girdle next to the meat stick. As he fastens it to the tree, he says: " With the sacrificial porridge, with the great *šuldeš*, we approach thee."

When both the meat and the shavings have been placed in the girdle, the congregation is called into the grove itself. In front of the altar, a great white cloth is spread on the ground, before which four assisting priests place themselves to pray for every person, who, with his sleeve over his hand, brings a sacrifice coin. While praying the priest also keeps the coin on the sleeve drawn over his hand, as the Cheremiss believe the naked hand defiles the coin. In these prayers, in which the donor is always named and kneels behind the priest, the words are as follows: " Good, great god! (then the person's name) comes with a sacrifice coin to the great sacrifice tree to worship, give him health, happiness and wealth, let him live happily in his house with his playful family! Give him family-luck — and all the different lucks up to money-luck — protect the cattle in the pastures from wolves, bears, evil sicknesses, and from the thieves who move in the night. Protect the seed from destructive frosts, from heat that might wither it, from heavy storms, from violent thunder-storms, and from all insects, that he might have bread to give also to the needy. Give all kinds of blessings to him! " As he finishes the prayer, the priest allows the coin to fall from his sleeve to the cloth. Those who have been hindered from coming to the festival send money by others, and prayers are read for them also. When each donor has been prayed for, which, although there are four priests, takes some time, the congregation fall on their knees in parallel rows behind the sacrificing priest. The essential festival-prayer of the day, often lasting half an hour, is now begun, the *kart* praying for all that is good in the eyes of the Cheremiss, chiefly for children in the house, cattle in the yard, but mostly for great stacks in the threshing-barn. Having prayed for all blessings, he prays to the god for

PLATE XXXV

In Government Vyatka the Cheremiss priest prays
to god with accompaniment of a stringed instrument
(küsle).   (See page 277.)
Water-colour by V. Soldan-Brofeldt.

many kinds of protection. Further, he thanks the god for having attended the sacrifices with fortune and accepted the offerings in good feeling. Finally he prays for pardon, should he have said last that which should come first, or *vice versa*. After each prayer the congregation bow their foreheads to the ground. The *kart* then makes a speech to the people, urging them to live in harmony, to avoid quarrels, not to take another's property, also not to lie, not to bear false witness, not to drink too much spirits, etc. The congregation then rises and the elder people go to shake the *kart's* hand in thanks.

Soon the congregation go on their knees again. The *kart* takes Jumo's drinking-bowl and two assistants the *šüvö*-bowls, after which they follow one another, keeping to the right, round the fire, stopping on the left side of the same, where the contents of the bowls are thrown into the fire. The *kart* pours twice from his bowl, the first time to Jumo, the second to the Fire god, to whom also the *šüvö*-bowls are sacrificed. As he sacrifices to Jumo he says: " O great, good god! the great sacrificial drinking-bowl, the great *šüvö*-bowls have we brought. Accept them with good feeling! " To the Fire god he says: " Fire god, thy smoke is high, and thy tongue sharp, take the sacrifice up with the smoke and steam and bear it to the great god! " Immediately afterwards a drink-offering and a *šüvö*-sacrifice is made in the same way to " Jumo's messenger," and the Fire god. From the great meat-trough, an assisting priest takes a piece also to the fire built on the place where the foal was slaughtered, and sheep's flesh to the fire on the place of the sheep's slaughtering. In both cases he turns to the Fire god and prays that the last drop of blood might be burned up, those also that possibly have spattered further.

The *kart* now gives to eight assisting persons (" goblet-bearers ") each his bowl, saying in which god's honour each shall cast the contents into the fire. The " goblet-bearers " pass round the fire in the direction of the sun, stopping to the left of the same. This round is made several times, the sacrificing priest refilling the bowls each time and naming new gods to be remembered. Thus, all the Cheremiss gods and spirits, from the highest to the lowest, obtain their share of this sacrifice. After this drink-sacrifice the bowls are replaced in their former order.

The *kart* now prays alone, with a bowl in his hand, casting three times from it also on to the sacred tree, saying: " Accept our prayer, give justice and peace to all the peoples under the heavens! " Repeating this prayer he throws soup from the trough on to the tree with a ladle. The assisting priest does the same also once.

The congregation then seat themselves on the grass. Two assisting priests go three times in the direction of the sun round the fire, shaking heartily all the sacrificial objects on the trough, the bowls, the dishes, the cloths, the "little" sacrifice tree, the animal's skin, etc., saying: " This is for thee."

It is nearly evening when the sacrificial meal is begun. First, the porridge and the honey-drink are tasted, everyone wishing each other happiness and prosperity. After this the bread and meat in the *šüvö*-dishes are shared out, and lastly the rest of the food, excepting the *orolek*, the people sitting on the ground and eating greedily after nearly a day's fast. All the remains and the bones are gathered together. When the meat from the head has been eaten, the *kart* places the bones in their natural order in the fire. The "little" sacrifice tree with the objects attached to it is also burnt up. More wood is then laid on the fire, and over the crackling flames assistants hold the skin by sticks fastened to the head, the tail and the feet. The *kart* goes round the burning skin with a fire-brand in his left, and a "resin-bowl" in his right, and stands to the left of the fire, saying, as he pours the contents of the bowl into the fire: " Say not, that we burned an empty hide; a great resin-bowl we set up on it." The already, mentioned "silver bridle" is also thrown upon the burning skin. Finally, the "stand" for the resin-bowls is also burnt up. The sheep-skin is not burnt by the Cheremiss, but given to the *kart*, who receives no other honorarium for his services; or it may be sold for the benefit of the sacrifice fund, or sometimes, the former owner of the animal may have reserved the right to it.

Together with the *orolek*-pieces, the candlestick, the other half of the "large" loaf, and three small ones without "noses" are left at the foot of the tree, as sacrifices have still to be made on the following morning. Neither is the fire extinguished with the fall of evening, but allowed to illuminate the grove through the night. Early in the morning, at sunrise, the so-called *orolek*-sacrifice is carried out, in which those who have passed the night in the grove, take part. From the pieces of meat left over to this day, a small piece is cut again into two bowls as on the preceding day. The rest is sliced into a larger dish. From the large half-loaf a piece is also added to each smaller bowl. Besides these a bowl of drink is placed on the cloth before the tree, together with three small loaves, and the coins which were dug up on the day before.

The candle is lit. The *kart* takes a brand in his left and a knife in his right hand, ringing as before three times on the axe, and reminding the god again of the shining sacrifice foal. Having encircled the fire and thrown in the brand, he stands before the tree and reads a prayer nearly as long as that said on the preceding day. After the prayer everyone shakes his hand in thanks. The priest himself now sacrifices the drinking-bowl, and two assistants the meat-bowls as on the day before, the prayers also being the same. The presenting of the sacrificial objects and the eating of the *orolek*-flesh follows, with the former expressions of good wishes. All remains, even the candlestick, are thrown into the fire. The coins dug up (*onapu-oksa*, "the sacrifice tree coins") to which a few copper coins have been added, are hidden again in the earth. While doing this, the *kart* says: " Sacrifice tree, do not say we left thee empty! "

The ceremonies at the other trees are similar, the gods of the sun, thunder, wind, or some other god being the object of worship to be sacrificed to either on the same day or later in the festival. The tokens of honour to the different gods do not end, however, with the sacrifices, but during the whole of the festival, the fires burn before the different trees, as well as those lit quite early, a long prayer being read at them each day. Sometimes the " messenger of Jumo " is not sacrificed to until the close of the festival. Then, from all the priests standing under the sacrifice tree, a peculiar murmur of prayer is heard, the echo of which in the centuries-old grove cannot but awaken reverence.

When the sacrificial fire, after the finish of the festival, is allowed to go out, the priest who has sacrificed at the same, sweeps together the ashes, saying: " Should a man blunder on to thee, may he become happy; if a dog, may he obtain a good weather-sense; if cattle, may they increase greatly." Those who wish, may still go to a specially reserved room in the village, where pancakes are eaten and mead and beer drunk, and the deities, to whom sacrifices have been made, are remembered.

It is only natural that divergences may occur in the different *mer*. This need not, however, depend on the distance between them; among the Western Cheremiss the same customs as were described in the foregoing are followed. As an example of different usages, it may be mentioned that in some places, the " girdle " is bound fast, together with the objects attached to it, to the living sacrifice tree, on which it remains as a pledge until the following festival. The number of shavings inserted in the *šuldeš*-branches also varies (cf. the Scandinavian *blotspån*). While the shavings are being whittled, it is noted in some places which side of them falls upward. Likewise the number of slices of meat and their order on the

PLATE XXXVI

CHEREMISS PRIESTS AT THE FESTIVAL TO
NATURE-GODS

Vyatka Government.   (See page 280.)
After photograph by U. Holmberg.

stick vary. Why the piece of liver should be placed on the
point of the stick, while the others are placed in some kind of
natural order, the Cheremiss could not explain. Could it be
connected with the custom in some places of commencing the
eating of sacrificial flesh with the liver? The most important
incident in all sacrifices among the Volga peoples, as among
the ancient Greeks, was the trial by water of the sacrificial
animal.

CHAPTER XVIII

THE SHAMAN

IN THE earlier beliefs of the Lapps, the shaman (*noidde*) played a part important enough to justify the application of the term "shaman religion." Everywhere, and in everything where the wishes of the spirits had to be consulted, the shaman was a necessary medium. In addition, he filled at times the post of sacrificing priest. His fame was therefore great and his position among the people a leading one. The more powerful shamans possessed titles such as "the ruler of the mountains" or "the king of the mountains." Their fame spread wide among the Lapp villages and their names were preserved from generation to generation.

The high reputation and position of the shaman among the Lapps appear also in an account from the beginning of the eighteenth century, in which it is stated that the shaman, on arriving at the tent of the Lapp, was met by the members of the family who, with heads bared, came out to meet him and thank him for the help he had already given them. He was given a new reindeer-skin to sit on, the best available food and drink were set before him, and when he remained overnight, the best sleeping-place was given up to him. It is further related that the shaman received a tax, paid biannually. Besides this, he received a special reward for each service, its size depending on whether his aid had been requested for the finding of some lost object, for the curing of the sick, or to offer up sacrifice. In addition to money, articles of silver, or clothes, he was also given reindeer. Were he not served and looked after in every way, it was believed he could bring about many kinds of misfortune.[1]

But though the office of shaman brought thus both honour and riches, it was not open to everybody to take up this profession, certain psychic qualities being necessary in its service. The gifts essential for a shaman often ran in the same family, appearing either early in childhood or also after some severe illness.[2] The Arctic peoples would seem to be specially inclined to nervous diseases. The merest trifle scares them, they faint on the slightest provocation or become furious, when they act like maniacs.[3] The shaman uses at times artificial stimulants to assist the coming of a trance. The Lapp shaman-drink was prepared of soda boiled from birch-wood ash, or of seal-fat, or from many other materials. By drinking such liquids it was believed that the shaman could harden his body so that not even the sharpest knife could penetrate it. Neither could fire or water destroy a great shaman. He could even seat himself naked on a glowing fireplace and scatter fire and burning cinders over his body without the least danger.[4]

People with shamanistic talent were believed to be able to converse with the spirits living under the ground, these last appearing also in material form to them, in particular on the occasion of their being first called to the office of shaman. When these spirits, called *noidde-gadse* (" shaman people ") by the Lapps, offered their help to a young shaman, they laid stress on the fact of having served also his father and his forefathers. Should he evince disinclination to accept their services, they would use threats and even force, stories being related in which spirits pressed the persons in questions to such an extent that an early decay and even death resulted. Where the Lapp listened to their call, the spirits were extremely devoted to him, helping him and teaching him the arts of shamanism. This schooling generally took place either on the ground in some lonely place, or the pupil was led to the underworld to imbibe there the wisdom of former shamans. At the first call of the spirits, the missionaries relate that the

Lapp behaved like one mentally afflicted, was unable to bear his wife, his children, or his servants, but forsaking these wandered around in the forests or on the mountains.[5]

The shaman could not, however, keep up his practice for the whole of his life. Generally he became unfit for office in his fiftieth year and was never employed afterwards in any important task. But he might lose his position even earlier, as a body free from any disfigurement was demanded of a shaman as sacrificer, even the losing of a tooth disqualifying him for office.[6]

As soon as a shaman had begun to practise, the spirits began to live more freely in his company. That these were the spirits of the dead is shown by the fact that they lived in the "holy mountains," from which the shaman could at will call them to his service. When travelling in strange districts they formed reliable guides. On hunting or fishing trips they were his trusty protectors, proving their allegiance by giving him rich hauls. Even his property and herds of reindeer were looked after by these willing servants. In addition, the shaman would seem to have possessed a special tutelary genius, as it is said that when about to proceed to a distant market-place, he would send a spirit to see whether the buyer had arrived. After a while this spirit would return and relate the circumstances there. In the same way, when the shaman was away, the spirit would bring news of his family and herds. Coming events were also foretold by it to its owner. This spirit, which procured all manner of news for the shaman, was obviously the shaman's own mobile "soul."[7]

This tutelary spirit the shaman could also use against his enemies. When two shamans quarrelled, e.g., at some fair when both were drunk, they would attempt to show one another which of them owned the more powerful spirit. They sat down opposite one another and began their arts. It was believed that their spirits fought with one another in the guise of reindeer-bulls. The one possessing the strongest "rein-

PLATE XXXVII

1. Lapp shaman's bowl-drum. Front, back and side views.

2. Lapp shaman's sieve-drum. Front, back and side views.

The drum was used as a medium of excitation by the shaman or of invoking a trance, and also for divination. (See page 287.)

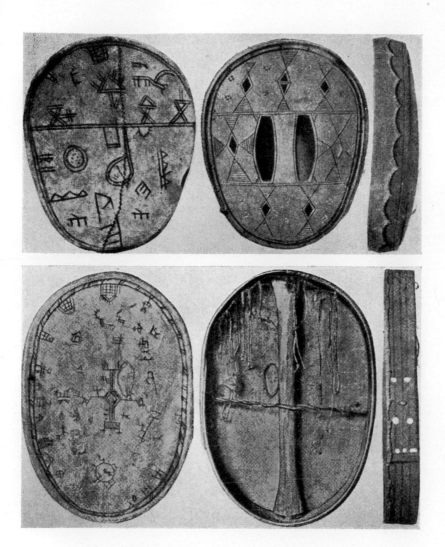

deer-bull " emerged from the contest as the winner. " Shaman-birds " were also used in these contests.[8]

The spirit of the shaman was called *sueje* (originally " shadow ") by the Scandinavian Lapps.[9] The fact that this is supposed to be able to take on the shape of a reindeer, a fish, a bird, or a snake shows that the *sueje*-animal in Northern Lapmark, corresponds with the shaman-animals which, according to the Southern Lapps, assist the shaman when, during a period of unconsciousness, he visits the underworld. Such animals were the " *saivo*-reindeer-bull," the " *saivo*-bird," the " *saivo*-fish " and the " *saivo*-snake." [10] The missionary J. Kildal, who assumes that these animals lived in the holy mountains, points out how they differed from the other inhabitants of the mountain, the shaman possessing several of the latter, but only, one " holy mountain bird," one " holy mountain fish " and one " holy mountain reindeer." [11] Another missionary draws attention to the fact that " the ' *saivo*-fish ' is not one of the gods of the underworld, although its services are called into account when journeying there." [12] One can plainly see that these animals were soul-animals, in the shape of which the shaman's soul moved during its separation from the body. Like a reindeer-bull it hurried over the land, like a bird it flew through the air, like a fish it swam through the water, and like a snake it wriggled into the earth. The same idea is contained in the following account by J. Kildal: " When two shamans send their ' reindeer-bulls ' to fight together, the result is that according as the competing ' reindeer ' win or lose, the shaman owning the same wins or loses; should one ' reindeer ' break off a horn from the other, the shaman owning the injured one becomes ill; should one ' reindeer ' kill another, the shaman, whose ' reindeer ' is killed, dies. In these combats it occurs also, that the shamans owning the ' reindeer ' become as tired and exhausted as their ' reindeer.' " The same author relates also that when the shaman falls into a trance, " he journeyed in his ' *saivo*-fish ' to the underworld, and when

he wakes from his trance, the ' fish ' has brought him back
uninjured to his body again." [13]   Jessen is able further to affirm
that " the louder a shaman can sing, the longer is his snake." [14]
The Finns also relate in their tales how the Lapps fly in the
shape of birds through the air; when one of these is shot
down, the Lapp tumbles to the ground.   These soul-animals
were sometimes pictured on the magic drums.

The power of thus taking on different forms is essential for
the shaman's soul to overcome difficulties particularly in the
underworld, and especially when bringing back the soul of
someone sick, which during the time it moved about without
a body has been carried off to the underworld by the spirits.
These last give back with great reluctance the souls falling
into their power.   The Lapps believed them to know beforehand when the shaman had decided to visit them.   On such
occasions they bolted their doors well, but a clever shaman
could always hit upon some little crevice through which his
soul could creep in.   Often a severe fight was waged between
the inhabitants of the underworld and the shaman, until the
former, against a fixed sacrifice, were willing to compromise.
When the bargain had been concluded, the shaman's soul
brought the soul in question back to its home " over mountains
and valleys, with such speed that the stones and sand flew
about." [15]

The shaman must also go to the underworld when accompanying the soul of some dead person, and when he had to
bring thence the soul of some departed relative, e.g., to herd
the cattle.[16]

Besides taking the form of the above mentioned animals,
believed also by the Samoyeds to be the method of supernatural journeying adopted by their shaman, the Lapps believed that the soul of the shaman could fly in the form of a
whirlwind, relics of a similar belief having also been noted
in Finland.

Of flying in the form of fire, an interesting report comes

from the Norwegian Lapp territory. When two Lapps quarrelled, they sat down on the ground and began to sing that
their *saivo* would send them their " light," which was believed
to be a flame of the Aurora Borealis. When these " lights "
met in the sky, they fought with one another, during which
battle the shamans lay on the ground, practising intensely their
art. A terrible noise and crackling in the sky accompanied
these duels. The one whose " light " gradually, faded, fell
ill; were it totally extinguished, the shaman died.[17] From this
method of flying through the air like a flame, the Finnish
term " Fire-Lapp " is derived.

The most important instrument of the shaman was his drum,
the skin of which during the close of the heathen period was
always furnished with numerous drawings and figures, painted
on with the juice from alder-bark or with reindeer blood.
Often, the heaven with the sun and moon and other gods,
the earth with tents and storehouses, forest and domestic
animals, fishing-waters, etc., and the underworld with its inhabitants were pictured on the drum. The pictures were not
always alike, neither was their order the same on all drums.
In the shape of the drum, not only in regard to size, but also
to construction, dissimilarities may be found. G. Hallström,
who has studied Lapp drums in many museums, classifies them
according to their construction into two chief groups, of which
one may be called sieve-shaped, and the other bowl-shaped.[18]

The sieve-shaped drum, which seems to have been much
more widely used than the bowl-drum, was prepared by
stretching the skin over a band of wood of about the width
of the palm of the hand. The wood had, if possible, to be
without knots, and the ends were bent together and fastened
with wooden plugs or twisted twigs. The form of the sieve-
drum was generally oval, one end being seldom broader than
the other. The handle was a narrow cross-piece of wood
fastened to the back.

The bowl-drum was fashioned out of a hollowed piece of

wood so that this formed a rounded bowl, over the open mouth of which the skin was stretched. Two long, narrow holes were cut in the bottom, leaving a handle between. It was further decorated with carved figures and small holes, which strengthened the sound. The body was oval in shape, of an egg-form. The size of the bowl-drum varied little, as it was always made of one tree, while the sieve-shaped drums were at times extremely large.

The variety of these drums appears also in the pictures on the skin. On the sieve-drum these usually formed a common circle in the midst of which the sun was placed. The latter is generally square, four fine rays reaching out from each corner; only seldom is its shape round. The surface of the bowl-drum is again divided by horizontal lines into two or more parts. Over these lines figures stand in a row, the upper being the Heaven gods. On these drums the sun does not take a dominating position as it does on the sieve-drums. Mixed forms are also to be found.

Further, the drums vary in their ornamentation. The sieve-drum, which resembles the Siberian drums, is, like the latter, often furnished with small metal-wire belts or chains, on which various silver, brass, and iron jingles are hung. These belts and chains are fastened to the back of the drums either to the wooden band or the handle. The ornaments fastened to the bowl-drum are generally the claws of wild animals, the ears or hair of forest animals, etc. Often these decorations are missing, when they are replaced by the figures cut in the handle. This last-named drum would seem to be a Lapp original, and according to our present knowledge, was known chiefly in Lule and Torne Lapmark.

Besides ornaments and bells, a beautifully carved hammer with two branches, made of reindeer-horn and often covered with skin, belonged with the drum, and at least in later times, also a ring or bunch of rings or another metal object called *arpa* (" die ") by the Finnish Lapps.

PLATE XXXVIII

In some places among the Cheremiss the sacrifice girdle is bound fast, together with the objects attached to it, to the living sacrifice tree, on which it remains as a pledge until the following festival. (See page 280.)

According to water-colour by A. Reinholm.

The shaman held his drum in great respect; to prevent it being looked on by anybody, it was often kept in a case of skin in the inner part of the tent. According to the Lapps, the drum was desecrated should a woman touch it. These last were not even allowed to go over a road, along which a drum had been transported, for the next three days. Were a woman to do this, the Lapps believed death or some other misfortune would follow. But, if for some reason or other, a crossing could not be prevented, the woman must sacrifice a ring of brass to the drum. As a matter of precaution, the drum was taken out

FIG. 12.

SHAMAN HAMMER.

through the backdoor and, in removal, it was placed in the last sleigh. Where possible it was taken along roads never travelled before by anybody. Were the sanctity of the drum violated in any way, it was regarded as useless. Were it angered, it was believed to be able to express its dissatisfaction by weeping or threats. The older a drum handed down from one generation to another became, the greater the honour accorded it.[19]

At the close of the heathen period, the magic drum became general in use. As Christians with the Bible, says Friis, so nearly every Lapp family possessed a drum. From the Lapps converted by him, von Westen received over a hundred magic drums. Yet every Lapp who owned a drum was not actually a shaman, but used it for purposes of divination, for his own benefit. Whatever the Lapp was about to engage in, removal, hunting, fishing, or if he desired to know the whereabouts of his reindeer lost in the mountains, or the source of some trouble in his life, or whenever he wished to appease his gods by sacrifice, he turned always to his drum, asking its advice.[20]

When a Lapp thus wished to divine the future in some matter or other, he clad himself as for a feast. He washed, combed his hair, and put on his best clothes. The same was done also by the others taking part in this holy act. The neighbours came in their red and blue jackets, ornamented with rings, gleaming neck-chains, etc. When beginning the act the questioner knelt down on his left knee, holding the drum horizontally in his left hand, and placed the above mentioned ring first on the picture of the sun, beginning then to tap carefully round it with the hammer so that the ring danced gently up and down. At the same time he sang a song. If the ring now moved round in the direction of the sun, it was regarded as a good sign, the opposite foreboding an accident, sickness, or other misfortune. From the figure on which the ring remained for a longer period towards the end, the answer to the question asked of the spirits was decided. On hunting or fishing trips a good haul was assured if the ring paused at the figures of a forest animal or a fishing-water. Where the ring paused at the drawing of a god, it was a sign that this god wished a sacrifice. In asking whether a sacrificial animal was pleasing to a god, a hair from the animal's neck was wound round the ring. Should the ring not pause now at the figure of the god in question, it was believed that the god would not accept the animal. Another was then chosen, and still others, the same procedure being gone through until the ring showed the sacrifice to be pleasing. When the ring moved over to the figures representing the underworld or jumped off the drum, it meant death or some other great misfortune.[21]

The above was not, however, the original purpose of the drum. Certain of the missionaries relate that when the sha-man earlier acted as above, he excited himself by banging violently on the drum with the hammer to such an extent that at last he would fall into a trance. In a description written down in Swedish Lapmark it is stated that when a Lapp wished to know of something happening in a distant neigh-bourhood, he laid the brass ring on the figure of the sun and commenced beating the drum with the forked drumstick. As the ring jumped from one figure to another, backwards and forwards, the shaman sang a peculiar song in which all the other Lapps present, male or female, joined in. The men had, however, to sing louder than the women. In the song, the name of the mountain in which the spirits capable of giving the desired information were supposed to dwell, was repeated every now and then; similarly, the name of the district from which news was desired. As the shaman beat longer on his drum and sang louder and louder, he became more and more excited until the ring paused at one spot, the face of the drummer darkened, and he sank on his knees still increasing the volume of his song, until finally he dropped to the ground like one dead. At this point care had to be taken that no article touched the shaman's unconscious body, as, if this happened, the Lapps believed that the spirit would no longer return to it. The men and women present had to continue singing until the shaman returned to consciousness. He was then reminded of the case in question and the matter concerning which knowledge was required. The shaman was at this time tired out and perspiring, as though he had performed some heavy task, and he now began to relate all he had discovered during his trance.[22]

According to this last description, the Lapps used the drum for two different purposes at the same time, but generally the two uses were kept separate. As an instrument of divination, the drum was used only for unimportant questions, e.g., success on hunting or fishing trips. For these, any male person could make use of his drum, without being an actual shaman. But in the case of serious misfortunes, such as severe sickness, the cause of these was sought in an unconscious condition, in the attaining of which the drum was used as an excitant. Here a real shaman had to be applied to, as he only could visit the spirits dwelling under the earth, from whom sickness and misfortunes in general were supposed to emanate. The cause of an illness was either the desire of some earlier departed person for the company of a relative, or a punishment for some misdemeanour or the omitting of a duty. The collapse of the sick person was due to the stealing of his soul by the underground spirits, or the carrying away of some article in close contact with him, e.g., a shoe, headgear, or a mitten. It was the duty of the shaman to discover what the spirits of the departed required, why they were angry, and by what means they could be appeased, so that the sick would be left in peace.[23]

When, in cases of sickness, the shaman was about to undertake a voyage to the underworld, he called together, according to Leem, his helping spirits, which latter arrived invisible to others. It was necessary that two women should be present in holiday costume, with kerchiefs over their heads but without belts, a man without cap and belt, and a half-grown girl. When all these were assembled, the shaman bared his head, opened his belt and unfastened his shoe-strings, covered his face, and placing his hands by his sides bent his body backward and forward, shouting: " Harness the reindeer! — Push out the boat! " Intoxicated with gin he began thereafter to pluck brands out of the fire with his naked hands, strike himself on the legs with an axe and swing the latter with both hands over his shoulders; then running three times round the assisting females with the axe, he sank unconscious to the floor. In this state, no one might touch him, and he must be watched over so closely that not even a fly could settle on him. The soul was believed to be wandering in the underworld, somewhere in the holy mountains, while the body lay unconscious. The women present whispered together, trying to guess where the spirit at that moment was. Should they hit on the exact place while going through the names of the holy places, the shaman moved either an arm or a leg. At the same time they tried by intensive concentration to follow all that the shaman might hear or see. When the latter at last began to awaken to life and with a weak voice faltered the beginning of the song, the women also raised their voices and joined in. Finally, the shaman declared the cause of the sickness, and the deity to whom sacrifice had to be made, and informed them of the nature of the animal and the place for the sacrifice, guaranteeing that the sick would recover within a certain period.[24]

Leem does not, however, make any mention of the magic drum, whereas Jessen expressly says that the shaman used this instrument as a means of invoking the trance.[25] In this way, the missionary Olsen also describes the Lapp shaman's falling into a trance, or " diving," as they themselves call it. The latter further points out that the shaman had always to have as assistant another person to awaken him out of the trance. This assistant was a woman, where possible, a virgin. The duty of the woman was to seek out the soul of the shaman as it wandered in the interior of the mountains or under the lakes, and lead it back to the body. Should the awakener be incapable of fulfilling this duty, the shaman would never wake again from his trance. Other antagonistic shamans could also lead the shaman's soul astray during its wanderings in the underworld and in this way prevent it from returning. Many shamans are said to have remained on their dangerous journey. It is not therefore surprising that the shaman, on his return to life, praised his awakener with many flattering terms.[26]

Like the Siberian shaman, the Lapp *noidde* used his drum originally only as a medium of excitation. The use of the magic drum as a method of divination is obviously of later origin.

In the oldest accounts of the shamanizing of the Lapps which have been preserved, dating from the thirteenth century, the magic drum is spoken of solely as a means of excitation. In these accounts the wonderful manner of the Lapps of prophesying coming events, of following events in distant places, of finding hidden treasures, of resisting sickness — even, at times, death, are all described. The following in-

cident is related as an example. Certain Norwegian merchants
had once visited the Lapps and were sitting at table when the
hostess was suddenly stricken by illness and died. While the
guests were expressing their fear that some envious shaman
had caused her death, and even the Lapps in their confusion
did not know what to do, a shaman rose, spread out a cloth
under which he placed himself, and began to shamanise.
Soon he lifted up an object like a sieve on which was portrayed
a whale, a reindeer with a sleigh, and a boat with oars, these
being the means used by the shaman's soul in hurrying over
the high snow-clad mountains and the deep seas. Having
sung and danced a long time on the floor, he finally fell down,
becoming black in the face. Foam appeared on his lips, his
stomach burst open, and, with a fearful cry, life left him.
The visitors then turned to another shaman for knowledge
of the fate of the two lying dead. This shaman accomplished
his task with such success that the hostess arose quite whole
and related the fate of the first shaman. When the first
shaman, in the shape of a whale, had hurried over a lake,
an antagonistic shaman had seized the opportunity to lie in
wait for his enemy in the form of a sharp post, with the result
that the belly of the whale was split. This accident had
shown itself on the body of the shaman.[27]

The objects mentioned in the above as being portrayed on
the drum are probably the very earliest pictures on the Lapp
drum, their object being originally, like the pictures on the
Siberian drum, to give wings to the shaman's fantasy by reminding him of the means of locomotion which his soul was
believed to need, and the forms of the animals in whose
shape he was supposed to make the journey to the underworld.
On some of the Lapp drums, these pictures may be seen to
occupy a central position, round which, during the development of the drum as an instrument of divination, later drawings have gradually been grouped.

Shamans, who with the help of magic drums have fallen

PLATE XXXIX

SAMOYED SHAMAN

(See chapter XVIII.)

After photograph by K. Donner.

into trances, have been met with also among the Ugrian peoples. Here also the shaman possesses a special protecting spirit, " head spirit," said to protect him on his journeys to the other world. In tales, the " bear-like spirit " of the shaman is often mentioned, this being doubtless a metamorphosis of his soul. Images of such " soul-animals " are very likely the animal-like objects of wood or metal found in the graves of shamans. The Ostiak shaman, like those of the Samoyeds and of the majority of the Siberian peoples, seems, at least in the more northern districts, to have attired himself for his functions in special apparel, a fact unknown in the very oldest accounts of the Lapp shaman. From the scanty existing accounts of the earlier Ostiak shamans it would seem that they, in general, and even in the matter of their drums, were nearly related to those of the Samoyeds and the other Siberian peoples.[28]

The other Finno-Ugric peoples who possibly possessed shamans at an earlier date have for a long period used more modern methods of prophesying their fate. Not even the earlier accounts contain any mention of the use of magic drums among them. And yet, the author of the " Life of St. Stephen " (d. 1396) mentions that the Siryan magicians could " on that same day, and at the very moment " know " what was happening in a distant neighbourhood, in another town, in the ninth land." [29] Most probably this happened in an ecstatic state. A similar condition is perhaps intended by the phrase in a Russian Chronicle, in which it is related how a Novgorodian visited a Chudic magician in 1071, the latter " lying dumb " while he invoked the spirits to his aid.[30] For the shaman's falling into a trance, the Finns have to this day a special expression (*langeta loveen*, " fall into trance ") which may, however, have been used originally with regard to the Lapp shaman. Further it may be pointed out that the Lapp name *noidde* (" shaman ") occurs also in the Finnish *noita*.

SIBERIAN MYTHOLOGY

BY

UNO HOLMBERG

PH.D.

DOCENT OF THE UNIVERSITY OF FINLAND, HELSINGFORS

INTRODUCTION

MOST dominant among the Siberian peoples is the great Altaic race, the original dwelling-place of which appears to have been in the vicinity of the Altai Mountains, but which at the present time is distributed over an enormous stretch of territory in Central and North Asia, the Near East and Eastern Europe. The languages spoken by these scattered peoples are divided into three large groups: Turco-Tatar, Mongolian, and Mandshu-Tungus.

Besides the Turks proper, or Osmans, the closely related Turkomans to the east of the Caspian Sea and in the Stavropol Government, and the Eastern Turkish tribes in East Turkestan, the Turco-Tatar group comprises further, the Tatars around the Volga, whence pioneers have migrated as far as to Western Siberia, the Tatars in the Crimea and other districts in Russia, the Bashkirs in the central Ural districts, the Nogaiyes in the Crimea and Northern Caucasia and other Tatar tribes up to south of the Caspian Sea, the Kirghis in Russia and Turkestan, the Altai Tatars in the neighbourhood of the Altai, where they form a number of smaller groups with different dialects, — Soyots, Karagass, the Abakan, Cholym, and Baraba Tatars, — the Teleuts, the Lebed Tatars and the Kumandines, and also the Yakuts by the River Lena in North Siberia, and the Chuvash from the bend of the Volga in Russia.

The Mongolians, whose original home was by Lake Baikal, and from whom Mongolia derives its name, have assimilated different Turkish tribes, which have appropriated the Mongolian language. In the course of raids of conquest the Mongolians have also overflowed to other districts, amongst others, extremely liberal in religious matters, tolerating all the different religious sects. His successors, notably Kubilai (1260–1294), whose capital became Pekin, were, however, more inclined towards Buddhism, which seems also to have exercised a great influence over the Mongolians. But with the fall of the Mongol dynasty in China in 1368, Buddhism appears to have gone out of fashion, and paganism blossomed anew, until Buddhism again, in the shape of Lamaism, won over in the seventeenth century fervent disciples among both Mongolians and Kalmucks, the last-named setting up during their war in Thibet the Dalai Lama as their spiritual leader. Eager missionaries arose also in the ranks of the people, and gradually, by fines and other punishments, the pagan sacrifices were overcome. For political reasons, however, many old folk-customs were tolerated by giving them a new meaning. At the present day, the orthodox people abhor their old shamanistic religion, the " Black Religion," which has almost entirely been supplanted by Lamaism, the " Yellow Religion," with Thibetan books of devotion. Since the beginning of the nineteenth century, the Buriats south and east of the Baikal, and a part of the Tungus dwelling there, have also been led to accept the " Yellow Religion." The older Buddhistic culture, which penetrated from China, has left among the Central Asian tribes a number of myths, in which the Buddhist names of the gods appear borrowed from the Sanscrit and not from the Thibetan.

Of the tribes belonging to the Turco-Tatar group, the majority have gradually declared for Islam, which had already in the eighth century penetrated to a Turkish tribe, forcing its way *via* Turan into the Near East. Only the Soyotes in Mongolia and the Uigurs, the latter lapsing little by little into Chinamen, are Buddhists; the Yakuts, part of the Tungus in Trans-Baikal and the Chuvashes, being, like many of the Tatars in the Minusinsk District and on the Volga, members of the Russian Orthodox Church.

PLATE XL

An Old Turkish Image and Memorial
Stone with Inscription in North
Mongolia

(See page 301.)
After photograph by S. Pālsi.

Traces of the religion conformed to at one time by the whole of the Altaic race, shamanism, have adhered to many of the converted tribes, such as the Yakuts, Buriats, part of the Kirghis, etc. In its primitive state, this religion still flourishes among the Tungus and the tribes related to them among the more Northern Yakuts, among the Buriats west of the Baikal, and among a few small Tatar tribes at the Altai.

An important field of investigation is moreover found among all the peoples who, in different ways, have been in close contact with the Altaic race. The peoples, related to the Finns, on the River Ob, the Ostiaks and Voguls, have been at least in their southern districts influenced by the Tatars. The Tungus, again, have transmitted many of their beliefs and customs to the eastern Samoyeds and to some Old Asian tribes, such as, for example, the nearly extinct Yenisei Ostiaks and the Yukagires. Asiatic shamanism exists still among the Chukchee, Koriaks and the Kamchadales. The Kamchadales have, however, to a great part become Russianised in recent times. Among the Tungus tribes by the Amur River, and equally among the East Mongolians, Chinese culture also has in some degree left traces.

Concerning the means of existence of the Altaic races, with which the religious beliefs stand in connection, the tribe most completely adhering to its primitive mode of life is the Tungus. They exist in the great primeval forests by hunting, or wander about with reindeer, riding on the backs of these; on the banks of rivers and on the sea-coasts, fishing is also an important means of existence On the same plane of civilization are also the other North Siberian peoples. The tribes dwelling on the great steppes of Central Asia have from prehistoric times been nomads; part of the Soyots near the Altai are reindeer-nomads. For the majority the horse and the sheep are the domestic animals of most importance. In some districts, chiefly in the south, agriculture has recently been taken up.

The oldest information concerning the Mongolian and

Tatar religions, is found in accounts of travels by certain Europeans, sent out in the thirteenth century to Central Asia. One of these was the Franciscan monk, Johannes de Plano Carpini, sent by Pope Innocent IV to the land of the Mongolians. He journeyed over the Volga as far as to Karakorum on the Orkhon, the capital founded by Ögedei, the son of Jenghiz Khan, in which town he remained over one winter. His experiences he describes in his *Historia Mongolorum*. Another important book of travel of the same period was written by the Franciscan Vilhelm Rubruquis (Ruysbroeck), who travelled in 1253–1255 as the ambassador of the French King, Louis IX, in nearly the same districts as did Carpini. Of the accounts mentioned above, a critical edition appeared in *Recueil de voyages et de mémoires publié par la société de Géographie*, tome IV, Paris, 1839. The well-known traveller, Marco Polo, sojourned also for a longer period among the Mongolians, going out in 1271 as the Pope's ambassador to visit Kubilai-Khan; serving the latter at one time in the capacity of governor, until in 1292 he was accorded permission to return to his native country. His *De regionibus orientalibus*, touching in some degree also on the religion of the Mongolians, has been translated into many languages. A few older fragments of knowledge concerning Mongolian religious beliefs are to be found in certain Chinese, Mohammedan, and Mongolian sources, amongst others, in the Mongolian Chronicle of Ssanang Ssetsen, translated into German by the Academician I. J. Schmidt (*Geschichte der Ost-Mongolen und ihres Fürstenhauses*, 1829).

The oldest reports are, however, so few and insignificant, that it is not possible to build up any clear representation of the ancient religion of the Altaic race by their aid alone. But as the majority of the scattered peoples have retained the old traditions handed down by their ancestors nearly to the present day, even in many cases right on to our time, it has still been possible to gather together an imposing mass of material for

investigation. The foundation of these, at present comparatively large, collections, was already laid in the seventeenth
century, and later, after the Russian migration to Siberia.
Among some of the tribes, notably the Buriats and Yakuts,
native investigators have played an important part in this work.
Some of the northern tribes, in particular the Tungus living in
their inaccessible primeval forests, are, however, up to the
present day, still very little known.

SIBERIAN MYTHOLOGY

CHAPTER I

WORLD PICTURES

THE VARIOUS streams of civilization, coming at different times and from different sources, which have crossed and recrossed Central Asia, have brought with them differing conceptions of the world we live in and the universe. The newest arrivals, usurping as they do the supreme authority, have either altogether brushed aside the old beliefs, or, finding in them some point of contact, have assimilated them. Matters being thus, it is often extremely difficult to decide which features represent older views, and what the original world picture of the Altaic race was like.

To obtain some idea of how primitive peoples form their idea of the world, we will examine the strange, but to them quite natural, conception of the world of the Yenisei Ostiaks. According to their ideas, the world is divided into three parts: Above, the sky; in the middle, the earth peopled by men; below, the kingdom of the dead; but all these parts are united by the "Holy Water," which, beginning in Heaven, flows across the earth to Hades. This water is the great Yenisei River.[1] The Samoyeds also, who have learned to speak of different storeys in the sky, declare the Yenisei River to flow from the lake in the sixth storey of Heaven. In their tales, the Yenisei Ostiaks describe how the shaman rows his boat in Heaven and how he returns along the river at such terrific speed that the wind whistles through him.[2] It may be difficult for us to understand these pictures, but to the Yenisei

Ostiak nothing can be more natural. Do they not know from experience that the earth is slanting, that the rushing river which is the dwelling-place of this fisher tribe comes from " above " and flows " down " into the depths of Hades? The south, like many other North Siberian peoples, they call " that above," the north " that below." The Yenisei is to them the centre of the world, as on its banks or tributaries they place all the peoples known to them, and thus would they draw a map of the world, had they a Ptolemy amongst them.

The peoples living in Central Asia imagine the world some-times as a circular disc, sometimes as a square. In an Altaic tale in which a Lama creates the earth with his staff, the world is said to have been originally circular but later to have altered, so that it is now square.[3] Thus do the Yakuts also imagine the world. In their folk-poetry the four corners of both Heaven and Earth are often mentioned. The winds, for ex-ample, are said to arise in the four corners of the sky.[4] Georgi relates how the Tungus made a picture of the earth which was in the form of a little square of iron plate.[5] This idea, common to many peoples, is closely connected with the four cardinal points. Even in the world pictures of the civilized peoples of Southern Asia it is quite general. In a certain Yakut tale, which speaks of the octagonal earth, the points of the compass have been doubled.[6]

Side by side with this idea of a square world, the idea of a circular one is equally common. It is often pictured as round, and as such it appears also to the eye. Similarly shaped is the sky stretching over the earth. In the hero tales of the Yakuts the outer edge of the earth is said to touch the rim of a hemispherical sky. A certain hero rode out once to the place where earth and sky touched. Simi-larly, in some districts, the Buriats conceive the sky to be shaped like a great overturned cauldron, rising and falling in constant motion. In rising, an opening forms between the sky and the edge of the earth. A hero, who happened at such

PLATE XLI

BOAT-GODS AND BOATS OF THE YENISEI
OSTIAKS

(See page 308.)
After photograph by U. Holmberg.

a time to place his arrow between the edge of the earth and the rim of the sky was enabled thus to penetrate outside the world.[7]

Between Heaven and Hades, the earth peopled by men forms the centre of the universe. Often the earth is called " The Middle Place." Sometimes this " Middle Place " is, in a more confined sense, the country of the people using the term. Mongolia, among other regions, is a world-centre of this description. The Chinese also call their country " the Central Empire." Examples of this belief, born in the beginning from the anthropocentric view of the world peculiar to man, are to be found also among the ancient civilized peoples.

From the fact that Mongolia is a plateau in which numberless rivers flowing in different directions have their sources, the Mongols derive their belief that they live on the peak of a world, imagined to be like a great mound, other peoples living on its sides below them.

In addition to the simplified idea that the world is three-storeyed: Heaven, Earth and Hades, Altaic folk-poetry speaks often of a many-storeyed world. Especially is the sky believed to contain hemispheres, one higher than another; generally three, seven, or nine are spoken of, but sometimes even more. Most common is the conception of a seven-storeyed Heaven, obviously derived from the Babylonian picture of Heaven, in which the sun and the moon and five planets are situated in hemispheres placed one over the other. As the complement to these seven heavens, an equal number of storeys are pictured down below. Where the sky is regarded as nine-storeyed, Hades is also divided into nine gradually descending parts. That a belief of this description has actually sprung from a belief in layers of stars, appears from an Altai Tatar tale, in which the sun and moon are placed in different storeys of the sky. The Moon old man lives in the sixth and the Sun mother in the seventh Heaven.[8] The primitive peoples of Siberia do not, however, know the reasons for this division, neither can they explain the significance of any Heaven. The most northern peoples place in the different storeys of Heaven, landscapes from the earth — mountains, lakes, tundras, snowfields, etc. The Samoyeds relate in their shaman tales that there is a lake in the first storey of Heaven, a flat plain in the second, the third is covered with numerous heights like little volcanoes, the fourth is formed like a roof of little icicles, the sixth contains a great lake, from which springs the Yenisei. Of the remaining storeys, of which there are in some districts altogether nine, they have very little knowledge.[9] The Yakuts believe that in the lower regions of the sky there are also animals, kept by the inhabitant spirits as food.

Although the conception of fixed storeys in the sky, among the primitive peoples of Siberia, bears without doubt the impress of foreign influence, we cannot with any certainty declare that the conception of higher and lower storeys in the sky might not also originate amongst a people living in a state of nature. The Chukchee speak of several Heavens, placed one above the other, so that the floor of the highest is the roof of the next. All these worlds are joined by holes situated under the Polar Star.[10]

Whatever the original idea of the edge of the earth may have been, later the idea became general that the earth is surrounded on all sides by an ocean. This is an essential feature in all the world pictures of the Asiatic peoples. The Greek Oceanos corresponds to it, and in Snorri's *Edda* we read: " The earth is circular in shape and outside it is the deep sea."

But if the flat earth has around and under it the deep, mysterious, primordial ocean, what is it that prevents the earth from sinking into the depths? To this question also, the folk-tales attempt to give an answer.

When the mighty Ülgen, so say the Altaic peoples, created the earth on the waters, he placed under the disc of the earth, in order to support it, three great fish, one in the centre and one at each side. The head of the middle fish is directed towards the north and thus, when it presses its head down, floods occur in the north. Should the fish sink too low, the whole earth will be inundated. A rope is attached to the gills of the fish, the end reaching to Heaven, where it is attached to three posts. In this way, whenever desired, the head of the fish can be lowered or raised. This is the special duty of the Bodhisattva Mandishire. When he takes the rope from the first post, the earth slants towards the north, causing floods there, but were he to slip the rope from the third post, the flood would reach over all the earth.[11]

In certain Buriat districts, one large fish only is mentioned as the supporter of the earth. When for any reason it changes its position, earthquakes occur.[12]

The idea of one or more giant fish as supporters of the earth is general also in East European legends,[13] while in Jewish myths the fish-shaped Leviathan bears the foundations of the earth. This belief, as the name Mandishire (= Manjucri) hints at, has come to Central Asia from India, where a similar belief has prevailed for ages.

Probably with a current of civilization from India through China, tales have reached Central Asia of a world-supporting frog, which animal here takes the place of the unknown turtle. If its " finger " even moves the earth quakes. This belief has spread even to the Tungus beyond the Baikal.[14]

In the tales of the Kirghis, and among the West Siberian, Volga, and Caucasian Tatars, it is related that the world is supported by a great bull. This idea has spread even among the Finnish tribes along the Volga. Under this bull there is often a support on which the bull stands. The Crimean Tatars say that in the world-ocean there is a great fish, and on the fish a bull which carries the earth on its horns.[15] A similar belief is found among the Votiaks of the Jelabuga District.[16] The world-bull is known also to the Votiaks of the Sarapul District, who believe that earthquakes are caused by the bull sometimes starting to move. It is said to be afraid of sunlight, as the light rays kill it.[17] The Kirghis relate that the world-bull stands on a stone arising out of the dense fog on the cosmic ocean.[18] According to the Cheremiss at Ufa, there is a giant crab in the ocean on which stands the bull, supporting the earth on its horns. Earthquakes are believed to occur when the bull shakes its head. The Cheremiss say that on account of the weight of the world, one of the bull's horns is broken and that when the other breaks, the end of the world will come.[19]

It is extremely probable that the idea of this world-supporting bull has reached the Tatars with Islam. In the tales of the Jews a bull-shaped Prince of the Depths is also spoken of.

The primitive peoples of North-East Siberia believe the underground mammoth to cause earthquakes and landslides. In the winter it is even supposed to break the ice of the rivers.[20] The local Tatars say that as the earth was not strong enough to bear the mammoth, God ordered this animal to bear the earth.[21] Possibly the "bull" has here changed into the "horned" mammoth.

For the sake of comparison it may be mentioned how the inhabitants of North-East Siberia, where earthquakes are common, explain these phenonema. The Kamchadales say that the dog of Tuila, on which this spirit rides under the ground, makes the earth tremble when it shakes the snow off its back.[22] According to this view, therefore, the actual supporter of the earth is not the causer of earthquakes.

In Central Asia the idea of a world-supporting being is generally connected with the belief in a cosmic ocean. Those tales, which seek to explain in a popular manner the origin of the earth, seem also to have been formed out of a similar world picture.

CHAPTER II

THE ORIGIN OF THE EARTH

TROŠČANSKIY says that, according to the original conception of the Yakuts, the earth has always existed, and that the question of its creation does not interest them.[1] Stories have, however, been gathered among all the Altaic peoples, the Yakuts also included, which tell that in the beginning there was no earth, only a deep and shoreless primordial ocean. This idea of a primordial ocean is common to most Asiatic creation myths, although the forming of a flat earth on the surface of the great water is described in different ways.

The most prolific cycle, possessing many variants, is that of the tales which relate how some being, diving into the water, brings up earth-matter from the depths of the ocean.

When the great Yryn-Ajy-Tojon ("White Creator Lord"), so runs a Yakut tale, moved in the beginning above the boundless ocean, he saw a bladder floating on the waters and inquired: "Who and whence?" The bladder replied that it was Satan and lived on the earth hidden under the water. God said: "If there really is earth under the water, then bring me a piece of it." Satan dived under the water and returned after a while with a morsel of earth. Having received it, God blessed it, placed it on the surface of the water and seated himself on it. Then Satan resolved to drown God by stretching out the land, but the more he stretched, the stronger it grew, covering soon a great part of the ocean's surface.[2]

The sharp dualism appearing in this tale, God and Satan as opposites, cannot represent the original beliefs of a primitive people. Clues showing which way to turn in tracing the origin of this myth are found in the name " Satan " and in the following variant noted down among this people: " Satan was the elder brother of Christ, but the former was wicked, the latter good. When God wished to create the earth he said to Satan: ' Thou boastest of being able to do everything and sayest thou art mightier than I. Good, bring me sand from the bottom of the ocean.' Satan dived immediately to the bottom of the ocean, but when he arrived again at the surface he saw that the water washed the sand out of his hand. Twice the devil dived without succeeding, but the third time he changed himself into a swallow and managed to bring up a little mud in his beak. Christ blessed the morsel of mud, which then became the earth, at first flat and smooth as a plate. Intending to create for himself a world of his own, Satan deceitfully hid a part of the mud in his throat. But Christ understood the wile of the devil and struck him on the back of the neck so that the mud squirted out of his mouth and formed the mountains on the originally smooth surface of the earth." [3]

When comparing these Yakut tales, in which the names " Christ " and " Satan " especially attract attention, with the apocryphal creation tales of Eastern Europe we see that they coincide in every detail. Knowing, besides, that exactly the same tales are to be found among the Russians who have migrated to Siberia, it seems probable that the Yakuts, who according to statistics are Christians, have learned at least the above mentioned tales direct from the Russians. Before beginning to prove the fact in detail, we will examine a few more Central Asian tales belonging to the same cycle, which contain interesting additions.

When there was no earth and no Heaven, but only water, Ülgen (" the Great "), according to an Altai Tatar tale, descended upon the water to create the earth. He thought and thought but could not conceive how to begin. Then " Man " came to him. Ülgen asked: " Who art thou? " " I also came to create land," answered Man. God became angry and

said: " Even I cannot create, how couldst then thou? " Man
remarked: " But I know where to get earth-matter from."
God urged him to get some, whereupon Man dived immediately into the water, finding at the bottom of the ocean a
mountain, from which he wrenched a piece and put it in his
mouth. Arriving again on the surface Man gave God a part
of it. The other part remained in his mouth between his
teeth. When at last he spat it out, the swamps and bogs appeared on the face of the earth.[4]

A creation tale in which God and the devil work together is
met with among the Alarsk Buriats. When Burkhan
(= Buddha) came down from Heaven to create the earth,
the devil (Sholmo) appeared beside him to give advice how
the earth was to be made from the earth-matter and stones
under the water, offering at the same time to fetch the earth-
matter. God scattered the earth-matter, which the devil had
brought him, on the surface of the ocean and said: " Let the
world be born! " As a reward for his trouble the devil begged
for a part of the land, receiving enough to plant his staff on.
The devil at once pushed his staff into this, and from the hole
there crept forth all manner of reptiles, snakes, etc. Thus
he created the harmful creatures of the world.[5]

In all the above tales, even before the creation of the world,
we meet with two beings of whom one was good, the other
wicked. This dualistic conception reaches its height in the
teachings of the Persian Zarathustra, in which Ahura Mazda,
the god of light and truth, is the promoter of all good and
happiness, and the devil, Angra Mainyu, of the evil and misery
which mar the good earth created by Ahura. Thus far back
must we trace the dualistic features of our tales. But for complete coincidence with these we search the sacred books of the
Mazda religion in vain.

Later, we meet with the same antagonistic original beings in
the teachings of the Persian Mani and in the legends of other
semi-Christian sects which have made their influence felt in

Northern Syria, Palestine and Caucasia, and in which, besides Iranian, old Babylonian fancies and beliefs are also mingled.

In a Yakut tale, Satan, appearing before God, declares that he lives under the water. This idea also seems to be of great age among the people of Caucasia and Asia Minor. With Zarathustra also the Evil One " arose from the depths."

According to the creation tales of a later period, in which the conception of a primordial ocean has become fixed, the devil appears on the surface of the water, sometimes in thick foam, as in a Galician tale, sometimes in a floating bubble, as in the Yakut. The Voguls explain that this bubble was formed by God spitting into the water while coughing. The bubble grew and grew until God heard the voice of Satanael inside it. The same story is told of the devil in a White Russian creation tale.[6]

An Altaic story relates in addition how Ülgen saw some mud with human features floating on the ocean. God gave a spirit to it, and to the being thus born he gave the name Erlik. In the beginning, Erlik was God's friend and brother, but became later his enemy. Mostly, the Altai Tatars call the being who helps God in creating the world " Man " or " First Man," but always, this Man develops into the devil, Erlik.[7] The reasons for his fall are his most obvious qualities, pride and boastfulness. On account of these God drives him down into the depths, where he now lives as the ruler of the spirits in the kingdom of death. This reflects the old Iranian conception of the first man, who, by falling into sin, was the first to die, and thus became leader of the spirits of the dead. In Caucasian tales also, the devil chooses the dead for his property, and in a Bulgarian creation story he says to God: " The living be thy property, the dead mine." [8]

In the legends of the Bogomil sect, formed in Bulgaria about the year 1000, God is said to have had two sons, of whom the elder was Satanael, the younger Christ. It is owing to this conception, which is met with already among earlier sects, that in Yakut tales Satan is called the elder brother of Christ. In the corresponding Votiak, as also in many Russian tales, God and the devil, Keremet, are brothers. A sect of the Iranians, the Zervanists, believed that Ormazd and Ahriman were born of the same mother, in whose womb they took shape at the same time, but that the latter was brought forth first.[9]

In all the above creation tales the devil appears in human shape, only in the Yakut variant he takes on the shape of a swallow in order to be able to hold mud in his mouth. In an Altaic tale the swallow is also the earth-bringer.[10] Mostly, however, the devil, in changing his shape, takes on the form of a water-fowl. A water-fowl is actually better adapted both for diving and for seeking earth on the bottom of the deep ocean. Again, in Eastern Europe the devil helps God both in human shape and as a diver-bird, loon, goose, or some other water-fowl. He appears in the form of a goose, as does God himself, in the following Altaic tale:

In the beginning when there was nothing but water, God and the " First Man " moved about in the shape of two black geese over the waters of the primordial ocean. The devil, however, could not hide his nature, but endeavoured ever to rise higher, until he finally sank down into the depths. Nearly suffocating, he was forced to call to God for help, and God raised him again into the air with the power of his word. God then spoke: " Let a stone rise from the bottom of the ocean! " When the stone appeared, " Man " seated himself upon it, but God asked him to dive under the water and bring land. Man brought earth in his hand and God scattered it on the surface of the water saying: " Let the world take shape! " Once more God asked Man to fetch earth. But Man then decided to take some for himself and brought a morsel in each hand. One handful he gave to God but the other he hid in his mouth, intending to create a world of his own. God threw the earth which the devil had brought him beside the rest on the water, and the world at once began to expand and grow harder, but with the growing of the world the piece of earth in Man's mouth also swelled until he was about to suffocate so that he was again compelled to seek God's help. God inquired: "What was thy intention? Didst thou think thou couldst hide earth from me in thy. mouth?" Man now told his secret intentions and at God's request spat the earth out of his mouth. Thus were formed the boggy places upon the earth.[11]

This story, in which God and the devil appear as birds, may be compared with a North Russian creation tale, in which God and the devil are in co-operation, the former as a white, the later as a black pochard.[12]

Even when appearing in the shape of a water-fowl, the devil does not quite lose his human features. Thus, among other things, his hands are spoken of. In the creation tales of the Voguls also it is often mentioned that the fetcher of earth, sometimes the devil, sometimes the son of the first people, dresses himself for the occasion in water-fowl's garb. When in one tale the devil makes three unsuccessful attempts to reach the bottom of the sea in a duck's skin, he winds a goose's skin about him and at last succeeds in bringing earth.[13] The Voguls, like the East Europeans, often imagine the earth-fetcher to be a real water-fowl, for which the bringing of earth in its mouth is much more natural than for a human-like being. But mostly, this bird is the antagonist of God, Satanael, who endeavours to deceive God by hiding a part of the earth in his mouth, where, like the earth of God's creation, it swells so terribly that the devil is forced to spit it out, thus forming sometimes mountains and hills, sometimes swamps and bogs on the smooth surface of the earth.

When the devil acts altogether in a human-like manner, the tales sometimes describe the hiding of the earth in a way more suited to men. Thus in a Buriat story, the devil hides it under his heel and thence scatters it as mountains on the smooth earth created by Burkhan. To God's question, why the devil wished to spoil his earth, the latter replies: "When man descends a mountain he is afraid and calls upon Thy name, but when he ascends he swears in my name. Thus he is ever mindful of us both." [14]   Similar words are uttered by the devil in both a Mordvin and a Russian creation tale. [15]

The devil mars the earth in a human-like manner in the following Yakut tale: In the beginning, God created a small, smooth and even earth, but the devil injured it sadly by kicking it with his feet and tearing it. God urged the earth to grow in spite of this and so the unevennesses caused by the devil became great mountains, valleys and lakes. [16]

In the first of the creation tales given, it is said that the devil intended to drown God, who had seated himself on the little earth-disc just formed upon the surface of the water. In a corresponding Bulgarian tale the devil has the same idea. He tries to coax God to lie down and sleep upon the earth-disc in order to be able to push him into the sea, and to become supreme in the world. Although God well knows the intentions of his enemy, he lays himself down and pretends to sleep. The devil then seizes him and begins to carry him to the edge of the earth in order to pitch him into the depths. But when he approaches the shore the earth begins to expand so that he is unable to reach its edge. He turns towards the other side but even there he can no longer see the ocean. The third and the fourth direction give the same result. [17]

This same story has been added to an entirely different creation tale in Central Asia. Here the earth is also brought from under the water and placed on the surface of the ocean, but the devil takes no part in the creation. The creator is Otshirvani (= the Buddhist Bodhisattva Vairapani) and his assistant Chagan-Shukuty. When these mighty beings descended from heaven they saw a frog (= turtle) diving in the water. Otshirvani's companion raised it from the depths and placed it on its back on the water. "I shall sit on the stomach of the frog," said Otshirvani, "dive thou to the bottom and bring up what thy hand finds." Chagan-Shukuty dived twice, and the second time he succeeded in bringing up some earth. Then Otshirvani told him to sprinkle it on the stomach of the frog (turtle), on which they sat. The frog itself sank out of sight and only, the earth remained visible above the surface of the water. Resting there, the gods fell asleep and while they were sleeping, Shulmus, the devil, arrived and saw the two friends lying on the earth which they had just created and which was yet so small that there was scarcely room for a third on it. The devil decided to make use of his chance and drown these beings together with their earth. But when he attempted to seize hold of the edge of the earth, he no longer saw the ocean. He took the sleeping friends under his arm and began to run towards the shore with them. But while he ran the earth grew. When he saw that his attempt was vain he dropped his burden and barely succeeded in escaping when Otshirvani awoke. The latter then explained to his companion how the devil had meant to destroy, them but how the earth had saved them.[18]

But although the devil did not succeed in destroying God, he was able to mar the earth, as we have seen, and, according to the Buriats, to create many useless and harmful animals on it. This last tale has also been recorded in other parts of Siberia, e.g., among the Voguls. Here the devil makes a hole in the earth with his staff, from which frogs, lizards, worms, beetles, gnats, wasps, mice, etc., arise, until God closes the hole with a fiery stopper. The same description is found even in East European creation tales.[19]

There would thus seem to be no doubt that these Asiatic stories of the origin of the earth, which correspond in all their details to the East European creation tales, are closely connected with a common cycle of tales, rich in variants. Outside the boundaries of the former Russian Empire, with the exception of certain Balkan States and the Gypsies who have been influenced by the Slavs of Austria, we do not meet in the west with this myth, which is unknown on Roman Catholic territory.

In the Greek Catholic Church, on the contrary, and especially among certain sects, it has been greatly favoured. This fact can also be proved in Finland, which has been a meeting-point for the currents of both Western and Eastern culture. Tales have been recorded only in Eastern Finland, in which the devil, sometimes with the aid of a diver-bird, fetches earth from the bottom of the sea, hides a part of it in his mouth, and adds the stones, rocks and mountains to the surface of the earth by being compelled to spit it out when it swells between his jaws. In one variant, where God sat in the beginning on a golden pillar in the middle of the sea, the devil is said to have appeared in the world when God told his reflection, which he saw in the water, to arise.[20] Bulgarian legends also relate that the devil was born of God's shadow.[21]

Veselovskiy, who has made comparative researches on a large scale into the legends of the last-named church, is of the opinion that this tale is a creation of the Bogomil sect in Bulgaria. We do not, however, meet with the story of the fetching of the earth in either the Bogomil literature or in the teachings of those Armenian Gnostics from whom the Bogomils inherited their dualistic conception. This tale of the origin of the earth appears first in a Russian manuscript of the fifteenth century, but seems already at that time to have been very widespread. Schiefner, who is acquainted with the stories of the Russian sectaries, assumes that our dualistic tale has wandered into Northern and Central Asia with Russian fugitives and settlers from Europe.[22] Sumcov doubts, however, whether the Russian newcomers could have implanted their tale so deeply into the beliefs of the Central Asian peoples in such a comparatively short time. He assumes, therefore, Nestorian influence, this sect having won much territory in Central Asia before Islam.[23] To Persian influence points the fact that God in one Altaic creation tale calls himself "the true Kurbystan" (= Ahura Mazda).[24] But in districts where Buddhism is common, names derived from this religion, such

as Burkhan, etc., are also met with, although the appearance
of the devil here hints at Iranian influence. Might it therefore
be assumed, as Dähnhardt also supposes, that the dualistic tale
of the bringing-up of earth has its origin somewhere in the
vicinity of the Iranians, e.g., among the Syrian Gnostics, whence
it has wandered both to Russia and Bulgaria and through
Persia to Central Asia? As no proof for this assumption can
be found in the literary sources on the subject, we should have
to add a further supposition, i.e., that in addition to the written
teachings, verbal stories corresponding with our tale have also
been handed down. However this may be, it is at least certain, as we have shown, that many features in this tale have
their origin in the Near East. It is also probable that this
cycle of tales is no single creation, but a collection of ideas
and stories of different content and gathered from various
places.

Especially interesting is the bird which fetches the earth
from the bottom of the primordial ocean. Whence has this
peculiar feature come into our tales and how shall we account
for it?

In some Russian legends and also in North-West Siberian
tales the fetching of the piece of earth is spoken of in connection with the story of the flood. The Samoyeds in the
District of Turukhansk relate the following: Seven people had
been saved in a boat and, when they saw that the water rose
and rose and that there was no help, they begged the diver-
bird to fly into the water and seek land there. After seven
days the diver-bird returned bringing a grassy piece of turf
in its beak, and of this they asked God to create for them an
earth.[25] Also in a Russian variant God sends the devil to bring
sand from the water when he wishes to make a new earth after
the flood.[26]

In the flood story of the Samoyeds, the diver-bird reminds
one of the bird sent by Noah from his ark, which brought him
news of the appearance of land in its beak, but from this we

cannot yet be certain that Noah's bird has been the original of the water-fowl appearing in our tales. For quite simple reasons, two myths, both treating of great floods and of a bird, may have become confounded.

In a Vogul creation tale, which mentions several birds, these have work of two kinds to perform The red- and the black-throated diver fetch earth, but the raven is sent out to see how large the earth has grown. On the first day the bird is away but a short time, on the second it returns toward midday, on the third not until the evening. Every day its journey takes a longer time and from this it may be guessed how the earth grows from day to day.[27] The raven in this tale has thus in some degree the same duty as the dove in the flood story of the Bible, but this feature can hardly be traced back to the Bible.

It is to be noted, in addition, that stories of the creation and of the flood are often met with separately among the same people.

Besides the preceding versions, in which God and the earth-bringer are antagonists, a creation tale without this dualistic idea is met with in Asia. In this the Creator uses quite simply an ordinary water-fowl in order to bring up earth from the waters.

The Yenisei Ostiaks related to me that in the beginning the water flowed everywhere. The Great Shaman Doh hovered over the waters in the company of swans, looms, and other water-fowl. As he could nowhere find a resting-place he asked the diver-bird to bring him a piece of earth from under the sea. The diver tried twice before it succeeded in bringing up some earth in its beak. Of this Doh made an island in the sea.[28]

According to Buriat tales, at the bottom of the shoreless primordial ocean, there were black earth and red clay. When Burkhan decided to create an earth he asked the white diver to fetch him earth-matter from under the water. The diver brought both earth and clay in his beak and sprinkled them on the water. Thus was created a world floating on the waves, on which trees and grass soon began to grow.[29]

The Buriats of the District of Balagan have the same story in the following form. In the beginning when there was yet no land, Sombol-Burkhan moved over the waters, where he saw a water-fowl swimming with its twelve young. God then said: "Water-bird, dive down and bring me earth — black soil in thy beak and on thy feet red clay!" Having thus obtained earth-matter, God scattered the red clay on the water, and upon it the black soil. Thus was made the earth which soon became covered with beautiful vegetation. Thankful, God blessed the water-bird saying: "Thou shalt have many young and shalt ever swim and dive in the water." That is how this bird has such a wonderful ability to dive deep and remain long under the water.[30]

In these tales we find no being akin to the devil appearing as God's opponent. We cannot, however, conclude from this, as Dähnhardt, who knows only the first mentioned Buriat tale, does, that this form of creation tale is only a deformed variant of the dualistic stories. Hardly, again, has the devil any part in the following story, which was recorded among the Northern Yakuts, although the "Mother of God" is mentioned in it: The Mother of God decided to create a world, but having no material she first created a diver-bird and a duck, both of which she commanded to dive under the ocean and fetch earth. The first to appear was the duck who brought some mud in her mouth. Then the diver came up, but without mud, explaining that it was impossible to find earth in the water. The Mother of God became angry and said: "Thou deceitful bird, have I not given thee more strength and a longer beak than the duck? But thou deceivest me and pitiest the ocean. For this thou shalt never live on the sacred surface of the earth, but shalt ever dive in the waters and seek all manner of refuse there for thy nourishment." Then the

Mother of God created the earth from the mud the diver had brought, and placed it upon the surface of the ocean. The earth did not sink under the water, nor could the waves move it or wash it asunder, but it remained fixed in a certain place like a floating island and grew gradually into a great world.[31]

In the tales of the Voguls also, we sometimes find two water-birds, the black- and the red-throated diver, acting as earth-fetchers.

A Buriat variant tells in addition how the water-fowl, which Sombol-Burkhan sent to fetch earth, met the "crab" in the depths. The latter inquired of the bird where it was going. The bird answered that it was diving for earth from the bottom of the sea. Then the "crab" became angry and remarked: "I am always in the water and have never yet seen its bottom, turn back quickly or I shall cut thee in two with my scissors!" The bird was forced to return to the surface. Seeing it, Sombol-Burkhan inquired why the bird had not brought him earth. On hearing how the crab had threatened it, he gave the bird magic words, by the help of which it at last succeeded in reaching the bottom.[32]

This interlude in the diving is mentioned also in the tales of the Votiaks of the District of Sarapul. God's assistant meets a crab in the water, who inquires where he is going and tells him that he, the crab, though a sea-dweller for one hundred and twenty years, has never yet met with land in the ocean. The story continues with the fetching of earth, and how an evil being hides sand in its mouth and then creates the mountains.[33]

Comparing these latter tales, we can scarcely remain in doubt as to which of them represents a more original stage. The crab as frightener in the dualistic story of the Votiaks is as unnatural and unnecessary as it is natural in the Buriat tale. This additional feature, which to the author's knowledge has not been met with further west, may have been added later to the dualistic creation story from a simpler and more primitive creation tale, which has perhaps been known also among the Votiaks.

If we assume, therefore, that the tales in which a natural water-fowl and not the Satanael of the Bogomils acts as earth-fetcher, are more primitive, we can easily explain the bird-like features of the devil, often appearing even in stories where the devil dives into the water in human shape. In this way, the problem of the fetching of earth, which can be explained in no other way, would be solved: an old primitive tale has later become embellished with the dualistic ideas of the sectarians of the Eastern Church.

All depends thus on whether we can take for granted that those Asiatic tales in which the devil is unknown, represent an earlier stage.

A proof of the fact, that the creation tales in this simpler form are both popular and original, is given by the innumerable stories of similar content gathered among the Indian tribes of North America. In these it is sometimes a water-fowl, sometimes a fish or some amphibian that brings up mud from the bottom of the primordial ocean, which mud is then placed on the surface of the water and soon grows into a big world for people to live in.[34]

Sometimes this earth-fetching tale is intertwined with the flood story even in America, where it is usually a musk-rat that saves the people floating on the ocean in a boat, on a raft, or on a tree-trunk, by bringing them mud from the bottom of the sea, from which mud a new earth then grows. Like the raven in the Vogul tale given earlier, so in the similar North American stories some animal, a fox or a wolf, is used for the purpose of reporting on the growth of the earth. When Nanabozhu, according to the Winnebago Indians, could no longer follow the growth of the land with his eyes, he sent a wolf to run round the earth in order to know its size. The first time the wolf soon returned, the second journey took him two years, the third time he returned no more.[35]

Noticeable, further, is the part played by the turtle in the tales of the North American Indians. There is a story among the Sioux Indians of how the turtle and some water-bird swam about in the primordial ocean with earth-matter in their mouths, the one with mud, the other with grass. The grassy earth formed by these was placed on the back of the turtle. The Hurons also say, that in the beginning there was nothing but water, until from the depths a turtle appeared and sent, one after the other, the otter, the musk-rat, the diver, and other water-dwellers to fetch earth-matter. But only in the mouth of the frog, the last to be sent, could the turtle find mud. This was then sprinkled round the edges of the turtle's shell, and before long formed the earth. When the earth grew, the turtle remained as its supporter, a duty it carries out even today.[36]

The part of the turtle in creating the world is especially interesting on account of the corresponding idea in the Central Asian stories.

In the beginning of time, so say the Buriats, there was nothing but water, and a great turtle who looked into the water. God turned this animal on its back and built the world on its stomach. In another connection we have already mentioned how, according to an Altaic story, the heavenly Otshirvani and Chagan-Shukuty notice a turtle diving in the waters, and how the latter dives down for earth while the former sits upon the animal's stomach, and how Otshirvani then sprinkled the earth on the frog.[37] In Central Asian tales we find in addition Mandishire (= the Buddhist Bodhisattva Manjucri) as creator of the earth, who changes himself into a large turtle and supports the earth he has made on the surface of the water.[38]

In these Central Asian tales we find an ancient Indian story in a form coloured by Buddhism. As is known, the Creator appears already in the ancient Indian tales in the shape of a turtle. In this form he fetches mud from the bottom of the primordial ocean and makes of it a rapidly expanding earth, which he supports on the surface of the vast surrounding ocean. In later Buddhist tales a Bodhisattva, mostly Manjucri, takes the place of the old and more primitive deity.

In Indian tales the earth-fetcher sometimes takes the shape of some other animal. As the supporter of the earth, as we have seen, a fish is also mentioned.

Our comparative research has thus at last brought us to India. This is actually the only country in Asia where the bringing of the earth from the bottom of the ocean is connected already with the beliefs of an unknown, far-distant past. The literatures of other ancient cultured Asiatic peoples do not possess a similar tale. It is also impossible to assume that the idea of a primordial ocean could have been born among the Central Asian prairie-dwellers. Although it is true that we can find among the information relating to India, no mention of a water-fowl as the bringer of earth, we are forced in the end to believe that this feature of our tales has its roots also in that land of countless stories.

Besides the above tales about the origin of the earth, in which the fetching of earth-matter from under the water is a common feature, stories have been recorded among the peoples of the Altaic race, which explain the appearance of the earth on the surface of the ocean in a different manner.

The following Mongolian story is probably a product of Lamaism: In the beginning, when there was yet no earth, but water covered everything, a Lama came down from Heaven, and began to stir the water with an iron rod. By the influence of the wind and fire thus brought about, the water on the surface in the middle of the ocean thickened and coagulated into land.[39] Certain syncretists of Nearer Asia also describe how the earth was formed when God caused the cosmic foam on the surface of the ocean to coagulate.[40] Closely corresponding to the Mongolian story is a Japanese tale: In the beginning one of the seven gods of Heaven stirred the chaotic waters with his staff. When he raised his staff, muddy foam dripped from it and, expanding and thickening, formed the islands of Japan.[41]

More than a hundred years ago a tale was written down among the Tungus beyond the Baikal, describing how God sent fire into the primordial ocean. In the course of time the fire vanquished the power of the water and burnt up a part of the ocean, so that it became quite hard. Thus the present land and sea were formed. With this tale is connected a dualistic conception of two antagonistic primitive beings. When God stepped down upon the earth he met the devil, Buninka, who also desired to create a world. Thus a dispute arose between God and the devil. The devil wished to destroy God's earth and broke the latter's twelve-stringed musical instrument. Then God was angry and said: " If thou canst command a pine-tree to grow out of the lake I will recognize thy power, but if I can do it, thou must admit that I am omnipotent." The devil agreed to God's proposal. At once, when God commanded, a tree arose from the water and began to grow, but the devil's pine would not stand erect but tottered from one side to the other. Thus the devil saw that God was mightier than he.[42]

In this story, which concludes with the creation of man, God and the devil as rivals, the stringed instrument, etc., are features which can by no means be reconciled with the original circumstances and beliefs of the Tungus. A feature corresponding to the tree-growing competition may be found in the Central Asian creation tale in which Otshirvani and his companion, Chagan-Shukuty, pour water into a vessel and wait to see on whose side a plant shall appear. Similarly in the Buriat tale, three Burkhans try which of them is to procure a spirit for the people whom they had created.

The Tungus believe that fire played a great part in the creation of the world. This conception appears already among the syncretistic Mandaean sect, the influence of which was felt in Mesopotamia in the first centuries of our era. Their tale had possibly been accepted by the Manicheans. It tells how fire is slung into the water and how, with the ensuing steam, dust rises into the air and in sinking again to the surface of the water forms into solid land.[43]

The presence of oriental learning is to be discerned also in a conception met with in Central Asia of a primitive chaos consisting of fire, water and wind. Burkhan-bakshi ($=$ Buddha-master; *bakshi* $=$ Mandshu *fakshi,* " master," Chinese *fashi,* " teacher ") separated them and scattered the dust thus formed on the surface of the water, where it gradually grew into an earth covered with grass and trees.[44]

In some Mongolian districts we meet also with an idea, common in China and Japan, that heaven and earth were joined together in the beginning, but later separated. At the parting of earth and sky fire appeared, or, according to some variants, the constellations in the sky.[45] This belief evidently originates in the Indian tale, which has spread especially to the eastward of India, of a world-egg, from whose halves earth and heaven have been formed.

Some of the most northern peoples of Siberia believe further that the earth came down from Heaven. Stories referring to this have been recorded both in the west, in the Vogul districts, and in the far east, among the Kamchadales. The Voguls tell that Numi-Tōrem let down an earth-disc from heaven as a dwelling-place for the people he had made.[46] The Kamchadales say that the god of Heaven, Kutku, brought the earth down from the sky and placed it on the surface of the ocean. The latter also relate how the wife of the god of Heaven bore a son while moving on the ocean, and that Kutku created an earth out of his body.[47]

The idea that the earth has come down from Heaven is closely connected with those tales in which sometimes fire, sometimes some animal, object, etc., is dropped or let down from the upper spheres. We may therefore assume that the letting down of the earth from Heaven is of the same origin. It is, however, to be noted that these tales take for granted the existence of a primordial ocean.

Just as the idea of a vast ocean surrounding the earth is natural to coast-dwellers, and the conception of the growing of the earth, i.e., the shore, is founded on the actual experience of years, so these same ideas seem unnatural and unexpected in the central parts of a great continent. How entirely different the conceptions of the nomads of the Altaic race have been, is to be seen from a story of the Kirghis, in which it is declared that in the beginning there was no water at all. Two people tended a great ox, but having long been without drink they were dying of thirst. The ox then determined to get them water by digging into the earth with his great horns. Thus were formed the lakes and the rivers on the surface of the earth.[48]

We cannot, then, consider any of the above mentioned creation tales to be the invention of the Altaic race. Without doubt the idea of the Yakuts: " The world has always been," probably represents the original belief of the whole Altaic race. By this we do not mean to say that the peoples of this race have not also had their own local myths, which try to explain the causes of certain changes on the surface of the earth. An example of this is the Kirghis tale already mentioned. The most northern peoples of Siberia, such as the Tungus, Samoyeds, Ostiaks, etc., who often find, in the neighbourhood of their homes, bones and teeth of the mammoth in the ground, say that this beast made the originally smooth earth uneven with his horns. The mountains and chasms at least are said to have been thus formed. The valleys and depressions were caused by the quaking of the earth under the weight of this former giant animal when it walked. The water, gathering into these depressions, afterwards formed the lakes and rivers. God is said to have at last become angry and to have drowned the mammoth in a lake where it still lives under the ground.[49]

Local also is another North-East Siberian tale of the origin of mountains and valleys. God lived in Heaven originally, but settled later upon the earth. When he then travelled, moving on skis, the thin earth bent under him like new, pliant ice. That is the reason why the surface of the earth is uneven.[50]

CHAPTER III

THE PILLAR OF THE WORLD

THE REGULAR diurnal movement of the stars round an axis at the North Star, the reasons for which neverending rotation were earlier unknown, gave birth to an idea that this apparent centre of the universe was formed by some object which could be represented in concrete form, and which was, in addition, believed to support the roof of the sky. This belief we have seen to be held by the Lapps, etc., and relics of a similar belief are to be found among most of the peoples of the Northern Hemisphere.

From this belief spring the curious names given by the Altaic stocks to the North Star. The Mongols, Buriats, Kalmucks, and the Altai Tatars and Uigurs call the star in question " The golden pillar "; the Kirghis, Bashkirs and certain other Siberian Tatar tribes call it " The iron pillar "; the Teleuts " The lone post," and the Tungus-Orotshons " The golden post." From the similarity of the names given it by these widely separated peoples we may conclude that the conception of a sky-supporting pillar reaches back among the Altaic race to a comparatively early period.[1] In a tale of the Yakuts in which the world is regarded as having gradually developed from a small beginning, this " iron tree " boasts: " When the heavens and the earth commenced to grow, I grew with them." [2]

Although none of the available sources mention directly that the peoples of the Altaic race made images of this great world-pillar, we can still be reasonably certain that they did so from the fact that several of the more northern peoples have kept up this custom even to our days. These peoples were under Turco-Tatar influence, and even offered up blood-sacrifices to these pillars. The Ostiaks call these wooden images of the pillar, " town-pillars " or " the strong pillars of the town's centre." Those more simple in construction are erected by being slightly sunk into the earth, and are hardly ever observed to be shaped at all in any way. The pillar of the village of Tsingala is about two fathoms in height, a squared, slender log, not very old. Nowadays these pillars, as the objects of reverential ceremonies, are here met with only in a few of the coast villages of Irtysh, those of the other villages having been swept along with landslides into the river. The " town pillar " of the village of Tsingala, although it stands among the buildings on a site incapable of awakening respect, is worshipped with offerings like a god. Karjalainen relates that " the inhabitants of this and other villages of the same district, gathered together for the paying of taxes, buy mutually a cow or a bull and sacrifice it at the foot of the pillar in order to obtain prosperity in their work and additions to their families." This pillar of Tsingala, which the Ostiaks of that place regard as a deity, is called by them " The iron

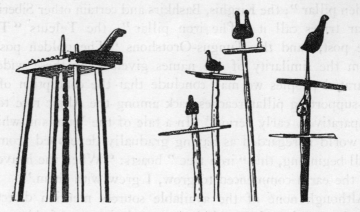

FIG. 13. DOLGAN SHAMAN-PILLARS WITH FIGURES OF BIRDS

pillar man," a similar name being given to the post of another village of Irtysh, resembling greatly the afore-mentioned " Iron pillar " of the Tatars. It is therefore obvious that

" the strong pillar of the town's centre " of the Ostiaks, which a certain tale describes as " the tree planted by God," cannot be, as Karjalainen assumes, intended merely for the tying of sacrificial animals and the hanging-up of offerings, but is a representation of the pillar supporting the sky.[3] This appears also from the prayers read at the post.

Some peoples in North-West Siberia, who have a similar custom, place on the world-pillar a wooden figure of a bird, which sometimes has two heads. What this bird, which is spoken of by the Dolgans as the " lord of the birds," and which hangs on the breast of the Yenisei Ostiak shaman-dress, is

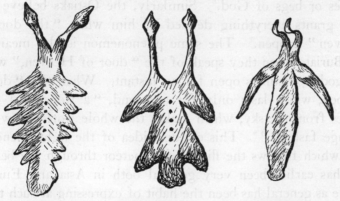

FIG. 14. TWO-HEADED BIRDS OF IRON WHICH HANG ON THE DRESS AND DRUM OF THE YENISEI-OSTIAK SHAMAN

intended to represent, the people themselves do not know; but it is probable that this bird has flown here from the mythology of the ancient peoples. The pillars, on which these birds are placed and which have sometimes cross-pieces like branches, are, according to the Dolgans, a symbol of the " never falling props " before the dwelling of the Supreme God. On the cross-pieces, so it is said, dwell the sons of God.[4]

It would be interesting to know what the sky, which this wonderful pillar was supposed to support, was originally believed to be. We can hardly be mistaken if we suppose it to have been pictured as some kind of a roof, the purpose of which was to protect the earth and life on the earth. To this points also the view still prevalent in some places, viz., that the sky is a kind of great tent-roof stretched over the earth. The Yakuts say that the sky consists of several overlapping tightly stretched skins. The Buriats see in the Milky Way " a stitched seam," and a certain being says with pride: " Long, long ago, when I was young, I sewed the sky together." [5] Sometimes the gods open slightly the sky-cover to see what is happening on the earth. In this way, the Chuvash, among others, explain the flight of meteors. Lucky the one who sees this " crack in the sky," as he obtains what he at that moment wishes or begs of God.[6] Similarly, the Ostiaks believe that God grants everything desired of him while " the door of Heaven " is open.[7] The same phenonemon is also meant by the Buriats when they speak of the " door of Heaven," which the gods sometimes open for an instant. When this " door " is open, which lasts only for a second, " a wonderful light shines from the sky, which makes the whole world glow in a strange fashion." [8] This childish idea of the light-phenomenon which follows the flight of a meteor through the belt of air, has earlier been very general both in Asia and Europe. Quite as general has been the habit of expressing at such times some wish, which it is believed will be fulfilled.

The sky having thus been regarded as a kind of tent-roof, which, stretched from a great post or pillar, covered the earth, it is comprehensible that the stars should then have been only a kind of hole in this cover. The worst hole was the Pleiades, from which winds and cold were believed to stream over the earth.[9]

This conception of the sky as a kind of roof, is, without doubt, of extreme age and the product of an extremely early culture. Obviously, the primitive dwelling-house of man himself gave direction to his imagination, when he attempted to create for himself a picture of the surrounding world. In some of the descriptions in the Old Testament the sky appears tent-like, e.g., in the 40th chapter of Isaiah, in which God is described as: " He who stretcheth out the heavens as a curtain and spreadeth them out as a tent to dwell in."

Besides the above conception, in which the world-pillar appears as the supporter of the sky, another is met with, according to which it is the tethering-post of the stars wandering in the sky. The fact that, seen from the earth, the stars seem to be eternally revolving round the sky-post, awakened the idea of bonds attaching these to one another. As the peoples related to the Turks sometimes imagined the stars to be a great drove of horses, we can understand why, in the tales of these people, the world-pillar is often called a mighty tethering-post for horses. As such the Yakuts call it " the horse-post ruler." [10] The Buriats have tales of the nine sons of a spirit named Boshintoi, living in the sky; these sons, as skilful blacksmiths, taught men to prepare iron, and are therefore worshipped and praised in the following words: " The nine white smiths of Boshintoi . . . made of the North Star a horse-post and of the golden lake a race course." [11] In the same way as the Nomads of Central Asia have a post for the tethering of their steeds before their buildings, the gods are said to fasten theirs to the heaven-post. Certain Siberian Tatar tribes believe the gods to live in a tent in the sky, in front of which is a " golden horse-post." [12] As Karjalainen remarks, the Ostiaks of Vasyugan, in their tales, have also adopted from the Tatars " the Iron post, the Stone post, on the side of the sun, created by Torem (the god of Heaven), in which there is an iron ring large enough to admit a sleeved arm," and to which the driving-reindeer is bound. Similarly, the Voguls speak of " The holy iron pillar of God erected for the tethering of the holy animal with many-coloured thighs," erected before the dwelling of the god of Heaven. [13]

In the folk-lore of the Ostiaks, as seen from the above, a " stone " pillar is also mentioned. A strange, rectangular, transparent pillar of stone, three fathoms in height, appears in the centre of an area of iron in the tales of the Yakuts.[14] Probably such world-pillars are hidden also among the stone pillars on the prairies of Central Asia. At any rate, traces have been found of high four-sided monuments which were erected upon the back of the world-bearing tortoise.

But especially interesting is the fact that many of these holy pillars of the Ugrians were imagined to be seven-storeyed. This was also true of the pillar at Tsingala, as although the object itself had no signs pointing to the fact, the words in the prayer, in which the god of Heaven is closely connected with the pillar god, run as follows: " My seven-divided high man-father thou art, a six-divided high man thou art. My iron pillar man-father, to the foot of the holy tree, my metal pillar man-father, to the foot of the holy tree, to partake of a generous dish of head-meat, to partake of a generous dish of breast-meat, we called thee." The word " six-divided " or " six-marked " is here only a poetic reiteration. Another prayer noted down in which a Heaven god called Sänke is addressed in addition to the post runs: " Seven-divisioned high man, Sänke, my father, my in-three-directions-watching man-father, my in-three-directions-protecting man-father. To the holy ground of my iron pillar man-father, to the innocent ground, at the foot of the holy tree erected by him, I stand my blood-animal blood-sacrifice." [15]

The significance of the number seven in the beliefs connected with the pillars of the Ugrians is especially apparent. The Ostiak tales relate how a person setting out on a courtship has to sacrifice at the foot of this " God-faced holy tree," or " to hold up there the sacrifice of seven reindeer-bulls tied to one rope," and to make " seven good bows of the head at the foot of the god-faced holy tree." The seven animals are mentioned also in certain advice given to a hero setting out on a dangerous journey: " Call together the village full of thy many men, the town full of thy many men; bring the seven animals

PLATE XLII

Tortoise-shell shaped stone representing the world-bearing tortoise and used as a foundation for an old Turkish monument. (See page 338.)
After photograph by S. Pālsi.

bound to one rope and tie them to the strong town-pillar." [16]
In the Yakut tales the seven reindeer at the " iron tree "
are also mentioned. [17]   Most probably these " seven animals " bound to one rope, like the pillar itself, have their
counterpart in the sky, and in this connection our thoughts
turn to the Great Bear, the " seven animals " of which are
imagined as being bound to the North Star " by one
rope."

But the number seven appears also in the names of the god
— " the seven-divisioned or seven-marked man," which points
possibly to the fact that the pillar itself was imagined to be
seven-storeyed.   And examples for this are not lacking.   Thus,
in sacrificing to a spirit called " the Roach lake old man " at
the sources of the Salym, the Ostiaks of that district erect on
the lake a pillar of fir-wood about a fathom in height, on
which they cut with a knife " seven marks at seven places."
To the head of the post they fix coloured cloths and place the
sacrificial runes before it, the sacrificial animal being also bound
to it for the duration of the prayers and genuflexions.   In
slaughtering, a stream of blood has to be directed on to the
post. [18]   Similar pillars were erected in earlier times by the
Yenisei Ostiaks on the banks of their rivers to give luck in
fishing.   Nowadays, to our knowledge, none are met with in
practice, although the older people still speak about them.   In
the museum at Krasnoyarsk several are preserved, these being
thin posts about two fathoms in height, on which seven deep
cuts have been made one above the other.   In the place of
these cuts, it was the custom in some districts to leave the
stumps of seven branches.   In the same way it is related of the
Irtysh Ostiaks that when sacrificing at a hole in the ice they
erected a post beside it on which seven branches had been left. [19]
Karjalainen assumes this to have been only an artificial sacrifice tree, but even these temporarily erected posts can probably
not be separated from the world-pillars.   In any, case, the
seven-divisioned " iron pillar man " has a heavenly counter-

part, as the Vogul tales tell of a " seven-divided pure silver holy pillar " to which the son of God ties his steed when visiting his father.[20]

On studying the Asian cosmography we find no difficulty in explaining what these seven divisions or stumps of branches signify. Without doubt, they represent the seven storeys of the sky, an idea general also among the Ostiaks. The " divisions " appear also in the shaman rites of the Altai Tatars, although here the storeys of Heaven are regarded as being nine in number. When about to shamanize, a special tent is erected on the Altai, in the centre of which a birch is erected so that the crown of the tree sticks out of the air-hole in the middle of the roof. Nine divisions are cut into the trunk of the birch, and are described as being the symbols of the nine-storied heavens. Rising by means of the tree into the highest Heaven the shaman has to travel through all the different storeys. This is done in such a manner that while exercising his magic the shaman climbs division by division upwards. When he places his foot on the lowest notch he has reached the first Heaven, and so on until he rises into the ninth.[21]

The tree, along which the Altai shaman rises into Heaven, though furnished with divisions, is not really a post, but a leaf-crowned birch-tree. Thus, we find here an intermediate stage between the above mentioned world-pillars and the branched world-tree supposed to rise from the centre of the earth. As the holy pillars of the Ostiaks had either seven divisions or seven branches, so an Abakan Tatar hero-poem tells of " the white, seven-branched birch-tree on an iron mountain in the centre of the earth." [22] But before describing in detail this mighty tree reigning over the earth's centre, we must first turn our attention to the mountain in this same region, from the summit of which, according to many tales, the tree arises.

CHAPTER IV

THE WORLD—MOUNTAIN

THE MAJORITY of the peoples of Central Asia have tales of a mighty world-mountain, which the Mongols and Kalmucks call Sumur or Sumer, and the Buriats Sumbur. In whatever form this mountain is imagined, it is connected always with the cosmography, of these peoples, forming its centre. Assuming that the world was formerly small and has gradually grown to its present size, the folk-tales tell of a distant time, when Sumur was only a very little hill.[1] Now its summit aspires to heights unattainable by man, offering thus to the gods a dwelling-place worthy of them.

Although the Altai peoples have worshipped their mountains, especially the Altai, adored in many tales, which they called the "prince,"[2] the conception of a central mountain of the earth-disc was not bound to any of the Central Asian mountains, but came from abroad, ready-shaped to a particular cosmography. It is worthy of note that this mythical mountain is often placed in Heaven itself. Thus, the Over-god Bai-Ylgön ("rich-great") lives in Heaven "on a golden mountain."[3] Similarly, the tales of the Yakuts tell of the "milky-white stone mountain" of Heaven.[4] Often this mountain is described as rising in storeys, the number of which varies, but is generally the same as the number of storeys into which Heaven is divided among that particular people. A certain Central Asian tale describes the central mountain of the earth-disc as "three-stepped."[5] The Ostiaks speak of the "seven-storied mountain" of Heaven.[6] Even Heaven itself is sometimes imagined as a mountain of this description; its underside, which we mortals see, is like a rounded arch. An Altaic creation tale relates how Ülgen when creating the earth, sat on a "golden mountain" where the sun and the moon always shine, and how this mountain later descended, hiding the earth; the edges of the sky did not, however, reach to the earth itself.[7]

The idea of a heavenly mountain appears also in the following tale of the Goldes living in North-East Siberia: "When the gods built Heaven, they made it of stone, but when it was ready the people below began to be afraid that it would fall down on them, wherefore the gods blew under the arch so that the air thus formed hid the arch from the sight of men."[8] Without doubt, this picture of Heaven is closely connected with "the mountain" and has developed from it. This idea of the stone arch cannot have arisen among the Goldes, as this structure is quite unknown to them, as it is to all other North Siberian tribes.

In the tales of the Mongols, Buriats, and Kalmucks the world-mountain — Sumbur, Sumur, or Sumer — has a name in which the central mountain of the inhabitants of India, Sumeru, is easily recognized, and the beliefs connected with the same have spread ready-formed along with a stream of civilization from India to the peoples of Central Asia. Whether this mountain Sumeru or Meru originated in India, in connection with some actual mountain there, is difficult to say. As far back as can be traced it has been a cosmologic belief.

Where then, is the summit of this earth-mountain? We might suppose it to be at the summit of Heaven, directly above us, and, as such, the apex of a hollow sky. It was not, however, envisaged thus, but instead, its peak rises to the sky at the North Star where the axis of the sky is situated, and where, on the peak, the dwelling of the Over-god and his "golden throne" are situated. To this idea points also the assumption, met with everywhere in Asia, that the world-mountain is in the north. This appears quite clearly in a Buriat tale reflecting Indian views of life: "In the beginning was only water and a frog (turtle), which gazed into the water. God turned this animal over and created the world on its belly. On each foot he built a continent, but on the navel of the frog he founded the Sumbur-mountain. On the summit of this mountain is the North Star." In another tale in which a temple is placed on the summit of Sumbur, the North Star is the golden spire of the tower of this temple.[9]

The cosmic mountain rising in this part of the sky was known long ago to the great civilized peoples of Nearer Asia. This idea appears also in the Bible. In the 14th chapter of Isaiah a proud being, who wished to "be like the most high," is described in the following words: "For thou hast said in thy heart, I will ascend into heaven, I will exalt my throne above the stars of God: I will sit also upon the mount of the congregation, in the sides of the north." As the throne of God is believed to be on the summit of the world-mountain in the north, this point of the compass was the direction of the prayers of the Mandeans.

Although the idea of this wonderful, cosmic mountain, as its name denotes, arose in India and travelled with a stream of civilization to the Mongol tribes, the same belief reached the Turco-Tatar peoples by other roads. The Sürö (" Majesty ") mountain, appearing in the tales of the Altai Tatars, has doubtless originated in Persia, as also the seven gods, who are believed to dwell on this heavenly mountain and whose name Kudai is a loan-word from the Persian.[10] That the idea of the heavenly mountain was known also far away in Europe, is shown by the Himinbjorg (heaven-mountain) of Scandinavian tales and by a Finnish poem on the origin of fire, in which it is asked where fire was born, the answer being: " There on the navel of the sky, on the peak of the famous mountain." [11]

In comparing the above traditions we notice in them two leading ideas, one in which this world-mountain is merely a giant mountain in the centre of the earth-disc with a summit touching the sky, another in which the mountain itself is situated in the sky, or the whole of the sky is imagined to be a mountain. Unless these ideas have a separate origin, the latter has in all probability developed from the former. The world-mountains of the ancient peoples — at least the Sumeru of India and the Hara Berezaiti of the Iranians — were cosmic, central mountains of the earth-disc. The *Bŭndahish* explains how all the stars, both fixed stars and planets, move round the mountain, to which they are bound as to the world-post. In a very interesting manner, both ideas are joined in the Sumeru of Chinese pictures, the mountain here resembling an hour-glass, comparatively narrow at its centre and widening both upwards and downwards; the upper part widens to a sky covering the earth.[12] Still stranger forms can be seen in Japanese art, where this rather narrow central mountain widens at measured intervals to represent the different storeys of Heaven.[13] In this shape Sumeru resembles a tree rather than a mountain, and is well designed to throw light on the manner in which the branched world-tree may have developed from the world-pillar.

A Central Asian tale places on this high, three-stepped central mountain a still greater world-tree. That this mountain, imagined as being three great steps, was rectangular, is shown by the fact that the summit, on which the world-tree stood, was " a square-shaped area." In addition, on each side of the mountain, there are said to be four mounds, which are called the four continents, believed by the inhabitants of India to be situated round Sumeru, one at each point of the compass. How impressive the view from the crown of the world-tree on the summit of the mountain is, appears from the fact, that looking from there, according to the tale, the earth floating in the ocean is no larger than the hoof of a horse. The height of the tree is pictured further by the idea that if a stone of the size of a bull is thrown down from there, it will reach the earth after the lapse of fifty years and then be no larger than a lamb.[14]

To this heaven-mountain idea, there is thus also connected
the idea of a world-ocean. In an Altaic creation tale the mountain and the ocean are said to have existed before the earth
peopled by men was created.[15]

The same mountain and ocean appear in the tales of the
Mongols, in which an evil giant snake called Losy is spoken of,
the home of which is in the ocean under the earth. By squirt-
ing poison on the earth, this being attempts to crush out life
by killing men and animals. At the request of God the hero
Otshirvani engaged this sea-monster in battle, but his powers
were not sufficient to overcome it, and he nearly fell victim
himself to the monster. Seeing this he fled from the earth and
ascended the Sumer mountain where he changed himself to the
mighty Garide bird. In this form he attacked the monster
again, seized its head with his claws, dragging it three times
round the world-mountain, and finally smashed in its head
with a great rock. This giant snake is said to be so large that
though its head is on the summit of the world-mountain, round
which its body is wound three times, its tail is still in the
ocean.[16]

This sea-monster, appearing in Central Asian tales also
under the name of Abyrga, was known already among the
ancient peoples of Asia. Along with Eastern myths and beliefs
it wandered to Europe. In Scandinavia there are tales of the
dreaded " Midgard snake," which " squirts poison " " scattering this over air and land." At the end of the world, " when
the sea will rise over the land " and " the giant snake squirms
in its wrath and crawls on to the earth," Thor will at last
succeed in killing it, falling dead himself from the poison
which the snake will have ejected against him.

As alien as the snake itself, is its vanquisher, the Garide
bird, which is said to live on Sumeru mountain and thus represents the heavenly powers in the tales of the Mongols. Its
name is identifiable with that of the Indian bird Garuda. The
hero Otshirvani, who changes himself into a bird, is the Bud-

dhist Bodhisattva Vairapani, and is only an addition, taken from legends, to this ancient tale.

Furthest developed is the cosmography with the Sumeru mountain in its centre, found at the present time in the teachings brought by Lamaism into Central and Eastern Asia. According to notes made among the Kalmucks the whole of the proportions of the universe is strictly fixed. The height of the central mountain is 80,000 leagues above the surface of the ocean, and at the same distance is its foundation in the world-ocean, where it rests on a stratum of gold, borne in its turn by a turtle. Round Sumeru there are seven circular " golden " mountain chains, divided from this and from each other by seven seas. Naturally these seas also are ring-shaped. The nearer a mountain chain is to the central mountain, the higher it is. The first is 40,000 leagues, the second 20,000, the third 10,000, the fourth 5,000, the fifth 2,500, the sixth 1,250, and the seventh, or last, 625 leagues above the ocean. As with the height, the distance between these mountain chains is also exactly defined. The higher the mountains become, the further they are from each other. The distance of each from the central mountain is the same as their height. The water of each of these inland seas is fresh, but the last mountain chain is surrounded by a salt ocean, which in its turn is ringed in with an " iron " mountain chain $312\frac{1}{2}$ leagues high. This iron chain, the circumference of which is 3,602,625 leagues and which is situated 322,000 leagues distant from the nearest mountain chain, forms the outer edge of the world. The circumference of the salt ocean is 3,600,750 leagues.

Sumeru itself is shaped like a pyramid slightly broken-off at the top. Its circumference at the surface of the sea is 2000 leagues and at its summit $3\frac{1}{2}$ leagues. The sides of the pyramid facing the different points of the compass glow with different colours. The southern side is blue, the western red, the northern yellow, and the eastern white. These different colours are said to come from the jewel or metal coverings of the different sides. On the south side there is a blue-gleaming and on the west a red-glowing jewel covering, the north side is golden and the east silver. These four colours are reflected in the parts of the world facing them, and for this reason the south is called the blue, the west the red, the north the yellow, and the east the white point of the compass.

In each direction there is a continent in the salt ocean, or as many as in certain tales already related. These continents are pictured as great islands, beside which there is on each side a smaller island, so that the total number of the islands surrounding the centre of the world is twelve. Without doubt, this conception, free from all geographical facts, reflects the beliefs connected with the twelve pictures of the cosmologic Zodiac. The Zodiac was already. imagined by the ancient Babylonians as the " land of Heaven." As above, so are there twelve lands below.

The people dwelling in these four continents differ from one another, above all, in the shape of their faces. The dwellers in the southern, or the continent in which India, China, Mongolia and many other lands are situated, have oval faces; those of the west round; those of the north square; and those of the east crescent-moon shaped faces. The continents themselves, as may be seen from the accompanying illustration, are of the same shapes.[17]

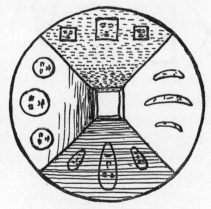

FIG. 15. A KALMUCK WORLD-PICTURE

This cosmography, which prevails in Tibet and in other Buddhistic districts, has its roots in the mists of antiquity. It is strange to find this colour idea connected with the four cardinal points also among certain

North American Indian tribes. Naturally, the colours of the different points vary among different peoples. The Chinese regard the east as blue, the south as red, the west as white, and the north as black. The colours of the cardinal points in America are black, white, yellow and blue, or, black, white, red and blue (green).[18] That these colour ideas have also had their counterparts in the sources of civilization in Nearer Asia is shown, e.g., by the belief, that when God created man he gathered differently coloured materials from the four quarters of the earth: i.e., red, black, white and brown.

CHAPTER V

THE TREE OF LIFE

AT THE navel of the earth, in the centre of the universe, according to Altaic tales, the highest tree on earth, a giant silver-fir, raises its crown to the dwelling of Bai-Ylgön.[1] Here we find the world-tree, situated in the earlier tales on the Sumeru mountain, removed to the navel or centre of the earth. Generally this tree is also imagined to grow on a high hill or mountain, especially on the central mountain of the earth, as appears from the words of a folk-poem already cited: "In the centre of the earth there is an iron mountain and on this iron mountain a white, seven-branched birch." But as this central mountain of the earth-disc is generally believed to hide its summit among the storeys of the sky, the tree itself, for very obvious reasons, has been raised into the sky, where, according to different beliefs and tales it continues to exist.

In the beliefs of the peoples related to the Turks this tree, which with the growth of the universe has grown from a small sapling to its present height, is intimately connected, like the world-mountain, with the construction of the universe.[2] And independently of whether it rises from the earth, a high mountain, or some storey in the sky, its position always resembles that of the world-pillar; like the former, the gods use this also to tether their horses to. In the fact, also, that it is often pictured as many-storeyed, it resembles the world-pillar. Thus, for example, in the shaman songs of the Vasyugan Ostiaks, which contain images obviously borrowed from the Tatars, this tree, like the heavens themselves, is said to be seven-storeyed.[3] More often, however, it is regarded as piercing the different floors of the sky, thrusting at the same time, like the central mountain which is its foundation, its roots deep into the underground depths.

This cosmic tree differs from the world-pillar chiefly in the fact that it is always regarded as a branched, living tree, an essential and at the same time most peculiar feature of which is its freshness and sappiness. In most of the tales it is situated on the brink of some spring, lake or sea, even at times in the water itself. The Ostiaks speak of " the watery sea of the heaven-centre " beside which this tree grows.⁴ The water from which the tree nourishes itself is described in a Minusinsk Tatar poem as follows:

> " Piercing twelve heavens
> On the summit of a mountain
> A birch in the misty depths of air.
> Golden are the birch's leaves,
> Golden its bark,
> In the ground at its foot a basin
> Full of the water of life,
> In the basin a golden ladle. . . ."

In the poem it is mentioned further that this " birch " is watched over by the forefather of the Tatars, the old Tata, who was given this post by the Creator himself.⁵

The same wonderful birch is met with in the tales of East European people. Thus, the Mordvins tell of a giant birch growing on a hill in the depths of the forest, the roots of which ring round the earth and whose branches surround the heavens. Its leaves are of the size of the palm of a hand, and its buds as long as the lash of a whip. At the root of the birch is a spring, roofed over with carved boards and white sheets, on its edge a red wooden can, in the can a sweet honey-drink, and in the liquid a silver ladle, the bottom of which is decorated with the sun and the moon, the handle with the smaller stars. As the sun moves in the heavens, the handle of the ladle turns with it.⁶

More interesting is this tree glowing with life in the folklore of the Yakuts.

On the yellow navel of the eight-edged earth, according to one of their tales, there is a dense, eight-branched tree. Its bark and knots are silver, its sap golden, its cones like nine-cornered goblets, and its leaves wide as the hide of a horse. From the crown of the tree runs foaming a heavenly, yellowish liquid. When passers-by drink of this, the tired among them are refreshed and the hungry become satisfied.[7]

This life-giving tree is, according to the Yakut tales, the dwelling-place of " the First Man "; and therefore some sort of paradise. When " the First Man," on appearing on the earth, wished to know why he had been created, he approached this giant tree, the crown of which " pierces through the three-storeyed Heaven " and " along the branches of which a light-coloured liquid flows " bringing blessedness to the one tasting it, and saw an opening appear in the trunk, from which opening a female, visible only to the waist, informed him that he had been created to become the father of the human race.[8]

A variant of this same tale describes " the First Man " as " the White Youth." " Above the wide motionless depths, below the seven storeys, the nine discs of heaven, in the central place, on the navel of the earth, in the quietest place, where the moon does not decline, nor the sun sink, where there is summer without winter and the cuckoo sings eternally, was the White Youth." He set out to walk to see where he had appeared, and what his dwelling-place was like. In the east he saw a wide, lightish plain, on the plain a mighty hill and on the hill a giant tree. The resin of the tree was transparent and sweetly perfumed, its bark never dried or cracked, its sap was silvery, its leaves never withered and its cones were like a row of reversed goblets. The crown of the tree rose over the seven storeys of Heaven, being the tethering-post of the Over-god Yryn-ai-tojon, and its roots went deep down into the underground depths where they were the dwelling-pillars of the strange mythical beings there. By means of its leaves the tree talked with the dwellers in Heaven.

Walking southward the White Youth saw a calm " lake of milk " in the centre of a green, grassy plain, which lake was never rippled by a breath of wind and on the shores of which were curdled swamps. In the north was a dark forest, where the trees rustled day and night and where all manner of animals moved. Behind the forest rose high mountains, bearing caps that resembled white rabbit-skin; the mountains leaned against the heavens, protecting these from cold winds. In the west grew a low tangle of bushes, behind these a high forest of firs, and behind the forest solitary blunt-headed mountains were just discernible.

Such was the world, in which the White Youth saw the light of day. Tired of his lonely existence he approached the tree of life and said: " Honoured High Mistress, Spirit of my tree and my dwelling-place, everything living moves in couples and gives birth to descendants, but I am alone. I wish to travel and seek a partner worthy of me, I wish to know other people and measure my strength against them, I wish to live as a man should. Do not refuse thy blessing, I pray to thee with humbled, bowed head and with bent knees."

Then the leaves of the tree commenced to rustle and a fine milk-white rain dripped from them upon the White Youth. A warm zephyr was felt, the tree creaked, and from under its roots a female being arose up to her waist. This spirit of the tree and of the place is described by the tale as a grave-eyed, middle-aged woman with flowing locks and naked bosom. The goddess offered the Youth milk from her swelling breasts, and having drunk, he felt how his powers had grown a hundred-fold. At the same time the goddess promised him every happiness and blessed him so that neither water, fire, iron nor anything else could harm him.[9]

It is obvious that this tale cannot have originated among the Yakuts in the cold atmosphere of North-East Siberia, but, as the glowing description of Paradise hints at, in the lap of a much richer and more fertile nature. With the help of the

PLATE XLIII

OLD TURKISH MEMORIAL IMAGE IN NORTH
MONGOLIA

(See page 301.)
After photograph by S. Pālsi.

description of nature in the tale, in which the mountains with white caps resembling rabbit-skin appearing in the north are obviously snow-clad mountains, we can endeavour to find the birthplace of this story, which pre-supposes the knowledge both of a fertile vegetation and of snow-clad mountains. We turn naturally then either to India or Nearer Asia. But the paradise landscape cannot, however, as such be used as a guide, as the " lake of milk " and other details belong to the beliefs connected with the navel of the earth. In addition the landscape differs somewhat in the different variants.

Before examining the above tale more minutely, we will glance at a few additional details throwing more light on the tree of life, these details being contained in the examples of the Yakut language published by Middendorff. In these the first man, " the ancestor of the Yakuts," is called Är-soghotoch (" the Lonely Man "). His dwelling also is spoken of, which is in the centre of the plain and has four silver-gleaming corners, forty windows, fifty pillars, and thirty roof-trees; the walls and the golden floor are fourfold and the silver roof threefold. Altogether this dwelling would therefore seem to have possessed seven storeys. The tree of life itself is described in the following words: " When he comes out of his dwelling on to the balcony towards the east to see the landscape, he has before him the king of trees, which grows among the grass. This tree over which swings the blue air, is so old that its age cannot be reckoned in centuries. Its roots stretch through Hades and its crown pierces the nine heavens. The length of each leaf is seven fathoms and that of the cones nine fathoms. From under its roots foams the ' eternal water.' When its aged, starved and weary, white or dark cattle, its flying or running game, drink or lick the sap and resin which drip from this tree's branches and cones, gathering and forming a brawling stream, they acquire again their former youth and overflowingness." It is further related that when the spirit of the tree, " a white-haired aged goddess," mottled of body like a woodcock and with breasts as large as "leather-bags," appears, the tree creaks and groans, growing smaller, until with the re-entrance of the goddess it regains its former size. From this spirit of the tree the Lonely Man receives the knowledge that his father is the Heaven god Ar-tojon ("The High Lord") and his mother Kybäi-Khotun ("Kybäi Mistress"), who had immediately after his birth lowered him from the third heaven to the earth so that he might become the forefather of the human race. At the same time the spirit takes water from under the roots of the tree and pours it into a bladder, which she gives to her ward, saying: "Fasten this under thy left arm, in the uttermost danger it will save thee." Later, according to the tale, the hero fights a duel on a courtship journey with a wicked dragon, receiving a blow in the heart, but the bladder bursting at the same time and its contents flowing on to the wound, his heart becomes immediately whole, giving him in addition his powers back ninefold.[10]

Where and how the tree of life ideas in this Yakut tale may have originated in the mists of antiquity, related tales are already met with among the ancient peoples in India, in Iran, in Mesopotamia, and in Egypt. As is well known, the corresponding beliefs of the ancient Semites are reflected in the Bible: "And out of the ground made the Lord God to grow every tree that is pleasant to the sight and good for food; the tree of life also in the midst of the garden. . . ." As in the Yakut tale the first man dwells here beside the tree of life. Similarly the nourishment afforded by the tree gives eternal life. The same conceptions appear from the following words from the *Book of Revelation:* "To him that overcometh will I give to eat of the tree of life, which is in the midst of the paradise of God." And for the belief that the water of life flows under the roots of the tree we find a counterpart in other words from the same book: "And he shewed me a pure river of water of life . . . and on either side of the river was there the tree of life which bare twelve manner of fruits and yielded her fruit every month: and the leaves of the tree were for the healing of the nations." Here we find also the health-giving properties of the tree of life mentioned. It is thus obvious that the Yakut tale and the images in the Bible are derived from a common foundation idea. In the former there are several additional details, such as the milk-breasted goddess, which are unknown to the Bible and cannot be regarded as having sprung from legends formed on the Bible stories, but must have had some other tale related to this as model.

Just as many of the Central and Northern Asian tales place the tree of life on a high hill or mountain, even in Heaven itself, so the Semitic paradise was imagined to be, sometimes on the central mountain of the earth, sometimes in Heaven. From the fact that the ancient Babylonians already in olden times knew of the paradise-mountain of the gods, the tree, and the water of life, we may conclude that this belief, relics of which have come down to us from ancient times, is of extreme age among the civilized peoples of Nearer Asia.

The corresponding beliefs in Indian mythology are pointed to further by the above mentioned Central Asian tale in which the mighty world-tree is situated on the Sumeru mountain. That this tree was the tree of life, the following tale, likewise from Central Asia, shows: " In the beginning was no land, only water out of which rose two great mountains. On the summit of one were three temples, harbouring thirty-three Tengeri or gods. At the foot of the mountain was a triangular plain, from which rose the extremely high Zambu tree, with its crown higher than the mountain. The Tengeri ate of its fruit, but the beings living under the tree, the Asuras, shouted to the Tengeri: ' Why do you eat from the tree growing on our land? ' The Asuras became at last so inflamed that they commenced to war against the Tengeri; in this war, however, they lost and were vanquished. The gods then threw down sand from the mountain, and even gold, and in this way the earth was created, on to which two gods, male and female, descended in order to people the earth with their descendants." [11]

In the beginning of the tale, two eternal mountains are thus mentioned, which appear thousands of years earlier in the cosmology of the ancient civilized peoples of Nearer Asia, but only one is described in detail, the Tengeri dwelling on the summit of which are the thirty-three gods of the Sumeru mountain of Indian mythology. Similarly, the beings dwelling at the foot of the mountain are the Asura giants of India, who were believed to dwell in the bottomless chasms of Meru, and from there warred against Indra and other gods. The Zambu tree also, from which the gods were nourished is, as the name shows, the Indian tree of life, Jambu. According to Buddhistic mythology this tree has sixteen large branches but a multitude of smaller ones. Its ruddy-grey leaves are as fine as the purest silk and its flowers glowing like gold. In its fruit there are hundreds of sweet lumps, of the size of goose-eggs, which drive away all diseases. The golden-yellow sap of the tree drips like melting butter. The beings living around procure their nourishment from this tree of life. [12]

It is probable that the idea of a tree of life among the Indians has its roots in distant ages, as already in the poems of the *Veda* the immortality-producing nourishment of Soma, which grew on a mountain, is mentioned. Corresponding to this is the Haoma of Iranian mythology, imagined as a fertile, golden-flowered tree of life and as such placed on the central mountain of the world, Hara Berezaiti. The Rauhina tree of the Indian poem *Suparnadhyaya*, from which a mythological eagle, the Garuda, known as the robber of Soma, breaks off a branch, is probably also a relic of a tree of life, in which the said bird, according to earlier ideas, was believed to live. In the folk-poetry of the Iranians we meet with this mythological bird in the crown of the tree of life.

The Indian tales cannot, however, be regarded as the model for the Yakut tale mentioned. Their tree of life resembles more the ancient Egyptian pictures, in which a date-palm described as being partly a tree and partly a woman, gives to its ward nourishment producing eternal life. Sometimes this tree is seen pictured on the brink of the spring of the water of life.[13]

The tree of life of the Yakuts with its goddess appearing from the roots resembles also the Yggdrasil of the Icelandic *Edda*, " Which is the greatest and best of all trees," whose " branches cover the whole earth and rise over the heavens," whose " tall trunk is hidden by a white fluid " and which will " stagger first when the world ends." Under this " openly flourishing tree, dripping honey-dew " is a wonderful spring, Urdarbrunn, beside which under the roots of the tree live the three deities of birth and fate, the Norns. If we compare Yggdrasil with the Yakut tree of life, it becomes obvious that they are identical, even to their details, with the exception that under the tree of life of the Scandinavian poem there are three, and under the Yakut, only one goddess.

The eagle also of the *Edda*, which sits in the crown of the tree, and the Nidhugg snake under its roots are details closely connected with the tree of life of Central Asia. The Kalmucks relate how a dragon in the sea at the foot of the Zambu tree lay in wait for the leaves dropping from Zambu. The leaves which it failed to catch, sinking to the bottom, turned into gold there.[14] In the Buriat poems a mythological snake called Abyrga is said to dwell at the foot of the tree in a " lake of milk." [15] In certain Central Asian tales the Abyrga snake twines round the tree itself, while at the same time the Garide eagle living in the crown attacks and pecks at it.[16] This Garide, which when flying furiously causes storms, is, as the name indicates, the Indian Garuda, the well-known robber of Soma.

The precursors of the Yakut tales have probably been the paradise ideas of the ancient Iranians, like the beliefs of the West Siberian peoples, who place this mighty tree on " the iron mountain " rising from the centre of the earth-disc. From ancient Persian literature we see that they also called the central mountain of the earth Hara Berezaiti, " the iron mountain," on the summit of which they believed the tree of life to be. On this mountain where, under the tree of life, is the spring of the water of life, Ardvisura, and the paradise of the Iranians, dwells the first man, Gajomartan, as in the Yakut paradise. Like the latter the Iranians also pictured him as a " white " being.[17] With the help of these facts we can assume that the tale in question has spread along with a current of civilization from the Iranians to the Turco-Tatar peoples, and with the Yakuts wandered to the distant River Lena, where their folk-lore was able to preserve it as near the original as has been shown, and thus to hand down to the present generation a valuable relic of the paradise ideas of the Iranians and the whole East, of which ideas only scanty and scattered fragments are to be found in ancient literature.

With the greater reason, therefore, do we turn our attention to the Yakut conception of the tree of life. From the preceding tales we have seen that besides " the First Man," the whole of the animals of creation dwell near the tree, and that it is regarded as the nourisher of them all. But in the beginning the tree would seem to have had a still more marvellous significance. A variant of the tale describes how the Over-god and the goddess of Birth and Fate, Kybäi-Khotun, the name also of the spirit dwelling in the tree, gave birth to the first man in the third heaven, from which he was lowered down to the earth; but despite this, the other version goes on to details showing how the ancestor of the human race really appeared in his life-giving surroundings. His curiosity as to where he has come from leads him to the conclusion that he has been born in those very surroundings. This appears, e.g., from his words: " If I had dropped down from heaven, I should be covered with snow and hoar-frost, if I had come from the south or the north, from the east or the west of the central place (the earth), I should bear marks of trees and grass and I should give out the scent of the wind; if I had risen from the bowels of the earth, I should have the dust of the earth on me." [18] It appears probable, therefore, that the milk-breasted goddess of the wonderful tree has given birth to him and that " the First Man " is right in saying to her: " Be my mother, as though thou hadst given birth to me; be my creator, as though thou hadst created me." Motherly care is also defined in the words: " Thou hast brought up me, an orphan, to man's estate, thou hast suffered me, the little one, to grow up." [19]

Further, we can hardly be mistaken in assuming that all the living beings crowded round this tree have the spirit to thank for their existence. Man at least confesses: " Thou hast brought up my white cattle, for my black beasts hast thou cared, protected my birds and my game, and kept together the fishes of my black waters." [20]

With the Central Asian ideas of the tree of life, as an essential feature, we have seen the belief connected that under the roots of the tree is a spring containing the water of life. In the tales of the Yakuts the tree itself is sometimes said to drip a sap-like fluid so copiously, that a foaming brook is formed. Under the Iranian tree of life there is a spring in which all the rivers of the earth have their source. Even the belief that the tree of life rises out of a lake or sea of wonderful water is met with.

Thus, e.g., the Kalmucks tell how the Zambu tree rises out of the Marvo Sea, which is as deep as it is broad and contains water of eight different elements. From this sea run four great rivers. These are said to flow towards the different points of the compass and, after having made seven turnings, to return to their source of origin. On their journey, each river receives the waters of five hundred tributaries. The sea itself is regarded as a mountain-lake, as each river pierces a rock, said to resemble some animal. The rivers flowing towards the east, south, west, and north emerge from rocks which are respectively like the mouths of an elephant, a bull, a horse, and a lion.[21] The animals in this tale represent the points of the compass, a belief extremely old among the civilized peoples of Asia, though the animals themselves may vary. Thus, in the Chinese tale the east is represented by a blue dragon, the south by a red bird, the west by a white tiger, and the north by a black turtle. To prevent diseases the Mongols are said to have built on the site of an old Chinese town a sanctuary (*obo*), at the four sides of which they erected wooden images of the points of the compass, i.e., a tiger, a lion, an eagle, and a dragon.[22]

That these four rivers of the Kalmuck tales have their source at the very centre of the earth, is shown by the fact that they are believed to carry with them the materials decorating the sides of the central mountain. The eastern river contains silver sand, the southern blue jewel sand, the western red jewel sand and the northern gold sand.

There can be no doubt of the fact that these ideas of the Kalmucks have come down to them from India along with the currents of civilization, even though these four rivers of paradise have, as the Bible shows, been known also to the Semitic race.

CHAPTER VI

DESTRUCTION OF THE WORLD

BESIDES the destruction caused by the subsidence of the pillar supporting the sky, other dangers also are believed to threaten the earth peopled by men. To the idea that the earth is situated on the bosom of a great cosmic ocean is attached the fear that the foundations of the earth may give way or that it may become inundated. The Asian tales of the different periods of the earth relate how a great flood once destroyed all life on it, and how a human being who escaped became the ancestor of a new race of men. Tales of this description are met with also among the Altaic peoples. Whether these are founded on ancient borrowings, and whether they contain any direct remainders of such loans, is difficult to conclude; in their present state, as known to us, they would seem to represent later currents of civilization. One may assume, however, that later arriving legends have been prone to sweep aside the more ancient forms of this tale.

A very common modern form is found in the following Buriat tale: Before the flood arrived, Burkhan advised a certain man to build himself a great ship. Following the advice of God, the man went to the forest, where he worked throughout the days. At last his wife, becoming curious, wished to know what her husband worked at so industriously in the forest. To keep his intention secret, the man replied that he chopped wood there. While the man was away, the devil, Shitkur, came to the woman explaining that her husband had deceived her and that he was building a great ship in the forest. And in the end the devil begged the woman to help him, saying: "The ship will soon be ready and thy husband will invite thee to enter it, but do thou refuse, and when he becomes angry and strikes thee, say to him: ' Why, dost thou strike me, Shitkur? ' When thou enterest the ship after this, I shall accompany thee." The woman promised to follow the advice of the devil. Soon a great flood threatened to destroy the whole earth and the builder of the ship exhorted his family to enter his vessel, but the wife resisted so long that the man became angry and began to beat her. The wife then said, as the devil had taught her: " Why, dost thou strike me, Shitkur? " When she finally went on board, the devil was enabled to accompany her. The tale tells in addition how, with the help of Burkhan, the man gathered specimens of all the animals into his ship with the exception of the Prince of animals (Argalan-Zon), which deemed itself so large that no flood could drown it. Having entered the vessel, the devil changed himself into a mouse and began to gnaw holes in the bottom of the vessel, until Burkhan created the cat to catch the mouse. As the flood was so great that it destroyed all the animals left on the earth, the Prince of animals, whose bones may be found in the earth today, was also drowned.[1] According to other tales the animal which failed to survive the flood was the mammoth.[2]

In a tale recorded among the Sagaiyes, in which the builder of the ship is called Noj, the devil tempts his wife to inquire what he is building in the forest, and having found out, begins to destroy by night what Noj builds during the day. Thus, when the flood begins, the vessel is not yet completed, and God is forced to send down to the man a vessel of iron, in which Noj with his wife and family and all kinds of animals are saved.[3]

In both tales, our attention is called to the part played by the devil; otherwise they resemble the Bible story of the flood. The Noj of these tales is unquestionably the Noah of the Bible.

The corresponding tales of the Irtysh Ostiaks and the Southern Voguls make the devil give the wife of the hero of the flood a strong drink, by the help of which she entices her husband to relate his secret. The Ostiaks call the man by a name borrowed from the Tatars, Pairekse.[4]

A legend corresponding in all its details is known also to the peoples of East Europe, where it is probably of literary origin. It is to be found at least in the Russian version of the *Revelations* of Pseudo-Methodius. With Russian settlers it may possibly have migrated in this form to Siberia, where told by these, it has been written down, e.g., in the territory behind the Baikal. In its chief points, this Russian legend is as follows: In order to find out why Noah is building his ark, the devil advises his wife to prepare a strong drink, having drunk of which Noah, in a state of intoxication, informs his wife of the secret entrusted to him by God. The devil disturbs Noah in his work, and when the ark is at last completed, he creeps into it in the company of Noah's wife, who has tempted her husband into pronouncing the devil's name. Arrived in the ark, in the guise of a mouse, he gnaws holes in the bottom of the ark.[5]

The flood tale of Pseudo-Methodius is without doubt a late Eastern apocryphal legend founded on the Bible story. That the wife of Noah, who is not especially mentioned in the Bible, was also the subject of tales among the Arabians, is suggested by the passage in the Koran, in which Noah's wife is mentioned, together with the wife of Lot, as being among the damned. Further, the manner in which the devil succeeds in entering the ark in the company of Noah's wife, greatly resembles the following Islamic tale, as already pointed out by Dähnhardt: When the ark was completed and all the animals hurried there in pairs, Noah saw that the ass lingered behind; annoyed, he shouted to it: " Come in, thou accursed! " This moment was taken advantage of by the evil Iblis, who answered, when the astonished Noah asked him how he had come into the ark: " I came at thine invitation, there being among the creations of God none accursed but I." [6] There are, however, no indications that the already cited tales could have spread into Siberia from Islam.

Nearer the Bible story than any other ancient flood tale known to us, is the following Altaic tale: "Up to the time when the flood (*jaik*) hid all the earth, Tengys (Sea) was lord over the earth. During his rule there lived a man called Nama, a good man, whom Ülgen commanded to build an ark (*kerep*). Nama, who had three sons, Sozun-uul, Sar-uul, and Balyks, was already failing of sight and therefore left the building of the ark to his sons. When the ark, which was built on a mountain, was completed, Nama told his sons to hang from its corners and walls eight cables of eighty fathoms each, by the help of which he could later determine ' how many days it takes for the water to rise eighty fathoms.' After this had been done, Nama entered the ark, taking with him his family and the various animals and birds which, threatened by the rising waters, gathered around him. Seven days later the cables attached to the earth gave way and the ark drifted free. This showed that the water had already risen eighty fathoms. When seven days had elapsed again, Nama told his eldest son to open the window of the ark and to look around. Sozun-uul looked in all directions and then said: ' Everything has sunk under the waters, only the summits of the mountains are in sight.' Later, when ordered by his father to look out again, he was able to answer: ' Nothing is to be seen, only the sky and the waters.' At last the ark stopped on eight closely situated mountains. Then Nama himself opened the window and set free the raven, which, however, did not return. On the second day he released the crow, and on the third the rook, but neither of these returned. On the fourth day he sent out the dove, which returned with a twig of birch in its beak. From this bird Nama also heard why the other birds had not returned. The raven had found the carcase of a deer, the crow that of a dog, and the rook that of a horse, which they had

stayed behind to devour. Hearing this, Nama became enraged
and laid a curse on these birds, saying: ' What they are doing
now, let them continue with to the end of the world! ' " The
tale goes on to relate that when Nama had become very old,
his wife exhorted him to kill all the men and animals he had
saved from the flood, so that, being transferred to the other
world, they would be under his power there also. Under the
ceaseless exhortations of his wife, Nama became restless and
did not know what to do. Then his son Sozun-uul, who knew
the intentions of his mother but did not dare to oppose her
openly, related to his father the following incident: " I saw
a blue-black cow devouring a human being so that only the
legs were any longer to be seen." Having understood this
fable, Nama seized his sword and cleft his wife in two, beginning at the head. Finally Nama removed to heaven, taking
his son Sozun-uul with him, and changing the latter into a
constellation of five stars.[7]

Thus, in this tale also, the wife of the hero of the flood
is pictured as a wicked person. Otherwise, the tale differs
greatly from the preceding dualistic tales and has obviously
reached Central Asia apart from these. Among some of the
Altaic peoples the hero of the flood has also become the object
of certain beliefs. As such he is often called Jaik-Khan (" the
Flood Prince ") and is prayed to as the intervener between
the Over-god and man, and as the protector of man. In some
places a white lamb is sacrificed to him annually in the spring.
The sacrifice is carried out on a high mountain. He is also
supposed to be the ruler of the dead, and as such is invited
to the house-purification ceremonies forty days after a death,
and begged to return the domestic animals, which the dead,
according to the people, sometimes take with them. In the
shaman rites also he is often spoken with and desired to con-
vey the prayers of the people to the Over-god.[8] His dwelling-
place is situated in the third heaven, where the paradise of the
blessed is, and from there, at suitable times, he sends his mes-

senger with a soul for a child born on the earth. In this capacity he is called Jajutshi (" the Orderer ").[9]

These ideas of the Altai Tatars correspond to those which the Irtysh Ostiaks have borrowed for their Pairekse from the Tatars. As we have already seen, the latter also is regarded as the hero of the flood, appearing besides in some tales as the " Writer man," who writes in heaven, in the Book of Fate, according to the dictation of God, how long and in what circumstances a human being is to live on the earth.

Not only as the ancestor of the present human race, but also as a kind of Creator does the hero of the flood appear in the flood tales of the Soyots: When the giant frog (turtle) supporting the earth happened to move once, the cosmic ocean began to flood the earth. A certain old man who had guessed that something of the kind would happen, built a raft strengthened with iron, placed himself upon it with his family, and was saved. With the decline of the waters the raft grounded on a high wooded mountain, where it is said to be still. After the flood, this Kezer-Tshingis-Kaira-Khan re-created everything we now see around us. He is especially mentioned as having taught people how to prepare strong drinks, an invention accredited also to the hero of the Bible story.[10]

How deeply the story of the flood has taken root in the beliefs of the peoples around the Altai, is shown by their obstinate belief that the raft or the ark is still today on the summit of one of the local mountains, where, however, it is not good for man to search for it, as none have returned from the spot alive. In other places, tradition tells that on the site of the grounding of the ark, great nails have been found, believed to be remains of the vessel of the flood.[11]

But in what manner can the hero of the flood have risen to godlike eminence, to be the object of worship, and have had ascribed to him so wide a field of action as he actually has among the Altaic peoples? Without doubt, the beliefs of the

Iranians may be regarded as having brought this about. Their
" First Man," Yima, who was worshipped as the ruler over
souls, was at the same time the hero of the flood. This ruler
is met with in Altai Tatar tales as Schal-Jime, the first part of
the name being a deformation of a Thibetan word meaning
" Prince of Death." In one Altaic creation-tale God says:
" Thou art my man, Schal-Jime; look well after the man who
has tasted strong drink, and little children, foals, calves and
lambs; those dying happily take to thee! " [12] According to the
preceding, Schal-Jime, like Jaik-Khan, is the ruler over infants and those dying happily.

Some of the more northern peoples of Siberia tell how the
flood brought about the origin of many races and many languages, a question dealt with in the Bible in connection with
the tower of Babel. The Ugrians tell how the people saved
on their rafts drifted in different directions, settling after the
flood in different parts of the earth.[13] In the same way, without mentioning any special hero, the Yenisei Ostiaks relate:
When the water rose continuously during seven days, part of
the people and animals were saved by climbing on to the logs
and rafters floating on the water. But a strong north wind,
which blew without ceasing for seven days, scattered the people
far from one another. And for this reason they began, after
the flood, to speak different languages and to form different
peoples.[14]

Original and unaffected as these tales appear to be, especially
in the frequently flooded Yenisei district, where the hated
north wind often causes trouble, we cannot even here, in this
primitive state, assume the story to have originated in North
Siberia. Above all, the influence of foreign flood tales seems
to be apparent in the seven-day periods of time. Compared
with the former tales, however, these latter would seem to
represent a new type.

Far away in the north, on the tundras of the Samoyeds,
a flood tale has also been recorded, in which, as in the ancient

Indian tales, seven persons are said to have been saved in a boat. The Samoyeds go on to relate how, after the flood, a terrible drought followed, so that these survivors were nearly dying of thirst. From this disaster, however, they were saved by digging a deep hole in the ground, in which water formed. More difficult was the finding of nourishment. This caused all but one young man and one maid to die of hunger, these two having started to eat the mice which came out of the ground. From this couple the present human race is descended.[15]

For the sake of comparison a flood tale from North-East Siberia may be given, according to which people were saved by binding together trunks of trees into great rafts. Establishing themselves on these, they took with them sufficient provisions for the duration of the flood. To prevent the rafts from drifting out to sea, the people fastened rocks to long ropes which were then dropped to the bottom as anchors. Finally, these log-rafts grounded on a high mountain.[16] In the above form this story is told, e.g., by the Kamchadales.

Besides a destructive flood, some of the North Siberian peoples speak also of a great conflagration, which once destroyed all life on the earth. The Tungus from behind the Baikal describe it as follows: In the beginning was the earth, but then a great fire raged for seven years and the earth was burned up. Everything became sea. All the Tungus were consumed except a boy and a girl who rose up with an eagle into the sky. Having wandered for a time in the air, they descended to a place where the water had dried up. With them the eagle also descended to the earth.[17]

Of an all-devouring conflagration the Voguls also speak, telling how God sent a sea of fire upon the earth in order to destroy the devil. The cause of the fire they call "the firewater." In the destruction of all creation, only the gods and a few mortals succeeded in saving themselves. The former placed themselves on an "iron ship," the latter on a "seven-bottomed beech-raft," which was provided in addition with a fireproof, sevenfold cover of sturgeon-skin. The tale gives thus the same means of escape as the ordinary flood tales, which the conflagration tales of the Voguls otherwise resemble.

The tales of the Voguls also tell of a recurring conflagration, the fearful thunder of which the " Earth-watching man " hears from afar. This hero decides to ride through the fire, " one side of which glows in the heights of the sky, the other burning at both corners of the sky." With the help of his magic horse he succeeds also in his attempt. Munkácsi believes the Aurora Borealis to have been the original source of these ideas.[18] This he assumes is meant by the " sea of fire " through which the hero rides for seven days. Obviously, this great phenomenon of North Siberia has played a great part in awakening the imagination of the people, the white streaks appearing among the Northern Lights being sometimes called " The track of the white horse of the Earth-watching man," but even then this tale can hardly have been born among the Ugrians. A hero riding across a sea of fire on a magic steed is a story-theme met with over a wide area. Neither can the steed be identified with the eagle of the Tungus tale, although the conflagration tales of the two peoples seem to have much in common. As mentioned before, the fire in the Tungus tale lasts for seven years, corresponding to the description in the Vogul tale: " Already for seven winters and summers the fire has raged, already for seven winters and summers it has burnt up the earth." [19]

Conflagration tales have also been noted down elsewhere in Asia. Thus, for instance, in East India it is told how God, as mankind sank deeper into sin, sent a flood of fire on to the earth, here also called " water of fire." Two people only, brother and sister, were saved by hiding themselves.[20] The ancient civilized peoples of Nearer Asia would also seem to have known these conflagration tales.

Quite obvious is the alien influence in such Central Asian

tales which tell how a great fire will occur at the end of the world and burn up the whole earth.

The Altai Tatars say that when Ülgen sends Maidere (a Buddhist Bodhisattva) from the sky, who will teach people the fear of God and convert the greater part of mankind, the evil Erlik will become angry and say to Maidere: "I am strong enough to kill thee with my sword." At the same time the devil will attack Maidere and fulfil his threat. The blood of Maidere, said to turn the whole world red, will take fire, the flames surrounding the earth and rising to the heavens. Then Ülgen will arrive and clapping his hands together shout: "Ye dead, arise!" And at once these will arise from their hiding-places, some out of the earth and some from the sea, others from the fire or the places in which they had hidden when overtaken by death. In the world-conflagration Erlik and all wicked people will be destroyed.[21]

This mighty drama of the end of the world, in which the powers of good and evil engage in a final contest and in which evil is completely destroyed, is probably Iranian eschatology, preached perhaps in Central Asia by the apostles of Manicheism in their time.

Comparable with the eschatology of the Bible is also the belief of the Buriats, that at the end of the world a great river of fire will flow from the east to the west, throwing its sparks everywhere so that the whole of creation will be set alight. In the place of this old earth it is believed, however, that a new one will appear with new inhabitants.[22]

CHAPTER VII

THE CREATION OF MAN

THE TRANS–BAIKAL Tungus relate how Buga (the Heaven god) made the first two people out of various materials which he gathered from the four quarters of the earth. From the east he brought iron, from the south fire, from the west water, and from the north earth. Out of the earth he created the flesh and the bones, out of the iron the heart, out of the water blood, and out of the fire warmth.[1]

According to a Yeside creation story God made the body of Adam by mixing the four elements, fire, water, air and earth. Old Jewish, Arabian and Syrian tales describe also how God, when creating the first man, gathered material from the four corners of the earth.[2] According to the Jewish story, these materials of which God made the body of Adam in the centre of the earth, were of different colours, red, black, white and brown, from which we may assume that, as in the Tungus' tale, each contained some element connected with some quarter of the earth. Thus the first man was a kind of microcosmos, closely related to the macrocosmos.

This ancient fancy is to be found also in Russian tales of creation. In one manuscript from the twelfth century the four quarters of the earth have been doubled, the story relating that God gathered material from eight directions. In later tales, of which one is from the sixteenth century, it is said that Adam's body, i.e., the flesh, was made of earth, his bones of stone, his ligaments of roots, his blood of water, his eyes of the sun, his thoughts of clouds, his spirit of wind and his warmth of fire. According to another tale God made the body of earth, the bones of stone, the ligaments of roots, the blood of water, the hair of grass, the thoughts of wind (clouds) and the spirit of clouds (wind).[3]

How close the connection is between man and nature according to this Asiatic conception appears also in Persian literature (*Būndahish*, 30) in which the resurrection is described in the following words: "At that time the bones will be demanded back from the earth, the blood from water, the hair from plants, and life from fire, all these having been at the time of creation ordered to return to their respective sources after death."

But this relation of man with nature appears also from a contrary conception, according to which the macrocosmos itself is born of man, the microcosmos. According to a tale of the Kalmucks the world was formed from the body of Manzashiri (= the Buddhist Bodhisattva Manjucri), the trees from his blood-vessels, fire from the warmth of his interior organs, earth from his body, iron from his bones, water from his blood, grass from his hair, the sun and the moon from his eyes, the seven planets from his teeth, and the other stars from his back.[4] In the same way is the cosmos formed when the Chinese demiurge Pan-ku expires: from his spirit is born the wind, from his voice the thunder, from his left eye the sun and his right eye the moon, from his blood the rivers, from his hairs the plants, from his saliva the rain, and from his vermin mankind.[5] Already the Vedic literature of India (*Rgveda*, X. 90) tells how the world was formed from the body of a human-shaped primordial being, Purusa. The Manicheans have a similar tale,[6] and even far in Europe, in Scandinavia, we find a variant of it. In the *Edda* of Snorri it is told how the sons of Bor slew the giant Ymir, and of his flesh created the earth, of his blood the water, of his bones the stones and rocks, of his skull the sky, of his brains the clouds, and of his eyebrows the circle surrounding Midgard. Doubtless all the above stories have some connection with each other and have not arisen separately.

PLATE XLIV

OLD TURKISH MEMORIAL IMAGE IN NORTH
MONGOLIA

(See page 301.)
After photograph by S. Pālsi.

In the tales of the Central and North Asian peoples the materials of which the first man's body was made, vary. The most common conception among the Buriats is that the flesh was made of red clay, the bones of stone, and the blood of water.[7] The Altaic peoples believe that bones were created from reeds and the rest of the body from clay.[8] The North-West Siberian peoples, like the Voguls, relate how God " took willow-twigs, bound them into skeletons, covered them with a layer of clay, set them before him and blew into them." In other tales they tell how God created man and animals from earth and snow.[9] The Yenisei Ostiaks relate how God rubbed a piece of earth in each hand for a long time and at last threw them away. The piece thrown by the right hand became a man, that from the left hand, a woman.[10]

Although some Siberian peoples seem to have partly shaped their own creation beliefs, we can in nowise decide from this that the idea of creation itself was their own. The tales themselves, to which these original fancies are connected as separate details, are the best proof of their being of foreign origin.

As in the stories about the origin of the earth, so also in tales telling of the creation of man we find two antagonistic beings, God and the devil, the latter in some way marring the work of the former. In most instances the devil succeeds in approaching man before God has had time to give him life. The dog, whom God sets to watch over man, has a very important part in these tales.

Among the Black Tatars there is the following story: When the great Pajana formed the first people from a piece of earth, he could not give them life. He was therefore compelled to go to Heaven to Kudai to seek a life-giving spirit for them. When going he left a dog to guard the people. While he was away the devil Erlik arrived and said to the yet naked dog: " Thou hast no fur-covering, I will give thee golden hairs, give thou to me those soulless people." The dog was delighted with Erlik's proposal and gave the people whom he was to guard into the keeping of the devil. Having thus come near the people the devil defiled them by spitting on them, but fled when he saw Kudai approaching to give them life. When God saw that the devil had befouled the bodies of the people and that it was impossible to make them clean again he turned them inside out. From that time the interior of man is full of filth and spittle.[11]

A similar explanation of the origin of the filth inside man is given by a Yakut tale. When God had created the world he built a great stone house in which he placed seven stone images and " Man " to guard them. Day by day the devil begged for entrance into the house, endeavouring to bribe the guardian without success, until he promised " Man " an indestructible garment, which he need never take off. He was then allowed to approach the images and to soil them with his evacuations. When God came to look at his images and saw what the devil had done in his absence he grew angry, reproached the guardian, and fulfilled his wish by changing him into a dog. The images he turned inside out and blew a spirit into them. For that reason the interior of man is full of filth.[12]

Corresponding tales are met with among the Volga Finns, the Cheremiss, Votiaks and Mordvins. The purport of these tales also is to explain why the interior of God-created man is unclean. The Mordvin tale tells in addition that internal diseases are caused by the spittle of the devil.[13] Certain diseases, a cough in particular, are given a similar origin in Russian tales. In the Samoyed tale which does not contain the turning inside out of man, serious eruptions, pox, and gatherings are the result of the devil's saliva. In this tale also appears a dog, naked as man himself, on whose body the devil causes hair to grow by stroking it.[14]

In another cycle of tales, in which the devil soils the people whom God had created by spitting on them, these people had originally some covering, hair or nail-matter.

The Buriats of the Balagan District tell how three creators, Shibegeni-Burkhan, Madari-Burkhan, and Esege-Burkhan made the first pair of human beings, using red clay for the flesh, stone for bones and water for blood. Doubtful as to which of them should procure a spirit for these as yet soulless beings, they determined to find out by placing a torch and a vessel of water before each and going to sleep beside them. The one whose torch took fire during the night and in whose water-vessel a plant appeared should have the honour of giving life to man and of being his tutelary genius. Shibegeni-Burkhan awoke in the night before the others and seeing that the burning torch and the plant were in front of Madari-Burkhan he stealthily lighted his own candle, putting out that of the other, and removed the plant into his own vessel. In the morning, when the Burkhans awoke and saw that the fire and the plant had appeared before Shibegeni-Burkhan they decided that fate had determined him to be the life-giver and the guardian of man. But Madari-Burkhan suspected Shibegeni-Burkhan of having acted deceitfully, and said: " Thou hast stolen the fire and the plant from me, therefore the people thou givest life to will ever steal from one another and quarrel together." [15]

This story, a product of Buddhism, which evidently endeavours to explain the origin of quarrelling and robbery in the world, is in itself a complete tale, although in this Buriat tale it appears only as a preface to another story. The tale tells further how Madari-Burkhan and Esege-Burkhan departed to heaven, leaving these earth-created beings, which at that time were covered with hairs, in the keeping of Shibegeni-Burkhan. When the latter also had to visit heaven to bring a spirit for man, he set a dog, which had then no hair, to guard the sleeping people. While he was away the devil Shiktur bribed the dog with a promise of hair resembling that of mortals, and was allowed to defile them by spitting on them. When Shibegeni-Burkhan came down from heaven and saw that the devil had succeeded in soiling the bodies of the people, he became angry and cursed the dog on whose body he saw the devil's hair-covering, saying: " Thou shalt ever suffer hunger, gnaw cold bones and nourish thyself with remains from man's repasts, and man shall beat thee." Then Shibegeni-Burkhan cleaned the peoples' bodies of the hairs which the devil had soiled, and they became naked except in those parts which the devil's saliva had not touched, such as the head, which they in sleeping had happened to cover with their hands.[16]

A corresponding tale of the Buriats of Alarsk, in which we do not meet with the preface mentioned above, also tells how Burkhan created a hair-covered man out of various materials, set the dog to guard him and went to heaven to fetch a spirit for him, and how the wicked Sholmo, having deceived the dog, deprived man of his hair, leaving only a remnant in some parts of the body. The tale tells at its close that had the devil never succeeded in touching man, man would never have known sickness or death.[17] In a tale recorded among the Voguls of the Losva, the covering of the first man was nail-matter or horn-matter. But while God was absent, seeking a spirit for man, the devil (Kul-oter) managed to spoil his body so that the nail-matter remained only on the ends of his fingers and toes. The surface of the body having thus become tender man was an easy prey for sickness and death.[18]

In this form the tale is known also to the Mordvins. By giving the dog a hair-covering the devil secures the opportunity of spoiling the first horn-covered man so that only the ends of the fingers and toes keep their coverings.[19]

This original hair-covering or horn-covering of the human body is met with even in other tales which remind one of the Biblical story of the fall of man. Seeing that the last mentioned covering is comparatively rare in creation tales, but in paradise-stories quite common, we may conclude that it has been taken from the latter into the former.

In some Central Asian creation tales in which the dog also

appears, the devil, during God's absence, blows a spirit into the man whom God has created.

The following Altaic tale relates that Ülgen created the first man, using earth for flesh and stone for bones, and made a woman of the man's rib. But he had no spirit to give them and was forced to go in search of one. On starting he created a hairless dog to guard the pair. This time the dog received its hair-covering by eating the excrement of the devil. The latter then blew a spirit into the people with a reed, which he inserted in the rectum of the sleeping bodies. When Ülgen returned and saw his people alive he was doubtful as to what he should do, whether to create new human beings or not. While he was considering, the frog came up to him and said: "Why shouldest thou destroy these beings. Let them exist for themselves. Who dies, let him die; who lives, let him live." And so Ülgen let the people live.[20]

In another tale two creators, Otshirvani and Chagan-Shukuty, built together a human body. The latter said to the former: "We have created a man, we must yet find him a spirit to make him alive." Otshirvani remarked that the devil might steal the body in their absence, and therefore they decided to set a naked dog to guard it. While they were away the devil arrived, bribed the dog by promising him hair, and lighting some flax blew the smoke into man's nostrils. Then man arose and began to walk. To their surprise the gods on returning saw that man had already begun to live.[21]

We find thus that in Central and Northern Asia two cycles of tales are known, in one of which the devil soils the human body which God has created, while in the other the devil gives life to a God-created man. The purpose of both these cycles of tales is to explain the unexpected deficiencies in a being of God's creation. The former tales represent perhaps a more materialistic conception, dwelling as they do on the weaknesses of the human body, and chiefly on the filth inside it and the diseases caused by this, although in certain East European variants wicked, sinful tendencies also are the result of the devil's touch. The latter cycle of tales endeavours to explain man's mental deficiencies. This appears even from the following Altaic story, in which, however, only the capricious character of woman is under consideration.

When Ülgen had created the earth he made seven masculine beings upon it and seven trees, one tree for each man. After that he created yet an eighth man named Maidere and a tree "upon the golden mountain." Having created these beings God left them to their own resources and departed. After seven years he returned and saw that each tree had grown seven branches, one branch each year, but the number of men had not increased. God said: "What is the meaning of this? The trees bring forth new branches but the number of men does not increase?" Then Maidere replied: "How could they increase when there is none able to procreate?" God now gave Maidere the power to rule freely over men and to take care that they increased, and so Maidere stepped down from the golden mountain, went to the men and began to create a woman, just as Ülgen had created him. On the third day, when he had finished, the woman was ready, but without a spirit, so Maidere went out to meet Ülgen and left the dog to guard the being he had made. The wicked Erlik, by bribing the dog, succeeded in approaching the woman. He blew at once into her nostrils with a seven-toned flute and played into her ear with a nine-stringed instrument, woman thus receiving a spirit and an intellect. But for this reason woman has seven tempers and nine moods. When Maidere hurried back, he saw the living woman and said to the dog: "Why didst thou let Erlik come so near, how did he deceive thee?" The dog replied: "Erlik promised me a fur-coat which should last unto my death and be neither hot in summer nor cold in winter." Then Maidere said to him: "The garment promised thee shall be a hairy covering which shall grow fast on to thy body." At the same time he cursed the dog, prophesying that people should always treat him ill, that he should be compelled to live under the sky, etc.[22]

Thus, even in this tale, the originally naked dog has an important part. The existence of this common feature in all the creation tales gives us reason to assume that they all have a common root, in whatever variants they may appear. To this common root both the devil as spoiler of the people whom God had created, and the dog which guards them, have belonged. The strictly dualistic conception of this original root, a conception which appears early in the religion of the Iranians, where also the dog, that originally sacred animal, the expeller of evil beings, and the creation of Ahura Mazda, had a very important place, raises the assumption that our tale, as Dähnhardt has indicated, is the outcome of an Iranian mental atmosphere, originating probably among the Syrian Christians, and from them wandering both to Eastern Europe and to Central and North Asia. The access into Western Europe for this, as for later oriental-syncretistic legends, was more difficult.

Our tale about the seven men continues by relating how Maidere inquires of these, which of them will take the woman to whom the devil has given life for his partner. Three of them at once refuse absolutely and escape to the golden mountain where they become assistant spirits to God, or Burkhans. The other four remain on the earth, and Ülgen takes two ribs from each side of one of them, Targyn-nama, and of them makes him a wife.[23]

An earlier mentioned Yakut tale also tells of the seven first men whom the devil marred before God had given them life. This tale also has a continuation in which the numbers three and four are specially noticeable. It tells how God gave a wife to four only, wherefore the other three were dissatisfied. They complained to God and, as he took no notice, adultery came into the world. These three got wives in the end when the daughters of the first four women grew up. One of the daughters, however, could find no husband and became therefore a prostitute.

More ancient than the fancies in these creation tales of the origin of man's deficiencies are those tales in which man first succumbs to evil suggestions after God has given him life.

CHAPTER VIII

THE FALL OF MAN

IN CONNECTION with the creation myths we have touched on many tales, in which already at his creation, man was corrupted by the devil and, therefore, never attained the perfection which God had intended for him. In the following we shall see how man, after his creation by God, has of his own accord drawn disaster on himself.

In most of the tales of this series, man was originally endowed with a special covering, which protected him from cold, moisture, wind and other matters liable to affect his health. Some of the tales provide him with a coat of fur, others with a nail-substance or horn covering. With the eating of the forbidden fruit man loses his natural, protective covering.

Very interesting is the following Altaic tale:

A lonely tree grew without branches. God saw it and said: "A single, branchless tree is not pleasant to look upon, let nine branches grow on it." The nine branches grew on the tree. God continued: "Let nine human beings appear under the nine branches; from the nine human beings nine races." Further on in this tale only two people are spoken of, man and wife, who were at first covered with fur. The name of the man was Töröngöi and of the wife Edji ("Mother"). God said to these people: "Do not eat of the fruit of the four branches growing towards the sunset, but eat of the five towards the sunrise." And God placed a dog under the tree as its guardian, saying: "If the devil comes, seize him." In addition he stationed the snake there, saying to it: "If the devil comes, bite him." Further, he said to both dog and snake: "If man comes to eat of the fruit towards the sunrise, let him approach the tree, but if he wishes to eat of the fruit of the forbidden branches, do not let him come near." Having said which God returned to Heaven.

The devil then arrived at the tree, where he saw the snake, which had just happened to fall asleep. He crept cunningly into the snake and with its help climbed the tree, from where he tempted first the woman and then, through her agency, the man, to eat of the fruit of the forbidden branches. Having eaten, the couple see to their astonishment how the hair begins to fall from their bodies. Ashamed, they hide frightened behind the tree.

When God came on to the earth and saw what had happened in his absence, he said to the man: " How is it with thee? " The man replied: " The woman has pushed into my mouth the forbidden fruit." God turned admonishingly to the woman: " Why hast thou done this? " The woman answered: " The snake tempted me to eat." God said to the snake: " Snake, what hast thou done? " It replied: " Not I, but the devil who had crept into me tempted her." God said: " How did the devil creep into thee? " The snake replied: " As I slept, the devil arrived." God turned then to the dog, saying: " How was it with thee, why didst thou not drive away the devil? " The dog answered: " Mine eyes saw him not." [1]

The introduction to this tale, in which nine people are mentioned, mystically connected with the nine branches of the tree, resembles greatly an earlier related tale of seven trees and seven men. In both tales these trees were at first branchless. The later tale goes on to relate that the first woman gave birth to nine sons and nine daughters, destined afterwards to become the ancestors of nine races. A few North Siberian tales speak of the seven ancestors of the human race. [2] The numbers seven and nine would seem, therefore, to have alternated in these tales.

In the Central Asian tales, our attention is drawn to the

fact that as the guardians of the forbidden fruit both the snake and the dog are mentioned. The latter, which is no longer mentioned in the punishments following on the disobedience, would seem to have been introduced only temporarily into this tale from the earlier related creation-tales.

Otherwise, the tale is very similar to the ancient Semitic story of the fall as known to us from the Bible. Only in details does it differ from the latter. In the paradise of the Bible, two trees are mentioned, the tree of life and the tree of knowledge of good and evil, both growing in the centre of paradise, the fruit of the latter being forbidden to man. The Central Asian tale mentions only one tree, the fruit of the five eastward branches of which were intended as nourishment for man, but the fruit of the four westward-growing branches of which was fraught with misfortune. This tree was at the same time the tree of life and death; in the Bible story life and death were represented by separate trees. The latter differs also from the former in the fact that it attempts to explain the origin of death spiritually, as a consequence of disobedience or the fall. The Central Asian tale would seem to represent a more primitive state by connecting the misfortune with the fruit itself. Starting from this, we may perhaps assume that the original form of the so-called story of the fall has come into being merely to explain how man, believed to have originally been created for eternity, could die. Death was thus not originally regarded in the light of a punishment, but as the natural consequence of eating of the fateful fruit, as, having lost its original covering, the power of resistance of the human body declined and diseases followed. Generally, primitive peoples tell how sickness and death, non-existent in the beginning, have since become the scourge of mankind.

The idea of an original covering of hair on the human body is widely-spread in Central and Northern Asia. The Voguls relate that in the beginning God created human beings covered altogether with hair, and that they were allowed to move everywhere and eat of everything but the "forest-spirit-berry" (*Vaccinium uliginosum*, growing in swamps). God then went off to Heaven, but returning to look at his creatures, he had great difficulty in finding these at all. In the end God found them hidden beneath some bushes. When they crept out at God's command, he saw that the human beings whom he had created had lost their covering of hair and shivered naked before him. This had come about by their eating of the fateful berries, against the express command of God, and thus becoming a prey to cold and moisture.[3]

In this tale of the Voguls, the mighty and beautiful tree of paradise of the ancient Semitic race has been transformed to a modest plant growing in the barren unfruitful north.

Besides the covering of hair, we have in the creation-tales met with another protective covering of the human body, i.e., the horn-covering, lost so completely by mortals that the only reminder of this primitive state is the substance of which our finger-nails and toe-nails are made.

This form of the tale, common also in Eastern Europe, appears already in old Jewish and Arabian tales, in which it is related how the bodies of Adam and Eve in paradise were covered with a horny substance so that they did not need clothes. Not until the fall did they, with the exception of the finger-nails and toe-nails, lose their covering.[4]

The idea of the hair-covering of the first human beings is also probably from Nearer Asia. It is related in an Arabian tale, how, on the diamond mountain of paradise, Adam and Eve had long hair reaching to the ground, protecting the whole body, and how this fell off when they had eaten of the forbidden fruit, so that their unprotected bodies darkened in the sun. The Bible story also obviously presupposes the existence of some covering, as it is expressly stated that when the first people had eaten of the forbidden fruit they saw themselves to be naked and in need of some garment.

The Astrachan Kalmucks relate further that during the time of paradise the first people were some kind of illuminated beings. At this time there was neither sun nor moon, these being unnecessary, as human beings then lighted up their surroundings themselves. The eating of the fruit extinguished their light altogether, all nature became dark, and God was obliged to give mankind the sun and the moon.[5] This belief is also founded on Nearer Asian tales.

Another consequence of the fall, according to the Kalmucks, was the shortening of the age of man and a reduction in his size. In the beginning men had been immortal or could at least live through a world-epoch, eighty thousand years, but gradually their age decreased, one year each century, so that their present average age is only sixty. This shortening will continue with the growth of sin until people will live to be only ten years of age. At the same time, after having originally been giants, they will decline to the length of a thumb. Then the messenger of the Bodhisattva Maidere and his apparition Berde-Gabat will arrive on the earth, and begin to better the state of men, increasing their age and size, until they have again attained their former age.[6]

With these Lamaistic beliefs may be compared the ideas of the modern Jews, reflected in the following words taken from a collection of their tales: "When Adam was created, his enormous volume filled all the earth, but when he fell into sin, he became very small." Concerning the shortening of the age of man we find comments in the Bible itself.

CHAPTER IX

THE ORIGIN OF THE MOSQUITO

A QUESTION of special interest to the Northern Siberian peoples is the origin of the myriads of mosquitoes, which during the light summer of the north are an unbearable plague for both men and animals.

The Yenisei Ostiaks declare that a cannibalistic demon woman, Khosadam, living in the farthest north, created the mosquitoes.[1] Many other Siberian peoples have a special myth to explain their origin.

The Ostiak Samoyeds tell of a hero named Itje, whose parents had been devoured by a man-eating giant named Pünegusse. He himself succeeded in escaping and making his way to a desert, where he was brought up by his relations. When he had grown to be a strong and heroic youth, he decided to free his people from this demon from the north. He succeeded in killing it, but the demon kept on being born again. He resolved therefore to burn up the carcase of the man-eater, but even in the fire the demon continued to exist. Its jaws ground against each other when the fire had burnt out, and its voice cried out that even when burnt up it would continue to plague mankind. The wind would scatter its ashes into the air, whence they would everywhere suck the blood of men. From these ashes the innumerable mosquitoes of Siberia arise each summer.[2]

In a Samoyed variant a small black bird is born of the flesh of Pünegusse. This bird is called " a bit of Pünegusse's flesh." [3]

Among the Ostiaks of the river Vach this story runs briefly as follows: A great bird once caught a great pike and gave it to its sister to cook. The latter prepared instead a meal of dog's offal, which so enraged the bird that it flew away until at last it came to the man-eater. Finding the hut empty, the bird ate its fill out of a large kettle of fat, but was caught by the man-eater. To save its own life the bird promised its sister in marriage to the giant and was set free. It then hurried home and to save its sister, fastened the door so that only a small hole was left. The man-eater, coming for his bride, tried to get through this hole, but stuck fast there. The bird then killed him with a great knife and set fire to the house. The body of the man-eater was burnt to ashes, but here also the spirit spoke, foretelling that its ashes would each summer be born anew as mosquitoes and would continue to live on the flesh of men.[4]

Corresponding myths, apparently of Indian origin, are to be found among the Altai Tatars. The evil Erlik created a water-giant named Andalma-Muus, who put out his long tongue to seize men, whom he then swallowed. Three of Ülgen's heroes, Mandyshire, Tyurun-Muzykay, and Maidere, decided to kill this demon. Tyurun-Muzykay declared himself to be the strongest giant-killer. Having said this, he came down from heaven, was given birth to by a virgin, and became a man. While he was still quite young he was running about once on the sea-shore when he saw the giant stick out his long tongue to seize him and drag him into the depths. The young hero, however, was not helpless in this danger, but grasped the demon's tongue and pulled so mightily that the earth was in danger of sinking under the water. To avoid this the hero drank so much of the sea that the water sank until he could see the feet of the demon. The youth then grasped his feet, pulled the giant out of the sea and beat him against the rocks so that his blood squirted out and his entrails were scattered over the rocks. From this originates the mixed colouring of rocks. After this, the hero cut the body into little pieces, out of which certain insects, including also mosquitoes, were born.[5]

According to a Yakut cannibal myth, the man-eating giant was burnt up, and from the fragments of his bones all kinds of destructive insects, and also frogs and snails were born.[6] Similarly, in Mongol tales it is related how a hero named Karaty-Khan vanquishes a demon, grinds it into fragments and throws these into the air, thus giving birth to mosquitoes and other insects.[7]

Far away to the east, among the Goldes, tales of a similar character are met with. These tell of two sisters who lived in the same hut. While one of them was away, the man-eater came to the other, enticed her from her hiding-place and tricked her into putting out her tongue, which the man-eater at once plucked out of her mouth. When the other sister came home, she found out what had happened in her absence and decided to avenge her sister's death. She sought a long time for the home of the man-eater, and at last she found four store-houses, of which one was full of human hands, another of human feet, a third of heads, and in the fourth numerous human tongues hung from the roof. Among these she discovered the still warm tongue of her sister. She wrapped this in a clean cloth and went on, until, in the depths of the forest, she found the man-eater's dwelling hidden away. The demon was away, but his sister, who was a good person, was at home and promised to help in killing him. In the evening he came home, bringing a human body with him and devouring this for supper, after which he went to sleep. The women now came forward and broke the demon into pieces with hammers, scattering the pieces in all directions. While doing so, they said: " Man-eater, thou fedst thyself on human flesh, may the pieces of thy flesh and thy bones change into small insects, which like thee shall eat human blood. Of the smallest fragments may gnats be born, of those a little larger mosquitoes, and of the largest flies, beetles, etc." Immediately great clouds of insects arose, which spread over the earth.[8]

The Goldes have still another tale related to this. A brother and sister lived in a hut in peace. Once when the brother came home from the forest, he noticed that his sister had altered considerably. He began to suspect that some one kept company with her. For this reason, he strewed ashes outside the hut when setting off again on a hunting-trip. Returning the next morning, he was astounded to see the foot-prints of a tiger in the ashes. He hid his suspicions, however, until it became apparent that his sister was *enceinte*. Then he decided to thrust a knife into her breast as she lay murmuring shaman songs to herself. While singing she said: " I have lived with the tiger, he is my husband, his spirit is in me; thou canst not kill me, but if thou wilt cut off my little finger, I shall die." The brother cut off his sister's little finger and when she was dead, built a large log-fire and threw the body on to it. While the body was burning, instead of sparks, all kinds of evil spirits in the form of birds and insects flew out of the fire.[9]

Cannibal myths of this description, which are to be found also among the Tungus, and are extremely characteristic of the more northern peoples of Siberia, have been noted down also on the other side of the Pacific Ocean. As in Siberia, North American Indian myths tell of the birth of blood-sucking insects from the ashes of a man-eater.[10] It seems probable, therefore, that these primitive tales have a common origin.

CHAPTER X

THE HEAVEN GOD

A S FAR back as the thirteenth century, Plano Carpini relates in his *Historia Mongolorum* that " The Mongols believe in one God, whom they regard as the creator of all things visible and invisible." Rubruquis also remarks that the Mongols acknowledge the existence of one God, but that despite this they prepare idols for themselves. Similarly, the Arabian historians mention the " one " God of the Mongols, whom, according to a decree of Jenghiz Khan, all the subjects of the Great Khan had to honour and worship.

We might perhaps assume the above reports of " one " God to have been coloured in some way or other, but on closer acquaintance with the beliefs of the Central Asian peoples, we find that the Heaven god has actually had an exceptional position among them. These reports are, further, of such late date, that alien, and, more particularly, Persian currents of civilization have long before their time exercised a considerable influence on them. As a relic of Mazdaism we find in the folk-lore of both the Mongols and the Tatars the name of Ahura-Mazda (Mongol Hormusda; Altaic Tatar Khurbystan). It is also a well-known fact that Manicheism and Nestorianism had by then spread their doctrines into this territory; the wife of Jenghiz Khan himself would seem to have been a Nestorian Christian. Matters being thus, we have no reason to doubt these old reports; they are trustworthy at least regarding the time of which they speak. Another question is whether they may be regarded as expressing the oldest beliefs of the Central Asian peoples concerning the god of Heaven.

A word of their own language, used by the Mongols as a name for their "one" god, is Tengri, a name used for the Heaven god in many other Altaic languages (Kalmuck Tengri, Buriat Tengeri, Tatar Tängere, Yakut and Dolgan Tangara, Chuvash Tura). This word meant originally, "Heaven." Among the Chuvash the meaning "Heaven" for Tura seems to have become extinct, and among the Yakuts also, Tangara appears only in folk-lore as meaning "the sky." Having acquired the meaning of a god living in Heaven, this word began to be used in many languages for "god" in general (= Latin *deus*). The Yakuts use it when speaking of their idols, i.e., wood, stone or birch-bark Tangara. The disappearing significance of the word, a "sky" appreciable by the senses, shows plainly that in the beginning the "Heaven god" of the peoples related to the Turks was the animated sky itself with its wonderful, mystical powers. At this stage, when as yet no humanlike or otherwise specially shaped being is thought of, with the sky merely as his dwelling-place, the heavens and the Heaven god do not require separate names as they did later. An irrefutable proof of this original point of view is the old title given by the Mongols to the Heaven god when worshipping him: "Blue Tengri."

Examples of the deification of the heavens themselves are met with among the other surrounding peoples. Herodotus already tells how the ancient Persians worshipped as their god (Zeus) "the whole area of the sky." The name Tien of the Chinese Heaven god meant originally "the sky." The Finnish races also used the word "sky" when speaking of their Heaven gods without any resulting confusion of thought. Similar examples are offered by the most northern peoples of Asia, the Samoyeds and the Yenisei Ostiaks.

In Mongolian folk-lore two expressions are met with: "Blue Tengri" and "Eternal Tengri," which, according to Banzarov, denote two different stages of development. The most common name, "Blue Tengri," for the power behind all the different phenomena of the sky, which gives to the earth fruitfulness and productivity, cannot, according to this investigator, apply to a spiritual being; but the " Eternal Tengri " who rules the world and decrees the fates of peoples and individuals, does seem to be a spiritual entity.[1] We cannot on our part, however, discern any such sharp division in the use of these qualifying terms, both being often used simultaneously.

In the beliefs of the Mongols the determining activities of the sky are extremely conspicuous. They speak frequently of the " Fate " (Dzajaga) of the heavens. In the Chronicle of Ssanang Ssetsen it is said that Jenghiz Khan, " that lion among men," appeared on the earth through " the Providence (Fate) of the blue, eternal sky." But not only rulers and princes, " sons of Heaven " in a special meaning, but also ordinary mortals were born into the world through the agency of the same " Providence." Everything that happens was believed to have been decreed by the sky. When the Mongol princes published their laws, they added to their authorization the words: " By the Providence of the eternal sky," in the same way as Christian monarchs exercise their power " by the grace of God."

As this Providence belief is not met with among the more northern peoples of the Altaic race, at least not in any such developed form, our attention is drawn to the Indo-Iranians, the proximity of whom to the Mongols cannot but have left some trace. The Dzajaga idea of the Mongols corresponds in fact with the Rita of the ancient Vedic poems and the Asha of the Avesta, by which a power watching over the world was meant. This Providence does not seem to have been personified, neither were sacrifices offered up to it in the beginning. The relations of men towards it may be compared with those of the Greeks of Homer's time towards Moira, under whose laws even the gods existed. But it is to be noted that this Providence or Fate, the decrees of which were unrecallable, was always connected with the sky, according to the ideas of the Central Asian peoples. In a similar way Fate was regarded by the Chinese, who call Fate Tien-ming (" the sky-order ") being in this respect entirely of the same opinion as the Mongols. Both these peoples see in the complete sub-ordination of Heaven to its own laws an example for all earthly order.

In the list of gods of the Chuvash living in Russia, a spirit named Käbä (" Fate," " Providence ") corresponds to the Dzajaga of the Mongols; from the former the Cheremiss have taken it as Kava-Jumo and the Votiaks as Kaba-Immar, and unaware of its origin, sacrifice nowadays to it as to a Heaven god. Among the Eastern Cheremiss even sacred groves (*Kawalan pumaš*) were consecrated to Fate.[2]

Obviously, Dzajaga, Käbä, Rita, Asha, Tien-ming and Moira, called Fatum by the Romans, are closely related to one another in their meaning. The question arises, therefore, as to whether this fatalistic belief is a general product of the human intellect, born among each of the separate peoples, or whether we have here a result of the so-called " migration theory." The dependence of fate on the heavenly rules pre-supposes so naturally a certain stage of development that we cannot avoid turning our glance to the cosmology of the ancient Babylonians. Nowhere else, in this early period, do we meet with such admiration of the constant order of the sky and such blind belief in its mechanically working powers, the latter affecting all life down to the smallest details. Here the sky has truly been " a Book of Fate " in which the wise can read future events. For this reason it is more than probable that just this star fatalism of the Babylonians has been the model and the source of the Providence beliefs of all the above mentioned peoples.

As the fate of everything is thus dependent on the sky, it is natural that one should say, like the Mongols: " The sky decrees " or " the sky commands." In the same way as the

Vedic poems speak of the " director of Rita," so the ruler of Providence, Dzajagatši (*dzaja* = " to decree," " allow," " order," or " command "), appears simultaneously with Dzajaga in the beliefs of the Mongols, meaning the god of Heaven. The qualifying attribute of the sky is often " Dzajagatši Tengri." In the inscriptions of Orkhon, where the " heavens " are mentioned also as the god of armies, we meet with the word *dzaja* with the meaning of " to command ": " The sky commanded our armies in the war and we were victorious."

The Dzajagatši of the Mongols has a counterpart in the Jajutši of the Altaic race, the Dzajan of the Minusinsk Tatars, and the Buriat Zajan (Mongol *dzaja* = Altaic Tatar *jaja* = Buriat *zaja*). The Buriats by Khudinsk call the Over-god of the heavens Zajan-Sagan-Tengeri (*sagan*, " white "). Another qualification of the Heaven god with the same meaning is the Tatar Bujuruktši (*bujur*, " to decree," or " order "), loaned also by the Ugrians (Ostyak Pairekse). The Voguls append to the name of their god in their own language, " Num-Tōrem-paireks." The same word is further met with in the god-name of the Chuvash, Pürdän-Tura, and in that of the Cheremiss, Puiršo-Jumo (Cheremiss *pujurem* = Chuvash *pür-* = Kazan Tatar *bojor-*).

We see thus how this idea of a Fate bound up with the heavens is common to all the Turk-related peoples. In addition to all the more fateful occasions of life, birth in especial is dependent on the providence of Heaven. Dzajagatši, Jajutši, Bujuruktši, etc., are often spoken of as the decreers of birth, and at the same time as a kind of gods of birth. Sometimes some other than the actual Heaven god is given this title. The Altai Tatars, who speak of several storeys in the heavens, believe Jajutši to live in the fifth of these.[3] Here he is thus a being apart from the Over-god. Each mortal having his own fate, each has been given a special ruler of fate, which follows him faithfully from the moment of birth. The Mongols call this spirit, which does not desert man as long as he is in favour with the heavens, Dzol- ("happiness") Dzajagatši.[4] It is said to watch over the health of its ward, his property and his prosperity in general, protecting him at the same time from all dangers. Similarly, each mortal has, according to the Altai Tatars, his own Jajutši, which, having received orders from above, brings down lifeforce from the wonderful "lake of milk" in the third storey of Heaven, then brings the embryo alive into the world, and follows the man thus born from his infancy onward as a kind of good spirit. Besides this, each mortal is supposed to have a lifelong evil companion, Körmös, which from his birth tries to harm him. The former, which writes down the good deeds done in life, is said to be on man's right shoulder, the latter, which notes down his evil deeds, at his left. These Jajutši, like the blessed dead, live in the lands of paradise in the third storey of Heaven.[5] It is hardly necessary to point out that these beliefs in good and bad angels reached the Tatars from the Iranians.

The belief that each mortal has a special arbiter of his fate in Heaven, seems to be closely related to the idea that each mortal has his own star in the sky. The appearance of a new star signifies birth, the "falling" of a star, death. When the Chuvash see a shooting-star they shout at once: "My star is still up above!"[6] Several North Siberian peoples also, e.g., the Tungus, speak of the stars of each mortal.[7]

Plano Carpini says that the Heaven god, according to the Mongols, is also the "avenger." This punishing activity of Heaven is closely related to its "providence" or "decreeing." When once Heaven has decreed anything, it is not good for men to show resistance. The Mongols believe that Heaven "sees" everything, and that therefore no one can conceal his actions from it. In taking an oath, the Mongols say: "May Heaven know!" or "May Heaven judge!" The revenge of the heavens has not, however, been regarded as something occurring beyond the grave, but is believed to fall on the guilty already in this life. In its judgments Heaven is completely neutral, punishing princes as effectually as peasants. Punishment is believed to follow crime as a kind of inner necessity.[8]

Without being in any way inconstant the sky can sometimes make troublesome demonstrations, reflecting in its own way disturbances on the earth. Neither were the ancient Babylonians unfailingly logical in their conception of the unwavering laws of Heaven, but saw at times " signs " in the sky, which were interpreted as showing the dissatisfaction of the gods. Heavenly demonstrations of this description were, according to the Mongols, comets, meteors, years of famine, floods, etc., at the threatening of which rulers and subjects had to review their plans and intentions and humbly submit to the will of the " eternal sky."

The Chronicles containing the history of the Mongols mention many illuminative examples. It is related in them how Mogan-Khan (during the Tukiu dynasty) having held ambassadors from China for a long time in captivity, freed them and made peace with their ruler after Heaven had by long storms shown its dissatisfaction at the tyrannous acts of the Khan. In the fifteenth century the Mongols seized the ruler of China and sentenced him to a long term of hard labour, but noticing once how the cup from which the emperor had drunk, glowed with a purple light, they sent him with all honours back to China, as they believed this to be the will of Heaven. Especially have the leaders of the people to follow closely all the " signs " of the sky. The Mongols regard Jenghiz Khan as having taught them the following wisdom: " The highest happiness, with which nothing can be compared, is for the ruler of a land to be in the favour of the eternal heavens." [9]

In crossing over to the most northern peoples of Siberia, we no longer find this deep belief in the Providence of Heaven.

PLATE XLV

PHALLUS ERECTED BEFORE A MONGOL MONASTERY TO FRIGHTEN AWAY A FEMALE DEMON

(See page 398.)

After photograph by S. Pālsi.

The Heaven god of the Tungus, Samoyeds and Yenisei Ostiaks is generally regarded as a being so apart, that he in no way directs towards men any action of a commanding or avenging character. It is therefore unnecessary to fear the heavens. It is also expressly said, concerning the Heaven god of the Yakuts, that he does not concern himself with doings on earth or the fates of men. A certain tale shows God as saying of mortals: " In letting them down upon the earth I did not say to them: ' Come back! ' If they increase, let them increase, if they die, let them die." [10] In other places, however, conceptions differing from the foregoing appear.

Extremely widespread among the peoples of Central Asia is, further, the belief that Heaven is some kind of a giver of life. As a life-creating god of this description the sky is imagined as male, though not anthropomorphic, with the earth, as its opposite, female. Both are then gods of birth, the former acting the part of father, the latter that of mother: the sky procreates, the earth gives birth. Doubtless, this conception is founded on observations made in nature. The effects of light, warmth, rain and wind on vegetation in particular, awakened in the mind of primitive man the idea of similar effects on all that has life. Thus the thought arose that the sky gives the spirit, the Earth Mother the material body.

In this same connection there is perhaps reason to point out that certain Central Asian peoples, as, for instance, the Buriats, have for the sake of fruitfulness worshipped a certain kind of stone, said to have dropped down from the sky. A very famous " fallen stone " is near the town of Balagansk. During a long drought the Buriats sacrifice to it in order to obtain refreshing rains. The stone, which is white in colour, is said by the people to have originally fallen on a mountain, whence it has later removed to several different places. Among the Buriats by Khudinsk, each village is said to possess a smaller " fallen stone," kept in the middle of the village in a trunk attached to a post. In the Balagansk District, where these stones are larger, they are generally placed on a platform supported by four posts. In the hope of a rainy and fruitful summer they are wetted in the spring and offerings are made to them. Probably, these stones dropped from Heaven, which in shape often resemble the longish weapons of the Stone Age, are, as Agapitov assumes, relics of a Mongol phallus cult.[11]

The belief in the procreative powers of the sky is reflected in numberless tales, in which it is explained how the children of men and the young of animals have come from Heaven to the earth. Generally, however, it is believed that only the souls of these come from Heaven. The Yakuts believe that the soul of a child comes down to its mother in the shape of a bird.[12] According to a Mongol tale the soul of the founder of the power of the Sjanbi tribe, Tanshikai, came down from above as hail, which fell on the lips of his mother. A certain ancestor of the Mongols was born in such a manner that a descending ray of light fructified his mother. Jenghiz Khan is said by the tales to have been born of a virgin, wherefore he could call the sky " father." [13] All these ideas spring from the same original idea, viz., that the sky is the giver of the spirit and life.

Whether the name of the Yakut Heaven god, Ajy-tangara (" Creator god," really " Creative Heaven "), springs from the preceding belief, which is doubtless extremely old, we do not know for certain. The Chuvash, however, seem to possess a counterpart, Šuratan-Tura (really " Birth-giving Heaven "), a name connected also with the Aurora Borealis. They believe that the sky, during this phenomenon, " gives birth to a son." Šuratan-Tura is said to ameliorate the agonies of a woman in child-birth.[14] Otherwise, the idea of this deity is somewhat confused. Among the Yakut gods we find also other names for the Creator god, Ajy (" Creator "), Yryn-Ajy (" White Creator ") or Yryn-Ajy-Tojon (*tojon* " lord ") and Aihyt-Aga (" Creator Father "). Although the same names may be used for the Creator of the Christian teachings, the ideas in question cannot be said to have arisen from these teachings. By the side of Ajy-Tojon, appears a special deity of birth, Ajysit, the name, like Ajy, being derived from the verb *ai* (" to give birth to," " to create "). Ajysit, of whom we shall speak later, is generally regarded as a feminine being (Ajysit-Khotun, " Ajysit-mistress "), and brings the soul from heaven to the child while being born, helping also the woman in the pains of child-birth. In prayers this deity is often referred to as Ajysit-Ijäksit (" Procreating-Nourishing "), a term corresponding to the qualifying term of the Votiak Heaven god, Kildis Vordis. Possibly from the Turco-Tatar peoples the Volga Finns obtained their Creator-god (Votiak Kildisin, Cheremiss Šatšektše or Šotšen, Mordvin Škaj), names derived from verbs denoting procreation and birth-giving.

It is certain that the conception of the creative power of the heavens of the Central Asian peoples is extremely old. Among the more northern tribes the conception does not appear quite as clearly, although they also, like the Yenisei Ostiaks, believe that not only men, but animals also, have the sky to thank for their existence: Heaven (Es) " gives," Heaven " sends," even " lets fall," what the earth needs.[15] A similar giver of everything good is the Buga or Šavoki of the Tungus, also called " the Lord " (Amaka).

The close connection between the Heaven god and light and the sun, appears from the sacrificial rites. Sacrifices to the Heaven god are offered always towards the direction of the " day " or the dawn, and at the same time the votive animal, when such is used, has to be white in colour. Sacrifices to the Heaven god among the most northern peoples are, however, comparatively rare. In some places it has been the custom to consecrate some live domestic animal, a horse or a reindeer, which is then never worked and is looked after well. In older times a consecrated animal of this description was driven far to the eastward.

A curious custom, which occurs among the Yakuts, is that several trees are erected before the victim, of which seven bear leaves and a few have figures of birds upon them. All these trees, which are ranged in a row, represent the different storeys of heaven, through which the victim is to wander to the Supreme God in the highest Heaven. A corresponding custom exists among the Dolgans, who, at the shaman ceremony set up, one behind the other, nine stumps, on which are figures of birds. There also these stumps represent the nine storeys of Heaven through which the shaman, with the help of these birds, will fly to God.[16]

The idea of the purity of Heaven would also seem to be of great antiquity. More even than the rest of nature, the sky loves cleanliness. Very widespread is a tale of how the clouds were at an earlier time lower down, but, after being soiled by the people, rose higher. An example of the purity of the sky, from which later sprang the belief in the holiness of God, is given by the Tungus of the North Siberian primeval forests. According to them, a woman, during her period of uncleanness, should not look up at the sky. Common also is the belief that the lightning strikes places where something evil or filthy is hidden.

Where the Heaven god has begun to be regarded as a kind of anthropomorphic being, the heavens have become merely the dwelling-place of this being. Countless tales relate how God has a magnificent home in the sky, sometimes also a wife and children, servants, cattle, and other property. In the brilliant palace of God a Tatar hero was once on a visit, and was received well and entertained with food, etc.[17] The special characteristics of these tales have, however, hardly been incorporated with the beliefs concerning heaven.

The old Babylonian idea of the seven or more storeys of Heaven gave rise to the thought that the Over-god dwells in the topmost storey of Heaven. The Yryn-Ajy-Tojon of the Yakuts dwells sometimes in the seventh, sometimes in the

PLATE XLVI

1. Dolgan shaman-pillars representing the nine storeys of heaven, with wooden figures of birds. With the help of these birds the shaman will fly through the heavens. (See page 400.)

2. Yakut custom of erecting trees, representing the storeys of heaven, before the victim offered to the god dwelling in the highest storey of heaven. (See page 401.)

PLATE XLVI

1. Dolgan shaman-pillars representing the nine
storeys of heaven, with wooden figures of birds.
With the help of these birds the shaman will fly
through the heavens. (See page 400.)

2. Yakut custom of erecting trees, representing the
storeys of heaven, before the victim offered to the
god dwelling in the highest storey of heaven. (See
page 401.)

ninth storey of Heaven, depending on the number of storeys
believed to be in the sky. The Es of the Yenisei Ostiaks lives
in a transparent palace over the seventh Heaven, and according to the Ugrians the dwelling-place of God is in the seventh
Heaven.[18] We see thus, that this belief has spread also among
the most northern of the Siberian peoples.

In the same way as the ancient Babylonians regarded the
navel of the sky as the throne of Anu, whence he ruled over
the earth, the Central Asian peoples place the abode of the
Over-god somewhere around the North Star.[19] Wherever
the belief in a Heaven-mountain has spread, God is regarded
as dwelling on the summit of this mountain, which touches the
North Star. In connection with the world-pillar it has already
been mentioned how some of the North Siberian peoples worship the Heaven god in connection with this pillar, as shown,
e.g., by the " seven-divisioned Sänke " of the Ostiaks. A more
suitable throne in the sky than the stationary, changeless region
of the sky-navel near the North Star, whence he can best
direct the countless, varying activities of the earth, can hardly
be imagined for the Over-god.

Many flattering attributes are given to their Over-god by
the Central Asian peoples. The Altai Tatars call him
" Great " (Ülgön, Ülgen), or " Rich and Great " (Bai-
Ülgön). " Merciful Khan " (Kaira-Khan) and other general
names are also given to him. The term Burkhan-Bakši (really
" Buddha-master "), which the Mongols, Buriats and Soyots
have begun to use for their highest god, was brought by Buddhists from China.

CHAPTER XI

THE SONS OF GOD

CLOSELY connected with the Heaven god, according to the Siberian peoples, are certain other gods living in the sky, the number of which is precisely fixed. Extremely common is a group of seven gods, said to act as the assistants of the Over-god.

More especially in the beliefs of the Kirghis and the Siberian Tatars, do these gods play an important part. In the Altaic tales mention is made of seven beings named Kudai (" god "), situated in the third storey of Heaven on the Sürö (" Majesty ") mountain.[1] The Yakuts call this group of seven gods, which they declare forms " the suite of the Over-god Ai-Tojon," Sättä-Kurö-Džüsägäi-Ai (*sättä*, " seven "); they are supposed to be the tutelary genii of horses, and a sacrifice of kumiss is poured into the fire for them at the spring festivals.[2] Often these grouped spirits are called the sons of the Over-god. Certain of the Altaic tribes can recount the names of these " seven sons ": Jashigan, Karshit, Bakhtagan, Kara, Kushkan, Kanym and Jaik.[3] Much cannot, however, be grounded on these names, as they vary greatly in the different districts. As little known as the names of this group are the spheres of activity ascribed to each. In the corresponding list of the Lebed Tatars, Kanym appears as the wife of Ülgen. Kara (" Black "), also Kara-Khan, according to these last, has left his father and, instead of the light-filled abodes of Heaven, has chosen the dark holes of the underworld as his lot. Jaik or Jaik-Khan is the prince of the flood and at the same time a kind of escort to the souls bound for Hades.[4]

Names for the seven " sons " of the Heaven god have also been invented by the Voguls and the Ostiaks, although these are for the most part the names of their own district gods. The list of the Voguls comprises, according to Gondatti, the following spirits: the god of Pelym, the god of the upper field of the Ob, the god of the Holy Ural, the Prince of the river Aut, the god of the Little Ob, the god of the Sosva centre, and the " Earth-watching Man." In the information obtained by Munkácsi from Sygva the following are named: the god of Pelym, the Old Man of the village Tek, the Holy Prince of the Lozva-water, the god of the Sosva centre, the god of the Little Ob, the Old Man of the village Lopmus, and the " Earth-watching man." Part of the corresponding catalogue of the Ostiaks by Tremyugan deserves mention: " The Forest-game-sharing man " and the " youngest son " of the Heaven god, Khan-Iki (" Prince old man "). The former is a deity living in the sky, from whom game is prayed for, and to whom, as to a Heaven god, a white animal has to be sacrificed.[5] The greatest interest is, however, awakened by the " youngest son " among this group, the Vogul " Earth-watching man," the Khan-Iki of the Ostiaks, to whom many tales are attached and who is certainly not an original Ugrian god.

The fact that these seven gods are but little known to the Siberian peoples, as is often true of their names also, draws our attention to their number. We know the Iranians to have had a group of gods of the same number, Amesha Spentas, and similarly the Adityas of the *Rgveda* were originally seven gods, the duties of whom, like that of the Siberian sons of God, was the watching over and the control of the heavenly laws of nature. We arrive thus at the assumption that these Asiatic gods, wherever they may be met with, have the same origin. But where and how did this heavenly group first take shape?

Light is thrown on the problem by the picture of Heaven of the Vasyugan Ostiaks, seen by the " eyes of the soul " of the shamans, and described by them in songs. From these we learn that the heavens are seven-storeyed, in the topmost of which the Over-god Num-Torem himself lives, and in the lower ones his sons. The dwellers in these storeys of the sky are called also by names borrowed from the Tatars, Torem-Talmas ("Heaven interpreter"; *talmas* = Tatar *tolmatš*) or Torem-Karevel ("Heaven watcher"; *karevel* = Tatar *karavel*). The names of the separate "Interpreters" are unknown to the Vasyugans, neither can their activities be explained, but they are believed to live one in each storey of the heavens. Usually, they are called after the sacrifices offered up to each. 1. "The arrow-sacrifice Torem" receives arrows shot anywhere into the sky; 2. "The cloth-sacrifice Torem," who receives a cloak of white cloth, which is hung up on forest expeditions in some birch in a primitive forest; 3. "The sable-sacrifice Torem," who is given a sable-skin, kept in a box taken on forest expeditions; 4. "The cup-sacrifice Torem," for whom a special tin cup is kept in the storeroom; 5. "The horned-deer-sacrifice Torem," for whom the hide of a deer killed in the forest is left, with horns and hoofs attached, hanging on a birch. This spirit is believed to let down game and fish upon the earth for men, and is the same being as the previously mentioned "Forest-game-sharing man." As the sixth a Russian saint, Nikolai the miracle-maker, is mentioned, the latter being the protective spirit of travellers by water, to whom the Ostiaks hang up the skin of a marten in their store-rooms as a sacrifice.[6]

As Karjalainen points out, this Karevel arrangement is not an invention of the Ostiaks, but has reached them in the first instance from the Tatars. It is unfortunate that we should know so little of the beliefs of the pagan period of the Tatar tribe geographically nearest to the Ugrians, a tribe from which these have acquired much interesting culture, but among the tribes further south, which have better preserved the beliefs of their forefathers we find a corresponding idea to the Ostiak Karevel arrangement, appearing in such a manner that each son of the Over-god is given a different storey of the heavens as dwelling-place. Radloff relates that he obtained from the Lebed Tatars on his travels the following description of their heaven: " The original Father, the Creator of everything, is Kudai Bai-Ülgön; he has four sons: Pyrshak-Khan, Tös-Khan, Kara-Khan and Suilap. The son of Suilap is Sary-Khan, and the son of Pyrshak-Khan is Kyrgys-Khan, the protective spirit of the local Tatars. All of these gods except Kara-Khan bring happiness to men. They give food and protection against dangers. To the highest god, Ülgön, white horses are sacrificed, to Pyrshak and his descendant brown ones; to all the gods, grain is further sacrificed. The gods live in Heaven, which according to these Tatars, is seven-storeyed. In the topmost lives Ülgön and his wife Kanym, in the next Pyrshak-Khan, in the third Tös-Khan, in the fourth Kyrgys-Khan, in the fifth Suilap, in the sixth Sary-Khan, and in the seventh the messengers sent by the gods down to men. Kara-Khan (" Black Prince ") is said to have deserted his father and removed from the light-filled dwellings of Heaven to the underworld." [7]

It is to be understood that this heavenly order is not an invention of the Turco-Tatar peoples, but has come to them from elsewhere. For this reason the signification of the different gods is so vague to the people; from the investigator, however, these gods dwelling in the seven storeys of the heavens cannot hide their origin, pointing plainly as they do to the Babylonian Planet gods, which, in their distant fatherland, ruled over seven discs of the sky situated one above the other.

In another description recorded by Radloff, in which seventeen storeys of heaven are spoken of, a detail that is only an accidental transformation found amongst a certain Altaic tribe, the sun is mentioned as dwelling in the seventh, and the moon in the sixth storey of Heaven.[8] Thus the sun and the moon govern two sky-discs situated one above the other. In the seventh storey, together with the sun, lives an omniscient

Mergen-Tengere ("Sharpshooter-god"), who reminds one of the Ostiak "Arrow-sacrifice Torem." Dare one assume this deity to reflect an ancient god of lightning?

As the spirit of the ninth Heaven, Radloff mentions Kysagan-Tengere. The corresponding Kisagan-Tengri of the Mongols was the god of war, believed to protect the army, to direct it in dangerous and difficult places, and to procure victory for it by vanquishing the enemy. In the fifth storey lived Kudai Jajutshi. If these, as seems probable, were originally Star gods, the counterpart of the former would be the Babylonian Nergal (Mars). Of the spirits of the upper storeys of heaven only Kaira-Khan ("merciful khan") and Bai-Ülgön ("Rich and Great") are mentioned, the former being placed in the seventeenth and the latter in the sixteenth storey of Heaven; according to the most general belief, however, these names apply to the same Over-god. The "black" Kara or Kara-Khan of the earlier lists, who descended from Heaven to Hades, being doubtless a Star god, deserves special attention; on account of his colour and other attributes he may possibly correspond to Saturn, called "the black star" by the ancient Babylonians.

Instead of the more original group of seven, a group of nine "sons" or "servants" of God appears in some districts. Thus, in the tales of the Mongols we often meet with "nine Tengeri, protectors and brothers," these words denoting attributes often ascribed to them.[9] The Buriats can give the names of the "nine sons" of the Over-god. These are, however, exceedingly artificial and vary in the different districts. Doubtless, these "nine sons" or "brothers" originally signified the Planet gods, from whom the names of the days of the week have been taken, although others have come later to join them as the storeys in Heaven were increased to nine. Banzarov says expressly that the Mongols worshipped "nine great stars, which corresponded to nine Tengeri."[10] The group of nine has not been as common in Asia as the group of seven, which is

known also in Eastern Asia. In ancient times the Chinese
worshipped the " seven rulers " or " directors " of the sky, by
which they are said to have meant the sun, the moon and five
planets. Where the numbers seven and nine have started to
compete among themselves, one notices that the former has
often given way to the latter.

These sacred numbers of the gods have in places left their
mark on the sacrificial cults. The descriptions of the sacrifices
among the Chuvash living on the Volga often mention nine
sacrificial priests, nine sacrificial animals, nine cauldrons, etc.[11]
Naturally the recipients of these sacrifices were formerly as
numerous; therefore the people even now try to arrange their
gods in a series of nine. Built on a similar foundation is the
custom of the Finnish tribes in East Russia, especially of the
pagan Cheremiss, of placing in some districts, when sacrificing
to the Heaven god, nine sacrificial loaves and as many bowls
of honey-drink on their altars.[12] On the sacrifice platform of
the Yakuts one may also see nine small bowls.[13]

But let us return again to the older group of seven gods,
the members of which the Ostiaks call " the Interpreters " or
" the Watchmen of Heaven." The conception of the Planet
gods as a kind of interpreters seems to be of great antiquity.
Diodorus already speaks of it in describing the Chaldean fore-
casting from the stars in the following words: " Most important to them is the examination of the movements of those
five stars, which are called planets. They call them the ' In-
terpreters ' ($\dot{\epsilon}\rho\mu\eta\nu\epsilon\tilde{\iota}s$); to the one we call Saturn they give a
special name, ' Sun-star,' as they have it to thank for their
newest and most important forecasts. They call the planets
' Interpreters ' because, while the other stars never deviate
from their routes, these go their own ways and thus interpret
the future and reveal to men the mercy of the gods."

The duties of these heavenly " Interpreters " is thus made
clear by Diodorus. According to the Chaldeans the starry
heavens are a book of fate, reflecting the path of life on earth,

and also affording to the wise an opportunity of reading the future. That the ancient Babylonians already knew the " Tables of Fate " and the " Book of Life " is known to us from the Bible. Founded on these ancient models is the belief of the Ostiaks, that the helpers of God write in the " Book of Fate," according to his dictation, each time a child is born, the length and all the varying fortunes of its life.[14] That these helpers or assistants are the previously described seven gods appears from the old tales of the western Tatar tribes of Siberia, in which seven Kudai live in a tent in the sky, before which is the " golden tethering-post." Here the gods sit in their abode behind a curtain, with the great " Book of Life " before them, marking down births and deaths and deciding the fate of men.[15]

Though these fatalistic beliefs may have spread with Islam wherever this religion obtained foothold, and thus among the Turco-Tatar peoples also, it is still evident that, even much earlier, they had taken deep root in the conception of life current among the Central Asian peoples. It is to be noted that the " Interpreters " and the " Sons of God " already appear in the pagan beliefs. The Kudai of the Tatar tribes already referred to have clearly come from Persia, as their name, a Persian loan-word, shows.

The most interesting of all the assistants of the Heaven god is a certain being, who, through the Turco-Tatar peoples, has reached the distant Ostiak territory. This being has a special duty to perform, as the name " Writer man " shows. On the Demyanka he is regarded as the " first assistant of the Heaven god " and is believed to live in heaven, a little lower than the Over-god himself. His duty is said to be " to write in the Book of Fate, according to the dictation of the Over-god, how long and in what circumstances a mortal may live on the earth." When a person dies, the Ostiaks say: " His days written by the ' Writer man ' have finished." In other Ostiak districts a deity of this name is unknown, and for this

reason Karjalainen assumes him to be of late origin and to
have sprung from the Heaven god himself, in other words,
he is a being developed from one of the Heaven god's attributes, as, according to an explanation recorded by the author
in question at Tsingala, the name " Life-time writing man "
is one of the names of the Heaven god.[16]   This assumption is
hardly correct, since besides being the writer of the Book of
Fate, this deity appears also as the bearer of God's commands.
The Irtysh Ostiaks call him by a name borrowed from the
Tatars, Pairekse, and believe that his duties are to come down
to the earth on reconnaissances as the messenger of the heavens,
and to write in the Book of Fate the length and circumstances
of the life of each person being born.   As the messenger and
spy of the Over-god he has been given the attribute " the Man
of many lands," " the Travelling man."   According to the
Ostiaks these journeys are often made in the shape of some
animal, occasionally as a goose.   As such he resembles more the
" younger son " of God, " the world-watching man " or Ort-
iki, who in the shape of a goose or " sitting on the wings of a
goose goes to the place he desires," and who, in tales, is called
the " goose spirit."   Further, the winged steed of the deity
under discussion, on which as the mediator between God and
man he flies through the air, and from " one nostril of which
fire darts out, from the other smoke," is spoken of.[17]   However
great the number of tales mixed up with these names may be,
it is probable that this messenger of God, the " Man of many
lands," the " Travelling man," did not originate among the
Ostiaks.   Still less can a " writing " god have had his birth
among people who have never been able to write.

The same being was known to the Chuvash living on the
Volga, in their belief that the god of Fate, Käbä, sends to the
earth at the birth of each child a being called Püleh, who
decrees the fate of the child and notes down its name.   Having
accomplished his task, he returns to heaven and relates the
matter to the god of Fate.[18]   Possibly, the same being is to be

found in the Cheremiss " Propounder of God," to whom, when sacrificing to the Heaven god, a special offering is prepared, in order that he may lay before his master the troubles of the Cheremiss people.[19] The Votiaks also, at their horse-sacrifices, have a custom of sacrificing a goose, without knowing any longer to which deity it is intended, remarking only that the goose escorts the sacrificial horse to heaven.

In searching for the origin of the Writing god, we must turn again to the land of the twin rivers, where the art of writing was known earlier than elsewhere in Asia, and where, from ancient times, the Tables of Fate and the Book of Life were known. A god corresponding to the " Writing man " of the Ostiaks is also to be found among the ancient Babylonians, who call this scribe of the gods Nabu. As the writer of the Book of Fate he is pictured with an object resembling a pen in his hand and the art of writing is itself called " the wisdom of Nabu." Among the planets he appears as Mercury. The same being is met with in another land where the art of writing was known, Egypt, where Thout is the counterpart of the Babylonian scribe. This ibis-headed deity is often pictured, like Nabu, with a tablet and writing materials in his hand.[20]

In addition to the groups of gods just mentioned, we meet in the mythology of Central Asia with more numerous groups, these forming also a closed ring, the origin of which the people can no longer explain. As in the Altaic tale of the Sumeru mountain, the thirty-three gods (Tengeri) believed to live on this world-mountain have come from India. Most probably connected with these gods is the information given by Verbitskiy regarding the cosmos of the Altaic peoples, that "in Heaven there are thirty-three discs, one higher than the other." [21]

Three times greater is the crowd of Tengeri in the Buriat Heaven. These were divided either according to their dispositions into good and evil, or according to where their habitations

PLATE XLVII

Hides of Buriat Offerings

(See page 404.)

were supposed to be, into " western " and " eastern." The
" western," friendly to man, were called " white "; the eastern,
bringing all kinds of evil, fogs, diseases, and other misfortunes,
were called " black " Tengeri. Of the former there are
fifty-five, of the latter forty-four. The Mongols have also
known these ninety-nine Tengeri of Heaven. The Buriats
relate how these gods, who formerly lived in peace together,
quarrelled among themselves. In the beginning there were
then fifty-four western, good Tengeri and forty-four eastern,
evil ones, one being on the border of each group but belonging
to neither. Being in the minority, the " easterns " begged
this solitary god, the name of whom is said to have been Segen-
Sebdek-Tengeri, to join their side, but the " westerns " put
up a resistance and tempted this god to their own side. In some
districts the source of the disagreement, and even of the war
among the gods, is mentioned as being the beautiful daughter
of Segen-Sebdek-Tengeri, whom both groups passionately
wished to own.[22]

That these ninety-nine gods are not the invention of either
Buriats or Mongols, appears already from the fact that these
peoples do not know the grounds for the above division, nor
do the names given by the Buriats to these gods throw light
on the question. To judge from all the data, this idea has
arrived complete from elsewhere.

More difficult is the explanation as to how this fancy has
originated. An idea has spread among the Altai Tatars, that
besides this earth of ours, the smallest and lowest, there are
ninety-nine other worlds.[23] It is further related that when
Ülgen thrust out the devil Erlik and his company from
Heaven, Erlik pronounced the following words: " Thou hast
cast out my servants and myself from Heaven to the earth,
these falling in forty-three different places. Therefore shall
I send out these forty-three kinds of servants (*etker*) and these
shall work evil each in the place where he has fallen from
Heaven, and trouble men up to their death." Counting Erlik

himself there are thus forty-four of these Altai Tatar evil spirits, or as many as the evilly-disposed Tengeri of the Buriats.[24] The placing of the evil spirits in the east and the good in the west by the latter is peculiar, all other peoples having a contrary opinion. Most probably some star-myth is at the back of these beliefs also. For the sake of comparison it may be mentioned that the Chinese know of seventy-two good and thirty-six evil Star gods.

CHAPTER XII

THE GREAT MOTHER

A MONG the eastern Finno-Ugric peoples we have already
met with a mighty goddess of birth, called by the Cheremiss and the Mordvins the "Great birth-mother," whose
dwelling-place these peoples, like the Votiaks and the Ugrians
living on the Ob, believe to be in the sky. The same goddess
is known to certain peoples of the Altaic race. When celebrating their spring-festival at the time when the flowers
break forth, the Altai Tatars, among other deities, remember
a goddess called " The Lake of Milk." In many prayers she
is referred to as the " Milk Lake mother " and worshipped as
the giver of all life.[1] That this great goddess was known
earlier over a comparatively wide area among the Turco-Tatar
peoples, is proved by the fact that the " Milk Lake mother "
appears also in the list of deities of the Chuvash living by the
Volga.[2] But according to the ideas of the peoples mentioned,
this mythical, deified lake is situated, as we have seen earlier,
beside the tree of life in the centre of the earth. Certain
Altaic tribes, who believe paradise to be situated in the third
Heaven, speak of the " milk lake " to be found there, from
which the god of birth, Jajutši (" the decreer "), takes " lifeforce each time a child is born into the world." [3]

A Central Asian tale would also seem to place the fabled
lake in Heaven, describing as it does how a certain mighty Khan
had promised his daughter in marriage to him who would procure him a wing of the Garuda eagle. To the heroes partaking
in this quest, a youth joins himself, who wishes to know where
this mythical bird dwells. When the heroes have arrived at a
high mountain, they notice how the sky above them begins to

grow white. The youth then asks: " What is behind that
sky? " The others explain that it is the lake of milk. . . .
" But what is the dark thing in its centre? " the youth asks
again, and is told that it is the forest, in which the bird dwells.[4]
Quite plainly, therefore, the " milk lake " of the story has
been imagined as situated on a mountain reaching to the
heavens, up which mountain the heroes have to climb. The
forest in the centre of the lake of milk answers to the tree of
life, in the crown of which other tales also declare the fabled
bird to dwell.

The conception of a lake of milk, believed to be the source of
all life, and worshipped as a female deity, is not a product of
Turco-Tatar mythology, but has drifted there from elsewhere.
A parallel to this belief is to be found in the ancient Iranian
paradise myths, where the lake of milk is represented by the
lake Ardvisura Anahita, which gleams from under the tree of
life on the Hara Berezaiti mountain, the said lake being regarded by the Iranians as a goddess of birth, to whom, in their
poetry, they ascribe anthropomorphic features. Without doubt,
the Yakut Kubai-Khotun, dwelling in the tree of life or under
its roots, is the same deity, and was regarded by them as the
great mother of both men and animals. As such she has
" breasts as large as leather sacks." [5] Sometimes she is mentioned as the wife of the Heaven god, the plenteousness of her
milk being described in a Buriat tale about the origin of the
Milky Way. This phenomenon is explained by them as having
been caused by the overflow of milk from the breasts of the
Heaven goddess (Manzan Görmö).[6] A corresponding myth
was known to the ancient Greeks, who declared the Milky
Way to have been formed when Hera snatched her breast
from the mouth of the infant Heracles, whom she hated, so
that drops of milk were scattered over the sky. From this,
the name met with in many European languages — the Milky
Way (cf. ancient Indian Soma-Dhara, " Soma Way ") — has
obviously been derived.

In Yakut prayers, the above-mentioned goddess of birth has most often the name Ajysyt (" Birthgiver," " Procreator ") or Ajy-Khotun (" Birth-giving mistress "), and children are prayed for from her, whom she is believed to present at her fancy to the woman who has gained her favour. As she is regarded at the same time as birth-giving and nourishing, she is referred to by a name with these significations, " Birthgiving Nourishing mother " (Ajysyt-Ijäksit-Khotun).[7] In some districts the great mother is believed to pour down from Heaven a white elixir of life to one who is in the throes of death.[8] Tales relate how a woman during severe birth-cramp directs a prayer to the Heavens and how, shortly afterwards, two Ajysyts sink down to the earth, and coming to the woman, give their assistance, after which she gives birth to a son.[9] Generally, however, the people speak only of one goddess, who is said to bring the soul of the child from Heaven, as according to the prevalent belief, mortals give birth to the embryo only, life being furnished by Ajysyt. In one prayer the child-bearing woman says to her protective genius: " Thou, my mild Creatress, the first day, on which thou didst let down me to the ' central place ' — i.e., the earth — thou didst say,: ' Be provided with a ceaseless breathing, with an eternal life. May the cattle brought up by thee flourish, may the children borne by thee be many.' " [10] Probably, connected with this belief is the conception that the souls of animals also are let down from the heavens.

Further light is thrown on the foregoing by the belief of the Ostiaks, that the great Birth-giving mother dwells in Heaven on a mountain with seven storeys, where she fixes the fate of all, by writing at the birth of each child in a golden book or on a " gold-ornamented seven-branch," i.e., the tree of life, the forthcoming events of its life.[11]

The Siberian peoples, after a successful delivery, have been in the habit of preparing a feast to the goddess of birth, in which only, women may take part. The Yakuts usually celebrate this feast three days after a birth, at which time the goddess of birth is believed to depart. Flesh of the votive animal is placed for the deity at the head of the bed, and especially butter, a little of which each one present throws laughing merrily into the fire; at the same time the women rub their hands and faces with butter " in order to become fruit-ful." In some districts, after the birth of a boy, a small tent of birch-bark is made by the fireside, and horses and cows and a bow and arrows made of the same material placed within it. The intention of this magic ceremony is the developing of the boy as a capable member of the community.[12]

CHAPTER XIII

THE STARS

THE NOMADS of the Altaic race, like most other peoples of the earth, early turned their attention to the stars and believed that they, in some mysterious way, occasioned the changes of season and weather. The stars were also most important guides for travellers on the prairies, in the forests, and on the tundra. For a thousand years the Great Bear, regularly moving round the Pole Star, that ever-stationary "pole" of the sky, and never disappearing below the horizon, has played an important part in the lives of all the peoples of the Northern Hemisphere. Not only the Altaic race but innumerable other peoples have used it, in addition to the sun and the moon, for measuring time. The ancient Finns are also said to have gone to "see the moon, to learn of the Great Bear." In Central and East Asia the Great Bear even determined the seasons. "When the tail of the Great Bear points eastward it is spring over all the world, when it points southward it is summer, when westward, autumn, but when it turns to the north it is winter over all the world." Some peoples foretell changes in the weather by this constellation. The Ostiaks on the Ob, who call it "the stag," say that when "the stag shrinks," i.e., when the stars of the Great Bear seem to draw together, there will be frost, but contrariwise, or when "the stag expands," mild weather and snowfalls may be expected.[1]

The greatest changes in the weather are believed, however, to be the work of the Pleiades. Even in other countries, such as America and the South Sea Islands, the rising and the setting of this constellation are considered as signs of the coming of cold or warm weather, a rainy or a dry period. In the beliefs of European peoples also, the influence of the Pleiades on the climate plays a certain part. In the question-forms which were used by Forbus as guides in gathering Lapp folklore there is a question: " Have you worshipped the Pleiades that they might give warm weather? " [2] The Turkish peoples believe the Pleiades to be chiefly the causers of cold. The Yakuts say that they " bring the winter." [3] The foundation of this thought is naturally to be found in the fact that a colder period follows the appearance of the Pleiades, whereas their setting takes place at the beginning of the warm season. The Yakuts say that the winter in former days was much colder and drearier than it is now, but since a shaman hacked in twain the binding-rod of the Pleiades, they have been able to move more quickly and thus the winter has become shorter. When the shaman struck, splinters flew into the air, which are now the innumerable stars. [4]

The idea of the Pleiades as the cause of cold weather is further reflected in the old name of this constellation, which is the same in several languages of Turkish origin: Urker, Ürgel, etc. Gorochov says that in Yakut Ürgel means " air-hole." [5] Further weight is given to this idea by a Yakut tale. This tells how a hero once gathered together thirty wolf-leg hides and from them made himself a pair of gloves with which to stop the Ürgel, as it " blew upon him endless frost and wind." [6] The Votiaks and even the Lithuanians and the Baltic Finns called this constellation " the sieve."

The Siberian peoples seem to have considered it impossible to solve the question of what the innumerable stars of the sky really are. The belief of the Yakuts that they are small holes through which heavenly light shines is easy to understand. In other places they are declared to be " the reflection of the heavenly ocean." [7]

THE SUN AND THE MOON

The Altaic peoples speak of a time when there was no sun and no moon. They say that people, who then flew in the air, gave out light and warmed their surroundings themselves, so that they did not even miss the heat of the sun. But when one of them fell ill God sent a spirit to help these people. This spirit commenced by stirring the primeval ocean with a pole 10,000 fathoms long, when suddenly two goddesses flew into the sky. He also found two metal mirrors (*toli*), which he placed in the sky. Since then there has been light on the earth.[8]

This tale is doubtless grounded on a previously-mentioned conception, that people living before the fall in paradise were a kind of luminous beings. The Kalmucks distinctly say that at the time of paradise there was yet no sun and no moon. It was only when the people, by eating of the forbidden fruit, fell into sin, and the world around them became dark, that the sun and moon were created.[9]

The idea of the sun and moon as metal mirrors in the above tale is also to be found in beliefs and customs connected with the prophesyings of Central Asian shamans. It is commonly supposed that everything that takes place on the earth is reflected in the sun and the moon and from these again in the magic mirrors of the shamans. There is a story of how a certain hero holds his magic mirror toward the sun and the moon in order to see in their reflections where the colt which he is seeking has disappeared.[10] This manner of finding out things has spread among the peoples of North Siberia. Even in Ostiak countries the sun is an important means of prophesying by sight; by watching it the magician can tell the life and the fate of a person far away.[11] Possibly the Siberian shaman's custom of fixing metal objects representing the sun and the moon on his dress originates in this belief. It is another question whether this belief and this custom are original with the

Altaic race, or whether they have wandered there from lands where prophesying from the stars has long been known and common.

Besides those tales which say that the sun and the moon were created comparatively late, there are others according to which the lights of the sky already existed when the vast primeval ocean yet covered all. In Mongolian tales the sun and the moon are called sisters, of whom the former says to the latter: " Travel thou in the day, I will travel in the night." The moon remarked: " There will be so many people about in the day, I shall be ashamed to walk abroad then." The sisters finally agreed, but the sun regretted that the earth was so smooth and that there were no hillocks or mounds above the water for the people to live on. The tale does not go on to tell how the earth on which the people dwell came to exist. We might suppose the moon to have had her share in its creation, the ebb and flow of the tide which she causes having early attracted the attention at least of coast-dwellers. A tale of the Votiaks says that the god of Heaven, Inmar, sent two people out during the flood to find earth and to scatter it on the surface of the ocean. The first went out in the day, wherefore he made the earth smooth, but the second, going out in the night, sowed the mountains and valleys on the earth.

In Central Asia tales have been taken down according to which there were three or four suns in primeval times. At that time it was unbearably hot upon the earth. The Buriats tell how a hero named Erkhe-Mergen shot three suns down into the sea with his bow so that only one remained to light and warm the earth.[12] In a legendary tale of the Torgouts it is said that the devil (Shulman) created three suns in order to burn the earth made by God (Burkhan-Bakshi). In answer, God covered the earth, on which there were as yet no dwellers, with a flood, so that the devil was forced to submit. Only one sun remained in the sky, the others God plunged later into the bottomless pit given to the devil for his dwelling-place.[13]

The following Buriat tale gives a description of the confining and liberating of the heavenly lights, a theme greatly favoured in the stories of many peoples. When Heaven and earth through the intermarriage of their children became related to one another, the " Lord of the Earth " once made a visit to the god of Heaven. On leaving he begged for the sun and the moon as presents. The god of Heaven, who wished to observe the sacred customs of hospitality, dared not refuse, and the " Lord of the Earth " took the lights of the sky with him and shut them into a box. Then all nature became dark. The god of Heaven had no other resource than to turn to the porcupine, asking him to help by bringing back the sun and the moon. The porcupine agreed to try and made a visit to the " Lord of the Earth." When the guest was about to depart, the host asked him what gift he wished as a token of hospitality. " Give me the mirage-horse and the echo-spear," answered the porcupine, and as the " Lord of Earth " could not fulfil so difficult a wish he gave his guest the sun and the moon. The porcupine put the lights back in their former orbits and the world became bright again.[14]

In the tales of Turco-Tatar peoples the porcupine appears as a wise and wily creature, sometimes as the inventor of fire, or the originator and teacher of agriculture.[15] Seeing that this animal also occupies an important position in the beliefs of the ancient Iranians, one might assume that the above mentioned tales have come to Central Asia from them.

The Altaic Tatars describe the nature of the sun and the moon by relating how Otshirvani took fire, placed it on his sword and slung it in the sky, and thus created the sun, and how he made the moon by striking the water with his sword. The reason why daylight is burning hot, say the people, is that the sun is made of fire, whereas moonlight is cold because this star came out of the water.[16] The Dolgans say that the sun was created in the day, the moon in the night.[17]

Most of the peoples of Turkish origin living in Siberia imagine, when addressing these heavenly lights, the sun to be feminine (Mother sun) and the moon masculine (Father moon, Old man moon). Often, especially in tales, we also hear of the Sun Khan and the Moon Khan. According to Chinese sources the Mongolian and the Old Turkish rulers used to worship the sun in the morning and the moon in the evening.[18] The Chuvash until quite lately brought the Sun god white sacrifices. Concerning moon-worship we have not much other information than that it has been a custom to greet the new moon and to utter a wish that he would bring good luck and prosperity. The most northern peoples of Turkish origin, who have eagerly retained their old customs, do not sacrifice to the sun or the moon, although these orbs seem to have played an important part in the rites of the shamans. Yet both are considered by them to be living beings. They believe that the sun sees all that people do, and therefore often appeal to it: " May the sun see! " or " May the sun know! " In swearing, the Yakut turns towards the sun and says: " If I have made a wrong oath may. the sun refuse me light and warmth." It is said that the Tungus believe the sun to watch their conduct and to punish their wicked actions.[19]

As is natural, the tribes of Turkish origin, like all other nations, keep account of time by the cycles of the sun and the changes of the moon. Plano Carpini says that the Mongolians never undertook a war expedition or any other important work except at the time of the new or the full moon. Weather prophesying by the sun is the same in Central and Northern Asia as in Europe. The Tungus and the Yenesei Ostiaks consider a ring round the moon in winter to be an omen of cold, in summer of rain, saying that the moon protects himself from the weather by making himself a tent. The Ostiaks on the Ob also know this saying.[20]

The spots on the sun and the moon, especially those on the latter, have always been interesting themes for tales among all peoples. The Yakuts tell of a poor orphan girl for whom life was so hard that the moon pitied her and determined to take her to him. One frosty night when the girl had gone out to get water the moon descended, raised the child to his breast, and ascended again to the heavens. Wherefore, we now see in the moon a girl bearing a yoke with two buckets on her shoulder. In other places there is a story of two children, a brother and a sister, who, having gone out to fetch water, stayed to watch the moon until he became angry and snatched them to him. The Yakuts never allow their children to watch the full moon.[21]

The Buriats see more than a girl with her yoke and buckets in the moon. They see also a willow-bush. The girl had had a strict and hard-hearted step-mother, who once when the child was a long time fetching water cried to her in anger: "Oh, that the sun and the moon took thee!" When she was bearing water the girl saw the sun and the moon descending towards her. In her fright she grasped a willow-bush. When the sun was about to take her the moon said: "Thou walkest in the day and I in the night. Give the girl to me." The sun agreed to the moon's request, who immediately lifted up the child with buckets, bush and all. The Yakuts also know this tale in the same form.[22]

This tale about the water-fetcher, of which we find a variant in the *Edda* of Snorri, is very widely known in Asia and in Europe.

The Altai Tatars tell of the old man of the moon, who in former times lived on the earth and caused great havoc as a man-eater. The dwellers of Heaven wished to save the people and gathered together to take counsel. The sun said: " I would willingly descend to free the poor people from that monster were not my heat harmful to them." On hearing this the moon remarked that they could well stand his coldness, and he descended to the earth, where he found the man-eater picking berries from a hawthorn. The moon at once seized the wretch and his tree and returned to the sky, where the man-eater and the hawthorn can still be seen in the moon.[23]

The primitive peoples of the District of Turukhansk see a shaman with his drum in the moon. This formerly mighty man undertook to fight against the moon, but scarcely had he drawn near it before the moon made him its prisoner.[24]

The Mongolians and the peoples of the Altai imagined also that a hare dwelt in the moon.[25]

The waning of the moon is said by the Yakuts to be caused by wolves and bears eating its disc. Every time the moon has grown to its ordinary size the beasts again attack it.[26]

According to Buriat tales an eclipse of the sun or the moon takes place when a certain beast, which is ever persecuting the lights of the sky, swallows the sun and the moon. Once when this monster, Alkha, again darkened the world, the gods became so angry that they cut his body in two. The hind part fell down, but the living forepart still haunts the sky. Every time Alkha now swallows stars they soon appear again, as the beast is unable to retain them in his body. The Buriats say that when Alkha is troubling the sun and the moon they pray for help, and the people have a custom of screaming and making a noise, throwing stones and even shooting up into the sky in order to drive away the monster.[27]

A tale recorded in another Buriat district relates that Arakho, as the beast is here called, formerly lived upon the earth and consumed the hairs off the people's bodies, which at that time were quite hairy. Seeing this, God became angry and inquired of the moon Arakho's hiding-place. On finding the beast he struck it in two, and the living forepart is forever eating the moon in consequence.[28]

It is also told that Otshirvani, wishing to sweeten life for people and animals, let the sun and the moon prepare water of life, but Arakho drank it up and soiled the cup. Having inquired the beast's dwelling-place from the moon, God hurried there and cut him in two. The forepart, having thus become immortal, pursues the moon. Some see the "body" of the monster in the moon-spots.[29]

The Arakho who causes eclipses of the sun and moon, and who has only a head but no body, is known to the Mongols also. The tale originates in India where the monster's name is Râhu. Arakho and Alkha are corrupt variants of this name.

The conception prevalent among the peoples of North-East Asia that the persecutor of the lights of heaven is a dragon has come from China. The Altai Tatars say that the eclipse of the moon is the work of a man-eater living in a star. The Russian Tatars and the Chuvash speak of a vampire which sometimes swallows the sun and the moon but soon leaves them in peace again, as the stars begin to burn his mouth.

THE POLE STAR AND THE LITTLE BEAR

The significance of the Pole Star in the universe has already been mentioned. The fact that other surrounding stars seem to circle round that "golden" or "iron pole" has given rise to a fancy that bonds exist between them. The Kirghis call the three stars of the Little Bear nearest the Pole Star, which form an arch, a "rope" to which the two larger stars of the same constellation, the two horses, are fastened. One of the horses is white, the other bluish-grey. The seven stars of the Great Bear they call the seven watchmen, whose duty it is to guard the horses from the lurking wolf. When once the wolf succeeds in killing the horses the end of the world will come.[30] In other tales the stars of the Great Bear are "seven wolves" who pursue those horses. Just before the end of the world they will succeed in catching them.[31] Some even fancy that the Great Bear is also tied to the Pole Star. When once all the bonds are broken there will be great disturbances in the sky. The Tatars by Minusinsk say that when the "seven dogs" are let loose the end of the world will come.[32]

The numerous tales about the one or more bound beasts, which are to be set free before the end of the world, were possibly originally similar star-myths. The Slavs have a story about a bound dog whose iron chains form the Little Bear. When the dog, who is ever endeavouring to bite his chains in two, once gets loose, the end of the world will be at hand.[33]

THE GREAT BEAR

Many North Siberian primitive peoples and even the Russians living in those parts call the Great Bear a "stag." The Samoyeds of the District of Turukhansk fancy that the Pole Star is a hunter chasing the stag and trying to kill it.[34] The Yenisei Ostiaks see a stag and three hunters in this constellation. The stars forming the square are the stag, those in the arch the hunters, the first of these being a Tungus, the second a Yenesei Ostiak and the little star, Alcor, glimmering by his side, his kettle, the third a Russian. In addition, the three stars forming the forepart of the stag are also specially explained: one is the beast's nose, the other two its ears.[35] This same tale is known among the Tungus of that district and it is possible that even the following Yakut variant, which is said in different places to refer to different stars, e.g., to Orion, also belongs to the same series. The Yakut variant is as follows: Once upon a time three Tungus chased a stag up into the sky, where they wandered long in hunger. In the end one of the hunters died, but the other two, together with the stag and the dog, were changed into stars (the stag-star).[36]

For the sake of comparison it may be mentioned that even the Indians of North America see an animal in the Great Bear, usually a bear, with three hunters at his heels.[37]

The Buriats call the seven stars of the Great Bear "seven old men." According to one tale they are the skulls of seven smiths. A hero once killed "seven blacksmiths" and prepared from their skulls seven cups, out of which he gave his wife to drink until she was intoxicated. When she had drunk she threw the cups into the sky, where they formed the seven stars of the Great Bear. All blacksmiths are said to be under the protection of these stars.[38]

The Mongols, who also call this constellation "the seven old men" or "the seven Burkhans," sacrificed milk and kumiss and even devoted some domestic animals to it.[39]

Very widespread is a tale in which the "seven old men" or the "seven Khans" as they are also called, are accused of theft. The Mongols tell that "the seven Burkhans" stole a star from the Pleiades, which numbered seven before but are now only six. This little stolen star (Alcor) is to be seen close to the central star of the arch of the Great Bear. With the Mongols it has developed into the god of thieves, to whom these always call on their predatory excursions to give luck in their wickedness.[40] It is in order to be revenged on the Great Bear, so say the Altai Tatars, that the Pleiades pursue the "seven Khans" although they never overtake them.[41] The Kirghis also call the Great Bear "the seven thieves," and accuse them of having stolen one of the two daughters of the Pleiades.[42] In Northern Caucasia there is a tale of how a certain Khan left his child in the keeping of "seven brothers" and how they were already on their homeward journey when the Pleiades attacked them, wishing to kill the child, but the "seven brothers" succeeded in saving it.[43]

The tales about the "seven brothers" and their "little sister" who was taken up into the sky, belong to the same series. That the "seven old men" of the Buriats also are originally robbers of a star-maiden appears from the following story, which has been recorded among them. There was once upon a time a poor man who received the gift of understanding the speech of birds. One day when he was resting under a tree he heard two ravens discussing how to heal the son of a Khan who had long lain ill. On hearing the method agreed upon by the ravens, he at once hurried to the Khan and healed

his son. Greatly thankful, the Khan presented him with seven
steeds. On his homeward journey he met six men, each of
whom attracted his attention in a peculiar way. The first was
so strong that he could lift a mountain from the ground. The
second had so keen a sense of hearing that he could tell what
was happening under the earth. The third was an archer of
such power that with his bow he could bring down a piece of
the " heavenly mountain." The fourth was so clever with his
hands that he easily transplanted the feathers from one kind
of bird to another. The fifth was able to suck a whole river
into his mouth and squirt it out again. The sixth was so
nimble of foot that he outran a wild-goat on the prairie. These
heroes now joined the poor man who understood the language
of birds. Then the one who had the keen sense of hearing
happened to hear how a certain Khan, wishing to choose a
husband for his daughter, set all the suitors-elect three difficult conditions to fulfill. The heroes, determining to try their
luck, went to the Khan and asked him for his daughter's hand.
Having easily fulfilled the most difficult tasks they took the
maiden with them. The servants of the Khan pursued them,
but the seven heroes escaped with their booty. In the end God
took them up into the sky where they were changed into the
Great Bear. The little star Alcor by the arch is the maiden
whom they won.[44] The same story-motif would seem to have
been known to the ancient Greeks also. They told how Elektra, one of the seven Pleiades, who is said to have been the ancestress of the Trojans, took the fall of Troy so much to heart
that she left her original place in the Pleiades. Hence, according to them, this constellation now has only six stars.
Elektra is said to have moved to the Great Bear where she
now glimmers as a little star beside the central star of the arch.
It is possible that the ancient Greeks had mixed up two tales,
viz., that of the robbing of the maid who caused the Trojan
war, and that of the robbing of the star, belonging to an earlier
period.

ORION

As with the Great Bear, a hunting-myth is also connected with Orion. Once upon a time, according to the Buriats, there lived a famous archer who hunted " three stags " and was just about to overtake them when the animals suddenly rose into the sky. The hunter had time, however, to send an arrow after them. The stags then suddenly changed into the three stars of Orion (" the three stags "), and a little lower down one can see the hunter's arrow as a star in the sky.[45]

In the district of the Altai this tale has been taken down in various other forms also. The Teleuts tell of a hero named Kuguldei-Matyr who chased three stags on horseback. Having speeded to and fro over the earth in all directions without finding a resting-place, the animals at last sprang into the sky. But the hero followed at their heels, shooting at them with two arrows. His steed appears as a great star in the east, near the " three stags " (the belt of Orion), and there also are his two arrows, the one white, the other red. The latter, having passed through the bodies of the stags, is bloody. The hero himself has also become a large star.[46]

Another tale tells how God cursed this hunter, who had intended to kill all the stags on the earth, and therefore changed the " three stags " into the belt of Orion, around which hunter, steed, hound and arrows now twinkle as stars. Some see in Orion, besides the stags, a hunter, a hound, a hunting-hawk and arrows. Some speak of two hounds. Hunters are said to worship this archer-hero and to pray to him for good luck in hunting.[47]

The Mongols also call the belt of Orion " the three stags." They see in addition, an archer, a horse, a hound and an arrow in this constellation.[48] According to a Buriat tale this hero was born of a cow, and had a human head and a horse's body.[49]

The Kirghis see in the belt of Orion three deer, the surrounding stars being the " three hunters " and their " arrow."

These hunters are said to have lived on the earth in former times, but as no animal could escape their well-aimed arrows God took the deer into the sky.[50]

The centaur of the Buriats brings into mind the ancient Greek tales in which Orion appears as a hero who was regarded as an exceedingly mighty hunter. The ancient Greeks believed, like the Siberian Tatars, that this hero intended to destroy all the animals on the earth. "The hunt of Orion" was reflected in the sky, where the hunter had even a hound (Sirius) with him.

The Yenisei Ostiaks call Orion "stag's head." Their ideas do not, however, appear to be connected with the series of myths just referred to. Thus they tell how this stag carried off a bride for the hero Alba.[51] For the Yenisei Ostiaks, Orion, and not the Great Bear, is the maiden-robber. Ideas corresponding to this are found among other peoples.

Orion has also many names taken from objects. The most common of these are: "the scales" or "the hand-scales" (Turkish, Kirghis, Tatar, Votiak, etc.) and "the yoke" (for buckets) (Volga Tatar, Cheremiss, Vogul, etc.).

THE PLEIADES

We have mentioned before that some peoples imagine the Pleiades to be air holes, a ventilator, or a sieve through which streams a cold draught from the upper air. With others this constellation has suggested a group of animals. The most northern peoples of Siberia call it a bird's nest, or a duck's nest (Yakuts, Voguls, Koriaks, etc.). Some Central Asian peoples call the Pleiades "monkeys" (*metshit*) or "monkey" (*metshin*). With this unexpected fancy, in a district where monkeys are unknown, stories are also connected.

The Altai Tatars relate that in olden times Metshin lived upon the earth. It was then terribly cold on the earth, and for this reason the camel and the cow determined to kill him.

Once, when he was hiding in the ashes of a log-fire and the camel had lifted his foot to crush him, the cow remarked: " Thy foot is too soft, let me try with my hard hoof." The camel stepped aside and let the cow stamp with its hoof into the ashes. Metshin was trodden in pieces, but through the cleft of the cow's hoof the pieces escaped and flew into the sky, where they now twinkle as six little stars.[52]

A variant of the tale is that as long as Metshin was on the earth it was exceedingly hot, but since the Pleiades rose into the sky the weather on the earth has grown colder.[53]

In connection with this tale, the Pleiades are mostly imagined to be a great insect. The Kirghis say that Urker was a great green insect that lived in the grass and ate cattle, especially sheep, for which it had a great liking. The camel and the cow grew angry and determined to kill it, but it escaped through the cleft of the cow's hoof into the sky. In the summer, when Urker cannot be seen in the sky, it is said to have come on the earth. If it alights in a watery district, the winter will be bad, but if in a dry spot, the Kirghis expect a good winter.[54]

In the district of the Altai the carrying-off of a star is connected with this tale. The Great Bear, which here appears as a mighty Khan, could not endure that Metshin should live on the earth as a great and wicked insect which ate up human beings and animals. Not knowing how he could destroy the monster, he asked his horse for advice. The horse replied: " I will crush him to powder with my hoof." The cow, happening to hear this, hurried to the ice where the insect was resting and stamped it into pieces with her foot. When the pieces escaped through the hoof to the sky the Khan managed to catch only one which he took with him. Metshin, which is now bereft of one of its stars, ever angrily pursues the Great Bear.[55]

A belief that the Pleiades originally formed one star, which afterwards was parted into many pieces, is suggested by many of the tales connected with this constellation from different parts of the globe, in which some creature is crushed into pieces. The idea, also, that the Pleiades formerly consisted of seven stars but now number only six is comparatively common.

VENUS

Of the planets Solbon (Turco-Tatar, Tsholbon = Venus), which " can be seen in the morning and in the evening," plays in the tales of the Buriats a considerable part. This star is said to be a famous horse-lover, who rides over the sky lasso in hand. He has in his possession a great troop of horses, watched over by a horse-herd named Dogedoi or Toklok. The Buriats consider Solbon to be the patron-god of their own horses, and for this reason they pray to and worship him. In the spring, when they cut the manes and tails of their horses and set the mark of the owner on the colts, they prepare a sacrifice for Solbon, cooking meat and cream-porridge (*sala-mat*) and making home-distilled spirits (*tarasun*) in his honour. The wine they throw into the air for Solbon and his groom Toklok, but the meat and the porridge they put into the fire. They then begin their own meal. In addition they have a custom of dedicating live horses to Solbon, as to many other gods, which horses are then no longer used in human service.[56] Georgi says the Buriats believe " that the gods and especially the shepherd-god Sulbundu (sic!) ride on these in the night when watching over the other horses, and for this reason they are believed to be covered with perspiration in the mornings." [57] Tales also tell how Solbon's groom teaches people to tend their horses well. Sometimes he informs them beforehand which persons will prosper with their horses during their lifetime. The Buriats regard as a good omen the birth of a colt in the autumn after Solbon has appeared in the sky, believing such a colt to become a very good horse afterwards.[58]

PLATE XLVIII

SHAMAN DRUMS FROM THE MINUSINSK DISTRICT

Both the outer and inner sides are shown. They are furnished with drawings and figures on the skin of the drum, and with hand-grip, bells and metal symbols on the inner side. (See pages 287, 520.)

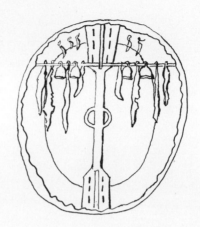

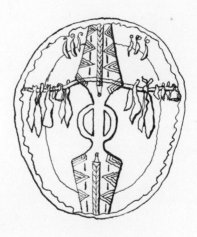

A certain tale relates how once when Solbon travelled to the western sky, his groom Dogedoi left the horses untended for three days, going out for a walk with his dog Burto. On returning, the groom saw to his surprise that the wolves had scattered his horses and even devoured some of them. Just as he was about to gather them together Solbon returned from the western sky and seeing the disorder punished his groom severely.[59]

It is easy to understand how Venus, as the morning and evening star, should have suggested the idea of a shepherd tending the flocks of stars. As a ruler over the stars, this planet appears also in the tales of the North American Indians. The Yenisei Ostiaks imagine Venus to be the oldest among the stars, and to guard them from dangers and watch that they do not disappear before their time. For this reason it is "first and last" in the sky.[60] Even the ancient Babylonians speak of the heavenly "sheep" that Ištar tended.

But whence have the Mongols obtained their horseman and his groom? One might assume that this horse-loving nomad tribe had of itself begun to imagine the stars to be a great flock of horses. And yet the Indo-Iranian peoples also seem to have had the same idea. Probably, as Oldenberg says, the twin gods Asvin ("the horsemen") of the *Veda* were originally the morning and the evening stars. The gods Asvin were worshipped together with the god of dawn in the early morning and they are mentioned also as "the givers of horses."

With this same star the Buriats connect a tale of the robbing of a bride. Solbon is said to have three wives, the third being a former Buriat girl, whom the hero carried off just as she was about to celebrate her wedding. Solbon descended to the earth, seized the girl, who was far-famed for her beauty, from the midst of the wedding-guests and took her with him to the sky. By his two first wives Solbon had no children, but the maid whom he carried off from the earth bore him a son.[61]

With the Yakuts Venus is feminine. They relate that she

is a beautiful maiden whom Ürgel (the Pleiades) loves. When these two meet in the sky it is a bad omen, foretelling storm and violent weather.[62]

The Kirghis say that " the Pleiades are the moon's son, and the evening star the moon's daughter." [63]

THE MILKY WAY

The imagination of the child of nature was early exercised also by the distant spectacle of the Milky Way. The most common name for it in the Turco-Tatar languages is " the birds' way " (Turkoman, Kirghis, etc.) or " the wild ducks' way " (Volga-Tatar, Chuvash, Votiak and Cheremiss), to which the corresponding term in Finnish and Esthonian is " the birds' road " and in Lapp " the birds' stair " (lodderaiddaras). What the origin of this comparatively old name is, appears from the beliefs of the Ostiaks and the Voguls: these say that the Milky Way, which they also name " the ducks' road " or " the southern birds' road," is the guide of birds of passage in the nighttime. The Esthonians explain the origin of this name in the same manner.[64]

Many other fancies have also been awakened by the Milky Way. We have already remarked that the Buriats and the Yakuts call it " the seam of the sky." The Samoyeds of the District of Turukhansk call it the " back of the sky." [65] These names evidently result from a conception of the sky as a kind of tent-roof.

In some Buriat districts, as mentioned, a tale has been recorded in which the Milky Way is said to have come into being when Manzan-Görmö milked herself and then threw away the milk.

In North-East Siberia the Milky Way is imagined to be a large river flowing across the sky.[66] This idea has perhaps its origin in China, where the idea of a " heavenly river " is also met with. Like the Japanese, the Koreans tell of two stars who

loved one another and whom God, because they neglected their
duties for the sake of their love, separated by placing the one
in the uttermost east, the other in the uttermost west. In
addition the broad heavenly river flows between them. Once
a year, in the seventh month, these lovers are said to meet,
the birds building a bridge for them over the river.[67]

With the Caucasian Tatars, the Turks, and many of the
Balkan peoples, a tale of Persian origin is connected with the
Milky Way, the tale telling of a man who stole straw or hay,
intending to hide his booty in the sky, but, as he journeyed,
sprinkled so much on the way that his path can yet be traced
in the sky. For this reason these stars are also called "the
straw-thief's track." [68]

Names of later origin are the "pilgrims' way to Mecca" of
the Mohammedan Tatars, and the "Burkhans' road" of the
Mongols. The Yakuts call the Milky Way "God's foot-
prints." He is said to have walked across the sky in creating
the earth.[69] More common is "the ski-track of the son of
God," [70] behind which name there is perhaps hidden some
hunting-story like the one written down among the Ostiaks
and the Voguls. When God (Numi-Tōrem), as the Voguls
relate, had created the earth, he sent a six-footed stag upon it.
An ordinary human being could not hunt this quick-footed
animal, and so he begged the Forest spirit to pursue it. But
even for this being, who glided at a terrific rate on his skis,
it was not easy to overtake his six-legged prey. When at last
he succeeded in killing the animal, which was so big that its
body "reached over thirty rivers," the Forest spirit broke off
the two additional feet, saying to his father Numi-Tōrem:
" Change this animal with the power of thy word into a four-
footed beast, as, seeing that the work of chasing and killing it
has been difficult even for me, how should an ordinary human
being have the strength necessary for it." This hunt was reflected in the sky. The stag became the Great Bear, in which
are to be seen the beast's head, its two eyes, its forefeet and

hindfeet, and in addition the chopped-off stumps of the other two feet. The Milky Way is "the ski-track of the Forest spirit." Even the Forest spirit's house can be seen in the sky in a shape which the Voguls call "the complete house of the Forest spirit," (i.e., the Pleiades). In this story also, the hero who attacks the Great Bear is from the Pleiades.[71]

The Ostiaks on the Irtysh River tell of a man named Tungk-Pok. who once when he was in the sky undertook to hunt this six-footed stag. Having chased it across the sky on his magic skis the hero overtook it at the mouth of the Irtysh, where the stag threw itself on to the earth. The hunter did not succeed in killing it, but could only cut off its two hindmost feet. He therefore declared: "Men will become more and more small and weak, how can they then overthrow a six-footed beast, which even for me is very difficult? May stags and other animals from this day onwards have only four feet!" The stag continued its flight towards the north until the hero again reached it near Obdorsk. The animal being then dead-tired, it begged God to save it from the hands of the hunter. God took pity on the stag and changed it into a great stone, but, as a memento of this heavenly chase, the Ostiaks see in the Milky Way two parallel ski-tracks ("the ski-track of Tungk-Pok" or "the way of Tungk-Pok") and in the Great Bear a "stag."

The Ostiaks of Vasyugan call this hunter "the son of the god of Heaven." [72]

THE SIGNS OF A TWELVE-DIVISIONED PERIOD

In connection with fancies relating to the stars it may be mentioned that the peoples of Central Asia divide time into periods of twelve, usually calling each of these units of time by the following animal names: mouse, cow, tiger, hare, dragon, snake, horse, sheep, monkey, cock, dog and sow.[73] Images of these animals in relief can often be seen decorating the edges of the circular metal mirrors (*toli*) hanging with other magic objects on the costume of the shamans and used as instruments of sorcery. Other objects, also decorated with the same images, for reckoning time can be seen here, most of which have been brought from China where, as in other parts of East Asia, this method of keeping account of time still prevails. From the Chinese pictures it will be seen that the animal-images there are the same as those of the Mongols. Only the sign of the mouse is called a rat by the Chinese, and that of the hare a rabbit. Although these animal signs are mainly the same with the different peoples of Central Asia, their order varies somewhat. Thus the Eastern Soyots are said to reckon the years in the following order — dragon, tiger, cow, sow, monkey, mouse, dog, frog, snake, cock, horse and hare.[74]

FIG. 16. SIGNS OF A TWELVE-DIVI-SIONED PERIOD

The Buriats, who begin their twelve-year and twelve-month periods with the mouse, say that they really ought to begin with the camel, but that the camel has lost this honour. Light is thrown on the subject by the following tale. The camel and the mouse quarrelled over which of them should rule over the first year of a period or the first month of a year. In the end they decided to solve the dispute in such a way that the one who first saw the rays of the rising sun should call the year or month in question by his name. The camel took his stand looking towards the east, but the mouse climbed on his hump and from there watched the west. At dawn the camel's eye had not yet caught the sun when the mouse had already seen the reflection of its rays on the western mountains. For this reason the first year and also the first month of the year are called after the mouse. From this tale the Buriats have a proverb: " In believing himself great the camel lost a year." [75]

Signs of animals representing a period of time divisible by twelve are already to be found side by side with the signs of the Zodiac on the marble tablets of the ancient Egyptians, found in the beginning of the last century. A period of twelve hours, which were represented by animal figures of the same description, was called Dodekaoros by the ancient Greeks. These pictures, which to some extent resemble the time-marks of the Mongols, are mentioned in the following order: cat, dog, snake, crab, ass, lion, goat, ox, hawk, monkey, ibis and crocodile. There can be no doubt that these time-marks, which, like the twelve-divisioned period itself, seem to have spread into East Asia from the west, are closely connected with the corresponding ideas of these civilized peoples. Later Greek texts call this method of reckoning time "Chaldean," which points to Babylonian astrology. The signs of the twelve-divisioned period are thus most probably explained by the twelve signs of the Zodiac.

CHAPTER XIV

THUNDER

LIKE most of the North American Indian tribes, the
peoples in the farthest north of Siberia imagine thunder
to be something resembling a large and mighty bird. The
Forest Tungus speak of it as such and explain that the rustle of
this mighty bird's wings is heard on the
earth, when it flies, as the terrific rumbling
of thunder. The Tungus never offer up
sacrifices to this being, nor do they worship it in any other way, but when weaving a magic spell they make a wooden
image of a bird to represent it, fixing this
outside their tent at the head of a long
pole. The Thunder bird is believed to
protect the soul of the shaman, who in
his flight through the air may encounter
many dangers. The shaman can even
send the Thunder bird against his enemies

Fig. 17. The Tun-
gus Thunder-bird

should he deem it necessary. The Tungus see a proof of the
gigantic powers of this bird of the upper air in trees struck by
lighting, which it has torn to shreds with its " claws of stone." [1]

A similar conception of the nature of thunder is found
among the Chukchee and all the primitive peoples of the District of Turukhansk. The Eastern Samoyeds liken the
Thunder bird to a duck, whose sneezing is the cause of rain.
It is also imagined as the Iron bird, probably on account of the
din it can create. [2] The Yurak Samoyeds of Northern Russia,
who make themselves an image of thunder in the form of a
goose, fancy, like the Tungus, that the Thunder bird attends

and protects the soul of the shaman. A certain shaman is even said to have wandered two or three years in the air accompanied by this giant bird.[3] The hero in a Yakut tale says: " Why should I not change myself into a bird and pretend to be the ruler of rain and thunder." [4]

In the beliefs of the Tremyugan Ostiaks, thunder appears as a black bird resembling a grouse and screaming very loudly.[5]

The Mongol tribes, many Altai peoples, and some Eastern Tungus tribes, such as the Goldes, believe that the phenomenon of thunder is caused by a large flying dragon. The Mongols say that this dragon has wings and a body covered with fish scales. At times it lives in the water, at times flies in the air. When it moves in the sky the rumbling of thunder follows. In some places the rumbling is explained to be the dragon's voice and every movement of its tail to be a flash of lightning. It never comes sufficiently near to the earth for people to see it, and in the winter it hides in lofty mountains where the hoar-frost on the crags is caused by its breath. Others say that it winters in dense forests, over which a perpetual mist then hovers, and a third opinion is that it spends the winter in the sea.[6]

The peoples of the Altai say that lightning and thunder follow when the dragon strikes two stones against each other, of which one is in its mouth, the other in its hand. It is also told that a certain Tengeri rides on the back of this monster, chasing a striped or flying squirrel.[7] The Tengeri desires to wreak vengeance on the squirrel, which, while in Heaven, tore out the eye of God's youngest son. It is dangerous during a thunder-storm to stand under a tree in which a squirrel is hiding, as the lightning always strikes such trees. This belief is also common among the Buriats.[8] The Goldes say that the dragon pursues evil spirits who will hide anywhere when a thunder-storm arises.[9]

This conception, in which the Creator of thunder is introduced in an exceedingly mythological shape, is not an original

Altaic one, but, as its geographical area already denotes, comes from China. As we know, the Chinese and, following their example, the Japanese, imagined the Thunder god to have the shape of a peculiar dragon, which is represented in their art in many different ways.

Both the above mentioned conceptions, the bird and the winged dragon, are evidently born of the swift movement of a thunder-storm and especially of the sudden flash of the lightning. Even where human features are attributed to the Thunder god, he is often regarded as a being with wings. The Ostiaks of Demyanka call him " the Winged old man." [10]

Among the Buriats a number of tales have been found relating how some human hero becomes transformed into a Thunder god by dressing himself in winged garments. One of these tales tells of a clever archer who came to heaven alive. On the earth he had had a wife and three sons with whom he lived happily until he became old. One day he told his sons that his days were numbered and asked them to prepare him a garment and saddle a horse. After wishing good-bye to his family he mounted the horse and departed. Coming to the meeting of three roads he chose the middle one, which led to the sky. There he arrived at an empty house where he was soon joined by four young men. These feasted the old man and asked him to remain there as guardian of that heavenly abode; at the same time they forbade him to open a chest which stood in the room or to put on a winged garment hanging on the wall. When he was alone, however, the man became so curious that he once opened the mystic chest and saw there strange, different-coloured stones shaped like arrow-points. Happening at the same time to turn his eyes to the earth, where at that moment a person was stealing vegetables from his neighbour's garden, he became so angry that he threw a red stone at the thief. A little later the four masters of the house returned home and scolded the old man for having set a whole village on fire because of one wicked man. Still later on, the old man conceived a desire to try on the winged clothes. When he had dressed himself in them he acquired a magic power of flying and thus he became the god of Thunder.[11]

There is another version of the same tale in a slightly different form. A man who had lost his way while wandering in great forests came to a place where a flight of stairs led up from the earth to the sky. Ascending the stairs he arrived at a fine house glittering and shimmering with gold and silver, where the old god of Heaven, Esege-Malan-Tengeri, was sitting. Hearing how the man had come to Heaven, God was delighted and begged him to be his servant, the man consenting to his request. One day God urged him to look down and see how people were living on the earth. On doing so, he saw a man leading a sheep stolen from another's flock, and he became so angry that he seized one of the stones which God kept in a chest and threw it on the earth. Instantly, God sent him down after his stone, so that he could see it fall on the earth as a great flash of lightning that slew the thief. From that day he remained with the god of Heaven and served him as the Thunderer.[12]

Notwithstanding all these tales, which evidently belong to a world-wide group of myths, the Buriats have no clearly-defined, anthropomorphic god of Thunder. They often call the rumble of thunder "the song of heaven."[13] As they have now, as mentioned earlier, a great number of different Tengeris, they cannot tell which of them is at the precise time the Thunderer. Therefore, when necessary, they consult a magician, sometimes even nine shamans, who endeavour to find out which god, one belonging to the eastern or one belonging to the western group, is the raiser of the particular storm. One of the mightiest Thunder gods is Asan-Sagan-Tengeri, who fights evil spirits with his fiery arrow.[14]

The Yakuts, on the contrary, have quite a distinct Thunder god whom they call Ulu-Tojon ("Great Lord") or Sygä-Tojon ("Lord with the axe"). Frequently he is only named

" the Thunderer." According to one source " the Lord with
the axe" lives in the eighth heaven. Other sources speak
separately of the gods of Thunder and of Lightning. In such
cases the Yakuts call the Thunderer " Bold Screamer " and the
Lightning-maker " the Lord with the axe." Both are supposed to pursue demons and evil spirits. In order to rid
their homes of the evil spirits which endeavour to hide
themselves there when a thunder-storm threatens, the
Yakuts smoke them out by burning pieces of a tree struck
by lightning, crying at the same time: " The Bold Screamer
shrieked, the Lord with the axe moved! Away, away! " They
then throw the bits of wood far out on the meadow. Thunderbolts, which the people believe they find in the earth, are
treasured in the houses as important talismans against lightning.[15] The Goldes call old stone weapons found in the
ground " thunder-axes." [16]

The Yakut " Lord with the axe," who pursues demons, is
most probably, like the corresponding figures in European
myths, derived from the ancient civilized peoples of Asia.

Of another origin also is the other conception of the god
of Thunder, met with already among the Finns, according to
which the Thunder god is a skilful archer. The Altai Tatars
tell of a mighty hero whose bow is the rainbow and whose
arrow the lightning.[17] In some Ostiak districts the rainbow is
explained to be the Thunder god's bow and ancient stone
weapons found in the ground his arrows, which he shoots in
order to kill the Forest spirit hiding in the trees.[18]

Generally the peoples of the Altaic race do not speak of
the rainbow as the Thunder god's weapon, nor do they call
it the thunder-bow. Very common is the fancy that the
rainbow is a kind of being that drinks water. The Tatars
have probably transmitted this idea to the Yenisei Ostiaks,
who call the rainbow: " The thunder drinks water." [19]
What this animated water-drinker, as the Votiaks also call it,
really is, does not appear from the beliefs of the Turco-Tatar

peoples. On the other hand the East European peoples, according to whom the rainbow sucks water from seas, lakes and rivers, sprinkling it anew on the earth as rain, imagine it to be a kind of giant snake. The Esthonians say that it has the head of an ox, which it lowers down to a river, emptying it of water.[20] Could this be the Vṛtra or Ahi (" snake ") of the *Veda,* from whose power the Thunder god Indra releases the waters?

The Yakuts believe that the rainbow can also raise people from the ground. A tale relates how it once lifted up a girl in the District of Verchoyansk and set her down again near Irkutsk.[21]

Both the Yakuts and Buriats call the rainbow also " the urine of the she-fox." [22] The southern Tatar tribes have several names for it, such as " rainbelt," " the half-bow of the pot," " God's sword " (Caucasus). The Kirghis name, " the old woman's sheep-halter," is explained by the following tale: A certain man had two wives who were always quarrelling. The mother-in-law cursed the older, who had three sons, so that she fled to the heavens with her sons and her cattle, and now tethers her sheep to the rainbow.[23]

The conception of the rainbow as the weapon of the Thunder god seems thus to be quite local to Middle and Northern Asia, where it occurs sporadically. Another tale written down somewhere in the district of the Altai belongs to a still more limited area. It tells of a camel moving in the sky with three persons on its back. The first beats a drum, whence the rumbling of thunder, the second waves a scarf, whence the lightning, the third pulls at the reins, causing water to run from the camel's mouth, whence the rain.[24] In other places it is said that a great shaman beats a drum in the sky when it thunders. The latter opinion, though only occasionally met with, belongs naturally to Siberia, the land of shamanism.

The Tatars, like many other of the peoples of the world, imagine the lightning, which for a moment draws a livid,

PLATE XLIX

SHAMAN DRUMS FROM THE MINUSINSK
DISTRICT

(See pages 287, 520.)

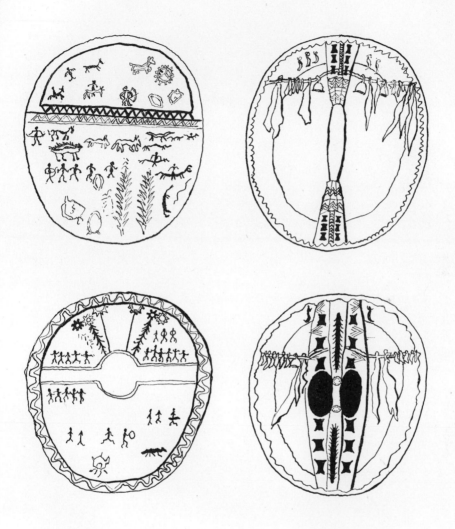

winding streak of light across the sky, to be a fiery snake falling down from Heaven.[25] The same idea has been earlier met
with in a Finnish poem on the origin of fire.

The most northerly peoples of Siberia, with the exception of
The Yakuts, do not sacrifice to the Thunder god. Some, e.g.,
the Yenisei Ostiaks, bid him during a storm pass by quietly
without raising a tempest. Records of Thunder worship are
found more among other Siberian peoples. Old Chinese
chronicles relate that the Northern Uigurs fear the thunder,
and cry out and shoot towards the sky at every crash. They
then leave the place and separate. The following spring they
assemble again at the spot where the lightning struck and
slaughter a ram there. A certain Persian historian mentions
that the Mongolians were greatly afraid of thunder and poured
milk and kumiss on the ground, begging it not to hurt their
dwellings or their cattle. It has been a custom with the Tatars
of the Altai to assemble village by village on high mountains,
when the first roll of thunder is heard in spring, and to sprinkle
milk towards the four points of the sky.[26]

Special attention is awakened by the thunder when it happens to kill a human being or a domestic animal. Such victims
of the lightning are regarded as sacred and so too is the spot
where the lightning has struck. According to the Buriats,
people and animals slain by lightning must always be buried
in the air upon a platform built on four posts. If the lightning strikes a house, the house must at once be removed to
another place, or certain rites, called " the raising," have to be
observed, the intention of which is the sending of the thunderbolt back into the sky. Unless this be done danger is believed to threaten. These rites, which must take place on the
third day after the thunder-storm, are conducted by a magician
and his eight assistants, who ride on horseback three times
round the dwelling in question, stopping before the door at
every round. The magician has a branch of a silver-fir in
his hand, the others a drinking-cup. While the magician re-

peats a prayer his assistants sprinkle liquid from their cups. The most important of these rites seems to be the raising of a felt carpet spread before the tent, on which some article resembling or intended to represent a thunderbolt has been laid. "The raising," from which the ritual gets its name, is performed by the eight assistants. Finally, molten tin is dropped into a liquid to test by the shapes thus obtained whether the raising has been successful. If the tin, on falling into a basin containing wine or milk, forms into a single lump, the sign is favourable.[27]

Exceedingly strange is the fancy of the Buriats that the Tengeris who are mentioned as the senders of thunderbolts sometimes pour down from the sky *urak* (the "first-milk," differing in colour from other milk given by a cow after calving). Although many such Tengeris are mentioned, e.g., Khan-Budal-Tengeri, Urak-Sagan-Tengeri, Kharan-Budal-Tengeri (*budal*, "to let down"), of which the last mentioned is fancied to belong to the black, i.e., the eastern Tengeris, it is probable that all these names originally meant one and the same being. According to tales, the *urak* dropped down from the sky is a thick yellowish-white liquid. The person who receives some of this "first milk" during a thunder-storm is deemed very fortunate and is believed to remain rich for ever. It is, however, an extremely rare event for a person to receive *urak*. When a Buriat perceives that he has been the recipient of special heavenly favour, *urak* appearing sometimes in his milk-foods, he turns to the magician, who witnesses the fact and examines from which Tengeri the *urak* has come. The liquid is then poured into a vessel made of birch-bark and placed on a high place, to prevent it from becoming defiled on the earth. The Buriats believe that the *urak* can rise into the sky again. According to the common custom, it must always, like a thunderbolt, be returned to heaven.[28]

This *urak*, which falls from the sky during a thunder-storm and must immediately be sacrificed to its sender again, reminds one of the Indo-Iranian tales about Haoma or Soma which an eagle brings down from the sky. The Soma, sometimes called " first milk " in the *Rgveda*, was originally the favourite drink of Indra, the god of Thunder. It provides the " Bearer of thunderbolts " with giant powers for his great deeds. Doubtless, the eagle itself, which, according to tales, procured this drink for its master, was the bird of Indra. Compared with Indo-Iranian legends, the beliefs of the Buriats seem to represent a more primitive standpoint. On the ground of these tales we may conjecture that the Indo-Iranians, like the peoples of Northern Siberia, orginally regarded thunder as a giant bird resembling an eagle. The fact that the liquid brought down from the sky by the Thunder bird is sacrificed to the Thunder god, may easily have given rise to an idea that there are two separate beings, of which the one brings and the other receives the Soma.

In a Yakut tale about how the son of Ulu-Tojon fought with a giant, even the thunder-bolt seems to appear personified. The tale begins with the description of a terrible storm and then goes on to relate how " suddenly pitch-black darkness covered the earth, a frightful roar, louder than the strongest peal of thunder, was heard, and at the same time a man three fathoms long, made half of fire, half of iron, came flying and twirling down in a mighty whirlwind. He sank over a yard deep into the earth, but bounced up again and stepped before the giant." [29]

That the Thunder god has not so prominent a place among the nomads, hunters, and fishers of Northern Siberia as in the mythology of the agricultural peoples of Nearer Asia, India and Europe is explained by the fact that the life of the farmers is in a much greater degree dependent on weather and rain. There are, it is true, even in the districts of the Altai, certain persons and even families, whose duty it is to bring about rain or drought as necessary, but these rainmakers (Jadatshy.) do not seem to appeal to any special Thunder god, but to the god of Heaven in general (Kaira-Khan), or to sundry gods living at the springs of certain rivers, who are believed to cause rain. Extremely famous in this respect are Mordo-Khan and Abakan-Khan, who are said to live at the spring of the Abakan river.[30]

The Buriats also speak of a separate Rain-god, Khuran-Nojon ("the Lord of Rain"), who is believed to have nine water-barrels in heaven. When he opens only one of them, a three days' rain ensues.[31] There is no information, however, as to whether this god has ever been worshipped with sacrifices.

CHAPTER XV

FIRE

WHERE did fire first appear to me, what is its purpose and its power, who has given it birth? " So cries in a Yakut tale a hero, supposed to be the ancestor of this tribe, arriving at last at the conclusion that fire is the son of Yryn-Ai-Tojon who sits on a milk-white throne to which three flights of silver stairs lead up.[1] The belief that the first fire came down from heaven is very common among the peoples of the Altaic race.

Tales gathered from different peoples show the origin of this belief. The Tungus told me that the Thunder bird brought down fire from the sky to earth. A fire caused by lightning is considered sacred by them and they dare not put out a forest-fire which has been lighted from Heaven. Among the Yakuts also the fancy is most common that the Thunder god Ulu-Tojon gave people the first fire.[2] The Buriats call the god of Fire, who was also the first sender of fire, Galta-Ulan-Tengeri; he is further the god of heat and drought, who " dries up the growing grass to the roots and the running rivers with their springs," and the sender of the lightning, who sets on fire all that he strikes.[3] The Altai Tatars declare that mankind originally lived on vegetables and fruits and therefore neither needed fire nor missed it, but with the change in their manner of nourishing themselves fire became necessary for the preparing of food. It was then that Ülgen took two stones, a white one and a black one, and struck them together so that the spark which flew from the sky to the earth set fire to the dry grass. From this man learned to strike fire.[4] Through the mouth of the Buriat shaman, fire declares itself to be "the middle son of the day-sky, the youngest son of the night-sky.." [5]

Certain other North Siberian peoples explain the origin of fire in the same way. The Ostiaks on the Yenisei give a more detailed account of how their ancestors received fire from lightning. The lightning kindled a tree, and some great shaman taught the people to make use of the fire. At first a great fire was kept burning, from which everyone could borrow a flame. Later on, fire-steel and tinder were placed beside it, and fire was thus transferred to these objects. [6]

In some tales about the origin of fire there figures also an inventor of fire, often an animal. In Buriat tales this wise animal is the porcupine, which has also in other ways already figured as an inventor. In the beginning, it is told, neither gods nor men could make fire, with one exception — the Porcupine, which was then a human being. One day a crowd had gathered round the Porcupine to hear the secret of fire-making. But the young maidens, seeing the strange shape of Porcupine, began to laugh, and this angered him so much that he decided to tell his secret only to his own wife, and even to her only against a promise of silence. But the hawk, whom the gods had sent out to steal his secret, happened to hear Porcupine explaining to his wife where flintstone was to be found and how steel could be made, with which two articles it was easy to strike fire, and the hawk told the secret to the gods. From these men learned the art of making fire. Later, the descendants of Porcupine became porcupines. [7]

In the tales of the Altai Tatars the frog advises Ülgen, who is in perplexity as to where men could get the necessities for striking fire, that "the mountains contain stones and the birch tinder." [8] The Mongols say: "Iron is the father of fire and stone its mother." [9] The above tales give thus two different explanations: fire has come down from heaven with the lightning, or its spark has sprung from a stone. Both fancies are also met with in Finnish poems on the origin of fire.

In Mongolian prayers, in which the birth of fire is related in many different ways, it is said that fire came from a tree or that it was born when in ancient times Heaven and Earth separated.[10]

Whether fires of different origin have been considered to be of unequal value does not appear from the sources at hand. Besides fire caused by lightning, which is esteemed holier than other fires, wood-fire or friction-fire has played an important part in the expelling of diseases. The Yakuts are said to have a custom, during an epidemic, of making a fire by rubbing two pieces of dry wood together, this sort of fire being supposed to have special protecting powers. The people, however, declare that they have learned this custom from the Russians, with whom epidemic diseases are also supposed to have come into their country.[11] The Tatars of Eastern Russia and the Chuvash also use friction-fire as a kind of purifying remedy during certain plagues either among people or cattle, and even at other times in the hot summer. On some previously fixed day the old fire in every home is put out and a great bonfire is lighted by friction outside the village. Over this the people spring in order to purify themselves and drive their cattle through it. Thus cleansed, each peasant carries a brand of " new fire " home.[12]

One might suppose this custom, known also to the Finno-Ugric peoples of the Volga, to have been learned from the Russians, as the Yakuts declare. But it appears from old sources that certain Turco-Tatar peoples already in ancient times used fire as a magic purifier. Byzantine Chronicles tell that when the messengers of the Emperor Justinian arrived at the court of the Turkish Great Khan at the springs of the Irtysh river, the Khan could not receive them until they had passed between two fires. The Tatars still observed this custom at the time when the Russians paid taxes to them. All people, animals, or objects that in some way, e.g., by touching some dead body, had become unclean, were thus purified.[13]

Whatever the origin of these customs may have been, the mystic, and more especially the heavenly birth of fire, its wonderful power and the part which it plays in the domestic life of the most primitive peoples, resulted in the fact that fire in general is esteemed holy. Many, of the peoples of Central and Northern Asia have indeed worshipped fire.

When worshipping the fire burning on the hearth the Mongols call it " Mother fire." According to their ideas the hearth is the sanctuary of the home and may on no account be desecrated. The Altaic tribes, the Kirghis, the Yakuts and other Turco-Tatar peoples also worshipped fire. The idea that fire must be kept pure and adored as a deity is common to all these and even to other North Siberian peoples. Nothing unclean or evil-smelling may be thrown into it, and nothing which could weaken its power or dim its brightness. For this reason it is wrong to spit into the fire or to extinguish it with water. It is also inadvisable to step over it unnecessarily or to hurt it with any, sharp weapon. Plano Carpini tells how the Mongolians deemed it a sin to hew wood in the vicinity of a fire, or to take meat with a knife from a pot under which a fire was burning; still more to put the knife into the fire. The Yakuts believe that the fire, which " takes as a gift the pine forest, consumes the damp wilderness, and spends the night in dry trees," understands speech and that it is therefore not well to scold or speak ill of it.[14]

Fire is believed to need nourishment as well as tender care. The pious master and mistress feed the fire on the hearth every time they begin a meal. The first morsels of food, the first spoonful of soup, the first cup of drink belong to the Fire god. Especially, at family festivals must the fire on the hearth be remembered. A fire-sacrifice is a special part of the wedding rites with most peoples of the Altaic race.[15] The Chuvash bride brings ashes or a fragment of stone from her parents' hearth to her new home, this custom doubtless expressing the thought that the fire on the hearth is to go in heritage

PLATE L

MONGOL SHAMAN WITH HIS DRUM

(See chapter XXI.)

After photograph by S. Pālsi.

from parents to children.[16] We have already seen that the Finno-Ugric peoples on the Volga observe rites akin to these. In worshipping the fire in their new home, a young Mongol couple sacrifice to it some yellow butter and a yellow-headed sheep. Yellow as well as red, in sacrifices to the Fire god, is intended to imitate the hue of the fire itself. The best sacrifices are those which intensify the burning of the fire, viz., butter, lard, gin, etc.[17]

A certain wedding-prayer, said beside the hearth, to some degree explains the beliefs of the Mongols. It begins with the following words: " Mother Ut (Turco-Tatar word, " fire "), Mistress of the fire, descended from the elms on the tops of the Khangai-Khan and the Burkhatu-Khan mountains. Thou, who wast born when Heaven and Earth parted, who camest forth from the foot-prints of Mother Ötygen (" Mother earth "), thou creation of Tengeri-Khan. Mother Ut, thy father is the hard steel, thy mother the flint, thy ancestors the elm-trees. Thy brightness reaches the heavens and spreads over the earth. Fire, struck by the Heaven-dweller, nursed by the Mistress Uluken. Goddess Ut, we offer thee yellow butter and a yellow-headed white sheep. Thine are this brave boy and the beautiful bride, the slender daughter. To thee, Mother Ut, who art always looking upward, we offer cups full of wine and handfuls of fat. Give luck to the son of the ruler (the bridegroom) and the daughter of the ruler (the bride) and all the wedding-folk. For this we pray." [18]

If fire is treated in an improper manner or left without food it is believed to take vengeance by sending a kind of skin-disease. In the worst case it burns the whole building.

There is no doubting the fact that the peoples of the Altaic race worship fire in itself. " Mother " and other such words are only names for the fire itself. Because of its numerous flames the Altaic shaman calls it the " Thirty-headed mother, the Forty-headed virgin-mother." [19] In the prayers of the

Chuvash there appears beside the " Mother fire " a " Father fire." The Yakuts and the Buriats also worship both a masculine and a feminine Fire god. The former name them " Old Man Ulakhany and Mistress Sabaga," the latter " Lord Säkhädai and Mistress Sakhala." Poetic denominations are further " the White-bearded Lord " and " White-haired Lady " of the Yakuts.[20]

Most Central and North Asian peoples speak in addition of the Ruler or Master of fire, who, according to the Yakuts, " lives right in the flames." [21] What they imagine him to be like appears from their legends which tell that the master of fire " eats raw wood," that he has " an ashen bed " where " the pillow is a glowing coal and the coverlet fine ashes " and that " the smoke is his breath." [22] They believe, however, that the Master of fire can extricate himself from the fire and appear in human shape. The Yakuts say that in a home where he is often remembered with sacrifices, the Master of fire is fat and thriving, but the Fire god of a mean and parsimonious household is thin and withered.[23] A Buriat legend relates how a man who had the power of seeing gods and understanding their speech once encountered two Masters of fire. One of them, though the god of a poor house, was well fed and dressed, but the other, the Fire master of a well-to-do house, looked very poor and wretched. The latter complained of having to live without food in the power of a mean master and mistress who at times even pierced his eyes by poking the fire with sharp irons. Because of this he threatened to punish his master, and very soon the grand house of the rich man was burnt down to the ground.[24]

Such tales, in which the Fire gods of different homes converse together and tell each other of their life, are quite common. In the tales of the Ugrian Ostiaks every hearth has its own " Fire maid," her outward appearance being said to show how the fire has been treated in that home.[25] Doubtless, these tales, some of which have been recorded even in Eastern

Europe, originate from the conception that the fire on the hearth must be tended and fed like a living being.

The Master of the fire may also appear to people before a disastrous fire or any other catastrophe which threatens the home. Then, also, the Fire god often takes on human shape. The Yakuts see him in the form of a " grey old man." [26] To a certain Buriat he appeared as a great, red, and therefore flame-coloured, man.[27] The Buriats even make themselves images of the Master of fire and keep them in a box near the hearth. In homes in the Balagansk District one may sometimes see two human-shaped figures covered with red cloth, of which the one represents the " Master," the other the " Mistress " of the fire. Two glass beads form their eyes; the headdress, the hands and the hem of the garment are covered with black sheepskin. The " Mistress " has beads for nipples and a tin ornament on her breast.[28] The red and the black in the image of the Fire god represent the colours of the glowing coal and the soot.

Besides the part played by fire in domestic life, most peoples of the Altaic race have given it another important duty to fulfil — the conveying to the various gods of the sacrifices destined for each. Thus every offering which is put in the fire is not intended to pacify the fire itself. More especially when a sacrifice is intended for some god of the upper spheres is fire used as the medium. It is in this capacity of mediator between man and the gods that fire is considered the most sacred, and for this reason it is especially worshipped at sacrificial festivals. The Finnish peoples of Eastern Russia also have this conception and the rites connected with it are met with among them.

If finally we attempt to compare the beliefs and customs prevailing in the different districts peopled by the large Altaic race, we find that these have not developed equally, being richer and more various in some districts than in others. The Tungus of the primeval forests of North Siberia are the most backward in this respect. It is true that these also worship fire after a fashion, keeping it clean and refraining from hurting it, but the offering up of sacrifices to the fire is not deemed so necessary by them as it is in Central Asia; and its use in wedding rites, equally with the idea of fire as a conveyer of sacrifices, is uncommon. We are therefore led to think that the mighty and much adored Fire god of the other peoples related to the Turks has developed under foreign influence and if we further remember that the Indo-Iranian peoples from ancient times have been zealous fire-worshippers and that their beliefs and customs coincide exactly with those of the Central Asian tribes, we cannot be unaware from whom the peoples of the Altaic race have, at least in its more developed form, inherited their fire-worship. Seeing that the Mongols, who in their own language call the Fire god Galai-Khan (" Ruler of the fire "), or, like their kinsfolk the Buriats, Gali-Edzin (" Master of the fire "), use in their prayers the Turco-Tatar name for fire, Ut, we can agree with Banzarov in his supposition that the Mongols learned to worship fire from the Iranians through the Turkish tribes.[29] This Iranian influence can also be traced in the fire-worship of the Finno-Ugrians in their idea of fire as a mediator of sacrifices, which conception does not seem originally to have been general among the Ugrians or the peoples of the Altaic race. Even at the present day, side by side with the later sacrifices by fire we find the older custom, known almost solely among the Northern peoples, of giving sacrifices to the gods untouched.

CHAPTER XVI

THE WIND

LIKE other phenomena of nature, the wind also was regarded as animated. Following the points of the compass, the Central Asian peoples speak of four winds, which arise at the " four corners of the earth." [1] A stranger idea is that the mountains are the home of the wind. The Yakuts say the winds " sleep " on the mountains, whence they can be called when needed by whistling.[2] The Yakuts and the Lamutes are said to have avoided loud conversation when passing by a high mountain, in order that the " Master " of the mountain might not become incensed and send a storm to hinder their journey.[3] The Goldes believe the winds to come from caves in the mountains, where the Wind spirit holds them captive. A shaman can persuade this spirit either to open these chasms, or keep them closed, according to whether wind is needed or not.[4] The Mongols call storms " running-days," as they believe the Mountain spirit runs from mountain to mountain during these times.[5]

Elsewhere than in Siberia, this belief is met with in mountainous districts, having probably its origin in observations made from nature. The Lapps also believe windy and stormy weather to arise out of the chasms in the fells. A certain fell at Inari is called Piegga-oaivi (" wind fell "). Possibly, also, the Finnish " birth of the wind " originates from the same idea, the wind being said in this poem to have been born " between two rocks." [6]

Among the Southern Turkish peoples a mythical idea of a grey bull has been recorded, the breath of which gives birth to the wind.[7] The majority of peoples believe some spirit to wander in the whirlwind.

Differing from ordinary winds, according to the Buriats, is the Zada, which has its own spirit, Zada-Sagan-Tengeri. By Zada they mean a short, intermittent wind, occurring several times on the same day. Often, it brings with it rain or snow. Generally, the Zada blows in the spring and the autumn. Zada-weather may be brought about by men with the help of a certain root, the Buriats believing that if one of these roots is pulled or dug up out of the ground, the weather will begin to change rapidly. Certain hunters, to whom this magic method is known, make Zada assist them in their hunting. Certain birds, also, such as hawks and swans, are said to know the properties of the said root and to conjure forth a so-called " bird-Zada " when migrating southward in the autumn. Similarly, some of the bigger inhabitants of the forest, notably the deer and the fawn, use this means for their own benefit (" deer-Zada "). It may also be brought about by the help of a special red stone, called " Zadan-ulan-shulun " by the Buriats. Further, Zada is sometimes born when a thunderbolt falls into the water, when nine days of this wind follow.[8]

This peculiar belief, met with also among the Kalmucks and the Turkomans, has spread to the Yakuts. They say that among the entrails of an animal a stone is sometimes found, which possesses the magic power, if taken into the yard on a calm summer day, of awakening a cold and severe wind. These stones the Yakuts call Sata (=Buriat Zada).[9]

PLATE LI

Mongol stone-heap on which each passer-by must throw a stone as an offering in order to have a lucky journey. (See page 470.)

After photograph by S. Pālsi.

CHAPTER XVII

THE EARTH

THE ALTAIC peoples early regarded the earth as being an animated, conscious and comprehending being. Even now the Central Asian peoples are afraid of being punished if they offend the earth. According to the Soyots the digging or the wounding of the earth with sharp instruments is a great sin.[1] The Altai Tatars declare the pulling up of plants out of the earth to be as improper as the pulling out of the hair or beard of a human being would be.[2] With ideas such as these, it is not to be wondered at that the nomads did not look with a favourable eye on the pioneers of agriculture. The agriculturist Cain, according to the Semites, was also less pleasing to God than the nomad Abel. Similar ideas were held, further, by the American Indians when the first whites penetrated into their territory.

As the producer of vegetation, etc., the earth was regarded as a female being. As the sky, which renders the earth fruitful, was called " the Father," the earth, which gives birth, was called " Mother." Already in the Orkhon stone inscriptions it is written: " The sky above is our father, the earth beneath is our mother, man is the child of both." In the ancient tales of the Mongols, the " Blue sky " and the " Brown earth " are two of the chief deities.[3] The Yakuts believe that the " Earth mother," also called " Mistress " (An-Darkhan-Khotun or An-Alai-Khotun) acts both as the producer of vegetation and as the birth-giver of children.[4] The Tungus lay to the merit of the earth, as Georgi points out, " all that it brings forth." [5] The Mongols say that the sky gives life to beings, but that the earth gives them their form.[6] Thus the Earth mother becomes also the deity of child-birth. As is well known, the ancient peoples of Asia had this same idea.

Concerning sacrifices to the earth there exist very old reports. The Chronicles of the Chinese relate that the Hunnu and Tukiu peoples sacrificed to the earth.[7] Marco Polo tells us that the chief object of Mongolian worship was the Earth god Natigai, to whom milk, kumiss and tea were sacrificed. When sacrificing, the people prayed to this deity for fruitfulness. The name Natigai mentioned by Marco Polo is probably a corrupted form of the name Ötükän, which appears in the Orkhon inscriptions as meaning the country of the old Turks, worshipped by them as a special deity.[8]

Even to-day the agricultural peoples, such as the Buriats, Tatars and Chuvashes, sacrifice to the Earth goddess. Generally, earth worship would seem to have gained in importance in places where agriculture had obtained foothold. The Buriats offer up a blood-sacrifice to the Earth spirit in the autumn when field-work is over.[9] The Chuvashes, like the Volga Finns, sacrificed black, "earth-coloured" animals to the Earth mother at their agricultural festivals. The most Northern Siberian peoples, however, such as the Tungus, do not see the necessity of sacrificing to the earth, as in the life of this hunting and fishing people the earth has not the same nourishing value as among these others.

Doubtless the earth as such was worshipped, as the Mongol prayer-name "Brown earth" shows. Illuminative are also the following words in the Yakut sacrifice ceremonies: "Ruler of vegetation (literally 'grass-tree'), earth moisture, eat, enjoy (*Ot-mas itšitä, sir-daidy sigä, asan, siän*)."[10] Later, the imagination of the people, especially in tales, created certain anthropomorphic features for the Earth mother. Chuvash fancy created an Earth old man to accompany the Earth mother.[11] The Buriats imagine the spirit of the earth as a whole (Daida-Delkhe-Edzhin) to be an old grey-bearded man, and his wife a white-haired old woman.[12] Generally, it seems to have been exceedingly difficult to give anthropomorphic features to the Earth mother.

The agricultural Chuvashes, when a field has lost its productive powers, carry out special ceremonies, called "The stealing of earth." The intention of these ceremonies is to procure productive earth from a field owned by someone else, in which the grain flourishes. A living "suitor" is chosen for the Earth mother, and arrayed precisely as for a real courtship; this suitor goes out to seek a bride. The suitor has to be young and strongly-built, as a marriage with the Earth mother, according to the Chuvashes, is so exhausting that in spite of his staying powers, the bridegroom hardly ever lives to a ripe old age. Although the wedding procession sets off with much jingling of bells and singing of wedding-songs and music, the participants all quiet down as the place whence the bride has to be fetched is reached. In the silence of the night the procession drives into the field, where the bridegroom, sitting in the first wagon, is lifted to the ground. The oldest man in the procession now acts as the agent for the bridegroom, saying, with glance fixed on the earth: "We have come to thee, rich and dear bride, with a young and beautiful bridegroom. We know that thy riches are endless, but undescribable is also the burning love of our bridegroom for thee." At this, the bridegroom bows down to the ground. The agent goes on: "Do thou also, dear bride, love our bridegroom, and refuse not to comply with our request." The bridegroom bows again. "Take with thee, dear bride, all thy property from the fields and meadows, the forests and rivers." After further deep bows, shovelsful of earth are lifted into all the wagons. The bridegroom is lifted into the first vehicle. When at last, with singing and music, clapping of hands and cries of delight, the home-village is reached, the "bridegroom," with a spade in his hand, goes first to his own and then to the other vehicles to welcome his "bride," saying: "Be welcome, my dear bride, I love thee more than gold, more, even, than my life. For the sake of my love, spread out thy property on our fields and pastures, our forests and rivers." Having said this, he takes earth from all the waggons with his spade, which also the other participants in the ceremony carry to their patches of field.[13]

Relics of similar weddings for the amusement and the enticing of the Earth mother, ceremonies alien to the nomad-culture of the Altaic peoples, are met with among certain other agricultural peoples. The " bridegroom " of the Earth mother is mentioned also in old Finnish poems.

Another Earth deity of whose origin there can be no doubt, is the Jär-Sub (" Land-water ") mentioned already in the Orkhon inscriptions.[14] " From the oldest times," say the Teleuts, " we have worshipped our Land-water and our Sky." [15] The " Land-water spirit " (Sir-šyv-Kudegen or -Kten) appears also in the list of deities of the Chuvashes side by side with the " Earth mother " and " Earth father." [16] The " Man of Land-water " is also known among the Voguls.[17] " Land and water " as a name for one's fatherland may, however, be originally an Iranian phrase. As Vambéry points out, the Persians are still in the habit of saying, for example, *ab-i-chak-i Isfahan* (" Isfahan's district," literally " Land and water of Isfahan.").[18] It is therefore easy to understand what Xerxes meant in demanding from the Greeks, as a sign of submission, " land and water."

PLATE LII

Dress with metal ornaments and symbols, and drum of a Mongol shaman. The inner side of the drum is shown with hand-grip with bells.

(See chapter XXI.)

After photograph by S. Pālsi.

CHAPTER XVIII

THE "MASTERS" OF NATURE

CONNECTED with the animating of natural objects and phenomena among the Altaic race, there is a conception that a " soul," corresponding to the soul of man, lies hidden within them, the name given to this being the same as that for the human soul. Thus, the Altai Tatars use the word *kut*, which appears in many Turco-Tatar languages, as signifying the soul of both human beings and natural objects. Just as the *kut* of the former leaves its dwelling for one reason or another, causing decline and sickness, so the earth, a tree, etc., wither when their *kut* leaves them. When expressing the fact that a field has lost its fertility, the people say: " The ground has lost its *kut* " (*jer kudun pardy*.) Similarly, the *kut* of a dwelling-place may depart, taking with it the feeling of homeliness. In cases like this last, *kut* is often translated as meaning " happiness," " health," " homeliness," etc.[1] A word with a similar signification in the Turco-Tatar language is *sür* (" appearance," " beauty," " comfort," " power," " soul "), used when speaking of the human soul, the haunting spirit of the dead, the health of cattle, the power of an army, the nourishing properties of bread, etc. Thus, for example, it is said that " when an army loses its *sür*, it cannot defeat its enemy." When food has lost its nourishing power, it is said that " its *sür* has departed." A soul of this description is believed to animate and to govern all the phenomena of nature and its parts, and thus a conception arises that these invisible souls, to use the words of M. A. Castrén, are " in respect of all visible nature, in a position of power resembling that of a master towards his property."[2]

That the metaphor " Master " used by Castrén is correct, is best proved by the names of like signification given by the peoples of the Altaic race to the invisible Nature gods. " Master," " Lord," or " Ruler " is expressed in the different Tatar dialects by the words Eä or Öjä, in Chuvash Hoza, Yakut Itshi and Buriat Edzhi. An invisible Ruler of this description is to be found in the sky and its phenomena, the stars, fire, land and forest, trees and grass, rivers and lakes, mountains and rocks, the different animals, and even in objects made by man, buildings, weapons, tools, vessels, etc. Especially in sharp or "living " weapons, with which it is easy to harm oneself, such as knives or axes, do the Yakuts see a Ruler (Itshi), and similarly in objects capable of motion, such as a spinning-wheel, or of noise, such as a magic drum or a musical instrument. The Yakuts even speak of a Ruler in the bundle of birch-branches with which they beat themselves in their baths.[3] The trade of blacksmith is held in great respect by both Yakuts and Buriats, and a Ruler is believed to dwell in all the tools needed for this work. Troščanskiy points out that each blacksmith's tool not bought from the Russians has its Itshi: the anvil and striking-hammer have theirs in common, the tongs and the forge have each their own, but the " Head-Itshi " is in the bellows.[4] Pripuzov speaks of a special tutelary genius of blacksmiths, called Kudai-Bakshy by the Yakuts, and whose dwelling-place is in the underworld. The smiths slaughter a brown cow in its honour and anoint themselves and their tools with the animal's blood, but the heart and the liver they roast in the forge and place them on the anvil, where they are beaten until nothing remains of them.[5]

The Buriats of the Balagan District worship a deity of blacksmiths called Boshintoi, with nine sons and one daughter, who are said to have taught the blacksmith's craft to men. In sacrificing to these, the smiths pour kumiss and other sacrificial liquids on to the glowing forge. A lamb is also sometimes slaughtered to them. Iron images are made of the aforesaid sons and the daughter, each with some blacksmith's tool in its hand, a hammer, tongs, an anvil, bellows, charcoal, etc.; these are called the corresponding "Masters" of these objects.[6]

The Master of a musical instrument (Khuri Edzhin) is said by the Buriats to teach people to become skilful musicians. The neophyte has to go out on a moonless night to the junction of three roads and there sit down on the skull of a horse fitted with silken reins. At midnight the skull is said to try to unseat its rider. Should the latter fall he loses his life, but if, being on his guard, he remains seated and continues to play, he becomes a very skilful player.[7]

Most often, the said "Masters" are believed to dwell in the phenomena or objects they, represent, the Master of fire in the fire, the Master of water in the water, the Master of a tree in the tree, etc., although at times they can separate from these. How close the connection between these Masters and their visible incarnations has actually been, appears from the habit of making images of the Masters of the sun and moon in the shape of these heavenly bodies. The Masters of animals appear to men in the shape of the respective animals. The Tungus make an image of the reindeer to represent the Reindeer's Master, and similarly certain North-East Siberian tribes make an image of a fish to represent the Fish Master. The Buriats speak of a Master-tree, which is recognized by the fact that its pith is blood-red; the tree is thus the body of the Master dwelling in it, from which, as from a human body, the blood can run.[8] This conception of Masters animating nature is not confined only to the Altaic race, but the same belief is met with among other Siberian peoples, the Yukagirs, the Chukchee, etc.[9]

The anthropomorphism of certain Masters, such as those of dwelling-places, forests and water would seem to have been helped by the spirits of the dead, who are said to dwell in these places. Often the dead can be seen to have become directly assimilated into these Masters. Thus the Master of the Yakut dwelling-place (Balagan Itshitä) sometimes appears in the shape of former dwellers in the place. Middendorff says that the oldest inhabitant becomes after his death the Master of a home.[10] The ancient Finns had the same belief. The Masters of forests and water are also said by the people to have originated in the spirits of those lost or drowned there. Buriat tales relate how a hunter was once lost in the forest, dying finally there of hunger, and how this unfortunate man became the Forest Master.[11] Similar tales are told of the origin of the Water Master. These tales make clear why the Masters of forests and water seek the company of men, and in tales aspire to marriage and other ties with them. We must not, however, from tales like those described, draw the conclusion that the Masters of natural phenomena and objects are generally the spirits of the dead.

The trees of the forest itself are imaged in the conception which causes the Master of the forest to be seen as a being of the height of a tree. As in Europe, this conception is general among the Asiatic peoples. The Mongols' Khan of the forest and of forest animals (Mani-Khan) is a being like a man of more than ordinary size.[12] A long, dark, human-like being is also the Forest Master of the Buriats, who halloes and weeps in the forest, leads wanderers astray, but gives also game to the hunter.[13] The large-sized Forest Master of the Tungus can at times take on the shape of a strange rock, resembling a man or an animal, the forest dwellers fearing to approach such rocks. A similar spirit is the Yakut Bajanai, who, as the owner of the valuable game of the forests, is called "rich," Bai-Bajanai. As the Master of forest animals it is also conceived as shaped like an animal. In the latter shape it has been seen by hunters and gatherers of berries. Sometimes, it is of the size of a year-old calf, with the muzzle of a dog, little moist eyes, long whiskers, a grey coat and forked hoofs. In some districts the Forest Master is said to

PLATE LIII

SHATTERED TOMB OF A YAKUT SHAMAN WITH
DRUM HANGING ON AN ADJACENT TREE

(See page 481.)

have two sons, one living in the depths of the primeval forests
and giving valuable game to the hunter, such as sable foxes,
blue foxes, etc., the other dwelling on heaths and giving brown
foxes, squirrels, and other animals of smaller value.[14]

Many North Siberian tribes, for whom hunting is an important means of subsistence, have a habit, at the beginning
of the autumn hunting season, of sacrificing a part of the first
" bag " to the Forest Master. The Yakuts are even said to
have sacrificed black bulls to Bajanai. In sacrificing, the
Tungus, the Yakuts, and other northern peoples make an
image of the Forest Master, either by carving human features
on the trunk of a living tree or by shaping a billet of wood
roughly into a human-like shape. The mouth of the image
is smeared with the blood of the sacrifice. At each sacrifice,
a new image is made.[15]

Comparing the Yakut Forest Master with the corresponding
Russian spirit, Šeroševskiy points out that beliefs brought by
the Russians have become connected with the former. According to his view, the Yakuts did not originally possess a
single spirit, comprising all forests, but each forest and thicket,
each separate tree even, had its own Master.[16] It is also
related of the Buriats, that they do not beg for game from
one general Forest spirit, but separately, from each local
Forest Master.

Among the European Tatars and Chuvashes the Forest
spirit has already received a strictly defined appearance, which
proves a more developed, more stable plane of thought. Here
the Forest Master, corresponding to Russian spirits, is chiefly
an evil being, which is seldom worshipped. In this respect
it differs from the Forest spirits of the most northern primeval
forests of Siberia.

The evil Shuräle of the Volga Tatars, which can increase or
diminish its height, has exceedingly large nipples on its
breasts, and kills its victims by tickling them, we have already
met with among the Volga Finns.[17]

A corresponding evil Forest spirit is the Chuvash Obyda, which wanders in the forest as a human being, but naked, long-haired, with large nipples, and with feet turned in the wrong direction. Having caused a man to lose his way, it tickles or dances its victim to death. The poor animal on whose back Obyda seats himself begins to run backward. According to folk-tales this spirit itself wanders backwards. The evil Forest spirit is also called the " Half-human " (Ar-sori) by the Chuvash.[18] Possibly this name signifies a being known also to the Votiaks, which has only half of a human body, viz., one eye, one arm, and one leg. The Yakuts speak also of an evil being with the same name, declaring it to live in an icy, mound with a door-opening at the top.[19]

Worse than Shuräle is the Tatar Albasta, which they believe to dwell in desert spaces, bogs and chasms. This also is human in shape but takes on the form of many objects belonging to the forests or fields. It is said to kill people by suffocating them.[20] The Kirghis imagine Albasta as a great woman, with a large head, and breasts reaching to the knee. She has long and sharp nails on her fingers. The Kirghis believe her to attack chiefly women who are enceinte, killing her victims by suffocation. They relate tales of how a certain Kirghis once saw her rinsing in a brook the lungs of a woman, whom she had deprived of these.[21]

Like the Forest Master, the Steppe Master also tries to lead travellers astray. The Mongols say that the Steppe Master Albin lights will-o'-the-wisps by the wayside. When the traveller, believing these to be the lights of dwellings, steps aside from the road, he finds that he has been deceived by Albin, who wishes him to lose his way.[22]

To the Forest spirits, the spirits of the forest animals are closely related. The latter, and even each species of animal, have, as has been said, their Masters or Khans, whom it is not always easy to separate from the respective animals. Sacrifices are even made to these Masters. The Tungus sacrifice to the Mammoth Master in order to find mammoth's teeth. The Reindeer Master is said to have received blood-sacrifices. Especially do the people fear to offend the Bear Master, for which reason this animal must not be called by its proper name. Women are afraid to touch bear-flesh with their naked hands and even the men have to treat the carcase of the bear with due respect, its skeleton being preserved on an erection of wood or branches, or, at least, its skull having to be hung up in a tree.[23]

The peoples living on the banks of rivers or lakes speak also of the Water Master. Each river, each lake, and each water has its Master, say the Yakuts. Most often this is imagined to be an anthropomorphic being, although it can also take on other shapes. The fishers of North Siberia sacrifice to it at the beginning of the fishing season in the spring. The Yakuts are said to have then offered up, through the agency of their shamans, a black bull, in order that the water-spirit (Ukulan Tojon) might give fish in plenty. More often, fish is sacrificed to the Water Master, sometimes also bread, salt or gin.[24] The Yenisei Ostiaks, who as a river and fisher people are dependent in a great degree on the bounty of the water, make images of the Water spirit.[25]

Although the spirits of the northern waters of Siberia are anthropomorphic beings, whom the shaman can visit and who choose wives and servants for themselves, from those drowned in the water, they have yet no strictly defined, unchangeable features. In many districts, however, the Russian Water spirit and Rusalka, as among the Volga Turks, have had time to settle in the rivers and lakes of Siberia. Especially among the Yakuts does one meet with purely. Russian ideas. They believe the Water spirits to rise on to the land in the time between New Year's Eve and Twelfth Night, when they wander along the roads, bearing on the backs of oxen their small children, of whom the Water spirits have many. While wandering from place to place the Water spirits make different noises, the people gathering to listen to these at cross-roads, openings in the ice, and near deserted huts. From what they hear, they decide on the events of the ensuing year.[26]

As we have seen earlier, the Russians also believe the Water spirits to wander on land at Christmas-time, until Twelfth Night, when according to the Orthodox Church ceremonies the Cross is lowered into the water, and they then return to their homes. Probably, therefore, the belief in the wandering abroad of the spirits of the drowned at Christmas-time has reached the Yakuts together with these holy-days themselves.

Over a large area in Central and Northern Asia a belief has been recorded, that in the lakes a bull dwells, which begins to roar before a storm or any other great event. When on frosty nights the ice begins to crack and rise, the water-bull is said to be breaking it.[27] Like the East European peoples, the Yakuts and Yukagirs celebrate the departing of the ice with a special ceremony. At such times they sacrifice food to the water, sometimes firing their guns. With their offerings they try to appease the Mother or Old Woman, as they call the stream, that it may refrain from doing damage to their lands during the spring floods.[28]

Once the belief in Nature spirits has originated, the number of these may easily become legion. Wherever a human being moves, some spirit accompanies him. Should an accident occur on a journey, e.g., a horse take fright or a cart break down, the Yakuts believe the Master of the spot to have occasioned the misfortune.[29] Especially in places traversed with difficulty, where the road runs along a steep mountain-ridge or precipitous pass, something, a piece of cloth or wool or a hair of the horse, is sacrificed to the Master of the place. The Mongols, Altai Tatars, etc., when crossing over a mountain, are in the habit of placing a stone at a certain spot, so that great heaps of stones (obo, "heap") have accumulated at such places.[30] Similarly, on journeys by water, the Siberian peoples, after safely passing a difficult stretch of water, offer up some small

PLATE LIV

MONGOL SEER PROPHESYING FROM A
SHOULDER-BLADE

(See page 488.)

sacrifice. On the Yenisei River, the author has even heard Russians speak of " the boiling of porridge " when a dangerous, swift rapid was being passed with great difficulty, the place being called the " bull " by the rowers. To deceive the Master of the place, the Yakuts, when making long journeys, speak in a secret language, in which the words have meanings differing from those of their everyday use, like the hunters and fishers, who also on their expeditions twist the significations of their words.[31]

CHAPTER XIX

DREAMS, SICKNESS AND DEATH

NATURAL causes of dreams, sickness and death, as with most of the peoples of the earth, were unknown to the Altaic race. The most usual idea is that man, in these states, has lost his "shadow." Of the varied souls that are commonly believed to be contained in man, it is just this "shadow" (Altai Tatar *kut*, *sür* and *sunä*, Mongol Buriat *sunäsun*, Yakut *kut*, etc.), which is the most important in myths.

A "shadow-soul" of this description, as already, mentioned, is owned also by animals, plants and lifeless objects.

The close connection between this soul and the shadow appears, e.g., from the idea that when a human being loses his soul, he loses also his shadow. According to the Yakuts men have three shadows; when all of these have disappeared, the one who loses them dies. Spirits are said to be beings without shadows.[1]

That the shadow-soul is received by a child at its birth from outside would seem to be a general belief. The idea of the Yenisei Ostiaks that all human beings born into the world receive, instead of new souls (*ulvei*, "shadow," "reflection in water"), such souls as have existed before, is enlightening in this respect. The shadow-soul is said to enter the sexual organs of a woman with child a little before confinement; the other life-spirits, on the other hand, which are believed to dwell in the heart, head, etc., are received by the child in the womb through its mother's food. From the moment of entry of the shadow-soul, birth pangs begin, as the soul (*ulvei*) is uncomfortable in the womb, where it is hot and suffocating. During life this shadow-soul is the faithful companion of man.

The Yenisei Ostiaks, like the Yakuts and Buriats, imagine it to be a little being which can be seen more especially by shamans.[2]

Among the Buriats, this belief in a previous existence of souls appears in a more developed form, of Indian origin. They explain that when the Tengeris lay themselves down to sleep (a slumber that may sometimes last a hundred years), their souls appear on the earth and are born here as human beings. If the soul of a Tengeri comes down a long time after the god has slept, the person within whom the soul has taken up its abode soon dies, as the soul has to return to its owner in heaven before the latter awakens from his sleep. Where the soul of the Tengeri comes down soon after its owner has fallen asleep, the person in question lives to old age.[3]

As has been said, the shadow-soul of a human being can leave its dwelling-place during life. In dreams it wanders unfettered by material means, visits distant places, strange races, passes through locked doors, and even keeps company with deceased companions. The Buriats say that what the soul has seen or heard during its journeys, remains in its memory, so that a person, when the soul has returned and awakened its owner, can relate to others the experiences of his soul. Dreams are thus believed to be actual truths, and for this reason are regarded as important.[4] But the wandering, released soul is also an actual and in some degree material being, which, e.g., may be both visible and audible to others. Besides its human form the soul of a sleeper can also take on the form of some animal. The Yakuts say that it wanders in space as a little bird or butterfly. In a Buriat tale the soul issued from the mouth of a sleeper in the form of a bee or a wasp. Such soul-animals must be left strictly in peace.[5]

Like dreams, sickness is caused also by the temporary absence of the soul from the body. But during sickness, the soul is believed to have been driven out of the body against its will.

Often a malicious spirit, for some reason or other, generally to obtain a sacrifice, carries off the soul. This may happen in different circumstances, and the soul is exposed to this danger, especially during its nocturnal journeys. In the stillness and darkness of the night all evil spirits are in motion and on the hunt for souls. To obtain help, the soul has to seek its deceased friends or other protecting spirits. Thoughtful souls can also help themselves by skilfully hiding, e.g., in the fur of animals, in leafy trees, or in other objects. Should a poor soul be pursued too long it loses itself in deep forests or other places strange to it, so that it can no longer find its way home. When a soul is seized by an evil spirit, one can sometimes hear its weeping and cries.[6]

Another very common belief is that the soul, against its will, may be driven by a shock from the body. The Buriats believe that the homeless soul then remains for some time at the place where this misfortune happens. Unless attention is given at once to this accident, the soul begins to wander about and flies further and further away, with the result that the victim becomes more and more seriously ill and in the end dies. The souls of little children can easily be driven away in this manner if they are frightened. The consequences of the absence of the soul soon show themselves as fatigue, paleness, tears, and restlessness during sleep, etc. One has then to seek out the place where the soul left its dwelling-place, where it may still possibly be found. Should one succeed in winning the soul back again by special ceremonies, the sick one becomes well again. Often, however, the soul may disappear without its owner being aware of the fact, and when he or she gradually begins to feel apathetic, weak, and in a decline, it is too late to find the soul again. The help of a shaman, who has the power of finding all lost and wandering souls, is then necessary.[7]

At times a sick person may recover his soul himself. He must recall to memory the place where his soul left him, dress in the clothes he wore on that occasion, and visit the scene of the disaster at a time corresponding to the time of his loss, viz., in the evening if his soul left him in the evening, and so on. The person seeking his soul has further to take with him such delicacies as his soul delights in, and call his soul to partake of them. If the soul happens to be still in the vicinity, it will return to its owner, who is said to feel the reunion by a violent shivering in the back. It is important to remember the exact time, as then the soul is most certainly to be met with, at first every day, later at ever-increasing intervals, until it comes at last only once a year to the place of its liberation. During a long absence from the body, a soul, however, seldom wins through all the dangers threatening it from the many malicious and cunning spirits.[8]

A further means of driving a soul from its home, said to be used by the spirits, is a tickling of the nose, which induces sneezing. This appears from the following Buriat tale, which in many other respects also throws light on the beliefs of the Mongols regarding souls.

Once, a man who had the power of seeing spirits and talking with them went on a journey. Meeting three spirits on the way he went on in their company. As they journeyed he ascertained that these spirits had formed wicked plans, intending to steal away the soul of a rich man's son. The man tried to worm himself into the spirits' favour by promising to help in the capture of the soul, and thus obtained an opportunity of accompanying them. This man, who wished to play the part of a spirit, could not, however, but awaken the attention of the spirits. When they had travelled awhile together, the spirits asked in astonishment: "Why dost thou walk so that the grass falls down and the dry leaves rustle under thy steps?" The man replied cunningly that he had died so recently that he had not yet learned to walk silently and without leaving a track as a spirit should. The spirits believed this. When they arrived at the rich man's house, one of the spirits placed itself at the door, the other at the chimney, the third went to the unlucky son, and by producing an irritation in his nose, caused him to sneeze violently. During the sneeze the son's soul jumped out of his body and tried to escape by the door, but the spirit watching there seized it at once and held it tight, although the soul wept bitterly. The spirits then took the captured soul away with them. On the way back, the man who had joined the spirits asked them if they had anything in the world to fear. The spirits answered that they were very much afraid of thistles and thorns. "But what art thou afraid of?" asked the spirits. "I," said the man, "am most afraid of fat meat." The spirits, unaware that the man intended to deceive them, travelled further and further. On the way the man begged to be allowed to help by carrying the soul, which was also granted. But just then they happened to come to a place where thorny bushes and thistles grew. The man jumped with the soul in his arms among the prickly bushes, where the spirits were afraid to come. Remembering that the man had expressed his dread for fat meat, they began to throw pieces of meat among the bushes to drive him out. But the man, who was very fond of meat, ate them without danger to himself, on seeing which, the spirits realized that they had been tricked and went their way. The man then hurried back to the rich man's house, taking the soul with him so that the son recovered.[9]

Sickness may also be caused by the soul injuring itself in some way on its travels. According to the Yenisei Ostiaks bodily pain is often closely connected with damage to the soul (shadow). Should the soul, e.g., hurt its foot, its owner will limp; should the soul catch cold, its owner begins to shiver, etc., etc. Similar ideas are met with among the Tungus, and are reflected in the general belief that everything done to the image of a person affects the person himself. The word "soul" originally meant both shadow and image.[10]

Should the shadow-soul have left its dwelling-place for

PLATE LV

YENISEI OSTIAK SHAMAN WITH DRUM

Front and back views.
(See chapter XXI.)
After photograph by U. Holmberg.

good, death follows, when also the spirit-soul (Altai Tatar *tün*, Mongol and Buriat *amin*, " breath ") disappears.   Among certain peoples, the Buriats and Altai Tatars, the belief prevails that when the soul of a sick person comes into the hands of the Prince of Death, fate has decreed that the person in question shall die, and then even the shaman can no longer be of any assistance.   The Buriats relate how Erlen-Khan (" Death-kingdom's Prince ") sends out his servants to capture wandering souls.   Without caring for the cries for help and the prayers of the souls, these servants put them into sacks and bear them to their hard master, who places the souls in captivity.[11]   In a tale about the first shaman, Mergen-khara, it is said that he possessed the power of freeing souls even from the prisons of the Prince of Death, where these sit with strong chains round their necks, hands and feet.   The Prince of Death complained to the Heaven god Esege-Malan-Tengeri, who decided to test the power of the shaman by taking a soul up to the heavens and hiding it there in a bottle, the mouth of which he stopped up with his thumb.   The person whose soul had been taken became now dangerously ill and the shaman, according to his wont, hurried to seek the soul.   He went down to the kingdom of the Prince of Death, but failed to find the soul there.   He then journeyed everywhere under the earth and the sea, in chasms in the mountains and deep forests, but without result.   Then he " sat himself on his drum," flew up to heaven and after much difficult searching found the soul of the sick one in the bottle.   But how to free it, as God kept his finger on the mouth of the bottle?   The shaman was equal to the task.   He changed himself into a wasp and stung God violently on the forehead, and as God tried to protect himself with his right hand the soul escaped from the bottle.   After a while God noticed that the bottle was empty and that the shaman, sitting on the drum with his prize, was already sinking towards the earth.   God then became very angry and decreased the power of the shamans, and

now no shaman can save a soul which has come into the hands
of the Prince of Death.[12]

After death, the soul is said to remain for a few days in the
home. According to the Altai Tatars, Buriats, Yakuts, and
others, the soul of a person recently dead cannot understand
at once that it has left the body, but wanders for three days
yet in its old home. Not until the soul notices that it leaves
no trace in the ashes of the hearth, does it realize that it now
belongs to the world of spirits.[13] Despite the last fact, however, the soul appears in stories with a material body. The
Yakuts believe it can burn or wound itself and that blood runs
from its wounds. By means of sharpened objects the soul of
a dead person can easily be prevented from returning to its
home. If the soul does not receive sufficient food, it feels
hungry; without the necessary clothing it feels cold.[14] The
soul can even die, according to a popular belief. Of later
origin is probably the belief held by the Yakuts, that the soul
is taken round by spirits on the night of burial, to the places
where its former owner sojourned during life, and punished
for misdeeds on the spot where these occurred, so that one can
hear its cries and plaints.[15]

According to a more northern idea, the soul remains among
the relatives for some time after death. During this period
the property of the deceased may not be touched, but the soul,
like a living person, must be provided with food and drink.
Many peoples, such as the Yakuts, Dolgans, Goldes, and, at
an earlier time, the Mongols, Kirghis, etc., who prepare images
of their deceased, or for longer or shorter periods look
well after and provide for the soul in connection with some
object owned by the deceased, believe that only at the end
of these periods does the soul remove to the kingdom of the
dead.[16]

Besides the souls living in peace and rest in the land of the
dead, there are also others, which wander restlessly around,
disturbing the living with all kinds of misfortunes, especially

sickness. A very common view is that the souls of childless or unmarried women, together with those whose owners either met with a violent death or died before their time, haunt their old homes, causing much trouble to their relations. Only a very clever shaman can drive out these spirits, which are especially dangerous for infants. The Yakuts call them Üör, the Buriats Anakhai.[17] According to the Yenisei Ostiaks the spirits of little children and unmarried women wander irritated around their graves for a whole year after death.[18] The longer a soul has been among the other dead, the more it begins to acquire the characteristics of an evil spirit. Such spirits of the long-ago deceased are the Abasy among the Yakuts, Buriat Bokholdoi, Altai Tatar Aina, Üzüt, etc.[19] Besides graves, certain deserted places, e.g., the deserts of Turan and Gobi, are the dwelling-places of these evil spirits, who from these centres set out on their destructive excursions. In mountainous districts places difficult of reach, the summits, etc., are the homes of all manner of spirits. The Mongols believe further that the souls of wicked people stop halfway between this and the next world, floating in the air and causing many kinds of misfortune.[20] The Buriats relate that the wandering spirits make fires at night in deserted huts. These fires are pale and bluish in colour. This fire can be stolen, the person succeeding in doing this becoming very rich. When the spirits gather round their fires to sit or dance, they never form a complete ring as human beings would. Men can sometimes see such spirits, and if they succeed in glancing at them before being noticed, the spirits become frightened and take to flight. The living are also said to be able to hear the song of these spirits.[21]

Like Odin of the Scandinavians, the ruler over the dead is said by the Buriats to have one eye in the middle of his forehead. In one of the tales of the latter, a man who had the power of seeing spirits kept watch while the spirits gathered at a deserted hut. There he happened to see also the ruler of the spirits. This was a roughly-built big man, with one eye in his forehead. The ruler seated himself in the place of honour and now and then announced which souls should be brought before him. Each time, certain of the spirits went to fulfil his command. The man approached the ruler of the dead and shot him in the centre of his forehead so that he fell down and was changed into a hip-bone.[22]

The idea that the soul of man is intimately connected with the bone-construction of the body, would seem to be a primitive belief among the Siberian peoples. Just as the preserving of the bones of animals — bears, reindeer, etc. — is said to

FIG. 18.   NORTH-SIBERIAN TOMB

be founded on the hope that these animals can preserve their lives as long as the skeleton is uninjured, so a similar belief was applied to the remains of human beings. In earlier times the dead were buried over the earth. According to Strahlenberg the Yakuts often left the body in the hut, removing themselves elsewhere.[23] Among nearly all the more northern

peoples, the custom of placing the bodies of children, sometimes also of adults, in hollow trees or on the branches of a
growing tree, has been preserved down to our day. At the
present time burial-erections are mostly made of wood. The
body of a shaman in particular, may not, among the Tungus,
Yakuts and others, be buried in the earth. For this reason it
is generally laid in a wooden box, borne on two or four posts.[24]
" Shamans," says Georgi, " will mostly dissolve in the free
air, as the devil lives in the earth." [25] A Tungus assured the
author that if a shaman is buried in the earth, his soul-bird
will never return again to a new shaman of the same family.
The following tale recorded among the Yenisei Ostiaks is
instructive: When the first man died, his relatives believed him
to be asleep, but when they were unable to awaken him they
became afraid and started to cry. The Heaven god, Es, then
sent down a dog to tell them that they had no reason to be
afraid, but that they should bind up the body with grass and
hang it in a tree, when the body would come to life within
seven days. But the dog deceived the people into burying
the body in the ground. The result was that afterwards men
began to die.[26]

Cremation, which occurs among certain peoples in the north-
east corner of Siberia (the Chukchee and Koriaks) and also
among the Buriats, cannot have been one of the earlier methods
of disposal of the dead among the Altaic peoples. A later
custom is probably also the Mongol method of throwing a
body into the fields as food for the dogs.[27]

Side by side with the thought that the soul wanders after
death in the other world, the idea appears that the souls of the
dead may after a time be born again on the earth in a child
of the same family. The Yenisei Ostiaks believe that the
soul can take up its dwelling, or live again in some animal,
especially in bears, and also *vice versa*.[28] This belief is not to
be confounded with that according to which the souls of the
dead are inclined to many temporary metamorphoses. A cer-

tain groping after explanations is already apparent in the view laid down by a Buriat, according to which human beings have three souls.   One is taken captive by the Prince of Death; the second remains as a ghost in this world, continuing to live as before; the third is born again as a living person.[29]

PLATE LVI

The illustration at the top (left) shows the tomb of a Buriat shaman, erected on posts. The others depict ongons or images of Buriat shamans.

(See page 499.)

CHAPTER XX

THE REALM OF THE DEAD

THE MANNER in which life beyond the grave is imagined appears plainly from the burial ceremonies, in
which the dead are furnished with food, clothes, implements
of labour, weapons and domestic animals. The most northern
peoples of Siberia have a custom of stabbing to death or binding reindeer and dogs alive to the grave. The rulers of the
Yakuts in earlier times received with them on their last journey, besides their horse, one of their slaves to serve his master
in the other world. "His servant followed him," say the
Yakuts even now, when a poor person dies soon after the death
of a wealthy man.[1] And even now sacrifices of slaves are said
to occur among certain Tungus tribes.

"In the other world," the Altai Tatars say, "we shall sow
our seed, herd our cattle, drink kumiss and eat beef, with this
difference only, that we shall live better there, as we shall
enjoy not only the possession of the cattle we owned on the
earth, but also of all the domestic animals that have died
earlier."[2] According to the tales of the Buriats, the dead have
food, raiment, etc., to the degree in which they were supplied
with these on their burial-day. Thus, depending on the property the relatives were able to present to the deceased, some
souls have to walk on foot, others to ride on horseback, the
most fortunate in carriages. The celebrating of weddings and
other merry festivals among the dead is also spoken of. The
dead shaman, who is supplied with his costume, his drum and
other sacred implements, continues his important calling in
the other world. In general, the dead are regarded as going
on with the work which each had done in this world. The

Buriat " manual labourer does not after death forget his skill, the scribe lives by his pen, and a woman who has been a skilful sempstress on earth, continues to work with her needle." Specially skilful workers are said to be short-lived, because the ruler over the dead needs their help.[3] The northern peoples, like the Tungus here, live in the world beyond the grave in tents of birch-bark, hunt and fish, and practise reindeer-keeping in the great, underworld, primeval forests.

That the world of the dead was originally a reflection of the earthly one is shown, further, by the scenes in the shaman ceremonies, when the latter escort the soul to the underworld. The Tungus believe this last journey to resemble in detail the difficult journeys of these nomads over mountains and valleys in their great forests. Those who drive here with reindeer, ride also to the underworld on the back of a reindeer; those, again, who use dogs, travel there behind dogs.

The shaman's business is to know the difficult path; the soul itself finds it difficult to reach its goal. Many dangers also threaten it on the way. Evilly-disposed spirits are often in motion, seeking to tempt the soul from its path; cannibal-spirits lie in wait to devour it. The Goldes say that the road to the underworld goes through certain particular places, which are many in number. At the commencement, the road is the same for all the dead, but later a point is reached where as many roads branch off as there are families among the Goldes. From here the road leads to the " steep slope " and then to the " river's crossing-place." This crossing is said to be so diffi-cult, that the soul nearly falls down with exhaustion. Still a few more places, and then from tracks and newly-chopped living branches and the barking of dogs one may conclude that the village of the dead is near. In the underworld each family has its own village, where the members of the family dwell together, continuing to live as on the earth. Life in the underworld is said, however, to be better and happier than here.   All the dangers and difficulties of the journey end at the village.   Should the soul go under on its last journey, the fault lies with the shaman, who has not been clever enough in his calling, and then the services of a better shaman must be called in, the latter, by his shamanizing, finding the point where the soul has succumbed, waking it to life again, and escorting it to the village of its earlier deceased relations.   For some families the last journey is said to be more difficult than for others.

Such of the Goldes as live by keeping reindeer, are escorted to the underworld by nine reindeer, eight of which bear the property of the deceased, the deceased himself riding on the ninth.   The saddle is constructed so that the soul cannot fall off though the reindeer moves rapidly.   As the shaman is said to take the form of this reindeer, or to represent its soul, he can carry the dead safely by avoiding and going round dangerous places.   All the districts passed during the journey are described by the shaman in his songs and ceremonies.   He leads the soul first to the source of the river, by which the clan in question dwells, then to the high range of mountains, and down this again into a primeval forest until another high mountain is reached.   Beyond this comes a great swamp which has to be crossed.   Further the road leads to a mountain torrent, on the open banks of which a level and beautiful forest grows.   Gradually, one begins to notice that the surroundings are populated, as the forest has been felled and there are marks of newly-timbered boats.   Finally one arrives in the village of the dead, where smoke rises, tents stand in rows, and reindeer feed as among the living Reindeer-Tungus.[4]

Such also the Yakut realm of the dead would seem to have been originally.   The spirits living there in similar circumstances to those of their earthly life are divided into six clans, according to information from one district.   In certain tales, the way to this realm is described as exceedingly. difficult to travel.   The soul has to go in at the throat of a snake-like monster, pass through its body, and come out from its tail, thus reaching the other world. The way is both painful and dangerous, as the gullet and the intestines of the monster are said to be covered with great, sharp spikes. For this reason the soul has to be provided with clothes and shoes, otherwise it would bleed to death. The custom of supplying the dead with a horse is said to have originated in the wish to make the journey through this dangerous pass as swift as possible. Especially in the shaman songs the way to the underworld is said to go through many dangers, over " stormy rivers " or " bloody streams," through " burning forests " or " icy winds." [5]

A very common idea among the Yakuts is that " the other world " lies beyond the " death-sea." [6] Most of the peoples of North Siberia consider the realm of the dead to lie somewhere in the north, most often at the mouths of rivers flowing into the Arctic Ocean. The point of the compass of the dead is said to be " towards the night " or " downwards." Down in the north, according to Yakut tales, lives the stern ruler over the dead, Arsan-Duolai, in a great chasm with winter frozen fields and cold summer-dwellings, where black chimneys arise from gloomy huts. This dreaded ruler is said to have his mouth in the middle of his forehead and eyes at his temples. The spirits serving him (Abasy) come sometimes to the villages of the living on depredatory raids, carrying off or swallowing people's souls, spreading sickness, etc. By appeasing them with bloody sacrifices, the shamans cause them to return to their dismal dwelling-place. [7]

Like the Yakuts, the Ugrians and the Yenisei Ostiaks speak also of an evil Prince of the dead living in the north, who carries off or devours souls. According to the latter, certain naked rocks in the Arctic Ocean are the dwelling-place of the dead. Side by side with this, another belief is met with among them, viz., that under the earth there is a great grotto, or seven grottoes under one another, in which the souls of the dead dwell, and where in the place of the sun and moon, only rotted trees give out a dim light. Strange fishes live in the underground rivers.[8] A third description noted down by the author among them relates how the underworld is a complete reflection of the Yenisei District. The underground Yenisei is said however to flow in the opposite direction.

The above seven grottoes are obviously closely connected with the seven or nine underground storeys, which according to the Altai Tatars and others are situated horizontally under the " middle place " or the earth and correspond to a similar number of planes of Heaven above.[9] The Central Asian people generally regard the underworld as populated by evil beings, ruled over by the stern Erlik-Khan, who is said to sit on his black throne, surrounded by a court consisting of evil spirits. At the command of their lord these spirits often make excursions, more especially in the night-time, to the world of the living, where they seize some poor soul and carry it off with them to their home. Extremely common is also the idea that this ruler over the dead has power only over those who were wicked in this life. Those mortals again, who have done more good than evil, are taken after death to the heavenly dwelling-places.[10] The path to both the underground dwellings and those above is believed to go through a hole in the middle of each plane, and according to this idea the Ostiaks call the seven-storeyed sky " seven-holed," [11] the Chukchee explaining that each hole is perpendicularly under the North Star.[12] As the hole leading to the underworld, which is often used by the shaman, is, of course, also in the centre of the earth, one may often see among his magic things a disc representing the earth, in the midst of which is a round hole. In travelling to the heavens, the Altai shamans use also a world-tree furnished with divisions, the Dolgans explaining that the shamans escort the souls of the dead to the tree in question, where they continue their life in the shape of a little bird.[13]

In Heaven also, life resembles that on the earth. According

to certain tribes living in the District Turuhansk, the souls in Heaven resemble little people, who catch little fishes in the lakes there.[14] The Buriats say that the souls living in heaven have cattle and houses, wives and children there. They even pay visits to one another, drink spirits and get intoxicated.[15] According to the Chukchee the heavens are peopled with spirits which live there in families and, like the people of the earth, exist by fishing and hunting. Often, however, the game they seek is human souls, which they carry with them to some storey of the sky, whence only a clever shaman can save them.[16]

How far these ideas of Heaven as the dwelling-place of the dead have originated among the above peoples, is hard to decide. In any case they are extremely old as they are connected with so many shamanistic customs. On the other hand the belief held by many peoples that those who have met their death in war or through an accident go to Heaven — a belief found among the most varying peoples all round the earth — is most probably of great antiquity. Like the Ugrians and certain Tatar tribes, the peoples of North-East Siberia, such as the Chukchee and the Gilyaks of the Amur country, believe that the souls of those who die a violent death go directly to Heaven, while those who die a natural death, remain on earth or descend underground. According to the Chukchee the Aurora Borealis is chiefly the home of those who die a violent death.[17]

The most original views do not regard the realm of the dead as a place of restitution, where the soul has to answer for the sins committed during life. Such Altaic peoples as have come under the influence of alien and more highly developed teachings, form exceptions in this respect.

In a Buriat tale the hero Mu-monto journeys on a commission from his father through the realm of the dead, to demand back the horse sacrificed by the latter at the burial of his father. To arrive there, one must first go due north. On the way there is a large, black stone. When the traveller

PLATE LVII

1. Buriat shaman with his hobby-horses. (See page 522.)

2. Hides of Buriat shaman-animals used in place of wooden images in shamanizing. (See page 512.)

has lifted up this and shouted: " Come here," a fox appears
in the opening under the stone and says: " Hold fast to my
tail." If one then obeys this request, the fox will lead him
into the land of the dead.   Mu-monto, travelling further and
further with the help of the fox, saw many mysterious things.
First he saw horses that were very fat on a naked rock.   Then
he met very thin and miserable cattle on a rich meadow.   In
another place he met women with their mouths sewn up.   In
a great cauldron full of boiling pitch he saw officials and
shamans writhing ceaselessly.   On his way he saw, further,
men whose hands and feet were bound fast, and women who,
although naked, embraced thorn-bushes.   In one place he saw
a woman who, although she appeared to be poor, lived luxu-
riously, and another, who, although rich, suffered from hunger.
Mu-monto soon learned the reasons for the fates of these
people.   The poor woman had been good during her life, and
out of her little had shared with the needy, therefore she had
everything in plenty now; but the other, albeit rich, had been
hard-hearted and parsimonious, and had therefore now to
starve.   The naked who embraced the thorn-bushes had been
frivolous and betrayed their husbands.   The bound men had
been thieves.   Those who were boiled in pitch had been false
in their professions.   Those whose mouths were sewn fast had
been liars during life and spread calumnies.   The thin and
miserable horses on the rich meadow had been so ill-treated by
their masters during life that they could not even now become
fatter, while the fat horses on the naked rock had been so
well-fed that even without food they were still flourishing.[18]

In a Tatar tale, recorded by M. A. Castrén from the neighbourhood of the Sayan steppes, life under the earth is described
in a somewhat similar manner.   The daughter of the ruler of
the dead, Irlek-Khan, once came to the earth in the shape of a
black fox and did all kinds of harm to human beings.   A hero
named Komdei-Mirgan was persuaded to hunt the fox, which,
however, ambushed him so that his leg was broken.   Shortly

thereafter, a monster (Yelbegen) with nine heads and riding on a forty-horned ox, arose out of the earth. This monster cut off the hero's head and carried it off to the underworld. When the hero's sister Kubaiko came to weep at her brother's corpse and saw that the head was lacking, she decided to go to the realm of the dead and seek the head there. The tracks of the ox of Yelbegen showed her the way. These led to an underground opening, through which she descended into Irlek-Khan's kingdom. Here she met with many marvellous things. By the wayside she saw seven clay vessels and an old woman who poured milk from one vessel to another without ceasing. Further on, a horse fastened with a long halter stood on a plain of sand where there was neither grass nor water, but in spite of this the horse was fat and in good condition. Not far off another horse, bound in the same manner, stood in a green field with running water, but this horse was lean and wasted. In another place she saw half of a human body forming a dam for a brook, while in another place a whole body was not sufficient to dam a similar brook. Kubaiko rode astonished past all these things and came deeper into the earth. Gradually she began to hear more and more distinctly the clang of hammers, and soon she saw forty men beating out hammers, another forty making saws, and a similar number making tongs. Following the tracks of Yelbegen's ox she travelled on without fear, until she reached the bank of a river running along the foot of a mountain. On the bank she saw Irlek-Khan's dwelling, a building of stone with forty corners. Before the entrance stood nine larches, all growing from the same root. To this tree the horses of the nine Princes of death were bound, one to each branch, and Kubaiko also bound her horse to it. While doing this she saw the following inscription on the tree: " When Kudai (God) created heaven and earth, this tree was also brought forth, and to this day no man and no animal has come living to the tree." Having read this Kubaiko entered the dwelling of the Princes of death and closed the door after her.   It was dark inside and Kubaiko was soon lost in the room.   She felt invisible hands take hold of her, her clothes were torn, she was dragged about and tormented, but when she tried to grasp her tormentors, she could not, as they were without bodies.   In her dread she shouted.   And then the door opened, the room became light and the Head (Ataman) of the Princes of death came in.   He noticed Kubaiko, but turned again and went out without a word.   Kubaiko followed closely at his heels.   She went first through many rooms that were empty and waited inhabitants, but afterwards came many rooms filled with human beings.   In one of them she saw old women sit and spin linen with great energy.   In another room also she saw old women, but these were without any occupation, except that they appeared to be continually swallowing something that would not go down their throats.   In a third room were middle-aged women, with great stones, which they were unable to move, round their arms and necks.   A fourth room was filled with men who had nooses round their necks fastened to great logs.   In a fifth room she saw armed men who had been shot through, and who sprang about shouting and groaning.   The same shrieking and groaning was heard from a sixth room where there were badly wounded men armed with knives.   Coming to the seventh room, she saw mad dogs and people bitten by them, mad and raving like the dogs.   This was followed by an eighth room in which husbands and wives lay in couples under their coverlets, but although these coverlets had been sewn together of nine sheepskins, they would only cover one member of each of the sleeping couples, and husbands and wives quarrelled unceasingly over the coverlets.   The ninth room also contained husbands and wives under coverlets, made of one sheepskin only, which were, however, sufficient to cover both. Finally, she entered a tenth room, large as a steppe.   In this room sat eight Princes of death and, in the midst of these, their Chief, Irlek-Khan.   Kubaiko bowed to them and asked why their servant Yelbegen had cut off and carried away her brother's head. The Princes replied that this had been done at their orders, but promised to give back the head if she could pull up a goat with seven horns which had grown fast in the earth and lay so deep that only the horns showed. Otherwise, she would lose her own head. Kubaiko, who was a heroine, did not hesitate to accept the proposal. The Princes then took her through nine other rooms, filled with human heads. Kubaiko burst into tears when she recognized her brother's head. In a tenth room the goat lay embedded in the earth. Kubaiko had now to show her strength and, at the third attempt, lifted the goat on to her shoulder. When the Princes saw that she was a mighty heroine, they gave her her brother's head and escorted her back to the larch. Here Kubaiko mounted her horse, but before riding off she compelled the Princes to show her the way back to the earth. During the journey she enquired about everything she had seen. The Princes gave her all particulars, saying: " The old woman whom thou sawest pouring milk, mixed water with the milk she gave to her guests on earth, and as a punishment for this bad deed has now to separate water from milk, a task she must keep on doing through all eternity. The half-body thou sawest damming a brook is not undergoing any punishment, but belonged instead to a wise man on the earth who could dam rivers and do anything he wished. Now, half of his body lies as a reminder to the passer-by that a wise man, even though bereft of his limbs, can accomplish great things with his will, while on the other hand, the complete body over which the brook flows serves to remind one that by strength alone man can do little. This body belonged formerly to a physically strong, but stupid man. As the water now runs over his body, so ran every matter past his understanding, without either being comprehended or turned to account through intelligence. The fat horse on the dry sand is a proof that a thoughtful man can keep his horse in condition even with poor fodder,

while the thin horse on the rich pasture shows that cattle cannot thrive on the best pastures unless well cared for." Thereafter Kubaiko asked: " Who were the beings that seized me
in the dark room, tore my clothes and tormented me, but were
without bodies? " The Princes replied: " They were our invisible serving-spirits that can injure and kill all wicked people,
but can do nothing to the good." Kubaiko continued to inquire into the sins of the people held captive in the dwelling
of the Princes, receiving the following answer: " The women
thou sawest spinning in the first room have been given this
work as a punishment for having spun during their lives after
sunset, when it is forbidden to work. Those again who sat
in the second room had been given threads to wind on spindles,
but had left the spindles hollow in the centre and hidden the
thread in their own bosoms. The spindleful which they thus
gathered of stolen wool, they are now doomed to swallow,
which is impossible, so that they must keep the spindle in their
throats through eternity. The younger women in the third
room had sold butter, in which they had hidden stones to
increase the weight. The men in the fourth room have nooses
round their necks, which are continually threatening to choke
them, because they hanged themselves on earth for weariness
of life. The men with shot-wounds are suicides, who shot
themselves on account of quarrels with their wives. Similarly,
the men in the sixth room are suicides, who cut themselves with
knives while drunk. The inhabitants of the seventh room
brought on their punishments by teasing mad dogs in life and
being bitten by them. In the eighth room were married
people who had quarrelled through their lives and looked only
to their own advantage; now they are doomed to bicker eternally over a covering which by good will and harmony would
be more than enough for both. The married people, on the
other hand, in the ninth room are there only as an example
of how even a little property can be sufficient for a family, if
there is harmony between the married couple. They are not

undergoing any punishment, but have been brought solely that the wicked, by seeing them, should feel their punishment more."

Having received all this information from the Princes of death Kubaiko separated from them, returned to the body of her brother with the head, and with water of life, procured from God, awakened her dead brother to life again.[19]

Alien influence can also be detected in an idea of the Tungus living near the Baikal, that each mortal will be weighed after death with a white and a black stone. If the white stone weighs less than the soul, the latter goes up to heaven, but if the black one is lighter than the soul, the soul goes to the underworld. The punishment there is that the soul is first thrown into a dark pit, where it is tormented by terrible cold, and afterwards roasted in never-ending flames.[20] The idea, met with among certain Tatar tribes, of a very narrow punishment-bridge, from which the soul overladen with sins falls into the depths below, has obviously come from Persia.

To true shamanism these ideas of restitution are completely alien. Certain terrible places are, however, met with in the cannibal-myths of the Northern peoples, into which the soul, regardless of its former life, may fall against its will.

In the cannibal myths of the Goldes, a gloomy place by a river is mentioned, on the sand-covered bank of which grows an enormously high poplar. The leaves of the tree prevent the rays of the sun by day and of the moon by night from falling on this deserted place. The spirit-birds, which fly about in the service of wicked shamans to torment and trouble poor souls, gather mostly in this tree. On the ground round about lie countless human bones. According to a tale, a girl who had happened to come there one evening saw two fires in the sky and heard the rustle of the wings of a great bird. The bird, which resembled a crane, bore a poor human being on its back, who pleaded the whole time: " Kill me quickly, why dost thou torment me." " Soon, soon," answered the bird, " see,

PLATE LVIII

Dress of a Yakut shaman (bird type), back view, with " feathers " or fringes. Dressed in this costume the shaman received the power of flying wherever he desired to go. (See pages 514, 519.)

there is my tree! " It then sat in the crown of the tree and slung the man on to a branch, where he remained hanging. Again and again he begged: " Kill me quickly, do not torture me! " When the girl, who was a heroine, saw how the bird began to tear off the man's garments with its beak, she became angry, aimed her bow at the bird and said: " If thou dost not take on thy shaman costume, I will kill thee." " Wait a little," said the bird, shaking its wings, which then became changed into iron feathers. " Shoot now," it said, " now thou canst not kill me, but thine own hours are counted." The heroine saw, however, a naked place in the evil being's breast between the feathers, and aiming her arrow at this shot the bird, which, falling to the ground, became a flame of fire.[21]

In its dream-voyages the soul may sometimes happen on such nests of evil spirits; an idea, the reason for which is probably to be found in the horrible nightmares and fever-visions of hysterical persons.

CHAPTER XXI

SHAMANISM AND TOTEMISM

AMONG nearly all primitive peoples, it is held that the chief cause of sickness is a temporary absence of the soul from its material envelope and that the only cure is the successful recovering of the soul. Connected with this is a belief in the existence of persons furnished with certain extraordinary powers, who, by different means and in different ways, generally, however, in a condition of ecstasy, can come into immediate touch with the spirit-world. Such persons are given different names by the separate peoples of Siberia. The Mongols and the Buriats nearly related to these, call them " bö," the Yakuts " ojun," the Altai Tatars " kam," and the Tungus " shaman." Through Russian ethnography the Tungusian name has been adopted by the literature of the science of religion. As the shaman is of the greatest importance in the nature-religion of the Siberian peoples, this form of religion has generally begun to be called shamanism.

It is not possible to become a shaman only by education or practice, a shaman having to possess special shamanic talents, which appear in varying forms with different individuals, often in early youth. The Tungus say no one can " take " this talent, but that it is " received " or, in other words, that " one is called " to the profession of shaman. A common idea is that a shamanic talent is " a difficult burden " for a beginner.

Dr. Sternberg, who, during his stay in East Siberia, made many interesting observations among the Giliak shamans, says that the preparation for the office of shaman forms a crisis in the life of the chosen, a crisis followed by extremely complicated psychic manifestations. A shaman of his acquaintance related that before he became a shaman he was ill for over two months, lying motionless and unconscious for this period. He was convinced that he would have died if he had not become a shaman. After the severe trials of these months he was reduced to complete exhaustion. During the nights, he started to dream that he sang shaman songs. Once a white owl appeared to him and placed itself close behind him, while a human being stood a little further off and said: " Make thyself a drum and everything a shaman needs, and sing songs. Thou wilt never more succeed in being an ordinary individual; but if thou acceptest the calling of shaman, thou wilt become a real shaman." He was unaware how long he had slept, but when he awoke, he saw that he was being held over a fire, his relatives believing that the spirit had killed him. He then commanded his relations to give him a drum and started to sing. During this singing he felt intoxicated but not as one dead.[1]

According to the Tungus a deceased shaman appears to the member of his own family whom he has chosen as his successor. This visit may take place in a dream, or during a severe illness. Anyone refusing to follow this call is tormented by the spirit to the verge of death. When the spirit has appeared to a shaman candidate, the latter begins to withdraw from the company of his fellows, has difficult nerve-attacks and fits of hysteria and epilepsy, behaving at times as though his mind were unhinged. The Tungus of the Turukhansk District call a shaman-spirit Khargi.[2]

A Yakut shaman describes his experiences as follows: " At the age of twenty I became ill and began to see and hear what other people do not see or hear. For nine years I resisted the spirit and told no one what was happening, for fear of being misunderstood or insulted. Finally, I became so ill that death was very near. It was then that I began to shamanize, recovering immediately. Even now, if I refrain from shamanizing for a long time, I become indisposed and fall ill." The spirit, which appears to the chosen, is said to be the soul of a dead shaman, and is called Ämägät by the Yakuts. The Ämägät of the shaman, which advises and protects him through life, is pictured in metal on his costume as a little man-like figure.[3]

Common to all the Siberian peoples is the view that only a member of a family or clan that has earlier contained shamans can become a shaman. The calling goes thus in inheritance. But individuals with shamanic talents do not appear in every generation. The Tungus at the Yenisei explained to the author, that if a shaman is buried in the earth and not on an erection in the air, the "loom" (*Cavia lumma*, a soul-bird of the shaman) of the deceased will return no more to his family. Often the "loom" appears first after a longer period. It is held that this "loom," the reappearance of which in the family is regarded as a great honour, is the wandering soul of the deceased shaman. When the "loom" has appeared to anyone, that is to say, when shamanic gifts become apparent in any individual, a wooden image is made of the bird and a reindeer sacrificed to it. This "loom" becomes the protective spirit of the new shaman. Here we meet with a conception, peculiar to shamanism, that besides the ordinary souls common to all men, the shaman possesses a special shaman-soul, lacking to others. From the beliefs connected with death it appears that this shaman-soul is immortal in a much higher degree than other souls. For this reason, special ceremonies are necessary at the burial of a shaman. Not even a chief, however many herds of reindeer he possesses, can compare in matters of religion with the poorest shaman, who, on account of his "loom" is honoured and feared already during his life, but still more after his death.

The Yakuts sometimes call the shaman-soul *sür*, which in other Turkish languages signifies soul in general. Its seat is said to be in the head of the shaman. It is related in a tale, how a great shaman received his head "in the Heaven of

Mänäriks " (*mänärik*, " nervy," " insane "; *mänärü*, " to lose one's sense ").⁴ According to the Buriats, a person who has been scared out of his wits by violent thunder receives a special shamanic talent.⁵ The Yakuts say such persons have received *sür* from Ulu-Tojon, the god of thunder.⁶

Besides male shamans, female shamans are also met with, though these can in no way be compared with the male in power and importance. Generally, they are called also by a different name from the male shamans (Yakut, Altai-Tatar, Buriat, Mongol, " udagan," " utagan," etc.). There have been, however, especially among the Buriats, many famous female shamans, worshipped after their death by their relatives. Each place, each family, and each tribe has, according to the Buriats, its individual Zajans or protective spirits of deceased shamans, both male and female, who after death were buried on adjoining heights, where their images (*ongon*) were also placed. At times even ordinary Buriat men or women become Zajans after death, and special ceremonies are gone through in their honour; but these are said to become Zajans " by the power of their shamanic origin and the protective powers springing therefrom for the survivors." ⁷

It is extremely important for each person to remember his shamanic origin, called Utkha by the Buriats. Each family, or clan, has its own Utkha, which imposes special duties on its members. It is said of the family Sartul, which dwells east of the Baikal, " that they do not devour the blood of animals, as their shaman-Utkha forbids this, and especially must they refrain from devouring the blood of the Sartul-family's shaman animals." An animal or a bird, regarded as protecting the shaman, is called *khubilgan* by the Buriats. In their opinion, each shaman has his own protectors, some a snake, some a vulture, some a frog, etc.⁸

Closely connected with the family Utkha are also the household spirits or household Ongons. These household spirits, worshipped by the members of the family and preserved in the tent, generally consist of a sheepskin on which tinplate figures of human beings and other things are fastened, or these figures may also be painted on the sheepskin or on a cloth. These Ongons are inherited with the tales and traditions attached to them. Among the Buriats of the Khangin clan one may see an Ongon, called Börtö, in nearly every dwelling, and of this it is said that the forefather of the clan, Khorton, a great shaman, had borne it on his back from Mongolia. Prayers to this Ongon begin: " Utkha of the thousands of Khangins, Sen-Serel bird (*sen*, a Siberian swan), Utkha of the Serel Mongols, Khun-Khorel bird (*khun*, a Siberian swan)." [9]

Animals, and especially birds, which play some part in shamanic beliefs, may. not be killed or even molested, otherwise sickness or some other misfortune will result. Among the Tungus, as among many other North Siberian peoples, certain birds, water-birds in particular, such as the loom, sea-gull, swan, crane, etc., are sacred. One may not even point a finger at them. Further, one tries to avoid mentioning their names. A Buriat tale tells how a swan, whose nest had been damaged, flew with a burning brand in its beak and dropped it on a house, so that the whole village was burnt up. Among the Yakuts and Buriats, the eagle is treated with extraordinary respect and dread. The Yakuts say that it is not a sign of good luck if an eagle flies over a village. The Buriats round the Baikal call the eagle " Olkhon island's master " or " the son of the god living on Olkhon island." Often the great shamanic powers of the eagle are praised, some myths calling it "the first shaman." There are countless tales of misfortunes which befell people who ill-treated this bird. A man once saw how an eagle plucked at the carcase of his cow, which had been killed on the steppes by a wolf. The man became angry and started to drive away the bird with a bough. Shortly afterwards he became seriously ill, and received the knowledge in a dream that his illness had been caused by his treatment of the eagle. The Buriats throw milk or kumiss into the air each time a swan or an eagle flies over their village.[10] If a Yakut finds a dead eagle or the skeleton of one, he regards it as his duty to bury the bird on a special erection of wood, or in a tree, in the manner in which human beings, particularly shamans, were earlier buried. While doing this, he utters the following words: "Lift up thyself, fly to thy birthplace, come not down on the earth. Thy bones of copper I have placed on the grave-erection, thy bones of silver have I lifted up." [11] With similar respect do the Tungus also treat shaman animals.

It is not always easy to define the difference between shaman animals and such as are regarded as the forefather or mother of a clan or a people. The myths of the Altaic peoples tell also of the latter. Among the Buriats tales have been recorded of three swans which once came down from the sky to bathe in a lake. They took off their swan-garments and became changed into three fair women. A hunter, who had hidden himself on the shore, took one of these swan-garments and hid it. When the swan-women had bathed for a time, they hurried to the shore to clothe themselves again, and when the others were ready to fly away the one who had lost her garment had to remain behind on the earth. The hunter married her later and she bore him eleven sons and six daughters. Once, after a long time, the wife remembered her former garment and inquired of her husband where he had left it. The man was so certain that she would not now leave him and her children that he decided to return the wonderful garment to her. With his consent, the woman then put it on to see how she would look in it. But no sooner had she got the swan-garment on, than she flew up through the smoke-hole and, floating high above her home, shouted to those left behind: "Ye are earthly beings and remain on the earth, I am from Heaven and fly back to my home." She added: "Each spring and autumn, when the swans fly northward and return, ye must carry out certain ceremonies in my honour." She then blessed her children, hoping that they would live happily on the earth, and disappeared in the sky. It is further related how one of the swan-woman's daughters tried to hinder her mother from flying by grasping her feet, which, as the daughter had dirty hands, became black and have remained so to this day..[12]

Tales related to the above, are met with also in Europe, having probably come there from Asia, but it should be noted that among the Buriats, certain ceremonies are connected with this belief. Generally speaking, tales of the supernatural origin of certain tribes and clans are not scarce among the Altaic peoples. According to the notes made by Potanin in the Altai territory the forefather of the Bersit clan was a wolf, which lived in the forest near a lake together with a deer (Cervus elaphus). Of these a son was born who became the ancestor of the said clan.[13] Regarding the origin of the Mongols there are several myths. In some it is related that their ancestor was a dog, or that he was given birth to by a tree and nourished by a dog. It is also related how two Khans warred together and destroyed all the people until only one woman was left. This last woman met with a bull by whom she had two children. From these the whole race of the Mongols was born. A variant of this tale describes how a woman gave birth to the son of a bull, the child walking on all fours. When the forefeet had been cut off this ancestor of the Mongols began to live like a human being, and ate meat in the place of grass.[14] The Kirghis believe themselves to be derived from a wild boar, and for this reason do not eat pork. According to one tale Jenghiz Khan's son lived at Gobi together with a wild boar, the latter bearing him several sons. Thus arose a great people, i.e., the Kirghis.[15]

Several myths have been recorded among the Buriats regarding their ancestor Bukha-Nojon (" Bull Lord "). South of the Baikal lived a king, Taizhi-Khan, who had a mottled bull. This, an exceptionally large and powerful animal, once said in its pride: " Whoever in the world dares to measure his strength against mine, may come and try." Then Bukha-Nojon was changed to a blue-grey bull and went to the kingdom of Taizhi-Khan to wrestle with the mottled bull. During the day-time he wrestled as a bull, but in the night he kept company as a fair youth with Taizhi-Khan's daughter. After a time the latter became enceinte and told Bukha-Nojon that she would soon give birth to a child. Then Bukha-Nojon ripped the child from her stomach and cast it with his horns over the Baikal. After he had vanquished the mottled bull, Bukha-Nojon swam over the lake, found the child on the shore and began to nourish it. A shaman woman found the child later sucking at a blue-grey bull, adopted it and called it Bulagat. This Bulagat, who had two sons, the ancestors of two clans, Khori and Buriat, of which the shamans sing that they are derived from " the resting-place of the blue-grey bull," found a playmate on the shore of the Baikal, Ekerit, also an ancestor, of whom it is said that " the burbot (*Lota lota*) was his father, the shore his mother." [16]

According to another myth, the forefathers of the Buriats came down from Heaven and were nourished by a wild boar. It is further related that Khurmusta's daughter, who became enceinte from some unknown cause, came down to the earth in the form of a goat and gave birth to two sons and a daughter. [17]

What appear to be relics of totemism were found in Siberia among the Yakuts in the eighteenth century. Strahlenberg says: " Otherwise, each family regards a particular creature as sacred, such as the swan, the goose, the raven, etc., and such animals as are held sacred by a family are not eaten among its members, though others are free to do so." [18] Similarly, in an appendix " Concerning the Yakuts," which is said to be taken from " two old manuscripts " and which appeared in a Russian book published in 1844, *A Journey to Yakutsk*, each clan has its own particular protector or mediator, represented by an image of a stallion with white lips, a raven, a swan, etc.

These animals were never used as food.[19]   According to a third source such animals are the eagle and the crane.[20]

Probably, the family-names derived from the animal kingdom and the ownership-marks of certain North Siberian peoples denoting animals, are connected with these totemistic ideas.   But during the centuries and thousands of years of their use, the original significance of these matters has faded from the consciousness of the people.

Certain investigators have attempted to trace the rise of totemism from an old custom, known over nearly the whole world, of giving names taken from nature to children, often from the animal kingdom.   The most northern peoples of Siberia give their children even today names taken from some object which, at the moment when the soul was believed to have taken possession of the child, awakened the interest of the mother or those around her.   The Yenisei Ostiaks give their children the name of the object " on which the shadow (*ulvei*) of the child fell first." [21]

Further, it has been pointed out that in early times the difference between man and the animals was not regarded as unsurmountable.   In countless Siberian tales it is related how certain animals were once men and *vice versa*.   The Buriats say of the bear that it was formerly, a hunter or a shaman, which was later changed into a bear.   Should the animal so wish, it could regain its human form.   The Tungus say that when the beaver was a human being, it was a skilful archer.   According to the Altai Tatars the owl was a great shaman.   The Yenisei Ostiaks told me that the swan was originally a woman, and from that time the bird has retained menstruation.   Even certain fish, such as the burbot, are, according to the Buriats, human beings drowned in the water. The Buriats tell of a land in the north-east, where the men are born as dogs, larger, however, than ordinary dogs, while the opposite sex are born as ordinary women.[22]

Just as there are tales describing the origin of ancestors

PLATE LIX

Left. Breast-cloth of a Yakut shaman with metal objects attached.

Center. Lebed-Tatar shaman.

Right. Drum of Lebed-Tatar shaman.

(See page 514.)

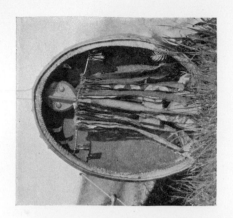

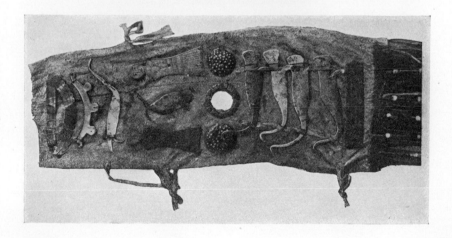

from certain animals, so it is related that the "power" of
the first female shamans was derived from an animal or a bird.
According to a Buriat myth the gods, when they created the
first people, sent a vulture to protect them against evil spirits.
But when the people did not understand its sacred mission,
and started to shoot at it, it returned to the gods complain-
ing: " I cannot protect mankind as they wish to kill me."
The gods then answered: " Go back and give thy wonderful power to some one of the earth's inhabitants." The
vulture flew down and saw a girl herding sheep. The bird
enticed her at once into a forest where it gave her its magic
powers. After this the girl began to see spirits and to keep
company with them. She received also a marvellous power
of foretelling both good and evil. When, after a time, she
returned home, her brother scolded her for having been out
so long with the sheep. The girl became angry and threatened
her brother, who shortly afterwards fell ill. The sister, who
had become a great shaman, was able, however, to cure him.[23]
According to another Buriat tale men knew nothing of sickness or death in the beginning, but were liable to these misfortunes through evil spirits. The gods then sent down an
eagle from heaven to protect the people. The eagle was
thus "the first shaman." The people did not, however,
understand the duty of the bird, so that it was forced to
return to heaven. The gods told the eagle to give its shaman
nature to the first person it should meet on the earth. The
eagle then approached a woman sleeping under a tree, who
had left her husband, and she became enceinte by the eagle.
The woman now returned to her husband, lived in complete
harmony with him, and gave birth to a son, who became later
"the first shaman." A variant of the same tale gives the
woman as "the first shaman." By receiving the eagle's powers,
she could see spirits and practise the profession of shaman.[24]

Among the Buriats one meets thus with two conceptions,
which might possibly throw light on the problem of totemism.

One is that the forefather of a clan originated from an animal; the other, that the magic powers of the first shaman woman or ancestress of the clan were obtained from some animal. Which of these should be regarded as the older conception? Judging from the Buriat myths, both are closely related. The "animal" which inspires the "first shaman woman" of the clan is also looked upon as a possible cause of her pregnancy. In this manner tales might arise of the animal-like ancestors of a clan. As the "animal's powers," according to an old belief, then go down in inheritance in the "first shaman woman's" clan (Yakut *ijä-usa*, "mother-clan"), or, in other words, lie dormant within the family, appearing only in its shamans, it becomes obvious that knowledge of their Utkha ("origin") is of importance to each clan and that it imposes certain duties on the clan. The animal whose "powers" or nature lie latent in a shaman clan becomes a special soul for the shaman. The Tungus conception of the "return of the 'loom'" points to a kind of migration of the soul. The Buriats call an animal of this description *khubilgan* ("metamorphosis," from *khubilkhu*, "to change oneself," "to take on another form"). In a variant of the myth of the "ancestor" of the Buriats, Bukha-Nojon ("Bull Master"), it is related that when this people still dwelt in the land of the Khalkha Mongols, a very large blue-grey ox appeared in their midst, the people accepting it as their *khubilgan*.[25] The conceptions of an "ancestor" and a *khubilgan* have thus been united in this myth.

One of the shaman's protective spirits in animal form is commonly regarded as being intimately connected with the shaman himself. Among certain Samoyeds in the Turukhansk District the shaman spirit has the shape of a reindeer which is bound by an invisible leather band to the shaman. This leather band can stretch to any length when the reindeer is sent out on a journey. It may happen, sometimes, that the spirit-reindeer of two shamans engage in warfare together (cf. the bull-fighting in the Buriat myth). Should one of the reindeer be killed in the conflict, the shaman owning the same dies.[26] That the "reindeer" is here a transformation of the shaman's soul, appears from a custom of the Yurak Samoyeds, after the death of a shaman, of preparing a wooden image of a reindeer, which is kept by the relatives wrapped up in the hide of a reindeer calf.

The Yakuts call a shaman animal of this description *ijä-kyl* ("mother-animal"). These may be of varying species. The mightiest shaman animals are said to be the stag, the stallion, the bear, the eagle, etc. Unlucky the shaman whose *ijä-kyl* is a wolf or a dog. The dog, it is said, never leaves the shaman in peace, but "gnaws with its teeth at his heart and tortures his body." When a new shaman has appeared, the others know this through having noticed the appearance of a new *ijä-kyl*. Only shamans can see these animals. When they quarrel, their "animals" fight together. An "animal war" may go on for several months or years. The one whose "animal" wins the fight emerges whole from the struggle, but, as said before, if one of the "animals" dies, its shaman owner dies too. The sickness of a shaman is often said to depend on a grave battle between shamans.[27]

Among the Dolgans standing under the influence of the Yakuts the same shaman spirit is met with under the same name. Although the shamans have many helping spirits in the shapes of different animals, each shaman has only one *ijä-kyl* upon which his life and death depend. This spirit-animal is said to appear to the shaman at the most three times in his life, viz., at his call to the office of shaman, in the middle of his shaman activity, and immediately before his death, when the spirit dies also. Should the animal die of any accidental cause, the death of the shaman follows soon after. The "mother animal" keeps always to the same place, for which reason it may happen that a strange shaman sees it while shamanizing. If the latter is an enemy of the animal's owner, he frightens the animal so that it dies, with fatal consequences to its owner (cf. similar beliefs of the Scandinavian Lapps).[28]

A further proof that the shaman's "animal," which is regarded as his necessary escort and means of conveyance to the other world, is intimately connected with his soul, is to be found in the description of the last journey of the Goldes, where the "reindeer" ridden by the soul of the deceased is the shaman himself.[29]

The forbidding of the killing of certain animals and the custom of burying them with ceremony where the body of one is found, would seem to depend on the fact that the animals in question are soul-animals of the types described above. For though soul-animals are often regarded as being invisible to the ordinary eye, they are most often connected with the corresponding material animals. This appears also from a Buriat tale about a great shaman and his nine sons. The father, who was blind, once sent his sons to a river to fish. " Ye will see there," he said, " seven fish, one of which is blind and is not to be touched, as it is my soul." The sons caught all the fish, however, but when they returned home, their father was dead.[30]

That all the " animals " regarded as helping the shaman are not *khubilgans,* but that there are numerous other helping-spirits is shown, further, by the following Buriat prayer: " Grey hare our runner, grey wolf our ambassador, bird Khon our *khubilgan,* eagle Khoto our messenger." [31]

Some light is thrown on the ideas of the different peoples regarding their shaman animals by the images prepared by them, those cut out of wood or, later, hammered also of iron, are more common than those which are drawn or painted. In the museum at Krasnoyarsk there is a Tungus shamanic object — a long chain of iron — the end of which is attached to a reindeer or deer made of ironplate, with birds' wings sticking out of its sides. On this animal sits a human being represent-

PLATE LX

Dress of a Yakut shaman (bird type). Front and
back views. (See page 514.)

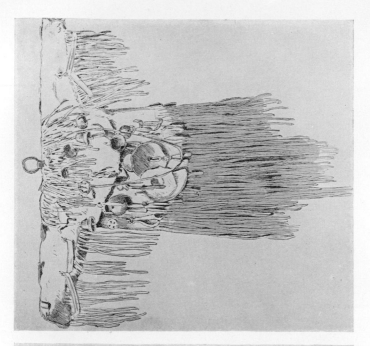

ing a shaman, with a square iron plate on his head, over which
a bird surrounded by nine small human-like objects is fastened.
The iron chain, to which, in addition, a bird and a reindeer
are attached, and which branches out into three thinner chains
with bells at their end, represents the spirit-journey of the
shaman.

When a Golde shaman intends to travel to the other world,
he must have the assistance of a mystic bird Koori and his
protecting spirit Buču. The bird resembles a crane, its image

FIG. 19. KOORI AND BUČU, SPIRIT-BIRDS OF A GOLDE SHAMAN

of wood being covered with the skin of a wild goat so that
only the head is uncovered. Buču is a human-like image with
a crooked leg and wings. The body and the wings of this
also are covered with wild-goat skin. Both these objects are
hung by the shaman in a shed erected specially for the occasion, the former in a horizontal, the latter in a vertical position. In these positions the spirit-animals are supposed to
make their journeys when they travel with the shaman. Koori
is said to carry the shaman's soul, while Buču is only an escort.
Even if the shaman could reach the world of the dead with-

out Koori, it would, as the people point out, be impossible for him to return without it.[32]

The Dolgans and the Tungus use a great many wooden images when shamanizing, which are prepared for one occasion only and which are regarded as being necessary helpers and protectors on the shaman's difficult spirit-journeys. According to the task and plans of the shaman, different images are made. When the Tungus on the Yenisei begin their shaman ceremonies, they always erect a special tent, in the middle of which a fire is lit. The shaman with his drum then takes up his position at the back of the tent, his face towards the fire, and before him, on the ground, a row of wooden objects is placed; on the right side a fish (*Stenodus leucichthus nelma*), a snake, a snail, and a bear; on the other side a fish (*Hucho taimen*), an otter, a wolf, and still another fish (*Lota lota*). The heads of these are pointed towards the fire. In addition, a snail is placed before him with its head towards the left. Outside the tent, on long poles erected round it, similar wooden figures are placed in the following order from the right: " the sun," a bird intended to represent the thunder, a cuckoo, and a swan. From the door opening to the left: a crane, " the moon," a loom and a duck. Each object has its special duty and all are necessary for each appearance of the shaman. During his song he lifts up in order the animals laid on the ground before him, drawing certain conclusions from the weight of each. For special tasks other images are also used, e.g., when the shaman has to escort the soul of some one deceased to the other world, he binds the " soul," that is to say, the image of a man, to a curious erection which would seem to be fitted with wings, and is erected behind the tent. The Dolgan shaman sometimes makes an image of his " mother-animal," *ijä-kyl*. Even at the sacrifices a wooden image is made both of the reindeer and the sacrificing shaman, who is to lead the sacrificed animal's soul to the gods. On the graves also of the Tungus, Dolgans and Yakuts, one

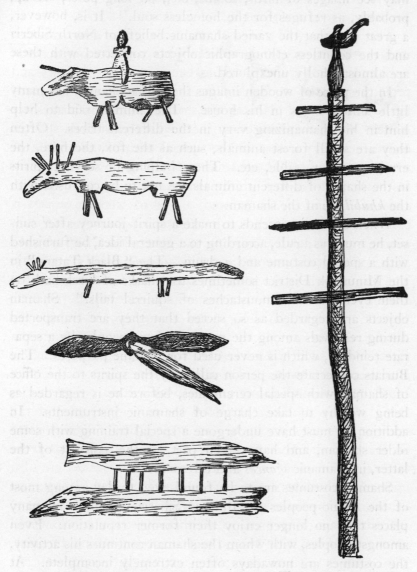

FIG. 20. DOLGAN SHAMAN-ATTRIBUTES AND THE WORLD-TREE WITH THE
TWO-HEADED LORD OF THE BIRDS

may see images of birds, looms, etc., on long poles, set up, probably, as refuges for the homeless soul.[33]   It is, however, a great pity that the varied shamanic beliefs of North Siberia and the countless ethnographic objects connected with these are almost wholly unexplored.

In the place of wooden images the Buriat shaman has many little animal-hides in his house.   The animals said to help him in his shamanizing vary in the different tribes.   Often they are small forest animals, such as the fox, the hare, the ermine, marten, sable, etc.   These helping or serving spirits in the shapes of different animals are not to be confused with the *khubilgan* of the shaman.

When a shaman intends to make a spirit-journey after sunset, he must, as a rule, according to a general idea, be furnished with a special costume and a drum.   The " Black Tatars " in the Minusinsk District sometimes use masks of birch-bark on their eyebrows and moustaches of squirrel tails.[34]   Shaman objects are regarded as so sacred that they are transported during removals among the more northern peoples by a separate reindeer, which is never used for profane purposes.   The Buriats consecrate the person called by the spirits to the office of shaman with special ceremonies, before he is regarded as being worthy to take charge of shamanic instruments.   In addition he must have undergone a special training with some older shaman, and have taken part, as the assistant of the latter, in shamanic *séances* and ceremonies.[35]

Shaman costumes are to be found even to-day among most of the Altaic peoples dwelling in Siberia, although in many places they no longer enjoy their former reputation.   Even amongst peoples, with whom the shaman continues his activity, the costumes are nowadays often extremely incomplete.   At times one sees shamans carrying out their duties in ordinary peasant dress, decorated perhaps for the occasion with a few ribbons or other objects from the real shaman costume.   Sometimes only the shaman head-dress has been retained.   The

PLATE LXI

Dress of a Tungus shaman (bird type) with metal decorations and fringes. Front and back views. (See page 514.)

FIG. 22. HEAD-DRESS OF
THE SOYOT SHAMAN
(BIRD TYPE)

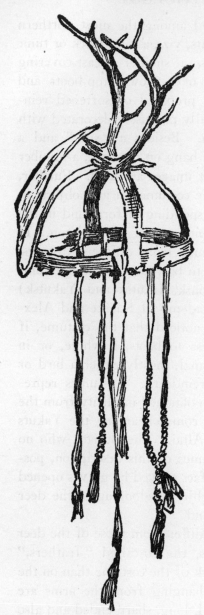

FIG. 21. HEAD-DRESS OF A YENISEI-
OSTIAK SHAMAN (REINDEER OR
STAG TYPE)

FIG. 23. TUNGUS SHA-
MAN-BOOT (BIRD TYPE)

complete costumes, best preserved among the most northern peoples, consist of several garments, viz., a long frock or tunic hanging down below the knees, a smaller breast-covering fastened under the chin, a cap or a crown, top-boots and gloves. All these garments are prepared of softened reindeer or other skin, and are generally profusely decorated with objects made of copper or iron. Besides a " sun " and a " moon," which in most costumes hang on the back, a number of human-like and bird-like spirit images are used. Further, in all the garments composing the costume, curious objects in beaten metal are sewn fast, corresponding in form and in the ideas of the people to the different parts of the skeleton. If one compares the shaman costumes from different districts, valuable collections of which are to be found in the museums of Siberia (Krasnoyarsk, Minusinsk, Irkutsk and Yakutsk) and, above all, in Petrograd (Academy of Science and Alexander III museums), it will be noticed that the costume, if complete, forms, from head-dress to boots, a whole, or in other words, represents some animal, mostly either a bird or a horned animal (a deer or a reindeer). Costumes representing both these types have been obtained in plenty from the Tungus. The bird type is most common among the Yakuts and many of the peoples at the Altai. The Buriats, who no longer seem to use shaman costumes of this description, possessed them at an earlier time, a fact proved by graves opened in their region, in which metal objects belonging to the deer type of shaman costume were found.

The costumes of the bird type differ from those of the deer type partly in the long fringes, the so-called " feathers," which are much longer on the back of the costume than on the front. Similar leather fringes hanging from the arms are said to represent " wings." Small, long, sharp-ended and also pipe-formed metal objects hanging in several rows on the back, are explained to be " bird's feathers." Naturally, the head-dress also is fringed with these. In the head-dress of

FIG. 24. TATAR SHAMAN (BIRD TYPE) IN MINUSINSK DISTRICT

this type in the Altai district one may at times even see the
head of a bird. The round brass buttons on the front of the
head-dress are " bird's eyes." The boots bear the same signs.
Tungus shaman boots of this type are decorated with bird's
feet sewn with yellow glass pearls, and having three or five
toes.

Specially characteristic of the deer or reindeer type is the
head-dress or crown with its high, upright, iron horns. The
fringes on the tunic are missing, or where these occur, are
shorter; the arms are altogether without them. Among the
Yenisei Ostiaks and the Dolgans the tail of the tunic ends
behind in a sharp point. Little pieces of iron sewn on to the
costume are called " hairs."

In the garments of each type, as may be seen from the
illustrations, there are numerous " bones " beaten in metal.
The skeleton plays, as is known, an important part in the
primitive soul-beliefs. On both sides of the front of the
tunic are seen " ribs " and, under the throat, " collar-bones."
Along the gloves, arms and boots the parts of the skeleton
belonging here are sewn. Naturally, the bird-type costume is
fitted with " bird's bones," the deer type with the deer
skeleton.

More difficult is the question, what bird the different bird-
costumes attempt to represent. It appears probable that although the dress represents an invisible spirit-bird, the people
see in it the counterfeit of some actual, living bird. A Yakut
shaman costume, described by Priklonskiy, is said to represent a vulture.[36] A Teleut shaman head-dress was covered
by the skin of an owl on which the head, wings and feathers
had been left intact.[37] Certain costumes bear also the identi-
fication marks of the hawk, eagle, etc.

Among the Yenisei Ostiaks, the shaman boots, the long
uppers of which reach over the thighs, are furnished with the
complete " bones " of the bear. This would seem to point to
a shaman costume representing a bear.[38] The crowns, how-

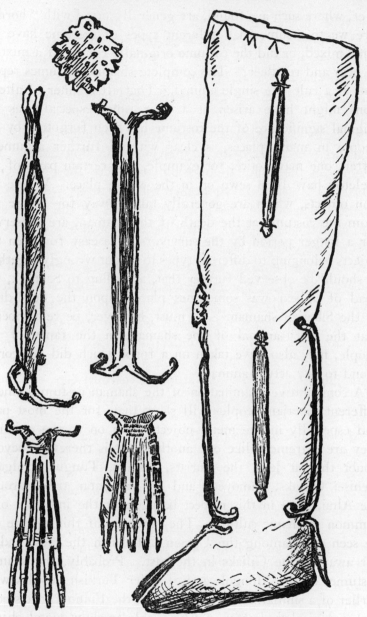

FIG. 25. LEFT BOOT OF YENISEI-OSTIAK SHAMAN (BEAR TYPE)
WITH ALL THE BONES OF BEAR'S LEFT LEGS

ever, where such are found, are generally fitted with "horns." Are we to assume that different types of costume have become mixed, or did the costume originally consist of a mixture of bear and reindeer? The complete shaman costumes represent as a rule one single animal. That all manner of alterations might have arisen at a later time, especially as the original significance of the costume has been forgotten by the people in many places, is clear without further argument. Often, one may notice, for example, that certain parts of the skeleton have been sewn on in the wrong place. Where the iron objects, which are generally taken away for future use from the costume at the death of the shaman, are preserved for a longer period by the survivors, it is easy for even the objects belonging to different types to be put wrongly together. It should be observed further that, according to Schrenk, the head of a bear was sometimes placed upon the head-dress of the Siberian shaman.[39] It must, however, be remembered that the spirit-animal of the shaman, in the fancy of the people, may also have taken on a form which did not correspond to any actual animal.

A comparative examination of the shaman costumes among different Siberian peoples will show that, for the most part, and especially in the metal objects sewn on to the costume, they are extremely like one another. It is therefore beyond doubt that at least the Buriats, Yakuts, Tungus, Dolgans, Yenisei Ostiaks, Samoyeds and certain Tatar tribes around the Altai, have in this respect been under the influence of a common shamanic culture. The influence of this culture can be seen even among the Ugrian Ostiaks in the west and as far away as the Giliaks in the east. Probably, the shaman costumes of the Mongols and of other Turkish peoples were earlier of a similar character. Among the Finno-Ugric stocks, archaeological finds have not been able to show metal objects which could prove the existence of similar shaman costumes among these peoples. Even in Siberia, however, shaman

PLATE LXII

Dress of a Yenisei Ostiak shaman (animal type). Back view. (See page 514.)

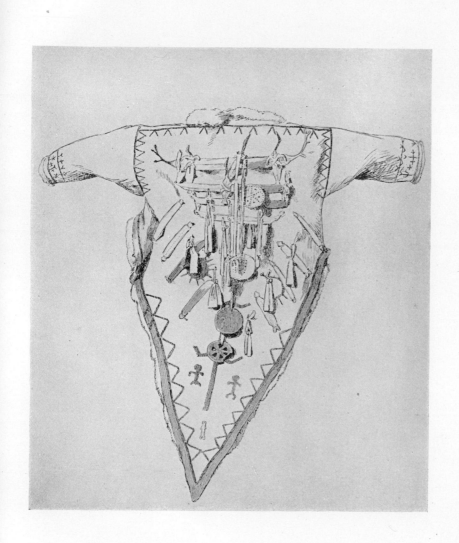

costumes seem to have existed at an earlier time, which in place of the metal objects were decorated with natural objects from the animal world. Thus, for example, among the Tatars of Minusinsk the wings of the owl have been seen on the back of a shaman costume and on the head-dress, and among the Yenisei Ostiaks the shamans formerly bore on their top-boots the natural paws of a bear instead of iron claws, and on their head-dress real horns.[40] Further, among the older types one may find costumes with "images" prepared in part from leather and bones. It would therefore seem probable that the shaman costumes of the Altaic race had practically the same form and purpose in a more primitive period.

But why should the shaman dress himself in the form of an animal for his mysteries? The answer to this question is given by the primitive peoples themselves. The Yakuts say that when the shaman takes on his bird-costume he himself receives the power of flying everywhere in the world. According to the Tungus, the costume of the shaman is his "shadow," or in other words, in this shape his soul travels on its spirit-journeys. Golde myths relate how a great bird came flying and alighted on a tree, and how by shaking its wings these became transformed into the iron feathers of the shaman costume.[41] The Yenisei Ostiaks call the shaman costume and the objects hanging on it, the "power" of the shaman. When the shaman puts on the long boots representing the feet of the bear, he believes himself to have acquired the "power" of the bear. While shamanizing he sometimes imitates the bear, regarded by the people in question as an extremely sacred animal.

It is probable that the shaman costume, which, at least regarding its form, goes in inheritance in the shaman's family and which is sometimes called "god" (Tangara) by the Yakuts, originally represented the shaman's soul-animal or *ijä-kyl*.

In his songs the shaman often calls his drum some animal,

on which he says he is travelling. Some call it their " horse " or their " deer," some their " loom " or their " eagle." The Karagass shaman from the Sayan mountain, who covers his drum with the skin of the Siberian deer, sings: " I am a shaman and ride on the wild deer." In certain myths it is said that the shaman " flies on his drum " or " rides " on it. The Yenisei Ostiaks, who use reindeer-calf skin for the cover of their drums, fasten iron " reindeer ribs " to the open side, adding to these each time a new cover has to be procured for the drum. In the inside of the wooden frame of the drum one may often see a picture of a reindeer, painted in alderbark juice, or carved with a knife.

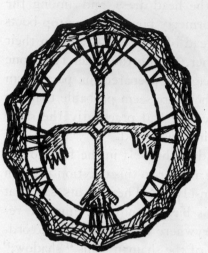

FIG. 26.   SHAMAN-DRUM WITH BIRD-SHAPED HAND-GRIP

It is on the whole an interesting feature of the art of the Siberian peoples, that objects in which the hide of some animal has been used, are often decorated with pictures of the same animal. Thus, for example, the end of a drumstick or the handle of a shaman hammer is engraved with the nose of the forest animal whose skin has been used for the cover of the hammer.

Like the shaman costume the inside of the drum is furnished with all kinds of spirit-pictures, among others, with small human- or bird-like images of metal, the number of which depends on the visions of its owner, becoming more numerous as the shaman becomes older. Certain peoples, such as the Abakan and Altai Tatars, also paint pictures, intended to represent the Heaven and the underground, with shaman animals, hunting trips, etc., on the skin of the drum.⁴² The Buriat

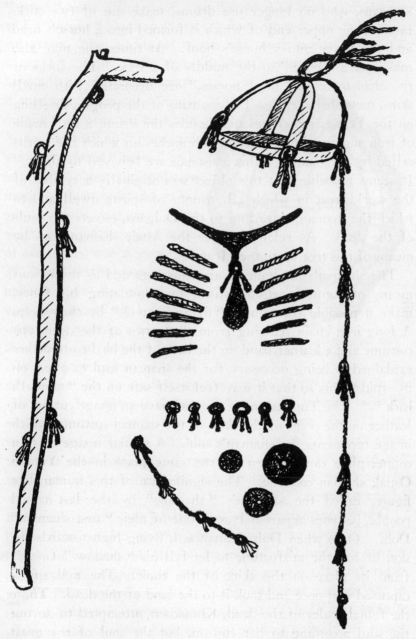

FIG. 27. HOBBY-HORSE OF A BURIAT
SHAMAN

FIG. 28. RELICS OF A BURIAT SHA-
MAN FOUND IN THE EARTH

shamans, who no longer use drums, make use of two sticks instead, the upper end of which is formed into a horse's head and the lower into a horse's hoof. At times one may also make out a " knee " in the middle of a stick. The sticks of the shaman, called his " horses," are decorated with small skins, metal bells, etc.[43] The shamans of the peoples dwelling on the Yenisei sometimes use, besides the drum, a staff made of iron and furnished with cross-branches on which the spirits called by the shaman to his assistance are believed to alight.[44] It seems probable that this object was originally a symbol of the world-tree, in which all manner of spirits dwell and to which the shaman, according to the Dolgans, escorts the souls of the dead. As related earlier the Altaic shaman rises by means of this tree up to the Heavens.

The shaman's implements are thus regarded as mysterious means of communication, which, by stimulating his fancy, make it possible for him to " fly and travel " by their help. A long iron chain hanging from the crown of the deer type costume and a leather band on the back of the bird costume are explained as being necessary for the shaman soul to grasp on its rapid flights so that it may feel itself safe on the " animal's back." [45] The Tungus on the Yenisei have an image cut out of leather on the point of the skirt of the shaman costume, which image represents the shaman's soul. A similar image of thin copper-plate can be seen on the same place in the Yenisei Ostiak shaman costume. The significance of this human-like figure, called the shaman's " shadow " by the last-named people, becomes apparent from a tale of their " first shaman," Doh. Once when Doh shamanized, flying high towards the sky, he had the misfortune to let fall his " shadow " (ulvei) from its place on the skirt of the tunic. The evil spirits captured it at once and took it to the land of the dead. There the female ruler of the dead, Khosadam, attempted to devour the soul according to her custom, but the soul of the great shaman was not so easy to destroy, and Khosadam broke a

PLATE LXIII

Drum of a Yakut shaman, showing inner and outer sides. (See page 522.)

PLATE LXIII

Drum of a Yakut shaman, showing inner and outer sides. (See page 522.)

tooth in trying. This made her angry and from spite she nailed the soul by its hands and feet to a tree, making it thus impossible for it to return to the shaman's body.[46]

With the assistance of the many objects already described, the shaman's soul is regarded as being able to move with the greatest ease anywhere on the earth, in heaven, and in the underworld. By its rapid journeys, it can procure supernatural knowledge, hidden to ordinary mortals. The latter are, therefore, in a very great degree dependent on the knowledge and power of the shaman. When they are going out to hunt or fish, the shaman has to find out what the weather will be like and where the fish or game are hiding just then. When an enemy draws near, he must discover beforehand the intentions of the latter. One of his most difficult tasks, however, is said to be the seeking after and recovery of the souls of the sick, which have too early left their suffering bodies. He must then undertake the difficult journey to the underworld, in order to propitiate the spirits and save the soul. Thither he must also, when fate has so decreed, escort the soul of the dead to the circle of those who have died at an earlier time.

In his songs, of which up to the present too few have been recorded, the shaman describes to those present the strange sights and adventures, the trials and dangers which he must experience and win through on his difficult journeys in the world of spirits. With tense attention the spectators follow his wild, fantastic song, when, as though drunk with the intermittent rattle and thunder of the drum, he dances and hops in the flickering light of a hearth-fire in the dark and mystic night of the primeval forest. These wild ceremonies, stimulated by a diseased imagination, form the most characteristic, though at the same time the least known and the most subjective part, of the mythology of these primitive peoples.

NOTES

FINNO–UGRIC

Citation by author's name or by title of a work refers to the same in the various sections of the Bibliography. Where an author has written several works, they are distinguished as [a], [b], etc. Where Roman numerals precede these letters they refer to the sections of the Bibliography.

CHAPTER I

1. Reuterskiöld [b], pp. 36, 59.
2. Charuzin, " Medv. prisyaga," pp. 32–3.
3. Graan, p. 19.
4. Bartenev, p. 86.
5. Länkelä, pp. 274–5.
6. Donner [b], pp. 140–1.
7. Holmberg [v b], p. 11.
8. Gondatti [b], p. 64.
9. Paasonen, " Über die urspr. seelenvorst," pp. 2, 27.
10. Novitskiy, p. 106; Karjalainen [c], p. 323.
11. Lundius, p. 7.
12. Holmberg [v b], p. 11.
13. Holmberg [vi a], pp. 14–15.
14. Patkanov, i. 148–9; ii. 32.
15. Munch, pp. 4–5.
16. Holmberg [iv b], p. 14.
17. Nalimov's Collections in the Archives of the Finno-Ugric Society.
18. Holmberg [vi a], pp. 14–16; cf. Gavrilov [b], pp. 124–5.
19. Holmberg [v b], pp. 29–30.
20. Turi, p. 150.
21. Nalimov [b], pp. 4, 8, 13–14; Popov, " Zyryane," p. 59; Kandinskiy, " Iz materialov," p. 107–8; Fuchs, p. 239.
22. Paasonen, " Über die urspr. seelenvorst.," pp. 19–20, 25.
23. Krohn [iii g], pp. 164–6.
24. Qvigstad [a], i. 49–50.
25. Cf. Wasiljev, " Übersicht," p. 102.
26. Jessen, pp. 34–9; Leem, p. 417; Holmberg [iv b], pp. 19–20.
27. Karjalainen [c], pp. 45–6.
28. Mainov [c], pp. 12–4; Wasiljev, " Übers.," pp. 101–2; Patkanov, i. 152.

Chapter II

1. Häyhä, p. 16; Varonen, *Vainajainpalv.*, p. 57; Wiedemann, p. 309.
2. Nalimov's Collections.
3. Holmberg [v b], pp. 12–13.
4. Lukkarinen [c], p. 1; Nikolskiy, p. 64.
5. Magnitskiy, p. 159; Nikolskiy, p. 65; Holmberg [v b], p. 15.
6. Varonen, *Vainaj.*, p. 77.
7. Holmberg [v b], p. 14.
8. Varonen, *Vainaj.*, p. 93; Lukkarinen [c], p. 2.
9. Reuterskiöld [b], p. 36.
10. Karjalainen [c], p. 64.
11. Nikolskiy, p. 65.
12. Högström, p. 207.
13. Molyarov [c], p. 741.
14. Varonen, *Vainaj.*, pp. 59–60.
15. Rheen, p. 46.
16. Charuzin [iv b], p. 324.
17. According to T. Lehtisalo.
18. Wiedemann, p. 310; Varonen, *Vainaj.*, p. 68.
19. Holmberg [vi a], p. 20, [v b], p. 13; Varonen, *Vainaj.*, p. 68.
20. Turi, p. 150.
21. Karjalainen [c], p. 77.
22. Holmberg [vi a], p. 26.
23. Gavrilov [b], p. 184; Holmberg [vi a], p. 26; Varonen, *Vainaj.*, p. 93.
24. Helland [a], ii. 315; Varonen, *Vainaj.*, p. 90.
25. Varonen, p. 96.
26. Smirnov [v b], xi. 538; Holmberg [v b], p. 17; Varonen, *Vainaj.*, p. 93; cf. Karjalainen, [c], pp. 85–7.
27. Varonen, *Vainaj.*, pp. 92–3, 94.
28. Charuzin [iv b], pp. 323–4; Leem, p. 499.
29. Karjalainen [c], pp. 84–6; Holmberg [vi a], p. 27.
30. Turi, p. 195.
31. Kolmodin, "Folktro," in *Lapparne*, iii. 16.
32. Karjalainen [c], p. 78.
33. Smirnov [v b], xi. 541; Varonen, *Vainaj.*, p. 94; Holmberg [v b], pp. 15–16.
34. Holmberg [v b], p. 16.
35. According to Lehtisalo's Collections.
36. Holmberg [vi a], p. 27.
37. Smirnov [v b], xi. 544; Holmberg [vi a], p. 27, [v b], p. 17; Varonen, *Vainaj.*, pp. 88–9.

38. Holmberg [v b], p. 17.
39. Magnitskiy, p. 166.
40. Holmberg [vi a], pp. 25–6, 45.
41. Varonen, *Vainaj.*, pp. 97–101.
42. Holzmayer, " Osiliana," in *VGEG* vii. 82; Varonen, *Vainaj.*, pp. 101–2. A corresponding custom is known among the Swedes (Nils Lithberg, " Allmogeforskningen och etnologin," *Fataburen*, 1919, Stockholm).
43. Hornborg, " Karsikoita," in *Vir.*, ii. 93–7; Holmberg [iii b], pp. 8–34.
44. Karjalainen [c], pp. 85, 89.
45. Gondatti [b], p. 67; Karjalainen [c], pp. 89–90.
46. Novitskiy, p. 45.
47. According to Prof. H. Paasonen.
48. Karjalainen [c], p. 65; Patkanov, i. 144.
49. Cf. Molyarov [c], p. 744.
50. Varonen, *Vainaj.*, p. 90.
51. ib., p. 94.
52. Karjalainen [c], pp. 70–1.
53. Varonen, *Vainaj.*, p. 61; Holmberg [v b], p. 13; Smirnov [v b], xi. 538.
54. Holmberg [v b], p. 14.
55. Molyarov [c], pp. 742–3; Holmberg [v b], p. 14.
56. Semenov, p. 34.
57. Holmberg [vi a], pp. 22–3.
58. Karjalainen [c], p. 65; Yakovlev, p. 66.
59. Folklore Collections in the Archives of the Kalevala-Society.
60. Holmberg [v b], p. 16.
61. ib., p. 16.
62. Karjalainen [c], pp. 74–6.
63. Holmberg [iv b], p. 15.
64. Varonen, *Vainaj.*, pp. 62–3.
65. Schwindt, pp. 185–8.
66. Karjalainen [c], pp. 66–7; 104–6.
67. Varonen, *Vainaj.*, p. 64.
68. Turi, p. 149; Vahl, p. 134.
69. Niurenius, p. 27; Tornaeus, p. 40; Aspelin, *Suom.-ugril. muinaist. alkeita*, p. 242; Patkanov, i. 142.
70. Setälä [b], p. 96.
71. Varonen, *Vainaj.*, pp. 103–7.
72. Holmberg [vi a], p. 24.
73. Ryčkov, p. 90.
74. Holmberg [v b], p. 16.
75. Leem, p. 407; Tornaeus, pp. 40–1; Charuzin [iv b], p. 323.

CHAPTER III

1. Holzmayer, pp. 81–2; Varonen, *Vainaj.*, pp. 34–5.
2. Lundius, pp. 34–40.
3. Qvigstad [a], i. 56–7.
4. Rheen, p. 47.
5. Graan, pp. 72–3.
6. Rheen, p. 47.
7. Lundius, p. 21.
8. Reuterskiöld [b], p. 91.
9. Qvigstad [a], i. 59.
10. Lundius, p. 29.
11. According to Lehtisalo.
12. Müller, *Das Leben*, p. 203.
13. Pallas, *Reise*, iii. 55.
14. Karjalainen [c], p. 81.
15. Gondatti [b], p. 67.
16. Karjalainen [c], pp. 90–1.
17. Munkácsi [vii d], p. 95.
18. Karjalainen [c], p. 92.
19. Novitskiy, *Kratk. opis.*, p. 46; cf. Müller, *Das Leben*, p. 204.
20. Castrén, *Reisen*, i. 296; Pallas, *Reise*, iii. 59–60.
21. Finsch, p. 547; Karjalainen [c], p. 92.
22. According to Lehtisalo.
23. Cf. Chapter xviii.
24. Karjalainen [c], pp. 116–8.
25. Rheen, p. 47.
26. Varonen, *Vainaj.*, p. 100.
27. Holmberg [vi a], p. 31.
28. Smirnov [vii b], p. 181.
29. Wasiljev, " Übersicht," p. 104.
30. Varonen, *Vainaj.*, pp. 81–2.
31. Nalimov's Collections.
32. Olearius, pp. 344–5.
33. Müller, *Sammlung*, iii. 144.
34. Varonen, *Vainaj.*, pp. 77–81.
35. Georgi [b], p. 57.
36. Dobrotvorskiy, pp. 577–8.
37. Holmberg [v b], p. 19.
38. Holmberg [vi a], p. 34.
39. Nalimov's Collections.
40. Smirnov [v b], xi. 545–6.
41. Groundstroem, p. 318; cf. Varonen, *Vainaj.*, pp. 109–11;
Lukkarinen [c], p. 7.

42. Krohn [iii g], p. 51.
43. Molyarov [c], pp. 745–7; Yakovlev, p. 72.
44. Holmberg [v b], p. 25.
45. Gorodskoy, p. 33.
46. Smirnov [v b], xi. 545–8.
47. Smirnov [vi a], pp. 243–4; Nalimov [b], p. 6; Rogov, p. 127.
48. Lukkarinen [c], pp. 9–10.
49. Forström, pp. 401–2.
50. Holmberg [vi a], p. 36.
51. Wichmann [a], p. 42.
52. Holmberg [v b], p. 26.
53. Wichmann [a], pp. 42–4; Gavrilov [a], pp. 40–1.
54. Smirnov [v b], xi. 550–1.
55. Nalimov [b], p. 5.
56. According to Paasonen.
57. Holmberg [vi a], pp. 50, 53–4.
58. Holmberg [v b], pp. 28–9.

Chapter IV

1. Holmberg [vi a], pp. 32–3.
2. Gavrilov [a], pp. 42–6; Holmberg [vi a], pp. 46–7, [v b], pp. 26–7.
3. Pervuchin, ii. 113–7.
4. Nurminskiy, p. 269.
5. Kallas, pp. 91–2.
6. Castrén, E., Beskrifning, p. 76.
7. Varonen, Vainaj., pp. 140–167.
8. Fellman, J., ii. 43, 113.
9. Turi, pp. 134–5; Helland [a], ii. 294; Jessen, p. 81.
10. Graan, pp. 67–8; cf. Rheen, pp. 27–8.
11. Fellman, I., i. 404.
12. Högström, pp. 188–9; cf. Leem, p. 482.
13. Fritzner, p. 157.
14. Krohn [iii g], p. 52.
15. Paasonen [v d], p. 843.
16. Holmberg [v b], pp. 29–30.
17. Qvigstad [a], ii. 27.

Chapter V

1. Charuzin [iv b], p. 324.
2. Holmberg [v b], p. 12.
3. Karjalainen [c], p. 124.

4. Paasonen [v d], p. 843; Smirnov [v a], pp. 117–21.

5. Karjalainen [c], p. 123.

6. According to Lehtisalo.

7. Karjalainen [c], pp. 130–1.

8. Smirnov [v b], xi. 550–1.

9. Paasonen [v d], p. 843; Holmberg [vi a], p. 19.

10. Karjalainen [c], pp. 121–2.

11. Lukkarinen [c], p. 17.

12. Holmberg [v b], p. 12.

13. Reuterskiöld [b], pp. 35–6, 67 etc.; Jessen, pp. 29–30, 71; Leem, p. 418.

14. Unwerth [c], pp. 29–36.

15. Reuterskiöld [b], p. 37.

16. Leem, p. 477.

17. Qvigstad [a], i. 49.

18. Wiklund, "Saivo," pp. 59–74.

19. Karjalainen [c], pp. 123–4.

20. Krohn [iii g], pp. 273–5; cf. Eisen [b], pp. 34–5.

21. According to Collections in the Archives of the Kalevala Society.

22. Vasilyev [b], x. 16.

23. Strahlenberg, p. 76.

24. Karjalainen [c], pp. 126–7.

25. Charuzin [iv b], pp. 197–8.

26. Holzmayer, pp. 48–9; Eisen [v b], pp. 32–3.

27. Brummer, "Über die Bannungsorte," *MSFO*, pp. 43, 44, 45 ff. and "Versverzeichnisse," *ib.*, pp. 19–20, 22–3.

28. *Suomen kansan vanhat runot*, i. 4, n. 870, (*Bor.* ii. 37).

29. Stadling, p. 26.

30. Veniaminov, I., *Zapiski ob atchinskich Aleutach i Kološach* (1840), iii. 56–60; cf. *The Mythology of All Races*, x. 249.

Chapter VI

1. Nalimov [c], pp. 5, 11

2. Karjalainen [b], p. 83.

3. According to Lehtisalo's Collections.

4. Genetz, *Wörterbuch*, p. 156.

5. Rheen, p. 15; Graan, p. 40.

6. Karjalainen [b], pp. 85–6.

7. Krohn [iii g], p. 147.

8. Tuderus, p. 12.

9. Lundius, p. 18.

10. Turi, p. 138; Kolmodin, p. 3.

11. Charuzin, "Medv. prisyaga," pp. 30 ff.
12. Wiklund [iv a], pp. 27–46.
13. Wiklund, ib., p. 30.
14. Qvigstad [a], i. 28.
15. Reuterskiöld [b], p. 37.
16. Wiklund [iv a], p. 46.
17. Rheen, p. 44.
18. Wiklund [iv a], p. 45.
19. Högström, p. 208; Wiklund [iv a], p. 39.
20. Niurenius, p. 18.
21. Reuterskiöld [b], p. 36.
22. Wiklund [iv a], p. 38.
23. ib. pp. 31–2.
24. Högström, p. 210.
25. Wiklund [iv a], p. 44.
26. Högström, p. 210.
27. Graan, p. 67, n.
28. Cf. Wiklund [iv a], p. 45.
29. Rheen, p. 46.
30. Lundius, p. 28.
31. Charuzin [iv b], p. 204.
32. Krohn [iii g], p. 163.
33. Karjalainen [b], pp. 85–7; cf. Patkanov, i. 125 ff.
34. Gondatti [a], pp. 74–87; Kannisto [a], pp. 213–37.
35. Karjalainen [b], pp. 86–7.
36. ib. p. 86, n. 2.
37. Krohn [iii g], p. 149 ff.
38. According to Lehtisalo's Collections.
39. Karjalainen [b], p. 88.
40. Fellman, I., i. 392.
41. Kolmodin, p. 5.
42. Niurenius, p. 19.
43. According to Lehtisalo's Collections.
44. Kolmodin, p. 4.
45. Högström, p. 183.
46. Wiklund [iv a], p. 37.

Chapter VII

1. Rosen, pp. 177–9.
2. Andersson, p. 31.
3. Tornaeus, pp. 26–7; Högström, p. 193; Rheen, p. 42.
4. Tuderus, p. 14.
5. Graan, p. 10.

6. Leem, p. 443.
7. Högström, p. 194.
8. Fellman, I., i. 405–6.
9. Holmberg [iv b], p. 32.
10. Andersson, p. 44.
11. Yaščenko, p. 31.
12. Fellman, J., ii. 146.
13. Schefferus, p. 100.
14. Högström, pp. 183, 197 n.
15. Tornaeus, p. 26.
16. Kildal, p. 455.
17. Jessen, p. 48.
18. Rheen, p. 39.
19. Holmberg [iv b], p. 35.
20. Qvigstad [a], ii. 89.
21. Tornaeus, p. 28.
22. Fellman, J., ii. 66.
23. Andelin, p. 274.
24. Yaščenko, pp. 31–2.
25. Charuzin [iv b], pp. 186–8; Yaščenko, p. 23.
26. Holmberg [iv b], p. 36; Graan, p. 63.
27. Rheen, p. 42.
28. Fellman, J., ii. 19–20.
29. Andersson, p. 44.
30. Tornaeus, pp. 26–7.
31. Appelgren, p. 50.
32. *ATPS*, xvii, 4 : 25; Fellman, I., i. 340, 342; Högström, pp. 190–1.
33. Högström, p. 192.
34. Rheen, pp. 39–40; Niurenius, p. 21.
35. Tuderus, pp. 14–5.
36. Qvigstad [a], ii. 9, 12, 34, 88–9.
37. Genetz, *Wörterbuch*, pp. xliv-xlv, 113.
38. Holmberg [iv b], pp. 41–2.
39. Rheen, p. 59; Jessen, p. 45; Düben, p. 260; Kolmodin, p. 27; Qvigstad [a], ii. 8 n.; Tuderus, p. 17.
40. Leem p. 441; Holmberg [iv b], pp. 42–3.

Chapter VIII

1. Donner [b], pp. 134–5.
2. Karjalainen [c], pp. 139–53; Patkanov, i. 106–8.
3. Charuzin, " Očerki," p. 262.
4. Hämäläinen, " Epif. Viis. tied.," pp. 39–40.

5. Ryčkov, p. 158.
6. Gavrilov [a], pp. 61–2; Wichmann [a], p. 25.
7. Aminoff, " Reseber.," p. 236.
8. Nalimov [b], pp. 4–5.
9. Lukkarinen [a], p. 6.
10. Wichmann [a], p. 25.
11. Bogayevskiy [b], p. 79.
12. Gavrilov, [a], p. 62.
13. Pervuchin, ii. 7–9; cf. Vereščagin [d], pp. 94–5.
14. Micheyev, p. 899.
15. Wichmann [a], p. 25.
16. Vereščagin [c], pp. 175–6.
17. Gavrilov [b], p. 152.
18. Ryčkov, p. 160.
19. Georgi [b], pp. 60–1.
20. Luppov [b], pp. 536–7.
21. Wasiljev, pp. 52–3; Bogayevskiy [a], p. 29.
22. Aminoff, " Reseber.," p. 236.
23. Bogayevskiy [a], p. 107.
24. Molyarov [a], p. 256.
25. Ryčkov, p. 160.
26. Ramstedt, p. 206.
27. Vasilyev [b], pp. 5–6.
28. Georgi [a], ii. 846, 843.
29. Buch, " Über den Tõnnis-cultus," pp. 5–13; Jürgens, pp. 1–9.
30. Voionmaa, p. 504.

Chapter IX

1. Veniamin, [b], pp. 116, 122–6.
2. Donner [d].
3. According to Lehtisalo.
4. Donner [b], pp. 61–3.
5. Pallas, *Reise*, iii. 61.
6. Karjalainen [c], pp. 158–207.
7. ib. p. 132.
8. Novitskiy, pp. 51, 83–5.
9. Karjalainen [c], pp. 214–36.
10. Hämäläinen, " Epif. Viis. tied.," p. 40.
11. Müller, iii. 345; Pallas, *Reise*, iii. 480; Georgi [b], p. 58.
12. Wichmann [a], p. 18.
13. Buch, " Die Wotjäken," p. 588; cf. Bogayevskiy [a], p. 25.
14. Gavrilov [a], pp. 32–3.
15. Buch, p. 588.

16. Bogayevskiy, *Očerki*, p. 161.
17. Miropolskiy, p. 362.
18. Bogayevskiy, *Očerki*, p. 161.
19. Bechterev, *VE* ix. 158.
20. Wasiljev, pp. 30–2.
21. ib. pp. 24, 121.
22. Hämäläinen, " Epif. Viis. tied.," p. 40.
23. Ostrovskiy, p. 37.
24. Bechterev, *VE* ix. 157.
25. Georgi [b], p. 59.
26. Wasiljev, p. 32.
27. Georgi [b], p. 59.
28. Wichmann [a], p. 16.
29. Cf. Hämäläinen, " Tšer. uhritap.," pp. 4–8.
30. Kuznecov [e].
31. Paasonen [v d], p. 847.
32. ib. pp. 843–4.
33. Krohn, J., *Suom. suv. pak. jumalanp.*, pp. 28–31.

Chapter X

1. Genetz, *Wörterb.*, p. xli; Charuzin [iv b], pp. 152, 240; Reuterskiöld [b], pp. 25, 107–8.
2. Pervuchin i. 89–91; Wichmann [a], p. 32; Miropolskiy, p. 353.
3. Holmberg [vi a], pp. 146–8.
4. Georgi [b], p. 62; cf. Gavrilov [a], pp. 58–9.
5. Wasiljev, pp. 77–80.
6. Pervuchin, i. 92–4; Wichmann [a], p. 32; Miropolskiy, pp. 354, 361.
7. Vereščagin [c], p. 85.
8. Gavrilov [a], p. 63; Pervuchin, i. 96.
9. Satrapinskiy, p. 21; Wichmann [a], pp. 29–30; Holmberg [vi a], p. 150.
10. Kandinskiy, pp. 108–9; Yanovič, pp. 54–5; Rogov, p. 102.
11. Fuchs, p. 242; Popov, p. 59; Smirnov [vi a], p. 281.
12. Holmberg [v b], pp. 34–6.
13. Paasonen [v d], p. 845.
14. Holmberg [v b], pp. 58–9.
15. Paasonen [v d], p. 845.
16. Lukkarinen [a], p. 4.
17. ib. pp. 1–2.
18. Krohn [iii g], pp. 86–7.
19. Lukkarinen [a], pp. 3–4.

20. Krohn [iii g], pp. 86–7.
21. ib. p. 95.
22. ib. pp. 95–6.
23. Holmberg [vi a], p. 151.
24. Lukkarinen [a], pp. 19–23.
25. Helland [a], ii. 304; Fellman, J., ii. 158–9.
26. Krohn [iii g], p. 97.
27. Eisen [b], pp. 133–43; Holzmayer, pp. 11–14, 16–17, 48.
28. Gavrilov [a], p. 45.
29. Krohn [iii g], p. 100.
30. ib. p. 99; corresponding beliefs are known also among the Volga-Finns.
31. Kallas, p. 82, cf. pp. 73, 80.
32. Ramstedt, p. 206.
33. Butuzov [b], p. 486; Yanovič, p. 55.
34. Šachmatov, p. 146.

Chapter XI

1. Reuterskiöld [b], pp. 14, 33; Qvigstad [a], p. 27.
2. Reuterskiöld [b], pp. 89, 37.
3. Charuzin [iv b], p. 152.
4. Genetz, *Wörterb.*, pp. xxxix-xl, 175.
5. Charuzin [iv b], p. 152.
6. Friis [c], p. 95; Reuterskiöld [b], p. 99; Helland [a], ii. 230.
7. Charuzin [iv b], p. 152; Genetz, *Wörterb.*, p. xli.
8. Qvigstad [a], i. 46; Wiklund, "Saivo," pp. 49–50, 51–3.
9. Helland [a], ii. 261, 318; Wiklund, "Saivo," pp. 50–1.
10. Turi, pp. 210–2; Wiklund, "Saivo," pp. 51, 59.
11. Donner [d].
12. Karjalainen [c], pp. 282–3.
13. ib. pp. 376–7.
14. ib. pp. 373–6.
15. ib. pp. 377–8.
16. Pervuchin, i. 76–86; Vereščagin [d], p. 80, [c], p. 86.
17. Wichmann [a], p. 31.
18. Vereščagin [d], p. 53 and [a], pp. 48–51.
19. ib. pp. 45–7, [d], p. 80.
20. Pervuchin, i. 88–9.
21. Wichmann [a], pp. 11–2.
22. Pervuchin, i. 88.
23. Smirnov [vi a], pp. 268–272, 276–281; Žakov, pp. 70–1; Fuchs, pp. 236–8; Yanovič, pp. 53–5.

24. Holmberg [vi a], p. 157.
25. Vasilyev [b], pp. 16–18.
26. Holmberg [v b], pp. 37–8.
27. ib. pp. 38–9.
28. Sněžnitskiy [a], p. 631.
29. Krohn [iii g], pp. 72–4.
30. Eisen [b], pp. 78–80.
31. Holmberg [ii b], p. 238 n.
32. Ramstedt, " Bergtscher. Sprachst.," p. 206.
33. Holmberg [v b], p. 39.
34. Aminoff, " Reseber.," p. 231.
35. Lukkarinen [d], p. 142–3.
36. Charuzin [iv b], p. 208.
37. Lundius, p. 18.
38. Holmberg [v b], pp. 54, 57.
39. Krohn [iii g], p. 130.
40. Milkovič, " Byt i věrov.," p. 5.
41. Setälä [a], pp. 46–7, n. 1; Yakovlev, p. 48.
42. Genetz, *Wörterb.*, p. xl.

Chapter XII

1. Andelin, p. 275; Leem, pp. 333–4; Friis, *Lex. lapp.*, p. 39, and [b], pp. 33–4.
2. Holmberg [ii b], pp. 36–7; Helland [a], ii. 291.
3. Fritzner, p. 159.
4. Fellman, J., ii. 125; Lindahl-Öhrling, p. 285.
5. Kildal, p. 458; Reuterskiöld [b], pp. 57, 98.
6. Genetz, *Wörterb.*, pp. xli-xlii; Holmberg [iv b], pp. 88–9.
7. Charuzin [iv b], p. 152; Kildal, p. 458.
8. Donner [b], p. 130, and [d].
9. According to Lehtisalo's Collections.
10. Patkanov, i. 111; Polyakov [a], p. 38.
11. Karjalainen [c], pp. 291–2.
12. ib. pp. 290–1.
13. Gondatti [b], p. 63; Holmberg [ii b], p. 60.
14. ib. pp. 58–9.
15. ib. pp. 64–74; Pervuchin, i. 72–6.
16. Fuchs, pp. 234–5; Žakov, pp. 72–3; Popov, p. 58; Yanovič, p. 55.
17. Setälä [a], pp. 10–23.
18. Holmberg [v b], pp. 39–42.
19. Smirnov [v b], p. 278, 282.
20. Eisen [g]; Holmberg [ii b], 160–73.

21. Holmberg, ib. pp. 191–211; 217–8.
22. Castrén, *Nord. Reisen*, iii. 85.
23. Lukkarinen [b], p. 49.
24. Krohn [iii e], p. 132.
25. Wiedemann, p. 419.
26. Holmberg [v b], pp. 41–2.
27. Paasonen, "Über d. urspr. Seelenvorst.," p. 13.
28. Kolmodin, p. 5.
29. Holmberg [ii b], p. 99.
30. Kolmodin, p. 32.
31. Donner [b], p. 95.
32. Žakov, p. 72.
33. Holmberg [ii b], pp. 189–90.
34. Saarimaa, p. 92.
35. Holmberg [ii b], p. 196.
36. Melnikov [c], x. 411.
37. Holmberg [v b], pp. 49–50.
38. Gutslaff, pp. 24–6, 32 ff.
39. Smirnov [v b], p. 322.
40. Holmberg [ii b], pp. 112–3, 149–52, 230–2.
41. Aminoff, "Reseb.," p. 234.
42. Wichmann, [a], p. 31.
43. Holmberg [v b], pp. 41, 58.

Chapter XIII

1. Veniamin [b], p. 116 n., 50.
2. Holmberg [v b], pp. 43–4; Karjalainen [vii c], pp. 296–306.
3. Donner [vii b], p. 129; Karjalainen [vii c], pp. 315–21.
4. Holmberg [vi a], p. 170.
5. Paasonen [v d], p. 844.
6. Karjalainen [c], p. 299.
7. Holmberg [vi a], p. 171.
8. Holmberg [v b], p. 44; Znamenskiy, p. 44; Karjalainen [c], p. 306.
9. Holmberg [vi a], p. 168, and [v b], pp. 43, 68; Karjalainen [c], p. 312.
10. Veniamin, [b], pp. 120–1.
11. Tretyakov, p. 201.
12. Holzmayer, p. 266.
13. Turi, p. 266.
14. Reuterskiöld [b], pp. 37, 94; Kildal, p. 471.
15. Leem, pp. 437–8.
16. Reuterskiöld [b], p. 112.

17. Olrik [a], pp. 1–9; Holmberg [ii d], pp. 15–18.
18. Holmberg [ii d], pp. 9–21.
19. Karjalainen [c], p. 416.
20. According to Lehtisalo's Collections.
21. Holmberg [vi a], pp. 172–3.
22. Holmberg [v b], pp. 46–7.
23. Paasonen [v f], p. 19, cf. pp. 157, 165, and [v d], p. 846.
24. Krohn [iii g], p. 115.
25. According to Paasonen.
26. Jessen, p. 47; Reuterskiöld [b], p. 23; Rheen, pp. 42–3.
27. Leem, p. 506.
28. Jessen, pp. 18–9; Leem, p. 411, Kildal, pp. 452–3.
29. Kildal, p. 472; Jessen, p. 49.
30. Qvigstad [a], i. 51.
31. Jessen, p. 81; Kildal, p. 452; Fellman, I., *Hand.*, i. 394.
32. *MO* (1912), p. 43.
33. Högström, pp. 179–80, 188.
34. Olrik, "Wettermachen und Neujahrsmond im Norden"
(*Zeitschrift des Vereins für Volkskunde*, 1910), pp. 57–61.
35. Holmberg, "Pakkasen synty," *Vir.*, 1919, pp. 73–4.
36. Qvigstad [a], i. 51.
37. According to Lehtisalo's Collections.
38. Karjalainen [c], pp. 327–8.
39. Yanovič, p. 123.
40. Holmberg [vi b], pp. 175–7, and [v b], pp. 45–6.
41. Paasonen [v d], p. 844.
42. Krohn [iii g], pp. 117–8.
43. Salmelainen, p. 130.
44. Lukkarinen [b], pp. 39–47.
45. Gutslaff, pp. 362–4.
46. Fellman, J., ii. 79, 147.
47. Setälä [a], pp. 39–48.
48. Reuterskiöld [b], pp. 23, 33, 81; Högström, pp. 177–8;
Qvigstad [a], i. 7; Jessen, pp. 19–20.
49. Rheen, pp. 35–7.
50. Reuterskiöld [b], p. 81.
51. Kildal, p. 453.
52. Fellman, J., ii. 84–5.
53. Holmberg [vi a], pp. 186–7; Aminoff, "Reseberätt.," p. 232.
54. According to Paasonen.
55. Eisen [b], pp. 109–10; Boecler, p. 146.
56. Rantasalo [a], iii. 48.
57. Qvigstad [a], i. 73.
58. ib. i. 13; Holmberg [iv b], pp. 74–5.

59. Qvigstad [a], i. 36; Reuterskiöld [b], p. 33.
60. Qvigstad [a], i. 13; Fritzner, pp. 201–2.
61. Karjalainen [c], pp. 419–20.
62. Holmberg [vi a], p. 187.
63. Holmberg [v b], pp. 64–5; Paasonen [v a], pp. 201–2.
64. According to Paasonen.
65. Reuterskiöld [b], pp. 23, 33, 113.
66. Holmberg [v b], pp. 47–8.
67. Pervuchin, i. 56; Vereščagin [d], p. 30.

Chapter XIV

1. Holmberg [v b], pp. 53–4.
2. Karjalainen [c], pp. 420–2.
3. Paasonen [v d], p. 846; Karjalainen [c], p. 422; Yakovlev, p. 38.
4. Holmberg [v b], p. 58.
5. Krohn [iii g], p. 88; Eisen [b], p. 119.
6. Karjalainen [c], pp. 421–2.
7. Holmberg [v b], p. 117, and [vi a], pp. 173–4; Vereščagin, [d], p. 78.
8. Smirnov [v b], p. 549.
9. Lukkarinen [b], p. 82.
10. Holmberg [v b], pp. 85, 104, 128; Karjalainen [c], p. 423.
11. Qvigstad [a], i. 39.
12. Krohn [iii e], pp. 101–2.
13. Holmberg, "Nykyaikainen tutkimus ja kansamme vanhat runot," *Aika*, 1918, pp. 29–31.
14. See *The Mythol. of All Races*, x. 256.

Chapter XV

1. Karjalainen [c], pp. 335–6.
2. Holmberg [v b], pp. 48–9.
3. Satrapinskiy, p. 30; Holmberg [vi a], pp. 177–8.
4. Paasonen [v d], p. 846.
5. Znamenskiy, p. 44; Paasonen [v d], p. 845.
6. Nalimov [b], p. 16; Holmberg [vi a], p. 179.
7. Holmberg [v b], pp. 59–60.
8. Magnitskiy, pp. 40–3.
9. Ostrovskiy, pp. 37–8.
10. Paasonen, "Mikä on jumala-sanan alkumerkitys," *Aika*, 1907, p. 190.
11. Holmberg [v b], p. 58.

12. Holmberg [vi a], p. 180.
13. ib. p. 180.
14. Paasonen [v d], p. 846.
15. Holmberg [vi a], p. 190; Magnitskiy, pp. 19, 25.
16. Holmberg [v b], p. 116.
17. Pervuchin, ii. 29–41.
18. ib. i. 87; cf. Wichmann [a], pp. 25–6.
19. Ganander, pp. 54, 97; Krohn [iii g], pp. 80–1, 139–40.
20. ib. pp. 137–9; Krohn, " Finns," *ERE* vi. 25.
21. *Suomen k. m. loitsur.*, p. 165; Hallström, G., " Halmstaffan," *Etnol. Studier tillägnade N. E. Hammarstedt* (Stockholm, 1921), pp. 227–31.
22. Krohn [iii g], pp. 136–7.
23. Gavrilov [a], p. 71.
24. Eisen [h], pp. 104–111, [b], pp. 128–32.
25. Krohn [iii g], pp. 137, 138 n.
26. Holmberg [vi a], p. 174, [v b], pp. 116–8; Magnitskiy, pp. 34–40.
27. According to Paasonen.
28. Nalimov [c], pp. 13–4; Kandinskiy, p. 110; Holmberg [iii c], pp. 1–12.
29. Holzmayer, pp. 19, 113.
30. Reinholm's Collections (Nat. Museum at Helsingfors).
31. Holzmayer, p. 107.
32. Rantasalo [a], iii. 54, cf. p. 33.
33. Holzmayer, pp. 73–4.
34. Nikander, G., " Fruktbarhetsriter," *Skrifter utg. av Sv. Litteratursällskapet i Finland*, cxxviii. *Folkloristiska och etnografiska studier*, i. 220–2 (Helsingfors, 1916).
35. Varonen, *Vainaj.*, p. 165.
36. Rantasalo [a], iii. 86–109.
37. Eisen [b], pp. 121–2; cf. Holzmayer, pp. 10–11.
38. Holmberg [v b], pp. 56–7.
39. Kildal, p. 452; Reuterskiöld [b], pp. 32, 56, 78, 95, 97; Jessen, p. 63.
40. Qvigstad [a], i. 10–1.
41. Graan, pp. 65–6; cf. Schefferus, p. 113.
42. Rheen, pp. 39–40; Qvigstad [a], i. 36.

Chapter XVI

1. Reuterskiöld [b], p. 57.
2. Jessen, p. 14.
3. Qvigstad [a], i. 25.

4. Jessen, pp. 14, 19; Reuterskiöld [b], pp. 8, 12, 103.
5. ib. p. 88; Setälä [a], pp. 49–50.
6. Reuterskiöld [b], pp. 24–5, 33–4, 105.
7. ib. p. 72.
8. Qvigstad [a], i. 24–5; Jessen, pp. 21–2; Reuterskiöld [b], pp. 24, 34.
9. ib. p. 72; Leem, pp. 493–5.
10. Jessen, p. 22.
11. Kildal, S., p. 470.
12. Reuterskiöld [b], pp. 37, 72.
13. ib. p. 25, etc.; Leem, pp. 414–5.
14. Leem, pp. 414–5; Qvigstad [a], i. 23–4.
15. Reuterskiöld [b], pp. 25, 27, 88–9; Jessen, p. 21.
16. Jessen, p. 22.
17. Qvigstad [a], ii. 11–3.
18. Reuterskiöld [b], p. 96.
19. Qvigstad [a], ii. 12–3.
20. Jessen, pp. 50–1.
21. Leem, p. 429.
22. Jessen, p. 48.
23. Qvigstad [a], p. i. 36.
24. Leem, p. 500.
25. Lund, Troels, Dagligt liv i Norden i det 16 : de Aarhundrede, viii (Copenhagen, 1903), pp. 38–9.
26. Samfundet för Nord. Museets främjande, (Stockholm, 1889), p. 38.
27. Fellman, J., ii. 119–21.
28. Reuterskiöld [b], p. 114.
29. According to Lehtisalo's Collections.
30. Krohn [iii e], p. 77.
31. Krohn [iii g], pp. 221, 232.
32. Boecler, p. 43; Eisen [b], pp. 200–1.
33. Ryčkov, p. 157.
34. Georgi [b], p. 58.
35. Holmberg [vi a], p. 165, and [v b], pp. 60–2; Znamenskiy, pp. 13–14.
36. Holmberg [vi a], p. 171.
37. Znamenskiy, p. 44.
38. Paasonen [v e], pp. 1–6, [v d], p. 844.
39. Znamenskiy, pp. 43–4.
40. Karjalainen [c], pp. 38, 248–9.
41. Krohn, J., [ii], pp. 72–3; Karjalainen [c], pp. 243–7.
42. ib. p. 43.

CHAPTER XVII

1. Cf. Yakovlev, p. 31 ff; Paasonen [v a]; Kuznecov [a]; Filonenko [b].

CHAPTER XVIII

1. Qvigstad [a], ii. 83, 89–90, 92–3.
2. Schefferus, p. 121; Tornaeus, p. 31; Högström, p. 156.
3. Lundius, p. 14.
4. Qvigstad [a], ii. 29.
5. ib. ii. 30–3; i. 43–5; Reuterskiöld [b], p. 2; Lundius, p. 7.
6. Jessen, p. 60; Fellman, J., ii. 27; Turi, p. 196.
7. Jessen, p. 55; Lundius, p. 6; Reuterskiöld [b], p. 90; Niurenius, p. 22.
8. Leem, pp. 415–6; Jessen, p. 26; Reuterskiöld [b], pp. 92, 67.
9. Lundius, pp. 6–9.
10. Leem, pp. 416–7.
11. Reuterskiöld [b], pp. 90–1.
12. ib. p. 65.
13. ib. pp. 92–3; cf. Leem, p. 416.
14. Jessen, p. 26.
15. Leem, pp. 416–7; Jessen, pp. 31–2; Lundius, p. 7.
16. Reuterskiöld [b], p. 35.
17. Qvigstad [a], i. 52.
18. Hallström [b].
19. Jessen, p. 21; Rheen, pp. 18, 35; Lundius, pp. 22, 26; Fellman, I., i. 396.
20. Friis [c], p. 23; Qvigstad [a], i. 29.
21. ib. ii. 43; Fellman, I., i. 396; Rheen, pp. 31–2, 34; Graan, p. 60; Tornaeus, pp. 30–1.
22. Graan, pp. 59–60.
23. Lundius, pp. 6–7.
24. Leem, pp. 475–8.
25. Jessen, p. 31.
26. Qvigstad [a], ii. 43–7.
27. Munch, pp. 4–5.
28. Karjalainen [c], pp. 546–601.
29. Hämäläinen, " Epif. Viis. tied.," p. 45.
30. Akiander, p. 21.

SIBERIAN

Chapter I

1. According to author's Collections.
2. Tretyakov, pp. 200, 217–8.
3. Potanin [b], ii. 160.
4. Troščanskiy, pp. 67–8.
5. Georgi, *Bemerkungen*, i. 276.
6. Chudyakov, pp. 112, 132.
7. "Skaz. bur.," p. 18.
8. Verbitskiy, pp. 73–4; Radloff [a], ii. 6.
9. Tretyakov, p. 200.
10. Bogoras, pp. 307, 330–1.
11. Verbitskiy, p. 90.
12. "Bur. skazki," p. 138; *Šaškov*, p. 30.
13. Afanasyev, *Poetičeskiya vozzrěniya slavyan na prirodu* (Moscow, 1868), ii. 162.
14. "Skaz. bur.," p. 72; Potanin [b], iv. 208, 221; Spasskiy, p. 36.
15. Potanin [b], iv. 799.
16. Holmberg [vi a], p. 179.
17. ib. pp. 179–80.
18. Potanin [b], ii. 153–4.
19. ib. iv. 799; Holmberg [v b], p. 49 n.
20. Potanin [b], iv. 799; cf. Middendorff, iv. 2: 1602.
21. Potanin [b], iv. 709–10; Munkácsi, *KSz*, ix. 3, 293.
22. Krašeninnikov, ii. 106.

Chapter II

1. Troščanskiy, pp. 22–3.
2. Priklonskiy [a], iv. 66.
3. Sěroševskiy, p. 653.
4. Potanin [b], iv. 218–9.
5. "Skaz. bur.," pp. 69–71.
6. Veselovskiy [b], v. 54, 65; Munkácsi, *KSz* ix. 3, 212 ff.; Dähnhardt, i. 66.
7. Veselovskiy [a], pp. 34–5.

8. Dähnhardt, i. 3, 32, 44.
9. ib. pp. 10–11.
10. Potanin [b], iv. 219.
11. Radloff [c], i. 175 ff.
12. Veselovskiy [b], v. 68.
13. Munkásci, *KSz*, ix. 3. 212 ff.
14. " Skaz. bur.," p. 69.
15. Veselovskiy [b], v. 13.
16. Middendorff, iv. 2 p. 1602.
17. Dähnhardt, i. 2.
18. Potanin [b], iv. 221–2.
19. ib. p. 219; Munkásci *KSz*, ix. 3. 219.
20. *Antero Vipunen*, (Helsingfors, 1908), pp. 25–6.
21. Dähnhardt, i. 44.
22. Radloff [c], i, Introd. p. x.
23. Sumcov, p. 5.
24. Radloff [c], i. 177.
25. Tretyakov, pp. 201–2.
26. Veselovskiy [b], v. 67.
27. Dähnhardt, i. 63–4.
28. Cf. Anučin, p. 14.
29. Šaškov, p. 30.
30. " Skaz. bur.," pp. 65–6.
31. Tretyakov, p. 207.
32. " Skaz. bur.," pp. 66–7.
33. Bogayevskiy, *EO* [1990] iv. 143.
34. See *The Mythology of All Races*, x. 279, and reff. there.
35. Dähnhardt, i. 74 ff.
36. ib. pp. 79, 77–8.
37. Potanin [b], iv. 220 ff.
38. ib. p. 224.
39. ib. ii. 166.
40. Dähnhardt, i. 19 n., 30.
41. ib. p. 19 n.
42. Spasskiy, pp. 33–4.
43. Dähnhardt, i. 23.
44. Potanin [b], iv. 268.
45. Troščanskiy, p. 43.
46. Munkásci, *KSz*, ix. 3. 209.
47. Krašeninnikov, ii. 100.
48. Potanin [b], ii. 153.
49. Tretyakov, p. 202; Munkásci, *KSz*, ix. 3. 293.
50. Krašeninnikov, ii. 101.

Chapter III

1. Potanin [b], iv. 137–8, 734–5; Vambéry [a], p. 154.
2. Chudyakov, p. 127.
3. Karjalainen [c], pp. 162 ff.
4. Vasilyev [a], pp. 285–7.
5. Gorochov [a], p. 37; "Skaz. bur.," p. 6.
6. Magnitskiy, p. 63 n.
7. Karjalainen [c], p. 303.
8. Changalov [a], p. 18.
9. Gorochov [a], p. 36.
10. Chudyakov, pp. 135, 153.
11. Changalov [a], p. 40.
12. Katanov, "Skaz. i leg.," p. 223 n. 6.
13. Karjalainen [c], p. 164.
14. Chudyakov, p. 202.
15. Karjalainen [c], pp. 162 ff.
16. ib. p. 163.
17. Chudyakov, p. 127.
18. Karjalainen [c], p. 165.
19. ib. p. 295.
20. ib. p. 164.
21. Radloff [a], ii. 20 ff; Verbitskiy, pp. 46, 63 ff.
22. Radloff [c], ii. 602.

Chapter IV

1. "Skaz. bur.," p. 1.
2. Verbitskiy, p. 168.
3. Radloff [a], ii. 6.
4. Chudyakov, p. 84.
5. Potanin [b], iv. 555.
6. Karjalainen [c], p. 332.
7. Landyšev, p. 7; Verbitskiy, p. 90.
8. Kotvič, p. 217.
9. "Skaz. bur.," p. 140.
10. Radloff [a], ii. 6.
11. Krohn [iii e], p. 106.
12. Grünwedel, *Altbuddhistische Kultstätten*, (Berlin, 1912), fig. 243, 482, 590, 604.
13. Smidt, "Der Tamamushischrein," *OZ*, 1914, p. 420.
14. Potanin [b], iv. 555–6.
15. ib. pp. 223–4.
16. ib. p. 228.

17. Žitetskiy, pp. 65 ff.
18. *The Mythology of All Races*, x. 286, and reff. there.

Chapter V

1. Radloff [a], ii. 7.
2. Potanin [b], iv. 226.
3. Karjalainen [c], p. 305.
4. ib. p. 305
5. Schiefner, pp. 62 ff.
6. Ahlqvist, A., *Versuch einer mokscha-mordwinischen Grammatik* (Petrograd, 1861), p. 133.
7. Chudyakov, pp. 112 ff.
8. "Skaz. bur.," p. 149.
9. Gorochov [b], pp. 43 ff.
10. Middendorff, iii. 79 ff.
11. Potanin [b], iv. 223–4.
12. Schott [c], p. 9; Grünwedel, *Myth.*, p. 50.
13. See *The Mythology of All Races*, xii. 36, fig. 23.
14. Žitetskiy, p. 66.
15. Changalov [a], p. 42.
16. Potanin [b], iv. 188.
17. See *The Mythology of All Races*, vi. 298–9.
18. Middendorff, iii. 1. 87–8; Gorochov [a], p. 43.
19. Middendorff, iii. 1. 87.
20. ib. p. 87.
21. Žitetskiy, p. 66.
22. Potanin [b], iv. 217.

Chapter VI

1. "Skaz. bur.," pp. 71–2.
2. ib. p. 79.
3. ib. pp. 140–1.
4. Munkásci, *KSz*, ix. 3. 262 f.; Patkanov, i. 134 f.
5. Dähnhardt, i. 258 ff.
6. ib. p. 266.
7. Verbitskiy, pp. 102–3.
8. ib. pp. 76, 103 n.
9. Radloff [a], ii. 6, 11.
10. Potanin [b], iv. 208.
11. ib. p. 208.
12. Radloff [c], i. 183.
13. Munkásci, *KSz*, ix. 3. 268.
14. Anučin, pp. 14–5.

15. Tretyakov, pp. 201–2.
16. Steller, p. 273.
17. Pekarskiy, p. 114.
18. Munkácsi, *KSz*, ix. 3. 258 ff.
19. ib. p. 260.
20. Andree, R., *Die Flutsagen*, (Braunschweig, 1891), pp. 25–6.
21. Verbitskiy, pp. 113–4.
22. " Skaz. bur.," p. 78.

Chapter VII

1. Spasskiy, p. 34.
2. Dähnhardt, i. 111–3; bin Gorion, M. J., *Die Sagen der Juden. Die Urzeit*, (Frankfurt a.M. 1913), p. 101.
3. Šaškov, p. 33; Dähnhardt, i. 111.
4. Žitetskiy, p. 67.
5. Grube, W., *Religion und Kultus der Chinesen* (Leipzig, 1910), p. 101.
6. Dähnhardt, p. 111 n.
7. " Skaz. bur.," p. 67.
8. Verbitskiy, p. 91.
9. Karjalainen, p. 19; Munkácsi, *KSz*, ix. 3. 227–8.
10. Anučin, p. 9.
11. Radloff [c], i. 285.
12. Middendorff, iv. 2. 1602.
13. Veselovskiy [b], v. 10.
14. ib. p. 18.
15. " Skaz. bur.," pp. 67–8.
16. ib. pp. 68–9.
17. ib. pp. 69–70.
18. Munkácsi, *KSz*, ix. 3. 228 ff.
19. Veselovskiy [b], v. 12.
20. Potanin [b], iv. 219–220.
21. ib. pp. 222–3.
22. Verbitskiy, pp. 91–2.
23. ib. p. 93.

Chapter VIII

1. Radloff [c], Prob., i. 177 ff.
2. Middendorff, iv. 2. 1602.
3. Munkácsi, *KSz*, ix. 3. 231 ff; Karjalainen [c], p. 19.
4. Veselovskiy [b], v. 12; bin Gorion, p. 95.
5. Žitetskiy, p. 68; cf. bin Gorion, p. 105.
6. Žitetskiy, p. 68.

Chapter IX

1. Anučin, p. 17.
2. Donner [a], pp. 6–7.
3. ib. p. 8 n. 1.
4. ib. p. 12.
5. Verbitskiy, p. 101.
6. Chudyakov, pp. 107, 124.
7. Potanin [b], iv. 373 ff.
8. Šimkevič, pp. 128–30.
9. ib. pp. 126–7.
10. *The Mythology of All Races*, x. 254, 291.

Chapter X

1. Banzarov, p. 6.
2. Magnitskiy, pp. 64, 85.
3. Radloff [a], ii. 6.
4. Banzarov, p. 27.
5. Radloff [a], ii. 11.
6. Magnitskiy, p. 64 n. 1.
7. Šaškov, p. 18.
8. ib. pp. 8, 10; Banzarov, p. 10.
9. Šaškov, p. 10; Banzarov, p. 10.
10. Troščanskiy, pp. 32–3.
11. Changalov [a], pp. 45–6; Šaškov, pp. 24–5; Agapitov-Changalov, p. 23.
12. Priklonskiy [a], iii. 65.
13. Šaškov, p. 9, Banzarov, p. 9.
14. Nikolskiy, pp. 71–2.
15. Anučin, p. 9.
16. Sěroševskiy, p. 645; Vasilyev [a], pp. 279–82.
17. Katanov, p. 233.
18. Šaškov, p. 11; Tretyakov, p. 200; Anučin, p. 3; Karjalainen [c], p. 303.
19. Cf. Bogoras, p. 319.

Chapter XI

1. Radloff [a], ii. 6.
2. Pripuzov [a], p. 48.
3. Potanin [b], iv. 218; Radloff [a], i. 361–2.
4. Verbitskiy, p. 103 n.
5. Karjalainen [c], p. 276 n.
6. ib. p. 331.

7. Radloff [a], i. 361–2; cf. Holmberg [a], pp. 121–126.
8. ib. ii. 6.
9. Banzarov, pp. 14, 28 f.
10. ib. p. 14.
11. Magnitskiy, pp. 48, 62, 93 etc.
12. Holmberg [v b], fig. 25.
13. Sěroševskiy, p. 647, fig. 161.
14. Karjalainen [c], p. 304.
15. Katanov, p. 223 n. 6.
16. Karjalainen [c], p. 326.
17. ib. pp. 325, 251 ff.
18. Nikolskiy, pp. 71, 72–3.
19. Holmberg [v b], p. 86.
20. See *The Mythology of All Races*, xii. fig. 16 and 51.
21. Verbitskiy, p. 91.
22. Changalov [a], pp. 1 ff.
23. Verbitskiy, pp. 90–1.
24. ib. p. 100.

Chapter XII

1. Potanin [b], iv. 70, 825; " Skaz. bur.," p. 98.
2. Magnitskiy, p. 91, cf. p. 64.
3. Radloff [a], ii. 11.
4. Potanin [b], iv. 389.
5. Middendorf, iii. 1. 87.
6. " Bur. skazki," p. 127.
7. Troščanskiy, pp. 83 ff.
8. Chudyakov, pp. 194–5, cf. p. 202.
9. ib. pp. 197–8.
10. ib. p. 194.
11. Karjalainen [c], pp. 38, 249.
12. Pripuzov [b], pp. 59–60; Priklonskiy [a], iii. 63 ff.

Chapter XIII

1. Potanin [b], iv. 712.
2. Reuterskiöld [b], p. 72.
3. Pripuzov [b], p. 63.
4. ib. p. 63.
5. Gorochov [a], p. 36.
6. ib. p. 36.
7. Sěroševskiy, p. 667.
8. Potanin [b], iv. 191.
9. Žitetskiy, p. 68.

10. Katanov, p. 227 n. 4.
11. Karjalainen [c], p. 416.
12. "Skaz. bur.," p. 151; cf. Potanin [b], iv. 179.
13. Ivanovskiy, p. 263; cf. Potanin [b], iv. 179.
14. Agapitov-Changalov, p. 22 n.
15. Magnitskiy, p. 18.
16. Potanin [b], iv. 225–6.
17. Tretyakov, p. 209.
18. Šaškov, p. 12.
19. Georgi [a], i. 275.
20. Anučin, p. 15; Karjalainen [c], p. 415.
21. Sěroševskiy, p. 667; Pripuzov [b], p. 62; cf. Tretyakov, p. 209.
22. Potanin [b], iv. 191; Šaškov, pp. 14–5; "Bur. skazki," p. 128; Gorochov [a], p. 39.
23. Potanin [b], iv. 190–1.
24. Tretyakov, p. 201.
25. Verbitskiy, pp. 73–4; Bergmann, iii. 40, 204; Potanin [b], iv. 270.
26. Sěroševskiy, p. 668.
27. "Bur. skazki," pp. 127–8.
28. Potanin [b], iv. 191–3.
29. ib. pp. 209–10.
30. Afanasyev, A., *Poetičeskiya vozzrěniya slavyan na prirodu* (Moscow, 1865), i. 609; Vambéry [a], p. 154.
31. Afanasyev, *op. cit.*, i. 762.
32. Potanin [b], iv. 736.
33. Afanasyev, *op. cit.*, i. 763.
34. Tretyakov, p. 201.
35. Anučin, p. 15.
36. Sěroševskiy, p. 660.
37. Cf. *The Mythology of All Races*, x. 278.
38. "Bur. skazki," pp. 126–7.
39. Banzarov, p. 14; cf. Agapitov-Changalov, p. 18.
40. Potanin [b], ii. 125; iv. 193.
41. ib. iv. 194.
42. ib. p. 200.
43. Afanasyev, *op. cit.*, i. 763.
44. Potanin [b], iv. 200–3.
45. "Bur. skazki," p. 126.
46. Potanin [b], iv. 204.
47. ib. iv. 204 ff.
48. ib. ii. 124.
49. ib. iv. 206.

50. ib. ii. 124.
51. Anučin, p. 16.
52. Potanin [b], iv. 203.
53. ib. pp. 203–4.
54. ib. ii. 125.
55. ib. iv. 194.
56. " Bur. skazki," pp. 125–6.
57. Georgi [a], i. 321.
58. " Bur. skazki," p. 126.
59. " Skaz. bur.," pp. 122–3.
60. Anučin, pp. 15–6.
61. Changalov [a], p. 7.
62. Sěroševskiy, p. 668.
63. Potanin [b], ii. 124–5.
64. Vambéry [a], pp. 55–6; Potanin [b], iv. 740–1.
65. Sěroševskiy, p. 667; Agapitov-Changalov, p. 18; Tretyakov,
p. 201.
66. Bogoras, p. 309; Jochelson [b], p. 123.
67. Dähnhardt, iii. 1. 13.
68. Vambéry [a], p. 156.
69. Sěroševskiy, p. 667.
70. Pripuzov [b], p. 62.
71. Munkásci, KSz, ix. 3. 251.
72. ib. p. 253 f.
73. Potanin [b], iv. 143, ii. 83.
74. Olsen, p. 47.
75. Potanin [b], iv. 143–4.

Chapter XIV

1. According to author's Collections.
2. Bogoras, p. 322; Tretyakov, p. 201.
3. According to T. Lehtisalo.
4. Troščanskiy, p. 26.
5. Karjalainen [c], p. 327.
6. Banzarov, p. 15; Potanin [b], iv. 138–42.
7. Potanin [b], iv. 141.
8. " Skaz. bur.," p. 76; Potanin [b], iv. 139, 141–2.
9. Šimkevič, p. 127.
10. Karjalainen [c], p. 327
11. Agapitov-Changalov, p. 7.
12. " Bur. skazki," p. 129.
13. Agapitov-Changalov, p. 6.
14. Changalov [a], p. 7.

15. Pripuzov [b], pp. 61–2; Troščanskiy, p. 48.
16. Šimkevič, p. 128.
17. Potanin [b], iv. 207.
18. Karjalainen [c], p. 327.
19. Anučin, p. 16; Potanin [b], iv. 742.
20. Holzmayer, p. 50.
21. Gorochov [a], p. 39.
22. Pripuzov [b], p. 62.
23. Potanin [b], ii. 172.
24. ib. iv. 139.
25. Afanasyev, *Poetičeskiya vozzrěniya slavyan na prirodu* (Moscow, 1868), ii. 511.
26. Troščanskiy, p. 165; Sěroševskiy, p. 655; Banzarov, p. 15; Šaškov, p. 94; Potanin [b], ii. 91–2.
27. " Bur. skazki," p. 130; Zatoplyayev, pp. 7–8; Changalov [a], p. 7.
28. Changalov, pp. 3–5.
29. Chudyakov, p. 213.
30. Šaškov, p. 27; Radloff [a], ii. 7.
31. Agapitov-Changalov, p. 8.

Chapter XV

1. Chudyakov, p. 135.
2. Sěroševskiy, p. 655, cf. Potanin [b], iv. 332.
3. Changalov [a], p. 8.
4. Verbitskiy, p. 97.
5. Agapitov-Changalov, p. 5.
6. Anučin, p. 16.
7. " Bur. skazki," pp. 130–1.
8. Potanin [b], iv. 220, cf. p. 331.
9. ib. p. 262.
10. Šaškov, p. 37; Troščanskiy, p. 43.
11. Troščanskiy, p. 51.
12. Magnitskiy, pp. 136–7.
13. Šaškov, pp. 36–8; Banzarov, pp. 22, 24.
14. Sěroševskiy, p. 665; Pripuzov [b], p. 61; Olsen, p. 141; Banzarov, pp. 23–4; Chudyakov, p. 135.
15. Troščanskiy, pp. 52, 178; Sěroševskiy, p. 665; Nikolskiy, pp. 73–4; Agapitov-Changalov, p. 6.
16. Magnitskiy, p. 203.
17. Banzarov, p. 23; cf. Šaškov, p. 37.
18. Banzarov, p. 25.
19. Radloff [a], ii. 29.

20. Chudyakov, p. 135; Agapitov-Changalov, pp. 4, 29.
21. Troščanskiy, p. 28.
22. Gorochov [b], p. 44.
23. Pripuzov [b], p. 61.
24. Agapitov-Changalov, pp. 5–6.
25. Karjalainen, [c], p. 422.
26. Pripuzov [b], p. 61; Priklonskiy [a], iv. 61.
27. Agapitov-Changalov, p. 30.
28. ib. pp. 29–30.
29. Banzarov, pp. 22–3.

CHAPTER XVI

1. Chudyakov, p. 213; cf. pp. 113, 198–9.
2. Sěroševskiy, p. 667.
3. Troščanskiy, p. 4.
4. Šimkevič, p. 57.
5. According to Prof. G. J. Ramstedt.
6. Krohn [iii e], p. 138.
7. Ivanovskiy, p. 263.
8. Changalov [a], p. 6.
9. Sěroševskiy, pp. 668–9; Pripuzov [b], p. 62; Potanin [b], iv. 189–90, 773–4.

CHAPTER XVII

1. Olsen, p. 143.
2. Potanin [b], ii. 98.
3. According to Prof. Ramstedt.
4. Troščanskiy, p. 47; Pripuzov [b], p. 62.
5. Georgi [a], i. 276.
6. Banzarov, p. 8.
7. ib. p. 16.
8. Thomsen, pp. 20, 152, 167.
9. Changalov [a], p. 44; Šaškov, p. 20.
10. Troščanskiy, p. 29.
11. Magnitskiy, pp. 29, 48, 62 etc.
12. Changalov [a], p. 44.
13. Magnitskiy, pp. 40–3.
14. Thomsen, pp. 144, 150.
15. Radloff [c], i. 139.
16. Magnitskiy, pp. 30, 48, 88.
17. Kannisto [b].
18. Vambéry [b], p. 36.

Chapter XVIII

1. Verbitskiy, p. 78.
2. Castrén, *Nord. Reisen*, iii. 160.
3. Sěroševskiy, pp. 651, 667; Troščanskiy, pp. 27 f., 47, 53; Gorochov [a], p. 39; V-skiy, p. 36.
4. Troščanskiy, p. 53.
5. Pripuzov [b], p. 62.
6. Changalov [a], pp. 38, 145.
7. "Skaz. bur.," p. 85.
8. ib. pp. 83–4.
9. Jochelson [b], p. 119; Bogoras, pp. 285–6.
10. Middendorff, iii. 1. 36.
11. "Skaz. bur.," p. 84; cf. Šaškov, p. 56.
12. Banzarov, pp. 21–2.
13. "Skaz. burjat.," p. 84.
14. Pripuzov [b], p. 63; V-skiy, pp. 38, 40.
15. Troščanskiy, p. 53; Pripuzov, p. 63.
16. Sěroševskiy, pp. 669–70.
17. Koblov, pp. 3, 11 ff; Maksimov, pp. 580–1, 607–9.
18. Magnitskiy, pp. 112, 247.
19. Gorochov [a], p. 39.
20. Koblov, pp. 18 ff.; Maksimov, p. 615.
21. Poyarkov, pp. 41–3.
22. Banzarov, p. 30.
23. Stadling, p. 18; Pekarskiy-Čvětkov, p. 113; Jochelson [a], pp. 120, 122–4; Maak [b], p. 110; Middendorf, iv. 2. 1610; Pripuzov [b], p. 62; Sěroševskiy, p. 658.
24. Troščanskiy, p. 178.
25. According to author's Collections.
26. Sěroševskiy, pp. 670 f.
27. Gorochov [a], p. 39; Potanin [b], ii. 98, iv. 186.
28. Troščanskiy, p. 178; Jochelson [a], pp. 120–2, 124.
29. Troščanskiy, p. 54, cf. Middendorf, iv. 2. 1568–9.
30. Banzarov, pp. 18–20; Hildén, p. 129; Verbitskiy, pp. 43–7.
31. Troščanskiy, p. 54.

Chapter XIX

1. Sěroševskiy, p. 666; Troščanskiy, p. 75.
2. Anučin, p. 10; Podgorbunskiy, p. 18.
3. Changalov [b], pp. 23–4.
4. Agapitov-Changalov, p. 58; Podgorbunskiy, pp. 19–20.
5. Pripuzov [b], p. 64; Agapitov-Changalov, p. 58.

6. Agapitov-Changalov, p. 59.
7. Changalov [a], pp. 135-7.
8. ib. p. 137.
9. Podgorbunskiy, p. 20.
10. Anučin, p. 11.
11. Podgorbunskiy, p. 20.
12. " Perv. bur. šam.," pp. 87 ff; " Perv. šam.," pp. 89-90.
13. Potanin [b], iv. 134; cf. Podgorbunskiy, p. 19.
14. Troščanskiy, p. 2.
15. Pripuzov [b], p. 64.
16. Šimkevič, p. 36; Banzarov, pp. 30-1; Potanin [b], iv. 699.
17. Sěroševskiy, p. 623; Vasilyev [b], pp. 34-5; Pripuzov [b],
p. 64; Zatoplyayev, p. 3; Batarov, pp. 10 ff.
18. Anučin, p. 13.
19. Troščanskiy, p. 85; Batarov, pp. 10 ff; Castrén, *Nord. Reisen,*
iii. 230; Potanin [b], iv. 63.
20. Banzarov, p. 32.
21. Agapitov-Changalov, p. 61.
22. ib. p. 61.
23. Strahlenberg, p. 377.
24. Šaškov, pp. 58 ff; Anučin, p. 12; Sěroševskiy, p. 619; Priklonskiy [a], pp. 76 ff; Troščanskiy, pp. 88-92; Potanin [b], ii. 88,
iv. 36-8; Pripuzov [b], p. 65; cf. Verbitskiy, p. 86.
25. Georgi [a], i. 266.
26. Anučin, pp. 11-2.
27. Šaškov, p. 59; Stadling, pp. 28 ff.; Podgorbunskiy, p. 27.
28. Anučin, p. 12.
29. Batarov, p. 13.

Chapter XX

1. Troščanskiy, p. 3.
2. Potanin [b], iv. 133-4.
3. Agapitov-Changalov, p. 60.
4. Šimkevič, pp. 15 ff.
5. Troščanskiy, pp. 2-3, 63.
6. Pripuzov [b], p. 64.
7. Troščanskiy, pp. 62-3, 68-9.
8. Anučin, p. 12.
9. Radloff [a], ii. 3.
10. Hildén, pp. 127-8.
11. Karjalainen [c], p. 313.
12. Bogoras, pp. 307, 331.
13. Vasilyev [a], p. 286.

14. Tretyakov, p. 200.
15. Podgorbunskiy, p. 27.
16. Stadling, p. 25.
17. Bogoras, p. 334.
18. Podgorbunskiy, pp. 23 ff.
19. Castrén, iii. 148 ff.; Šaškov, pp. 68–73; Potanin [b], iv. 287–8.
20. Spasskiy, p. 35.
21. Šimkevič, pp. 62–3.

Chapter XXI

1. Stadling, pp. 56–7.
2. Tretyakov, p. 211.
3. Stadling, p. 63; Sěroševskiy, pp. 625 ff.
4. Troščanskiy, pp. 76, 78, 119–20.
5. Agapitov-Changalov, p. 45.
6. Troščanskiy, pp. 66, 76.
7. Changalov [a], pp. 83 ff; Agapitov-Changalov, pp. 27 ff.
8. Changalov [b], p. 21; Potanin [b], iv. 57 n.; Batarov, p. 10; Zatoplyayev, p. 9.
9. Georgi [a], i. 314; Agapitov-Changalov, pp. 32–3; Potanin [b], iv. 93 ff; Changalov [a], pp. 74–6, cf. p. 90.
10. "Skaz. bur.," pp. 80–1; Changalov [c], pp. 15–6.
11. Sěroševskiy, pp. 656–8; Troščanskiy, p. 56.
12. "Skaz. bur.," pp. 114–7, 125–6; cf. p. 81.
13. Potanin [b], ii. 161.
14. ib., pp. 161–2.
15. ib., pp. 164–5.
16. "Skaz. bur.," pp. 94 ff.; Potanin [b], iv. 264 ff.; O proischoždenii, pp. 187 ff.
17. "Skaz. bur.," pp. 97–8.
18. Strahlenberg, p. 378.
19. Ščukin, p. 276.
20. Šaškov, p. 43.
21. Anučin, p. 10.
22. Potanin [b], ii. 151; iv. 168, 183; "Skaz. bur.," pp. 80, 82; Changalov [b], p. 19; "Bur. skazki.," p. 119, cf. Pripuzov [a], p. 50.
23. "Skaz. bur.," pp. 123–4.
24. Agapitov-Changalov, pp. 41–2.
25. "O proischoždenii," p. 188; cf. Šaškov, pp. 42–3.
26. Tretyakov, p. 212.
27. Sěroševskiy, p. 626, Troščanskiy, p. 138.

28. Vasilyev [a], p. 277.
29. Šimkevič, p. 18.
30. Zatoplyayev, p. 9.
31. Changalov [a], p. 95.
32. Šimkevič, pp. 15, 17.
33. Vasilyev [a], pp. 271 ff.; Priklonskiy [a], iv. 88–9; Troščanskiy, p. 141.
34. Potanin [b], iv. 54.
35. Agapitov-Changalov, pp. 44 ff.
36. Priklonskiy [a], iv. 54; cf. Troščanskiy, fig. 1–3; Vasilyev [b], pp. 1 ff.; Pekarskiy, *Plašč*, pp. 93 ff.
37. Potanin [b], iv. 53; cf. Lankenau, p. 279.
38. Cf. Holmberg [b], pp. 12–20; Anučin, pp. 44 ff.
39. Schrenk, i. 408; cf. Kulikovskiy, "O kultě medvedya," *EO*, 1890, no. 1, p. 110.
40. Tretyakov, p. 214; Mordvinov, p. 64; cf. Širokogorov, p. 33, n. 2.
41. Šimkevič, p. 63.
42. Klemenc, pp. 25 ff.
43. "Perv. bur. šam.," p. 88 n.; Agapitov-Changalov, pp. 42–3.
44. Anučin, pp. 60 ff.
45. Tretyakov, p. 214; Pekarskiy, "Plašč," p. 112.
46. Anučin, pp. 7–8.

BIBLIOGRAPHY

FINNO—UGRIC

I. ABBREVIATIONS

ASSF	Acta Societatis Scientiarum Fennicae.
AASF . . .	Annales Academiae Scientiarum Fennicae.
ATPS . . .	Archives des Traditions Populaires Suédoises.
DNR	Drevnaya i Novaya Rossia.
EMU	Ethnologische Mitteilungen aus Ungarn.
EO	Etnografičeskoe Obozrěnie.
ERE	Encyclopædia of Religion and Ethics.
ES	Etnografičeskiy Sbornik.
FFC	Folklore Fellow Communications.
FUF	Finnisch-Ugrische Forschungen.
GI	Geografičeskiya Izvěstiya.
IAOIRS . .	Izvěstiya Archangelskago Obščestva Izučenie Russkago Sěvera.
IKE	Izvěstiya no Kazanskoy Eparchii.
IO	Inorodčeskoe Obozrěnie.
IOAIE . . .	Izvěstiya Obščestva Archeologii, Istorii i Etnografii pri Kazanskom Universitetě.
IOLEAE . .	Izvěstiya Obščestva Lyubiteley Estestvoznaniya, Antropologii i Etnografii pri Moskovskom Universitetě.
IOORGO . .	Izvěstiya Orenburskago Otděla Russkago Geografičeskago Obščestva.
IRGO . . .	Izvěstiya Russkago Geografičeskago Obščestva.
JSFO	Journal de la Société Finno-Ougrienne.
KGV	Kazanskiya Gubernskiya Vědomosti.
KSz	Keleti Szemle.
KV	Kalevalaseuran Vuosikirja.
MO	Le Monde Oriental.
MSFO . . .	Mémoires de la Société Finno-Ougrienne.
NGV	Nižegorodskiya Gubernskiya Vědomosti.
NS	Novoe Slovo.
PEV	Penzenskiya Eparchialnyja Vědomosti.
PS	Pravoslavnyj Sobesěnik.
RV	Russkiy Věstnik.
S	Suomi.
SEV	Samarskiya Eparchialnyja Vědomosti.

SGEG . . . Schriften der Gelehrten Estnischen Gesellschaft.
SGV . . . . Simbirskiya Gubernskiya Vědomosti.
SM . . . . Suomen Museo.
SMA . . . Suomen Muinaismuistoyhdistyksen Aikakauskirja.
SSU . . . . Suomen Suvun Uskonnot.
TEV . . . . Tambovskiya Eparchialnyja Vědomosti.
TOEA . . Tomskiya Eparchialnyja Vědomosti.
TOEKU . . Trudy Obščestva Estestvoispytaleley pri Kazanskom Universitetě.
VE . . . . Věstnik Europy.
VEV . . . Vyatskiya Eparchialnyja Vědomosti.
VGEG . . . Verhandlungen der Gelehrten Ehstnischen Gesellschaft.
VGV . . . Vologodskiya Guberskiya Vědomosti.
Vir . . . . Virittäjä.
VOUO . . . Věstnik Orenburskago Učebnago Okruga.
VRGO . . . Věstnik Russkago Imperatorskago Geografičeskago Obščestva.
ZAN . . . . Zapiski Akademii Nauk.
ZRGO . . . Zapiski Russkago Geografičeskago Obščestva.
ŽMVD . . . Žurnal Ministerstva vnutrennich děl.
ŽST . . . . Živaya Starina.
ZZ–SORGO . Zapiski Zěvero-Sibirskago Otděla Russkago Geografičeskago Obščestva.

II. GENERAL SOURCES AND TREATISES

ABERCROMBY, J., *The Pre- and Protohistoric Finns both Eastern and Western with the Magic Songs of the West Finns*. London, 1898.

AHLQVIST, A., *Muistelmia matkoilta Venäjällä vuosina 1854–1858*. Helsingfors, 1859.

AKIANDER, M., " Utdrag ur ryska annaler," in *S.*, 1848. Helsingfors.

ASPELIN, J. R., *Suomalais-ugrilaisen muinaistutkinnon alkeita*. Helsingfors, 1875.

CASTRÉN, M. A., *Nordische Reisen und Forschungen*, 5 vols. Petrograd, 1853–1862.

ERDMANN, J. F., *Beiträge zur Kenntniss des Innern von Russland*. 2 vols. Riga, 1822–26.

ERMAN, G. A., *Reise um die Erde durch Nord-Asien und die beiden Oceane in den Jahren 1828, 1829 und 1830, I. Historischer Bericht*. 3 vols. Berlin, 1833.

GEORGI, J. G., [a] *Bemerkungen auf einer Reise im Russischen Reiche in den Jahren 1773 und 1774*. 2 vols. Petrograd, 1775.

—— [b] *Beschreibung aller Nationen des Russischen Reichs.* Petrograd, 1776.

GMELIN, J. G., *Reise durch Sibirien von dem Jahr 1733 bis 1743.* 4 vols. Göttingen, 1751–2.

GUAGNINO, A., *Sarmatiae Europeae descriptio.* Spirae, 1581. (Editio princeps. Cracow, 1578.)

HERBERSTEIN, S. von, *Moscowiter wunderbare Historien.* Basel, 1567.

HOLMBERG, UNO, [a] *Gudstrons uppkomst.* Uppsala, 1917.

—— [b] " Die Wassergottheiten der finnisch-ugrischen Völker," in *MSFO* xxxii, Helsingfors, 1913.

—— [c] "Suomalais-ugrilaisten kansain pakanallinen uskonto," in *Tietosanakirja,* ix. Helsingfors, 1917.

—— [d] "Der Baum des Lebens," *AASF* xvi. Helsingfors, 1922–23.

KROHN, JULIUS, *Suomen suvun pakanallinen jumalanpalvelus.* Helsingfors, 1894. (The Hungarian translation, with further additions by A. Bán, appeared in Budapest, 1908).

LEPECHIN, I., *Tagebuch über seine Reise durch verschiedene Provinzen des Russischen Reichs in den Jahren 1768 und 1769.* 3 vols. Translated into Germ. by C. H. Hase. Altenburg, 1774–83.

MÜLLER, G. F., *Sammlung Russischer Geschichte.* 5 vols. Petrograd, 1732–60.

OLEARIUS, A., *Ausführliche Beschreibung der kundbaren Reyse nach Muscow und Persien.* Schleswig, 1646.

PAASONEN, H., " Über die ursprünglichen seelenvorstellungen bei den finnisch-ugrischen völkern und die benennungen der seele in ihren sprachen," in *JSFO,* xxvi. 4. Helsingfors, 1909.

PALLAS, P. S., *Reise durch verschiedene Provinzen des Russischen Reichs.* 3 vols. Petrograd, 1771–6.

RYČKOV, N., *Žurnal ili dnevnyja zapiski puteštviya po raznym proviniyam Rossiyskago gosudarstva 1769 i 1770.* Petrograd, 1770. (Translated into German by C. H. Hase, Riga, 1774.)

SETÄLÄ, E. N., [a] "Studien aus dem gebiet der lehnbeziehungen," off-print of *FUF* xii. Helsingfors, 1912.

—— [b] "Zur frage nach der verwandtschaft der finnisch-ugrischen und samojedischen sprachen," off-print of *JFSO* xxx. Helsingfors, 1915.

STRAHLENBERG, Ph. J. von, *Das Nord- und östliche Theil von Europa und Asia.* Stockholm, 1730.

VARONEN, M., *Vainajainpalvelus muinaisilla suomalaisilla.* Helsingfors, 1898.

WITSEN, N., *Noord en Oost Tartarye.* 2 vols. Amsterdam, 1705.

III. BALTIC FINNS

Aspelin, J. R., "Kalevalan sankarikuvaston aiheita," in *SM* xxiii. Helsingfors, 1916.

Blomstedt, Y., "Venäjän Karjalan kalmistoista ja hautapylväistä," in *SM* ii. Helsingfors, 1895.

Boecler, J. W., *Der Ehsten abergläubische Gebräuche, Weisen und Gewohnheiten*. Mit auf die gegenwart bezüglichen Anmerkungen beleuchtet von Fr. R. Kreutzwald. Petrograd, 1854. (Editio princeps, 1685).

Boubrig, J. S., [a] "Volkssagen und Traditionen aus dem eigentlichen Estlande, besonders aus Harrien und der Wieck," in *VGEG*, ii. 3. Dorpat, 1850.

———— [b] "Zur nähern Kenntniss der Volkssagen und des Aberglaubens der Ehsten aus dem Kirchspiele Odenpä," in *VGEG*, i. 2. Dorpat, 1843.

Brummer, O. J., "Über die Bannungsorte der finnischen Zauberlieder." Helsingfors. (*MSFO* xxviii. 1909.)

Buch, M., "Ueber den Tõnnis-cultus und andere Opfer-gebräuche der Esthen," in *JSFO* xv. Helsingfors, 1897.

Castrén, E., *Beskrifning öfver Cajaneborgs län*. Åbo, 1754.

Comparetti, D., *Der Kalewala oder die traditionelle Poesie der Finnen*. Halle, 1892.

Eisen, M. I., [a] *Eesti muistsed jumalad ja wägimehed*. Dorpat, 1913.

———— [b] *Eesti mütoloogia*. Reval, 1920.

———— [c] *Esivanemate ohverdamised*. Dorpat, 1920.

———— [d] "Haldijad," in *Eesti Ülioplaste Seltsi Album, iii*. Dorpat, 1895.

———— [e] *Kodukäijat*. Reval, 1897.

———— [f] *Krati raamat*. Dorpat, 1895.

———— [g] *Näki raamat*. Reval, 1897.

———— [h] "Über den Pekokultus bei den Setukesen," in *FUF* vi. Helsingfors, 1906.

Fählmann, Dr., "Wie war der heidnische Glaube der alten Ehsten beschaffen? " in *VGEG* ii. 2. Dorpat, 1852.

Forström, O. A., "Kuvaelmia Itä-Karjalasta," in *Valvoja*, 1886. Helsingfors.

Ganander, Chr., *Mythologia fennica*. Åbo, 1822.

Groundstroem, O., "Berättelse öfver en under sommaren 1861 gjord runosamlingsvandring inom en del af Ingermanland," in *S* ii. Helsingfors, 1866.

Gutslaff, J., *Kurtzer Bericht und Vnterricht von der Falsch-heilig genandten Bäche in Lieffland Wöhhanda*. Dorpat, 1644.

Häyhä, J., *Kuvaelmia Itä-Suomalaisten vanhoista tavoista, II. Maahanpaniaiset (Kansanvalistusseuran toimituksia, 98)*. Helsingfors, 1894.

Henricus Lettus, *Origines Livoniae (Scriptores Rerum Livonicarum*, i). Riga and Leipzig, 1853.

Hertzberg, R., *Vidskepelsen i Finland på 1600–talet*. Helsingfors, 1889.

Holmberg, Uno, [a] "Suomalaisten haltioista," in *KV* i. Helsingfors, 1921.

—— [b] "Suomalaisten karsikoista," in *KV* iv. Helsingfors, 1924.

—— [c] "Suomalaisten muinaisuskosta," in *Tietosanakirja*, ix. Helsingfors, 1917.

—— [d] "Virolaisten viljaneitsyet," in *MSFO* xxxv. Helsingfors, 1914.

Holzmayer, J. B., "Osiliana," in *VGEG* vii. Dorpat, 1873.

Hornborg, K. H. "Karsikoista," in *Virittäjä*, ii. Helsingfors, 1886.

Hurt, J., [a] "Beiträge zur Kenntnis estnischer Sagen und Überlieferungen," in *SGEG* ii. Dorpat, 1863.

—— [b] *Über estnische Himmelskunde*. Petrograd, 1900.

Itkonen, T., "Suomalaisia mytologisia sanoja Inarista," in *Virittäjä*, 1912. Helsingfors.

Jürgens, E., "Ein weiterer beitrag zum Tõnnis-cultus der Esten," in *JSFO* xviii. 3. Helsingfors, 1900.

Kallas, O., "Kraasna maarahvas," in *S* iv. 10. Helsingfors, 1903.

Kreutzwald, Fr. R., [a] *Eestirahwa ennemuistsed jutud*. Helsingfors, 1866.

—— [b] "Beitrag zur Mythologie der Esthen," in *Inland*, 1838, no. 9. Dorpat.

—— [c] "Esthnische Gebräuche bei Sterbenden und Todten," ib. 1837, no. 18.

—— [d] "Ueber den Character der Estnischen Mythologie," in *VGEG* ii. 3. Dorpat, 1850.

—— [e] "Ueber einige festliche Gebräuche bei den Esthen," in *Inland*, 1837, nos. 12, 25 and 27. Dorpat.

Kreutzwald und Neus, H., *Mythische und magische Lieder der Ehsten*. Petrograd, 1854.

Krohn, Julius, *Suomalaisen kirjallisuuden historia i. 2. Kalevalan synty*. Helsingfors, 1884.

Krohn, Kaarle, [a] "Finns," in *ERE* vi. 23 ff. Edinburgh, 1913.

—— [b] "Kalevalankysymyksiä," in *JSFO* xxxv-xxxvi. Helsingfors, 1918.

—— [c] *Kalevalan runojen historia*. Helsingfors, 1902–10.

——— [d] "Kaleva und seine sippe," in *JSFO* xxx. 35. Helsingfors, 1915.

——— [e] *Suomalaiset syntyloitsut.* Helsingfors, 1917. Translated into Germ. in *FFC* no. 51–52. Helsingfors, 1923.

——— [f] "Suomalaisten pakanalliset jumalat," in *Oma Maa*, i. Borgå, 1907 and 1920.

——— [g] "Suomalaisten runojen uskonto," in *SUU* i. Borgå, 1914.

KUNDER, J., *Eesti muinasjutud.* Rakwere, 1885.

LÄNKELÄ, J., "Matkakertomus," in *S* 1860. Helsingfors.

LENCQVIST, H. G., *De superstitione veterum fennorum theoretica et practica* (Porthan, *Opera selecta*, iv). Helsingfors, 1870.

LUCE, J. W. L. VON, *Wahrheit und Muthmassung.* Bernau, 1827.

LUKKARINEN, J., [a] "Inkeriläisten kotijumalista," in *SMA* xxvi. Helsingfors, 1912.

——— [b] "Inkeriläisten praasnikoista," in *S* iv. 11. Helsingfors, 1912.

——— [c] "Inkeriläisten vainajainpalveluksesta," in *MSFO* xxxv. Helsingfors, 1914.

——— [d] "Tietoja susi-ihmisistä Inkerissä," in *Virittäjä*, 1914. Helsingfors.

MANSIKKA, V. J., "Taikojen aarreaitasta," in *Virittäjä*, 1914. Helsingfors.

MURMAN, J. W., "Några upplysningar om Finnarnes fordna vidskepliga bruk och trollkonster," in *S* 1854. Helsingfors.

RANTASALO, A. V., [a] "Der Ackerbau im Volksaberglauben der Finnen und Esten mit entsprechenden Gebräuchen der Germanen verglichen, I–III," in *FFC*, no. 30–32. Helsingfors, 1919–20.

——— [b] *Suomen kansan muinaisia taikoja, iii. Maanviljelystaikoja.* Helsingfors, 1912.

RUSSWURM, C., *Eibofolke oder die Schweden an den Küsten Ehstlands und auf Runö.* 2 vols. Reval, 1855.

SAARIMAA, E. A., "Liiviläisten mytologisia uskomuksia," in *Virittäjä*, 1914. Helsingfors.

SALMELAINEN, E., "Vähänen kertoelma Muinois-Suomalaisten pyhistä menoista," in *S* 1852. Helsingfors.

SAXÉN, RALF, *Finsk guda- och hjältetro.* Helsingfors, 1916.

SCHWINDT, TH., *Tietoja Karjalan rautakaudesta.* Helsingfors, 1898.

SETÄLÄ, E. N., "Wäinämöinen und Joukahainen," in *MSFO* xxxv. Helsingfors, 1914.

SKOGMAN, D., "Kertomus matkoiltani Satakunnassa muistojuttuja keräämässä," in *S* ii. 2. Helsingfors, 1862.

Suomen kansan muinaisia loitsurunoja. Helsingfors, 1880.

Suomenkansan vanhat runot. Helsingfors, 1908 ff.

TUNKELO, E. A., " Eräistä vainajainpalvontaan liittyvistä suomalaisista nimityksistä," in *MSFO* xxxv. Helsingfors, 1914.

VARONEN, M., *Suomen kansan muinaisia taikoja.* 2 vols. Helsingfors, 1891–1892.

VOIONMAA, V., *Suomen karjalaisen heimon historia.* Helsingfors, 1915.

WIEDEMANN, F. J., *Aus dem inneren und äusseren Leben der Ehsten.* Petrograd, 1876.

WIKLUND, K. B., " Mytologi (Finsk)," in *Nordisk Familjebok,* xix. Stockholm, 1913.

IV. LAPPS

ACERBI, J., *Travels through Sweden, Finland and Lapmark to the North-cape.* 2 vols. London, 1902.

ÄIMÄ, FR., " Muutamia muistotietoja Inarin lappalaisten vanhoista uhrimenoista," in *Virittäjä,* 1903. Helsingfors.

ANDELIN, A., " Kertomus Utsjoen pitäjästä," in *S* 1858. Helsingfors.

ANDERSSON, G. A., *Tietoja Sodankylän ja Kittilän pitäjien aikaisemmista ja myöhemmistä vaiheista.* Kemi, 1914.

APPELGREN, Hj., " Muinaisjäännöksiä ja tarinoita Kemin kihlakunnan itäisissä osissa," in *SMA* v. Helsingfors, 1882.

B[ERGMAN], E. W., " Anteckningar om Lappmarken, särskildt med hänseende till kristendomens införande därstädes," in *Historisk Tidskrift,* xi. Stockholm, 1891.

CHARUZIN, N., [a] " O noydach u drevnich i sovremennych loparey," in *EO* i. 1889. Moscow.

—— [b] " Russkie lopari," in *IOLEAE* lxvi. Moscow, 1890.

DRAKE, SIGRID, " Västerbottens-lapparna under förra hälften av 1800–talet," in *Lapparna och deras land,* vii. Uppsala, 1918.

DÜBEN, GUST. VON, *Om Lappland och Lapparne.* Stockholm, 1873.

FELLMAN, ISAK, *Handlingar och uppsattser angående Finska Lappmarken och Lapparne,* i. Helsingfors, 1910.

FELLMAN, JACOB, *Anteckningar under min vistelse i Lappmarken.* 2 vols. Helsingfors, 1903.

FJELLSTRÖM, P., *Berättelse om Lapparnes björnafänge samt deras dervid brukade vidskepelser.* Stockholm, 1755.

FRIIS, J. A., [a] *En sommer i Finmarken, Russisk Lapland og Nord-Karelen.* Christiania, 1871.

—— [b] *Lappiske Eventyr og Folkesagn.* Christiania, 1871.

—— [c] *Lappisk Mythologi.* Christiania, 1871.

FRITZNER, J., " Lappernes hedenskap og trolddomskunst sammenholdt med andre folks isaer nordmaennenes tro och overtro," in *Historisk Tidskrift*, i. 4. Christiania, 1877.

GENETZ, A., *Wörterbuch der kola-lappischen Dialekte*. Helsingfors, 1891.

GRAAN, O., " Relation Eller En Fulkomblig Beskrifning om Lapparnas Vrsprung, så wähl som om heela dheras Lefwernes Förehållande," in *ATPS* xvii. 2. Uppsala, 1899.

HALLSTRÖM, G., [a] " Gravplatser och offerplatser i ryska Lappmarken," in *Etnologiska studier tillägnade N. E. Hammarstedt*. Stockholm, 1921.

——— [b] " Lapptrumman," in *Fataburen*, 1910. Stockholm.

HAMMOND, HANS, *Den Nordiske Missions-Historie*. Copenhagen, 1787.

HELLAND, A., [a] *Norges Land og Folk. Topografisk-statistisk beskrivelse over Finmarkens amt*. 2 vols. Christiania, 1906.

——— [b] *Norges Land og Folk. Topografisk-statistisk beskrivelse over Nordlands amt*. 2 vols. Christiania, 1908.

HÖGSTRÖM, PEHR, *Beskrifning öfver de til Sweriges Krona lydande Lapmarker*. Stockholm [1747].

HOLMBERG, UNO, [a] " De fornnordiska nornorna i lapparnas religion," in *Argus*, 1915. Helsingfors.

——— [b] " Lappalaisten uskonto," in *SSU*, ii. Borgå, 1915.

——— [c] " Lapps," in *ERE*, vii. 797 ff. Edinburgh.

JESSEN, E. J., *Afhandling om de Norske Finners og Lappers Hedenske Religion*. (Printed in Leem's work) Copenhagen, 1767.

KILDAL, S., " Efterretning om Finners og Lappers hedenske religion," in *Det skandinaviske Litteraturselskabs Skrifter*, iii. 2. Copenhagen, 1807.

KOLMODIN, T., " Folktro, seder och sägner från Pite Lappmark," in *Lapparne och deras land*, iii. Stockholm, 1914.

KROHN, KAARLE, " Lappische beiträge zur germanischen mythologie," in *FUF* vi. Helsingfors, 1906.

LEEM, KNUD, *Beskrivelse over Finmarkens Lapper*. Copenhagen, 1767.

LINDAHL, E., and ÖHRLING, J., *Lexicon Lapponicum*. Stockholm, 1780.

LUNDIUS, N., " Descriptio Lapponiae," in *ATPS* xvii. 4. Uppsala, 1905.

MUNCH, T. A., *Symbolae ad Historiæm antiquiorem rerum Norvegicarum*. Christiania, 1850.

NIURENIUS, O., " Lappland," in *ATPS* xvii. 4. Uppsala, 1905.

OLRIK, AXEL, [a] " Irmensûl og gudestdtter," in *Maal og minne*, 1910. Christiania.

—— [b] "Nordisk og lappisk gudsdyrkelse," in *Danske Studier*, 1905. Copenhagen.

—— [c] "Tordenguden og hans dreng," ib. 1905–6.

—— [d] "The sign of the dead," in *FUF* xii.   Helsingfors, 1912.

QVIGSTAD, J., [a] "Kildeskrifter til den lappiske mythologi, i–ii," in *Det kgl. Norske Videnskabers Selskabs Skrifter*, nos. 1 and 4. Trondhjem, 1903 and 1910.

—— [b] "Lappischer Aberglaube," in *Kristiania Etnografiske Museums Skrifter*, i. 2.   Christiania, 1920.

REUTERSKIÖLD, E., [a] "De nordiska lapparnas religion," in *Populära etnologiska skrifter*, 8.   Stockholm, 1912.

—— [b] "Källskrifter till lapparnas mytologi," in *Bidrag till vår odlings häfder utgifna af Nordiska Museet*, 10.   Stockholm, 1910.

REUTERSKIÖLD, E., and WIKLUND, K. B., "Linnés lappska trolltrumma," in *Fataburen*, 1912.   Stockholm.

RHEEN, S., "En kortt Relation om Lapparnes Lefwarne och Sedher, wijdskiepellser, sampt i många Stycken Grofwe wildfarellser," in *ATPS* xvii. 1.   Uppsala, 1897.

ROSEN, ERIC VON, "En nyupptäckt lappsk offerplats vid Vidjakuoika," in *Ymer*, 1911.   Stockholm.

ROSÉN, HELGE, "Om lapparnas dödsrikesföreställningar," in *Fataburen*, 1919.   Stockholm.

SAMZELIUS, H., "Sagor och sägner, skrock och öfvertro från finnbygder och lappmarker, i–ii," in *Meddelanden från Nordiska Museet*, 1902–3.   Stockholm.

SCHEFFERUS, J., *Lapponia*.   Frankfurt, 1673.

TORNAEUS, J., "Berättelse om Lapmarckerna och Deras Tillstånd," in *ATPS* xvii. 3.   Uppsala, 1900.

TUDERUS, G., "En kort underrättelse om the österbothniske lappar, som under Kiemi gebit lyda," in *ATPS* xvii. 6.   Uppsala, 1905.

TURI, J., *Muittalus samid birra*.   Copenhagen, 1910.

UNWERTH, W. VON, [a] *Namensgebung und Wiedergeburtsglaube bei Nordgermanen und Lappen*.   Off-print of *Festschrift für Alfred Hillebrandt*.

—— [b] "Ódinn und Rota."   Off-print of *Beiträge zur Geschichte der deutschen Sprache und Litteratur*.   Published by W. Braune.   1913.

—— [c] *Untersuchungen über Totenkult und Ódinnverehrung bei Nordgermanen und Lappen*.   Breslau, 1911.

VAHL, J., *Lapperne og den lapske mission*.   Copenhagen, 1866.

WIKLUND, K. B., [a] "En nyfunnen skildring af lapparnas björnfest," in *MO* 1912.   Uppsala.

—————— [b] "Saivo.   Till frågan om de nordiska beståndsdelarna i lapparnas religion," in ib. 1916.   (Translated into Germ. in *Beiträge zur Religionswissenschaft,* ii. 1918.)

—————— [c] "Mytologi (Lapsk)," in *Nordisk Familjebok,* xix. Stockholm, 1913.

YAŠČENKO, A., "Něskolko slov o Russkoy Laplandiy," in *EO* xii. Moscow, 1892.

V. VOLGA FINNS

ANDRIEVSKIY, A. A., "Děla o soveršenii yazyčeckich obryadov i žertvoprinošeniy kreščenymi inorodcami Vyatskoy gubernii," in *Stolětie Vyatskoy guberni,* 1780–1880. ii.   Vyatka, 1880.

AUNOVSKIY, V., "Etnografičeskiy očerk Mordvy Mokši," in *Pamyatnaya kniga Simbirskoy gubernii na* 1869.   Simbirsk.

BAGIN, S. A., "Gadateli i znachari u carevokokšayskich čeremis," in *IOAIE* xxvi. 3.   Kazan, 1910.

BENEVOLENSKIY, G., "Mordovskiya molyany," in *SEV* 1868, no. 21. Samara.

BUTUZOV, F., [a] "Iz byta mordvy sela Živaykina Žadovskoy volosti, Karsunskago uyezda Simbirskoy gubernii," in *IOAIE* xi. 5. Kazan, 1893.

—————— [b] "Věrovaniya i kult mordvy (Erzi) sela Sabančeyeva Alatyrskago uyezda Simbirskoy gubernii," in *IOAIE* xi. 4. Kazan, 1893.

DUBASOV, I., *Očerki iz istorii Tambovskago kraya,* i.   Tambow, 1890.

ERUSLANOV, P., [a] "Očerk byta i predaniy vostočnych čeremis," in *IOORGO* iv. 1894.   Orenburgh.

—————— [b] "Žertvoprinošeniya čeremis Birskago uyezda po slučayu neurožaya," in ib.

EVSEVYEV, M. E., "Bračnyj i drugie religiozne obryady mordvy Penzenskoy gubernii," in *ŽS* xxiii.   Petrograd, 1914.

FILIMONOV, A., "O religii nekreščennych čeremis i votyakov Vyatskoy gubernii," in *VEV* 1868, no. 8, and 1869, nos. 7–8 and 21. Vyatka.

FILONENKO, V., [a] "Pogrebalnye i svadebnye obryady čeremis Ufimskoy gubernii," in *VOUO* 1912, no. 2.   Ufa.

—————— [b] "Prazdnik 'Kysö' u vostočnych čeremis," in ib. 1912, nos. 7–8.

FUKS, ALEKSANDRA, *Zapiski o čuvašach i čeremisach Kazanskoy gubernii.*   Kazan, 1840.

FUKS, K., "Poyezdka iz Kazani k Mordve Kazanskoy gubernii v 1839 godu," in *ŽMVD* 1839, x.   Petrograd.

GENETZ, A., "Ost-tscheremissische sprachstudien," in *JSFO* vii. Helsingfors, 1889.

GORODSKOY, G., "O čeremisach proživayuščich v Kransnoufimskom uyezdě Permskoy gubernii," in *ES* 1864, vi. Petrograd.

HÄMÄLÄINEN, A., " Tšeremissien uhritapoja," in *JSFO* xxv. 3. Helsingfors, 1908.

HOLMBERG, UNO, [a] " Tsheremissien mytologia," in *Tietosanakirja*, ix. Helsingfors, 1917.

——— [b] "Tsheremissien uskonto," in *SSU* v. Borgå, 1914.

ILLUSTROV, N., "Obryady mordvy pri pogrebenii i pominovenii umeršich" in *PEV* 1868, no. 3. Penza.

IVANCEV, S., " Iz byta mordvy derevni Dyurki Paraněevskoy volosti Alatyrskago uyezda Simbirskoy gubernii," in *IOAIE* xi. 6. Kazan, 1894.

KUZNECOV, S. K., [a] "Četyre dnya u čeremis vo vremya Surema," in *IRGO* xv. 2–3. Petrograd, 1879.

——— [b] "Kult umeršich i zagrobnyja věrovaniya lugovych čeremis," in *EO* 1904. Moscow.

——— [c] "Očerki iz byta čeremis, ii. Čeremisskie prazdniki," in *DNR* ii. Petrograd, 1879.

——— [d] "Ostatki yazyčestva u čeremis," in *IRGO* xxi. 6. Petrograd, 1885.

——— [e] "Poyezdka k drevney čeremisskoy svyatyně, izvyectnoy so vremen Oleariya," in *EO* liv. Moscow, 1905.

——— [f] *Zagrobnyja věrovaniya čeremis.* Kazan, 1884.

MAINOV, W., [a] "Les restes de la mythologie Mordvine," in *JSFO* v. Helsingfors, 1889.

——— [b] "Mordvankansan häätapoja," in *S* ii. 16. Helsingfors, 1883.

——— [c] "Mordvankansan lakitapoja," in ib. iii. 3. Helsingfors, 1888.

MELNIKOV, P. J., [a] "Nižegorodskaya Mordva," in *SGV* 1851, nos. 25–6. Simbirsk.

——— [b] "Obščestvennoe molenye Erzyan," in *SGV* 1851, no. 31. Simbirsk.

——— [c] "Očerki mordvy," in *RV* 1867, ix–x. Moscow.

MENDIAROV, V., "O čeremisach Ufimskoy gubernii," in *EO* xxii. Moscow, 1894.

MILKOVIČ, " Byt i věrovaniya mordvy Simbirskoy gubernii v konce xviii-stolětiya," *SGV* 1851, no. 32. Simbirsk.

MINCH, A., "Narodnye obyčay, obryady, suevěrii i predrazsudki krestyan Saratovskoy gubernii," in *ZRGO* xix. 2. Petrograd, 1889–90.

MITROPOLSKIY, K., "Mordva. Religioznyja vozzrěniya ich, npavy i obyčay," in *TEV* 1876, nos. 12–13. Tambow.

MOLYAROV, I., [a] " Besĕdy k čeremisam Kuznecovskago prichoda," in *IKE* 1873, nos. 7–9. Kazan.

—— [b] " Narodnyja vĕrovanya lugovych čeremis Kazanskoy gubernii," in ib. 1877, no. 9. Kazan.

—— [c] " Pochoronnye obyčay i povĕrya gornych čeremis," in ib. 1876, pp. 740–747.

MOŽAROVSKIY, A., " Mordovskoe selo Kakino, Sergačskago uyezda Nižegorodskoy eparchii," in *NEV* 1890, no. 24. Nižni-Novgorod.

NURMINSKIY, S., " Očerk religioznych vĕrovaniy čeremis," in *PS* 1862. Kazan.

Obrazcy mordovskoy narodnoy slovesnosti, i. Kazan, 1882.

PAASONEN, H., [a] " Beiträge zur Kenntnis der Religion und des Cultus der Tscheremissen," off-print of *KSz* ii. pp. 30–8, 122–33 and 198–210. Budapest, 1901.

—— [b] " Matkakertomus mordvalaisten maalta," in *JSFO* viii. Helsingfors, 1890.

—— [c] " Mordvalaisten mytologia," in *Tietosanakirja*, vi. Helsingfors, 1914.

—— [d] " Mordvins," in *ERE* viii. Edinburgh.

—— [e] " Mythologisches, etymologisches," in *MSFO* xxxv. Helsingfors, 1914.

—— [f] " Proben der mordwinischen Volkslitteratur," in *JSFO* ix and xii. Helsingfors, 1891 and 1894.

PETROV, A. A., " Zamĕtki po etnografii čeremis Krasnoufimskago uyezda, Permskoy gubernii," in *IOORGO* 1895, vi. Orenburgh.

PORKKA, V., " Tscheremissische texte mit übersetzung," in *JSFO* xiii. Helsingfors, 1895.

PRIMĔROV, A., " Religiozyne obryady i suevĕrnyja obyčay mordvov Krasnoslobodskago uyezda," in *PEV* 1870, no. 16. Penza.

RAMSTEDT, G. J., " Bergtscheremissische sprachstudien," in *MSFO* xvii. Helsingfors, 1902.

RYABINSKIY, K., " Ardinskiy prichod Kozmodemyanskago uyezda," in *IOAIE* xvi. Kazan, 1900.

ŠACHMATOV, A., *Mordovskiy etnografičeskiy sbornik*. Petrograd, 1910.

SEMENOV, T., " Čeremisy," in *Pravoslavniy Blagovĕstnik*, 1893. Moscow.

ŠESTAKOV, " Byt čeremis Uržumskago uyezda," in *Cirkulyar no Kazanskomu Učebnomu Okrugu*. Kazan. 1866.

SMIRNOV, I., [a] " Čeremisy," in *IOAIE* vii. Kazan, 1889.

—— [b] " Mordva," in ib. x–xii. Kazan, 1892–5.

SMIRNOV, N., Mordovskoe naselenie Penzenskoy gubernii," in *PEV* 1874, nos. 1–24. Penza.

SMOLENCOV, O. I., " Yazyčeskiya žertvoprinošeniya i obyčai u pravoslavnych čeremisov," in *Ogonek*, 1914, no. 19. Petrograd.

SNĚŽNITSKIY, I., [a] " Mordovskiy prazdnik ' Vermavy ' (Verbnoe voskresenie) i ' Viryavy,' " in *PEV* 1871, nos. 19–20.

———— [b] " Prazdnik ' Petrooskos ' — Petrov molyan v dyen sv. apostolov Petra i Pavla v. Mordoyskom selě K-sě," in ib. 1870, no. 22.

TROITSKAYA, N., " Čeremisy Arbanskoy volosti," in *IOAIE* xi. 1 Kazan, 1893.

TROITSKIY, S., " Zamětki o vetlužkich čeremisach," in *NGV* 1863, nos. 19–20. Nizhni-Novgorod.

VASILYEV, V. M., [a] " Ceremisy-yazyčniki," off-print of *IO* xii. 1915. Kazan.

———— [b] " Materialy dlya izučeniya věrovaniy i obryadov čeremis," off-print of *IO* x. 1915. Kazan.

———— [c] " Materialy dlya izučeniya věrovaniy i obryadov čeremis," off-print of *IO* v. 1915. Kazan.

YAKOVLEV, G., *Religioznye obryady Čeremis*. Kazan, 1887.

ZNAMENSKIY, P., " Gornye čeremisy Kazanskago kraya," in *VE* iv. 1867. Petrograd.

ZOLOTNICKIY, N., *Nevidimyi mir po šamanskim vozrěniyam čeremis*. Kazan, 1877.

VI. PERMIANS

AMINOFF, T. G., " Reseberättelse," in *Öfversigt af Finska Vetenskapssocietetens Förhandlingar*, xxi. Helsingfors, 1879.

APTIEV, G. A., " Iz religioznych obyčaev votyakov Ufimskoy gubernii Birskago uyezda," in *IOAIE* ix. 3. Kazan, 1891.

BECHTEREV, V., " Votyaki, ich istoriya i sovremennoe sostoyanie," in *VE* viii–ix. Petrograd, 1880.

BLINOV, N., *Yazyčeskii kult votyakov*. Vyatka, 1898.

BOGAYEVSKIY, P., [a] " Očerk byta Sarapulskich votyakov," in *Sbornik materialov po etnografii izd. pri Daškovskom etnograf. muzeě*, iii. Moscow, 1888.

———— [b] " Očerki religioznych predstavleniy votyakov," in *EO*, 1890. Moscow.

BUCH, MAX, " Die Wotjäken," in *ASSF* xii. Helsingfors, 1883.

CHARUZIN, M., " Očerki yuridičeskago byta narodnostey sarapulskago uyezda Vyatskoy gubernii," in *Yuridičeskii Věstnik*, 1883. Petrograd.

CHARUZINA, VERA, " K voprosy o počitanii ognya," in *EO* lxx–lxxi. Moscow, 1906.

CHLOPIN, V., " Několko slov o Permyakach," in *GI*. Petrograd, 1849.

DOBROTVORSKIY, N., " Permyaki," in *VE* iv. Petrograd, 1883.

Drevnie Akty otnosyaščiesya k istorii Vyatskago kraya. Vyatka, 1881.

FROLOV, A., " Svadebnye i pochoronnye obyčay žiteley sela Ustnemskago, Ustsysolskago Uyezda," in *VGV* no. 21. Vologda, 1885.

FUCHS, D. R., " Eine Studienreise zu den Syrjänen," in *KSz* xii. 3. Budapest, 1911.

FUKS, A. A., " Poyezdka k votyakam Kazanskoy gubernii," in *KGV* no. 14 ff. Kazan, 1844.

GAVRILOV, B., [a] " Pověrya, obryady i obyčay votyakov Mamadyškago uyezda, Uryasučinskago prichoda," in *Trydy IV archeologičeskago sězda v Rossii*, ii. Kazan, 1891.

———— [b] *Proizvedeniya narodnoy slovesnosti, obryady i pověrya votyakov Kazanskoy i Vyatskoy gubernii*. Kazan, 1880.

HÄMÄLÄINEN, A., " Epifanij Viisaan tiedot Pyhästä Tapanista ja syrjääneistä," in *Vähäisiä kirjelmiä*, xli. Helsingfors, 1908.

HOLMBERG, UNO, [a] " Permalaisten uskonto," in *SSU* iv. Borgå, 1914.

———— [b] " Syrjäänien muinaisuskonto," in *Tietosanakirja*, ix. Helsingfors, 1917.

———— [c] " Votjaakkien mytologia," in ib. x. 1919.

KANDINSKIY, V., " Iz materialov po ethnografii sysolskich i vyčegodskich zyryan," in *EO*, iii. Moscow, 1889.

LUPPOV, P. N., [a] *Christianstvo u votyakov so vremeni pervych istoričeskich izvěstiy o nich do XIX věka*. Petrograd, 1899.

———— [b] *Christianstvo u votyakov v pervoy polovině XIX věka*. Petrograd, 1911.

LYTKIN, G., *Zyryanskiy kray pri episkopach permskich i zyryanskii yazyk*. Petrograd, 1889.

MICHEYEV, I., " Iz religioznoy žizni kazanskich votjakov," in *IKE* 1900. Kazan.

MIROPOLSKIY, A., " Kreščenye votyaki kazanskago uyezda, ich yazyčeskie pověrya, obryady i obyčai," in *PS* 1876. Kazan.

MUNKÁCSI, B., [a] *Lexicon linguae votiacorum*. Budapest, 1896.

———— [b] *Votják népköltészeti hagyományok*. Budapest, 1887.

———— [c] " Votják nyelvtanulmányok," in *Nyelvtudományi Közlemények*, xviii. Budapest, 1884.

NALIMOV, V., [a] " Někotoryia čerti iz yazyčeskago mirosozercaniya zyryan," in *EO* lvii. Moscow, 1903.

———— [b] " Zagrobniy mir po věrovaniyam zyryan," in ib. lxxii-lxxiii. Moscow, 1907.

———— [c] " Zur Frage nach den ursprünglichen Beziehungen der Geschlechter bei den Syrjänen," in *JSFO* xxv. 4. Helsingfors, 1908.

OSTROVSKIY, D., "Votyaki Kazanskoy gubernii," in *Trudy Obščestva Estestvoispytateley pri Kazanskom Universitetě*, iv. Kazan, 1874.

PERVUCHIN, N., *Eskizy predanii i byta inorodcev Glazovskago uyezda*, i–v. Vyatka, 1888–90.

POPOV, N., "Zyryane i zyryanskiy kray," in *IOLEAE* xiii. 2. Moscow, 1874.

POTANIN, G., "U votyakov Elabužskago uyezda," in *IOAIE* iii. Kazan, 1884.

ROGOV, N., "Materialy dlya opisaniya byta Permyakov," in *ŽMVD* xxix. Petrograd, 1858.

SATRAPINSKIY, K. A., *Votyaki i Besermane* (Manuscript in Archives of Geogr. Society in Petrograd. x. 49).

SMIRNOV, I., [a] "Permyaki," in *IOAIE* ix. 2. Kazan, 1891.

—— [b] "Votyaki," in ib. viii. 2. Kazan, 1890.

TEZYAKOV, I., Prazdniki i žertvoprinošeniya u votyakov yazyčnikov," in *NS* 1896. Petrograd.

VEREŠČAGIN, GR., [a]"Starye obyčai i věrovaniya votyakov," in *EO* lxxxiii. Moscow, 1910.

—— [b] "Votskie bogi," in *IAOIRS* 1911, no. 7. Archangelsk.

—— [c] "Votyaki Sarapulskago uyezda Vyatskoy gubernii," in *ZRGO* xiv. 3. Petrograd, 1889.

—— [d] "Votyaki Sosnovskago kraya," in ib. xiv. 2. Petrograd, 1886.

WASILJEV, J., "Übersicht über die heidnischen Gebräuche, Aberglauben und Religion der Wotjaken," in *MSFO* xviii. Helsingfors, 1902.

WICHMANN, YRJÖ, [a] "Tietoja votjaakkien mytologiiasta," in *Vähäisiä Kirjelmiä*, xvii. Helsingfors, 1893.

—— [b] "Wotjakische sprachproben," i–ii, in *JSFO* xi and xix. Helsingfors, 1893 and 1901.

ŽAKOV, K., "Yazyčeskoe mirosozercanie zyryan," in *Naučnoe Obozrěnie*, viii. 3. Petrograd, 1901.

YANOVIČ, M., "Permyaki," in *ŽSt* 1903. Petrograd.

VII. UGRIANS AND SAMOYEDS

ABRAMOV, N. A., "Opisanie Berezovskago kraya," in *ZRGO* xii. 1857. Petrograd.

AHLQVIST, A., "Unter Wogulen und Ostjaken," in *ASSF* xiv. Helsingfors, 1885.

BARNA, F., *Ösvallásunk föistenei*. Budapest, 1881.

BARTENEV, V., *Na kraynem sěvero-zapadě Sibiri. Očerki obdorskago kraya*. Petrograd, 1896.

BĚLYAVSKIY, F., *Poyezdka k Ledovitomu moryu*. Moscow, 1833.

Bröms, P., *De religione siberiensium.* Uppsala, 1728.

Bucinskiy, P., *Kreščenie Ostyakov i Vogulov pri Petrě Velikom.* Harkow, 1893.

Charuzin, N., "Medvězya prisyaga i totemičeskiya osnovy kulta medvědya u Ostyakov i Vogulov," in *EO* 1898. Moscow.

Donner, Kai, [a] "A Samoyede epic," in *JSFO* xxx. 26. Helsingfors, 1914.

———— [b] *Siperian samojedien keskuudessa vuosina 1911–1913 ja 1914.* Helsingfors, 1915. (Publ. also in Swed. 1915.)

———— [c] "Eteläisten ostjakki-samojedien luona," in *Joukahainen,* xiv. Helsingfors, 1913.

———— [d] "Samojedien mytologia," in *Tietosanakirja,* viii. Helsingfors, 1916.

Dunin-Gorgavič, A. A., *Tobolskiy sěver. Etnografičeskiy očerk městnych inorodcev.* Tobolsk, 1904–11.

Finsch, O., *Reise nach West-Sibirien im Jahre 1876.* Berlin, 1879.

Gluškov, I., "Čerdynskie voguly," in *EO* xlv. Moscow, 1900.

Gondatti, N., [a] "Kult medvědya u inorodcev sěvero-zapadnoy Sibiri," in *IOLEAE* xlviii. 2. Moscow, 1888.

———— [b] "Slědy yazyčeskich věrovaniy u Mansov" in *IOLEAE* xlviii. 2. Moscow, 1888.

Gorodkov, N., "Religioznyja yazyčeskiya vozzrěniya Ostyakov," in *TOEA* 1890, no. 2. Tomsk.

Grigorovski, N., "Opisanie Vasyuganskoy tundry," in *ZZ–SORGO* vi. Petrograd, 1884.

Hofmann, E., *Der nördliche Ural und das Küstengebirge Pae-Choi.* Petrograd, 1853.

Islavin, V., *Samoyedy v domašnem i obščestvennom bytu.* Petrograd, 1847.

Jackson, F. J., "Notes on the Samoyeds of the Great Tundra," in *Journal of the Anthrop. Institute of Great Brit.* xxiv. London, 1908.

Kandra, K., *Magyar mythologia.* Eger, 1897.

Kannisto, A., [a] "Über die wogulische schauspielkunst," in *FUF* vi. Helsingfors, 1906.

———— [b] "Vogulien mytologia," in *Tietosanakirja,* x. Helsingfors, 1919.

Karjalainen, K. F., [a] "Alte bilder zur Ob-ugrischen mythologie," in *MSFO* xxxv. Helsingfors, 1914.

———— [b] "Eteläostjakkien karhumenoista," in *Virittäjä,* 1914. Helsingfors.

———— [c] "Jugralaisten uskonto," in *SUU* iii. Borgå, 1918.

———— [d] "Ostjaakkien mytologia," in *Tietosanakirja,* vi. Helsingfors, 1914.

——— [e] "Ostjakkeja oppimassa," in *JSFO* xvii. Helsingfors, 1900.

KATONA, L., " Allgemeine Charakteristik des magyarischen Folklore," in *EMU* i. Budapest, 1887–8.

KUŠELEVSKIY, Y. I., *Sěvernyj polyus i zemlya Yalmal.* Petrograd, 1868.

KUZNECOV, N. N., " Priroda i žiteli vostočnago sklona sěvernago Urala," in *IRGO* xxii. 6. Petrograd, 1887.

LEHTISALO, T., " Entwurf einer Mythologie der Jurak-Samojeden," in *MSFO* liii. Helsingfors, 1924.

LYADOV, V., "Zauralskie finny," in *Razsvět,* vii. 1860. Petrograd.

MIECHOV, M. VON, *Descriptio Sarmatiarum.* Krakow, 1521.

MÜLLER, J. B., *Das Leben und die Gewohnheiten der Ostjacken.* Berlin, 1720.

MUNKÁCSI, B., [a] "Ältere Berichte über das Heidenthum der Wogulen and Ostjaken," i–v, in *KSz* iii–v. Budapest, 1902–4.

——— [b] " Die Weltgottheiten der wogulischen Mythologie," in ib. vii–x. Budapest, 1906–9.

——— [c] " Götzenbilder und Götzengeister im Volksglauben der Vogulen," in ib. vii. Budapest, 1906.

——— [d] " Seelenglaube und Totenkult der Wogulen," in ib. vi. Budapest, 1905.

——— [e] " Über die heidnische Religion der Wogulen," in *EMU* iii. Budapest, 1893.

———[f] Vogul népköltési gyüjtemény, i–iv. Budapest, 1892–1902.

NOVITSKIY, GR., *Kratkoe opisanie o narodê ostyatskom.* Petrograd, 1884.

PÁPAY, J., *Osztják népköltési gyüjtemény. Budapest,* 1905.

PATKANOV, S., *Die Irtysch-Ostjaken und ihre Volkspoesie.* 2 vols. Petrograd, 1897 and 1900.

PAVLOVSKIY, V., *Voguly.* Kazan, 1906.

POLYAKOV, I., [a] "Ostyaki i rybopromyšlennost v dolině r. Obi," in *Priroda i Ochota,* ii. Petrograd, 1878.

——— [b] " Pisma i otčety o putešestvii v dolinu r. Obi," in *ZAN* xxx. 2. Petrograd, 1877.

RAMSAY, W., " Ein Besuch bei den Samojeden auf der Halbinsel Kanin," in *JSFO* xxiii. Helsingfors, 1906.

ŠAVROV, V., "O šamanach ostyatskich," in *Moskvitanin,* 1844. Moscow.

SCHRENCK, A. G., *Reise nach dem Nordosten des europäischen Russlands im Jahre 1837.* 2 vols. Dorpat, 1848 and 1854.

SIRELIUS, U. T., "Ostjakkien ja vogulien hautaustavoista ja heidän käsityksestään elämästä kuoleman jälkeen," in *SM* 1902–3. Helsingfors.

SOMMIER, S., *Un' estate in Siberia.* Firenze, 1885.

SOROKIN, N., "Putešestvie k vogulam," in *TOEKU* iii. 4. Kazan, 1873.

TRUBETSKOY, N., "K voprosu o zolotoy babĕ," in *EO* lxviii–lxix. Moscow, 1906.

VENIAMIN, [a] "O obraščenii v christianstvo mesenskich samojedov," in *Christianskoe Čtenie.* Petrograd, 1850.

—————— [b] "Samoyedy Mezenskie," in *VRGO* xiv. Petrograd, 1855.

WLISLOCKI, H. VON, [a] *Aus dem Volksleben der Magyaren.* München, 1893.

—————— [b] *Volksglaube und religiöser Brauch der Magyaren.* Münster, 1896.

ŽITKOV, B. M., "Poluostrov Yamal," in *ZRGO po Obščey Geografii,* xlix. Petrograd, 1913.

SIBERIAN

I. ABBREVIATIONS

(See also Abbreviations under Finno-Ugric)

IV–SORGO . . Izvěstiya Vostočno-Sibirskago Otděla Russkago Geografičeskago Obščestva.
MER . . . . Materialy po Etnografii Rossii.
OZ . . . . Ostasiatische Zeitschrift.
SMAEAN . . Sbornik Muzeya po Antropologii i Etnografii pri Akademii Nauk.
SS . . . . . Sibirskiy Sbornik.
SV . . . . . Sibirskiy Věstnik.
TIVAS . . . Trudy IV Archeologičeskago Sězda v Rossii.
VO . . . . Vostočnoe Obozrěnie.
ZAO . . . Zapiski Archeologičeskago Obščestva.
ŽMNP . . . Žurnal Ministerstva Narodnago Prosvěščeniya.
ZPORGO . . Zapiski Priamurskago Otděla Russkago Geografičeskago Obščestva.
ZRAO . . . Zapiski Russkago Archeologičeskago Obščestva.
ZVORAO . . Zapiski Vostočnago Otděleniya Russkago Archeologičeskago Obščestva.
ZV–SORGO . Zapiski Vostočno-Sibirskago Otděla Russkago Geografičeskago Obščestva.

II. BIBLIOGRAPHY

AGAPITOV, N. N., and CHANGALOV, M. N., "Šamanstvo u buryat Irkutskoy gubernii," in *IV–SORGO* xiv. 1–2. Irkutsk, 1883.

Altayskaya cerkovnaya missiya. Petrograd, 1865.

ANUČIN, V. I., "Očerk šamanstva u yeniseyskich ostyakov," in *SMAEAN* ii. 2. Petrograd, 1914.

BANZAROV, D., *Černaya věra ili šamanstvo u mongolov.* Petrograd, 1891.

BATAROV, P. P., " Buryatskiya pověrya o bocholdoyach i anachayach," in *ZV–SORGO* ii. 2. Irkutsk, 1890.

BERGERON, PIERRE, *Voyages faits principalement en Asie dans les XII, XIII, XIV et XV siècles par Benjamin de Tudele, Jean du Plan-Carpin, N. Ascelin, Guillaume de Rubruquis, Marc Paul Venitien, Haiton, Jean de Mandeville et Ambroise Contarini.* 2 vols. La Haye, 1735.

BERGMANN, B., *Nomadische Streifereien unter den Kalmücken*. Riga, 1804–5.

BOGORAS, W., *The Chukchee*. (*The Jesup North Pacific Expedition*, vii.) New York, 1904.

BRAIG, C., "Eine mongolische Kosmologie," in *Philosoph. Jahrbuch*, ii. 1890.

"Buryatskiya skazki i poverya," in *ZV–SORGO*, i. 1. Irkutsk, 1889.

CHANGALOV, M. N., [a] "Novye materialy o šamanstvě u buryat," in *ZV–SORGO* ii. 1. Irkutsk, 1890.

—— [b] "Predaniya i pověrya unginskich buryat," in *ZV–SORGO* ii. 2. Irkutsk, 1890.

—— [c] "Sud zayanov nad lyudmi," in *ZV–SORGO* ii. 2. Irkutsk, 1890.

CHUDYAKOV, I. A., "Verchoyanskiy sbornik," in *ZV–SORGO* i. 3. Irkutsk, 1890.

DÄHNHARDT, O., *Natursagen*. 3 vols. Leipzig and Berlin, 1907–10.

FRAEHN, CH. M., "Die ältesten arabischen Nachrichten über die Wolga-Bulgaren, aus Ibn Foszlan's Reiseberichten," in *Mémoires de l'Académie Imp. des Sciences*, vi. Sc. politiques, histoire et philologie, i. St. Petersburg, 1832.

GALSAN-GOMBOYEV, "O drevnich mongolskich obyčayach i suevěriyach," in *ZAO* xiii. Petrograd, 1859.

GILMOUR, J., *Among the Mongols*. London, 1883.

GOROCHOV, N., [a] "Materialy dlya isučeniya šamanstva v Sibiri," in *IV–SORGO* xiii. 3. Irkutsk, 1882.

—— [b] "Yuryung-Uolan. Jakutskaya skazka," in *IV–SORGO* xv. 5–6. Irkutsk, 1885.

GRÜNWEDEL, A., *Mythologie des Buddhismus in Tibet und der Mongolei*. Leipzig, 1900.

HARLEZ DE, CH., *La Religion nationale des Tartares orientaux: Mandchous et Mongols*. Paris, 1887.

HELMERSEN, G. VON, *Reise nach dem Altai im Jahre 1834 ausgeführt*. Petrograd, 1848.

HILDÉN, KAARLO, "Om shamanismen i Altai, speciellt bland lebedtatarerna," in *Terra*, 1916. Helsingfors, 1916.

Historia Orientalis Haythoni Armenii: et hvis svbiectvm Marci Pavli veneti Itinerarium. Helmaestadii, 1635.

HOLMBERG, UNO, [a] "Der Baum des Lebens," in *AASF* xvi. Helsingfors, 1922–1923.

—— [b] "The shaman costume and its significance," in *Annales Universitatis Fennicae Aboensis*, i. no. 2. Turku, 1922.

HUC, E. R., *Souvenirs d'un voyage dans la Tartarie, le Thibet et la Chine*. Paris, 1850.

Ionov, V. M., " Duch-chozyain lěsa u yakutov," in *SMAEAN* iv. 1. Petrograd, 1916.

Ivanovskiy, A., " Dyavol-tvorec solnca," in *EO* no. 4. Moscow, 1890.

Jochelson, W., [a] *Materialy po izučeniyu yukagirskago yazyka i folklora*, i. (*Trudy Yakutskoy Ekspeditsii*, iii. 9. 3). Petrograd, 1900.

———— [b] *The Koryak*. (*The Jesup North Pacific Expedition*, vi.) New York, 1905.

Kamenskiy, N., *Sovremennyja ostatki yazyčeskich obryadov i religioznych věrovaniy u čuvaš*. Kazan, 1869.

Katanov, N., " Skazaniya i legendy minusinskich tatar," in *SS* 1887. Petrograd.

Klemenc, D., " Něskolko obrazcov bubnov minusinskich inorodcev," in *ZV–SORGO* ii. 2. Irkutsk, 1890.

Koblov, Y., " Mifologia kazanskich tatar," in *IOIAE* xxvi. 5. Kazan, 1910.

———— *Religioznye obryady i obyčai tatar magometan*. Kazan, 1908.

Kotvič, V., " Materialy dlya izučeniya tungusskich narečiy," in *ŽSt* 1909, ii–iii. Petrograd.

Krašeninnikov, S., *Opisanie Zemli Kamčatki*. Petrograd, 1819.

Landyšev, S., " Kosmologiya i Feogoniya altaycev yazyčnikov," in *PS* 1886. Kazan.

Lankenau, H. v. " Die Schamanen und das Schamanenwesen," in *Globus*, xxii. Braunschweig, 1872.

Lassy, Ivar, *The Muharram mysteries among the Azerbeijan Turks of Caucasia*. Helsingfors, 1916.

Ledebour, C. F. von, *Reise durch das Altai-Gebirge und Soongorische Kirgisen-Steppe*, 2 vols. Berlin, 1829–30.

Maak, R., [a] *Putešestvie na Amur*. Petrograd, 1889.

———— [b] *Vilyujskiy okrug yakutskoy oblasti*. Petrograd, 1887.

Magnitskiy, V., *Materialy k obyasneniya staroy čuvašskoy věry*. Kazan, 1881.

Maynagasev, S. D., " Žertvoprinošenie nebu u beltirov," in *SMAEAN* iii. Petrograd, 1916.

Maksimov, S., " Ostatki drevnich narodno tatarskich (yazyčeskich) věrovaniy u nyněšnich kreščenych tatar Kazanskoy gubernii," in *IKE* 1876. Kazan.

Mészáros, Gyula, *A csuvas ösvallás emlékei*. Budapest, 1909.

Mészáros, J., " Osmanisch-türkischer Volksglaube," in *KSz* vii. Budapest, 1906.

Michailov, V. I., " Obryady i obyčai čuvaš," in *ZRGO* xvii. 2. Petrograd, 1891.

MICHAYLOVSKIY, V. M., "Šamanstvo," in *IOLEAE* lxxv. *Trudy etnografičeskago otděla*, xii. Moscow, 1892.

MIDDENDORFF, A. Th. v., *Reise in den äussersten Norden und Osten Sibiriens*, iii. 1 and iv. 2. Petrograd, 1851 and 1875.

MILKOVIC, "Byt i věrovaniya čyvaš Simbirskoy gubernii v 1783 godu," in *SGV* 1851, no. 42. Simbirsk.

MORDVINOV, A., "Inorodcy obytayuščie v Turuchanskom kraě," in *VRGO* 1860, ii. Petrograd.

NANSEN, F., *Gjennem Sibirien*. Copenhagen, 1915.

NASYROV, K., "Pověrya i priměty kazanskich tatar," in *ZRGO* vi. Petrograd, 1880.

NIKOLSKIY, N., *Kratkii konspekt po etnografii čuvaš*. Kazan, 1911.

NORDENSKIÖLD, A. E., *Vegas färd kring Asien och Europa*. Stockholm, 1880–81.

OLSEN, ØRJAN, *Et primitivt folk. De mongolske rennomader*. Christiania, 1915.

"O proischošdenii sěvero-baykalskich buryat." *Pamyatnaya knižka Irkutskoy gubernii za 1881 g*. Irkutsk, 1881.

PALLAS, P. S., *Sammlungen historischer Nachrichten über die mongolischen Völkerschaften*. 2 vols. Petrograd, 1776–1801.

PARKER, E. H., "Mongols," in *ERE* viii. 806 f.

PEKARSKIY, E., "Plašč i buben yakutskago šamana," in *MER* i. Petrograd, 1910.

PEKARSKIY, E. K. and CVETKOV, V. P., "Očerki byta priayanskich tungusov," in *SMAEAN* ii. 1. Petrograd, 1913.

"Pervyi buryatskiy šaman ' Morgan Chara,' " in *IV–SORGO* xi. 1–2. Irkutsk, 1880.

"Pervyj šaman Bocholi-Chara," in *IV–SORGO* xi. 1–2. Irkutsk, 1880.

PODGORBUNSKIY, S. I., "Idei buryat šamanistov o dusě, smerti, zagrobnom miře i zagrobnoy žizni," in *IV–SORGO* xxii. no. 1. Irkutsk, 1891.

POTANIN, G. N., [a] "Gromovnik po pověriyam yužnoy Sibiri i sěvernoy Mongolii," in *ŽMNP* 1882, no. 1. Petrograd.

—— [b] *Očerki sěvero-zapadnoy Mongolii*, vols. ii and iv. Petrograd, 1881 and 1883.

POYARKOV, F., "Iz oblasti kirgizskich věrovaniy," in *EO* 1891, no. 4. Moscow.

POZDNĚYEV, A., [a] "Kalmytskiya skazki," in *ZVORAO* vols. iii, iv, vi, vii, ix and x. Petrograd, 1889–1897.

—— [b] *Mongoliya i mongoly*. Petrograd, 1896.

PRIKLONSKIY, V. L., [a] "Tri goda v Yakutskoy oblasti," in *ŽSt* 1891, iii–iv. Petrograd.

—— [b] "Yakutskiya narodnyja pověrya i skazki," in *ŽSt* 1891. Petrograd.

Pripuzov, N. P., [a] "Melkiya zamětki o yakutach," in *ZV–SORGO* ii. 2. Irkutsk, 1890.

—— [b] "Svěděniya dlya izučeniya šamanstva u yakutov Yakutskago okruga," in *IV–SORGO* xv. 3–4. Irkutsk, 1885.

Prokopyev, K., "Pochorony i pominki u čuvaš," in *IOAEI* xix. 5. Kazan, 1903.

Radloff, W., [a] *Aus Sibirien*. 2 vols. Leipzig, 1884.

—— [b] "Mifologia i mirosozercanie žiteley Altaya," in *VO* 1882, no. 7.

—— [c] *Proben der Volkslitteratur der türkischen Stämme Süd-Sibiriens*. 3 vols. Petrograd, 1866, 1868 and 1870.

Recueil de Voyages et de Mémoires, publ. par la Société de Géographie, i–iv. Paris, 1824–1836.

Šaškov, S., "Šamanstvo v Sibiri," in *ZRGO* 1864, 2. Petrograd, 1864.

Sboyev, V., *Čuvaši v bytovom, istoričeskom i religioznom otnošeniyach*. Moscow, 1865.

Schiefner, A., *Heldensagen der minusinskischen Tataren*. Petrograd, 1859.

Schmidt, I. J., [a] *Forschungen im Gebiete der älteren religiösen, politischen und literarischen Bildungsgeschichte der Völker Mittel-Asiens, vorzüglich der Mongolen und Tibeter*. Petrograd and Leipzig, 1824.

—— [b] *Geschichte der Ost-Mongolen und ihres Fürstenhauses, von Ssanang Ssetsen*. Petrograd, 1829.

Schott, W., [a] *Altaische Studien*. Berlin, 1860.

—— [b] *Älteste Nachrichten von Mongolen und Tataren*. Berlin, 1845.

—— [c] *Über den Buddhaismus in Hochasien und in China*. Berlin, 1846.

Schrenk, L. v., *Die Völker des Amur-Landes*. (*Reisen und Forschungen im Amur-Lande*, iii. 2, 3.) Petrograd, 1891–95.

Ščukin, N., *Poyezdka v Jakutsk*. Petrograd, 1844.

Sěroševskiy, V. L., *Yakuty*. Petrograd, 1896.

Šimkevič, P. P., "Materialy dlya izučeniya šamanstva u goldov," in *ZPORGO* i. 2. Chabarovsk, 1896.

Širokogorov, S. M., *Opyt izslědovaniya osnov šamanstva u tungusov*. Vladivostok, 1919.

"Skazaniya buryat, zapisannyja raznymi sobiratelyami," in *ZV–SORGO*, i. 2. Irkutsk, 1890.

Sofiyskiy, I. M., "O kiremetyach kreščenych tatar," in *TIVAS*. Kazan, 1891.

Solovyev, F., "Ostatki yazyčestva u yakutov," in *Sbornik gazety "Sibir,"* i. Petrograd, 1876.

Spasskiy, G., "Zabaykalskie tungusy," in *SV* xix–xx. 1822. Petrograd.

Špicyn, A. A., "Šamanizm v otnošenii k russkoi archeologii," in *ZRAO* xi. Petrograd, 1899.

Stadling, J., "Shamanismen i norra Asien," in *Populära etnologiska skrifter,* 7. Stockholm, 1912.

Steller, G. W., *Beschreibung von Kamtschatka.* Frankfurt and Leipzig, 1774.

Sumcov, N. F., "Otgoloski christianskich predaniy v mongolskich skazkach," in *EO* no. 3. Moscow, 1890.

Tchihatcheff, Pierre de, *Voyage scientifique dans l'Altai oriental et les parties adjacentes de la frontière de Chine.* Paris, 1845.

Thomsen, Vilh., "Inscriptions de l'Orkon," in *MSFO.* Helsingfors, 1896.

Tretyakov, P. I., *Turuchanskiy kray, ego priroda i žiteli.* Petrograd, 1871.

Troščanskiy, V. F., *Evolutsiya černoy věry u yakutov.* Kazan, 1902.

Vambéry, H., [a] *Die primitive Cultur des turko-tatarischen Volkes.* Leipzig, 1879.

—— [b] "Noten zu den alttürkischen Inschriften der Mongolei und Sibiriens," in *MSFO* xii. Helsingfors, 1899.

Vasilyev, V. N., [a] "Izobraženiya dolgano-yakutskich duchov kak atributy šamanstva," in *ŽSt* 1909. Petrograd.

—— [b] "Šamanskiy kostyum i buben u yakutov," in *SMAEAN* viii. Petrograd, 1910.

Verbitskiy, V. I., *Altayskie inorodcy. Sbornik etnografičeskich statey i izslědovaniy.* Moscow, 1893.

Veselovskiy, A., [a] "K voprosu o dualističeskich kosmogoniyach," in *EO* 1890, no. 2. Moscow, 1890.

—— [b] *Razyskaniya v oblasti russkago duchovnago sticha* (xi–xvii), v. Petrograd, 1889.

V-skiy, N., "Materialy dlya izučeniya šamanstva u yakutov," in *ZV–SORGO* ii. 2. Irkutsk, 1890.

Zatoplyayev, N., "Někotoryja pověrya alarskich buryat," in *ZV–SORGO* ii. 2. Irkutsk, 1890.

Žitetskiy, I. A., "Očerki byta Astrachanskich Kalmykov," in *IOLEAE* lxxvii. 1. *Trudy etnografičeskago otděla,* xiii. 1. Moscow, 1893.

Zolotnitskiy, N. I., *Kornevoy čuvašsko-russkiy slovar.* Kazan, 1875.

PRINCIPAL ARTICLES ON FINNO–UGRIANS AND SI-BERIANS IN THE ENCYCLOPÆDIA OF RELIGION AND ETHICS

BEVERIDGE, J., " Kalevala," vii. 641–2.

BILLSON, C. J., " Names (Lapp)," ix. 270–1.

———— " Prayer (Finns and Lapps)," x. 181–2.

CZAPLICKA, M. A., " Ostyaks," ix. 575–81.

———— " Samoyed," xi. 172–7.

———— " Siberia, Sibiriaks, Siberians," xi. 488–96.

———— " Tungus," xii. 473–6.

———— " Turks," xii. 476–83.

———— " Yakut," xii. 826–9.

HOLMBERG, U., " Lapps," vii. 797–800.

———— " Priest, Priesthood (Ugro-Finnish)," x. 335–6.

KLEMENTZ, D., " Buriats," iii. 1–17.

KROHN, K., " Ancestor-Worship and Cult of the Dead (Ugro-Finnish)," i. 467.

———— " Birth (Finns and Lapps)," ii. 647–8.

———— " Finno-Ugrians," vi. 22–3.

———— " Finns (Ancient)," vi. 23–6.

———— " Kalevala," vii. 639–41.

MacCULLOCH, J. A., " Shaman," xi. 441–6.

MacRITCHIE, D., " Images and Idols (Lapps and Samoyeds)," vii. 148–50.

PAASONEN, H., " Mordvins," viii. 842–7.